［例解］**現代英語冠詞事典**

樋口昌幸＝著　マイケル・ゴーマン＝協力　大修館書店

An
Illustrative
Guide to
English Article
Usage

Higuchi Masayuki
with
Michael Gorman

TAISHUKAN

はしがき

　本書は，英語の冠詞はどのように用いられるか，その用法の背後にはどのような原理があるか，ということをできるだけ包括的にまとめたものである。第1部では，6つの原理に基づいて，どのような場合に名詞部が不定冠詞 (a/an) をとり，どのような場合にとらないかを説明する。第2部では「同定可能性」という観点から定冠詞 (the) の用法を詳述する。第3部では，冠詞など限定詞の省略を論じる。

　近年，外国人用のすぐれた英英辞典があいついで出版され，多数の例文に基づいて英語の名詞が可算名詞であるか不可算名詞であるかを調べるのが容易になった。だが，見出し語の説明ではしばしば例文なしに [C] と [U] とが併置されているため，説明を読んでも [C] と [U] との使い分けは不明のままであることが多い。さらに，[U] 表示の名詞も文脈によっては a/an が必要とされるという事実がある。このため，すぐれた辞書の助けを借りても，英語の冠詞の使用法が日本人にとって理解しにくいことに変わりはない。
　他方，日本人による英語の冠詞に関する論文あるいは著書も出版されてはいるが，ほとんどは有益とは言いがたい。この原因を突きつめれば，冠詞の包括的な実態調査がきちんと行われていないことによると断ぜざるをえない。本書が理論的または実用的に貢献するところがあるとすれば，豊富な一次資料を基に英語の名詞が無冠詞で使われる場合と冠詞つきで使われる場合とを対比することによって，両者の相違を明らかにしようとしたこと，および，これまで個々別々に列挙されてきた冠詞の諸用法をできる限り統一的に説明するための原理を明らかにしたことであろうか。
　本書の説明法は，記述的であると評されるかもしれない。たしかにそうであるが，筆者としては，「厳密な」記述的・説明的アプローチであると補足したい。この名詞には冠詞がつく場合もつかない場合もあるというような，例文の羅列で終わってはいないからである。本書は，無冠詞用法も冠詞つき用法も意味的，構造的もしくは文体的な必然性から生じるという前提に立つ。この前提なしには，冠詞の本質をかりそめにもとらえることは不可能であろう。本書では統計的処理はいっさい行っていない。意味に違いがあるとき頻度を求めても無意味だからである。

本書は，Appendix も含め，例文が多すぎるという印象を与えるかもしれない。しかし，実用面を考えれば，外国語の使い方に関しては説明を読むだけでは十分には理解できないし，英語母語話者の書く英文にも誤用が皆無ではないので，多すぎるほどの用例をあげることが必要である。学問的にも，本書中の原理が有効であることを実証するためには，適切な例文を広範囲に提示しなければならない。加えて，インターネットの世界的な普及にともない英語が変化していくことが予想されるので，現時点における英語の冠詞の用例を記録しておくことは決して無意味なことではないであろう。僭越な比較であることは承知の上で，*MEG*（第7巻，第12−16章）の豊富な例文が20世紀初期までの冠詞の実態を記録して有益であるのと同様に，本書も2000年前後の英語における冠詞の実態を示すのに貢献するところがあると期待したい。(もちろん，*MEG* の価値は冠詞論だけにとどまるものではない。)

　本書中の例文の多くは筆者自身が過去数年に *Reader's Digest*（主として，Asian Edition; RD と略す）から集めたものであるが，文脈なしでも理解可能な例として各種の英英辞典から補ったものもある。ほかに，BNC などコーパスから採取した例文，草稿がほぼできあがった段階で入手した CD-ROM 版の *Encyclopaedia Britannica 2001*（EB 01）および *Grolier Multimedia Encyclopedia*（GME）から補った例文，あるいは，少数ながら，母語話者と相談して作った例文もある。

　無冠詞の用例と冠詞つきの用例との意味的・文体的な相違に関しては，広島大学外国人教師 Michael Gorman 氏とのメールによる頻繁な議論をとおして説明をより正確にすることができた。関西外大教授・安藤貞雄博士からは，第1部の構想段階で，諸事実を原理としてまとめるようご助言いただいた。大修館書店の米山順一氏は，出版にご尽力くださった上に，編集上の助言を惜しまれなかった。以上の方々のご厚意に深謝したい。私ごとながら，家族の協力にも感謝のことばをささげたい。

　筆者が，日本人にとって1番むずかしい英語の品詞は冠詞だということを初めて聞いたのは大学1年のときだった。しかし，当時は英語で長文を書いたことがなかったため，そのことばを十分には理解できなかった。卒業論文を拙い英語で書いたころから冠詞の難解さを実感するようにはなったが，研究対象にしようという気持ちは起こらなかった。ところが，授業や研究のかたわら冠詞に関する概説書を読むうち，疑問を解決してくれる説明がないことに気づき，自分で冠詞の用法を調査研究するしかないと思うようになった。本書は，筆者が英語母語話者によって書かれた英文を読んで資料を集め，それらの一次資料

との格闘をとおして，現時点までに到達した冠詞研究のエッセンスを，利用しやすい形で，まとめたものである。格闘はまだ継続中であるが，従来のどの研究書よりも英語の冠詞の本質に迫ることができたと自負している。本書が日本人のための冠詞理解の一助になることを願ってやまない。

2003年9月

樋口 昌幸

◆本書の利用法

1. **索引から調べる**
   特定の語が冠詞をとるかどうか急いで調べたい場合は、索引からその語の用例を見る。
2. **目次から調べる**
   冠詞の使い分けの原理や構文的タイプは目次に網羅されているので、当該箇所を見る。
3. **関連項目から調べる**
   同じ語の別の文脈における用法やより詳しい説明、類似の用法に関しては関連箇所が "☞" および「参照」によって言及されているので、その項目を見る。
4. **全体を通読・精読する**
   英語の冠詞の用法を総体的に理解するためには本書を最初から最後まで読む。1回目は、例文は適宜飛ばしながら、説明に集中して読み、再読のときは例文もすべて検討する。
5. **見つけた例を書き込む**
   英文を読書中に本書の説明と合致する表現、あるいは例外的な表現を見つけた場合は、関連箇所に書き込む。

◆凡　例

1. ☞ は関連箇所を表す。
2. φ は無冠詞を表す。
3. * は後続する表現が非文法的または不適切であることを表す。
4. 大文字のローマ数字とアラビア数字の組み合わせは章と例番号を示す。たとえば、(I-45, c) は第1章の例文 (45, c) を表す。
5. 例文の出版年は、誤解の恐れがない場合、最初の2桁を省略する。たとえば、(RD 99/2: 129) は (*Reader's Digest*, 1999年2月号, p. 129) であることを表す。
6. 訳文中の固有名詞は、紙面節約のため、原則として頭文字のみ表記する。

目 次

はしがき ……… iii
本書の利用法 ……… vi
凡　例 ……… vi

第1部　無冠詞と不定冠詞 ……………………………………………… 3

序　章　不定冠詞使用の条件 ……… 5

第1章　原理Ⅰ──意味の有無 ……… 11

1 原理Ⅰ──意味の有無／11
 1.1 冠詞をとる条件／11
 1.2 固有名詞／11
 1.3 肩書き・称号／13
 1.4 呼びかけ／18
 1.5 数字・文字つき名詞／19
 1.6 記号／21
 1.7 「擬態普通名詞」／21

第2章　原理Ⅱ──姿かたちの有無 ……… 27

2 原理Ⅱ──姿かたちの有無／27
 2.1 解体と統合／27
  2.1.1 素材と個体／27
   2.1.1.1 食材／27
   2.1.1.2 素材・構成物／31
   2.1.1.3 におい／33
   2.1.1.4 音／34
   2.1.1.5 毛皮／34
  2.1.2 タイプ：NP_1 of NP_2／35
  2.1.3 タイプ：birds of a feather／42

2.2 ジャンルと作品／42
2.3 無定形が組み込まれている語／48
　2.3.1 物質集合名詞／48
　　2.3.1.1 植物／48
　　2.3.1.2 精神活動／50
　　2.3.1.3 創作物・製品／50
　　2.3.1.4 その他／50
　2.3.2 物質名詞の普通名詞化／51
　2.3.3 抽象名詞／57
　　2.3.3.1 ゲーム名／57
　　2.3.3.2 学問名／60
　　2.3.3.3 その他の抽象名詞／60
　　　2.3.3.3.1 「混乱」／60
　　　2.3.3.3.2 laughter／61
　　　2.3.3.3.3 traffic／61
　　　2.3.3.3.4 advice／61
　　　2.3.3.3.5 evidence/identification／61
　　　2.3.3.3.6 information/news／62
　　　2.3.3.3.7 progress／62
　　　2.3.3.3.8 weather／62
2.4 メタ言語用法／62
2.5 言語と話し手／63

第3章　原理 III ──働きの有無 ……… 65

3 原理 III ──働きの有無／65
　3.1 (準)補語／65
　3.2 job/position/rank/role／67
　3.3 enough/half/more／68
　3.4 play／71
　3.5 楽器名／73
　3.6 turn／76
　3.7 by＋名詞句／77
　　3.7.1 輸送・移動手段／77
　　3.7.2 通信手段／82
　　3.7.3 その他の手段・方法／83
　　3.7.4 by＋複数形／87
　3.8 施設名／88
　3.9 能力・機能／96

3.10 慣用的表現 (1)／103
　　3.11 慣用的表現 (2)／107

第 4 章　原理 IV ──限定と非限定 ……… 113

　4 原理 IV ──限定と非限定／113
　　4.1 空間的限定／114
　　4.2 時間的限定／126
　　4.3 種類／132
　　4.4 共起する語句による限定／133
　　　4.4.1 前置詞句／134
　　　　4.4.1.1 数値による限定／134
　　　　4.4.1.2 感情・能力などの対象／140
　　　　　4.4.1.2.1 感情／140
　　　　　4.4.1.2.2 能力／143
　　　　　4.4.1.2.3 その他の名詞類／143
　　　　　4.4.1.2.4 対象をともなう名詞に関する注意／147
　　　　4.4.1.3 「助数詞」扱い／148
　　　4.4.2 関係詞節／150
　　　4.4.3 形容詞／152
　　　　4.4.3.1 食事名／152
　　　　4.4.3.2 色彩語／157
　　　　4.4.3.3 挨拶ことば；擬音；発話／160
　　　　4.4.3.4 形容詞による，その他の名詞類の限定／162
　　　4.4.4 that 節／167
　　　4.4.5 不定詞および動名詞／173
　　4.5 否定と存在／177
　　　4.5.1 否定／177
　　　4.5.2 存在文／181

第 5 章　原理 V ──抽象概念と個別事例 ……… 185

　5 原理 V ──抽象概念と個別事例／185
　　5.1 犯罪名と事件／186
　　5.2 治療法と施術／170
　　5.3 病名と症状／196
　　　5.3.1 病名 [U]／197
　　　5.3.2 病名 [C]／204
　　　5.3.3 病名 [U, C]／205

5.4 その他の個別事例／215
　　　　5.4.1 具体物指示および同定構文／215
　　　　　　5.4.1.1 具体物指示／215
　　　　　　5.4.1.2 同定構文／216
　　　　5.4.2 個別行為／217
　　　　5.4.3 状態・精神活動／219
　　　　5.4.4 内容／220
　　　　5.4.5 その他／221

第6章　原理 VI ──a/an＋複数形 ········ 225
　　6 原理 VI ──a/an＋複数形／225

第7章　不定冠詞に関するその他の問題 ········ 233
　　7.1 タイプ：a cup and saucer／233
　　7.2 一見同義表現／235
　　7.3 総称用法／239
　　　　7.3.1 総称用法の不定冠詞／240
　　　　7.3.2 総称用法の複数／241

第2部　定冠詞 ·· 245

第8章　定冠詞使用の文脈および環境 ········ 247
　　8 定冠詞の選択原理／247
　　8.1 文脈内限定／248
　　　　8.1.1 形容詞的修飾語句／248
　　　　8.1.2 関連語句／250
　　8.2 複数構成物／251
　　　　8.2.1 年代／252
　　　　8.2.2 一族／一門／252
　　　　8.2.3 グループ名／チーム名／253
　　　　8.2.4 国民；部族／民族／254
　　　　8.2.5 大陸／国家／山脈／平原／群島／256
　　　　8.2.6 病名／259
　　　　8.2.7 その他の複数構成物／261
　　8.3 状況的同定／261

　　　　8.3.1　場面依存／261
　　　　8.3.2　唯一物／262
　　　　　　8.3.2.1　天体／地点；聖典／262
　　　　　　8.3.2.2　競技大会／264
　　　　　　8.3.2.3　祭り／266
　　　　　　8.3.2.4　賞／267
　　　　　　8.3.2.5　単位／268
　　　　　　8.3.2.6　その他／270
　　　　8.3.3　流行病／272
　　　　8.3.4　the＋形容詞／分詞／273
　　8.4　文化的了解／274
　　　　8.4.1　換喩的限定／274
　　　　　　8.4.1.1　内面的特徴／274
　　　　　　8.4.1.2　娯楽／276
　　　　　　8.4.1.3　タイプ：play the clown／277
　　　　　　8.4.1.4　タイプ：the perfect pizza／277
　　　　　　8.4.1.5　タイプ：the Mona Liza／278
　　　　8.4.2　その他の文化的了解／279
　　　　　　8.4.2.1　同格／279
　　　　　　8.4.2.2　ダンス名／泳法名／282
　　8.5　対立／284
　　　　8.5.1　二項対立／284
　　　　8.5.2　身体部位／287
　　　　8.5.3　交通機関／291
　　8.6　総称／292
　　　　8.6.1　総称用法／292
　　　　8.6.2　(play＋) 楽器名／296
　　　　8.6.3　発明品／297
　　8.7　the＋固有名詞／298
　　　　8.7.1　同定可能性と the の有無／298
　　　　　　8.7.1.1　海／299
　　　　　　8.7.1.2　湾／海岸／300
　　　　　　8.7.1.3　海峡／303
　　　　　　8.7.1.4　河川／運河／303
　　　　　　8.7.1.5　滝／306
　　　　　　8.7.1.6　環礁／307
　　　　　　8.7.1.7　半島／307
　　　　　　8.7.1.8　峡谷／渓谷；海溝／308
　　　　　　8.7.1.9　山／峰／310

        8.7.1.10 道路／312
        8.7.1.11 トンネル／316
        8.7.1.12 橋／317
        8.7.1.13 船／318
        8.7.1.14 塔／320
        8.7.1.15 宮殿／322
        8.7.1.16 公園／庭園；植物園／325
        8.7.1.17 病院／330
        8.7.1.18 一般化困難な固有名詞／332
      8.7.2 the をとる固有名詞／335
        8.7.2.1 砂漠／荒野；高原；森林／335
        8.7.2.2 電車／バス／宇宙船／338
        8.7.2.3 ホテル／レストラン／パブ；劇場／映画館／341
        8.7.2.4 動物園；博物館／図書館；研究所／大学／341
        8.7.2.5 新聞／雑誌／349
  8.8 the をとらない施設／352
    8.8.1 刑務所／352
    8.8.2 駅／空港／352
    8.8.3 娯楽施設／353
  8.9 修飾語句＋人名／地名／355
    8.9.1 定冠詞／355
    8.9.2 不定冠詞／356
    8.9.3 無冠詞／358
    8.9.4 年齢＋人名／360
  8.10 the が随意的に見える場合／361
  8.11 タイプ：this the 最上級／序数／362

第3部　限定詞の省略 ……………………………………………………………… 365

第9章　限定詞の省略 ……… 367

  9.1 等位接続詞のあと／367
    9.1.1 and による並列／367
    9.1.2 or による並列／370
  9.2 ペア／371
    9.2.1 between; both; neither...nor／371
    9.2.2 その他の文脈／374
  9.3 列挙／377

9.4　構造的省略／378
　　9.4.1　タイプ：three times a day／378
　　9.4.2　文頭／379
　　　　9.4.2.1　タイプ：Fool as [that, though] I am／379
　　　　9.4.2.2　タイプ：Fact is, ／379
　　　　9.4.2.3　タイプ：Same＋名詞／副詞的語句／380
　　　　9.4.2.4　間投詞扱い／381
　　　　9.4.2.5　その他の文頭位置／381
9.5　付帯的表現／382
　　9.5.1　タイプ：with pen and notebook／382
　　9.5.2　タイプ：pen in hand／383
　　9.5.3　タイプ：belly down/up／385
　　9.5.4　タイプ：engine running／386
9.6　省略的文体／389
　　9.6.1　見出し／キャプション／ト書き／かっこ内／注／389
　　9.6.2　その他の省略構文／390

Appendix 1（a/an＋物質名詞）／393
Appendix 2（a/an＋修飾語句＋名詞）／403
Appendix 3（具体物指示および同定構文）／435
Appendix 4（個別行為など）／445

参考文献 ……… 479
索　　引 ……… 481
　欧文索引／481
　和文索引／505

［例解］現代英語冠詞事典

第 1 部
無冠詞と不定冠詞

第1部では，不定冠詞が用いられるための条件を概説し，
つづいて6つの原理に基づいて
英語の不定冠詞がどのような理由によって
選択されるかを示す。

序章　不定冠詞使用の条件

> 英語の不定冠詞は，名詞部が完結を表すときに用いられる。

上の 1 文に英語の不定冠詞の用法のすべてが凝縮されている。まず用語の定義をしておこう。「名詞部」(nominal part) とは名詞句 (noun phrase) から限定詞 (determiner)(= 冠詞や所有格，指示形容詞など) を除いた部分を指す。たとえば，(1) において，

(1) a. This book is *a treasure chest* of information. (本書は情報の宝庫だ) (CCED³)
    b. This book will give your students *a firm grasp* of English grammar. (本書は生徒たちに英文法をしっかり理解させるだろう) (OALD⁶)

名詞句は this book; a treasure chest of information; a treasure chest; information [1 語から成る名詞句]; this book; your students; a firm grasp of English grammar; a firm grasp; English grammar であり，名詞部は book; treasure chest of information; treasure chest; information; book; students; firm grasp of English grammar; firm grasp; English grammar である。

他方，上の文に言う「完結」とは，たとえば，「完結した論理」と言うときのように，「それ自体でまとまった形にととのっていること」の意味である (広辞苑)。

名詞部が完結を表す最も明白なケースは，名詞自体が完結を含意する場合である。たとえば，fox/lamb/house など普通名詞は，通例，それ自体でまとまった姿かたちを表すので，不定冠詞をとる。しかし，これらの語も姿かたちを表さない文脈では不定冠詞は不要である。

(2) a. There was *a fox* on the prowl near the chicken coop. (ニワトリ小屋の近くをキツネがうろついていた) (OALD⁵)
    b. Mary had *a little lamb*. (M は子羊を飼っていた) (nursery rhyme by Sarah Josepha Hale, 1830; CIDE)
    c. *Fox* and *lamb*, for instance, do not need to be altered in nature to be represented as vicious deceiver and innocent victim. (たとえば，狐と羊とは性質を変えるまでもなく邪悪な嘘つきと無辜の犠牲者

として描かれる）(Cooper, *The Structure of the Canterbury Tales*, p. 181) [姿かたちではなく，性質を表すので無冠詞（☞ 2-3章）；ペアで用いられていることも無冠詞の一因（☞ 9.2）; deceiver/victim が無冠詞であることに関しては3.1 [as のあと] 参照]

(3) a. They've bought *a* new *house*, but it'll need a lot of work before they can move into it/move in. (新居を買ったが，入居できるまでには大仕事が必要だろう) (CIDE)

   b. We recruited some friends to help us move *house*. (転居を手伝ってもらうのに友人を数人雇った) (OALD5; 主に〈英〉) [家屋を動かすのではない]

普通名詞と異なり，抽象名詞は，通例，それ自体ではまとまった姿かたちをもたないので不定冠詞をとらない。だが，抽象名詞も，修飾語句をともなうことにより，その抽象名詞に関する意味あるいは情報が完結するならば，不定冠詞をとる。たとえば，(4, b; 5, b-c) のような場合である。

(4) a. The relationship of brain size to *intelligence* is a matter of dispute. (大脳の大きさと知性との関係は議論のあるところだ) (CIDE)

   b. Compared to monkeys, dogs have *a* fairly low *intelligence*. (サルに較べれば，イヌはかなり知性が低い) (CIDE) [形容詞による intelligence の程度限定（☞ 4.4.3）]

(5) a. Even here there is room for some variation, for metal surfaces vary in *smoothness*, absorptive capacity, and chemical reactivity. (ここでさえ多少の差が生じる余地がある。金属の表面は，なめらかさ，吸収力，化学的反作用に差があるからだ) (Brown)

   b. The unearthed pot has *a smoothness* that is rare in ancient times. (発掘された壺は古代にはまれなほどなめらかだ) [関係詞節による smoothness の様態限定（☞ 4.4.2）] [注：様態 = もののあり方や，行動のありさま。状態。様相。（大辞林）]

   c. Everyone stood up with *a* choreographed *smoothness*. (全員が一糸乱れずなめらかに立ち上がった) (OALD5) [形容詞による様態限定（☞ 4.4.3）]

以上の例が示すように，不定冠詞の選択は，名詞自体に可算性あるいは不可算性が内在しているために決定されるというわけではなく，名詞部が完結を表すか否かによって決定されるのである。

NB 複数形

　複数形が，通例，不定冠詞をとらないことはよく知られている。しかし，その理由は明白ではない。不定冠詞と複数形語尾とは「±individual の標識として相互補完的に機能している」（織田 2002: 35）という説があるが，これら両者は必ずしも相互補完的ではない。なぜなら，(i) 上記 (4, b; 5, b-c) の名詞は不定冠詞はとっても複数形語尾をとることはない（つまり，*low intelligences / *choreographed smoothnesses は非文法的である），逆に (ii) surgery などいくつかの語は，通例，a/an はとらないが，複数形はとる（☞ V-38; Ap.4.1-20)，さらに，(iii) 下記 iv) のように，"a/an＋複数形" という構造も可能だからである（☞ 6章)。試案であるが，a/an と複数形とが，通例，両立しないのは，複数形が「完結以上」を表すためと推測される。（「超過」ではなく「以上」とするのは iv) のような表現を含む可能性を残すためである。）

 i) (= 4, b) Compared to *monkeys*, *dogs* have a fairly low intelligence. (CIDE) [複数回完結]

 ii) (= 5, b) The unearthed pot has a smoothness that is rare in ancient *times*. [完結を超えて延びる時間的広がり]

 iii) For the first half of this century, no right whale sightings were reported in Australian *waters*. (今世紀前半，豪海域ではセミクジラの目撃は報告されていない) (RD 99/10: 49) [完結を超えて延びる空間的広がり（または完結を超える多量)]

 iv) To date, they have sold *an* astonishing 41 million *copies*. (現在までに驚異的な4千百万冊も売れている) (RD 01/4: 48) [完結した姿をもつものとしてとらえられた量]

不定冠詞の用法と完結性との関係は次のように一般化できる見込みが高い：無冠詞の名詞部は完結未満を，不定冠詞つきの名詞部は完結を，複数形の名詞部は完結以上を表す。

　ここで注意すべきは，修飾語句があれば自動的に名詞部は完結した情報を表し自動的に不定冠詞がつけられるというわけではない，ということである。たとえば，(6)-(7) では名詞部は形容詞を含んでいるにもかかわらず不定冠詞はつけられていない。

 (6) I have great *sympathy* for you. (あなたにとても同情します) (CIDE)

 (7) Urgency lent sudden *strength* to his weary body. (緊急さゆえに，疲れ

ていた体に突然力が湧いた) (RD 00/1: 79) [(IV-209, b; Ap.4.2-5, b) [a sudden cheerfulness/impulse] と比較せよ)

これらの例が無冠詞であるのは，名詞部が完結を表さないから，つまり，完結性あるいは具象性を表すには great/sudden という形容詞は情報不足だからである。類例を追加するならば，OALD[6] には φ flowery perfume [以下，φ は無冠詞を表す] / a lemony perfume; at φ high speed / at a blindingly fast speed; in φ complete silence / in a companionable silence という例があげられている (s.v., flowery, lemony, pursue, blindingly, complete, companionable)。「花の香り／高速／まったくの沈黙」は具象性に欠けるので（つまり，それらの姿かたちを想像しがたいので）冠詞をとらないのに対し，「レモンの香り／目もくらむほどの高速／いっしょにいて楽しい沈黙」は限定の度合いが高いので完結した情報とみなされ，それゆえ，冠詞が要求されるのである。これまでも「冠詞の問題は形容詞と関係がある」（金口 1970: 175）ことは指摘されていたが，どのような場合に不定冠詞をとるかは明らかにされていない。名詞部という概念も完結性という視点も欠けていたため，不定冠詞の選択は，形容詞など修飾語句が名詞の意味を補って名詞部全体として完結した意味（あるいは，情報）を表すか否かによって決定されるという事実が気づかれていなかったのである。（不定冠詞の選択には，このほか，前置詞および動詞，文体も関与する（☞ 2章 NB 4-2; 3章 NB 6, 8; 4章 NB 7-2; 5章 NB 7; Ap.4.2, NB 2; 3.1; 3.7.1; 3.10; 3.11; 4.4.3.3; 5.3.3; 9)。)

「名詞部が完結を表す」ということは，「名詞部がイメージ化可能である」と言い換えてもよい。あるいは，そのほうがわかりやすければ，名詞部が具象性もしくは個別性を表す，ととらえなおすことも可能である。あるいは，「完結」を認知言語学で言う「境界性」(boundedness) に読み替えても支障ないであろう（☞ 1.1)。大事なのは，名詞部が不定冠詞をとるためには，その名詞部はまとまった姿かたちを表さなければならない，そのためには，名詞部をイメージとしてとらえるに足る，あるいは，名詞部を具象的・個別的な存在として表すに足る，情報が与えられていなければならない，ということである。

後章への予告として，それぞれの原理によって説明される典型的な例を紹介しておきたい。原理 I は名詞の意味の有無にかかわるものであり，これによって固有名詞や愛称が無冠詞で用いられることの理由が説明される。原理 II および原理 III は，主として，物体を表す名詞を対象とする。原理 II は物体を外形からとらえる。この原理により集合名詞・物質名詞・抽象名詞が，通例，a/an をとらないことが予測され，a chicken（「ひなどり」）と φ chicken（「鶏肉」）との相違が説明される。他方，原理 III は物体をその働きにおいてとら

えるものであり，これにより，先にあげた move φ house のほか，by a bus 対 by φ bus, in a school 対 in φ school のような対比が説明される。原理 IV は，名詞部の指示範囲限定という観点から不定冠詞の有無を説明する。上記の例 (4, b; 5, b–c) の名詞部が不定冠詞をとる理由は，原理 IV によって説明可能である。原理 V は，典型的には，動詞から派生した名詞にかかわる。この原理により，たとえば，be arrested for φ burglary と be wanted for a burglary という相違が理由づけられる。最後に，原理 VI はこれまで最も無視されていた表現形式を扱う。すなわち，上記 NB 中の例 iv) の an astonishing 41 million copies のように，a/an が複数形の名詞とともに用いられる場合である。

第1章　原理Ⅰ——意味の有無

1　原理Ⅰ——意味の有無

周知のように，固有名詞は，通例，冠詞をとらない。これは，次のような一般的な原理に還元することが可能である。

> 原理Ⅰ：英語の名詞部は，意味をもたないときは冠詞をとらない。

以下，本章では，なぜ固有名詞は a/an をとらないかについて考察する。

1.1　冠詞をとる条件

名詞が冠詞をとるためには，その名詞はなんらかの「限界」(limit) を表す名詞でなければならないという条件がある。これは，すでに前世紀前半に Christophersen (1939: 69) によって指摘されているにもかかわらず，しばしば忘れられている条件である。限界を表すということは，なんらかの区切りをもち，他から区別可能であるということである。つまり，本書のことばで言い換えれば，それ自体で完結した姿かたちをもつ，ということである。以下，本書では完結もしくは限界を表すことを，コンテクストに応じて，「画定」(= 区切りをはっきりと定めること (広辞苑))，あるいは「囲い込み」，「(指示範囲／程度／内容) 限定」と呼ぶことにする。(筆者は独立に「完結」という考えに到達したのであるが，認知言語学でいう "boundedness"（または "bounded region")（「境界性」，または「境界領域」）も Christophersen の "limit"，本書の「完結」，「画定」あるいは「囲い込み」とほぼ同じ概念を指すようである。Langacker (1991: 63)，山梨 (1995: 121)，石田 (2002: 17); 樋口 (1993, 1998) 参照。)

1.2　固有名詞

人名・地名などが，通例，冠詞をとらないのは，これらの語には意味がないためである。すなわち，固有名詞は認知のための符帳 (tag) にすぎないので (Ullmann [池上 (訳)] 1969: 86 参照) 意味をもたず，それゆえ，意味が画定されることもないからである。伝統的な説明に従うならば (Ogden & Richards 1969: 324 参照)，他の名詞は，図1のように，意味をとおして指示物と間接的

に結びついているのに対し，固有名詞は，図2のように，指示物と直接的に結びついているため意味をもたないのである。(冠詞の用法を論じる上では，図2のような，冠詞をとらない固有名詞は「本来固有名詞」(primary proper noun) と呼んで，「派生固有名詞」(derived proper noun) (= 構造的に冠詞が必要な固有名詞，例: the Gulf of Mexico, the Tower of London) から区別するのが有効であろう (☞ 8.7.1.2)。)

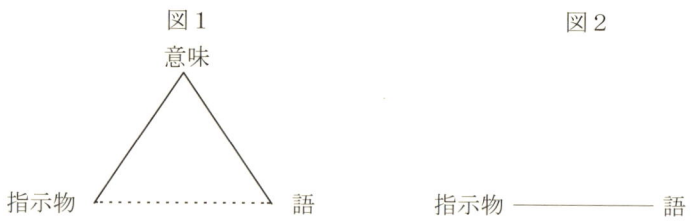

固有名詞の例を若干あげておこう。
(1) What's the 'S' for in *A S Hornby*? (A. S. Hornby 中の 'S' は何を表すか) (OALD[5])
(2) Where is *George Washington* buried? (GWはどこに埋葬されているか) (OALD[5])
(3) Within six months, *Caesar* had established his authority over *Gaul*. (半年以内でシーザーはガリアに対する支配権を確立した) (McED)
(4) *London, Paris* and *Washington DC* are capital cities. (L, P, Wは首都だ) (OALD[5])

> NB 1 「親密度の度合い」
> Jespersen (正確には, Niels Haislund) (*MEG*, vol. 7, 12.4$_2$ff.) は「親密度の度合い」(stages of familiarity) という考えに基づいて冠詞の用法を説明しようとした。しかし，"familiarity" という用語で無冠詞用法を一般化することには無理がある。なぜなら，固有名詞が無冠詞で用いられる理由は2種類あるからである：(i) 仲間内で familiar な名称が符帳 (愛称) として無冠詞で用いられる場合と，(ii) 広域的に unfamiliar な固有名詞が無冠詞で用いられる場合とである (例：φ mother; φ Tokyo Bay)。同時に，(ii) とは逆に，広域的に familiar な固有名詞は the をとる傾向が強い (例: the Persian Gulf) (☞ 1.7; 8.7)。

さらに，著者自身が言及しているように (12.7₁, 12.7₂, 12.8₄)，次のような表現中では familiarity 説は無効である：abandon φ ship / I am not φ philosopher enough / φ Brother and φ sister were at breakfast. (これらの例に関する本書の見解は 1.7 (I-45, c); 3.3 (III-25-27); 9.2.2 (IX-9) 参照。)

1.3 肩書き・称号

固有名詞に先行する肩書きあるいは称号は固有名詞の一部とみなされるので冠詞をとらない。*Mother* Teresa, *Uncle* Tom, *first lady* Hillary Rodham Clinton [the 不要], *Mt* Everest, *Lake* Victoria などに見られるとおりである。

(5) I even made a bet with *Dr.* Steinschneider that *baby* Noah would not come back. (Nちゃんは帰って来ないだろうとS博士に賭けまでした) (RD 99/2: 129)

(6) In the 1992 Presidential campaign, *candidate* Bill Clinton accused *President* Bush of coddling China by refusing to use economic pressure on Beijing to ease its domestic oppression. (1992年の大統領選キャンペーンで，[中国] 国内の弾圧緩和のために北京に経済的圧力をかけないのは中国に対して甘いとBC候補がB大統領を非難した) (RD 98/12: 71)

(7) "There's a UFO!" *co-pilot* John Middleton kidded to *pilot* Larry Campbell. (「UFOだ」と副操縦士JMは操縦士LCにふざけて言った) (RD 99/8: 116)

(8) One day the doctor got a call from *Detective* Frank Budzielek of Syracuse. (ある日同医師はS市のFB刑事から電話をうけた) (RD 99/2: 131)

(9) According to *economist* Richard Thaler, people are more likely to take a risk if they paid for the ticket. (経済学者のRTによれば，チケットの代金を払っている人は[会場に行くために] 危険をより冒しやすいとのことだ) (RD 96/3: 93) [risk は take と共起して個別事例を表す]

(10) Having lampooned Europe and the US with his earlier works, *travel writer* Bill Bryson is currently working on a book about Australia. (旅行作家BBは，初期の作品で欧州と合衆国を風刺したが，現在は豪に関する著書を執筆中だ) (RD 99/6: 1)

(11) *Mechanic* Tim Molloy gave US Air Flight 427 from Chicago to Pittsburgh a final safety check. (TM整備員はC発P行きのUSAF

14

427便に最後の安全点検を行った) (RD 00/2: 89)

(12) In the cockpit, *Captain* Peter Germano and *First Officer* Charles Emmett were flying on autopilot and settling in for the 55-minute flight. (操縦室では PG 機長と CE 副操縦士とは自動で操縦中であり，55分間のフライトに入ろうとしていた) (RD 00/2: 89f.)

(13) When *Typhoon* Sam hit the city in August 1999, a ferry heading from Hong Kong island across the harbour to Kowloon had already loaded when her master received an order from maritime officials halting all boat traffic. (台風サムが1999年8月その都市を襲ったとき，香港島から港を渡って九龍に向かうフェリーはすでに乗客を乗せていたが，船長は海事当局からすべての船舶の航海を中止せよという命令をうけた) (RD 01/4: 63)

このような例は枚挙にいとまがない。以下，"肩書き＋固有名詞"の箇所のみ列挙する。

a) 肩書きのみ

(単数形) *art historian* E. H. Gombrich (RD 99/12: 112); *artist* Andrew Wyeth (RD 97/5: 77); *author* Joan Didion (RD 00/4: 8); *Blackhawk pilot* Mike Ellis [Blackhawk はヘリコプタの名前 ; (VIII-122, f) 参照] (RD 97/5: 115); *bodyguard* Luis Valero (RD 99/3: 34); *cartoonist* Tad Dorgan (RD 99/8: 13); *cellist* Yo-Yo Ma (RD 99/4: 79); *charter pilot* Scott Sterritt (RD 99/10: 65); *co-founder* Jerry Yang (RD 99/10: 42f.); *comedian* Corbett Monica (RD 97/5: 28); *construction engineer* Ng Kok Seng of Kuala Lumpur (RD 00/1: 110); *crewman* Ronald So Chi-yip (RD 97/5: 115); *Crown Prince* Naruhito and *Princess* Masako (P. A. Goldsbury, Chugoku Shimbun, May 8, 99); *crusading lawyer* M. C. Mehta (RD 99/9: 46); *daughter* Kimberly (RD 00/3: 116); *designer* Oliver Scholl (RD 99/4: 74); *dietitian* Robyn Flipse (RD 99/9: 75); *director* Roland Emmerich (RD 99/4: 74); *eating-behaviour-expert* John Foreyt (RD 99/9: 76); *emergency-management coordinator* Woody Odom (RD 00/2: 143); *ex-Member of Parliament* Girver Fretz (RD 99/4: 116); *farm owner* Jean-Charles Lung (RD 00/1: 69); *federal prosecutor* David Irwin (RD 00/2: 36); *fellow crew member* Kevin Dingle (RD 99/12: 59); *fellow student* Bob Bradshow (RD 00/2: 36); *fire-effects specialist* Joe Viskocil (RD 99/4: 75); *fisherman* John Copik (RD 00/1: 124); *flight attendant* Annabelle (RD 99/6: 126); *Florida highway patrol Trooper* Marisa Sanders (RD 99/3: 65); *general manager*

Frankie Yick (RD 99/6: 41); *geneticist* Stephen O'Brien of the US National Cancer Institute (RD 00/1: 71); *geochemist* Chris Romanek (RD 97/5: 72); *golfer* Lee Trevino (RD 00/2: 80); *graduate student* John Santini (RD 99/9: 5); *heart surgeon* Michael DeBakey (RD 00/2: 17); *Homicide Detective Sergeant* Rick Gilliam (RD 97/5: 57); *husband* Glenn (RD 99/8: 6); *Judge* Jaime N. Salazar, Jr. (RD 99/3: 104); *Justice* Neil Butterfield (RD 00/1: 142); *leader* Kim Jong-il (RD 99/6: 67); *local coastguard* Ken Richards (RD 99/12: 57); *Londoner* Dave Brooks (RD 99/4: 46); *managing director* Bill Cakebread (RD 99/3: 109); *marketing manager* Judith Galas (RD 00/3: 26); *microbiologist* Siri Wickremesinghe (RD 99/5: 54); *NBI agent* Benito [NBI = National Bureau of Investigation] (RD 99/3: 104); *neurosurgeon* William Chadduck (RD 99/3: 19); *Nobel prize-winning author* Toni Morrison (RD 99/4: 78); *nutritionist* Jamie Pope (RD 97/5: 11); *ocular oncologist* John Hungerford (RD 00/7: 28); *Oscar-winning actress* Mira Sorvino (RD 00/2: 72); *owner* Jay Handlin (RD 99/9: 86); *pal* Rusty [Rは犬の名前] (RD 00/3: 118); *park ranger* Yohanes Rawi (RD 99/6: 29); *pediatric oncologist* H. Stacy Nicholson (RD 99/3: 20); *Princeton sociology professor* Sara McLanahan (RD 99/2: 71); *project-director* Dr Edward Condon (RD 99/8: 117); *public relations specialist* Robert T. Henkel (RD 99/3: 54); *Pulitzer Prize-winning historian* David McCullough (RD 00/1: 94); *scholar* Julian Boyd (RD 99/5: 94); *sculptor* Don Gummer (RD 00/2: 105); *shire president* Kevin Fong (RD 00/2: 118); *shot-putter* Heidi Krieger (RD 99/11: 95); *singer* Celine Dion (RD 99/10: 64); *soft-tissue surgeon* Dr Heidi Hottinger (RD 99/9: 82); *son* Hunter (RD [U.S. Edition] 02/8: 110); *song writer* Jimmy Chi (RD 00/2: 118); *study leader* Dr Dennis Maki (RD 99/9: 6); *swimmer* Karen Königm [sic; Königの誤植 ; cf. König and Knacke survived. (p. 96)] (RD 99/11: 95); *Sydney University electrical engineering honours student* David Shanahan (RD 99/10: 51); *teacher* Lalitha Jayalath (RD 99/12: 66); *teammate* Tiffany Milbrett (RD 99/12: 113); *thriller writer* James Herbert (RD 01/4: 23); *US-based Editor-at-Large* Henry Hurt (RD 00/2: 1); *whale biologist* Steve Burnell (RD 99/10: 47); *whaler Captain* Ahab (RD 99/10: 48); *whale specialist* John Bannister (RD 99/10: 49); *wife* Maggie (RD 97/5: 83); *writer* Sebastian Junger (RD 00/3: 11); *zoo keeper* Helen Shewman (RD 00/4: 39)

(複数形) *daughters* Erin and Camryn (RD [U.S. Edition] 02/8: 110); *doctors* Harold Koenig and David Larson (RD 01/9: 100); *dramatists* Shakespeare, Kyd, Beaumont and Fletcher, Congrete and Shreridan (*Cambridge History of the English Language* [*CHEL*], Vol. III, p. 2); *researchers* Robert H. Colvin and Susan C. Olson (RD 97/5: 10); *movie stars* Demi Moore and Arnold Schwarzenegger (RD 99/3: 55)

b) 国籍名・地名＋肩書き

American astronaut Gus Grissom's awestruck words (RD 99/12: 119); *American football player* Chris Zorich (RD 99/6: 48); *American sports editor* Dan Cook (RD 00/2: 114); *Australian-born contributing editor* Peter Michelmore (RD 00/3: 1); *Australian folk poet* C. J. Dennis (RD 00/3: 45); *Australian wine entrepreneur* Len Evans (RD 00/2: 114); *Barrow Mayor* Jim Vorderstrasse [バロウ市長] (RD 99/3: 28); *British entrepreneur* Richard Branson (RD 99/3: 110); *Dutch historian* Johan Huizanga (RD 99/10: 42); *Italian talk-show host* Maurizio Costanzo (RD 97/5: 88); *New Zealand operatic superstar* Dame Kiri Te Kanawa (RD 00/4: 24)

c) 修飾語句（国籍名・地名以外）＋肩書き

convicted rapist Jalosjos (RD 99/9: 65); *famous French baker* Lionel Poilâne (RD 99/9: 67); *former Canadian Minister of Fisheries and Oceans* John Crosbie (RD 99/6: 94); *former primary-school student* Walter Winger (RD 99/4: 114); *former racing driver* Jackie Stewart (RD 99/4: 46); *former Chicago White Sox baseball pitcher* Saul Rogovin (RD 00/2: 12); *frequent contributor* Anita Bartholomew (RD 99/3: 1); *legendary Australian cricketer* Donald Bradman (RD 00/5: 36); *local restaurateur* P. J. O'Flaherty (RD 99/9: 31); *moustached artisan* Christian Vanderkerken (RD 01/5: 73); *retired FBI agent* John Cook (RD 01/4: 26); *seven-year-old son* Nicholas and *four-year-old daughter* Eleanor (RD 97/5: 83); *"This Morning" host* Michael Enright ["This Morning" はテレビ番組名] (RD 00/3: 117); *veteran foreign correspondent* Joseph Reaves (RD 99/9: 1); *48-year-old Detective Chief Inspector* John Morse (RD 99/11: 44)

d) 肩書き and 肩書き

dancer and director Tommy Tune (RD 99/4: 80); *married TV writer and producer* David Kelley (RD 99/5: 111); *mountaineer and author* Peter Potterfield (RD 99/4: 1); *neighbour and colleague* Idzi Kusiak (RD 99/12:

103)

NB 2 肩書きと同格
1) 原則的に，肩書きは無冠詞で用いられ，同格は無冠詞または冠詞つきで用いられる (8.4.2.1 も参照)。

 i) a. "Without a schedule, students can easily forget what they have to do. If there's an assignment that requires a lot of work, they need to get going on it early," says *award-winning teacher* Jose F Llarinas of Manila. (「計画なしでは生徒は何をすべきかすぐに忘れてしまう。たくさん勉強しなければならない宿題があれば，早く取りかかる必要がある」と受賞歴のある M 市の教師 JFL は言う) (RD 99/9: 90) [肩書き]

  b. "Parents who are not educated may feel they cannot approach a teacher, who seems to know everything," says Anthony Lim, *an award-winning teacher* and now principal of Stanford College in Petaling Jaya, Malaysia. (「教育をうけていない親は教師に近づくことができないように感じるかもしれない。何でも知っているように思われるので」と AL は言う。彼は受賞歴のある教師であり，現在は M の PJ 市の S 大学の学長をしている) (RD 99/9: 89) [同格]

2) 次の Winner ... 1995 が，肩書きであるにもかかわらず，コンマを従えているのは，読みやすくするための表記上の工夫であると思われる。

 ii) *Winner of Malaysia's National Teacher Award in 1995,* Mohamad Radzi decided to make a game of learning. (1995 年の M 国教師賞の受賞者，MR は勉強をゲームにしようと決めた) (RD 99/9: 88)

参考：次のように表現することも可能。

 iii) As a result, the boy would often cry in class, says Javier, *a 1995 Metrobank Foundation Teachers Award winner.* (その結果，少年は授業中によく奇声を発した，と 1995 年の M 基金教師賞の受賞者である J は言う) (RD 99/9: 91)

3) 次の表記は eldest son Joel (コンマなし) と their/the eldest son, Joel との混同と見るべきであろう。

iv) The Smiths' home in suburban Riderwood, Maryland, "was a zoo," says *eldest son, Joel*, who dropped out of university and drove a truck. (長男のJ——大学中退後、トラックの運転手——が言うには、M州Rの郊外にあるSの家は「動物園だった」) (RD 99/12: 77)

1.4 呼びかけ

　呼びかけが無冠詞であるのも、普通名詞が、先の図2のように、目前の指示物と直接的に結びついているためである。つまり、呼びかけの語は普通名詞としての意味が希薄になり、2人称代名詞の代用という働きをしているのである。呼びかけの対象が複数ならば、冠詞なしで複数形をとる (19-20)。

(14) Yes, *officer*, I saw it happen. (はい、お巡りさん、それが起きるのを目撃しました) (OALD⁵)

(15) I've had enough of your impudence, *young lady*! (君の厚かましさにはもううんざりだ) (OALD⁵)

(16) Where did you come from, *poor bird*? And how are you going to feed yourself when the waterways freeze over? (どこからやって来たんだい、かわいそうな鳥よ。川が凍ったらどうやって餌をとるつもりなんだ) (RD 99/4: 93)

(17) Hurry, *driver*, hurry! (急いで、運転手さん、急いで) (Dahl, "The Ways up to Heaven")

(18) "Hold on, *house*," Jen pleaded, squeezing her dad. (「家よ、もちこたえて」、Jは父親の手を握りしめて祈った) (RD 01/6: 93)

(19) You *girls*, stop talking! (女の子たち、おしゃべりはやめなさい) (OALD⁵)

(20) "Listen, you *guys*," said Mr. Mahoney to our class of eleven-year-olds. (「みんな、よく聞いて」と11歳児のクラスにM先生は言った) (RD 98/3: 47)

　　NB 3　呼びかけが2人称の代用である統語的証拠
　　　(19)-(20) のように、呼びかけがyouとともに用いられているのは、呼びかけの語が2人称の働きをしていることの裏づけと見てよいかもしれない。より強力な統語的証拠は次の引用である。この例では、be は、先行詞である Our Father ではなく、2人称単数の thou と一致している。呼びかけにおいて、名詞が2人称の代用であることを示す決定的な証拠である。

Our Father which *art* in heaven, Hallowed be *thy* name.（天にましますわれらの父よ，み名があがめられますように）(Mat. 6:9 [Authorized Version])

1.5 数字・文字つき名詞

数詞や文字を含む名詞句が無冠詞であるのも，数詞および文字が符帳にすぎないからである。

(21) Saul entered Yale at *age 14*.（Sは14歳でY大学に入学した）(LDOCE³)

(22) When we reached *Camp 2*, the sun was strong enough for us to strip off a few layers of clothes.（第2キャンプに着いたとき，日射しは衣類を数枚脱がなければならないほど強烈だった）(RD 95/1: 61)

(23) He played miserably in the first round and even worse on *day two*.（第1ラウンドでのプレーは悲惨であり，2日目はもっとひどかった）(RD 00/2: 78)

(24) All four terrorists moved to the rear of the plane, opened *Door 4-left* and fired outside.（4人のテロリスト全員が機体後部に移動し，第4ドア左を開け，外に発砲した）(RD 99/6: 138)

(25) Four months after Sputnik the United States responded with *Explorer 1*.（S［の打ち上げ］から4か月後，合衆国はE1号で応えた）(RD 99/3: 120)

(26) *Flight AF8969*, bound for Paris, was fully booked: 292 passengers were expected to board the plane.（P行きのAF8969便は満席であり，292人の乗客が搭乗する予定だった）(RD 99/6: 125)

(27) In June of 1965 *Gemini 4* flew a four-day journey, highlighted by Ed White's walk in space.（1965年6月G4号が4日間飛行し，そのハイライトはEWの宇宙遊泳だった）(RD 99/3: 123)

(28) In 1959 the Soviets launched *Luna 2*, an 860-pound projectile that became the first man-made object to hit the moon.（1959年にソ連はL2号を打ち上げた。これは，860ポンドのロケットであり，月に衝突した最初の人工物体となった）(RD 99/3: 120)

(29) As they were busy working on *patient Y*, I went to see *patient X*.（他の者たちが患者Yを忙しく治療していたので，私は患者Xを見に行った）(RD 00/2: 83)

(30) The train on *platform 1* is for London, calling at Didcot and Reading.（1番フォームの電車はL行きで，DとRに停車する）(OALD⁵)

(31) This is *Room 33*, and in here you will do your best. (ここは33教室だ。ここでみんなベストをつくすのだ) (RD 98/3: 47)

(32) Marengo County is intersected by *US Highway 80* . . . (M 郡は国道80号線と交差している) (RD 00/5: 127)

(33) Dairy products, eggs and fortified yeast extracts provide *vitamin B12*. (乳製品や卵、強化イーストエキスにはビタミンB_{12}が含まれている) (RD 99/11: 35)

(34) It was *week 18*. Normal gestation is an average of 40 weeks. (18週目だった。通常の妊娠期間は平均40週なのに) (RD 99/5: 19)

類例：Act 2; Air Force One [米大統領専用機]; Channel 4; Chapter 6; Figure 8; Grade A; Ground Zero; line 24; page 9; Psalm 77; Route 101; runway 32; Scene 3; Unit 10; World War II, etc.

ここで注意すべきは、名詞に数字あるいは記号が2つ以上つけられれば、不可算名詞の場合は単数形のままであるが、可算名詞の場合は複数形になる、ということである。

(35) The new drugs seem to work against both *influenza A and B*. (新薬はA型およびB型両方のインフルエンザに効き目があるようだ) (RD 99/2: 14)

(36) ally: a group of countries fighting on the same side in a war, esp those which fought with Britain in *World Wars I and II* (連合国 ＝ 戦争で同じ側に立って戦う一団の国、特に、第1次および第2次世界大戦で英国とともに戦った国) (OALD[5])

NB 4

1) the number 7 と number 7

標記の2表現において、number と 7 との関係は前者では同格 (appositive;「7という数」) であり後者では限定的 (attributive;「第7（番）」) である。言い換えれば、the は number のみにつくのであり、number 7 全体につくのではない。

2) 製品名

製品名が数字を含むときは不定冠詞をとる。

  i) He was taller and had *an AK-47* slung over his shoulder. (彼はもっと背が高く、自動小銃 AK 47 を肩に掛けていた) (RD 99/6: 125)

  ii) He looks up to see a silver silhouette on the horizon, *a Boeing*

747-400.（視線を上げて水平線上に銀色のシルエット，ボーイング 747-400，を見る）(RD 98/3: 73)

1.6 記号

例 (37)–(40) は，記号が独立的に用いられる場合である。無冠詞の A/'A' や B/'B' はそれぞれの字形につけられた符帳であるので，「（文字である）A/B」を表すにすぎない。これに対し，冠詞つきの an A/'A' や a B/'B' は「A/B という文字/評価」を表す。もう1歩踏み込んで言えば，冠詞をつけることによって，文字体系あるいは評価体系のなかにおける A/B の位置づけが与えられ，「アルファベット内の最初［2番目］の文字」/「成績評価の最上位［第2位］」という意味をもつのである。言い換えれば，φ A/'A' は意味をもたないので（説明は可能であっても）翻訳は不可能であるのに対し，an A/'A' は意味を有するので翻訳可能である。

(37) 'Ann' begins with *(an) A / 'A'.* (Ann は A（という文字）で始まる) (OALD[5])

(37') a. 'Ann' begins with *A*. [i.e., 'Ann' begins with letter A (or the tag A).] [文字 A]

b. 'Ann' begins with *an A*. [i.e., 'Ann' begins with the letter A (or the first letter in the alphabet).] [最初の文字]

(38) get *(an) A/'A'* in biology (生物学で A（という成績）をとる) (OALD[5])

(38') a. get *A* in biology [i.e., get grade A (or a grade called A) in biology] [評価 A]

b. get *an A* in biology [i.e., get the grade A (or the best grade) in biology] [優]

(39) get *(a) B/'B'* in English (英語で B（という成績）をとる) (OALD[5])

(40) 'Moscow' starts with *(an) M/'M'.* (Moscow は M（という文字）で始まる) (OALD[5])

無冠詞の記号は不特定のものを指すときにも用いられる。次の例文中の A/B が人間を指すことは knows という動詞から推論されることであり，A/B そのものは無意味な符号にすぎない。それゆえ，a/an は不要である。

(41) Let's assume *A* knows *B* is guilty. (甲は乙が有罪であることを知っていると仮定しよう) (OALD[5])

1.7 「擬態普通名詞」

固有名詞の最初の文字は，通例，大文字が用いられるが，小文字のまま固有

名詞として扱われていると判断される語がいくつかある。意味も表記法も普通名詞と同様であるが, 限定詞なしで用いられ, 文法的には固有名詞の働きをする名詞である。たとえば, 次のような場合である。

(42) a. Algiers *airport* is probably one of the safest in the world. (A の空港はたぶん世界で 1 番安全な空港の 1 つだ) (RD 99/6: 127)　類例：Beijing airport (RD 98/12: 62); Heathrow airport (RD 96/3: 23); Kai Tak airport (RD 96/3: 17); Kai Tak international airport (RD 97/5: 120) (☞ 8.8.2)

　　b. The villagers have reacted with alarm to news of *a* proposed new *airport*. (村人たちは新空港提案のニュースに対して不安の反応を示した) (CIDE) [普通名詞；広がりを含意するので冠詞つき (以下同様)]

　参考：At Algiers *Airport* an Air France Airbus was about to take off for Paris. (A 空港では AF のエアバスがパリに向けて離陸するところだった) (RD 99/6: 124) [大文字表記]

(43) a. "We've got an incident in the north end of *town*," the dispatcher says. (「町の北端で事故があった」と運転指示員が言う) (RD 96/3: 42)

　　b. the west/east end of *a town* (ある町の西／東の端) (OALD5)

(44) a. They'd sit in Archie's truck, parked on *main street*, on Friday nights. (金曜日の夜は, 本通り上に駐車した A のトラックによく乗り込んだ) (RD 99/5: 67)

　　b. We walked down *a* broad *street* lined with trees. (並木のある広い通りを歩いた) (CIDE)

　参考：The bank, post office, and library are all on *Main Street* in our town. (銀行や郵便局, 図書館はみなわが町では本通りぞいにある) (NHD) [大文字表記]

airport/main street は大文字で書かれることもあるが, town は小文字で書かれ, 話し手が住んでいる町を指す (*MEG*, vol. 7, 15.2$_5$ 参照)。身近な, なじみのある地名であるため固有名詞化 (= 愛称化) が進んだのである。

deck/ship も乗船中の, つまり, 最も身近な, 船およびその甲板を指すときは無冠詞で用いられる。

(45) a. When we've eaten, let's go up on *deck* and get some air. (食事をしたら, デッキに出て風に当たろう) (CIDE)

　　b. We sat on *deck* until it was dark. (暗くなるまでデッキに座っていた) (CIDE)

　　c. We were sinking fast, and the captain gave the order to abandon

ship.（急速に沈んでいたので，船長は棄船命令を出した）(CIDE)
　次の family/mama bear が無冠詞であるのも，Mother/Father など身近な親族名称の場合と同様に，固有名詞化されているためである。
- (46) a. But I occasionally took shots on compacts owned by *family* and friends, and many of them turned out very well.（ときどき家族や友人のコンパクトカメラで写真を撮ったことがあるが，多くはとてもよく写っていた）(RD 01/3: 70)
  b. During the evening I managed to hit *mama bear* about three times in the rump.（夕方，母グマのお尻を3度ほど [ゴム銃で] 撃った）(RD 99/1: 128)
  比較：*A mama bear* and her two cubs were at the corn pile.（母グマと2頭の子グマがトウモロコシの山にいた）(RD 99/1: 128)

次は，「かかりつけ」の医者を指す。
  c. *Doctor* prescribed some pills and tests, and his stomach improved.（主治医が薬と検査を指示して，彼の胃はよくなった）(RD 01/8: 30)

　Parliament/Congress（通例，大文字表記）が無冠詞で用いられるのも「自国の国会」を指すので，それぞれ，英国および米国で固有名詞化されたためである。
- (47) a. Television cameras are now being allowed into the chambers whilst *Parliament* is in session.（今では英議会会期中テレビカメラを議場に持ち込むことが許されている）(CIDE; 'U not after *the*'（*the* に後続しないときは不可算名詞 [固有名詞扱いの意]）と注記)
  b. *Congress* has rejected the president's plan.（米議会は大統領の計画案を拒否した）(CDAE)
  比較：Japanese politics in the second half of the 20th century has revolved around *the Diet*.（20世紀後半の日本の政治は国会を中心として行われた）(EB 01) [英米以外の国会は，通例，the が必要]

(43)–(47) に共通なのは，「身近」ということである。この観点から earth の無冠詞用法が説明可能となる（8章 NB 6-2 も参照）。
- (48) a. Mission control ordered the spacecraft to return to *earth*.（宇宙管制センターは宇宙船に地球への帰還を命じた）(OALD⁵)
  b. extraterrestrial: of or from outside the planet *Earth* and its atmosphere（地球外の ＝ 惑星地球およびその大気の外部に関する，あるいは外部に由来する）(OALD⁵)

(48, b) のように Earth が大文字で表記され，かつ無冠詞で用いられる場合は，

Mercury/Venus/Mars/Jupiter などと同様に，惑星として位置づけられている（強いて訳せば「地星」）。これに対し，小文字で始められる場合は，1番身近な星として扱われているのである。

ちなみに，副詞として扱われている downtown も，次のように前置詞に後続する場合には，固有名詞的であるかもしれない。

(49) The hotel is situated two miles north of *downtown*. (ホテルは中心部から北に2マイルのところにある) (CIDE)

専門用語がしばしば無冠詞で用いられるのも，符帳扱いされているためと考えられる (☞ 8.10)。

(50) Boiling will destroy most of the harmful bacteria, but not <u>the Bacillus cereus</u>, a nasty little character that causes vomiting and diarrhoea. *Bacillus* will thrive and grow in any cooked rice stored above seven degrees. (煮沸すればほとんどの有害なバクテリアを殺菌するが，Bcはそうはいかない。これは，嘔吐(おう)や下痢を引き起こすやっかいな悪玉だ。Bは7度以上で保存されていれば，ご飯の中で繁殖し成長するのである) (RD 01/4: 25) [正式な学名としては the がつけられる]

(51) a. If a patient's voice is hoarse, I may think *thyroid*. (患者の声がかすれていれば，甲状腺を考えるかもしれない) (RD 96/3: 99) [専門用語，または「(代謝調節) 機能」(☞ 3.9)]

b. Hypothyroidism (having *an* underactive *thyroid*) is surprisingly common, especially in women. (甲状腺機能減退症 (甲状腺の働きが不十分なこと) は，特に女性では，驚くほどありふれている) (RD 00/1: 27)

(52) a. As soon as we were sure it was *hantavirus*, we knew how it was spread. (ハンタウイルスだと確信すると，どのように広まったかはすぐにわかった) (RD 97/6: 140) [専門用語]

b. Finally we showed our test results to a panel of disease experts. To a man, they said, "Looks like *a hantavirus*." (ついにテスト結果を病理専門の医師団に示した。一人に彼らは言った「ハンタウイルスのようですね」) (RD 97/6: 142) [姿かたちの認識]

参考：This was a new viral family. It became known as *Marburg virus*. (これはウイルス科の新種だった。Mウイルスとして知られることになった) (RD 97/6: 124) [大文字表記；固有名詞 (符帳) 扱い]

(53) You get *(a)* 10% *commission* on everything you sell. (売るものすべてから10パーセントの手数料が入る) (OALD[5]) [無冠詞は専門用語扱い；a

つきに関しては 4.4.1.1 参照]

参考：She gets $10 commission on each sale. / He gets commission on top of his salary. (以上 OALD[5]); The dealer takes a 20% commission on the sales he makes. (LDOCE[3]) [専門的用法と一般的用法]

第2章　原理 II ——姿かたちの有無

2　原理 II ——姿かたちの有無

英語の名詞の多くは姿かたちを表すか表さないかによって冠詞の有無が決定される。このことを次のように定式化して原理 II と呼ぶことにする。

> 原理 II：英語の名詞部は，指示物の姿かたちが認識されるときは a/an（あるいは他の限定詞）をとり，認識されないときは a/an をとらない。

以下，具体的に例文を見ながら，この原理がどのように適用されるかを見ていこう。

2.1　解体と統合
2.1.1　素材と個体
2.1.1.1　食材

『新英和中辞典』（第6版，研究社）はいくつかの植物名に関して，[食べ物には [U]] あるいは [食品には [U]]（第5版では，[食べ物としては [U]]）と注記している（s.v., cabbage, carrot, cauliflower, cucumber, onion, melon, potato, pumpkin, turnip）。これらは食用植物なので，この辞書の利用者は，たとえば，cabbage が可算名詞か不可算名詞か調べようとして，「キャベツが食べ物としては不可算名詞だって？　キャベツが食べ物でない場合とはいったい何だろう？」ととまどうかもしれない。だが，次のような無冠詞用法と不定冠詞つき用法とを見れば，この説明の意味するところが理解できるであろう。

(1) a. feed the baby some more stewed *apple* (赤ん坊に煮リンゴをもっと食べさせる) (OALD[5])

　　b. Eve plucked *an apple* and offered it to Adam. (イブはリンゴをもいでアダムに与えた) (LDOCE[3])

(2) a. Decorate the dessert with sliced *banana*. (スライスしたバナナでデザートを飾りなさい) (CIDE)

　　b. Have *a banana*, Roger. (R君，バナナをどうぞ) (CIDE)

(3) a. Children never seem to like eating *cabbage*. (子供は好んでキャベツ

を食べることはなさそうだ)(CIDE)

b. I shouted throwing *a cabbage* at them. (キャベツを投げつけながら叫んだ) (BNC, ACK 1091)

(4) a. Add *carrot*, mushrooms, beans, courgettes. (ニンジン，マッシュルーム，マメ，ズッキーニを加えなさい) (CCED[3])

b. We used *a carrot* for the snowman's nose. (雪だるまの鼻にはニンジンを使った) (OALD[6])

(5) a. Boiled *cauliflower* tastes good with melted cheese on it. (ゆでたカリフラワーに溶かしたチーズをのせればおいしい) (NHD)

b. Many of us might never be able to distinguish one variety of seed from another, but we have no trouble in telling an apple from a pear, or *a cauliflower* from a cabbage. (種の変種を識別することは多くのものにはできないかもしれないが，リンゴとナシ，カリフラワーとキャベツはなんなく区別できる) (BNC, C8V 1325)

(6) a. Heat oil, add onion, salami, garlic and fresh *chilli* and cook until onion is soft. (油を熱し，タマネギ，サラミ，ガーリック，それに新鮮なチリを入れて，タマネギがやわらかくなるまで調理しなさい) (CCED) [onion も食材扱いなので無冠詞であることに注意；salami/garlic は，通例，[U]]

b. Add *a*/some *chilli* to the mixture. (混ぜあわせたものにチリを1さや／いくらか加えなさい) (CIDE)

(7) a. Be careful not to add too much ground *clove*. (粉末クローブを加えすぎないよう注意しなさい) (CIDE)

b. I like to put *a clove* or two in the sauce. (ソースにクローブを1，2個入れるのが好きだ) (CIDE)

(8) a. Anne, is there *coconut* in this sponge? (A，このスポンジケーキにはココナツが入っていますか) (CIDE)

b. I bought *a coconut* in the market. (マーケットでココナツの実を1つ買った) (CIDE)

(9) a. It tastes something like *melon*. (いくぶんメロンのような味がする) (OALD[5])

b. scoop out the inside of *a melon* (メロンの中身をすくい出す) (OALD[5])

(10) a. Though the ingredients may vary, a battuto is usually a combination of very finely chopped *onion*, garlic, carrot, celery, and

　　　 parsley and either pork fat or olive oil. (材料は異なることもあるが, ソフリットは, ふつう, 細かくみじん切りにしたタマネギ, ニンニク, ニンジン, セロリ, パセリ, およびポークの脂身またはオリーブオイルの取り合わせだ) (GME)
　　b. Chop *an onion* into pieces. (タマネギをみじん切りにしなさい) (LDOCE³)
(11) a. Ingredients including pettigrain, lemon and *bergamot orange*, together with pepper leaf, nutmeg and cinnamon contribute to this elegant fragrance. (ペティグレイン, レモン, ベルガモット・オレンジ, それにペパーの葉, ナツメグ, シナモンを含む成分がこの優雅な芳香のもとだ) (CCED³) [lemon/pepper leaf/nutmeg/cinnamon も食材扱いなので無冠詞]
　　b. Would you peel me *an orange*? (オレンジの皮をむいてください) (OALD⁵)
(12) a. We tried *peach*, peppermint, chocolate, blueberry and even cinnamon-honey. (試しに [アイスクリームに] ピーチや, ハッカ, チョコレート, ブルーベリー, はては, シナモン入り蜂蜜を加えてみた) (RD 99/9: 9) [blueberry も食材扱いなので無冠詞]
　　b. *a* blemished *peach* (いたんだ桃) (OALD⁵)
(13) a. "Sure, you can put *pineapple* on your pizza if you want to," says Antonio Pace with a shudder. "But it's not Neapolitan pizza." (AP は身を震わせながら言う, 「もちろん, ピザにパイナップルを入れたければ入れてもかまいません。でも, それはナポリタンピザではありません」) (RD 99/2: 94)
　　b. If you use *a* whole *pineapple*, increase the other ingredients in proportion. (パイナップルをまる1つ使うのなら, それに応じて他の材料も増やしなさい) (LDOCE³)
(14) a. Centuries ago pizza was a circle of baked dough without *tomato* and often eaten in the morning. (数世紀前ピザは, トマトを入れないで, パン生地を丸形に焼いたものであり, しばしば午前中に食べられた) (RD 99/2: 94)
　　b. I sliced up *a tomato* for my salad. (サラダ用にトマトを薄切りにした) (NTC)

NB 1 mashed potato(es)/grated carrot(s)

次のように単複両形が可能な場合もある。(ただし,〈米〉用法では無冠詞の単数用法はまれ。すなわち, a scrambled egg; scrambled eggs は可であるが, φ scrambled egg は不可 ; cf. OALD⁶ (s.v., potato): '(BrE) mashed potato, (AmE) mashed potatoes')

grated carrot (OALD⁵) / grated carrots (CIDE); a dish of meat topped with mashed potato (OALD⁵) / mashed potatoes, turnips, etc (OALD⁵); Take a slice of bread and dip it in beaten egg. (CIDE) / mix in beaten eggs; eat scrambled egg for breakfast (OALD⁵) / We sat in a booth and ate scrambled eggs and bacon. (RD 97/5: 144)

小さくきざまれて姿かたちが失われるにもかかわらず複数形をとることもある。

Finish by sprinkling some chopped *almonds* over the cake. (仕上げにきざみアーモンドをケーキにふりかけなさい) (CIDE)

上のような例文中で複数形が用いられるのは, きざまれたり混ぜられたりしたのは複数個のニンジンや卵であったことを明示的に表すためである。個別性が失われる以前にさかのぼって数を表しているので,「加工前の複数」と呼んでもよい用法である。

(1)-(14) の例からわかるように, 食用の植物を表す名詞の多くは,「食材」としては無冠詞であり, 本来の姿かたちを保っているときは [C] である。このことは動物とその肉に関しても同様である。

(15) a. We had fried *chicken* for dinner. (ディナーにトリの唐揚げを食べた) (NHD)

b. *A* male *chicken* is called a cock and *a* female *chicken* is called a hen. (オスの鶏はおんどりと呼ばれ, メスの鶏はめんどりと呼ばれる) (CIDE)

(16) a. We ate *crab* (or) crab meat. (カニ/カニ肉を食べた) (NHD)

b. *A crab* moves sideways. (カニは横に動く) (OALD⁵)

(17) a. We usually have *fish* for dinner on Friday. (金曜日にはたいてい夕食に魚を食べる) (CIDE)

b. An expert angler was casting his line and catching *a fish* every time. (ベテランの釣り人は釣り糸を投げ込み, そのたびに魚を釣っていた) (CCED³)

(18) a. John ordered *halibut* for dinner. (J はディナーにハリバットを注文した) (NTC)
　　 b. *A halibut* is a large flat fish. (ハリバットは平べったい大きな魚だ) (CCED³)
(19) a. I chose *lamb* for the meat course. (肉料理にラムを選んだ) (CIDE)
　　 b. The hyenas would sneak up and snatch *a lamb* or kid that had wandered off. (ハイエナは，はぐれた子ひつじや子やぎに忍び寄ってかっさらう) (RD 99/10: 124)
(20) a. We had *lobster* for dinner. (ディナーにロブスターを食べた) (CDAE)
　　 b. crayfish: an animal like *a* small *lobster* that lives in rivers and lakes (ザリガニ＝ロブスターを小さくしたような動物。川や湖に生息する) (OALD⁵)
(21) a. *Octopus* is eaten in many parts of the world. (タコは世界じゅうの多くの地域で食用とされている) (NHD)
　　 b. My little daughter was telling me that her teacher had read the class a story about *an octopus*. (娘は，先生がタコのお話をクラスのものに読んでくれたことを話していたところだった) (CCED³)
(22) a. I like to eat grilled *salmon* with potatoes. (焼いたサーモンにポテトを添えて食べるのが好きだ) (NHD)
　　 b. but somebody had hauled *a* very good *salmon* out of the Spey... (だれかが S 川でとても立派なサケを釣り上げた) (ConCD-ROM)
(23) a. Have you ever eaten smoked *trout*? (燻製(くんせい)にしたマスを食べたことがありますか) (CIDE)
　　 b. Last time we went fishing I caught *a* huge *trout*. (前回釣りに行ったとき大きなマスを釣った) (LDOCE³)

2.1.1.2　素材・構成物

上のような名詞の無冠詞用法は「食材」にとどまらない。本質的なのは，動植物などが本来の姿かたちを保ち，個体として認識されるときは a/an（または他の限定詞）をとり，何かの「素材」として用いられ，姿かたちが認識不可能（あるいは不要）なときは a/an をとらない，ということである。このことは以下の例によって実証される。

(24) a. Baseball bats are made from *ash*. (野球用バットはトネリコから作られる) (NHD)
　　 b. The cuckoo was perched amongst the upper branches of *a* tall *ash*. (カッコウはトネリコの高木の高枝のあいだに止まっていた) (CIDE)

(25) a. Their linen chest was made from sweet smelling *cedar*. (リンネル収納箱は芳香のするスギで作られていた) (CIDE)

b. *A cedar* is a large ever-green tree with wide branches and small leaves shaped like needles. (スギは大きな常緑樹で，枝は広がり，葉は小さく針のような形をしている) (CCED[3])

(26) a. [T]he wooden boards upon which images were painted were at first in *oak* or pitch pine. In the eighteenth century beech, pearwood and mahogany were alternatives. (像が描かれた木製のボードは当初はオークまたはヤニマツだった。18世紀にはブナ，ナシ，マホガニーが代用された) (Brown) [pitch pine ほかも素材を表すので無冠詞]

b. Here *a* giant *oak* stood. (ここにはオークの大木があった) (Brown)

(27) a. This drill can bore through *rock*. (このドリルは岩をくりぬくことができる) (OALD[5])

b. The ship struck *a rock*. (船は岩礁に乗り上げた) (OALD[5])

参考： They drilled through several layers of *rock* to reach the oil. (幾層もの岩をくりぬいて油に達した) (OALD[5]) [layers を構成する「素材」を表すので無冠詞 (☞ 2.1.2)]

(28) a. The statue was carved out of *stone*. (その像は石を彫ったものだった) (OALD[5])

b. She threw *a stone* into the pond and watched the ripples spread. (池に石を投げ込んでさざ波が広がるのを見た) (OALD[5])

(29) a. They converted vacant lots into a big courtyard inlaid with *tile*. (空き地を，タイルをちりばめた大きな中庭へと変えた) (RD 98/6: 107)

b. If you've seen *a tile*, pick it up straight away and come back. (タイルを見つけたら，ただちに拾って戻りなさい) (BNC, H0R 1124)

(30) a. A fire can bring down a building of *brick* and timber after just 20 minutes. (火事になれば木造レンガの建物はわずか20分で崩れ落ちてしまう) (RD 98/7: 28)

b. Someone had thrown *a brick* through the shop window. (だれかが店の窓からレンガを投げた) (CIDE)

次の諸例では，辞書には [U] 表示はないけれども，指示物の姿かたちが個体として認識されていないので冠詞は不要である。

(31) *Alligator* tastes like *chicken*. But I like *wild boar* best. (アリゲータの肉は鶏肉のような味だが，1番好きなのはしし肉だ)

(32) There was *cat* all over the road. (道路いっぱいにネコが [つぶれて] 散乱していた) (Chen, *A Study of the Article System in English*, p. 38)

(33) Emmy finds squashed *spider* more nauseous than the thing alive. (E は生きているのよりつぶれたクモのほうがもっといやだ) (Allen, "Nouns and Countability") [Chen]

(34) the face of another seemed to consist entirely of *nose* (もう 1 人の [小人の] 顔は，全く鼻だけで出来ているように思われた) (Irving, *Rip Van Winkle*)

今や容易に推測できるように，次例中の冠詞の有無は意味の相違を反映しているのである。

(35) a. a squeeze of *lemon* (juice) (レモン果汁少量) (OALD[5])
   b. squeeze the juice out of *a lemon* (レモンをしぼって果汁をとる) (OALD[5])

(36) a. I ordered pork *loin* for dinner. (ディナーにポークロインを注文した) (NTC) [料理されて出るのは豚の腰肉の一部]
   b. Mary roasted *a loin* of beef in the oven. (M はオーブンで牛のロインを焼いた) (NTC) [焼いたのはひと塊としての腰肉]

(37) a. Today millions of people eat *roast turkey* [i.e., slices of the turkey's meat] on December 25. (今日では何百万人もの人が 12 月 25 日にローストターキーを食べる) (RD 98/12: 54) [通例，スライスされた肉片]
   b. Traditionally, many North Americans have *a roast turkey* [i.e., an entire turkey] for Thanksgiving dinner. (伝統的に，多くの北アメリカの人々は感謝祭のごちそうに七面鳥の丸焼きを食べる) (NHD) [姿かたちを認識可能]

2.1.1.3 におい

動植物などを表す名詞がその「におい」を表すときも，姿かたちは認識されないので，無冠詞で用いられる。

(38) Caracas, Venezuela, is clammy and smells of old *dog*. (V の C は，じめじめしていて老犬のようなにおいがする) (RD 98/9: 56)

(39) The Silverback has an odour like *skunk* and vinegar, only very faint. (S は，非常にかすかではあるが，スカンクや酢のようなにおいがする) (RD 00/6: 43) [S はゴリラの名前；普通名詞の意味を残しているので the をとる (☞ 8 章 NB 18-1)]

(40) When I smell bourbon, all I can smell is bourbon. It could have vanilla, chocolate or *strawberry* in it for all I know. (私がバーボンを嗅

げば，バーボンの香りがするだけだ。私にはわからないが，バニラ，チョコレート，ストロベリーも含まれているのかもしれない）(RD 99/10: 117)

(41) and sniffing *banana, green apple* or *peppermint* could help people lose weight. (バナナや青リンゴ，ペパーミントの匂いを嗅ぐのも減量の助けになる) (RD 98/3: 119)

2.1.1.4 音

(42)–(43)で斜字体の名詞が無冠詞であるのは，姿かたちのない「音」を表すためである。(drum が複数形であるのは複数のドラムから発せられる音であることを表す（☞ 本章 NB 1 [加工前の複数]）；無冠詞の楽器名に関しては 3.5; 8.6.2 も参照）。)

(42) a. At first just two women waltz uninhibitedly to drums, *flute,* banjo and accordion. (最初は女性 2 人だけがドラムやフルート，バンジョー，アコーディオン [の音色] にあわせて奔放にワルツを踊る) (RD 99/9: 32) [banjo/accordion も音色を表すので無冠詞]

　b. *A flute* is played by blowing over one hole near the end and covering and uncovering other holes along the pipe with one's fingers. (フルートの演奏は，管頭の 1 つの歌口を吹き，管の側口を指で塞いだり空けたりすることによる) (NTC)

(43) a. The sounds of *tango* filled the air. (タンゴの音が空中に満ちていた) (CCED³)

　b. And when she played – always *a tango* – she seemed transported to another world . . . (演奏するときは――いつもタンゴの曲だった――彼女は別世界に移動するかのようだった) (RD 99/9: 60) (8章 NB 13 参照)

2.1.1.5 毛皮

動物の毛皮を指すときも，姿かたちは認識されないので，冠詞は不要である。

(44) My tsarer was made from thick black fabric in the shape of a long coat, trimmed with *snow leopard*. (私のツァレル [一種のローブ；チベットの民族衣装] は黒い厚めの生地で作られ，長いコートの形をしていて，ユキヒョウ [の毛皮] の飾りがつけられていた) (RD 01/9: 123)

(45) Artificial fur is increasingly replacing natural furs such as *mink* and *fox*. (人造の毛皮がミンクやキツネといった天然ものの毛皮にますます取って代わってきている) (CIDE)

NB 2

1) a mink/horn — φ mink/horn — a mink/horn

mink は動物を指すときは [C] であり、その毛皮を指すときは [U]、毛皮製品を指すときは [C] である（織田 1982: 4f.; 2002: 12)。同様に、horn も、「角」(つの) を指すときは [C]、角が素材として用いられれば [U]、角で作られた製品を指すときは [C] である。

 i) unicorn: an imaginary animal like a white horse with *a* long straight *horn* growing on its head （一角獣 = 想像上の動物。白馬に似る。長いまっすぐな角が頭にある）(LDOCE[3])

 ii) The decorative buttons were made of *horn*. （装飾用ボタンは角製だった）(NTC)

 iii) The piercing sound of *a* hunting *horn* reverberated through the forest. （狩猟用角笛の鋭い音が森じゅうに響いた）(OALD[5])

2) いくつかの語では素材と個体とが分化している。

 iv) a. Bolognaise sauce consists of minced *beef*, onion, tomatoes, garlic and seasoning. （ボロネーズソースは細かく切った牛肉、タマネギ、トマト、ニンニクおよび調味料でできている）(LDOCE[3])

  b. beef: the meat from *a cow* （beef ＝ 牛の肉）(LDOCE[3])

 参考：I've ordered *a* steak. （ステーキを注文した）(OALD[5]) [cow/bull/ox（個体）— beef（素材）— steak（製品／物質）]

 v) a. Muslims do not eat *pork*. （イスラム教徒は豚肉を食べない）(OALD[5])

  b. pork: the flesh of *a pig* eaten as food （pork ＝ 食料として食べられる豚の肉）(OALD[5])

これらのほか venison/deer; mutton/sheep; ivory/tusk も同様である。

2.1.2　タイプ：NP$_1$ of NP$_2$

姿かたちの有無という基準を取り入れるならば、a slice of φ lemon, a piece of φ cake, a dish of φ pudding, a kind/sort/type of φ house のような慣用的な無冠詞用法が説明可能となる。なぜなら、"NP$_1$ of NP$_2$" という構文において NP$_2$ は個別性を失い NP$_1$ の素材（あるいは、構成物）として扱われているからである。(46, a) の gown は scraps の「素材」として扱われているので無冠詞であり、(46, b) の gown はガウン全体を指し「個体」として捉えられているので不定冠詞つきである。

(46) a. The butterflies shimmer like scraps of ball *gown*. (蝶は舞踏会のドレスの切れ端のようにきらきら輝く) (RD 98/9: 59)

　　b. By 10 a.m. the heat, which began as a sheen on the skin, clings to you like *a* wet dressing *gown*. (暑さのため，初めは肌で [汗で] きらきらしていたが，午前 10 時には濡れたガウンが体に張りつくかのようだ) (RD 98/9: 59)

類例をあげよう．

(47) a. He cut himself a great thick slice of *cake*. (自分用にケーキを分厚く切った) (OALD⁵)

　　b. I'm baking Alex *a* birthday *cake*/baking *a* birthday *cake* for Alex. (A に誕生ケーキを焼いているところだ) (OALD⁵) [まるごとのケーキ 1 個]

(48) a. She cut up some bits of old *carpet* for the children's playhouse. (子供のおもちゃのおうち用に古いカーペットを数切れ切った) (CCED³)

　　b. We've just had *a* new *carpet* fitted/laid in our bedroom. (新しいカーペットを寝室に敷いたばかりだ) (CCED³)

(49) a. Bumboret, a valley nearly hidden in a cleave [sic; cleavage ?] cut by a glacial river, is between two steep mountains lined with dense stands of *cedar* and holly-oak. (B は，氷河の川によって切りとられた裂け目の中にほとんど隠れた谷間であり，2 つの険しい山のあいだにある．山にはスギとトキワガシとの鬱蒼(うっそう)とした樹木群が筋状に植えられている) (RD 00/4: 104) [holly-oak も stands の素材]

　　b. The soaring grey-blue of *a* magnificent Atlantic *cedar* took his eye. (壮大なタイセイヨウスギの上空に伸びゆく灰青色が彼の目を引いた) (ConCD-ROM)

(50) a. Ellis now understood their deadly predicament. Their rope was pulled taut over a fulcrum of icy *glacier*. (今や E は彼らが絶体絶命の窮地にあることがわかった．彼らのロープは氷河をテコとして [両側に] ピンと張っているのだ) (RD 00/1: 55)

　　b. The ten-mile, six-hour hike would take them up the mountain and across *a glacier* to the lodge. (10 マイル，6 時間歩けば，山を登り，氷河を横切って，山小屋に着くだろう) (RD 97/5: 31)

(51) a. The experience left me with a feeling of deep *hurt*. (その経験は私に深く傷ついたという感情を残した) (OALD⁵)

　　b. There would be *a hurt* in her heart for a while, but in the end she would get over it. (彼女の心にはしばらく傷が残るだろうが，最終的には乗り越えるだろう) (CCED[3])

(52) a. A bungalow is/Bungalows are a type of *house*. (バンガローは1種の家だ) (OALD[5])

　b. They changed the little cottage into *a* splendid *house*. (小屋を豪邸に変えた) (OALD[5])

(53) a. Would you like a slice of *lemon* in your tea? (紅茶にレモンを1切れいかがですか) (CIDE)

　類例：What's in this drink?　It's got a tang of *lemon*. (この飲み物には何が入っているのか。レモンの香り[味]がする) (CIDE)

　b. *A lemon* is an acid fruit. (レモンは酸っぱい果実だ) (OALD[5])

(54) a. The old man wore an eyeglass attached to a piece of *ribbon*. (老人はリボンにつけられた単眼鏡をかけていた) (OALD[5])

　b. Her hair was tied back with *a* black *ribbon*. (彼女の髪は後ろで黒いリボンで結わえられていた) (OALD[5]) [4.1 も参照]

(55) a. The police often clock motorists on this stretch of *road*. (この道路区間では警察がよく速度検査をしている) (OALD[5])

　b. If you're walking along *a* badly-lit *road* at night you should wear conspicuous clothes. (夜間に照明の悪い道路を歩くのなら，目立つ服装をすべきだ) (OALD[5])

上の例ほど顕著ではないが，ascent/beach/coast などは可算名詞でも用いられることを考えれば，(56–60, a) 中の ascent など斜字体の名詞も「素材」扱いである。

(56) a. Every few hundred feet of *ascent* offers a fresh vista. (数百フィート登るごとに新たな眺望が開ける) (RD 96/10: 13)

　b. Three decades later, in 1888, British zoologist John Whitehead made *a* full *ascent*. (30年後の1888年に英国の動物学者 JW が完全に登頂した) (RD 98/6: 78)

(57) a. Our final camp is on a small crescent of *beach* just above kilometre 380. (最後の基地は380キロ地点を少し過ぎたところの小さな三日月型の砂浜にある) (RD 00/2: 59)　類例：an expanse of pristine white beach (汚れなき白い浜辺の広がり) (RD 00/2: 116)

　b. Lying on *a beach* doing nothing begins to pall after a while. (何もしないで浜辺に寝そべっているのもしばらくすると飽きてくる) (OALD[5])

(58) a. A scrap of *coast* near Marseille was in sight, with a layer of flat cloud blanketing the country-side 12,000 feet directly below. (M 近くの海岸の 1 端が視界に入った。平らな雲の層が 12,000 フィート真下の田園地帯をおおっていた) (RD 98/10: 37)

b. This is *an* artificial *coast* with a natural hinterland. (人口海岸ではあるが，天然の内陸地がつづいている) (ConCD-ROM)

(59) a. In case of *emergency*, break the glass and press the button. (緊急時にはガラスを割ってボタンを押してください) (OALD[5])

b. There is no fire department or firetruck in Ambler, only a few coils of hose and a large chemical extinguisher. In *an emergency* people must depend on their neighbors and themselves. (A には消防署も消防車もない。ホース数本と大型の化学消火器があるだけだ。緊急時に頼りとするのは隣人と自分だ) (RD 97/5: 104)

(60) a. Anemia can be a sign of serious *illness*, such as kidney failure or colon cancer, and pills won't solve the problem. (貧血は腎不全とか結腸ガンといった大病のしるしであることがあるので，ピルは問題解決にはならない) (RD 96/3: 100)

b. One day when he was ten years old, Mark Fletcher's mother had to go to the hospital for *a* serious *illness*. (彼が 10 歳のある日，MF の母は大病のため病院に行かなければならなかった) (RD 98/3: 67)

次の 2 例で automobile; basset hound, Labrador が無冠詞であるのは，これらが新型車および雑種犬を構成する「素材」として提示されているためである。

(61) a. The Prius and Insight are the first of a new breed of *automobile*, the petrol-electric "hybrid." (P と I とは自動車の新種，ガソリンと電気の「交配種」，の第 1 号だ) (RD 02/2: 102)

b. *An automobile* is a car; used especially in American English. (自動車とは車のことであり，特にアメリカ英語で用いられる) (ConCD-ROM)

(62) Picture a ten-month-old cross of copper-coloured *basset hound* and *Labrador*. His face, ears and body said *Labrador* – more or less. His legs were unadulterated *basset*. A "basslab" was what he was. (生後 10 か月の，銅色のバセットハウンドとラブラドールとの掛け合わせを想像してごらんなさい。顔，耳，胴体は，多かれ少なかれ，ラブラドールであることを表していた。足は純粋なバセットだった。「バスラ

ブ」というのが彼の姿だったのだ) (RD 01/6: 86) [3 章 NB 2 の例 ii) と比較せよ]

比較：One was Elizabeth, who had *a Labrador* named Kiri.（1 人は E であり，K という名前のラブラドール犬を飼っていた）(RD 01/6: 88) [個体]

　次例中の standard orthography の冠詞の有無は先行する語を考慮することによってのみ説明可能である。すなわち，a form of NP では NP は form の素材であるが，the beginnings of NP では，主語－述語関係があるので，NP は素材にはならないからである。

(63) a. Less than a decade later, the scribes of the Royal Chancery in Westminster began to send out official documents in English nation-wide, thus providing a form of *standard orthography* which could, and to a large extent did, become a model for imitation throughout the kingdom.（10 年もしないうちに，W の王立公文書館の書記たちは英語で書かれた公文書を全土に送るようになり，標準的書記法の形式を提供することになった。それは国土全体で模倣されるモデルになりうるものであり，事実，かなりの程度そうなったのだった）(*CHEL*, III, p. 15)

b. When William Caxton set up the first printing-press in England in 1476, there was no generally recognised standard form of English speech, and only the beginnings of *a standard orthography*.（1476 年にカクストンが英国で最初の印刷所を設立したとき，英語に関する広く認められた標準的形式はなく，初期段階の標準的書記法があるのみだった）(*CHEL*, III, p. 15)

NB 3　NP of NPs

"NP_1 of NP_2" の構文中でも NP_1 が集合体を表し，かつ NP_2 の名詞に個別性が認められるときは複数形をとる（*MEG*, vol. 7, 12.6_{10} も参照）。

a flock of *birds*（鳥の群）; a herd of *goats*（ヤギの群）; a pack of *hounds*（一群の猟犬）; a string of *pearls*（真珠の首飾り）

次例のように be composed of につづく場合も同様である。

Stonehenge is composed of about 80 massive standing *stones*, each weighing 20 to 50 tonnes.（ストーンヘンジはおよそ 80 個の直立巨石から成り，それぞれの重さは 20〜50 トンである）(CIDE)

素材という考えをもう1歩押し進めるならば，a man of ability/importance のようなパタン中の "of + NP" が無冠詞であることの理由が説明可能となる。このパタンでは of-phrase が先行する名詞を構成する素材とみなされているため冠詞は不要なのである。

(64) a. We don't want Einstein, just someone of average *ability*. (E は望まない。ただの平均的な才能の人でいい) (CIDE)

b. But she has *an* uncanny *ability* to win over gifted professionals willing to take up the cause. (彼女には，主張を積極的に支持してくれる有能な専門家を味方にするという不思議な才能がある) (RD 99/6: 21) [形容詞および不定詞による限定 (☞ 4.4.5)]

(65) a. He is a man of fierce/ruthless *determination*. (断固とした／非情な決断力の男だ) (CIDE)

b. She conveyed in her demeanour *a* steely, defiant *determination*. (行動で断固とした，反抗的な決意を示した) (RD 00/3: 131)

(66) a. This is an issue of great *importance* to all disabled people. (これはすべての障害者にとって非常に重要な問題だ) (LDOCE³)

b. Later in the following year, he had another experience which was to take on as great *an importance* in his personal mythology as his beating by Miss Long. (翌年の後半，彼は別の経験をしたが，それは彼の個人的神話において L による敗北に劣らず大きな重要性をもつことになるものだった) (ConCD-ROM)

(67) a. A secret foe of the Soviet system . . . , he had provided the United States with information of enormous *value*. (ソ連の体制に対し秘密の敵として彼は莫大な価値のある情報を合衆国に提供した) (RD 99/1: 104)

b. Ronnie put *a* high *value* on his appearance. (R は彼の外観を高く評価した) (CCED³)

of-phrase 内に名詞が2つ含まれることもある。

(68) He is very quick-thinking and very much a man of *decision* and *action*. (頭の回転が速く決断力と行動力のある男だ) (CCED³)

NB 4

1) 次の例では of an excessive thinness は形容詞的に a tall man を修飾するにもかかわらず不定冠詞がつけられている。これは，thinness が excessive に修飾されることに加えて，of . . . thinness が

a tall man から離れているので，素材という概念が弱められているためである．事実，long-bearded ... がなければ，ii) のように，an が落とされる．

　i) On the little plateau which crowned the barren hill there stood a single giant boulder, and against this boulder there lay a tall man, long-bearded and hard-featured, but of *an* excessive *thinness*. (禿山の天辺をなすその小さな平地に 1 個の巨岩があり，この巨岩に寄りかかって 1 人の背の高い，長い顎ひげを蓄えたいかつい顔の，極度にやせこけた男が身を横たえていた) (Doyle, *Study in Scarlet*)

　ii) On the little plateau there stood a single giant boulder, and against this boulder there lay a tall man of φ excessive *thinness*.

2) 同義的でも of 以外の前置詞に後続するときは NP₂ は素材扱いされないので，冠詞が必要とされる．

　iii) The members of the committee described Gates as a man of keen *intellect*. (委員会のメンバーたちは G のことを鋭い知性の男だと言った) (CCED³)

　iv) a woman with *a* keen *intellect* and exceptional qualities of leadership (鋭い知性と類いまれな指導力をそなえた女性) (OALD⁵)

素材を表す "of＋NP" が be 動詞に後続するときも同様である．たとえば，先にあげた (66–67) 中の *of*-phrase が補語の位置に現れるときも次のように無冠詞で用いられる．

(66) c. The building is of historical *importance*. (その建物は歴史的に重要だ) (OALD⁶)

(67) c. Rain forests support half the world's species, whose medical importance is of inestimable *value*. (雨林は世界の種の半分を支えており，それらの医学的重要性は計り知れないほど価値がある) (CIDE)

(69) a. He was of noble *countenance*. (気品の高い顔つきだった) (CIDE)

　b. He met each inquiry with *an* impassive *countenance*. (どの問い合わせにも無表情な反応が返った) (CCED³)

2.1.3　タイプ：birds of a feather

"NP₁ of NP₂" との関連において，次例のような表現に言及しておきたい。

(70) a. Birds of *a feather* flock together. (類は友を呼ぶ) [諺]
　　 b. Two of *a trade* can never agree. (同業者同士は意見が一致することはない) [諺]
　　 c. They're both of *a size*. (両者ともほぼ同じ大きさだ) (OALD⁵)

これらの例においては，a は「同じ」を意味すると言われる。だが，大事なのは，"Ns of a N" という脈絡における a/an の意味は決して例外的な意味ではないということである。なぜなら，この文脈でも，不定冠詞は後続の名詞部の姿かたちを示すという本来の働きを果たしているにすぎず，複数の事物の姿かたちが示されれば「同一の」姿かたちを表すことになるからである。もしも (70, a) が無冠詞ならば「羽でできた鳥」という意味になる (a building of brick (レンガ造りの建物) と同様である)。

2.2　ジャンルと作品

これまで姿かたちが認識されるか否かという観点から，無冠詞用法と不定冠詞つき用法とを見てきた。この基準によって説明可能な別の語類をさらに見ておきたい。文学および修辞学関係の用語は無形のジャンルや修辞法を指すときは無冠詞であり，当該のジャンルもしくは修辞法の具現としての有形の作品あるいは表現を指すときは [C] である。

(71) a. The play can be read as *allegory*. (その戯曲はアレゴリーとして読むことが可能である) (CIDE)
　　 b. Saint Augustine's 'City of God' is *an allegory* of the triumph of Good over Evil. (聖アウグスティヌスの『神の国』は善が悪に勝利することのアレゴリー作品である) (CIDE)

(72) a. She specialized in nineteenth century *autobiography*. (19世紀の自伝文学を専攻した) (CIDE)
　　 b. His novel is *a* thinly disguised *autobiography*. (彼の小説はわずかに脚色されただけの自伝だ) (OALD⁵)

(73) a. Do you prefer *biography* or fiction? (伝記が好きですか，それともフィクションですか) (CIDE)
　　 b. He wrote *a biography* of Lincoln. (Lの伝記を書いた) (CDAE)

(74) a. Does the study of history require an emphasis on *chronology*, a clear sense of the sequence of events in time? (歴史の研究は年代順の重視，つまり，出来事の時間的連続に関する明確な感覚，を要求するか)

第 2 章　原理 II ——姿かたちの有無　43

(CIDE)

b. According to *a chronology* later released by the Cuny family, the group was detained by masked gunmen outside a small Chechen town on April 4. (C 家がのちに公開した年代記によると，一団は 4 月 4 日覆面をして銃をもった男たちにより Ch の小さな町のはずれに監禁されていたのだった) (RD 98/10: 74)

(75) a. I prefer *comedy* to tragedy. (悲劇より喜劇のほうが好きだ) (OALD⁵)

b. They're filming *a* new *comedy*. (新しい喜劇作品を撮影中だ) (OALD⁵)

(76) a. She studied English and *drama* at college. (大学で英語と演劇を専攻した) (CIDE)

b. Our theater group is producing *a drama* by Shakespeare. (演劇グループは Sh の戯曲作品を演出中だ) (NHD)

(77) a. The article made so much use of *euphemism* that often its meaning was unclear. (その記事には婉曲語法が多用されているのでしばしば意味不明だった) (CIDE)

b. 'Pass away' is *a euphemism* for 'die'. (「亡くなる」は「死ぬ」の婉曲表現だ) (OALD⁵, LDOCE³)

(78) a. Take them each month, and you'll strengthen your immune system against awkward *expression*, boost your fitness for correct speech and develop a healthier, more robust vocabulary. (毎月 [語彙のビタミンを] 摂れば，ぎこちない表現 (法) に対する免疫系統を強化し，正しいことばづかいへの体力を高め，より健康的で，より逞 (たくま) しい語彙を築くことになる) (RD 99/10: 7) [方法・様式]

b. When you tell s.o. to "break a leg," it is just *an expression* meaning "good luck." (だれかに「足を折れ」(break a leg) と言えば，それは単に「成功を祈る」という意味の表現だ) (NHD) [文言・語句]

(78) a. The plot often borders on *farce*. (そのプロットはしばしば笑劇まがいだ) (CCED³)

b. After writing light romantic comedies, I decided to write *a farce*. (軽いロマンティックコメディを書いたあと，笑劇を書くことに決めた) (NTC)

(80) a. It's a shame that the later chapters of the book degenerate into *hagiography*. (その本の後半の章が聖人伝に堕しているのは残念だ) (CIDE)

b. This latest book about the queen is more than just *another hagiography.*（女王に関するこの最新書は単なる聖人伝以上だ）(CIDE)

(81) a. I have come to see the pygmies before their way of life passes into *history.*（彼らの生活様式が歴史にならないうちにピグミーを観察に来たのだ）(RD 98/12: 106)

　　b. writing *a* new *history* of Europe（ヨーロッパに関する新しい歴史書を執筆中）(OALD⁵)

(82) a. Although he's not given to *hyperbole*, Ron says we are light-years ahead of our time.（Rは誇張しがちではないが、彼が言うには、我々は数光年時代に先んじているとのことだ）(CDAE)

　　b. *A hyperbole* such as "It made my blood boil" constitutes a violation, in some degree, of the Maxim of Quality, and a litotes such as "I wasn't born yesterday" constitutes in some degree a violation of the Maxim of Quantity.（「血が煮えるほど私を怒らせた」のような誇張表現はある程度質の原則違反であり、「昨日やそこら生まれたのではない」のような緩叙（かんじょ）表現はある程度量の原則違反である）(Leech, *Principles of Pragmatics,* p. 145) [litotes も「作品」扱い]

(83) a. Cleopatra seduced Mark Antony amid heaps of rose petals, *legend* says.（伝説の伝えるところでは、Cはバラの花びらに囲まれた中でAを誘惑した）(RD 98/3: 119) [伝説というジャンル]

　　b. What should *a legend* contain? Should it be of happiness or of dispute?（伝説は何を含むべきか。幸せに関するべきか、言い争いに関するべきか）(ConCD-ROM) [具体的作品]

　　c. According to *family legend*, Long Wolf joined his nation's tribes camped along the banks of the Little Bighorn River.（部族の伝承によれば、LWはLB川の土手に野営していた部族連合隊に加わった）(RD 98/12: 90) [口承文芸の1ジャンル]

　　d. The incident has since become *a family legend.*（その出来事はそれ以後家族の語りぐさになった）(CCED³) [具体的な顛末（てんまつ）・表現等を含意]

(84) a. *Metaphor* and simile are the most commonly used figures of speech in everyday language.（隠喩法と直喩法は日常言語で最もよく用いられる比喩的表現だ）(CIDE)

　　b. The sporting term 'being on the inside track' is used in business as *a metaphor* to mean 'having an advantage'.（スポーツ用語の「インコー

スにいる」は商取引では「有利な立場にいる」の隠喩表現として使われる) (CIDE)

(85) a. *Rhyme* is just one of the elements of his poetry. (脚韻法は彼の詩の1要素にすぎない) (LDOCE³)
b. Time is *a rhyme* for lime. (time は lime の脚韻語だ) (NTC)
c. "Rhyme" and "time" form *a rhyme*. (rhyme と time とは脚韻 [カプレット] を形成する) (NHD)

(86) a. Since taking up writing *romance* in 1967 she has brought out over fifty books. (1967年に恋愛小説を書きはじめて以来, 50冊以上を創作した) (CCED³)
b. This movie is *a* beautiful *romance* about two college students. (この映画は2人の大学生に関する美しい恋愛物語だ) (NTC)

(87) a. With typical *understatement*, Streep refers to herself as "an actress who goes home to her family when I'm finished working." (いかにも彼女らしい控えめな口ぶりで S は自分のことを「仕事が済めば家族のもとに帰宅する女優」と言う) (RD 00/2: 105)
b. It ["We have a slight problem"] was *a* massive *understatement*. (それははなはだしく控えめな表現だった) (RD 97/2: 130)

    NB 5   φ fiction / a novel
    類義語であるが, fiction は不定冠詞をとらず, novel は不定冠詞をとる。
    i) This scenario is not science *fiction*. (このシナリオは SF 小説ではない) (RD 99/2: 50)
    ii) She wrote *a novel* about the Civil War. (南北戦争に関する小説を書いた) (NHD)

chorus/opera/song の無冠詞用法もジャンルを表すととれば納得できるであろう。

(88) a. "Yes," we replied in *chorus*. (「そのとおり」と一斉に答えた) (RD 99/7: 49)
b. *A chorus* of disapproval greeted my suggestion. (提案には反対の大合唱が返ってきた) (CIDE)
(89) a. She's a natural athlete; I love *opera* and ballet. (彼女は生まれつきの運動家だが, 私はオペラとバレエが好きだ) (RD 98/3: 37)

b. *a* one-act *opera* about contemporary women in America（米現代女性に関する1幕のオペラ）(CCED³)

(90) a. Inspired by their success, Jandu holds up a carcass and bursts into excited *song*, immediately joined by the other women.（彼らの成功に高揚して，Jはしとめた獲物をもち上げ，興奮して歌い出す。すぐに他の女たちも加わる）(RD 98/12: 108)

b. They ended the play with *a song*.（歌で芝居を締めくくった）(OALD⁵)

    NB 6 a chorus of NP

    chorus が「作品」になるのは *of*-phrase により限定されるときだけである。別例：

    i) They burst into *a chorus* of Happy Birthday.（突然ハッピーバースデイの合唱を始めた）(CIDE)

    次例は「合唱団」という別語義であり，「ジャンルと作品」という区別は当てはまらない。

    ii) She sang in *a chorus*.（彼女は合唱隊で歌った）

「ジャンルと作品」という区別に従えば，prayer の用法も説明可能である。なぜなら，prayer が不定冠詞をとらない場合は行為としての「祈り」を表し，不定冠詞をとる場合は表現としての「祈りのことば」を表すからである。

(91) a. "Does *prayer* really work?" he asks. "Would it really get us out of here?"（彼は尋ねた。「お祈りは本当に効くの？　お祈りで本当にここから出られるの？」）(RD 98/10: 81)

b. I'm not sure anything I said would qualify as *a prayer*.（私の言ったことが多少なりとも祈りのことばに値するのか確信はない）(RD 98/10: 84)

    NB 7 「祈り（のことば）」に関する LDOCE³ (s.v., prayer) の定義：

1 [countable] words that you say when praying to God, especially a fixed form of words: ...（[C] 神に祈るときに言うことば，特に，定型の文言）

2 [uncountable] the act of praying or the regular habit of praying（[U] 祈るという行為，または定期的に祈る習慣）

次の hiss/V-sign の用法の区別も，「ジャンル」対「作品」によって説明可

第2章　原理Ⅱ──姿かたちの有無　47

能である。
- (92) a. *Hiss* on tape recordings can be reduced using the Dolby system. (録音テープのシューシューいう雑音はドルビーを用いることによって減らすことができる) (CIDE)
    - b. She silenced him with a glare and *a hiss*. (にらんでシッと言って彼を黙らせた) (CIDE)
- (93) a. He raised his arms in the air and spread his fingers in the V for *victory sign*. (両腕を空に突き上げて，勝利のしるしに指をV字型に広げた) (RD 98/12: 136) [「表す」の意味の for に後続して意味としての「Vサイン」; cf. Red roses are *for* love. (赤いバラは恋を表す) (McED)]
    - b. The driver shouted rudely at the cyclist and gave her *a*/the *V-sign*. (ドライバーはサイクリストに乱暴に叫んで，Vサインをした) (CIDE) [形としての「Vサイン」]

次のような例における相違は「技法と作品」と呼ぶほうが適切であるが，使い分けの原理は「ジャンルと作品」と同じである (3.5 も参照)。

- (94) a. I found *wood carving* satisfying and painting fun. (木彫りは満足できるし，絵画はおもしろい) (CCED[3])
    - b. There's *a wood carving* of a man's head on my table. (テーブルの上に木彫りの人の頭部がある) (NHD)
- (95) a. She frequently uses *collage* in her work. (作品中でしばしばコラージュ[の手法]を用いる) (CIDE)
    - b. The children made *a collage* of postcards. (子供たちははがきでコラージュを作った) (CIDE)
- (96) a. After finishing secondary school in 1986, Engel studied graphic *design*, specializing in film animation at the State Academy of Fine Arts in Stuttgart. (1986年に中等学校を修了後 E はグラフィックデザインを学び，S市の州立美術アカデミーで映画のアニメを専攻した) (RD 99/4: 74)
    - b. wall paper with *a floral design* (花の図案のある壁紙) (LDOCE[3])
- (97) a. Nonetheless, he stayed on and did four columns in *mosaic*. (それでもとどまって，モザイク模様の円柱を4本仕上げた) (RD 98/6: 106)
    - b. The church window was *a mosaic* made of colored glass. (教会の窓はカラーガラス製のモザイク画だった) (NTC)
- (98) a. The old lady sat in the corner doing *patchwork*. (老婦人は隅に座っ

てパッチワークをしていた) (CIDE)
 b. The blanket was *a patchwork* made from many older blankets. (その毛布はたくさんの古毛布のパッチワークだった) (NHD)

(99) a. Tom teaches *sculpture* at the local art school. (T は地元の芸術学校で彫刻術を教えている) (CIDE)
 b. With a pick, Mary made *a sculpture* from a block of ice. (アイスピックで，M は氷の塊から彫像を造った) (NTC)

上述の「ジャンルと作品」および「技法と作品」という区別をより包括的に再解釈するならば，「形式」(または「制度」) と「実現形」として一般化することができる。「実現形」は，第5章で詳述する「個別事例」と同じことなので，本章は第5章の下位区分である。本章と第5章との相違は，本章であげた不定冠詞つきの例は具体的・即物的であり触知可能であるのに対し，第5章で見る不定冠詞つきの例はそうではないということである。

2.3 無定形が組み込まれている語

いくつかの語類は，指示物が無定形であるため (つまり，完結した姿かたちをもたないため)，不定冠詞をとらない。よく知られているのは，物質名詞および抽象名詞である。

2.3.1 物質集合名詞

furniture (家具) のような名詞は，従来の名詞分類に従えば，物質名詞に入れてよいか，あるいは集合名詞に入れてよいか判断に苦しむ (広瀬 1973: 259)。本書では，furniture, bedding (寝具類), baggage/luggage (荷物), coffee (コーヒー豆) などの名詞を「物質集合名詞」(material collective noun) と呼ぶことにする。

これらの名詞が [U] であるのは，その構成物が不定であるため，姿かたちを思い描けないからである。たとえば，furniture は desk と chair だけを指すこともあるし，bed や table を含むこともある。以下，物質集合名詞を意味分野ごとにあげよう。

2.3.1.1 植物

CIDE および OALD[5] によると，通例，野菜に分類されている asparagus, broccoli, chicory, cress, garlic, okra, parsley, spinach, sugar cane などは [U] である。同様に，ハーブあるいはスパイスに含められる ginger, marjoram, mint, mustard, rhubarb, rosemary, sage, sesame, thyme なども [U] である。文中での用例をあげよう。((Ap.1-3, b) [veronica/rue] も参照。)

(100) Cabbages, brussels sprouts, *cauliflower*, *kohlrabi*, *kale* and *broccoli* all

originated from one botanical species. (キャベツや芽キャベツ, カリフラワー, 球茎カンラン, ケール, ブロッコリーはすべて同じ植物種から生じた) (RD 00/2: 63) [注：cauliflower は [C] 用法もある (II-5, b)]

(101) Fat-free chilies, *garlic*, *ginger* and onions – each with only one or two calories – guiltlessly add zing to noodles, rice and vegetable salads. (無脂肪のチリ, ガーリック, ジンジャー, オニオンは, いずれも1～2カロリーしかなく, なんら体に悪影響なくめん類, ライス, 野菜サラダに風味を添える) (RD 98/6: 57)

(102) Silk, porcelain, *tea*, *ginger*, pearls and *rhubarb* – prized in Europe as a laxative – were shipped through the port ... (絹, 磁器, 茶, 生姜, 真珠, 大黄——欧州では下剤として珍重されていた——は [マカオ] 港から積み出された) (RD 99/11: 52)

　ここで, これらの野菜やハーブが不可算名詞であることの理由として, 一年草であるとか多年草であるとか花の部分が目立たないといった植物学的な特徴をあげてもあまり有意義ではない。重要なのは, これらの名詞は grass と同様に [U] である, つまり, 英語では「草」と同類のものとして認識されているということである。では, なぜ上記の名詞は英語では, 可算性に関する限り, 「草」扱いされるのか。おそらく, これらの植物は共通の根から発芽して増殖し (Biard [厨川 (訳)] 1957: 13 参照), やがては枯れていくので季節によって姿かたちが異なるため, 無定形なものとして認識されていると推測される。このように解釈してはじめてこれらの名詞が英語のなかで占めている統語的・意味的な位置が説明可能になるのである。

　上記の asparagus などに対して, cabbage, carrot, cauliflower [(II-5) 参照], cucumber, onion, pepper, potato, pumpkin, radish, turnip などは, 個体としては [C] である (「食材」としては 2.1.1.1 参照)。これは, これらの野菜は, 上記のものに比べ大形なので, その姿かたちが一目瞭然だからであろう。

　　　NB 8　an asparagus
　　　　上述のように asparagus は辞書では [U] として扱われているが, 次のような用例もある。
　　　　He resembled, to an extraordinary degree, *an asparagus*. (彼は [極端ななで肩なので] 異様なほどアスパラガスに似ていた) (Dahl, "Mr Botibol")

　植物名以外の名詞も, 集合的に用いられれば中身が不定なので, 無冠詞で用

いられる。このことは訳語からでも容易に推測可能である。以下の語群に関して見落としてならないのは, 個別的な事物を表すためには [C] 用法の別語が用いられるということである (訳語のあとに例示)。(grass/leaf/treasure のように, 同一の語が [U, C] 両用法をもつ場合もある。)

2.3.1.2 精神活動

balladry (バラッド類 ; ballad), epigraphy (碑文 ; epigraph), imagery (像 ; image), statuary (彫像 ; statue), poesy/poetry (詩 ; poem), beefcake/cheesecake (男性／女性写真集 ; photo(graph)), cinema (映画 ; movie), correspondence (往復文書 ; letter/card), e-mail (電子メール), fiction (フィクション ; book/novel), mail/post (郵便物 ; letter/card), pornography (ポルノ ; film/magazine/picture); reading (読み物; book/magazine/newspaper/reading)

2.3.1.3 創作物・製品

apparel/clothing/gear/garb (衣類 ; garment), underclothing/underwear (肌着類 ; vest, pants), outerwear (アウトウェア ; coat), sportswear (スポーツウェア ; swimsuit/sweatpants), footgear/footwear (はきもの類 ; shoes/boots), earthenware (土器 ; cup/plate), hardware (ハードウェア／武器類 ; machine; tank/missile/weapon), software (ソフトウェア ; program), silverware (銀(めっき)食器類 ; knife/fork/dish), kitchenware (台所用品 ; dish/pan), tableware (食卓用器具 ; plate/glass/knife), woodwork (木工(部) ; door/stairs), basketry (かご細工品 ; basket), cutlery (食事用器具類 ; knife/fork/spoon), jewelry (宝石類 ; ring/necklace), laundry (洗濯物, linen (リネン類 ; sheet/tablecloth), machinery (機械類 ; machine), millinery (婦人帽子類 ; (women's) hat), pottery (陶器類 ; pot/dish), property (所有物 ; land/building), gadgetry (小道具類 ; gadget), stationery (文房具類 ; pen/pencil/paper), weaponry (兵器類 ; weapon), baggage/luggage (手荷物 ; bag/box/case), carpeting (敷物類 ; carpet), delicatessen (デリカテッセン ; cheese/salad), equipment (装具), furniture (家具 ; table/desk/chair/bed), glass/glassware/glasswork (ガラス製品 ; glass/dish/mug), gold (金製品), merchandise (商品), mintage (貨幣 ; mint), porcelain (磁器類 ; cup/plate/ornament), shrapnel (榴散(りゅうさん)弾)

2.3.1.4 その他

brier (イバラの茂み ; bush/rose), scrub (低木林 ; tree), gravel (砂利 ; stone), shingle (小石 ; pebble), clutter/litter (散らかしたもの), fauna (動物群 ; animal), flora (植物群 ; plant), fruit (果物類 ; apple/banana/strawberry), game (獲物 ; animal/bird), grain (穀類 ; corn/wheat/rice), grass (草(類)), grass/marram (grass)/reed/rice), greenery (緑樹 ; plant/leaf), hair (毛),

herbage (草木類 ; herb/grass/plant), leaf/leafage/foliage (葉 ; leaf), plankton (プランクトン), poultry (家禽 ; chicken/duck/goose), scenery (風景 ; scene), seed (種), spawn (はららご ; egg), straw (むぎわら／ストロー), treasure (財宝 ; treasure/jewel), vegetation (草木 ; plant), vermin (害虫 ; flea/louse/insect), wildlife (野生動物 ; animal/bird)

NB 9　a poetry
　　物質集合名詞も修飾語句により指示範囲が限定されれば（☞ 4章），不定冠詞をとる。

　　Imagistic free verse presents sharp, clear images and aims at concentration as being 'the very essence of poetry'. This is largely *a poetry* of exact word-pictures, often of concrete things well observed, but also perhaps of emotions. (イマジストの自由[韻律の]散文は鋭い明晰なイメージを提示し，「詩のまさに本質」として集中することを目的とする。これは主として正確なことばによる絵画――しばしば十分に観察された具象的事物に関してであるが，ことによると感情に関することもある――の詩歌である) (Boulton, *Anatomy of Poetry*) [*of*-phrase による限定（☞ 4.4.1）]

2.3.2　物質名詞の普通名詞化

物質名詞は無冠詞で用いられるが，ほとんど同義のままで不定冠詞をとることもある。以下にあげる例は，通例は，物質名詞扱いであるが，完結した個体として認識されれば普通名詞として扱われる（別例は Appendix 1　参照）。

(103) a. The body is made up primarily of *bone*, muscle, and fat. (身体は，主として，骨組織と筋肉と脂肪から成る) (CCED[3]) [骨を構成する物質・組織]

　　　b. Stephen fractured *a* thigh *bone*. (S は大腿骨を骨折した) (CCED[3]) [骨組織から成る「製品」]

(104) a. The top of the mountain was covered in *cloud*. (山頂は雲でおおわれていた) (OALD[5])

　　　b. There wasn't *a cloud* in the sky. (空には雲ひとつなかった) (OALD[5])

(105) a. Gas-fired electricity is cheaper than *coal*. (ガス発電のほうが石炭よりも安上がりだ) (CCED[3])

　　　b. In her rage she threw *a* burning hot *coal* (= single piece of coal) at him. (カッとなって，熱く燃えている石炭をひとかけら彼に投げつけ

た) (CIDE)
　　c. The iron tea-kettle was hissing splendidly over fire *coals*. (鉄製の茶瓶が，燃えている石炭の上でさかんにシューシューと音をたてていた) (CCED[3])
(106) a. My jacket is lined with *fleece* / is fleece-lined. (私のジャケットにはフリースの裏地がつけてある) (CIDE)
　　b. *A fleece* is the fur of a sheep cut off in one piece. (フリースとは五体つなげたまま刈られた羊の柔毛のことだ) (CIDE)
(107) a. These exercises build *muscle* and increase stamina. (これらの運動は筋肉をつけ，スタミナを高める) (CIDE)
　　b. My leg hurts – I think I've pulled *a muscle*. (脚が痛い。筋肉を痛めたのだと思う) (LDOCE[3]) [痛む部分の筋肉]
(108) a. houses built of *timber* (木造家屋) (OALD[6])
　　b. The main beam is *a* very sturdy *timber*. (主柱は非常に頑丈な桁だ) (NTC)

　物質名詞の普通名詞化の例としてよく知られているのは glass/iron であろう。これらは物質名詞と普通名詞とで指示物が明らかに異なるので，冠詞の選択は日本人にも容易である。

(109) a. The sculpture was made of *glass*. (その彫刻はガラス製だ) (CIDE)
　　b. She poured some milk into *a glass*. (ミルクをグラスについだ) (CDAE)
(110) a. Anne ate a healthy meal rich in *iron*, zinc, and vitamin. (A は鉄分，亜鉛，ビタミンが豊富な健康的な食事をとった) (NTC)
　　b. My mother uses *an iron* to press my cotton shirts. (母は私の綿のシャツをプレスするのにアイロンを使う) (NHD)

　glass/iron ほど明白ではないが，次の b-文中の名詞も人工の「製品」を指しているので，不定冠詞（または他の限定詞）をとる (4.3 および Appendix 1 も参照)。

(111) a. *Aspirin* is a mild analgesic. (アスピリンは穏やかな鎮痛剤だ) (OALD[5])
　　b. Do you want to take *an aspirin* for your headache? (頭が痛いならアスピリンを 1 錠飲みますか) (LDOCE[3])
(112) a. I prefer drought *beer* to keg *beer*. (樽ビールよりも生ビールのほうが好きだ) (CIDE)
　　b. After a hard day's work I enjoy *a beer* or two. (きつい 1 日の仕事の

第 2 章　原理 II ──姿かたちの有無　53

あとはビールを 1, 2 杯 [本] 楽しむ) (CIDE)

(113) a. Harry took a sip of *bourbon*. (H はバーボンを 1 口飲んだ) (CCED³)
　　　b. I'll have *a bourbon* on the rocks/and water/and soda. (バーボンをオンザロックで／水割りで／ソーダ割りで飲もう) (CIDE) [意味的には a (bourbon on the rocks) / a (bourbon and water/soda)]

(114) a. a cup of hot frothy *cappuccino* (泡立っている熱いカプチーノ 1 杯) (LDOCE³)
　　　b. Those who want to get a taste of the Internet can visit a cybercafé to make an electronic journey around the world while enjoying *an aromatic cappuccino*. (インターネットを味わってみたい人は電脳カフェーを訪れて，薫り高いカプチーノを楽しみながら，電子世界旅行をすることができる) (RD 97/5: 25)

(115) a. Five thousand years ago, unimaginably poor Stone Age women living in Swiss swamps were . . . using fruit pits to create beaded *cloth*. (5 千年前 S の湿地帯に住んでいた，想像を絶する貧しさの石器時代の女性たちでさえも果実の種を用いて布に珠飾りをつけていた) (RD 99/10: 43)
　　　b. After we returned home, I . . . saw the table was covered with *a white cloth*, our best dishes, crystal and silver. (帰宅したところ，テーブルは白いクロス，とっておきのクリスタル製および銀製の皿でおおわれていた) (RD 99/12: 136)

(116) a. a small cafeteria where the visitors can buy tea, coffee and *chocolate* (お茶，コーヒー，ココアを買うことのできる小さなカフェテリア) (CCED³)
　　　b. I'll have *a* hot *chocolate* please. (ホットココアをお願いします) (CCED³)
　　　c. We'd like two coffees and two (hot) *chocolates* please. (コーヒー 2 杯と (ホット) ココア 2 杯，お願いします) (CIDE)

(117) a. Black *coffee* leaves a bitter taste in the mouth. (コーヒーをブラックで飲むと口に苦味が残る) (OALD⁶)
　　　b. Can I get you *a coffee*? (コーヒーを 1 杯いれましょうか) (CIDE)
　　　c. Two black *coffees*, please. (コーヒー，ブラックで 2 杯お願いします) (OALD⁶)

(118) a. She had a glass of *cognac* after dinner. (ディナーのあとコニャックを 1 杯飲んだ) (NHD)

b. Phillips ordered *a cognac*. (P はコニャックを注文した) (CCED³)

(119) a. The dancers dressed in national *costume*. (踊り子たちは民族衣装をまとっていた) (CDAE) [cf. dress]

b. Our host was wearing *a* clown *costume*. (ホストはピエロの衣装をまとっていた) (CIDE) [特定の一式]

(120) a. Do you like *curry*? (カレーはお好きですか) (OALD⁵)

b. I went for *a curry* last night. (昨晩はカレー料理を食べに出かけた) (CCED³)

(121) a. *Diamond* is the hardest material known. (ダイヤモンドは知られているなかで1番硬い物質だ) (CIDE)

b. Her ring was set with *a* large *diamond*. (彼女の指輪には大きなダイヤがはめ込まれていた) (CIDE) [カットされたダイヤ]

c. In San Francisco, Kozlenok and his men were soon opening pouch after pouch of polished Siberian *diamonds*. (SFで, Kと彼の部下は早速キラキラ輝くシベリア産ダイヤの入った袋を次々と開いていた) (RD 99/4: 53)

(122) a. The *Rules* advised modest *dress*, and undue attention to appearance was deplored: "Play not the peacock." (『ルール集』は質素な服装を勧め, 外観への過度な注意は咎められた:「見栄を張るなかれ」) (RD 99/2: 114) [cf. costume]

類例 : wear formal/traditional dress (CIDE); in full ceremonial/military dress (CIDE, NHD); harsh restrictions on . . . dress (RD 98/10: 46) [不定冠詞をつけるには情報不十分]

b. Early in the evening nurse Corrine Dower dressed the baby in *a* pink *dress* that another colleague had brought in for her. (その日の夕方早く, 看護師のCDは赤ちゃんに, 同僚がもってきたピンクの服を着せた) (RD 99/2: 126) [関係詞節 (☞ 4.4.2) により限定された, 新生児用の特定の衣服]

(123) a. Too much *drink* is bad for your health. (飲み過ぎは健康に悪い) (CCED³) 類例 : run out of drink (CIDE)

b. She felt like *a drink* after a hard day. (きつい1日のあと1杯やりたかった) (CCED³)

(124) a. My jacket is lined with *fur*. (ジャケットには毛皮の裏地がついている) (CDAE)

b. I wear *a fur* in the winter because it's very warm. (とても暖かいの

で，冬には毛皮の服を着る）(NTC)

(125) a. Would you like a glass of orange *juice*? (オレンジジュースを1杯いかがですか) (NTC)

b. 'I'm driving,' he said. 'A tomato *juice* will be fine.' (彼は言った，「運転中なので，トマトジュースで結構です」) (ConCD-ROM)

(126) a. Make your corrections in *pencil*. (訂正は鉛筆で行うこと) (CDAE) [塗料としての，鉛筆の芯を指す]

b. You cannot sign this contract with *a pencil*; it must be signed in ink. (本契約に鉛筆で署名はできない。インクで署名されなければならない) (NTC) [木の軸に芯をはめた筆記用具を指す]

(127) a. Would you like some more pork *pie*? (ポークパイをもっといかがですか) (CIDE) [分量に重点；物質名詞扱い]

b. He bought *a pie* for lunch. (昼食用にパイを買った) (LDOCE³) [製品；(47, b) [cake] 参照]

c. Make *a pie*. Real *pie*, homemade *pie*, is a work of art and an act of love. (パイを作りなさい。本物のパイ，つまり，ホームメードのパイは芸術作品であり愛の行為なのだから) (RD 00/9: 76) [まるごとのパイ1個 vs. ケーキやパンに対してパイ]

(128) a. *Pizza* may be the first truly global food. (ピザは最初の真に世界的な食物かもしれない) (RD 99/2: 92)

b. We went for *a pizza* together at lunch-time. (昼食時間にピザを食べにいっしょに出かけた) (CCED³) [製品；まる1個ずつ，または全員で1個]

c. You can't beat our local Italian restaurant for *a* good *pizza*. (うまいピザに関しては地元のイタリア料理店にはかなわない) (CIDE) [品質限定（または製品）]

(129) a. Outside the camp gates, standing before the British soldiers on duty, I sweated cold *sweat* when I bowed to them, as I had done to the Kempeitai, showed them my sensei's letter, and signed my particulars into their formidable book. (収容所の門の外で，勤務の英国兵の前に立って冷や汗をかきながら，憲兵隊にしたように，お辞儀をして，先生の手紙を見せ，ものものしい台帳に個人的詳細を記入した) (RD 99/5: 9) [広がりも量も含意しないので無冠詞]

b. I break out in *a* (cold) *sweat* when I think how near to death I was. (もう少しで死ぬところだったと考えると冷や汗が出る) (OALD⁵) [break out in (= to suddenly become covered in sth) が，最大で，体をおおう程度という姿かたちを含意するので不定冠詞をとる] 類例：I break out in *a rash* if I eat chocolate. (OALD⁵)

(130) a. bronze: a metal made by mixing copper and *tin* (青銅 = 銅と錫を混ぜてつくられる金属) (OALD⁵)

b. Reuben found *a* rusty baking-soda *tin* and dropped his coins inside. Then he climbed into the loft of the barn and hid the tin beneath a pile of sweet-smelling hay. (R は錆びた重曹のブリキ缶を見つけ，硬貨を入れた。そして，納屋の屋根裏に上り，甘い匂いのする干し草の山の下にそのブリキ缶を隠した) (RD 00/9: 116)

比較：He ran into the barn, climbed to the hayloft and uncovered the *tin can*. (彼は納屋に駆け込み，干し草のある屋根裏に上り，ブリキ缶を開けた) (RD 00/9: 117)

(131) The Pet Shop Guy told me to take a seven-litre bucket and place an apple inside. Douse *a towel* in apple juice. Put the bucket a few hamster steps from the hole and drape the towel over the side – a kind of hamster ramp, if you will. Just enough *towel* should stick into the bucket to allow the hamster to fall in but not crawl out. (ペットショップのお兄さんは次のように言った。7リットルサイズのバケツを用意して，その中にリンゴを入れる。タオルをリンゴジュースに浸す。やる気があるなら，バケツを［ハムスターが逃げ込んだ］穴からハムスターの足で数歩離れたところに置いて，ハムスター用の一種のスロープとして，［バケツの］側面からタオルを掛ける。タオルは，ハムスターがなかに落ちるが這(は)い出すことはできないという長さだけ，バケツの中に垂らす) (RD 00/1: 38) [最初の towel はタオル1枚を指すので不定冠詞つき；最後の towel はタオル生地の部分的な長さを指すので無冠詞 (☞ 3.3)]

上例からわかるように，しばしば物質名詞として用いられる名詞が冠詞つきで用いられるとき，その名詞は多くの場合なんらかの姿かたちをもつ「物体」または「製品」を表している。名詞に物質名詞とか普通名詞という性質が本来的に内在しているというより，指示物の姿かたちが認識不可能または不要なときは [U] 扱いされ，認識されるときは [C] 扱いされると考えるほうが現実的である。

次のように，辞書で a/an がかっこに入れられている例では不定冠詞があってもなくても意味は同じだと思われるかもしれない。だが，実は，「無形の液

体」と「容器に入った製品」(または「種類」) という区別が観察されるのである。(4.3 も参照)。

(132)　*(a) fruit cocktail* (フルーツカクテル (1 杯)) (OALD5)
(133)　*(a) face/hand/antiseptic cream* (化粧／ハンド／防腐クリーム (1 瓶)) (CIDE)
(134)　I won't have any wine – I'll just have *(a) soda water.* (ワインは飲まない。ソーダ水を (1 杯) 飲もう) (OALD5)
(135)　a. If you want *good emerald* you go to Zambia, Brazil, Colombia. (上質なエメラルドが欲しければ、Z とか B, C に行くことだ) (RD 02/2: 67) [物質名詞としての，無定形のエメラルド原石]
　　　 b. *a good emerald* is far more rare than a diamond (上質なエメラルドはダイヤモンドよりもはるかに稀少だ) (RD 02/2: 66) [かたまりとしてのエメラルド原石]

2.3.3 抽象名詞

　抽象名詞が無冠詞であるのは，物質名詞と同様，完結した形状を表さないためである。抽象名詞は，抽象概念 (= 具体的な経験内容から，ある性質，関係，状態などを抜き出して考える場合の，その性質，関係，状態をさすもの (国語大辞典)) を表すので，姿かたちそのものが存在しない。たとえば，beauty/goodness/knowledge などは，物理的外形はもちろん，意味の範囲にも明確な区切りは設定されえない。つまり，抽象名詞が，通例，冠詞をとらないのはそれが指す範囲が不定であるためである。逆に言えば，抽象名詞も関係詞節などにより指示 (あるいは意味) 範囲が限定されれば，不定冠詞を必要とする (☞ 4章)。
　本節では，以下，不定冠詞をとらない抽象名詞のうち主としてゲーム名と学問名との例をあげたい。

2.3.3.1 ゲーム名

　baseball/basketball/chess などゲーム名が無冠詞で用いられるのは，様態が無指定だから，つまり，進行具合が試合ごとに異なるからである。たとえば，野球の試合において，たとえ先発メンバーが固定されている場合でも，試合ごとに投手の配球は異なるし，打者の打球も異なり，得点経過も異なる。つまり，ゲームには一定の姿かたちがないので，不定冠詞は要求されないのである。

(136)　I get quite a charge out of watching *baseball.* (野球を観戦するとかなり興奮してくる) (OALD5)
(137)　He coached *basketball*, a sport Hakeem had never played. (彼はバスケットのコーチをした。H 自身は 1 度もしたことのないスポーツである) (RD 97/2: 88)

(138) There was little money to spare; the few pounds she planned to spend on *bingo* that evening of December 6, 1972, was a rare indulgence. (まわすべきお金はほとんどなかった。1972年12月6日の夕方ビンゴゲームに使うつもりの数ポンドはめったにない贅沢だった) (RD 98/3: 82)

(139) "Sheso licked Khayam's fur clean and played *throat bite* with her," Marker says. (「S [犬の名前] は K [チーターの名前] の毛をなめてきれいにしてやり，喉咬みごっこをした」と M は言う) (RD 00/1: 70) [ゲーム]

比較： The dog gave me *a* playful *bite.* (犬はふざけて私を咬んだ) (OALD[5]) [個別行為]

(140) We were invited for *bridge* at the home of an acquaintance – our first visit. (知人宅にブリッジに招待された。最初の訪問だった) (RD 01/6: 88)

(141) The children are playing *catch* in the playground. (子供たちは運動場でキャッチボールをしている) (NHD)

(142) When the parents who have always been strong for you are suddenly incapacitated, it is as though someone has played *cat's cradle* with the world, turning it inside out and taking it from their hands and putting it into yours. (いつも強かった両親が突然体が不自由になれば，まるでだれかが世界を相手にあやとりをしたかのようだ。外側にひっくり返して手から取って，あなたの手に押しつけてくるのだ) (RD 96/3: 140)

(143) The aim in *chess* is to win by attacking the other player's king in such a way that it cannot avoid being taken. (チェスの目的は，取られるのを避けられないようなやり方で相手のキングを攻撃して勝つことだ) (CIDE)

(144) My father used *cribbage* to teach me number theory. (父は私に数の原理を教えるのにクリベッジを利用した) (RD 99/2: 100)

(145) I watched *football* on TV with my son, which is about as exciting as watching a moth sleep. (息子とフットボールをテレビで見たが，面白さはガが眠るのを見るようなものだった) (RD 98/3: 13)

(146) People who love *golf* have a big advantage over people who fish. When golfers lie, at least they don't have to show anything to prove it. (ゴルフの好きな人たちは釣りをする人たちよりもずっと有利だ。ゴルファーは嘘をついても，少なくとも証拠を見せる必要はないから) (RD 97/5: 42)

(147) In 1980, 17-year-old Olajuwon, now six-foot-eight, was playing *handball* when a man called over to him. (1980年，17歳で，すでに6フィート8インチになっていたOがハンドボールをしていたとき，ある男が彼に声をかけた) (RD 97/2: 88)

(148) After my husband received an injury playing *hockey*, I drove him to the hospital to have his shoulder looked at. (夫がホッケー中に負傷したとき，彼の肩を診てもらうため車で病院に連れて行った) (RD 99/11: 23)

(149) The 53-year-old housewife had played *mahjong* in the afternoon with friends, then had supper with her husband, Ling Takgay, at their home in eastern Hong Kong Island. (53歳の主婦は午後友人と麻雀をしたのち，香港島東部の自宅で夫のLTと夕食をした) (RD 97/2: 81)

(150) Tina has challenged me to beat her at *poker*. (Tはポーカーで勝てるものなら勝ってごらんと言った) (CIDE)

(151) She went home to southwest England and started playing *polo*. (英国南西部の自宅に帰って，ポロをしはじめた) (RD 01/7: 22)

(152) He likes to play *pool* once a week. (週に1度玉突きをするのが楽しみだ) (NHD)

(153) One dieter has kept 50 pounds off for nearly four years by spending six hours a week playing *racquetball*, *tennis* and other sports, and generally eating meat only on weekends. (ダイエット中のある人は4年近く50ポンド減のままでいる。週に6時間ラケットボールやテニス，他のスポーツをして過ごし，肉はふつう週末にしか食べない) (RD 97/5: 10)

(154) If there was a defect, it would be like *Russian roulette*: countless 737s could fly without a problem, but someday another one would go down. (欠陥があれば，ロシアンルーレットのようなものだ。無数の[ボーイング]737が問題なく飛行できていて，ある日もう1機が墜落するのだ) (RD 00/2: 91)

(155) *Hockey, volleyball, football* and *tennis* are all sports. (ホッケー，バレーボール，フットボール，テニスはみなスポーツだ) (OALD5)

NB 10　複数形のゲーム名
　　ゲーム名には，限定詞なしで，複数形で用いられるものもある。
　　i) They enjoy themselves drinking wine, smoking and playing

cards. (ワインを飲んだり，葉巻をくゆらせたり，トランプをしたりして楽しむ) (CCED[3])
  ii) Let's play *charades.* (シャレードをしよう) (OALD[6])
  iii) *Checkers* is easy to learn and fun to play. (チェッカーは覚えやすいし，遊んで楽しい) (NHD) [単数一致]

2.3.3.2 学問名

学問名も不定冠詞をとらない。学問の諸分野は，本来，無限に深化・拡散すべきものだからである。少数例をあげれば十分であろう。

(156) Unlike *astronomy*, *astrology* cannot be described as an exact science. (天文学と異なり，占星術は厳密な科学とは言えない) (CIDE)

(157) *Biology* and *botany* are life sciences. (生物学と植物学は生命科学だ) (OALD[5])

(158) He flunked me in *chemistry*. (化学で落とされた) (OALD[5])

(159) She studied European *history* at college. (大学でヨーロッパ史を学んだ) (NHD)

(160) In this chapter, the author surveys recent developments in *linguistics*. (本章で筆者は言語学における最近の発達を概観する) (OALD[5])

(161) She majored in *math* and *physics* (at Yale). ((Y 大で) 数学と物理学を専攻した) (OALD[5])

(162) The proposition that the individual is more important than society is common in Western *philosophy*. (個人のほうが社会より大事だという命題は西洋哲学では一般的だ) (OALD[5])

(163) Would you classify this book under/as *sociology* or *politics*? (この本を社会学に分類しますか，それとも政治学ですか) (CIDE)

(164) She's studying *statistics* at university. (大学で統計学を専攻している) (OALD[5])

2.3.3.3 その他の抽象名詞

以下，抽象名詞のうち，「ゲーム名」と「学問名」以外の例をあげておきたい。

2.3.3.3.1 「混乱」

anarchy/chaos/confusion が a/an をとらないという事実は，「混乱」には一定の姿かたちはないという意味的理由により説明可能である。

(165) If law and order break down, *anarchy* will result. (法と秩序が崩壊すれば混乱が生じる) (OALD[5])

(166) *Chaos* in the middle of *chaos* is not funny, but *chaos* in the midst of order is funny. (混乱のなかの混乱は滑稽(こっけい)ではないが，秩序のなかの混乱は滑稽だ) (Steve Martin, quoted in RD 02/9: 81)
(167) This complicated situation has led to considerable *confusion*. (複雑な状況のため相当な混乱が生じた) (LDOCE³)
(168) *Pandemonium* erupted among the three hijackers. (3人のハイジャッカーのなかで大混乱が生じた) (RD 98/8: 30)

turbulence が不定冠詞をとらないのも，「動揺，騒乱」に一定の姿かたちはないから，という理由により説明される。

(169) The era was characterized by political and cultural *turbulence*. (その時代の特徴は政治的文化的動揺だった) (CIDE)

2.3.3.3.2 laughter

grin/laugh/smile が [C] であるのに対し，laughter は無冠詞で用いられる。この相違は，意味の相違の反映である。すなわち，前者には様態の指定が組み込まれている (歯(茎)を見せて笑う；声に出して笑う；口の両端を上向きにして笑う) のに対し，laughter は様態が無指定だからである。

2.3.3.3.3 traffic

traffic が不定冠詞をとらないのも，ゲームの進行と同様 (☞ 2.3.3.1)，同じ状況の反復はないという理由による。

(170) I was driving in rush-hour *traffic* when, without warning, the driver in front of me slammed on his brakes. (ラッシュアワーの往来の中を運転中，私の前の運転手が，警告もなく，急ブレーキを踏んだ) (RD 00/1: 9)

以上のほかに日本人が間違って可算名詞として扱いやすい語には次のようなものがある：advice, evidence, information/news, progress, weather. これらの語が a/an をとらない理由は次のように説明される。

2.3.3.3.4 advice

日本語でも「冷や酒と親の意見はあとで効く」というように，advice はその場限りではなく，将来にもわたって有効であるべきものである。つまり，advice が a/an と相いれないのは，その内容に終わりがないことによると推測される。これに対し，類義語の admonition/exhortation が [C] としても用いられるのは，これらの内容は即物的だからであろう。

2.3.3.3.5 evidence/identification

evidence は，定義上，証明という目的を達成するための手段である。したがって，何であれ evidence になりうる。それゆえ，この語は一定の姿かたちをもたない抽象概念を表すので，冠詞をとらない。これに対し，類義語の proof は，

集合的に用いられるときは[U]あり，「証拠品」という意味のときは[C]である。日本人がしばしば evidence を[C]として誤用するのは，日本語では「証拠」と「証拠品」との区別が判然としていないことに起因すると思われる。

「身分証明(書)」の意味の identification も，通例，無冠詞で用いられる。これは，この語が「働き」(☞ 3章)を表すためである。

2.3.3.3.6　information/news

これらが不可算名詞であることの理由は，一方では axiom/proverb/saying (a/an をとる)と，他方では，hearsay/rumor/word (a/an をとらない) と，対比すれば理解しやすい。すなわち，axiom などは表現に重点が置かれ，一字一句たりとも変更できないのに対し，hearsay などは(あやふやな)内容に重点が置かれていて人から人に伝わるときに語句は変更され，尾ひれがつけられることさえある。hearsay などと同様に，information/news も同一内容を種々の表現で伝えることが可能であり，決まった表現形式はない。このため，information/news; hearsay/rumor/word は a/an をとることはないのである ((IV-236) [rumour] も参照)。

2.3.3.3.7　progress

progress は数で測るものではなく，質または量で測るものである。言い換えれば，progress は限定された期間内でとらえられるのではなく，長期間においてとらえられる(希望的には，いつまでもつづく)のである。advice と同様に終わりがないのだから，progress は a/an とは共起しえない。

2.3.3.3.8　weather

天気は本来地球全体をおおう連続体である。「東京の天気」とか「横浜の天気」という言い方は便宜的な区分にすぎない。rainy weather とか snowy weather という場合，雨や雪が文字どおり馬の背を分けることはなく，その天気がどこから始まりどこで終わるかを特定することは不可能である。それゆえ，weather は形容詞がついてもその範囲を画定できないので不定冠詞をとることはない。

2.4　メタ言語用法

ここで，姿かたちが明らかなために，冠詞が必要とされる場合に言及しておきたい。語が，メタ言語的に(つまり，「〜という語」という意味で)用いられるとき，その語は，意味よりも，語形を表すので，冠詞や他の限定詞をとる。

(172) So we could replace *Stella's mother* in the original sentence with *a who* or *whom*. (かくして，原文の S's mother を who あるいは whom [という語]に換えることも可能であろう) (Jacobs, *English Syntax*, p. 95)

(173) It may also be an object anticipated by *a* formal *it*. (形式的 it から予期

される目的語であることもある）(Söderlind, *Verb syntax in John Dryden's Prose*, I, p. 134)

参考：By Malory's time it may well be that *the thou* of intimacy was becoming less common. (M の時代［16世紀後半］までには親密さを表す thou は以前ほど普通ではなくなりつつあったのであろう) (*CHEL*, III, p. 538) ［以上，冠詞以外の斜字体は原文］

人名の場合も同様である。(人名の複数形に関しては 8.2.2 参照。)

(174) We're looking for *a* Mr (= a man called) *George Smith*. (GS ［という名前の人］を探しているところだ) (CIDE)

2.5 言語と話し手

本節では，本章と次章とのつなぎとなるケースを見ておきたい。よく知られているように，一人ひとりの人間は冠詞つきの a Chinese, a Japanese, a German, an Italian, a Russian であるが，彼らの話す言語は無冠詞の Chinese, Japanese, German, Italian, Russian である。次はややめずらしい例である。

(175) a. You won't hear much real *Cockney* spoken unless you go to the East End of London. (L のイーストエンドに行かなければ本物のコックニーが話されるのを聞くことはあまりない) (CIDE)

　　　b. My father is *a Cockney*. (父はロンドン子だ) (CIDE)

言語は，本来，新しい文を無限に産み出しうるものであり，特定の表現に限定されてはいないので原則的に a/an をとらない。このことを念頭において (176) を読めば crow が無冠詞である理由が納得されるであろう。

(176) Charlie was perched at the top of a tall tree, holding court with about 20 fat crows. They had become friends through the years – Charlie spoke fluent *crow* and allowed them to share his apples. (C ［オウムの名前］は高い木のいただきにとまって，およそ 20 羽の太ったカラスと会議中だった。彼らは長年月のあいだに友達になっていたのだ。C はカラスのことばを流暢に話し，彼らにリンゴを食べさせてやっていた) (RD 98/7: 89)

言語は表現の可能性であり，一定の姿かたちはないと考えれば，上例は原理 II (姿かたちの有無) により説明可能である。言語を話し手の性質・能力と見るならば，次に述べる「働き」と「個体」という基準により説明可能である。

第3章 原理 III ——働きの有無

3 原理 III ——働きの有無

原理 III は，名詞の「働き」（機能，効力，役割，身分，性質，関係を含む）に関するものである。

> 原理 III：英語の名詞部は，「働き」を表すときは a/an をとらず，「個体」として認識されるときは a/an（あるいは他の限定詞）をとる。

この原理は原理 II（姿かたちの有無）の下位原理と言ってよい。なぜなら，名詞が「働き」を表すとき，その名詞は姿かたちを指示してはいないので，原理 III は原理 II から予測可能だからである。（ここで，原理 III を原理 II とは別の章とするのは，英語の名詞には「働き」を表すために無冠詞で用いられる事例が多いので，独立した項目とするほうが論じやすく，かつわかりやすいという実際的理由による。）

以下，本章では，「個体」とその「働き」という区別に基づいて冠詞の有無が選択される例をあげる。

3.1 （準）補語

まず，従来の文法書でも扱われている例から始めよう。

(1) The feat so impressed Hershey that he appointed Murrie *general manager*, and later *president*, of the chocolate company. (その快挙は H に感銘を与えたので，彼は M をチョコレート会社の総支配人に，のちには，会長に，任命した) (RD 99/7: 132)

(2) However, Camilla is emphatic: she wants no part of Charles's life of public duty and has no desire to be *queen*. (だが，C はきっぱりと言う。Ch の公的義務をともなう生活を望まず，王妃になることも願わない，と) (RD 00/3: 63)

(3) There is a very real possibility that Primakov will become *president* of Russia. (P がロシア大統領になるという可能性は非常に現実的であ

る) (RD 99/5: 46)

(4) They elected her *mayor*. (彼女を市長に選んだ) (CDAE)

(5) Would you like to nominate anyone for/as *director*? (管理職に指名したい人がいますか) (CIDE)

(6) He returned to *Searchlight* as *editor* in 1983. (1983年に編集者としてS誌に戻った) (RD 98/12: 99) [*Searchlight* 斜字体は原文]

(7) They had to travel everywhere by *bus*. (どこにでもバスで移動せざるをえなかった) (CCED[3])

以上のような身分や機能を表す語が補語であるとき，あるいは as/by に後続するとき，冠詞は不要であるということはよく知られている。だが，次のような，いわば，「準補語」の場合も冠詞が不要であることはあまり知られていない（慣用句 (3.10; 3.11) も参照）。

(8) Beginning as a kitchen helper while still a teen-ager, he had advanced to *second cook*. (まだ十代に調理場助手からスタートして，第2料理人に昇った) (RD 94/4: 26)

(9) In July 1996 he was promoted to *sergeant*. (1996年7月巡査部長に昇任した) (RD 97/5: 60)

(10) He was demoted to *patrol officer* and transferred to a low-crime precinct. (警ら巡査に降格され，低犯罪地区に飛ばされた) (RD 00/7: 133)

(11) Tran became a cook's helper in a Mexican fast-food restaurant, and quickly rose to *manager*. (Tはメキシコ料理のファーストフード店の調理助手になり，すぐに支配人に昇進した) (RD 97/2: 58)

(12) At the end of his long career as a policeman, Davis had decided to run for *sheriff* of Marengo County. (警官としての長い経歴ののち，DはM群の保安官に立候補することに決めた) (RD 00/5: 123)

(13) Jeff got a factory job and worked his way up to *superintendent*. (Jは工場に職を得て監督にまで出世した) (RD 99/4: 9)

ここで指摘しておかなければならないのは，無冠詞用法は構造的に決定されるのではない，ということである。つまり，名詞が（準）補語の位置にある場合でも，あるいは as/by のあとに現れる場合でも，必ずしも無冠詞ではない。なぜなら，名詞をその「働き」においてとらえるか，「個体」としてとらえるかは，文の意味による場合もあるし（例 (14-15)），話し手あるいは書き手にゆだねられる場合もあるからである (16-19)。

(14) a. Prince William is *heir* to the British throne. (W皇太子は英国王室の

王位継承者だ)(NHD)[身分]

b. Primarily interested in biology and medicine, Canguilhem was in many ways *an heir* to Bergson's vitalism.(主として生物学と医学に関心があるので，CはBの生気論の後継者だった)(ConCD-ROM)[補語ではあるが，身分というよりも，複数の後継者のうちの1人を表すので冠詞がつけられる]

(15) a. In 1948, Gandhi fell *victim* to a member of a Hindu gang.(1948年Gはヒンズー教徒団の1員の犠牲になった)(CIDE)[負わされた役割]

b. The best way to avoid becoming *a victim* of violence is to acquire the ability to defend oneself.(暴力の犠牲になるのを避ける最良の策は自らを守る能力を身につけることだ)(CIDE)[(14, b) と同様]

(16) She was made *(a) professor* at the age of 40.(40歳で教授になった)(OALD[5])

(17) He's *(a) part owner* of a racehorse.(競走馬の共同オーナーだ)(CIDE)

(18) The hijackers kept the pilot as *(a) hostage* on board the plane.(ハイジャッカーたちは操縦士を人質として機内に監禁した)(OALD[5])

(19) She was commissioned (as *a) lieutenant* in the Women's Army Corps.(女性部隊の副官に任命された)(OALD[5])

3.2 job/position/rank/role

名詞が the job/position/rank/role of に後続する場合，その名詞が「働き」を表すことはすでに job などにより明示されているので，通例，冠詞は不要である (2.1.2 も参照)。

(20) As the weeks in the Academy slip by, the job of *firefighter* becomes clearer.(学院で数週間過ぎるうちに消防士の仕事が明らかになってくる)(RD 98/5: 125)

(21) "This is going to be difficult. . . . " said Berlyn, a quiet young man and talented pilot who had advanced rapidly to the position of *commander*.(「やっかいな仕事になるだろう。……」とBは言った。彼は物静かな若者であり有能なパイロットであり，またたく間に部隊長の地位に昇進していた)(RD 02/6: 29)

(22) I graduated from Purdue in 1956 with a degree in electrical engineering and the rank of *ensign*.(電気工学の学士号と海軍少尉の階級とを得て 1956 年に P 大学を卒業した)(RD 99/3: 120)

類例:[Ray Canuel] promoted his coveted officer from constable to the newly created rank of *detective inspector*. (RCは引き抜きの話がある巡査を警察官から新設された階級である捜査警部に昇進させた) (RD 01/9: 77)

(23) At one end of the street there's a four-bed hospital supervised by the islands' one doctor, who also fills the role of *veterinarian* when required. (通りの端には4床の病院があり、島でただ1人の医者が取り仕切っている。彼は、求められれば、獣医の役割も果たす) (RD 99/12: 28)

次の例では、先行する work により veterinarian はその仕事内容を指すことが示されるので、veterinarian は無冠詞である。

(24) But he would never consider any other line of work than critical-care *veterinarian*. (だが、彼は救急獣医以外の仕事には目もくれなかった) (RD 00/9: 126)

NB 1
1) role のあとでも、個別性が明示されるときは冠詞がつけられる (本章 NB 3 も参照)。
  i) Accompanied by fellow DEA agent Helmut Witt, Brant was playing the role of *an offloader*, a greedy small-town fisherman out for a big payday. (同僚の麻薬取締局員 HW につきそわれて、B は沖仲仕、小さな町の一攫千金をねらっている強欲な漁師、の役を演じていた) (RD 99/9: 122)
  ii) the role of *a trainer* these days seems to be something of a moot point. (今日のトレーナーの役割は議論の余地がある問題のようだ) (ConCD-ROM)
2) 名詞部が by occupation/trade/vocation と共起するときは、「類」を表し、「働き」を表すわけではないので、冠詞が必要である。
  iii) He was *a carpenter* by trade. (職業は大工だった) (OALD⁶)
  iv) She's *a doctor* by vocation. (医者が天職だ) (CIDE)

3.3 enough/half/more

これらの語が「働き」の程度を表すとき名詞部は冠詞をとらない。たとえば、(25) 中の mouth は enough とともに用いられることにより、口の外形というよりも話すという機能を表し、(28) 中の machine/snake は half と共起することにより、それらの動き方を表すので、冠詞は不要である。もしも (28) で不定冠詞がつけられれば、半分に切断された機械あるいは蛇が動いていることに

第 3 章　原理 III ──働きの有無　69

なる．

(25) 'How are you going on?' said the Cat, as soon as there was *mouth* enough for it to speak with.（「どうだね？」と猫は，ものが言えるだけの口が現れるとすぐに言った）(Carroll, *Alice's Adventures in Wonderland*)

(26) And so no longer do I pray that we be delivered of the "perfect" child. Instead I ask only that I am *man* enough to be father to the girl whom God in his wisdom, mysteriously and against all evidence, believes needs me.（だから，私はもはや「完璧な」子供を授かることを祈りはしない．私が求めるのは，私を必要としている──知恵深き神は，不可思議にも，そしてあらゆる反証にもかかわらず，そう信じたまう──この子にとって父親たりうるよう十分に男らしくあることだけだ）(RD 98/6: 85) [father も「働き」（厳密には「関係」）を表すので無冠詞 ; the perfect child に関しては 8.4.1.4 参照]

(27) Soy's power against cholesterol and the strong suggestion that it can lower cancer risk are *reason* enough to make it a regular guest at your table.（大豆はコレステロールに効力があり，ガンの危険を下げることを強く示唆しているので，定期的に食卓にのせるのは十分理由があることだ）(RD 01/4: 20)

(28) It wriggles in a way that is half *machine*, half *snake*, in a manner Tilden terms "animal-like plasticity."（半ば機械のように半ば蛇のように，「動物的可塑性」と T の呼ぶ様子でうごめく）(RD 98/8: 57)

(29) Once wrapped in the trim column of lush black fabric, I became half *sophisticated lady*, half *siren*.（いったんきらびやかな黒い生地のぴったりとした筒型 [のドレス] に身を包めば，半ば上流婦人に，半ば魔女に変身する）(RD 98/3: 4)

(30) Most of his conversations were serious, but not the one with Wayne, who is half *sage*, half *joker*.（彼の会話の大半は真面目だったが，W とは別だった．W は半ば賢者で，半ば道化師だから）(RD 99/12: 125)

(31) Half *spiritual guide*, half *drill instructor*, Passoff, the author of *Lighten Up! Free Yourself From Clutter*, has made a career of helping people pare down their stuff.（『軽くいこう──ゴミからの解放』の著者であるPは，半ば精神的案内人，半ば訓練指導者として，所持品の減量を手伝うのを仕事としている）(RD 02/8: 44)

比較 : If you are serving it on a half-shell, leave the oyster on the bottom shell and serve on ice with half *a lemon*, brown bread and butter and a glass of chilled, dry white wine. (貝殻にのせて出すのなら，カキは下側の殻の上に置いたままにして，氷にのせて出し，レモン半分，バターを塗った黒パン，冷やした辛口の白ワイン1杯を添えなさい) (ConCD-ROM) [half の無冠詞用法は half A, half B というパタンで用いられる；2分の1の個体を表すときは冠詞が必要]

　more を含む次の例もここに含まれる。たとえば，(32) の dog はイヌの性格を指しているので無冠詞である。

(32) People can fall in love with a cute puppy, then find out six months later that they got more *dog* than they bargained for – or one whose personality is different from what they imagined. (かわいい子犬が気に入ったものの，6か月後には，予期していた以上のイヌを，あるいは思っていたのとは違う性格のを，買ってしまったことに気づくことがある) (RD [U.S. Edition] 00/1: 84)

(33) は，体重4.3キロの新生児を平均的体重の新生児と比較したときのジョークであるが，baby が無冠詞であるのは，赤ちゃんを体重 (あるいは成長) という「働き」においてとらえているからである。

(33) It's thirty-six percent more *baby*! (36パーセントも余分に赤ちゃんなのだ) (RD 02/4: 55)

　次例は，「働き」というよりも「血筋」に関する記述なので原理 II により予測可能であるが，「個体」を表してはいないという点では (25)-(33) と共通である。

(34) Frank – half *Danish* and half *Inuvialuit* – was himself a fiddler. (F は――半分デンマーク人で半分イヌヴィアルイト族――彼自身フィドル奏者だ) (RD 00/8: 92)

　　NB 2
　　1) 血筋に関する表現でも両親を個体として述べるときには不定冠詞が必要である。
　　　i) She was a first breeze from that world, a honey-skinned migrant daughter of *a French father* and *a German mother*, exotic in our rural town. (彼女はそのような世界からの最初のそよ風だった。フランス人の父親とドイツ人の母親とのあいだの，蜂蜜色の肌をした移住者の娘であり，田舎町ではエキゾチックだった) (RD 01/5: 122)

ii) A mule is a cross between *a horse* and *a donkey*. (ラバはウマとロバのかけあわせだ) (OALD⁵)

参考：A mule is a cross between *horse* and *donkey*. [between のあとで関係を表し無冠詞 (☞ 9.2.1)]

A mule is a cross of *horse* and *donkey*. [素材扱い] 類例：II-62

2) more NP₁ than NP₂

　名詞が more . . . than/as much . . . as と共起するときも，iii)–iv) のように，無冠詞でも用いられうるが，冠詞をとることのほうが多いようである．

iii) He is more *(a) teacher* than *(a) scholar*. (学者というより教師だ)

iv) For some, the *feng shui* expert may be as much *management consultant* as *wizard*. (ある人々にとっては，その風水専門家は魔法使いであると同程度に経営コンサルタントであるのかもしれない) (RD 97/2: 75)

v) "I've always said I was more *an adventurer* than I was *a businessman*," he drawled. (「いつも言ってきましたように，私はビジネスマンというより冒険家でした」と彼はとつとつと言った) (RD [U.S. Edition] 98/9: 207)

vi) But he understood that, 30 years earlier, David Evans would have been more *a spectator* than *a participant* in the birthing process. (DE は気づいた，30 年前には自分は出産の参加者というより傍観者だったのだ) (RD 00/3: 34)

次例も同様．

vii) She was more of *a hindrance* than *a help* (to me). (彼女は (私には) 助けよりむしろ邪魔だった) (OALD⁵)

viii) "I was not so much *a doctor* as *a policeman*," Glod says. (医者よりも警官だった，と G は言う) (RD 99/12: 104)

3.4　play

「演じる」の意の play のあとでは「役割」が演じられるのだから，名詞はしばしば無冠詞で用いられる．("play the N" に関しては 8.4.1.3 参照．)

(35) When you are in a public space and one person is violating the most basic rule, whose job is it to play *cop*? (公共の場にいてだれかが最も基本的なルールを破っているとき，警官役を演じるのはだれの仕事だろう

か) (RD 01/8: 80)

(36) The Gila, a rugged wilderness in south-west New Mexico, was a perilous place to play *cowboy*. (ヒーラは NM 南西の岩だらけの荒れ地であり、カウボーイを演じるには危険な場所だった) (RD 99/8: 60)

(37) And all I've got to do to get money is to play *doctor* again. (お金を稼ぐにはまた医者役をしさえすればいいんだ) (McCarthy, *Rakugo!*, p. 38)

(38) We were playing *host* to a Japanese exchange student, and I planned to take him to a rodeo to see calf roping and steer riding by real cowboys. (日本人の交換学生のホスト家庭をしていたので、ロデオに連れていって、本物のカウボーイによる子牛へのなわ投げや牛乗りを見せようと計画した) (RD 01/5: 53)

(39) My fiancée called and offered to come over, fix dinner and play *nurse* to me. (婚約者が電話してきて次のように申し出てくれた。来て、夕食を作り、ナース役をしてくれる、と) (RD 99/8: 88)

(40) During one game, I was playing *third base* when a batter ripped a shot over my head. (ある試合で三塁を守っていたところ、頭上を越えるホームランを打たれた) (RD 98/10: 95) [序数詞の前で the がつかないことに注意]

(41) So, playing *truant* from lackluster lectures one day, I flicked through an atlas in the college library, searching for inspiration for a new challenge. (こういう次第で、ある日つまらない講義をさぼり、大学の図書館で地図帳をめくって、新しい挑戦のインスピレーションを求めた) (RD 97/2: 122)

比較 : *A truant* is a pupil who stays away from school without permission. (無断欠席者とは許可なく学校を欠席する生徒のことだ) (CCED[3])

次の例が無冠詞であるのは、名詞が「役割」を表すためでもあり、ゲーム名 (☞ 2.3.3.1) を表すためでもあり、2つの名詞がペア (☞ 9.2) になっているためでもある。

(42) At speeds up to 50 knots, the two boats played *cat and mouse* [i.e., played a cat-and-mouse game] for ten minutes across the Adriatic Sea. (2隻の船は最大50ノットのスピードで10分間にわたってA海で追跡を演じた) (RD 99/10: 104)

NB 3

1) "play＋無冠詞名詞" のパタンには「人」以外の名詞も現れる。

第3章 原理 III ──働きの有無　73

 i) My four-year-old son, Austin, and I spend a lot of time playing *school*. (4 歳の息子の A と私はよく学校ごっこをする) (RD [U.S. Edition] 02/8: 60A)　類例：play house (ままごとをする) [(III-107, a) 参照]

2) 役割や典型例 (☞ 8.4.1.3) ではなく，1 人の人物を演じるのであれば，"play a 名詞部" という構造をとる。

 ii) Three weeks later I was in Canada playing *a scientist*. (3 週間後，私 [Martin Kemp] はカナダにいて，科学者の役を演じていた) (RD 01/9: 132)

3) 演じられるのが複数であれば，名詞は複数形をとる。

 iii) I can still picture, a few years later, Roger and Lee playing *soldiers*. (数年経った今でも R と L とが兵隊ごっこをしていたのが目に焼きついている) (RD 99/8: 127)

3.5　楽器名 (2.1.1.4; 8.6.2 も参照)

play につづく楽器名もしばしば無冠詞で用いられる。これは，このとき楽器名はジャズバンドなどにおけるパート，つまり，「役割」，を表すので，原理 III により，冠詞をとらないからである。(以下の例文の多くにおいて in a/the band (または類義語句) が共起していることに注意されたい；"play the 楽器名" に関しては 8.6.2 参照。) 他方，learn/study/teach の目的語としての楽器名は「演奏法」を表し，「技法」(☞ 2.2) に属するので無冠詞で用いられる。

(43) a. Also, for all the years I had known him, he practised his guitar every day – he played *bass* in a band – but in the last couple of months he had stopped. (また，知り合ってからずっと，彼は毎日ギターを練習していた。バンドでベースギターを担当していたので。でも，ここ数か月やめていた) (RD 99/12: 124) [バンド内での役割]

 類例：Carol's on *bass* (ie She is playing the bass guitar in the band). (C はベース担当だ) (OALD5); Crandall had played *bass guitar* in all-girl rock bands in Toronto, but that was more than 25 years ago. (C は T で女性ばかりのロックバンドでベースギターを弾いていたが，それは 25 年以上も前のことだ) (RD 00/9: 98); An accomplished classical musician, Bradley played *bass* for local symphonies . . . (クラシック音楽の名手なので，B は地元の交響楽団でコントラバスを演奏していた) (RD [U.S. Edition] 02/8: 92)

 b. They had *a bass* and a piano and a sax and percussion. (ベースにピ

   アノ, サックス, 打楽器をそろえていた) (CCED³)

  c. Then the "manager" . . . suggested I learn *bass guitar* so I could play in the band. (そこで「マネージャー」は, バンドで演奏できるように, ベースギターを習うことを提案した) (RD 01/9: 134) [learn の目的語として「演奏法」]

(44) a. The piece is scored for *violin*, *viola* and *cello* (その曲はバイオリン, ビオラおよびチェロ用に作られている) (OALD⁶) [曲内での主要楽器という役割]　類例: a piece for solo cello (OALD⁵)

  b. *A cello* is a musical instrument with four strings that looks like a large violin. (チェロとは弦が4本ある楽器であり, 大型のバイオリンのような形だ) (CCED³)

  c. Invited to study *cello* at the Moscow Conservatory at the age of seven, Nina practised endlessly, until her fingers bled and her head pounded. (7歳でチェロの勉強にM音楽学校に招待され, Nはいつまでも練習し, ついには指からは出血し, 頭はくらくらした) (RD 01/10: 108)

(45) a. She played *clarinet* in the band, sang in the choir and served on the student council. (バンドでクラリネットを演奏し, コーラスで歌い, 学生自治会で委員を務めた) (RD 96/3: 67) [クラリネット担当という, バンド内での役割]

  b. *A clarinet* is a musical instrument of the woodwind family in the shape of a pipe with a single reed. (クラリネットとは, リードが1枚で円筒形をした木管類の楽器のことだ) (CCED³)

(46) a. He used to play *guitar* and wear outlandish costumes in a punk band. (パンクロックのバンドでギターを弾いて派手な服装をしていた) (LDOCE³) [バンド内でギターというパートを担当]

  b. My brother plays *a guitar* in a rock band. (兄はロックバンドでギターを弾いている) (NTC) [ある (古い／新しい／重い) ギター]

  c. When the knock came at the door, Arlo was practising *guitar* . . . (ドアがノックされたときAはギターの [演奏法の] 練習中だった) (RD 02/2: 10)

(47) a. She [Actress Diane Keaton] once had played *piano* for silent films. (無声映画用にピアノを弾いたことがあった) (RD 99/10: 27) [ピアニストの役割]

 類例: written for piano and violin (CCED¹); arranged the score for piano

(CIDE); a piece transcribed for piano (LDOCE³) [曲内での主要楽器という役割]

  b. We're going to buy *a* new *piano*. (新しいピアノを買う予定だ) (CIDE)

参考: Mommy came home from a meeting of parents and teachers one evening and mentioned that someone's child had played *a piano piece*. (ある日の夕方母は父兄会から帰ってきて，だれかの子供がピアノ曲を弾いたと言った) (RD 96/3: 130)

(48) a. He plays *saxophone* in a little-known jazz band. (ほとんど無名のジャズバンドでサックスを吹いている) (LDOCE³) [バンド内での役割]

  b. The singer performed with a musician playing *a sax*. (歌手はサックス奏者のミュージシャンと共演した) (NTC) [外形としてのサックス]

(49) a. She studied *oboe* and *saxophone* at the Royal Academy of Music. (王立音楽院でオーボエとサクソフォンを学んだ) (Swan 1995: 66)

  b. *An oboe* is a musical instrument shaped like a tube which you play by blowing through a double reed in the top end. (オーボエとは上端の2枚のリードを吹くことによって演奏する筒型の楽器のことだ) (CCED³)

(50) a. He studied *piano* with the same teacher he'd had since age six. (6歳のときから同じ教師についてピアノを習った) (RD 98/8: 16)

  b. Bob taught himself *piano* before moving on to *acoustic guitar*. (Bはピアノを独習し，その後アコースティックギターに移った) (RD 02/2: 9)

  c. (= III-47, b) We're going to buy *a* new *piano*. (CIDE)

(51) a. Soon Catherine was studying *violin*. (間もなくCはバイオリンを習っていた) (RD 99/2: 28)

  b. the neck of *a* bottle/*violin* (瓶／バイオリンの首) (OALD⁵)

今や辞書で the がかっこに入っている例に遭遇しても，the がある場合とない場合とが同義でないことは明らかであろう。the の有無は，典型的には，バンドでのパートを表すか否かによって決定されるからである。

(52) He plays *(the) bass (guitar)*. (彼はベース（ギター）を弾く) (CIDE)

NB 4

1) play piano

Heaton & Turton (1987: 198) は次の例は〈米〉用法であり，〈英〉用法では the が必要であると言う。

i) I've been playing *piano* since I was eight. (8歳のときからピアノを弾いている)

しかし、上掲の例文や下記 3) で引用する Swan の解説から判断するならば、無冠詞用法は地域差のみに帰せられるとは思われない。

なお、楽器名の無冠詞用法は in the band のほか、しばしば *for*-phrase とも共起する。

ii) She has played *clarinet* for thirty years. (30年前からクラリネット奏者をしている)

2) bagpipe はパイプが複数個 (the Great Highland bagpipe の場合は5本; chanter, blowpipe, bass drone, two tenor drones) あるので複数形で用いられるか、the が選ばれるかのいずれかである (8.6.2 も参照)。

iii) How is playing *bagpipes* like throwing a javelin while wearing a blindfold? (なぜバグパイプの吹奏は、目隠しをして槍投げをするがごとしか) (RD 01/6: 43)

drum も、通例、複数個たたかれるので、複数形をとる。

iv) We always said we would have the reception at the Hotel Royal in Budapest where . . . Richie used to play *drums* in a dance band. (披露宴はブダペストのホテル R でしようといつも話していた。R がそこのダンスバンドでドラムを演奏していたから) (RD 01/8: 9)

3) Swan (1995: 66) は楽器名の前の the の省略に関しての次のように解説している。

v) But *the* is often dropped when talking about jazz or pop, and sometimes when talking about classical music. (しかし、ジャズやポップスを話題にするとき、ときにはクラシック音楽を話題にするときでも、the はしばしば省略される)

この解説は、楽器名が無冠詞で用いられるのは「役割」を表すときであるという本質を見逃していると言わざるをえない。

3.6 turn

「〜になる」という意味の turn のあとの名詞は、通例、無冠詞で用いられる (OED, s.v., turn 39b)。この意味は 'change or reverse the course' (OED, s.v., turn IV) という意味から比喩的に派生し、姿かたちよりも方針の転換、つまり、「変節」、に重点が置かれているためである。

(53) a. Sykes had turned *informer* and told the police where to find his fellow gang members. (S は密告者になって，仲間のギャングはどこで見つかるかを警察に教えた) (CIDE)
   b. A lead from *an informer* enabled the police to make several arrests. (密告者からの通報により警察は数件逮捕できた) (CIDE)
(54) a. You aren't suggesting he'd turn *traitor*, are you? (彼が裏切り者になると言っているのではないだろうね) (CCED¹)
   b. In Poland, Kuklinski was branded *a traitor*. (P では K は裏切り者という烙印を押された) (RD 00/4: 141)

NB 5
1) turn into のあとでは a/an がつく。
   i) He watched in alarm as his son turned into *a harsh critic* of the government he had once served. (息子が，かつて勤務した政府の激しい批判者になっていくのを驚いて見つめた) (RD 01/6: 129)
2) 類義語であるが，become のあとでは a が必要とされる。
   ii) turn *traitor*: to become *a traitor* (OALD⁵)

3.7 by ＋名詞句

先に触れたように (☞ 3.1)，by のあとでは名詞句はしばしば無冠詞で用いられる。以下，もう少し詳しく "by ＋名詞句" の例をあげておきたい。このパタンが最も頻繁に用いられるのは「輸送手段」または「移動手段」を表すときであり，「通信手段」がこれにつづく。

3.7.1 輸送・移動手段

以下の a-文と b-文とには救急車／はしけ／船などという「輸送手段」と救急車／はしけ／船などという姿かたちをもつ「物体」という意味の相違が見られる。

(55) a. After examining Nicholas, now in a coma, doctors at the local hospital in Polistena recommended that he be taken by *ambulance* to an intensive care ward at a larger hospital in Messina, Sicily. (P 市の地元の病院の医師たちは，今や昏睡状態の N を検査して，S 島 M 市の大きな病院の集中治療室に救急車で搬送することを勧めた) (RD 97/5: 84f.)
   b. Richburg, less severely hurt, went in *an ambulance* to a different hospital. (R は傷がそれほどひどくなかったので，救急車で別の病院

に行った) (RD 99/3: 70)

(56) a. Carrying goods by train costs nearly three times more than carrying them by *barge*. (列車で荷物を運ぶのははしけで運ぶよりも3倍近く費用がかかる) (CCED³) [手段；1艘のはしけが1回で，または往復して，運搬；train も輸送手段を表すので無冠詞]

　　 b. The load of wheat was carried up river by *a barge*. (小麦の荷は1艘のはしけで川の上流に運ばれた) (NHD) [物体；1艘のはしけが1回で運搬]

(57) a. In fact, for countless centuries this range shut out the New Territories – except to the few who trudged over its passes, rode by *bicycle* or pony along the narrow "carriage road" from Kowloon, or went by boat around the coast. (事実，何百年もこの高山地帯のため新領土は遮断されていた。ただ，少数のものが峠を歩いて越えるか，九龍からの狭い「運送路」を自転車か小馬で行くか，海岸ぞいに船で行くのを除いて) (RD 97/5: 120) [pony/boat も移動手段を表すので無冠詞]

　　 b. Can you ride *a bicycle*? (自転車に乗れますか) (OALD⁵)

比較： A child came wobbling along (the pavement) on *a bicycle*. (子供が自転車に乗ってふらふらしながら (歩道を) やってきた) (OALD⁵); She goes to work on *her bicycle*. (自転車で職場に行く) (LDOCE³) [by 以外の前置詞のあとでは限定詞が必要]

(58) a. The island may be reached by *boat* from the mainland. (その島には本土から船で行ける) (CCED³)

　　 b. Rose Hwang escaped Vietnam with her family in *a tiny boat*. (RH は家族とともに小さなボートに乗って V から脱出した) (RD 99/4: 104)

(59) a. (= III-7) They had to travel everywhere by *bus*. (CCED³)

　　 b. Since she was run over by *a bus* when she was four, Ragama Rehabilitation Hospital on the outskirts of Colombo has been her home. (4歳のときにバスに轢(ひ)かれて以来 C の郊外にある R リハビリ病院が彼女の家だった) (RD 00/1: 17)

比較： ride in *a bus* (OALD⁵) [by 以外の前置詞のあとでは限定詞が必要]

(60) a. It will save time if we go by *cab*. (タクシーで行けば時間の節約になる) (CIDE)

　　 b. Let's take *a cab* to the office. (会社までタクシーにしよう) (NHD)

(61) a. While seconded to the Jordanian Army some years earlier I'd retraced, by *camel*, Lawrence of Arabia's journeys. (数年前にJ軍に転勤になっていたが，アラビアのロレンスと同じ行程を，ラクダで，たどったのだ) (RD 97/2:122)

b. It is easier for *a camel* to go through the eye of a needle than for a rich man to enter the Kingdom of God. (金持ちが神の国に入るより，ラクダが針の穴を通るほうがやさしい) (Luke 18: 25)

(62) a. Cars are prohibited, so transportation is by *electric cart* or by horse and buggy. (車は禁止されているので，輸送手段は電気自動車か馬車だ) (CCED[3]) [horse and buggy も輸送手段を表すので無冠詞]

b. [H]e toured out from the city in *a pony cart* at weekends, searching for his ideal spot. (理想の場所を求めて，週末には小馬に引かせた荷車で市外に出かけた) (ConCD-ROM)

(63) a. I hate travelling by *coach*. (バスで旅行するのはきらいだ) (CCED[3])

b. Imagine yourself hurtling down a mountain road in *a coach*. (バスで山道を猛スピードで下って行くところを想像してごらんなさい) (ConCD-ROM)

(64) a. To get there takes three days by *Jeep*. (そこに行くにはジープで3日かかる) (RD 00/4: 104)

b. *A Jeep* pulled up to the dump and a marine jumped out. (ジープが集積場に登って行き，海兵隊員が飛び降りた) (CCED[1])

(65) a. When Moseley checked out the situation he saw it was impossible to reach Sims by *ladder*. (Mは状況を調べて，はしごでSのところまで行くのは無理だとわかった) (RD 00/5: 41)

b. A carpenter climbed *a ladder* to fix the roof. (屋根屋は屋根を修理するためにはしごを上った) (NHD)

(66) a. but one Sunday her friends hid Catherine's long blond hair with a scarf and took her by *motorbike* to their homes far from the city. (ある日曜日友人たちはCの長い金髪をスカーフで隠して，町から遠く離れた彼らの家にオートバイで連れていった) (RD 99/2: 31)

b. One morning in October he was wiping the counter down when he heard *a motorbike* approaching. (10月のある朝カウンターを拭いていたとき，オートバイが近づいてくるのを聞いた) (BNC, C86 2958)

(67) a. We went by *ship* over to America. (船で渡米した) (CCED[3])

b. *A ship* appeared on the horizon. (船影が水平線上に現れた) (OALD[5])

比較：stow away on *a ship* bound for New York (NY 行きの船で密航する) (OALD⁵) [by 以外の前置詞のあとでは限定詞が必要]

(68) a. In Le'opoldville we began a journey of more than 1600 kilometres by *paddle steamer* up the Congo through the great equatorial rainforest. (L から外車船で 1,600 キロ以上の旅を始めた。C 川をさかのぼって，赤道直下の広大な雨林を抜けるのだ) (RD 00/3: 125)

b. *A paddle steamer* (US side-wheeler) is a large boat that uses steam and a paddle wheel to move through the water. (外車船 (〈米〉side-wheeler) とは，蒸気と外車を用いて，水上を移動する大型船のことだ) (CIDE)

(69) a. While forming their plans, they had decided to cross South America from the west coast to the east, on foot and by *raft*. (計画を立てているうちに，徒歩と筏(いかだ)とで，南米を西岸から東岸に横断することに決めた) (RD 01/7: 88)

b. We lashed together anything that would float to make *a raft*. (筏を作るために浮くものはなんでも結びあわせた) (CIDE)

(70) a. When Orky's mate, Corky, gave birth, the baby did not thrive at first, and keepers took it out of the tank by *stretcher* for emergency care. (O [シャチの名前] の連れ合いの C が出産したとき，赤ちゃんは最初元気がなかったので，飼育係は緊急治療のため担架で水槽から取り出した) (RD 00/4: 39)

b. It was a strange experience to see my father being taken to hospital on *a stretcher*. (父親が担架に乗せられて病院に運ばれるのを見るのは奇妙な経験だった) (LDOCE³)

(71) a. We'll go by *train* as far as London, and then take a coach. (L まで列車で行って，そこからバスに乗ろう) (OALD⁵)

b. I was disgusted to read that when a girl was attacked on *a train* in broad daylight, no one went to her rescue. (少女が白昼電車内で襲われたときだれも助けに行かなかったということを読んでうんざりした) (ConCD-ROM)

(72) a. By noon I was nearly 50 kilometres into the walk and reached the first of four caches, which I had left weeks earlier by *truck* and which I hoped would sustain me for the entire trip. (正午までに歩きだしてほぼ 50 キロ進み 4 つの貯蔵所のうちの 1 つに達した。数週間前にトラックで出た場所であり，全旅程中私に補給してくれると期

待している場所だった) (RD 00/9: 87)
 b. She was knocked down/over by a hit-and-run driver/*a truck*. (轢き逃げ運転手/トラックにはねられた) (CIDE)

以上の "by＋乗り物名" の用法に関して注意すべきことは，これらの名詞が a/an をとらないのは，名詞がその本来の役目・目的である輸送または移動の手段として用いられるときのみである，ということである．(59, b)，(72, b) に見られるように，人を轢いたりはねたりすることはバスやトラックの本来の働きではないので，そのようなときは冠詞 (または他の限定詞) が必要である．このことは次の4例が明白に示している．

(73) a. She was transported to hospital by *helicopter*. (ヘリコプターで病院に搬送された) (OALD5)
 b. rescued from the sea by *(a) helicopter* (ヘリコプターで海から救助される) (OALD5)
 c. a sailor plucked from a sinking ship by *a helicopter* (沈没する船からヘリコプターで釣り上げられた船員) (OALD5)
 d. The tower was collapsed by *a helicopter*. (その塔はヘリコプターによって倒された)

「搬送」(transportation) はヘリコプターの本来の目的だから無冠詞で用いられる．「救助」(rescue) も，通例，病院など安全な場所への搬送を含意するので無冠詞で用いることが可能である．ところが，pluck の場合は，救出活動ではあるが，a が要求される．これは，「引っ張り上げる，リフトする」('to pull something from some place' (NTC)) という行為が強く意識され，搬送は含意されないためである (1度で完了という読みも可能 (III-56, b [by a barge] 参照))．これらに対し，「倒壊させる」(collapse) ことはヘリコプターの本来の目的ではないので，helicopter は物体として認識され，a/an (または他の限定詞) がつけられる．(by φ helicopter と共起する他の主な動詞：visit, be lifted to safety, be taken off (以上 OALD5); be landed, be flown to land (以上 LDOCE3); be flown in, be rescued, be ferried to hospital, be hoisted to safety, be picked up (= saved from the sea) (以上 CIDE); be evacuated (RD 99/6: 92) [(III-105) 参照]; be carried (NY Times, Feb. 22, 02))

helicopter の場合と同様に，コンピュータにとって計算することは本来の働きなので冠詞は不要であるが，小説を書くことは本来の働きと見るには (現時点では) 時期尚早なので冠詞が必要である．ところが，働きが何であれ，by hand と対照的に用いられれば，表現の並行性のため冠詞をとらず，computer に形容詞がつけられれば，冠詞が必要となる．

(74) a. The work of calculating tax deductions is done by *computer*. (減税の計算という仕事はコンピュータで行われる) (OALD5)

　　b. The novel was allegedly written by *a computer*. (その小説はコンピュータによって書かれたとされている) (OALD5) [行為者ともとれる]

　　c. Books were previously set by hand but much of the work is now done by *computer*. (本は以前は手組みだったが、現在ではその仕事の大部分はコンピュータでなされる) (OALD5)

　　d. This vision assumes that functions that have been customarily performed by *a PC*– Web surfing, scheduling, note-taking – will be handled by specialised information appliances that can simplify our lives. (この未来像が想定するところは、慣例的にパソコンで行われている機能——ウエブサーフィン、予定管理、メモ——は特殊化された情報処理機によって扱われるようになり、生活を簡素化することが可能になる、ということだ) (RD 00/4: 98)

3.7.2　通信手段

乗り物の場合と同様、名詞が「個体」(または、「物体」)としての通信機器そのものを指示するときは冠詞をとり、機器の「働き」を表すときは冠詞をとらない。

(75) a. I'll send you the agenda by *fax*. (議題をファックスで送ろう) (CIDE)/ send a letter by *facsimile* (ファックスで手紙を送る) (OALD5)

　　b. I've got a phone and *a fax*. (電話機とファックス機を入手した) (BNC, KGK 436)

(76) a. By *phone*, Tite now contacted Karen. (電話で今やTはKに連絡した) (RD 99/2: 111)

　　b. A nurse handed me *a phone*. (看護師が電話機を手渡した) (RD 99/12: 134)

(77) a. The police communicate with each other by *radio*. (警察は互いに無線で連絡をとる) (OALD5)

　　b. He cannibalized *an* old *radio* to repair his cassette-player. (カセットプレーヤーを修理するために古ラジオの部品を取り外した) (OALD5)

(78) a. Television stations around the world are linked by *satellite*. (世界じゅうのテレビ局は衛星で結ばれている) (OALD5)

　　b. *A* test *satellite* was launched from Cape Canaveral. (実験衛星がCCから打ち上げられた) (LDOCE3)

(79) a. You can always reach me by *telephone*. (いつでも電話で連絡できる) (OALD5)
　　 b. Esther ran for *a telephone* and called Rockford. (E は電話機に走り，R に電話をした) (RD 99/11: 134)

3.7.3　その他の手段・方法

種々雑多な例を含むため 1 つにまとめることは困難だが，輸送や通信以外の手段・方法にも，上記と同様，「働き」と「個体」という区別が見られる。本節中の大多数の a- 文とは異なり，多くの b- 文は形容詞や不定詞，*of-/as*- phrase，関係詞節など修飾語句をともなっている。これは，名詞部が「働き」を表す場合と「個体」を表す場合との相違の反映である (4-5 章も参照)。

(80) a. Viewing is by *appointment* only. (見物は予約制のみです) (CCED3)
　　 b. I have *an appointment* to see the manager. (支配人に会う予約をとっている) (LDOCE3)
(81) a. You can only withdraw money from this account by (prior) *arrangement* with the bank. (本口座からの換金は当行との (前もっての) 取り決めによってのみ可能とする) (CIDE)
　　 b. Her class teacher made *a* special *arrangement* to discuss her progress at school once a month. (クラス担任は学校での進度について月に 1 度話し合うという特別な取り決めをした) (CCED3)
(82) a. The painting will be sold at/(Br also) by *auction* next week. (絵画は来週競売で売られる) (CIDE)
　　 b. They're holding *an auction* of jewellery on Thursday. (木曜日には宝石類の競売会が開かれている) (CIDE)
(83) a. When it became more difficult to buy cocaine by *catalogue*, Fletcher found a dealer. (カタログでコカインを買うのがもっとむずかしくなると F は売人を見つけた) (RD 98/3: 68)
　　 b. In 1974 he ordered his first quarter-ounce from a pharmaceutical *catalogue*. (1974 年に薬品のカタログで初めて 4 分の 1 オンス注文した) (RD 98/3: 68)
(84) a. I'd like to pay by *cheque*. (小切手で支払いたい) (CCED3)
　　 b. He wrote them *a cheque* for ￡10,000. (1 万ポンドの小切手をきった) (CCED3)
(85) a. Human perception is highly imperfect and by *definition* subjective. (人間の知覚は非常に不完全であり，定義上，主観的である) (CCED3)
　　 b. Can you give me *a* good *definition* of 'harsh'? ('harsh' をちゃんと定

義してくれないか) (CIDE)

(86) a. Keep in mind that they learn by *example*. (彼らは実例によって学習するということを念頭に置いておきなさい) (RD 99/7: 48)

b. Let me give you *an example* of what I mean. (意味することの具体例をあげよう) (CDAE)

(87) a. By conservative *estimate*, the Caspian holds at least 50 billion barrels of oil, and the real figure could well be twice that much. (控えめに見積もっても、カスピ海には少なくとも500億バレルの原油がある。実際の数字はその2倍であってもおかしくない) (RD 99/4: 18)

b. How many people live in Chicago? Three million would be *a reasonable estimate*. (Cの人口は何人か。300万人というのが妥当な見積もりだろう) (RD 97/2: 24)

(88) a. My primary responsibility is to the company, and by *extension* to the people who work for it. (私の第一義的な責任は会社に対してであり、拡大的に、その社員に対してである) (LDOCE[3])

b. The work they do now is *an extension* of this tradition. (現在やられている仕事はこの伝統の延長だ) (RD 97/5: 21)

(89) a. Can you imagine your teenage son copying out 110 rules about good manners, by *hand* and of his own choice? (手書きで、しかも自分から進んで、10代の息子が礼儀作法に関する110ものルールを書き写しているのを想像できるだろうか) (RD 99/2: 113)

b. 'Oh, dear!' she cried, clapping *a hand* to her forehead. (額に手を当てながら、「まあ」と叫んだ) (OALD[5])

(90) a. In studies, zanamivir (Relenza), taken by *inhaler*, was found to significantly reduce the length and contagiousness of a flu attack if taken daily and within 48 hours of the onset of symptoms. (研究で、zanamivir (Relenza) [薬品名?]——吸入器から取り込む——は、連日、かつ症状が現れて48時間以内に、摂取すれば、感冒の期間と感染を顕著に減じることが発見された) (RD 99/2: 14)

b. Aspiration of a foreign body during use of *an inhaler* has been infrequently reported since the first report in 1981. (吸入器使用中の異物の吸入に関する報告は、1981年の最初の報告以来まれだ) (BNC, FT1 1396)

(91) a. My collection was formed partly by *inheritance* and partly through my own purchases. (私のコレクションは幾分は相続によって、幾分

は私自身の購入によって形成された) (CIDE)

b. She has *an inheritance* to live off (US also live off of) so she doesn't need to get a job. (暮らしていける遺産があるので仕事に就く必要はない) (CIDE)

(92) a. The letters are sorted by *machine*. (手紙は機械で仕分けされる) (LDOCE³)

b. It's *a machine* for slicing bread. (パンをスライスするための機械だ) (OALD⁵)

(93) a. Someone must have left the door open by *mistake*. (だれかが誤ってドアを開けたままにしたにちがいない) (LDOCE³)

b. A week after the wedding she realized she had made *a* terrible *mistake*. (結婚から1週間後ひどい間違いをおかしたことに気づいた) (OALD⁵)

(94) a. Vaccination by *mouth* – on a lump of sugar – is the most common way of administering the polio vaccine, though others are usually given by *injection*. (経口による──砂糖のかたまりで──ワクチン接種が, ポリオワクチンの投与方法では1番ふつうなやり方だが, 他[のワクチン]は, 通例, 注射によって行われる) (CIDE)

b. The lion had *a* cavernous *mouth*. (ライオンは巨大な口をしていた) (CIDE)

c. The doctor gave her *an injection* to alleviate the pain. (医者は痛みを和らげるため彼女に注射をした) (OALD⁵)

(95) a. She was by *reputation* a good organiser. (評判によると, 彼女はすぐれたまとめ役だ) (CCED³)

b. She had already begun to establish a *reputation* as a writer. (すでに作家としての名声を確立しつつあった) (LDOCE³)

(96) a. Long ago a handful of bones had been carried *by river* to the coast, where they settled at the bottom of shallow seas. (はるか昔に数片の骨が川によって海岸に運ばれ, 浅瀬の底に堆積したのだ) (RD 01/9: 110)

b. They continued until they came to *a river*. (行きつづけて川に着いた) (OALD⁶)

(97) a. It takes three hours by *road*. (陸路で3時間かかる) (LDOCE³)

b. (= II-55, b) If you're walking along *a* badly-lit *road* at night you should wear conspicuous clothes. (OALD⁵)

(98) a. Many kinds of insect find their mates by *scent*. (多くの種類の昆虫はにおいで相手を見つける) (CCED³)

b. So, if I've got this right, *a scent* that doesn't work is the national anthem sung by Roseanne, and an aroma that sings is Pavarotti at La Scala. (正しく理解していれば，効果のないにおいは R が歌う国歌であり，歌う香りはスカラ座での P だ) (RD 99/10: 119)

(99) a. The results showed that breech babies delivered by *C-section* were three to four times less likely to die or have serious problems in the first six weeks of life than those delivered vaginally. (結果的にわかったのは，帝王切開で生まれた逆子は，経腟出産児よりも，生後6週間で死亡率も深刻な問題も3〜4倍低い，ということだ) (RD 01/7: 18) [5.2 も参照]

b. A Canadian study has proven that *a caesarean section* is the safest method of delivering full-term breech babies. (カナダのある研究は，臨月の逆子を分娩する1番安全な方法は帝王切開だということを証明した) (RD 01/7: 17)

(100) a. Let's search by *sound*. (音で調べよう) (RD 99/2: 110)

b. There was not *a sound* from Jimmy. (J からは寝息さえなかった) (RD 99/2: 122)

(101) a. The new show took London by *storm*. (新しいショーは L で大成功だった) (LDOCE³)

b. They had the misfortune to be hit by *a* violent *storm*. (激しい嵐に襲われるという不運に遭った) (OALD⁵)

(102) a. Her lab determined that the infectious agent was Influenza A, but the virus resisted identification by *subtype*. (彼女の研究室は感染源は A 型インフルエンザであると特定したが，下位タイプによるウイルスの同定はできなかった) (RD 98/10: 107)

b. Shortridge's lab had discovered that *an* Influenza A *subtype* known as H5 had killed the chickens. (S の研究室は，A 型インフルエンザの下位タイプである，通称，H5 がニワトリの死因であることを発見した) (RD 98/10: 109)

(103) a. In the past seven years, Motivation has set up self-sustaining projects in 12 countries, many plagued by civil *war*, such as Afghanistan and Cambodia. (過去7年間に M [英国の慈善団体] は12か国で自立計画をうち立てた。多くは，A や C のように，内乱で

疲弊した国である）(RD 00/1: 18)
- b. If *a war* breaks out, many other countries will be affected. (戦争が起これば，他の多くの国も影響をうける) (OALD5)

3.7.4　by＋複数形

あまり知られていないが，"by＋名詞句"が名詞本来の働きを表す場合でも，複数の器機が用いられていることを明示するときは，複数形が用いられる。

(104) This was one of the homes of Cable & Wireless, the company that connects my computer to the Internet by *telephone lines*. (ここはC&W社——私のコンピュータを電話回線でインターネットに接続する会社——の支所の1つだった) (RD 00/7: 32)

(105) Last December, 93 workers were evacuated by helicopter to a nearby drilling platform when gas was accidentally released within the GBS [Gravity Base Structure] and detected by *sensors*. (昨年12月，93人の労働者がヘリコプターで近くの海底石油掘削作業台に避難した。GBS内で，誤ってガスが漏れ，センサーで探知されたのだ) (RD 99/6: 92)

(106) It was also swept day and night by *infrared cameras*, *movement sensors*, radar and *armed patrols*. (日夜，赤外線カメラや動作センサー，レーダー，武装巡視隊員によっても監視された) (RD 98/9: 69) [radar は本来的に無冠詞]

> **NB 6　by 以外の前置詞**
>
> 名詞が「働き」を表せば，by 以外の前置詞のあとでも無冠詞で用いられる。
>
> i) With nothing more than a computer and a telephone linkup via *modem*, more and more people such as McNeil are tapping into an international network of health resources. (コンピュータとモデムによる電話接続以上には不要なので，Mのように，健康資源に関する国際的ネットワークに加入する人が増加しつつある) (RD 98/5: 24)
>
> ii) receive a programme via *satellite* (衛星からプログラムを受信する) (OALD5)
>
> iii) Jack's voice was crisp on the radio in my helmet as he read off the data from *computer* and radar. "You're 31 feet per second, going down through 500. That's a little high, Geno." (Jの声が無線でヘルメットにきびきびと響いた。コンピュータとレーダー

からデータを読みとっているのだ。「秒速 31 フィート, [高度] 500 を通過して降下中。G, 少し高い」) (RD 99/3: 137)

iv) In the Hollywood remake nine out of ten special effects featuring the primeval monster, for example the underwater scenes, were simulated on *computer*. (H のリメイクでは, 原始怪獣 [ゴジラ] を主役とする特殊撮影, たとえば, 水中シーン, の大部分はコンピュータでシミュレートされる) (RD 99/4: 77)

比較: In time, members of a pain-management unit arrived and attached an I.V. bag containing a painkiller to my stand. Its flow was regulated by *a* small *computer*. (やがて痛み管理部門の人たちが到着し, 鎮痛剤入りの点滴用バッグを私 [患者] のスタンドにとりつけた。流れは小型のコンピュータで制御されていた) (RD 97/5: 139) [特定のコンピュータを指すので冠詞をとる]

3.8 施設名

court/church/school/hospital/jail など建造物の無冠詞用法に関しては, 公共施設 (institution) が本来の目的で用いられるときは無冠詞であると伝統的に説明されている (松本・松本 1976: 82; Berry 1993: 43f.)。

この説明が日本で流布しているのは institution が「公共施設」と訳されているためであろう (研究社英和中辞典 (4 版), 三省堂新コンサイス英和辞典)。たしかに, institution は次のように定義されるので, この訳語は間違いではない: 'an organization devoted to the promotion of a cause, program, etc., esp. one of a public or educational character' (福祉, 計画などの推進を目的とする機関, 特に, 公的または教育的性格をもつもの) (*Random House Webster's Dictionary of American English*)。

しかし, 無冠詞用法の理由を説明するに当たって「公共性」を強調するならば, 公共的であるべき orphanage (孤児院) や poorhouse (救貧院), workhouse (救貧院／感化院), library (図書館) が冠詞をとるという事実を説明できないことになる。むしろ, 身分・機能の場合と同様に, これらの場合も「働き」対「建物」(=「個体」) という区別に基づいて冠詞の選択が決定されると考えるほうが矛盾なく説明可能である。事実, house は公共施設とは言いがたいが,「居住」あるいは「生活」, つまり, 家屋にとっての「働き」, を表す場合は, 次のように無冠詞で用いられる。

(107) a. You go from, 'Gee, we're going to have this little baby – it will be like playing *house*,' to 'Here's this huge problem.' (「この [障害のあ

る］赤ちゃんを育てることになるんだ。ままごとみたいなもんだろう」から「これは大問題だ」へと変わっていく）(RD 96/3: 76)
   b. He lives with an aunt who keeps *house* for him. (伯母と住んでいて，家事をしてもらっている) (CCED[3])
   c. He used to keep open *house* on Sundays. (日曜日には自宅を開放していた) (CCED[3])
   d. In fact, I have just moved *house* in order to accommodate my birds with ease. (事実，容易に鳥の世話ができるように転居したばかりだ) (ConCD-ROM) [生活空間の移動；主に〈英〉]

比較：
(108) a. So they had moved into *a house* near the end of Owlstone Road. (こういう次第で，O 通りの端近くの家に移り住んだ) (ConCD-ROM) [建物への入居]
   b. She lives in *a* little *house* (Br and Aus) in/(Am) on Cross Street. (C 通りの小さな家に住んでいる) (CIDE)

同様に，shop も，姿かたちをもつ「店舗」を表すときは冠詞をとるが，店舗の働きである「営業活動」を表すときは冠詞をとらない。

(109) a. But he made his way back to the subcontinent, setting up *shop* in Calcutta, India. (だが，彼は亜大陸に戻り，インドの C で開業した) (RD 00/9: 95) [営業]
   b. He never opens up *shop* on a Sunday. (日曜日には決して営業しない) (OALD[5])
   c. They were forced to shut up *shop* because they weren't getting enough customers. (十分に集客できなかったので閉店せざるをえなかった) (CIDE)

比較：
(110) a. Their plans to open *a* new *shop* have been stymied by lack of funds. (新店舗をオープンするという計画は資金不足のため挫折した) (OALD[5]) [建物]
   b. There's *a shop* at the bottom of the street. (通りの端に店屋がある) (LDOCE[3])
   c. I work in *a* machine *shop* making wire. (ワイヤーを作る機械工場で働いている) (CDAE)

さらに，office は，公共の建物というよりむしろ私的な建物である場合が多いが，仕事・任務という「働き」を表すときは無冠詞であり，「事務室・建物」

を表すときは冠詞をとる。

(111) a. Four years later he was elected district attorney, and after taking *office* in 1992, he called in his chief investigator. (4年後地区検事長に選ばれ、1992年に就任したのち、捜査主任を訪ねた) (RD 99/2: 132)

b. In his first year in *office*, Davis bought an expensive Christmas present for his 16-year-old daughter: a $3000 four-wheeler... (就任して最初の年にDは16歳の娘に高価なクリスマスプレゼントを買った。3千ドルの4輪車だ) (RD 00/5: 125)

c. After levelling corruption charges against Hun Sen and others, he was dismissed from *office*. (腐敗の責任をHSほかに向けたが、解任された) (RD 99/11: 22)

比較：

(112) a. He had *an office* big enough for his desk and chair, plus his VDU. (机、椅子とコンピュータ1式を置くには十分な広さの事務室があった) (CCED[3])

b. I'd hate to work in *an office*, but I could use a regular income. (オフィスビルで働くのはいやだったが、定期的な収入を使うことが可能だった) (LDOCE[3])

class も施設とは呼びがたいが、school と同様に用いられる。

(113) a. I was told off for talking in *class*. (授業中おしゃべりをしていたため叱られた) (CIDE)

b. "Sir," the student responded solemnly, "every time I went to the library to listen to it, someone else from *class* was already using the recording." (「先生」、その学生は勤勉げに答えた、「いつ図書館に聞きに行っても受講生のだれかが録音を使用中でした」) (RD 98/12: 117) [教授の質問に対し、他の学生全員は図書館に行く時間がなかったと答えたのに、遅刻してきた学生が上記のように言い訳をしたというジョーク]

c. But Carolyn had cut *class* that day. (だがCはその日さぼっていた) (RD 99/2: 65)

d. Students began gravitating towards him after *class*, clustering around on the walk to his car. (学生たちは授業後彼のまわりに集まるようになり、歩道に群れながら彼の車まで行った) (RD 00/4: 118)

比較：

(114) a. He had to spend about six months in *a class* with younger students.

(年下の学生たちと同じクラスで約6か月過ごさなければならなかった) (CCED³) [特定のクラス]
  b. Form 4 is/are *a* difficult *class* to teach. (4組は教えにくいクラスだ) (OALD⁵)
  c. I have *a* maths *class* at 9 o'clock. (9時に数学の授業がある) (OALD⁵)

逆に, mosque/synagogue は, イスラム教徒/ユダヤ教徒にとっては, キリスト教徒の chapel/church と同様に, 公共の建物であるにもかかわらず, 無冠詞では用いられない。

(115) a. That Friday the man led him to a modest Houston building. Olajuwon had passed it many times without realizing it was *a mosque*. (その金曜日その人はOをH市内の粗末な建物に案内した。Oは何度もそこを通っていたが, それがモスクだとは気づかなかった) (RD 97/2: 90)
  b. Hakeem looked forward to Fridays because he got out of school early to attend *the mosque*. (Hは金曜日を楽しみにしていた。モスクに出るために早退していたのだ) (RD 97/2: 87)
(116) a. When Todd first saw the chapel turned into *a synagogue* for one of these occasions, he was shocked. (礼拝堂がシナゴーグに変わっているのをあるとき初めて見て, Tはショックをうけた) (ConCD-ROM)
  b. Every Sabbath he reasoned in *the synagogue*, trying to persuade Jews and Greeks. ([パウロは] 安息日ごとに会堂で論じては, ユダヤ人やギリシャ人の説得に努めた) (Acts 18: 4)

house/shop/office/class; mosque/synagogue の例からわかるように, 公共施設名だから無冠詞で用いられるというわけではなく, 英語話者の目から見て「働き」を表すとき施設名に冠詞は不要である, と言うべきである。

以下, 施設名が「働き」を表すために無冠詞で用いられている例をあげる。

(117) a. Once, while crossing *campus*, he encountered a former student and greeted him with the question, "Jim?" (あるときキャンパスを横切っていたとき, 以前の学生に出会い, 「J君だったっけ」と声をかけた) (RD 00/7: 143)
  b. College statutes forbid drinking on *campus*. (学則により学内での飲酒は禁止されている) (LDOCE³)
(118) a. I was taken to *casualty* at St Thomas's Hospital. (聖T病院の緊急治療室に運ばれた) (CCED³) [<米>では the emergency room]

b. He had to wait for more than an hour in *casualty* before seeing a surgeon. (外科医に診てもらうのに1時間以上も緊急治療室で待たされた) (CIDE)]

(119) a. On Sundays, the family went three times to *chapel*. (日曜日にはその家族は3度礼拝に行った) (CCED[3])

b. It did not stop there – there's more – every Wednesday everyone in the college had to attend *chapel*. (それで終わったのではなく，つづきがある。毎水曜日には大学の全員が礼拝に参加しなければならなかったのだ) (ConCD-ROM)

c. My dear friend got up in *chapel* to share his experience of the previous night, saying that God had spoken to him and he was terminating his training and going to Switzerland to share his experience. (私の親愛なる友人は，前夜の経験をみなに伝えるために礼拝中に立ち上がって言った。神が語りかけたので，訓練を終えて，スイスに行って，自分の経験をみなに伝えることにした，と) (ConCD-ROM)

(120) a. *Church* begins/is at 9 o'clock. (礼拝は9時からだ／始まる) (OALD[5])

b. They go to/attend *church* every Sunday. (毎週日曜日には礼拝に行く／出席する) (CIDE)

c. I'll see her before/after *church*. (礼拝の前／後に彼女と会おう) (CIDE)

d. He went on a walking trip with some of his friends from *church*. (教会の友だち数人と徒歩旅行に出かけた) (CIDE)

e. I didn't see you in *church* on Sunday. (日曜日，礼拝で君を見かけなかった) (CCED[3])

f. They are in/at *church*. (礼拝中だ) (OALD[5])

(121) a. Stephanie took up making jewellery after leaving *art college* this summer. (Sは今夏芸大を中退したのち装身具の製作を始めた) (CCED[3])

b. She wants to do social work when she finishes *college*. (大学の課程を終えたらソーシャルワークをしたいと思っている) (OALD[5])

c. Her eldest boy is at *college*. (長男は大学に在学中だ) (OALD[5])

d. You have to go to *college* for a lot of years if you want to be a doctor. (医者になりたいのなら何年も大学に行かなければならない) (CIDE)

(122) a. It is after *court*, however, that Cherie's real priorities come to the

fore... (C の真の優先権が表面化したのは閉廷後だ) (RD 00/7: 111)

    b. He was summoned to appear in *court* as a witness. (証人として出廷するよう召喚された) (LDOCE³)

    c. When the company would not pay the money it owed us, we went to *court* to get it. (貸している金を会社が払おうとしなかったので、取り戻すために提訴した) (NHD)

    d. The case was settled out of *court*. (その件は示談で解決された) (OALD⁵)

(123) a. He was rushed to *hospital* to have his eyes flushed. (目の洗浄のため病院へ急送された) (RD 99/6: 60) [hospital の無冠詞用法は、主に〈英〉; 8 章 NB 35-1 参照]

    b. A week after his admission to *hospital*, he discharged himself to fly home to Britain to see his family and to undergo skin grafting. (入院から 1 週間後、退院して英国に飛び家族に会い、皮膚移植をうけた) (RD 99/2: 22)

    c. I wanted to get my husband out of *hospital* and away from the chemotherapy. (夫を退院させて化学療法をやめさせたかった) (RD 99/12: 138)

    d. Cherie visited him in *hospital* every week. (C は毎週病院に彼を見舞った) (RD 00/7: 110)

(124) a. The financier was released from *jail* last week. (金融業者は先週拘置所から釈放された) (CIDE)

    b. Though never charged, she spent the next 15 months in *jail*. (起訴されなかったにもかかわらず、その後の 15 か月を拘置所で過ごした) (RD 99/3: 36)

    c. The thief was sent to *jail*. (泥棒は拘置所に送られた) (NTC)

(125) a. "In my grandfather's school of acting, I'm still in *kindergarten*," she says. (「祖父 [Henry Fonda] の演劇学校では、私はまだ幼稚園課程だわ」と彼女 [Bridget Fonda] は言う) (RD 99/12: 115)

    b. The children took naps every day when they went to *kindergarten*. (子供たちは幼稚園に行ったときは毎日お昼寝をした) (NTC)

(126) a. Many criminals offend again within a year of their release from *prison*. (犯罪者の多くは出所から 1 年以内にふたたび罪を犯す) (LDOCE³)

    b. After a trial, which her family was prohibited from attending, she was sentenced to six years in *prison*. (家族は出廷を拒否されたが，裁判ののち，彼女は懲役6年の判決をうけた) (RD 99/3: 36)

c. He was flung into *prison*. (刑務所にぶち込まれた) (OALD5)

d. Instead, she was taken to *prison*, where she spent five months before Chinese authorities charged her with "spying and illegally providing state secrets." (ところが，彼女は拘置所に連行され，5か月間過ごしたのち，中国当局により「スパイ行為を行い国家機密を不法に提供した」として起訴された) (RD 99/3: 36)

(127) a. She wasn't very academic and hated *school*. (あまり勉強好きではなく，学校がきらいだった) (OALD5)

b. He wanted to quit, just as he had quit *secondary school* and his family. (放りだしたかった。ちょうど中等学校 [の教育課程] と家族を放りだしたように) (RD 96/3: 76)

c. I was told to stay behind after *school*. (放課後残っておくようにと言われた) (OALD5)

d. We had the basic rules of grammar drilled into us at *school*. (授業で文法の基本的ルールを鍛え込まれた) (OALD5)

e. Some children do a paper round before *school*. (登校前に新聞配達をする子供もいる) (OALD5)

f. I loved sports and started playing football in *primary school* in my hometown of Paris, Texas. (スポーツが好きだったので，故郷のT州，Pで小学校 [の教育課程] のときフットボールを始めた) (RD 98/12: 120)

g. Tom is habitually late for *school*. (Tは常習的に授業に遅刻する) (OALD5)

h. It was Preminin's second cruise since graduation from *engineering school*, but he took his job very seriously. (Pには工学課程を卒業以来2度目の巡航だったが，自分の仕事を非常に真剣にうけとめていた) (RD 98/3: 132)

i. Have you got the all-clear from Mum to be off *school*? (学校を中退するのにお母さんの許可を得ていますか) (OALD5)

j. She had to work her way through *law school*. (法科大学院課程を修了するのに自分で学費を稼がなければならなかった) (OALD5)

k. Going to *graduate school* had been a dream come true for her. (彼女にとって大学院課程に行くことは夢の実現だった) (RD 00/6: 121)

(128) a. My sisters and I left home as soon as we could, marrying young or attending *university* across the country. (姉たちも私も可能になるとすぐ家を出た，若くして結婚したり，国内の［東西］反対側の大学に行ったりして) (RD 98/10: 12)
　　b. She's going to study law at *university*. (大学で法学を専攻する予定だ) (CIDE)
　　c. Since that was where I had gone to *university*, I thought he was going to ask for a donation. (私はその地の大学に行っていたので，彼は私に寄付を要求するつもりなのだと思った) (RD 98/12: 125)

冠詞つきの例：

(129) a. It is *a* lively, friendly *campus*, home to people from all sorts of backgrounds, with a wide variety of interest. (活気と親しみにあふれるキャンパスであり，あらゆる背景の人々の家庭であり，多種多様な関心に満ちている) (ConCD-ROM)
　　b. Sara and Mike were married in *a* little Methodist/Baptist *chapel* in Swansea. (SとMとはSのメソジスト派／バプティスト派の小さなチャペルで結婚した) (CIDE)
　　c. The village had 200 inhabitants and *a* wooden *church*. (村には200人の住人がいて，木造の教会があった) (RD 96/10: 124)
　　d. Their daughter Joanna is doing business studies at *a* local *college*. (娘のJは地元の大学で実務研究を学んでいる) (CCED[3])
　　e. The murder trial took place in *a court* of law. (殺人事件の審理が司法裁判所で行われた) (NHD)
　　f. When the man was taken to *a hospital*, doctors found that one of his coronary arteries was more than 95 per cent blocked. (病院に運ばれたとき，医師の診断では，冠状動脈の1つは95パーセント以上詰まっていた) (RD 00/4: 22)
　　g. Three prisoners escaped from *a jail*. (3人の囚人がある刑務所から脱走した) (CCED[3])
　　h. After a court hearing in November 1996, he was sentenced to 37 months and sent to *a prison* in Pennsylvania. (1996年11月の公判ののち，懲役37か月を申し渡されP州の刑務所に送られた) (RD 99/8: 76)
　　i. Paul had no-nonsense views on discipline, pocket-money and education – [Stella] McCartney went to *a* public *school*. (Pはしつけ，

小遣い，および教育に関して堅実な見解をもっていた。M は公立校に通った）(RD 99/5: 51)

上の諸例からわかるように，無冠詞の建物名は建物本来の目的のための活動（本書で言う「働き」）を表し，a/an つきの建物名は話し手／書き手にはわかっている，特定の建物を表している。

NB 7
1)「場所」と「場」
　日本語の「場所」と「場」とは類義語であるが，前者が囲い込まれた空間を表すのに対し，後者は働きを含意する。
　i) 家庭は安らぎの場（？ 場所）だ。
　ii) 競技会は練習の成果を発揮する場（× 場所）だ。
この区別は，英語の冠詞の用法を判断する際にも，ある程度，有効である。例：a house（生活する場所）/ φ house（生活の場）; a church（礼拝のための建物）/ φ church（祈りの場）; a market（販売［売買］する場所）; φ market（交易の場）［空間的認識と機能的認識］（☞ 3.9; 3.10）

2) library/hospital
　特定の目的をもつ建物であるにもかかわらず，library/orphanage が無冠詞では用いられないのは，建物としての囲いが意識されているためと思われる（☞ 4.1)。〈米〉で hospital/university が the をとるのも (Swan 1995: 64) 同様な理由によると推測される。

3) the X School
　School は固有名詞の一部のときしばしば定冠詞をとる（☞ 8.7.2.4)。

3.9 能力・機能

上記の諸例以外にも名詞部が能力，機能など広義の「働き」を表すために冠詞をとらない例がある。ここではそのような例をあげたい。（本節中の無冠詞の例のいくつかは慣用的表現（☞ 3.10; 3.11）と見ることも可能であろう。他方，本節中の冠詞つきの例の多くは指示範囲限定もしくは個別事例を表す（☞ 4-5章)。）

(130) a. When I explained to Mark and Lucy that there are safe new medications that can potentially help restore *erection*, no matter what the primary cause of the problem, they were skeptical. (M と L とに，安全な新薬があり，問題の主因が何であれ，勃起力を回復させるかもしれないと説明したとき，彼らは懐疑的だった) (RD 98/10:

77)［能力］

b. A few months later Mark reported that occasionally he didn't require the medication to achieve *an erection*. (数か月後，M は勃起するのに薬を必要としないことも時々あると報告した) (RD 98/10: 78)［個別事例］

(131) a. "There was a tremendous pressure to keep up *face*," says Chung. "A few months after IMF, people started throwing *face* away." (C が言うには，「面子を保つのに途方もない圧力があった。［しかし］IMF から数か月後には，みんな面子をかなぐり捨てはじめた」) (RD 99/12: 46)

b. He had *a face* like thunder (He looked very angry). (雷のような顔をしていた(とても怒っているようだった)) (CIDE)

(132) a. Vitamin E is believed to play an important role in immune *function*. (ビタミン E は免疫機能において重要な役割を果たすと信じられている) (RD 98/12: 85)［抽象概念］

b. The advice service performs *a* useful *function*. (助言サービスは有益な役目を果たしている) (LDOCE[3]) ［形容詞による限定（☞ 4.4.3)］

(133) a. His companions nervously stood *guard* as the stocky Australian lay unconscious for 30 minutes, his face half-buried in soggy mulch. (その大柄なオーストラリア人が，湿った落ち葉のなかに顔を半分埋めて，30 分も意識を失って横たわっていたとき，彼の仲間たちは心配そうに立って見張っていた) (RD 96/10: 4)［役割 ; cf. on/off/under guard］

b. So we want *a* twenty-four hour police *guard*, please. (警察の 24 時間の見張りをお願いします) (CCED[3])［個別事例 ; 4 章 NB 4 参照］

(134) a. We reached/entered (the) *harbour* at sunset. (日の入りどきに入港した) (OALD[5])［無冠詞のときは，囲い込まれた場所というよりも，船が安全に停泊可能な場という働きを表す ; cf. port］

b. After being at sea for so long, seeing *harbour* was wonderful. (長期間の航海後に，港を見るのはすばらしかった) (CIDE)［同上］

c. Our hotel room overlooked *a* pretty little fishing *harbour*. (ホテルから美しい小漁港が見えた) (CIDE)［囲い込まれた場所 (= 空間的限定 ; ☞ 4.1)］

(135) a. She has great *influence* with the manager and could probably help you. (マネージャーに大きな影響力をもっているので，たぶん助けて

くれるだろう）(OALD⁵)

    b. Everyday activities at home can have *a* big *influence*. (家庭での日々の行動が大きな影響を及ぼすことがある) (RD 99/9: 89) [個別事例]

(136) a. His work shows originality and *insight*. (彼の作品は独創性と洞察力とを示している) (CDAE) [能力]

    b. The article gives us *a* real *insight* into the causes of the present economic crisis. (その論文は現在の経済危機の原因に対する真の洞察を与える) (LDOCE³) [洞察された内容・事実]

(137) a. She does excellent work because she has good *judgment* on what is important and what is not important. (彼女はすばらしい仕事をする。何が重要で何が重要でないかに関してすぐれた判断力があるからだ) (NHD) [能力]

    b. He encourages such playfulness because he thinks it bypasses rational *judgment* and elicits truer reactions. (そのような冗談ぽさを彼は勧める。合理的判断を飛び越えて，より真実の反応を引き出すと考えるからだ) (RD 96/3: 28) [抽象概念]

    c. She made *a judgment* to buy a new car. (新車を買おうと判断した) (NHD) [不定詞による内容限定 (☞ 4.4.5)]

    d. What do you think we should do about this problem[?] – I'm finding it hard to come to/form/make *a judgment*. (この問題に関してどうすべきだと思いますか。私は判断しがたいと思いつつあるところです) (CIDE) [個別事例]

    e. The industry was awaiting *a judgment* from the European Court. (経営者側は欧州裁判所の判決を待っている) (CCED³) [個別事例]

(138) a. He had lost *movement* on his right side. (右半身の運動能力を失った) (RD 99/12: 138) [能力]

    b. Straining to see, he perceived *a* slight *movement* and crawled towards it. (見ようと懸命に努めて，わずかな動きを感知したのでその方向に這(は)って行った) (RD 00/1: 78) [個別事例]

(139) a. Ross shows unusual *perception* for a boy of his age. (Rは彼の年齢の少年としては異例の認識能力を示している) (LDOCE³)

    b. This drug alters *perception*. (この薬物は認識方法を変える) (LDOCE³)

    c. "There is *a* growing *perception*, regardless of the reality, that cigars are back," said a 1985 CAA memo, "and that the momentum is in place for a better climate for our industry." (1985 年の CAA のメモには次のように書いてあった。「現実とは無関係に葉巻が復活しており，わが業界に追い風の勢いがあるという認識が高まりつつある」) (RD 99/3: 55) [that 節による限定 (☞ 4.4.4)]

(140) a. Steroids have a bad name, and although the corticosteroids used in asthma are quite different from anabolic steroids – which some athletes take illegally to improve *performance* – parents often confuse them. (ステロイドは悪名をこうむっており，喘息(ぜんそく)に用いられるコルチコステロイドはアナボリックステロイド——運動選手が競技能力を向上させるために違法に摂取する——とはまったく別物であるにもかかわらず，親たちはそれらを混同することがしばしばある) (RD 99/6: 84) [能力]

b. I arranged for tickets to *a* Toronto *performance* of the Peking Opera for a friend, her father and me. (友人とその父親と私のために北京歌劇団の T 公演のチケットの手配をした) (RD 98/9: 85) [能力の実現 (= 個別行為)]

(141) a. "How much longer before we get to *port*?" he asked weakly. (「港に着くまでもうどのくらいだい」と彼は弱々しく尋ねた) (RD 99/2: 20) [(III-134) [harbour] の注参照]

b. We had a good view of all the ships coming into/leaving *port*. (入港／出港する船がよく見えた) (CIDE)

c. A docker is a person who works at *a port*, loading and unloading ships. (港湾労働者とは，船に荷を積んだり降ろしたりして，港で働く人のことだ) (CIDE) [囲い込まれた場所 (= 空間的限定 ; ☞ 4.1)]

d. New York City is *an* important *port*. (NY 市は重要な港湾都市だ) (NTC)

(142) a. He seemed to have the gift of *prophecy*. (彼には予言の能力があるようだった) (OALD[5])

b. But if you keep saying how good your husband is with the kids, he'll want to be good with the kids. It's *a* self-fulfilling *prophecy*. (だが，夫が子供たちにどんなに優しいか言いつづければ，彼は子供たちに優しくしたいと思うようになる。これは自己実現的予言なのだ) (RD 99/3: 61) [内容限定 (☞ 5.4.4)]

(143) Leave your key at *reception* before departing. (出発の際はキーを受付

にお返しください) (OALD⁵) [仕切られた場所というよりも，客への対応を目的とする場を表すので無冠詞]

比較：Please leave your key at the *reception desk*. (キーは受付にお返しください) (LDOCE³) [空間的限定]

(144) a. His powers of *recollection* are extraordinary. (彼の記憶力は抜群だ) (CIDE)

　　b. I have *a* clear *recollection* of what you said during our meeting. (会談中に君が言ったことをはっきりと記憶している) (NHD) [*of*-phrase による内容限定 (☞ 4.4.1)]

(145) The patient is in *recovery*. (患者は回復室にいる) (OALD⁵) [治療を目的とする場を表すので無冠詞]〈英〉

比較：After the operation, the doctor watched his patient in the *recovery room*. (手術後医師は患者を回復室で診た) (NHD)

(146) a. He showed great *resolution* in facing the robbers. (強盗に出くわしたとき強い決断力を示した) (CIDE)

　　b. On New Year's Day, John made *a resolution* to lose ten pounds. (元旦に J は 10 ポンドやせるという決意をした) (NTC) [不定詞による内容限定 (☞ 4.4.5)]

(147) a. Because trees have taken firm *root*, the soil of terraced fields has stabilized and once-dry streams are flowing again. (木々がしっかりと根を張っているので，ひな壇状の野原の土は固まっていて，涸れていた小川にふたたび水が流れている) (RD 97/5: 117) [take に後続して「安定」という働きを表すので無冠詞；cf. take wing]

　　b. He caught his foot on *a* tree *root* and fell. (木の根に足を取られてころんだ) (OALD⁵) [姿かたちをもつ，物体としての根]

(148) a. To be a counselor or psychiatrist requires great *sensibility*. (カウンセラーや精神科医になるにはすぐれた感性が必要だ) (NHD) [感知する能力]

　　b. The author has applied *a* modern *sensibility* to the social ideals of an earlier age. (著者は往時の社会的理想に対して現代的感性を用いた) (CIDE) [形容詞による種類限定 (☞ 4.4.3.4)]

(149) a. Scouting ahead, he found three huge pines that could provide *shelter*. (前方を探して，[身を] 守ってくれそうな 3 本の大きな松を見つけた) (RD 99/3: 90) [役割]

　　b. The cave provided *a* primitive *shelter* from the storm. (洞窟は粗末

ながらも嵐から守ってくれた) (OALD⁵) [形容詞による種類限定 (☞ 4.4.3.4)]

c. It is completely dark when we finally reach *a* simple *shelter*. (真っ暗になってやっと粗末な避難場所に着く) (RD 99/7: 87)

(150) a. At 7.30 p.m. Briers reported that the Volvo, parked facing a two-metre-high fence, had just flashed its lights in *signal*. (B からの午後 7 時半の報告によると，ボルボが高さ 2 メートルのフェンスに向けて停めてあったが，合図にライトを点けた，とのことだ) (RD 99/11: 19) [合図という「働き」]

b. She flashed the torch as *a signal*. (合図に懐中電灯を点けた) (OALD⁵) [個別事例]

(151) a. Long dismissed as the basest of the five senses, *smell* may be the most powerful. (長いあいだ五感のうち 1 番低いものとして片づけられてきたが，嗅覚は最も強力なものかもしれない) (RD 98/3: 119) [能力; cf. touch]

b. *An* enticing *smell* came from the kitchen. (おいしそうなにおいが台所からて漂ってきた) (OALD⁵) [形容詞による限定 (☞ 4.4.3.4)]

c. There's *a smell* of cooking. (料理のにおいがしている) (OALD⁵) [*of*-phrase による対象限定 (☞ 4.4.1)]

d. Have *a smell* of this egg and tell me if it's bad. (この卵のにおいを嗅いでみて腐っているかどうか教えてくれ) (OALD⁵) [個別行為]

(152) a. Children usually develop *speech* in the second year of life. (子供は通常 2 歳のとき言語能力を発達させる) (CIDE)

b. I was grateful that they didn't ask me to make *a speech*. (ありがたいことに，スピーチをするよう頼まれなかった) (OALD⁵)

(153) a. Swearing, Osborne slammed the automatic brake valve, throwing the train into full emergency *stop*, but he knew it was too late. (チクショーと言いながら，O は自動ブレーキバルブをギュッと締めて，列車を緊急完全停止させようとしたが，手遅れだとはわかっていた) (RD 00/7: 101) [stop は通例 [C] だが，ここでは緊急停止という機能を表すので無冠詞]

b. Our negotiations have come to *a* full *stop*. (交渉は全面停止している) (CIDE) [現在の様態]

(154) a. My boat was tied stern to *stream*, and a glance over the side at water speeding past the hull alarmed me. (船は逆向きに潮流に乗っ

ており，海水が船体を勢いよく越えて行くのを舷側からちらっと見た
だけで怖くなった) (RD 99/3: 44) [範囲や速度などに関して非限定の
「流動」を指すので無冠詞]

  b. There's *a stream* not far from here. (ここから遠くないところに小川
がある) (OALD⁵) [具体物]

(155) a. When Diamond checked their brains, she found that the rats
treated to toys had a significantly thicker cerebral cortex – the part
of the brain largely concerned with *thought*. (大脳を調べたところ，
玩具を与えられたネズミの大脳皮質──思考に深くかかわる大脳部分
──は太くなり，有意差があることに D は気づいた) (RD 99/2: 99) [能
力]

  b. I thought: something's wrong with these people; they lack *thought*
and dignity. (私は思った。この人たちはどこかおかしい。思索と威厳
に欠けているのだ) (RD 99/4: 99) [抽象概念]

  c. *A thought* flitted through my mind. (ある考えが心をよぎった)
(OALD⁵) [特定の考え (= 個別事例)]

  d. It is *a* consoling *thought* that there are others in a much worse
position. (もっとずっと悪い立場の人たちもいると思えば慰めにな
る) (OALD⁵) [that 節による内容限定 (☞ 4.4.4)]

(156) a. Blind people rely a lot on (their sense of) *touch*. (目が不自由な人た
ちは触覚に頼るところが大きい) (OALD⁵) [能力; cf. smell]

  b. I felt *a* cold *touch* on my arm. (腕に冷たい感覚を感じた) (CIDE) [形
容詞による種類限定 (または個別事例)]

  c. At *a*/the *touch* of the button, the door opened. (ボタンに触るとドア
が開いた) (CIDE) [能力行使 (= 個別事例)]

(157) a. The latest model is equipped with five-speed manual *transmission*.
(最新モデルには5速手動変速機能が装備されている) (CIDE) [機能]

  b. The car had *a* faulty *transmission*, so I took it in to the garage. (そ
の車の変速装置は欠陥品だったので修理工場にもって行った)
(CIDE) [製品]

(158) a. People who work at computer terminals for hours at a time often
complain of blurred *vision*. (コンピュータの端末で何時間も連続して
働く人たちはしばしば眼がかすむと訴える) (RD 97/2: 106) [範囲非限
定 (または視力)]

  b. I have *a vision* of a society that is free of exploitation and injustice.

(搾取と不正のない社会の未来図を描いている) (CCED[3]) [*of*-phrase による内容限定 (☞ 4.4.1)]

  c. It was on 24th June 1981 that young villagers first reported seeing the Virgin Mary in *a vision*. (若い村人たちが幻視で聖母マリアを見たと初めて報告したのは 1981 年 6 月 24 日だった) (CCED[3]) [個別事例]

(159) a. It turns out that when my younger self thought of taking *wing*, she wanted only to let her spirit soar. (より若い自分は，翔ぼうと思ったとき，精神だけを舞い上がらせようとしたのだ，ということがわかる) (RD 00/2: 87) [飛翔能力；cf. take root]

  b. The bird had *a* broken *wing* and couldn't fly. (鳥は羽が折れていて飛べなかった) (NHD) [具体物]

　無冠詞で用いられる季節名もここに含めてさしつかえない。季節名が無冠詞で用いられる場合は，温かさ，暑さ，寒さ，芽吹き，収穫など季節の特徴を表し，不定冠詞をとる場合は（通例，形容詞をともなう），種類または期間を表すからである (8.5.1 も参照)。

(160) a. Leaves change colour in *autumn*. (秋には黄葉する) (OALD[6])

  b. It's been *a* very mild *autumn* this year. (今年はとても穏やかな秋だった) (OALD[6])

(161) a. In *summer* we have to mow the lawn once a week. (夏には週に 1 度芝生を刈らなければならない) (OALD[5])

  b. They say we're going to have *a* hot *summer*. (暑い夏になるそうだ) (OALD[5])

(162) a. *Winter* was grudgingly giving way to *spring* in Minnesota's remote Northwest Angle. (M の片田舎の NA でも冬はしぶしぶ春に移りつつあった) (RD 99/11: 25)

  b. We had *a* very hard *winter* last year and some of the plants died. (昨年はとても厳しい冬だったので植物のいくつかは枯れてしまった) (CIDE)

  c. *A* cold *spring* will provide a natural check on the number of insects. (春が寒ければ自然により虫の数は抑制される) (OALD[6])

3.10　慣用的表現 (1)

　慣用的表現の多くも原理 III「働きの有無」によって説明される。以下の例で冠詞が不要なのは，名詞は前置詞または動詞との関連において，名詞本来の

役目あるいは目的，つまり，「働き」，を表しているからである。

(163) a. The boat rode/lay/was at *anchor*. (船は停泊中だった) (CIDE) [船舶を停止させるという機能]
   b. We cast *anchor* off a small island. (小さな島の沖に停泊した) (OALD5)
   c. We dropped *anchor* in the bay. (湾に停泊した) (CIDE)
   d. A heavy *anchor* prevented our boat from drifting from that spot. (重い錨(いかり)のおかげで船はその地点から漂流しなかった) (NTC) [物体]

(164) a. Which team is at *bat*? (どちらのチームが攻撃中ですか) (NHD)
   b. A baseball *bat* has a handle at one end. (野球バットは一方に握りがある) (NHD)

(165) a. I want to go to *bed*, but there is too much work to do. (床につきたいのだが，しなければならない仕事が多すぎる) (NTC)
   b. He lived in a room with only two chairs, *a bed* and a table. (彼が住んでいた部屋には椅子2脚，ベッド1台，テーブル1台しかなかった) (CIDE)

(166) a. She paints with oil on *canvas*. (画布上に油絵を描く) (NHD) [上に絵を描くものという役割においてとらえられた canvas; cf. on cassette]
   b. Pierre Bonnard often painted on *a canvas* much larger than he knew the final painting would require. (PBはわかっていても絵の出来上がりが要求するよりもずっと大きい画布に描くことがよくあった) (CCED3) [限定された広がりをもつ物体としての canvas]

(167) a. His two albums released on *cassette* have sold more than 10 million copies. (カセットでリリースされた2枚のアルバムは1千万部以上売れた) (CCED3) [録音機能 ; cf. on canvas]
   b. I put *a cassette* in the tape player and listened to some jazz. (テーププレーヤーにカセットを入れてジャズを聴いた) (NHD) [具体物]

(168) a. She is with *child* now. (現在妊娠中だ) (NHD) [old use) CIDE [胎児の姿かたちではなく，その「生命」を論じているので無冠詞]
   b. When she was *a child* she was always healthy. (子供のころいつも元気だった) (CIDE)

(169) a. They've been on *court* now for 3 hours. (もう3時間もコートにいる) (OALD5) [試合または練習中]

b. We played on *a* tennis (volleyball, handball, etc.) *court*. (テニス(バレー／ハンドボール) コートでプレーした) (NHD) [空間的限定 (☞ 4.1)]

(170) a. A worker stood the table on *end* so that he could paint its underside. (作業員は裏側に塗るためテーブルを立てた) (NHD) [末端部（四隅のどの部分かは無指定）; cf. on foot]

b. She waited for days on *end* before his letter finally arrived. (彼の手紙がやっと来るまで彼女は何日もつづけて待った) (NHD) [上の転用的用法]

c. A good speech needs a fine beginning, *an* excellent *end* – and as little as possible in-between. (良いスピーチは立派な始まりとすぐれた終わりが必要だ。中間はできるだけないほうがよい) (RD 99/2: 115)

(171) a. The city is best explored on *foot*. (町の探索には歩くのが1番だ) (OALD6) [歩行機能]

b. He dragged *a foot* when he walked, a leftover from polio. (歩くとき片足を曳いていたのはポリオの後遺症だ) (CCED3)

(172) a. Searching the fringes of the fire for his wife and two children, Greg Herman began to lose *heart*. (妻と2人の子供を求めて火事の周辺を探していたが，GH は希望を失いかけた) (RD 01/8: 134) [生の原動力]

b. But the man I knew, someone who virtually became part of my family, was always at *heart* a gentleman. (だが，私の知っている男は，事実上，私の家族の一部になっていたのであるが，心底はいつも紳士だった) (RD 99/6: 72) [感情の湧く場；サイズ非含意]

c. He has *a* hard/cold/cruel *heart*. (彼は無情な／冷たい／残酷な心をしている) (CIDE) [形容詞による限定 (☞ 4.4.3)]

(173) a. Desperate to save what was left to sell at *market*, he put up a sign with a skull and crossbones that read, "One of these melons is poisoned." (残り[のメロン]を市場で売るためにどうしてもとっておこうとして，どくろマークつきで「メロンの1つは毒入り」という掲示を掲げた) (RD 98/11: 14) [交易の場；広がりの範囲には関知せず]

b. Once in the city, I got directions to my sister's neighborhood and asked some women at *a market* if they knew Aman. (いったん街に入ると，妹[宅]の近くに向かい，市場で何人かの女性にAを知っているか尋ねた) (RD 99/10: 128) [空間的に限定された場所 (☞ 4.1)]

(174) a. The builders were on *site* early this morning. (建築業者たちは今朝

　　　　早く現場にいた) (OALD⁵) [仕事遂行の場]

　　b. The monument was moved bodily to *a* new *site*. (記念碑はまるごと新しい場所に移された) (OALD⁵) [空間的限定 (☞ 4.1)]

(175) a. She often forgot her lines on *stage* but she was very good at ad libbing. (舞台でよく台詞を忘れたが，アドリブを言うのがとても上手だった) (OALD⁵) [舞台活動の場]

　　b. Near the end of my stay, as dusk falls and an orange sun plunges towards the ocean, several hundred people stream along Cable Beach towards *a stage* set on a lawn. (滞在の終わり近く，夕暮れが落ちオレンジ色の太陽が海原に沈むころ，数百人の人々が芝地の上に設けられた舞台へと CB ぞいにやってくる) (RD 00/2: 122) [空間的限定 (☞ 4.1)]

(176) a. Children must learn to behave at *table*. (子供たちは食卓のマナーを学ばなければならない) (OALD⁵) [食事の場]

　　b. They sat down at *a* corner *table*. (隅のテーブルに座った) (LDOCE³) [具体物]

(177) a. A dedicated pilot, I was totally focused not on space, but on putting the dummy nuclear bomb strapped to the belly of my FJ-4B Fury precisely on *target*. (パイロットの仕事に没頭していたので，宇宙のことには目もくれず，FJ-4BF 機の胴体にくくりつけられた偽装核爆弾を狙いどおりに落下させることにひたすら集中していた) (RD 99/3: 120) [比喩的に「正確さ」]

　　b. dive-bomb: (of an aircraft, a pilot, etc) to drop bombs on *a* target after diving steeply downwards (急降下爆撃する＝(航空機，操縦士などが) 急角度で降下したのち標的に爆弾を落下させること) (OALD⁵) [具体物]

(178) a. She works in *theatre*, following in her father's footsteps. (父親の足跡に従って演劇界で働いている) (OALD⁵) [演劇活動の場]

　　b. This hall would make *an* excellent *theatre*. (このホールは立派な劇場になるだろう) (OALD⁵) [空間的限定 (☞ 4.1)]

(179) a. The orchestra is currently on *tour* in Germany. (オーケストラは現在ドイツ国内を旅行中だ) (OALD⁵) [抽象概念；期間には関知せず (noncommittal)]

　　b. Janina took me on *a tour* of Radom the next day. (翌日 J は R の旅に連れていってくれた) (RD 01/7:124) [期間・場所を含意]

類例：go on a fact-finding tour（事実探しの旅に出る）(OALD⁵); be/go on a whistle-stop tour of the country（地方遊説旅行中だ／に出る）(OALD⁵) [修飾語句による限定（☞ 4.4)]

(180) a. "I always give *way* to the other vessel," he says.（「いつも他の船に航路を譲ることにしている」と彼は言う）(RD 99/6: 41) [give に後続して通行の許可・権利・能力などを表し，広がりの範囲には関知しないので無冠詞]

　　b. He has got *a* long *way* to go before he can present the scheme to the public.（その計画を大衆に発表できるまでには長い道のりがある）(CIDE) [空間的限定の転用（☞ 4.1)]

3.11 慣用的表現 (2)

本章で述べてきた原理 III により，from flower to flower や house after house, face to face, century upon century, hand in hand のように，前置詞句中で名詞が無冠詞であることの理由も説明可能である。まず，無冠詞用法が「働き」に起因することを明白に示すケースとしては，(181)–(184) のような，地位・身分を表す例があげられる（本章の例 (8)–(13) も参照）。

(181) As I shifted perspectives from *writer* to *friend*, my reporting became a means not only to document Samantha's joy of living, but also to try to enhance it.（書き手から友人へと見方が移行していくにつれて，私の報告は S の生活の喜びを記録するための手段というだけでなく，それを高めようとするものとなった）(RD 01/5: 44)

(182) It was the ideal job, and for 15 years I had thrived – moving from *freelancer* to *foreign correspondent* and finally to *senior editor*.（理想的な仕事であり，15 年間順調だった。フリーランサーから外国特派員に，そして最終的には編集主任へと昇っていった）(RD 01/5: 120)

(183) It's like watching her grow from *baby* to *child* all over again.（まるで彼女がもう 1 度赤ちゃんから子供へと成長するのを見るようだった）(RD 02/2: 55)

(184) It takes at least 10 years to become a master pizzaiolo, he explains, for you must climb up the ladder from *dishwasher* to *dough maker* and then *oven hand*.（彼の説明によると，親方のピザ師になるには最低 10 年かかる。皿洗いから生地ねり，そして，焼き職人へと階段を登っていかなければならないからだ）(RD 99/2: 96)

さらに，Quirk et al. (1985: 280) があげる次の非文も，副詞的用法における名

詞が「独立した名詞としての資格を大部分失っている」(they have largely lost their independent nominal status) ことの証拠となるであろう。

(185) a. *They talked old man to young man.
　　　b. *They stood toes to toes.

以下の, 同様な構文中の名詞も, 本来的には, 位置関係 (または時間関係)(「働き」の下位区分) を表しているのであり, 広がりや高さに関する限定はなく, 特定の事物・物体を指示しているのではない。

(186) a. Then he tenderly transfers the eggs from *bucket* to *hole*. (それから卵をバケツから穴にそっと移す) (RD 98/4: 124)
　　　b. "Good morning!" Dad said as he stepped into the kitchen, smiling from *ear* to *ear*, obviously pleased. (父は台所に入ってきたとき「おはよう」と言った。満面に笑みをたたえて, 明らかに喜んでいた) (RD 00/2: 38)
　　　c. To keep him from being swept overboard, his safety harness was tethered to a wire "jack line" that ran from *bow* to *stern*. (船外に流されないように安全ベルトは, 針金状の「ジャックライン」につながれていて, それは船首から船尾まで伸びていた) (RD 99/8: 17f.)
　　　d. She is covered, *head* to *toe*, with blue paper, exposed only at her abdomen. (頭から足の先まで青い紙におおわれ, 腹部だけが出ていた) (RD 00/9: 122)

(187) a. *House* after *house* and *town* after *town* were engulfed by its frigid waters. (次々と家が, 町が, 冷たい水に呑み込まれた) (RD 98/10: 120)

次の例では, 慣用的表現が *of*-phrase をともなっている ((III-191, b) も参照)。

　　　b. To battle dehydration he consumed *mug* after *mug* of hot water and soup. (脱水症状と闘って, 何杯も何杯も湯やスープを飲んだ) (RD 99/4: 134)
　　　c. (= II-121, c) In San Francisco, Kozlenok and his men were soon opening *pouch* after *pouch* of polished Siberian diamonds. (RD 99/4: 53)

(188) a. Some natives say the influx is corrupting Inishmore's heritage of insular self-reliance, turning *neighbour* against *neighbour* as a handful of locals profit from the visiting hordes. ([観光客の]殺到は島内の自立自給というI島の遺産を腐敗させ, 一握りの地元民が訪問者団体から利益を得るにつれて, 隣人同士が対立するようになっている, と言う現地人もいる) (RD 99/9: 31)

b. They hunted us, infiltrated us, and turned *friend* against *friend*. (我々を探しだし、我々のなかに侵入し、友と友とを背反させた) (BNC, CDA 1700)

c. Skirmish is the 'game' that pits *friend* against *friend*, *brother* against *sister* and *husband* against *wife* – a great way to let off steam. (いざこざは、友人対友人、兄対妹、夫対妻を争わせる「ゲーム」であり、ガス抜きのための見事な方法だ) (BNC, HP6 716)

(189) a. *Hand* in *hand* Micha and I walk to the protruding spit of rock where pilgrims once waited for the "sign of Buddha." (Mと私とは手に手を取って岩の突き出た先端へと歩く。かつて巡礼者たちが「仏陀のしるし」を待った場所である) (RD 99/7: 87)

b. stroll *arm* in *arm* (腕を組んで散歩する) (OALD5)

(190) a. We put two tables *end* to *end* to make one long table. (ひとつの長いテーブルにするために2つのテーブルの端と端をくっつけた) (NHD)

b. He turned the corner and found himself *face* to *face* with a policeman. (角を曲がったら警官と面と向き合っていた) (OALD5)

c. *Shoulder* to *shoulder*, often on their hands and knees, they scoured great swathes on either side of the fire trails, sieving hundreds of square yards of earth and ground cover. (肩をつきあわせ、しばしば四つんばいになって、火事の跡の両側を広範囲に調べ、何百平方ヤードもの泥や地被を篩(ふるい)にかけた) (RD 99/5: 127)

d. On average it takes about seven minutes, *portal* to *portal*, to cover the 1.24 kilometres of water at the narrowest section of the harbour. (港の1番狭い箇所の1.24キロの水域を橋門から橋門まで行くのに、平均で約7分かかる) (RD 99/6: 40)

(191) a. Because there was nowhere for the graveyard to expand in the crowded Quarter, the dead were buried *layer* upon *layer*, *generation* upon *generation*, *century* upon *century*. (混み合った地域ではどこにも墓地を拡げられないので、死者は何層も重ねられ、何世代も重ねられ、何世紀もつづけて埋葬された) (RD 00/4: 59)

b. A video screen is really *row* upon *row* of dots called pixels, each one identified in the computer's memory by a number. (ビデオの画面は実際にはピクセルと呼ばれる点が何列も重なったものであり、それぞれの点はコンピュータのメモリにおいて数で識別されている) (RD 98/11: 89)

(192) a. The apple trees are in (full) *bloom* at the moment. (リンゴの木はいま花盛りだ) (CIDE) [状態]
　　　b. All along the road the trees are in (full) *blossom*. (道路にそって木々は花盛りだ) (CIDE)
　　　c. In the garden most of the plants are in *bud*. (庭のほとんどの植物は蕾(つぼみ)だ) (CIDE)
　　　d. Some of the daffodils are still in *flower*. (水仙のいくつかはまだ咲いている) (CCED³)
　比較： One day my mother showed me how a daisy seemed to have a face, while *an* upside-down azalea *bloom* looked like a flouncy evening gown. (ある日母が教えてくれたのは, アザレアは, 逆さにすれば, すそひだ飾りをつけたイブニングドレスのように見えるけれども, デージーはどうすれば顔があるように見えるか, ということだった) (RD 99/12: 98); Once, just once, he had been careless, and a leg had slid into a crack just as he had stretched to *a* high *blossom*, putting his weight on that corner. (1度, 1度だけ, 彼は注意が不十分だった。高い花に[手を]伸ばして, 隅に体重をかけたとき脚が割れ目に滑り込んだのだ) (ConCD-ROM); Trim to approx. 4″ long, cutting just below *a bud* at the base and just above *a bud* at the top. (根本は蕾のすぐ下で, 先は蕾のすぐ上で切って, 約4インチに刈り込みなさい) (ConCD-ROM); *a flower* with five petals (花弁が5つある花) (OALD⁵)

NB 8　in a clutter
clutter は, in に後続するときは不定冠詞とともに用いられる。
　i) a. My desk is full of *clutter*. (私の机はがらくたでいっぱいだ) (CIDE)
　　 b. How can you work with so much *clutter* on your desk? (机の上をそんなに散らかしていてどうして仕事ができるんだ) (OALD⁵)
　ii) a. My room is always in *a clutter*. (私の部屋はいつも散らかっている) (OALD⁵)
　　 b. He always leaves his office in *a clutter*. (事務所をいつも散らかしている) (CIDE)
前置詞に後続するときは冠詞が不要なことが多いにもかかわらず (た

とえば，(III-192))，in a clutter では冠詞が必要となるのは，clutter が空間的に限定されるためと思われる。すなわち，in は，部屋や事務所に関して用いられれば，広がりが有限であることを示すので，clutter は姿かたちをもつことになり，不定冠詞が必要となるのである。in a hurry/panic/rage が a をとることによって一時的であることを示すのと同様である (in haste は 'careless' という意味的限定を含意するので無冠詞 [CCED³ (s.v., haste) 参照]；in panic/rage は抽象概念を述べるときには無冠詞で用いられる)。他方，in fear/terror/need などにおいては in に後続する名詞が抽象概念を表し，限界を含意しないので不定冠詞は不要である。(clutter の類義語である mess は，通例，不定冠詞をとる。clutter が単位を表す場合に関しては 4.4.1.3 参照。)

第4章　原理 IV ——限定と非限定

4　原理 IV ——限定と非限定

　本節では，名詞部の表す時間，空間，様態，内容，数量，種類などに関して「指示範囲限定」という見方を取り入れることによって，同一の名詞が不定冠詞をとる場合ととらない場合との相違を説明したい。この原理は，次章で紹介する辞書の定義の不備を補うものである。(注：「指示範囲」というよりも「適用範囲」あるいは「意味範囲」というほうが適切な場合もある。多くの場合，指示範囲あるいは適用範囲，意味範囲と使い分ける必要はないので，以下，文脈に応じて単に「範囲」と呼ぶことにしたい。)

> 原理 IV：英語の名詞部は，指示範囲が限定されるときは a/an (あるいは他の限定詞) をとり，指示範囲が限定されないときは a/an をとらない。

　原理 IV により説明可能なケースの具体例をあげるに先だって，なぜ指示範囲が限定されるとき a/an がつけられるかということの理由を考察しておきたい。名詞部の指示範囲が十分に限定されるということは，名詞部の姿かたちが具象化される，つまり，その名詞部が完結された情報を表す，ということである。cord/rope; eternity/time など物質名詞や抽象名詞は，修飾語句なしでは，姿かたちを想像不可能なので，冠詞はつけられない。特に，distance/length など「段階的形容詞」(gradable adjective) から派生された抽象名詞は，単独では絶対的な値や明確な段階がないので，不定冠詞をとることはない。ところが，修飾語句がつけられれば，これらの名詞も指示範囲が一定範囲内に限定され，それゆえ，イメージ化可能となり，a/an が共起可能となるのである (安井 2000: 26 参照)。(注：段階的形容詞 = beautiful/tall/tired などのように，段階的な性質を表し，rather/very など程度を表す副詞をとることができる形容詞。これに対し，dead/impossible/perfect など非段階的な形容詞は程度を表す副詞をとらない。)

　以下，限定方法が明白なものから順に見ていこう。

4.1 空間的限定

原理 IV が特に有効なのは，長さに関する場合である．

(1) a. tie sth up: to fasten sth with *cord*, rope, etc (捕縛する ＝ コードやロープなどで縛ること) (OALD[5]) [物質]

　　b. We need *a* longer *cord* for this telephone. (この電話用にもっと長いコードが必要だ) (CIDE) [具体物；長さ限定]

(2) a. Quickly he cut off a length of *hose* to use a makeshift stethoscope. (素早くホースを切って，間に合わせの聴診器にした) (RD 00/4: 48) [素材]

　　b. Water in the engine compartment is sucked away by *a hose*. (エンジン室の水はホースで吸い出される) (CCED[3])

(3) a. Copper *pipe* is sold in lengths. (銅管は様々な長さで売られる) (OALD[6])

　　b. Our kitchen flooded when *a pipe* burst. (水道管が破裂したとき台所が水浸しになった) (NTC)

比較：The baby is currently being fed via *a tube*. (赤ちゃんは目下のところチューブを通して栄養を与えられている) (CIDE) [pipe と類義語であるが，tube は一定の長さや太さを含意するので，通例，[C]]

(4) a. The thieves had trussed the guard (up) with *rope*. (賊は守衛をロープで縛った) (OALD[5])

　　b. We let the bucket down by *a rope*. (バケツを1本のロープでつるした) (OALD[5])

(5) a. a robe embroidered with gold *thread* (金糸で刺繡(しゅう)されたローブ) (OALD[5])

　　b. pass *a thread* through the eye of a needle (針の目に糸を通す) (OALD[5])

(1-5, a) のように，長さに関してノーコメントである場合は無冠詞で用いられるが，(1-5, b) のように，一定の長さをもつこと，つまり，どこからどこまでという両端の区切り，が含意される場合は冠詞がつけられる．

以上は一次元的に囲い込まれた線的長さに関する例であるが，名詞が二次元的に囲い込まれた空間的広がりを表す場合も「範囲限定」という概念は有効である．

(6) a. There's a gorge right in front of us, but all we can see is *desert* with mesas the shape of crushed cowboy hats. (すぐ眼前は峡谷だが，見えるのは砂漠だけであり，つぶれたカウボーイハット型のメサ [台地

が点在している）(RD 96/10: 77)

 b. It now looked almost as if we were flying over *an* Arizona *desert*, but no desert has ever had such terrain. (今やまるでAの砂漠の上を飛んでいるかのようだったが，どんな砂漠もそんな地形であったことはないのだ) (RD 99/3: 133) [月面上での描写；アリゾナ州（特に，南半部）にある多くの砂漠のうちの任意の１つを指す]

(7) a Feminine forms – circles and ovals that suggest completeness, receptiveness and *enclosure* – provide the underlying theme for many packages, because these forms have the most positive associations. (女性的な姿――完全性や受容性，囲い込みを示唆する円形および卵形――は，多くの容器に潜在的テーマを提供する。これらの姿は最も積極的な連想をともなうからである) (RD 96/3: 27)

 b. The dogs are in *a* fenced *enclosure* in the backyard. (犬は裏庭の柵をめぐらした囲みのなかにいる) (CDAE)

(8) a. And yet, if I lifted my gaze, I could see down past the periphery of the park, right into Rwandan *farmland*, which rolled bare and treeless up to the very edge of the forest. (それでも，視線を上げれば，公園の周辺の彼方にRの農地が見えた。それは地肌がむきだしで，木々はなく，うねって森の端までつづいていた) (RD 00/6: 44) [farmland は，通例，無冠詞；b-文の farm と相補的]

 b. His family bought *a* two-hectare dairy *farm*, ostensibly to provide milk and eggs for the paper mill's canteen but really to support the wounded soldier and his children. (彼の家は２ヘクタールの酪農場を買った。表向きは製紙工場の簡易食堂にミルクや卵を供給するためだったが，実際にはその負傷兵と子供を養うためだった) (RD 99/10: 100) [farm は，通例，限定詞つき]

(9) a. Some of his ideas are way out in left *field*. (彼の考えのいくつかはまったく風変わりだ) (LDOCE[3])

 b. He hit a long ball to right *field*. (右翼側に長打を放った) (LDOCE[3]) [どこからどこまでが right/center/left field なのか範囲がはっきりしないときは無冠詞；範囲が含意されるときは対立の the (☞ 8.5) がつけられる]

 c. The pilot had to make an emergency landing in *a field*. (パイロットは畑に緊急着陸をせざるをえなかった) (OALD[5]) [野原／畑は囲い込みが明確なので，この意味では [C]]

(10) a. Both engines landed in dense *forest* below. (両エンジンとも下の密林に落下した) (RD 98/10: 35) [広がりの範囲には関知せず]

b. Shortly after 9 P.M. on December 29, 1980, Betty Cash, 52, was driving through *a* pine *forest* on a deserted rural road to her home in Dayton, Texas. (1980年12月29日午後9時をわずかに回ったころ BC, 52歳, は T 州の D の自宅へと寂れた田舎道を車で走って松林を抜けていた) (RD 99/8: 118) [囲い込み含意 (= 空間的限定)]

c. The trip took us through ancient, primordial *rain forest*. (その旅で我々は古い原始時代の多雨林を通り抜けた) (CIDE)

d. Plants grow quickly in *a rain forest*. (植物は多雨林内では成長が速い) (NHD)

参考: Large areas of *rain forest* are being destroyed. (広範な多雨林が破壊されている) (CIDE) ["NP₁ of NP₂" の形式で素材扱い (☞ 2.1.2)]

(11) a. Lifting her up, Tom carried her onto dry *ground*. (T は彼女を抱え上げて, 乾燥した地面まで運んだ) (RD 98/12: 80)

b. The area was all broken concrete and it was being used as *a* dumping *ground*. (一帯は瓦礫(がれき)の山であり, ゴミ捨て場として使われていた) (ConCD-ROM)

c. a design of pink roses on *a* white *ground* (白地にピンクのバラのデザイン) (OALD⁵)

(12) a. To plot a rescue program, Miquelle knew he would have to capture at least ten of the tigers, place radio collars on them and track their movements – vital information for identifying the tiger population and determining how much *habitat* they need. (M にはよくわかっていたが, 救済計画を立てるには, 少なくとも10頭のトラを捕獲し, 無線機つきの首輪をつけ, 彼らの動きを追跡しなければならなかった。トラの数を特定し, どれだけの生息範囲を必要とするかを算定するために不可欠な情報だからである) (RD 98/9: 28)

b. The polar bear lives in *a* cold *habitat*. (シロクマは寒冷の生息地にいる) (NTC)

(13) a. Either side of the river is dense, impenetrable *jungle*. (川の両側は足を踏み込めない密林だ) (CIDE)

b. Our garden is *a* real *jungle*. (わが家の庭はまったくジャングルだ) (CIDE)

(14) a. Amphibians live both in water and on *land*. (両生類は水中にも陸上

第 4 章 原理 IV ―― 限定と非限定　*117*

にも生息する) (NTC)
　　b. My uncle was from *a land* across the sea. (伯父は海の向こうの国の生まれだ) (NTC) [cf. wasteland]
(15) a. garden: especially BrE a piece of land around or next to your house where there is usually *lawn* (= area of grass) and an area where you grow flowers, plants, or vegetables (庭 ＝ 特に〈英〉，家のまわりまたはすぐそばの土地，通例，芝地 (= 芝生の地面) および花や植物，野菜を育てる地面がある) (LDOCE[3])
　　b. There was *a lawn* of sorts . . . (名ばかりの芝地があった) (CCED[3])
　参考：The house is surrounded by several acres of *lawn*. (その家は数エーカーの芝地に囲まれている) (CIDE) ["NP$_1$ of NP$_2$" の形式で素材扱い (☞ 2.1.2)]
(16) a. To the east there is a dense date plantation bounded by *marsh*. (東には鬱蒼(うっそう)としたナツメヤシの農園があり沼地と接していた) (Con-CD-ROM) [沼地状態の場所；広がりの範囲には関知せず]
　　b. Rain was falling fairly steadily and most of the ground had become *a marsh*. (雨がかなり連続的に降っていて地面のほとんどは沼地になっていた) (CIDE) [空間的限定]
　参考：At the mouth of the river is a large area of *marsh*. (河口には広大な沼地がある) (CIDE) ["NP$_1$ of NP$_2$" の形式で素材扱い (☞ 2.1.2)]
(17) a. This area used to be *meadow* but it was ploughed up during the war. (この一帯は牧草地だったが戦争中に耕作された) (CIDE) [状態；広がりの範囲には関知せず]
　　b. At noon, the villagers gather at *a meadow*. (正午に村人たちは牧草地に集まる) (RD 00/4: 107) [空間的限定]
(18) a. Rare remnants of the ancient world have been shepherded into our own times by the forbidding guard of desert and *mountain*: whole cities, dry as tamarisk; tiled domes; a thousand Buddhas on a cliff face at Dunhuang, China. (古代世界のまれな遺物が砂漠と山という人を寄せつけない番人により現在まで守られてきている：乾燥した都市全体，瓦葺(かわらぶ)きの丸屋根建造物，中国，敦煌の千もの磨崖仏) (RD 99/1: 71)
　　b. The plane flew into *a mountain* and disintegrated on impact. (飛行機は山に激突し，衝撃で分解した) (OALD[5]) [空間的限定]
(19) a. His success was due in *part* to luck. (彼の成功はいくぶん幸運によ

  る) (OALD⁵)
- b. Little Bit had become *part* of our family. (LB[クマの名前]はわが家の家族の1員になっていた) (RD 99/1: 135) [家族の生活のどこからどこまでを占めるかは限定不可能]
- c. "There's something in there that looks like a piece of glass." The doctor pointed to *a part* of the X ray that was black. (「そこにガラス片のようなものがあります。」医師はX線の黒い部分を指した) (RD 98/12: 129) [特定の部分に限定]
- d. This region has only recently become *a* constituent *part* of the republic. (この地域は共和制国家の構成部分にほんの最近なったばかりだ) (CIDE) [特定の部分に限定]
- e. There was still *a* missing *part* in Hutchinson's family . . . (Hの家庭にはまだ欠けている部分があった) (RD 01/9: 47) [父子家庭なので母親が欠けていることを指す]

(20) a. Lost in its lyrical beauty, he would remain rooted in *place* until the last haunting tones faded into silence. (その叙情的な美しさに我を忘れて，耳に残る最後の音が消えて静かになるまでその場に立ちつくしていた) (RD 97/2: 87) [広がりの範囲には関知せず (a–f)]
- b. I felt completely out of *place* among all those smart rich people. (洗練された金持ちの人たちのなかでまったく場違いに感じた) (LDOCE³)
- c. It all began to fall into *place* when detectives found her will. (刑事が彼女の遺書を発見したときすべてのつじつまが合いはじめた) (OALD⁵)
- d. Houses and factories gave *place* to open fields as the train gathered speed. (列車がスピードを上げるにつれて家屋や工場は開けた野原に変わった) (OALD⁵)
- e. The next meeting will take *place* on Thursday. (次回の会議は木曜日に開催される) (LDOCE³)
- f. The swimmer who won first *place* got a gold medal. (優勝した泳者は金メダルを得た) (NTC) [本来的には位置関係 (= 働き)]
- g. I couldn't find *a place* to park. (駐車する場所を見つけられなかった) (LDOCE³) [空間的限定]
- h. Make sure you keep it in *a* safe *place*. (必ず安全な場所に保管しなさい) (LDOCE³) [形容詞による限定 (☞ 4.4.3)]

　　　　i. He's been offered *a place* at York University. (Y 大学から勤め口の申し出があった) (LDOCE³) [1 人分の場所]

(21) a. But first Blair had to put himself in *position* to make such changes. (だが，そのような変革をするためには B はまず立場を固めなければならなかった) (RD 98/3: 55) [広がりの範囲には関知せず]

　　b. Now it pops out of *position* every once in a while. (今でもときどき [膝が] はずれる) (RD 00/6: 42)

　　c. Sit quietly in *a* comfortable *position*, close your eyes and relax your muscles. (心地よい位置に静かに座って，両目を閉じて，筋肉を緩めなさい) (RD 99/10: 58) [特定の場所]

(22) a. Flat *prairie* gave way to the rugged landscape of the West, and Hutchings's company traveled by starlight to avoid the daytime heat. (平坦な草原は西部のごつごつした風景へと変わった。H の一行は昼間の暑さを避けるため星明りによって進んだ) (RD 98/6: 51) [状態；広がりの範囲には関知せず]

　　b. The farms of Illinois were once *a* vast *prairie*. (I の農園はかつては広大な草原だった) (NTC) [空間的限定]

(23) a. This vehicle has been parked on private *property*. (この車は私有地に停められている) (CCED³) [私有地の広さには関知せず (= 抽象概念)]

　　b. Cecil inherited *a* family *property* near Stamford. (C は S 近くの家産を相続した) (CCED³) [空間的限定] 類例：a beachfront property (CIDE); own a property in the West Country (OALD⁵)

(24) a. James took the books off the little table to make *room* for the television. (J は，テレビを置くスペースをつくるために，小机から本を取りのけた) (CIDE)

　　b. I'd like *a room* with a shower, please. (シャワー付きの部屋をお願いします) (OALD⁵)

(25) a. The tuatara also live in these burrows, which give *sanctuary* from predators like hawks. (ムカシトカゲはこういった穴にも住んでいる。タカのような捕食動物から保護してくれるからだ) (RD 99/11: 108) [保護という働き；広がりの範囲には関知せず]

　　b. She left a large sum of money in her will to found *a* wildlife *sanctuary*. (野生動物の保護区域を設立するように遺言で多額のお金を残した) (CIDE) [空間的限定]

(26) a. Write the letter on the computer, then you can make changes easily on *screen*. (コンピュータで手紙を書けば、画面上で簡単に変更できる) (CIDE) [表示という働き；広がりの範囲には関知せず]

b. I spend most of the day working in front of *a* computer *screen*. (コンピュータの画面の前で仕事をしてその日の大半を過ごした) (CIDE, CDAE)

(27) a. The sun was hot, and there were no trees to offer us *shade*. (太陽は暑く、陰を与えてくれる樹木はなかった) (CIDE) [日よけという働き；広がりの範囲には関知せず]

b. When I arrived, the children were drawing pictures and learning English in a makeshift school Dr Cynthia had set up under *a shade* of woven leaves. (到着したとき、子供たちは仮校舎で絵を描いたり英語の勉強をしたりしていた。それは編んだ木の葉の陰にC博士が建てたものだった) (RD 99/10: 37) [陰の範囲限定]

(28) a. This corner of the room is always in *shadow*. (部屋のこの隅はいつも陰になっている) (CIDE) [陰の範囲には関知せず]

b. The house next door casts *a shadow* over our garden. (隣家のためわが家の庭が陰になる) (CIDE) [隣家が作る陰]

(29) a. When he reached *shore*, Gorrell felt almost euphoric. (岸に着いたとき、Gは幸福感のようなものを感じた) (RD 98/9: 35) [岸の範囲には関知せず]

b. As he returned home, the apparition of Christina, "crawling like a crab on *a* New England *shore*," stirred Wyeth's imagination. (帰宅したとき、Cの亡霊が「NEの岸のカニのように這(は)って」Wの妄想を刺激した) (RD 97/5: 78) [場所的に限定された岸]

c. We are on *a shore* of white sand too hot to stand still for a moment... (我々は暑くていっときもじっと立っていられない白い砂の岸辺にいた) (BNC, AOL 1344) [修飾語句による限定 (☞ 4.4.1)]

(30) a. Elephants were often to be found in *swamp* in eastern Kenya around the Tana River. (象は、東ケニアのT川周辺の沼沢地でしばしば見かけられた) (CCED³)

b. Certain they had dropped into *a swamp*, he waited for the water to pour in. (沼地に落ちたのはたしかだった。[車両に] 水が入り込んでくるのを待った) (RD 00/7: 103)

参考：And the silence across 300 square kilometres of northern *swamp* and woods that cold Friday, May 15, 1998, was absolute. (その寒い金曜日，1998年5月15日，300平方キロにわたる北の沼地と森の静けさは絶対的だった) (RD 99/11: 25) ["NP_1 of NP_2" の形式で素材扱い (☞ 2.1.2)]

(31) a. We're in uncharted *territory*. (未知の領域に入っている) (RD 02/9: 69) [territory の広さには関知せず]

  b. The island of Guam is *a territory* of the USA. (G島は合衆国の領土だ) (NHD) [空間的限定]

比較：As this is Aboriginal *territory* unaffected by commercial fishing, the sea teems with fish. (ここは先住民の領地であり，商業的漁業の影響をうけていないので，海は魚であふれている) (RD 00/2: 120) [territory の広さには関知せず；an をつければ aboriginal territory が他にもあることを示す；(VIII-48, a) [wife] も参照]

(32) a. Rain forests are being transformed into barren *wasteland*. (雨林は不毛の荒地へと変えられている) (CDAE) [状態；広さの範囲には関知せず]

  b. All that was left in the tornado's direct path was *a wasteland* – house after house, street after street irrevocably demolished. (竜巻がじかに通過したあとに残っていたのは荒廃した土地だった。家という家，通りという通りが再興できないほど破壊されていた) (RD 00/2: 143) [空間的限定；cf. land]

(33) a. *Wilderness* is protected in many of our national parks. (未開地が国立公園の多くで保護されている) (NHD) [状態；広さの範囲には関知せず]

  b. The garden had been neglected for years and was now *a wilderness* of weeds. (庭園は長年手入れされていなかったので今では雑草の荒れ野だ) (OALD5)

(1)–(33) の例ほど明白ではないが, distance/space も有限であることが指定されるときは，冠詞がつけられる。

(34) a. *Distance* is no problem with modern telecommunications. (現代の遠距離通信にとって距離は問題ではない) (OALD5) [無冠詞のときは「距離」という抽象概念]

  b. At *a distance* of 30 feet the buffalo stopped and gazed at Alistair. (30フィート離れたところでバファローは立ち止まってAをじっと見た) (RD 98/11: 35) [数値による距離限定 (☞ 4.4.1.1)]

  c. There is *a distance* now between those two friends. (現在2人の友人のあいだには隔たりがある) (NHD) [*between*-phrase による個別性含意]

  d. The police are out in force, keeping people *a* safe *distance* from the site. (警察が出動し，人々を現場から安全な距離に隔離する) (RD 99/1: 45) [形容詞による距離限定 (☞ 4.4.3.4)] 類例：a short distance from camp (RD 99/3: 90)

(35) a. The world exists in *space* and time. (世界は空間と時間とのうちに存在する) (OALD⁵) [範囲には関知せず]

  b. There's *a space* here for your signature. (こちらが署名欄です) (OALD⁵) [書面上の限定された空間]

  c. His world, the submarine's Central Command Post, was a hot, low-ceilinged compartment where as many as 20 men worked in *a* confined *space*. (彼の世界である潜水艦の中央指令所は，蒸し暑く，天井の低い仕切り部屋であり，その狭い空間のなかで20人もの男が働いていた) (RD 98/3: 124) [空間的限定] 類例：a curtained space (RD 99/12: 126)

  d. It may explain why my husband can park a van in *a space* the size of a postage stamp. (それで，夫が郵便切手ほどのスペースにバンを駐車できることの説明がつく) (RD 99/7: 79) [空間的限定]

community/society も，広がりもしくは種類が限定されないときは無冠詞で用いられ，限定されるときは不定冠詞（または他の限定詞）がつけられる。

(36) Because it's a mistake to take for granted *a* good *community*, or to assume we'd luck into one somewhere else. In the end, good and lasting *community* arises from a commitment to it. (なぜなら，住みよい地域を当然のものと考えたり，どこかよそに運よく入り込むと思ったりするのは間違いだからだ。結局，住みやすく永続的な共同体はそれに関与することから生じるのだ) (RD 00/6: 12) [a good community は同類が存在するという前提のもとに任意の1つを指すので不定冠詞をともなう；good and lasting community はこれから形成されるべき共同体を指し，まだ姿かたちをもっていないので無冠詞]

(37) a. If you can stir children to want to learn, you're improving *society*. (子供たちに勉強したいという気持ちを起こさせることができれば，社会を改善していることになる) (RD 99/12: 115)

  類例：wives in Vietnamese society (RD 98/12: 19); live in mainstream

society (RD 99/3: 82); expelled from Soviet naval society (RD 98/3: 143); give something back to society (RD 99/3: 83); reintegrated into Cambodian society (RD 99/11: 19); many insights into panda society (RD 00/2: 26)
b. She worries her people have forgotten what it means to build *a society* instead of destroy it. (彼女の心配は，国民が社会を，破壊ではなく，建設するとはどういうことかを忘れてしまった，ということだ) (RD 99/10: 35)

類例：in a society where personal, political and religious beliefs are muzzled for fear of offending (RD 98/3: 117); in a society that degrades moral values (RD 98/12: 20); in a society in which people blame everyone from their parents to the government for their failure to get ahead (RD 99/12: 41); a peaceful society (RD 99/8: 36); a technocrastic society – a society of orderly drones (RD 99/10: 42); an affluent society (RD 99/10: 43)

NB 1 「歩いて行ける距離」
walking/driving/jogging distance は漠然としているため，距離の限定とはみなされないので無冠詞で用いられる。
  i) Does she live within walking/driving *distance* of her parents? (彼女は両親のもとから歩いて／車で行ける距離内に住んでいますか) (CIDE)
  ii) [One suspect] lived within jogging *distance* of the area suggested by Rossmo's profile... (容疑者の1人はR作のプロフィールが示す地域からジョギングで行ける距離内に住んでいた) (RD 01/9: 78)
類例：
  iii) [C]igarettes and ashtrays on low tables are within easy *reach*. (タバコや灰皿を低いテーブルに置けば[幼児でも]簡単に手が届く) (RD 96/3: 55) [(IV-89, a) [range] も参照]
  iv) Keep those medicines out of *reach* of the children/out of the children's reach. (薬は子供の手の届かないところに保管しなさい) (OALD[5])
  v) Mark was out of *earshot*, walking ahead of them. (Mは彼らの先を歩いて，声が聞こえないところにいた) (CCED[3])

次の例文は，範囲含意と非含意 (= 空間的限定と非限定) とを明示している。
(38) a. All we could see was blue *sky*. (見えるのは青空ばかりだった) (RD 99/3: 126) [範囲非含意；一面の青空]
　　 b. In sharp contrast to her mood, the clouds were breaking up to reveal *a* blue *sky*. (彼女の気分とは著しく対照的に，雲が切れて青空が出はじめていた) (OALD6) [範囲含意；雲の切れ間]

上例ほど明示的ではないが，fog/haze/mist が不定冠詞をとれば，広がりが一定範囲内であることが含意される。(いずれも，通例，形容詞をともなう。)
(39) a. The car and the van collided head-on in thick *fog*. (乗用車とバンとが濃霧のなかで正面衝突した) (OALD6) [状態]
　　 b. Sailing in *a* thick *fog*, the ferry hit another passenger ship, split in two and sank. (濃霧のなかを航海中，フェリーは別の客船とぶつかり，2つに折れて沈没した) (RD 01/4: 59) [航路周辺の濃霧]
(40) a. The engine was throwing off so much heat that the air above it shimmered with *haze*. (エンジンは多量の熱を発していたのでその上の空気はもやで揺らめいていた) (LDOCE3) [形状不定の物質]
　　 b. *A* brownish *haze* hung over the field. (茶色っぽいもやが野原の上にかかっていた) (CDAE) [野原の上のもや]
(41) a. Thick *mist* made flying impossible. (濃霧のため飛行は不可能になった) (CCED3) [状態]
　　 b. The sleet disappears, and *a* thick *mist* suffuses the mountain. (みぞれは消え，濃い霧が山をおおう) (RD 98/10: 84) [山の周りの濃霧]

heaven/paradise/hell が不定冠詞をとる場合も範囲含意と非含意という区別によって説明可能である。無辺の世界は無冠詞であり，限定された世界は不定冠詞（または他の限定詞）を必要とするからである。
(42) a. Mary told her children that their grandfather was up in *heaven* with the angels. (Mは子供たちにおじいさんは天国にいて，天使といっしょだと言った) (NTC)
　　 b. If there's *a heaven* on earth, this is it! (地上に天国があるなら，ここがそうだ) (OALD5)
(43) a. "Oh, my God!" screamed one woman. *Hell* had come to Alabama. (「うわあ」と1人の女性が叫んだ。地獄がAにやって来たのだ) (RD 00/2: 133)
　　 b. Josh felt trapped in *a* living *hell*. (Jはこの世の地獄にはまったよう

に感じた) (LDOCE³)

(44) a. They believe they would all go to *Paradise* after they died. (彼らは死後はみな天国に行くと信じている) (CIDE)
　　b. Hawaii is *a paradise* for surfers. (Hはサーファーたちには楽園だ) (LDOCE³)

utopia も同様である。

(45) a. But will it really be *utopia* for Black people? (しかし，本当に黒人にとってユートピアになるだろうか) (CCED³)
　　b. We weren't out to design *a* contemporary *utopia*. (何がなんでも現代のユートピアを設計しようとしていたのではない) (CCED³)

以上の例とは異なり，paddy (水田); parking lot/car park (駐車場); reservation (保護地) などは囲い込みを含意するので，可算名詞扱いされる。

(46) a. Sophal ... was found two weeks later, face down in *a* rice *paddy*. (Sは2週間後水田でうつぶせの状態で発見された) (RD 99/11: 18)
　　b. *A parking lot* is *an* outside *car park*. (屋外駐車場とは外にある駐車場のことだ) (CIDE) [主に, parking lot は〈米〉, car park は〈英〉; (8章 NB 23-4, vii, 比較) 参照]
　　c. The family lives on *a* Native American *reservation*. (その家族は米先住民保護地に住んでいる) (CIDE)
　　d. He's the chief warden of *a* big-game *reservation*. (大型動物禁猟区の管理主任だ) (CIDE)

厳密な意味では空間的限定ではないが，business/enterprise/industry/service もここに含めてさしつかえないであろう。いずれも活動分野が限定されるときは不定冠詞をとるからである。

(47) a. People flocked to the street, and *business* in the dying downtown boomed. (通りには人が群がり，斜陽の町の景気が急に活気づいた) (RD 98/6: 61)
　　b. His parents, Salam and Abike, operated *a* small cement *business*. (彼の両親のSとAとは小さなセメント会社を営んでいた) (RD 97/2: 87)

(48) a. Those were the years of private *enterprise*, when lots of small businesses were started. (当時は民間企業の時代であり，多くの小企業が設立された) (CIDE)
　　b. Horse breeding is indeed *a* risky *enterprise*. (馬の飼育繁殖はまったく危険な事業だ) (CCED³)

(49) a. *Industry* grew quickly after the discovery of electricity. (産業は電気の発見後急速に発達した) (NHD)
   b. England was warm enough to support *a* thriving wine *industry*. (英国は盛況なワイン産業を支えるには十分温暖だった) (RD 99/9: 24) [特定分野を指す；参考：NTC (s.v., industry 2): 'the business activity concerning a specific class of product or service']
(50) a. When *service* was finally resumed, I noticed that one sleeping passenger had scribbled a note on a serviette and attached it to a button on his shirt. (業務がやっと再開されたとき，居眠りしていた1人の乗客がナプキンにメモを走り書きして自分のシャツのボタンにくっつけているのに気づいた) (RD 00/9: 45)
   b. Sterritt has recovered from his injuries and is once again flying planes for *a* charter *service*. (Sは怪我から回復して，ふたたび飛行機に乗ってチャーター業をしている) (RD [U.S. Edition] 98/9: 93)
   c. We offer *(an)* excellent after-sales *service*. (すぐれたアフターサービスをやっております) (OALD[5]) [褒めことばと様態限定 (☞ 4.4.3.4)] [「便」という意味の service に関しては『英語教育』(2000, 12月号, p. 67f.) 参照]

4.2 時間的限定

時間を表す名詞も，いつからいつまでという限定なしに抽象的意味を表すときは無冠詞で用いられるが，時間が限定されるときは不定冠詞がつけられる。

(51) a. That's why we group people by *age*. (こういう理由で人々を年齢ごとに分けるのだ) (RD 99/11: 63)
   b. One Christmas season, however, his life is altered after he gets to know an old woman whose only child died at *a* young *age*. (しかし，ある年のクリスマスの季節に，一人息子が若くして亡くなった老婦人と知り合って以来，彼の人生は急変した) (RD 00/3: 30) [死亡した年齢に限定 (☞ 4.4.3)]　類例：an early age (RD 00/3: 18)
   c. He was only 13, *an age* when peer approval means everything. (ほんの13歳だから，友だちに認められることがすべてなのだ) (RD 99/8: 124) [関係詞節による限定 (☞ 4.4.2)]

   NB 2　age 補足
   次例で age が無冠詞であるのは，in depth/length; in terror/haste

などと同様，in に後続するとき age は範囲に関して無指定であるためと思われる（3 章 NB 8 参照）。

 i) To test this idea, Sheldon Cohen . . . and his colleagues . . . recruited 276 healthy volunteers ranging in *age* from 18 to 55. (この考えを試すために SC と彼の同僚は年齢が 18 歳から 55 歳の健康な自発的参加者を 276 名集めた) (RD 99/11: 8)

 ii) Our powers decay in old *age*. (老齢になるとパワーが落ちる) (OALD⁵) [上限無制限]

次の例では golden により種類が限定され，かつ一時的であることが含意されているので，不定冠詞が必要である（☞ 4.3; 4.4）。

 iii) The Jewish community experienced *a* golden *age* during the reign of the Hapsburg king Rudolf II, who recognised them as valuable members of society, not to mention a useful source of revenue. (ユダヤ人社会は H 家の王 R 二世の御代に黄金期を謳歌(おうか)した。王は彼らを，有用な収入源であることは言うにおよばず，社会の貴重な成員として認めたのだ) (RD 00/4: 59)

(52) a. You're grounded for three weeks for staying out after *curfew*. (門限後外出していたので 3 週間の地上勤務だ) (RD 99/1: 54) [curfew を時間的な広がりをもたない 1 点としてとらえる；cf. at noon/high tide]

 b. There's *a curfew* from eleven at night until seven in the morning. (夜の 11 時から朝の 7 時まで外出禁止令が敷かれている) (CIDE)

参考：The village was placed under *curfew*. (村は戒厳令下に置かれた) (CCED³) [「拘束力」という働きを表すので無冠詞 (☞ 3 章)]

(53) a. The trip will bring to an end years of *estrangement* between the two countries. (その旅は 2 国間の長年の断絶を終わりにするだろう) (CCED³)

 b. The misunderstanding had caused *a* seven-year *estrangement* between them. (誤解のため 7 年間仲違いしていた) (OALD⁵) [数値による期間限定 (☞ 4.4.1.1)]

(54) a. Many people wonder about *eternity*. (多くの人は永遠とは何かと思う) (NHD) [限界非含意]

 b. The wait seems like *an eternity*. (待ち時間はまるで永遠のようだ) (RD 96/3: 46) [限界含意]

(55) a. At *present* children under 14 are not permitted in bars. (目下のと

ころ 14 歳未満の子供はバーには入場禁止だ) (CCED³)

  b. Marriage exists in a continuum, with time past and time future embodied in *an* endless *present*. (結婚は連続体であり, 果てしない現在のうちに具現化された過去の時間と未来の時間とを含むのだ) (RD 99/4: 110) [endless は強調的に長時間を表す]

(56) a. For a girl who had never been aware of *time*, I learned to watch the clock closely – and live by it. (時間というものを知らなかった少女として, 時計をよく見て, それに従って生活することをおぼえた) (RD 99/10: 130) [抽象概念]

  b. There comes *a time* when sons test their fathers. (息子が父親を試すときが来る) (RD 97/5: 6) [関係詞節による限定 (☞ 4.4.2)]

hour/day/week/year も, 60 分/24 時間/7 日/365 日という長さの画定がなされるかなされないかによって, 冠詞の選択が決定される.

(57) a. On a journey on the subway during rush *hour*, my train stopped at a popular station. (ラッシュアワー時に地下鉄に乗っていると, 乗降客の多い駅で電車が停まった) (RD 99/1: 54) [60 分間に限定されるわけではない]

 類例: I had to drive eight miles at rush *hour*. (ラッシュアワー時に 8 マイル運転しなければならなかった) (CCED³)

  b. The exam lasted *an hour*/three hours/half *an hour*/a quarter of *an hour*/*an hour* and a half. (試験は 1 時間/3 時間/半時間/15 分/1 時間半つづいた) (CIDE)

(58) a. Operation *day* had arrived. (手術の日が来た) (RD 94/4: 51)

 類例: There is no such thing as family *day* either. (家族[面会]の日などというものもない) (RD 02/3: 52)

  b. I'm taking *a day* off next week. (来週 1 日休暇をとる) (LDOCE³)

(59) a. During exam *week* at university, dinners tend to get longer and longer as students put off going back to their studies. (大学の試験週間中, 学生は自習室に戻るのを遅らせるので, 夕食はだんだん長くなりがちだ) (RD 00/3: 143)

  b. I spent *a week* gathering the courage to say no. (断る勇気をふるいおこすのに 1 週間かかった) (CIDE)

(60) a. This time of *year*, weather usually moved northwest to southeast. (1 年のこの時期, 天気はふつう北西から南東へ移動した) (RD 99/11: 26)

  b. The earth takes *a year* to make a circuit of the sun. (地球は太陽を 1 周するのに 1 年かかる) (OALD⁵)

 season が不定冠詞をとるかとらないかも，期間が画定されるかされないかによる．

(61) a. Apple *season* is the time for harvest mischief. (リンゴの季節は収穫量に関する戯(たわむ)れ口のときだ) (RD 99/9: 100)

  b. Now British asparagus is in *season*. (今は B アスパラガスが旬だ) (CCED³)

  c. Still, while the summer is a celebration of endless light, winter is *a season* of darkness. (だが，夏が果てしない光の祝典であるのに対し，冬は暗闇の季節だ) (RD 99/3: 30)

  d. His haul of 40 goals in *a season* is a record. (1 シーズン 40 ゴールという彼の総得点は記録だ) (OALD⁵)

 day/night も，明るさ／暗さという「働き」(☞ 3 章) を表せば無冠詞であるが，時間的長さを表せば冠詞をとる．

(62) a. *Day* became evening, and he had barely stirred from the couch. (昼は夕方になったが，彼は長椅子からほとんど動いていなかった) (RD 99/12: 132)

  b. We had *a day* by the sea. (海のそばで 1 日過ごした) (OALD⁵)

(63) a. When we reached about 3400 metres, *night* gained on us. (およそ 3,400 メートルに達したとき，夜になった) (RD 01/4: 40)

  b. Downcast, Johnson prepared for *a* fourth lonely, dream-haunted *night*. It was *a night* that would be followed by another. And another. And then two more. (がっかりして，J は 4 日目の孤独で悪夢につきまとわれる夜の準備をした．まだつづく夜だった．その翌日も．そしてもう 2 夜も) (RD 99/11: 30)

 holiday/vacation の冠詞の有無も，「期間非含意」(休養・娯楽という「働き」を表す) 対「期間含意」という区別によって決定される．

(64) a. On *holiday*, I stopped at a small village shop for some food and postcards. (休暇中，食料品とはがきを買うために小さな村の店屋に立ち寄った) (RD 00/6: 79) [主に＜英＞]

  b. Thanksgiving is *a* national *holiday*, and most businesses are closed. (感謝祭は国民の祝日であり，ほとんどの会社は閉まっている) (NTC)

(65) a. I gazed at it, aware for the first time since *vacation* began that I'd treated the children more as interruptions than family members

whose lives I wanted to share and enjoy. (私は [挿し絵を] 見つめ，休暇になってから初めて気づいたのだが，子供を，生活を共有し楽しみたい家族の成員というより，妨害者として扱っていたのだ) (RD 98/10: 116)

 b. Harold used to take *a vacation* at that time. (H はその時期には休暇をとっていた) (CCED[3])

absence/silence/sleep も期間を表すときは冠詞がつけられる。

(66) a. *Absence* makes the heart grow fonder. (会えないと恋しく思われる) (CIDE)

 b. Now 31, Davies has recently returned to senior rugby following *a* long *absence* due to a shoulder injury that required surgery. (現在 31 歳であるが，D は手術が必要だった肩の怪我による長い欠場期間ののちシニアのラグビーに最近復帰した) (ConCD-ROM)

(67) a. "He was killed by his own father!" Aguilar listened in stunned *silence* as the woman told onlookers that the boy's father regularly tied him up and beat him. (「実の父親に殺されたんです！」婦人がまわりの人たちに少年の父親が普段から縛ったりたたいたりしていたと話すのを A は唖然（あぜん）としてことばもなく聞いた) (RD 99/3: 100) [in に後続して沈黙状態を表す；期間には関知せず]

 b. After *a* stunned *silence*, the daughter piped up, "Mommy, do hookers have children?" (びっくりしてことばが出なかったが，やがて娘は「ママ，夜の女にも子供がいるの」とかん高い声で言った) (RD 99/2: 47) [期間含意；after が一定期間のあとであることを表す]

(68) a. During *sleep*, kilojoules are converted and stored as fat. (睡眠中に数キロジュールが変換され脂肪として蓄えられる) (RD 99/9: 78)

 b. After *an* all-too-short *sleep*, I began the final, and toughest, part of the climb at 2 a.m. (短すぎる一眠りののち午前 2 時に, 登山のうち最後で 1 番厳しい部分を開始した) (RD 98/6: 77)

(69, b) で history が不定冠詞をとる理由も，中世から現代までという範囲の限定によって説明される。

(69) a. (= II-81, a) I have come to see the pygmies before their way of life passes into *history*. (RD 98/12: 106)

 b. The village has *a history* going back to the Middle Ages. (その村には中世にまでさかのぼる歴史がある) (OALD[5])

時間の長さが組み込まれていない語は無冠詞で用いられるという条件によ

り，exile/travel が，原則的に a/an をとらず，excursion/journey/trip などが a/an をとることが説明される。前者は帰還を必ずしも含意しないのに対し，後者は帰還が含意されているからである。(tour に関しては III-179; Ap.2.2-125 も参照。)

(70) a. *Exile* is the state of being forced to live away from your country, especially for political reasons. (追放とは，特に，政治的理由で，自国外への居住を強いられている状態のことだ) (ConCD-ROM) [state と定義されていることに注意]

　　b. Khan, now living in *exile* in Europe, fears most for the children. (K は現在ヨーロッパで亡命生活をしているが，子供たちのことを最も心配している) (RD 97/5: 22)

　　c. Cheap air *travel* is at last taking wing in Europe. (低価格の空の旅が欧州でもやっと飛び立ちかけている) (RD 99/3: 107)

　　d. The whole point of *travel* is to take things easy. (旅行で肝心なのは気楽にやることだ) (RD 99/2: 18)

比較：*An exile* of 28 years had ended. (28年の追放が終わったのだった) (RD 02/7: 16) [数値による限定 (☞ 4.4.1.1)]

(71) a. They've gone on *an excursion* to York. (小旅行で Y に行った) (OALD⁶)

　　b. During *a* recent *expedition* to Mount Kinabalu in Borneo, a number of local climbers met a group of foreign climbers as they were coming down from the peak. (BのK山への最近の遠征中，地元の多くの登山者は山頂から降りてくるとき1団の外国人登山者に出会った) (RD 99/2: 24)

　　c. She had invited her parents on *a jaunt* to California, and they were now returning home. (彼女は両親をCへの小旅行に招待し，いま両親は帰宅中だった) (RD 99/5: 25)

　　d. It's been *a* fascinating *journey*. (すばらしい旅行だった) (RD 97/5: 4)

　　e. And so I began *an odyssey* common to young writers, who search the world in the hope that somewhere an editor is waiting for them. (こうして若い書き手によくある長旅が始まった。どこかで編集者が待っているという希望をもって世界を探すのだ) (RD 97/2: 113)

　　f. (= III-120, d) He went on *a* walking *trip* with some of his friends from church. (CIDE)

　　g. I suggest *a tour* of the museum. (美術館巡りを提案する) (OALD⁵)

h. It's our final stop on *an* ethnic *whirl* that began this morning...
(今朝始まった民族［料理］旅行の終点だ) (RD 99/3: 72)

NB 3　safari/pilgrimage
1) safari は不定冠詞をとることもあるし，とらないこともある。本来は狩猟のための旅を意味するので，野生動物に逆襲されて生還しないこともまれではないからであろうか。
  i) They're currently on *safari* in Kenya [they may or may not come back from the safari]. (現在 K に冒険旅行中だ) (CIDE) [滞在期間非含意]
  ii) For his winter vacation this year, he's decided to go on *a safari* [he will come back from the safari]. (今年の冬休みは冒険旅行に行くことに決めた) (CIDE) [期間・帰還含意]
  iii) return from *(a) safari* (冒険旅行から帰る) (OALD5)
2) pilgrimage は「巡礼（という行為）」を意味するときは無冠詞で用いられ（しばしば place/site of に後続），「巡礼の旅」を指すときは不定冠詞をとる。
  iv) After Mao's death in 1976... this mountain in the province of Sichuan was once again able to function as a place of *pilgrimage*. (1976年の毛［沢東］の死後，四川省にあるこの山 [Emei Shan (峨眉山)] はふたたび巡礼の地として機能するようになった) (RD 99/7: 84)
  v) Since then, he has hiked up Africa's tallest mountain 38 times in *a* yearly *pilgrimage* that restores his spirit. (それ以後，毎年魂を取り戻す巡礼の旅をして，アフリカの最高峰 [Kilimanjaro] に 38 回登った) (RD 99/11: 68)

4.3　種類

次のような不定冠詞の用法は「種類」(type) を表すと言われる (Berry 1993: 12)。
(72) I was impressed by *a wine* from Friuli. (F 産のワインに感銘した)
(73) When boiled to setting point with an equal weight of sugar, they make *a* very fine *jam*. (同じ重さの砂糖といっしょに凝結温度にまで煮込めば，とても上等なジャムができる) [以上 Berry]
いま，もう1歩踏み込んで，なぜこれらの物質名詞に不定冠詞がつけられるの

かを考えるならば，修飾語句によって名詞の指示範囲（この場合，産地，品質）が限定されるため，名詞の姿かたちが想像可能となるからである。

　液体であれ固体であれ，姿かたちをもたない物体を指すときは無冠詞であるが，指示範囲が限定されるときは冠詞つきである。これは，範囲が限定されることにより，その名詞は宇宙における位置づけを獲得し，したがって，他の類義の名詞から区別された「個別性」を獲得するからである。この種の例は豊富にあるので，多数の実例は Appendix 1 であげることにして，ここでは物質名詞として使われる語が不定冠詞をとる場合ととらない場合とで，意味が異なるという事実の指摘にとどめたい。

　(74)–(76) のように，辞書の例文中で不定冠詞がかっこに入れられている場合は，冠詞の有無が意味に関与しないように思われるかもしれない。だが，すでに触れたように (II, 131–133)，物質と種類（または製品）という区別があると想定すべきである。この想定が言語事実の反映であることは (76, b-d) によって証明される。

(74) treat the fence with *(a) wood preservative* (柵に木材用防腐剤を施す) (OALD[5]) [防腐剤である液体 vs. 限定された（たとえば，A 社の／B という製品名の）防腐剤]

(75) treat the garden fence with *(a) wood preserver* (庭の柵に木材用防腐剤を施す) (OALD[5]) [同上]

(76) a. With repeated applications of *weedkiller*, the weeds were overcome. (除草剤を繰り返し使用して雑草を駆逐した) (CCED[3]) [製品名非限定]

　　b. Check weeds, not by hoeing which can tear through surface roots, but by applying *a weedkiller* such as paraquat or glyphosate. (雑草を防ぐには，根を途中で切ることがあるので鍬で除草するのではなく，パラコートやグリフォセートのような除草剤を使用しなさい) (CCED[3]) [製品名限定；(Ap.1-19, b)も参照]

　　c. ?? Check weeds, not by hoeing which can tear through surface roots, but by applying *weedkiller* such as paraquat or glyphosate.

　　d. Check weeds, not by hoeing which can tear through surface roots, but by applying *weedkiller*.

4.4 共起する語句による限定

　前節で見たように，従来「種類」を表すとされていた不定冠詞の用法は，実は，「産地」や「品質」に下位区分可能である。しかし，空間・時間を除いて

は，意味概念に基づいて名詞部の限定の仕方を下位区分するのは困難であり有益でもないので，構造を手がかりに例示していくことにしたい。名詞の指示範囲を限定する語句には前置詞句，関係詞節，形容詞，that 節，不定詞および動名詞がある。

4.4.1　前置詞句
4.4.1.1　数値による限定

(77–97, b) では of 625.6 square kilometers/of 40 weeks 等々により area/average 等々の範囲が限定されて姿かたちが浮かび上がってくる——つまり，完結した情報が与えられる——ので，不定冠詞が必要となる (52–53, b および 4.4.1.3 も参照)。

(77) a. Although large in *area*, the flat did not have many rooms. (床面積は広いが，そのアパートの部屋数は多くない) (CCED[3])

　　 b. The islands cover *a* total *area* of 625.6 square kilometers. (群島は全部で 625.6 平方キロの面積がある) (CCED[3])

(78) a. A normal pregnancy lasts *an average* of 40 weeks. (通常の妊娠は平均 40 週間継続する) (RD 01/4: 122) [(I-34) も参照]

　　 b. A normal pregnancy lasts 40 weeks on *average*. [同上]

(79) a. There is no more room in the bottle; it is filled to *capacity*. (瓶にはもう余裕はない。容量限度までいっぱいだ) (NHD)

　　 b. My computer has *a capacity* of 400 megabytes. (私のコンピュータの容量は 400MB だ) (LDOAE)

(80) a. There was enough *clearance* for the big truck to go under the bridge. (橋の下には大型トラックが通るのに十分なゆとりがあった) (NHD)

　　 b. It was difficult getting the piano through the doorway because we only had *a clearance* of a few centimetres. (数センチの余裕しかなかったので，戸口からピアノを入れるのは難儀だった) (CIDE)

(81) a. three feet in length/*depth*/diameter (長さ／深さ／直径 3 フィート) (OALD[5])

　　 b. Water was found at *a depth* of 30 feet underground. (地下 30 フィートの深さで水が発見された) (OALD[5])

(82) a. (= IV-81, a) three feet in length/depth/*diameter* (OALD[5])

　　 b. We need a pipe with *a diameter* of about six inches. (直径 6 インチ程度のパイプが必要だ) (CDAE)

(83) a. Average life *expectancy* is 50 years, compared with 69 for a Thai

and 65 for a Vietnamese. (タイ人の 69 歳，ベトナム人の 65 歳に比べ，平均余命は 50 歳だ) (RD 99/11: 22)

b. She read that the author had been told ten years earlier he had lung cancer and was given *a* life *expectancy* of 30 days. (彼女が読んだところでは，著者は 10 年前に肺ガンを告知され，余命 30 日と言われたのだった) (RD 99/3: 20)

(84) a. Some of the pyramids are over 200 feet in *height*. (ピラミッドには高さ 200 フィート以上のものもある) (LDOCE³)

b. The rattan survived intact to *a height* of about 18 inches. (トウは無事に生き延びて約 18 インチの高さになった) (RD 97/2: 134)

(85) a. Vehicles of over 3 metres in *length* pay an additional toll. (3 メートルを超える長さの車両は超過料金を払う) (LDOCE³)

b. The fish can grow to *a length* of four feet. (その魚は 4 フィートもの長さになる) (LDOCE³)

(86) a. She didn't care to pay full *price* because she didn't really want such a large tree. (本当はそんな大きな木は欲しくなかったので，全額は払いたくなかった) (RD 99/12: 9) [a をつければ同じ商品に全額が 2 つ以上あることになり論理矛盾]

b. They agreed on *a price* of £2000 for the car. (車代として 2 千ポンドという価格で同意した) (LDOCE³)

(87) a. The company is ruthless in its pursuit of *profit*. (その会社は利潤の追求に情け容赦もない) (CIDE)

b. The restaurant chain brings in *a profit* of millions of pounds a year. (そのレストランのチェーン店は年に数百万ポンドの利益を上げている) (CIDE)

参考： The intersection of the lines on the graph marks the point where we start to make *a profit*. (グラフ上の線の交差点は利益が出はじめる点を示している) (CIDE) [a profit は不定の量を表す。つまり，a profit (of some amount) と解釈可；LDOCE³ (s.v. profit) には make (a) profit の小見出しがあるが，この文脈では不定冠詞をとるほうがふつうのようである]

(88) a. *Rainfall* is about average for the time of year. (降雨量はこの時期としてはほぼ平均的だ) (OALD⁵)

b. Those 150 days deliver *an* annual *rainfall* of more than 78 inches. (その 150 日が 78 インチ以上の年間降雨量をもたらすのだ) (RD

96/10: 47)

(89) a. We are now within *range* of enemy fire. (今や敵の砲火が届く範囲にいる) (OALD⁵) [本章 NB 1 [歩いて行ける距離] 参照]

b. The life detector picks up vibrations through solids and can detect the scratching of a pin within *a range* of 25 metres, and up to a depth of nine. (生命探知器は固体を通してでも振動を拾い，幅25m，深さ9mまでの範囲なら針のかすかな音でも探知することができる) (RD 00/4: 49)

(90) a. They paid over $2 million in *ransom* (money). (身代金に2百万ドル以上払った) (OALD⁵)

b. He paid the kidnappers *a ransom* of £50 000 for his son. (息子のために5万ポンドの身代金を誘拐犯に支払った) (OALD⁵)

(91) a. A specially placed camera, protected against the fire, worked at high *speed*. (特別に設置された，耐火性のカメラが高速で作動した) (RD 99/4: 75)

b. Dorine felt her pulse quicken and synchronise with the rhythm of the propellers, slicing through the milky vapour at *a speed* of 200 kilometres an hour. (Dは鼓動が速まり，時速200キロという速度で白っぽい霞を切り進むプロペラのリズムと重なるのを感じた) (RD 00/7: 72)

(92) a. *Staff* are trained to treat customers with civility at all times. (スタッフは顧客にいつも丁重に対応するように訓練をうける) (OALD⁵) [集合的]

b. I was assigned as project manager, with *a staff* of ten. (10人のスタッフの企画部長を命ぜられた) (OALD⁵)

(93) a. *Temperature* varies in relation to pressure. (温度は気圧との関連で変化する) (OALD⁵)

b. The thermometer recorded *a temperature* of 40℃. (温度計は摂氏40度という温度を記録した) (OALD⁵)

参考: This wine cellar stays at *an* even *temperature* all year round. (このワイン貯蔵室は1年じゅう一定温度に保たれている) (OALD⁵) [数値は明記されていなくても，特定の温度なので不定冠詞をとる]

(94) a. calipers: a tool used for measuring *thickness*, the distance between two surfaces, or the diameter of something (カリパス＝厚さ，2つの表面間の幅，あるいは何かの内・外径を測るための道具) (LDOCE³)

b. Snow fell to *a thickness* of several centimetres. (雪が数センチの深さに積もった) (OALD⁵)

(95) a. Shares can go down as well as go up in *value*. (株は価値が上がることも下がることもある) (CIDE)

b. John's watch has *a value* of $75. (Jの時計は 75 ドルの価値がある) (NTC)

(96) a. The term 'dialect' refers to *vocabulary* and grammar. (「方言」という用語は語彙と文法とを指す) (OALD⁶)

b. The result is *a vocabulary* of maybe two million words. (その結果, [英語には] たぶん 200 万語の語彙がある) (RD 02/4:94)

(97) a. He's lost ten pounds in *weight*. (体重を 10 ポンド落とした) (OALD⁵)

b. a lorry with *an* unladen *weight* of 3,000 kilograms (空荷時の車体重量 3 トンのトラック) (OALD⁵)

(98) During a five-day work week, if you got six hours of sleep each night instead of the eight hours you needed, you would build up *a sleep debt* of ten hours (five days times two hours). Because *sleep debt* accumulates in an additive fashion, by day five your brain would tend towards sleep as strongly as if you'd stayed up all night. (平日の 5 日間に毎晩, 必要な 8 時間でなく, 6 時間の睡眠をとるならば, 10 時間の睡眠負債をためることになる (2 時間×5 日)。睡眠負債は加算的に蓄積するので, 5 日目には, 脳は徹夜したときのように眠くなる傾向が強い) (RD 00/6: 20)

(99, c) のように, *of*-phrase 以外の修飾語句が指示範囲を限定することもある。

(99) a. The following day I ran my first race at high *altitude*. (翌日初めて高地でのレースを走った) (CCED³)

b. Our ration of five pints of water a day was hopelessly inadequate for walking up to ten hours at *an altitude* of 5000 feet above sea level, in temperatures reaching as high as 43 degrees Celsius. (1 日につき水 5 パイントという割り当ては, 43℃にもなる温度のなかで, 海抜 5,000 フィートの高地を 10 時間も歩くにはどうしようもなく不足していた) (RD 97/2: 121)

c. Three hours into their journey, at *an altitude* just above 6000 feet, they climbed over a ridge and came to an alpine meadow above the tree line. (登りはじめて 3 時間後, 標高 6,000 フィートを少し越えた

ところで尾根を登って，樹木限界線よりも上にある高山の草地に着いた）(RD 97/5: 32)

数値が名詞の前に置かれるときも，通例，冠詞がつけられる。

(100) a. Life *expectancy* in Europe has increased greatly in the 20th century. (欧州の平均余命は 20 世紀に大幅に延びた) (CIDE)
 b. "We based ourselves on *a* 90-year life *expectancy*," Poilâne explains. (「平均余命 90 歳 [という計算] に基づいている」と P は説明する) (RD 99/9: 67)

(101) a. The shop said they would replace the television as it was still under *guarantee*. (まだ保証中なのでテレビを取り替えるとその店は言った) (CIDE)
 b. The video recorder comes with/has *a* two-year *guarantee*. (ビデオレコーダーは 2 年間の保証つきだ) (CIDE)

(102) a. Two basic types of internal *memory* are used in digital computers: Read-Only Memory (ROM) and Random-Access Memory (RAM). (デジタルコンピュータの内部メモリには 2 種類の基本的タイプが用いられている：ROM と RAM だ) (CIDE)
 b. My computer has *a* 500-megabyte *memory*. (私のコンピュータは 500MB のメモリがある) (NHD)

(103) a. Should public transport be run for *profit*? (公共輸送機関は利潤を求めて運行されるべきだろうか) (OALD[5])
 b. *A* two million pound *profit* is not to be sniffed at. (200 万ポンドの利益を小ばかにすべきではない) (CIDE)

(104) a. (= IV-90, a) They paid over $2 million in *ransom* (money). (OALD[5])
 b. The kidnappers have demanded *a* £1 million *ransom*. (誘拐犯は百万ポンドの身代金を要求した) (OALD[5])

(105) a. *Reduction* in government spending will necessitate further cuts in public services. (政府歳出を削減すれば必然的に公的サービスをさらにカットすることになる) (CIDE)
 b. The budget was subject to *a* 20% *reduction*. (予算は 20 パーセント縮小することになっていた) (NTC)

(106) a. As she came off *shift*, Woodward tucked it inside her BA hat, jumped into her car and drove to the Harrison house. (交代勤務が終わって出てきたとき，W はそれを British Airways の帽子のなかにはさみこんで車に飛び乗り H の家まで運転して行った) (RD 99/1:

28)
　b. I had almost finished *a* busy 12-hour *shift* as a casualty officer in a large government hospital in London when the emergency "red phone" rang. (L市内の大規模公立病院で緊急外来係として忙しい12時間勤務がほとんど終わったころ，緊急の「赤電話」が鳴った) (RD 00/2: 81)

(107) a. Grant Warren Beaucage will soon stand *trial* in Ontario for the murder of Aileen O'Brien-Beaucage. (GWBは間もなくAOB殺人のかどでOで裁判をうける) (RD 00/2: 8)
　b. After *a* two-and-a-half-week *trial* in October and November 1997 Judge Brian Pryor sentenced six gang members to between nine and 18 years' imprisonment. (1997年の10月と11月との2週間半にわたる裁判ののち，BP裁判長は6人の強盗に懲役9年から18年を言い渡した) (RD 99/11: 48)

(108) a. (= IV-95, a) Shares can go down as well as go up in *value*. (CIDE)
　b. This book is *a* ten-dollar *value* that is now on sale for five dollars. (この本は10ドルの価値があるが，今5ドルでセールに出ている) (NHD)

(109) a. In the dark I can barely see the SWAT officers who lie in *wait* in front of me. (暗闇のなかで，私の前で待ち伏せしている特別機動隊員たちがかろうじて見える) (RD 96/3: 46)
　b. We had *a* three-hour *wait* before we could see the doctor. (診察までに3時間待たされた) (CIDE)
　参考：We had *a* long *wait* for the bus. (バスを長い間待った) (OALD⁵) [個別行為]

(110) a. (= IV-97, a) He's lost ten pounds in *weight*. (OALD⁵)
　b. *a* 2 lb *weight*（2ポンドの重量）(OALD⁵)

　　NB 4　φ　数値＋名詞
　　次例中の"数値＋名詞"は under に後続して状態を表すので，冠詞をとらない。
　　　Placed under 24-hour police *guard*, she complained that she could not do her job: chasing crooks. (24時間警察の保護のもとに置かれたため，自分の仕事——悪人の追跡——ができないとこぼした) (RD 99/3: 38) [(III-133, b) と比較せよ]

4.4.1.2　感情・能力などの対象
4.4.1.2.1　感情

hatred/love/preference/reverence など感情を示す語は抽象概念を表すので，通例は無冠詞で用いられるが，その対象を明示する語句が後続するときは a/an と共起する傾向が強い。

(111) a. The poor guy was in *agony*. (気の毒にその男は苦しんでいた) (LDOCE³)

　　b. I was in *an agony* of doubt/indecision/suspense. (疑惑／ためらい／不安の苦しみのなかにあった) (CIDE)

(112) a. I dreaded going home to face another night of unrelenting *craving*. (帰宅してまた [喫煙の] 仮借のない渇望の夜を迎えるのが怖かった) (RD 97/5: 42)

　　b. The experience had planted in me *a craving* for the freedom of a vast desert landscape. (その経験は私に広大な砂漠の光景のなかを自由に旅することへの渇望を植えつけた) (RD 97/2: 122)　類例：have/develop a craving for chocolate/oranges (CIDE, OALD⁵)

(113) a. Low pay is the main cause of job *dissatisfaction* among teachers. (安月給が教師の職業的不満の主原因だ) (CCED³)

　　b. The first two are *a dissatisfaction* with the status quo and a willingness to change. (最初の２つは現状に対する不満と変革への意欲だ) (RD 00/5: 82-84)

(114) a. *Fear* cramped his muscles. (恐怖のため筋肉が痙攣(けいれん)した) (RD 97/6: 95)

　　b. I had been kicked by a mule in vet school and developed *a fear* of mules and horses. (獣医学校でロバに蹴られて，ロバやウマへの恐怖が生じた) (RD 99/6: 99)

　参考：Many people live in *fear* of violence. (多くの人々は暴力の恐怖のなかで暮らしている) (McED) [fear は, of-phrase をともなっていても，in に後続して状態を表すので無冠詞 (☞ 3 章 NB 8)]

(115) a She spoke with *feeling* about the plight of the homeless. (感情を込めてホームレスの惨状を語った) (OALD⁵)

　　b. (= II-51, a) The experience left me with *a feeling* of deep hurt. (OALD⁵)

(116) a. He looked at me with *hatred*. (憎しみを込めて私を見た) (OALD⁵)

　　b. Cromwell had *a hatred* of Roman Catholics ... (C はローマカトリッ

ク教徒に憎しみをもっていた)(CCED³)

(117) a. *Hope* gradually returned during the operation. (手術中，希望が徐々に戻ってきた) (RD 96/10: 138)

　　　b. We haven't *a* chance/*hope* in a million of winning. (勝つ見込み/望みは百万に１つもない) (OALD⁵)

(118) a. "Jump!" Gorrell yelled.　Horton looked toward him and saw *horror* on his face. (「跳べ」と G は叫んだ。H は彼のほうを向き，表情に恐怖を見てとった) (RD 98/9: 34)

　　　b. Joanne has *a horror* of spiders. (J はクモに恐怖心をもっている) (CIDE)

(119) a. He fainted from *hunger*. (飢えのため気を失った) (OALD⁵)

　　　b. All her life, Mary has had *a hunger* for affection. (これまでずっと M は愛情に飢えていた) (NTC)

(120) a. He gazed with *longing* and apprehension into the future. (憧れと不安をもって将来を見つめた) (CCED³)

　　　b. *a longing* for hearth and home (家庭への憧れ) (OALD⁵)

(121) a. "*Love* always hopes," she said. (「愛は希望を捨てないものなの」と彼女は言った) (RD 99/4: 11)

　　　b. They shared *a love* of the sea and often played guitar together. (2 人とも海が好きで，しばしばギターをいっしょに弾いた) (RD 99/12: 56)

　　　c. [T]he seminar . . . is open to anyone with an interest in or *a love* for some of the greatest dancing traditions in the world. (当セミナーは世界じゅうの偉大な伝統を有するダンスのいくつかに関心あるいは好みがあればだれにでも開かれている) (CCED³)

(122) a. While Cliff treated the girls as extended family she demanded *loyalty*. (C は少女たちを家族の延長として扱ったが，忠誠を要求した) (RD 99/11: 76)

　　　b. But Chaudhuri also has a lovely tenderness, *a* deep *loyalty* towards his subjects. (しかし，C はすばらしい繊細さ，主題に対する深い誠実さもあわせもっている) (ConCD-ROM)

(123) a. Perhaps he was not sure whether I had now come as a friend, or out of reluctant duty, or even *pity*. (私がいま友人として来たのか，いやいや義務から，さらには同情から，来たのかたぶん彼にはわからなかっただろう) (RD 99/5: 9)

b. He felt *a* sudden tender *pity* for her. (突然彼女にやさしい哀れみを感じた) (CCED³)

(124) a. The most popular pets, in order of *preference*, are: dogs, horses, cats. (最も人気のあるペットは，好まれる順に，犬，馬，猫だ) (OALD⁵)

b. I must admit I have *a preference* for younger men. (若者びいきだと認めざるをえない) (LDOCE³)

比較：After people develop *a preference*, they often distort additional information to support their view. (好みが定着すると，付加的情報を歪曲して自分の見解を支持することがよくある) (RD 96/3: 95) [個人個人に特定の好みを指す]

(125) a. The wife considered the picture was in bad *taste* and moved on quickly, but the husband lingered, completely transfixed. (妻はその絵画を悪趣味だと思ってすぐに移動したが，夫は立ち止まり，まったく釘づけになった) (RD 99/7: 28)

b. The edible tuber was brought to Africa from Brazil 400 years ago and the forest-dwelling pygmies developed *a taste* for it. (食用の芋類は 400 年以前に B から A に持ち込まれ，森に住むピグミーはその味が好きになった) (RD 98/12: 109)

(126) a. She nursed her father with devotion and great *tenderness* during his long illness. (父親が長患いしていたとき，献身的にかつ深い愛情をもって看病した) (CIDE)

b. When McCorkell rode in and heard his sons' stories at the campfire, each crediting the other, he felt *a* great *tenderness* towards them. (M は [野営地に] 馬でやって来てキャンプファイア中の息子たちが互いに相手をたたえている話を聞いたとき，彼らに深い愛情を感じた) (RD 99/8: 64) [対象が明示され a-文よりも具体的]

(127) a. The news of the epidemic struck *terror* into the population. (伝染病のニュースで人々は恐怖に襲われた) (OALD⁵)

b. Lots of people have *a terror* of spiders/drowning. (多くの人はクモ／溺死に恐怖をもっている) (CIDE)

比較：They lived in *terror* of capture by enemy soldiers. (敵兵に捕らえられるのではないかという恐怖のなかで暮らした) (CIDE) [感情や知覚を表す語が in に後続するときは，範囲非限定なので無冠詞 (☞ 3 章 NB 8)]

4.4.1.2.2 能力

aptitude/capacity など能力を表す名詞も同様である。

(128) a. Evidence of mathematical *aptitude* is important and some physics or electronics background is most useful. (数学的能力を証明できることが肝心であり，物理学あるいは電子工学の背景的知識がいくぶんあればきわめて有益である) (ConCD-ROM)

b. Clark then returned to the Navy's classroom, and found that he had *an aptitude* for mathematics. (その後 C [Netscape Navigator の設立者] は海軍の教室に戻り，数学の能力があることに気づいた) (RD 00/4: 26)

(129) a. The purchase of 500 tanks is part of a strategy to increase military *capacity* by 25% over the next five years. (戦車 500 台の購入は軍事能力を次の 5 年間で 25%増強しようとする戦略の一部だ) (CIDE)

b. She has *a* great/*an* enormous *capacity* for hard work. (つらい仕事もやる能力が大いにある) (CIDE, OALD[5])

(130) a. It is rare to find such *genius* nowadays. (今日そのような才能を見いだすのはまれだ) (OALD[5])

b. She has *a genius* for raising money. (資金集めをする才能がある) (CIDE)

(131) a. Though she had never migrated before, *instinct* told the flamingo to head for a warmer climate. (以前渡りをしたことはなかったが，本能的にそのフラミンゴは温暖な気候のほうへと向かった) (RD 99/4: 91)

b. You seem to have *an instinct* for getting into trouble. (トラブルに巻き込まれる本能があるみたいだ) (NTC)

(132) a. His work shows great *talent*. (彼の作品は大きな才能を示している) (OALD[5])

b. She possesses *a* remarkable *talent* for music. (彼女には音楽に著しい才能がある) (OALD[5])

比較：I've always been able to learn languages easily; it's *a gift*. (ことばを学習するのはいつも簡単だった。天与の才だ) (OALD[5]) [類義語の gift は可算名詞]

4.4.1.2.3 その他の名詞類

上記以外にも多数の名詞が，対象を表す前置詞句に後続されるときは不定冠詞をとる（空間的・時間的限定 (☞ 4.1; 4.2) も参照）。

(133) a. On further *acquaintance* he seems quite pleasant. (もっと親しくなると，彼はなかなか愉快な男のようだ) (ConCD-ROM)
   b. Nurses have *an* intimate *acquaintance* with the male body. (看護師は男性の体をよく知っている) (CCED³)
(134) a. Reporters must be impartial and not show political *bias*. (報道記者は公平でなければならず，政治的偏見を見せてはならない) (CIDE)
   b. There has always been *a* slight *bias* in favour of/towards employing arts graduates in the company. (その会社にはずっと以前から芸術系の卒業生を採るという偏りが少しばかりある) (CIDE)
   c. He has *a bias* against people who wear glasses. (眼鏡をかけている人に対して偏見がある) (NHD)
(135) a. The symphony is admirable in *conception*. (そのシンフォニーは概念的にはすばらしい) (CCED³)
   b. She has *a conception* of people as being basically good. (人間は基本的に善だという考えをもっている) (CIDE)
(136) a. He's in excellent *condition* for a man of his age. (彼の年齢としてはきわめて良好な状態だ) (OALD⁵)
   b. The garden was in *a condition* of total neglect. (庭はまったく手入れされていない状態だった) (LDOCE³)
(137) a. His public statements have always been in marked *contrast* to those of his son. (彼の公的発言はいつも息子のそれと顕著な対照をなしていた) (CCED³) [in に後続して範囲非限定 (☞ 3 章 NB 8)]
   b. There's *a* marked *contrast* between the standard of living in the north of the country and the south. (国の北部と南部との生活水準には顕著な相違がある) (CIDE) [*between*-phrase による範囲限定]
(138) a. We seem to be perpetually in *debt*. (年がら年じゅう借金しているみたいだ) (CDAE)
   b. I owe all those who offered me support *a debt* of gratitude. (支援してくれたみんなに恩義がある) (CIDE)
(139) a. Vitamin *deficiency* can lead to illness. (ビタミンの欠乏は病気につながることがある) (OALD⁵)
   b. High homocysteine coincides with *a deficiency* of the B vitamin folic acid and, in some cases, vitamins B-6 and B-12. (高ホモシステインはBビタミン葉酸，場合によっては，ビタミンB_6およびB_{12}の欠乏と重なる) (RD 99/5: 99)

(140) "Tears aren't a sign that you're simply feeling sorry for yourself but are *an expression* of sadness or emotion that must find an outlet."
　　　And it doesn't matter if the grieving takes a while to surface, as long as it finally finds *expression*. (「涙は自分に対してただ悲しんでいるというしるしであるのではなく，出口を見いださなければならない悲しみや感情の表出なのです。」嘆きが表面に現れるのにしばらくかかっても，最終的に感情表出を見いだすならば，問題はない) (RD 97/5: 52)

(141) a. In Arab countries *generosity* must be boundless because your honour is at stake. (アラブ諸国では気前のよさは無制限でなければならない。名誉がかかっているからだ) (ConCD-ROM)

　　b. Characteristics such as a strongly independent spirit, *a generosity* of personality, and an appreciative warmth are assets. (強い独立心，人格の寛大さ，感謝に満ちた暖かさといった特徴は財産だ) (BNC, CGD 327)

(142) a. (= IV-101, a) The shop said they would replace the television as it was still under *guarantee*. (CIDE)

　　b. California's state Constitution includes *a guarantee* of privacy. (Cの州法はプライバシーの保証を盛り込んでいる) (CCED³) 類例：a guarantee of quality (CCED³)

(143) a. The bonds between immigrant and native are forged in the workplace, Salins says, where hard work counts for more than *heritage*. (Sが言うには，移住者と地元民との絆は職場で生じる。そこでは刻苦精励のほうが遺産よりも大事だからだ) (RD 99/4: 107)

　　b. That family has *a heritage* of wealth and power. (あの家は富と権力という遺産がある) (NHD)

(144) a. (= II-81, a) I have come to see the pygmies before their way of life passes into *history*. (RD 98/12: 106)

　　b. Hendigham, with *a history* of heart attacks, was exhausted but vainly continued to pound away at the bear. (Hは心臓発作の病歴があり，疲れきっていたが，効果はないにもかかわらず，クマを追い払おうとたたきつづけた) (RD 99/9: 72)

(145) a. Based on a tip, they had staked out the dwelling, thinking Robert Cloud lived there.　After a month, they had positive *identification*. (通報に基づき，RCが潜伏しているとにらんでその家に張り込んだ。1か月後はっきりと身元が確認された) (RD 99/3: 103) [構造的には

identification は内容非限定；だれを指すかは先行の文から推論]
- b. The police officer made *an identification* of the criminal after talking to witnesses. (警官は目撃者と話したのち犯人の身元を確認した) (NHD) [*of*-phrase による内容限定]
- c. Marilyn had *an* intense *identification* with animals. (M は動物に強い一体感をもっていた) (CCED³) [*with*-phrase による対象限定]

比較：Correct *identification* of needs is vital. (ニーズの正確な確認が不可欠だ) (LDOCE³) [一般論 (＝ 抽象概念) なので *of*-phrase がついていても無冠詞]

(146) a. In prison people often suffer from a loss of *identity*. (刑務所内ではしばしば自己喪失にさいなまれる) (CIDE)
- b. I felt *an identity* now with the words he wrote. (今や彼の書いたことばに一体感を感じた) (RD 00/3: 45)

比較：develop a sense of *identity* with the organization (組織との一体感をはぐくむ) (OALD⁵) ["NP₁ of NP₂" の形式で素材扱い (☞ 2.1.2)]

(147) a. Puglia, in southern Italy, provides graphic *illustration* of what can be done and what needs to be done. (南イタリアの P は何がなされうるか，何がなされる必要があるかを生き生きと例示している) (RD 99/10: 109) [例示されるものの数には関知せず]
- b. *An illustration* of China's dynamism is that a new company is formed in Shanghai every 11 seconds. (中国の活力を示す実例は上海では 11 秒ごとに新会社が設立されているということだ) (CCED³) [多くの実例のうちの 1 例]

(148) a. The war shattered Prague's Jewish community – and the communists, who took power in 1948, tolerated Judaism in *name* but repressed it in fact. (戦争で P のユダヤ人社会は粉砕された。1948 年に権力を握った共産主義者たちはユダヤ人を名目上は許容したが，実質上は抑圧した) (RD 00/4: 61) [抽象概念]
- b. Sony has *a name* for producing high-quality electrical equipment. (ソニーは高品質の電気製品を製造することで名声を得ている) (CIDE) [個別事例]

(149) a. Tim had been saving for an engagement ring – but he was in graduate school and in dire *need* of a computer. (T は婚約指輪のために貯金していたが，大学院在学中でありコンピュータがどうしても必要だった) (RD 98/12: 103) [感情・知覚を表す語が in に後続すると

きは，範囲非限定なので無冠詞）[☞ 3 章 NB 8]
b. The company has *a need* for computer programmers. (その会社はコンピュータプログラマーを必要としている) (NHD) [対象限定]

(150) a. After she read the letter I could see she was in fighting *spirit* and determined to have the decision changed. (手紙を読んだのち，彼女は目に見えて闘志が湧いてきて，決定を変更させることに決めた) (CIDE) [spirit の様態非限定；cf. (VII-50)]
b. We acted in *a spirit* of co-operation. (協調の精神で行動した) (CIDE) [様態限定]

(151) a. He has come to know her well, and now the panda, exhibiting amazing *trust*, allows him to gently stroke her. (彼はそのパンダのことがよくわかるようになった。今では彼女は驚くほどの信頼を示し，優しく撫(な)でられるがままにしている) (RD 00/2: 24)
b. Moreover, he had violated *a* sacred *trust* with his wife. (さらに，彼は妻との聖なる信頼関係を裏切ったのだ) (RD 99/3: 49)

4.4.1.2.4 対象をともなう名詞に関する注意

ここで注意しなければならないのは，対象が明記されても a/an がつけられない場合もある，ということである。

(152) a. She felt great *affection* for the child. (子供に好意を感じた) (CIDE)
b. Bart felt *a* great *affection* for the old man. (B は老人に大きな愛情を感じた) (LDOCE³)

(152, a–b) の相違に関しては，無冠詞の great affection は，抽象概念（または，一般論；抽象概念に関しては 2.3.3 参照）としての愛情であり，話し手は great を「褒めことば」（または「枕詞」）として用いている。これに対し，a great affection は Bart がそのとき，その場で感じた，彼に特有な愛情であり，話し手は affection の程度を記述している，と説明可能である (4.4.3.4 も参照)。以下の (153)–(155) でも，抽象概念と個別事例 (☞ 5 章) という区別に基づいて不定冠詞の有無が決定されている。

(153) a. dote on/upon sb: to feel and show great *love* for sb, ignoring their faults (溺愛(できあい)する = 欠点を無視して，大きな愛情を感じ，かつ示すこと) (OALD⁶) [抽象概念]
b. The dynamic Knowles had felt *a* special *love* for the Mongolian horse since he'd obtained his first one 25 years earlier. (精力的な K は蒙古馬に対して，25 年前に最初の馬を得たとき以来の特別な愛情を感じていた) (RD 96/10: 92) [個別事例；K に特有な愛情]

(154) a. You have to have *passion* for your work because that's what's going to drive you at the end of the tenth consecutive 15-hour day. (仕事に対して情熱をもたなければならない。それこそが連続15時間［労働］の10日目の終わりに君を駆り立てるものだからだ) (RD 00/4: 25) [抽象概念；情熱の具体的内容に関しては限定なし]

b. Lumiére had *a passion* for progress and soon set himself up as a photographer in Lyon. (L は進歩に情熱をもっていて，まもなく L で写真家として身を立てた) (RD 96/3: 8) [L に特有な情熱]

(155) a. He claims that *prejudice* against homosexuals would cease overnight if all the gay stars in the country were honest about their sexuality. (彼の言い分は，国じゅうのゲイのスターたちが彼らの性行動に関して正直に話せば，同性愛者に対する偏見は一晩で消えるということだ) (CIDE) [抽象概念]

b. The judge seemed to have *a prejudice* against the lawyer. (裁判官は弁護士に偏見をもっているようだった) (NTC) [個別事例；当該の裁判官に特有の偏見]

4.4.1.3 「助数詞」扱い

これまで修飾語句である前置詞句に重点をおいて述べてきたが，ここで被修飾語句である名詞句を中心として考察しておきたい。英語の名詞には *of*-phrase をともなって，日本語の「助数詞」(auxiliary numeral) に相当する働きをするものがある。(注：助数詞＝「2本のペン／本を3冊」における「本／冊」のように，数量を表す語に添えられることば。）明白な例は次のようなものである。

(156) Bring me *a glass* of water/Bring *a glass* of water for me. (水を1杯もってきてくれ) (OALD[5])

(157) Let's indulge ourselves with *a bottle* of champagne. (シャンペンを1本楽しもう) (OALD[5])

(158) *A convoy* of trucks containing food supplies has been sent to the areas worst hit by famine. (食料を載せた1団のトラックが飢饉(きん)に最もひどく襲われている地域に送られた) (CIDE)

上例ほど明白ではないが，次例のb-文中のabundance/airなどは *of*-phrase の「助数詞」，つまり，wine/confidence などの大まかな量を表わす単位，として用いられている。

(159) a. We had wine in *abundance*. (ワインがたっぷりあった) (CIDE)

b. There was *an abundance* of wine at the wedding. (結婚式ではワイ

ンがたっぷりあった) (CIDE)

(160) a. *Air* consists mainly of nitrogen and oxygen. (空気は主として窒素と酸素から成る) (CIDE)

b. She has *an air* of confidence about her. (彼女にはどこか自信めいた雰囲気がある) (CIDE)

(161) a. Caroline prefers her worktops to be clear of *clutter*. (C は調理台に散らかりものがないのが好みだ) (CCED[3])

b. There is *a clutter* of papers on his desk. (彼の机の上には書類の山がある) (NHD)

(162) a. *Fog* came rolling in from the ocean. (霧が海から寄せてきた) (CIDE)

b. For a few moments Jason had drifted off into *a fog* of resentment at the way things were going. (しばし J は事態の進み方に対するもやもやとした憤りに思いをはせた) (ConCD-ROM)

(163) a The mountain range stretched away into *infinity*. (山脈は無限へと連なっていた) (CIDE)

b. The names go on and on, almost 80,000 of them, in *an infinity* of tragedy. (莫大な悲劇における[犠牲者の]名前は連綿とつづき, ほとんど 8 万名もある) (RD 00/4: 59)

(164) a. The metre is a measure of *length*. (メートルは長さの単位だ) (OALD[5])

b. He used *a* short *length* of steel pipe as a weapon. (短いスチールパイプを武器として使った) (CIDE) 類例：a length of rope/string (McED)

(165) a. The goods are now ready for *shipment*. (商品は今や出荷の準備ができている) (LDOCE[3])

b. Authorities learned from the informant that *a shipment* of drugs was about to leave Vietnam. (当局は通報者から薬物が船荷として V から輸送されようとしているということを知らされた) (RD 99/9: 122)

(166) a. The lightning was quickly followed by heavy *thunder*. (稲妻のすぐあとに激しい雷鳴があった) (OALD[5])

b. *a*/the *thunder* of applause (雷鳴のような喝采(かっさい)) (OALD[5])

(167) a. *Wealth*, like power, tends to corrupt. (富は, 権力と同様, 腐敗しがちだ) (CCED[3])

b. a book with *a wealth* of illustrations (イラストがふんだんにある本)

(OALD⁵)

of-phrase に先行する名詞が単位を表す場合があることが認められるならば，(168) のような，通例は無冠詞で用いられる名詞が a/an をとる理由が納得されるであろう．a knowledge of は知識の「量」を表すのである．

(168) a. *Knowledge* of French is a plus in her job. (フランス語の知識は彼女の仕事にプラスだ) (OALD⁶) [i.e., If she knows French, it is a plus in her job.]

  b. *A knowledge* of Italian is crucial in establishing relationships with the Italian commercial sector, which has a reputation for insularity. (イタリアの商業部門と関係を結ぶにはイタリア語の知識が必須だ，閉鎖性で評判のところだから) (CCED³) [i.e., An amount of knowledge of Italian is crucial . . .]

NB 5
1) 次は上例と，一見，類似の構文であるが，冠詞の有無は形容詞の解釈の相違に帰すべきものである (褒めことば (または枕詞) vs. 事実記述；☞ 4.4.1.2.4)．

  i) He has *(a) good command* of the French language. (フランス語がよくできる) (OALD⁵)

2) 助数詞扱いされるのは存在を表す名詞であり，「非存在」を表す名詞には当てはまらない．存在しないものの姿かたちは想像不可能だからである (☞ 4.5.1)．

  ii) His work displays *(a) poverty* of imagination. (彼の作品は想像力の貧困を示している) (OALD⁵) [母語話者の判断では，冠詞の有無による意味の相違なし]

  iii) His policies show *(a) lack* of foresight. (彼の政策は先見の明の欠如を示している) [同上]

4.4.2 関係詞節

普段は無冠詞で用いられる名詞であっても，それらの多くは限定用法の関係詞節によって修飾されれば，指示範囲が限定されるので，冠詞をとる．この種の例は多数あるので，ここでは数例のみあげ，他は Appendix 2.1 に回したい．(以下の例文中の名詞の多くは「段階的形容詞」(☞ 4) と関連づけられることに注意．)

(169) a. Some species . . . move among rocks with *agility*, using the flippers

第4章　原理 IV ——限定と非限定　*151*

　　　　for balance. (ヒレでバランスをとりながら，岩のあいだを素速く移動する種もいる) (EB 01)
　　b. Then, with *an agility* I would not have thought possible, they slithered under the barbed-wire fence and disappeared into the forest. (それから，可能と思いもしなかった敏捷さで，彼ら [象] は有刺鉄線の柵の下を滑り抜けて森へと消えた) (RD 00/3: 127)
(170) a. There is no absolute standard for *beauty*. (美には絶対的な基準はない) (OALD5)
　　b. She has *a beauty* that comes from within. (内から湧きでる美しさがある) (RD 00/5: 113)
(171) a. E-mail helps ease the isolation, but *boredom* is still a problem. (Eメールは孤独感を癒すのに役立つが，退屈さは依然として問題だ) (RD 98/3: 27)
　　b. Joss could see *boredom* pulling at the corners of her painted mouth, *a boredom* which he knew would soon give way to malice. (Jは退屈のため彼女の紅を塗った口の端が引きつっているのを見た。おなじみの，やがて悪意に変わる退屈だ) (ConCD-ROM)
(172) a. I had never seen diamonds shine with such *brilliance* before. (これまでダイヤがそんなにきらきらと輝くのを見たことがなかった) (CIDE)
　　b. There is a clarity, *a brilliance* to space that simply doesn't exist on Earth... (宇宙には地上にない輝き，光輝さがある) (RD 99/12: 119)
(173) a. *Confidence* flows from her. (自信が溢(あふ)れでている) (OALD5)
　　b. When Hanna and her son leave, arm in arm, there is *a confidence* about her that seems complete. (Hと息子とが手に手を取って出ていくとき，彼女には完璧と見える自信が漂っている) (RD 98/5: 101)
(174) a. He spoke with great *depth* of feeling about how kind they had been to him. (彼らがいかに親切にしてくれたかをとても深い感情をこめて話した) (CIDE)
　　b. "How bad is it going to be?" she asked, with *a depth* of concern I had never heard before. (「どのくらい悪くなるの」と，これまで聞いたことのない深い心配をこめて尋ねた) (RD 97/5: 128)
(175) a. In *desperation*, they jumped out of the window to escape the fire. (火事から逃れるために，必死の思いで窓から飛び降りた) (CIDE, CDAE)

b. My daily walk, lengthened every day, saved me from despair and fueled my recovery. That walk was a lifeline, and I grasped it with *a desperation* only Margaret truly understood. (日々の散歩は毎日伸びていき，私を絶望から救い，回復を促進した。その散歩は生命線であり，私は M だけが真に理解してくれる必死な気持ちでしがみついていたのだった) (RD 97/5: 143)

次の b-文中の修飾語句は定動詞を含まないので，厳密に言えば関係詞節ではないが，ここにあげてもさしつかえないであろう。

(176) a. The storm (wild animal, soldier, etc.) attacked with *ferocity*. (暴風 (野生動物，兵士，など) はどう猛に襲いかかった) (NHD)

b. It is a distinct place notorious for storms that seem to arrive out of nowhere and blow with *a ferocity* unparalleled anywhere on the planet. (そこは暴風で知られている独特の場所であり，暴風はどこからともなく突然起こり，地上のどこにも類のない猛烈さで吹きまくる) (RD 98/7: 120)

(177) a. I understood what incredible *strength* the women in Somalia possess. (S の女性が何という信じがたい力をもっているかがわかった) (RD 99/10: 138)

b. With *a strength* born of anger, he smashed at the bear's head, all the while screaming for help. (怒りから生じる力でもってクマの頭をたたきながら，大声で助けを求めた) (RD 99/9: 71)

4.4.3　形容詞

直前の例 (176)–(177) が示すように，関係詞節は文法単位であって，意味単位ではない。話し手にとって a strength which/that was born of anger と a strength born of anger とのあいだには，冠詞の選択に関しては，なんら違いはない。本節では，形容詞によって名詞の指示範囲が限定されるために不定冠詞が必要となる場合を示す。まず，食事名から始めよう。これは形容詞 (相当語句) の有無によって冠詞の有無がほとんど自動的に決定される語類だからである。

4.4.3.1　食事名

breakfast/lunch/supper など食事名は，単独では，その構成物が指示されていないために (つまり，おかずが何であるか不定なので) 無冠詞で用いられる。しかし，形容詞など修飾語句がつけられれば，どのような食事であるか想像可能になる (やや専門的に言えば，食事の様相が限定される) ので，a/an をとる。

無冠詞の例:

(178) a. *Breakfast* is served between 7 and 9 a.m. (朝食は午前7時から9時まで出される) (LDOCE[3])

b. I often skip *breakfast*. (よく朝食を抜く) (OALD[5])

c. We got off immediately after *breakfast*. (朝食後すぐに出かけた) (OALD[5])

(179) a. Sue and I have had *lunch*. (Sと私はお昼を食べた) (OALD[5])

b. I suggested we share the cost of *lunch* and he eventually assented. (昼食代を割り勘にすることを提案したところ, 最終的には彼も同意した) (OALD[5])

c. I was relieved when we broke for *lunch* at noon. (正午に昼食をとるため休憩になったときはほっとした) (RD 98/6: 130)

(180) a. Could you entertain the children for an hour, while I make *supper*? (夕食を作るあいだ1時間ほど子供の相手をしていてくれないかしら) (OALD[5])

b. What's for *supper*? (夕食は何ですか) (OALD[5])

c. We've invited friends to *supper* and it's too late to put them off now. (友人を夕食に招待しているので, 先延ばしにするにはもう遅すぎる) (OALD[5])

(181) a. I haven't had *dinner* yet. (まだ夕食をとっていない) (McED)

b. I'm not averse to a drop of whisky after *dinner*. (食後にウィスキーを1杯やるのはきらいなほうじゃない) (OALD[5])

c. The atmosphere over *dinner* was relaxed and friendly. (ディナー中の雰囲気はくつろいで友好的だった) (OALD[5])

(182) a. On Sundays *brunch* is served between 1 pm and 3 pm. (日曜日にはブランチは午後1時から3時まで出される) (ConCD-ROM)

b. One beautiful Sunday, I took a few hours from my university studies to meet friends for *brunch*. (ある好天気の日曜日, 大学の勉強を数時間割いて友人と会ってブランチをとった) (RD 00/7: 143)

(183) a *Dessert* is the last course of a meal. (デザートは食事の最後のコースだ) (NTC)

b. During *dessert*, Tim suddenly reached into his pocket and pulled out an engagement ring. (デザートのときTは突然ポケットに手を入れて婚約指輪を取りだした) (RD 98/12: 103)

c. He wanted *dessert*. (デザートをほしがった) (RD 00/7: 36)

(184) a. *Tea* is always served at 5 o'clock. (いつも5時にティーが出される) (LDOCE³)

b. have (your) *tea* as soon as you get home from school (学校から帰ったらすぐにティーにしなさい) (OALD⁵)

冠詞つきの例:

(185) a. Dave Crocker awoke around 7.30 the next morning and prepared *a* leisurely *breakfast*. (DC は翌朝7時半頃に起きて、ゆったりととる朝食の用意をした) (RD 00/1: 76)

b. Every weekend Jon Levine, a university professor, makes *a* special pancake *breakfast* for his wife, Claudia Cryer, and their three children. (毎週末、大学教授の JL は妻の CC と 3 人の子供のためにホットケーキの特別朝食を作る) (RD 98/3: 96)

c. Rising at 5 a.m., he downs *a* simple *breakfast* of rice, soup and kimchi, then heads off to meet his students. (午前 5 時に起きて、ご飯とスープとキムチのつましい朝食をかき込み、学生に会いに出かける) (RD 00/2: 49)

類例: a full breakfast (RD 00/1: 5); a high-fibre breakfast (RD 01/9: 18); a hot breakfast (RD 99/6: 51); a prayer breakfast (RD 99/4: 100); a Sunday breakfast (RD 99/11: 139); a 6 a.m. breakfast of bacon and eggs (RD 00/3: 106); [*of*-phrase] a breakfast of minced meat (RD 99/3: 75)

(186) a. I was going out to *a* business *lunch* with two other people, one of whom volunteered to drive. (もう2人とビジネスランチに行こうとしていたとき、そのうちの1人が運転を買ってでた) (RD 98/3: 52)

b. That was quite *a* decent *lunch*. (なかなかの昼食だった) (OALD⁵)

c. They stopped for *a lunch* of sandwiches and coffee in a lay-by near Alresford and by three-thirty that afternoon their coach had reached Tanniford. (A 近くの一時駐車所に停まって、サンドィッチとコーヒーの昼食をとり、その日の午後3時半までにバスはTに着いた) (ConCD-ROM) [*of*-phrase による限定 (☞ 4.4.1)]

(187) a. We'll have *an* early *supper* before we go out. (出かける前に早い夕食をとろう) (OALD⁵)

b. I'll just throw together *a* quick *supper*. (急いで夕食を作ろう) (OALD⁵)

c. In apartment 324, after cooking himself *a* frugal hamburger *supper*, 46-year-old Dave Crocker turned on the television to keep his mind off pressing personal problems. (324号室で，つましくハンバーガーの夕食を作ったのち，46歳の DC はひっ迫した個人的問題から気を紛らすためにテレビをつけた) (RD 00/1: 75)

(188) a. One evening, my friend Tim took his girlfriend, Mary, out for *a* romantic *dinner* where conversation turned to marriage. (ある日の夕方，友人の T はガールフレンドの M とロマンチックなディナーに行き，会話は結婚のことにおよんだ) (RD 98/12: 103)

b. My friend Don was preparing *a* macaroni and cheese *dinner* for his young family. (友人の D は若い家族のためにマカロニとチーズの夕食を準備中だった) (RD 99/10: 110)

c. Esther and her boss delivered *a* complete Thanksgiving *dinner* to the family. (E と上司とはその家族に申し分のない感謝祭のディナーを届けた) (RD 99/11: 125)

(189) Lena Gusinsky has *a* champagne *brunch* at the Metropol. (LG は M でシャンペンつきのブランチをとる) (ConCD-ROM)

(190) Chefs differ in their idea of what makes *a* good *dessert*. (シェフたちは何がよいデザートになるかに関して考えが異なる) (LDOCE[3])

類例：a light/pineapple/scrumptious chocolate dessert (LDOCE[3], OALD[5])

(191) Lily had eaten *a* hearty *tea*: sandwiches, tea-cakes, scones and a handsome wedge of chocolate cake. (L はこってりしたティーをとった。サンドイッチ，ティーケーキ，スコーンパン，それに，チョコレートケーキをたっぷりである) (ConCD-ROM)

NB 6

1) a＋meal

meal は「1回分の食事」('The food served and eaten in one sitting.' (AHD)) を指し，開始と終了が前提とされているので，冠詞をとる。

 i) When you pay that much for *a meal* you expect the best. (食事にそんなにたくさん払うのなら最高が期待できる) (OALD[5])

 ii) After the movie we went for *a meal* in a Chinese restaurant. (映画のあと中華料理店に食事に行った) (LDOCE[3])

2) a＋dessert/nightcap

dessert が，主食のあとという順序ではなく，食べ物自体を指すときは，製品扱いされるので (☞ 2.3.2)，修飾語句なしでも冠詞をとる。

iii) If you make the main course, I'll make *a dessert*. (メイン料理を作ってくれるのなら，デザートを作ろう) (CIDE)

nightcap も同様：

iv) Jock, Scott and Andrew had *a nightcap* at a cafe on the Champ-Elysées. (J と S，A はシャンゼリゼの喫茶店でナイトキャップをとった) (RD 00/7: 40)

3) a+dinner

dinner が 'social gathering, dinner party' (晩餐会) を表すときは修飾語句なしでも a/an をとる．

v) The prime minister attended *a dinner* given in his honour. (総理大臣は彼のために開かれた晩餐会に出席した) (OALD⁵)

vi) *A dinner* was held to celebrate the opening of the new hotel. (新しいホテルの開業を祝って晩餐会が開かれた) (CIDE)

4) φ Sunday lunch

Christmas/Saturday/Sunday lunch などは，lunch の下位分類を成すので (☞ 8.9.3)，修飾語句がなければ，無冠詞で用いられる．

vii) replete with turkey and plum pudding after *Christmas lunch* (クリスマスの昼食のあと七面鳥とプラムプディングとで満腹である) (OALD⁵)

viii) Would you like to come to *Sunday lunch*? (日曜の昼食に来ませんか) (OALD⁵)

ix) It serves . . . the very best style of food to eat . . . for *a* light *Saturday lunch*. (土曜日の軽い昼食に最良の食事を提供する) (ConCD-ROM)

5) (a) diet

diet は治療法としては無冠詞で用いられるが，治療の実践としては，通例，冠詞がつけられる (☞ 5.2)．形容詞がつけられるときも冠詞をとる．

x) *Diet*, medication and exercise helped me, and I became more active. (食事療法と薬，運動が役に立ち，より行動的になった) (RD 98/3: 62)

xi) Some people never seem to put on weight while others are always on *a diet*. (決して体重がつかないような人もいるし，いつもダイエット中の人もいる) (OALD⁵)

xii) Maintaining *a* low-fat *diet* and exercising will also minimize the risk of heart disease. (低脂肪の食事と運動をつづけることも心臓病の危険を最小化する) (RD 97/2: 85)

xiii) The question I'm most often asked is, "Can I prevent cancer with *diet*?" Clinical trials are still examining whether *a* more healthful *diet* can prevent a recurrence of breast cancer. But studies have shown that colon cancer is associated with *a diet* high in red meat, animal fat and calories. Researchers continue to investigate a possible link between *diet* and other kinds of cancer. (私が一番よくうける質問は「食事療法でガンを予防できるか」というものである。臨床試験ではより健康的な食事で乳ガンの再発を予防できるかどうかをまだ調査中であるが，これまでの研究から，結腸ガンは，赤身肉や動物性脂肪が多く，高カロリーの食事と結びついていることが判明している。研究者たちは食事と他の種類のガンとの関連を継続して調査中である) (RD 98/11: 82)

4.4.3.2　色彩語

色彩語も形容詞により色彩の幅が限定されれば，ほぼ例外なく，a/an をとる。(一見例外に関しては (193, b) [blue] および本章 NB 7 参照。)

(192) a. She nearly always dresses in *blue*. (ほとんどいつも青をまとっている) (LDOCE³)

b. His face had turned *a* dirty *blue*. (彼の顔は汚れた青色に変わった) (RD 99/8: 122)　類例：a brilliant blue (RD 00/2: 41; 01/6: 114); a deeper blue (RD 99/3: 128); a deep turquoise-blue (RD 02/9: 143); a metallic blue (RD 02/2: 56); a perfect blue (CIDE); a soft blue (RD 00/2: 58)

比較：They came in all sizes and hues, from deepest *blues* to brilliant *yellows*, *scarlets* and shimmering emerald *greens*. ([蝶の見本には]あらゆるサイズと色彩があった。深い青色から鮮やかな黄色，緋色，輝くエメラルドグリーンにいたるまで) (RD 02/7: 32) [いろいろな明度・彩度・色調の blue など]

(193) a. The lady is dressed in *gray*. (その婦人はグレーの服をまとっている) (NHD)

b. Pure darkness gave way to *a* ghostly *mist-gray*; then a thin, pale band of fragile blue appeared along the horizon. (漆黒(しっこく)がおぼろ

にかすんだ灰色に変わり，それから，かすかな青色の薄いぼんやりした筋が地平線ぞいに現れた）(RD 99/3: 128) [fragile blue が無冠詞であるのは band に後続して素材扱いであるため (☞ 2.1.2)]

(194) a. Yellow and *green* together make *a* pale *green*. (黄色と緑色をいっしょにすれば淡い緑色になる) (CCED³)

b. It was hot and tinged *a* luminous *green*. ([水は]熱く，明るい緑色を帯びていた) (RD [U.S. Edition] 98/9: 132)　類例：an unfetching pale green (RD 97/5: 144); an ugly mud-green (RD 99/12: 37); a dark, liquid green (RD 01/5: 87f.); a bright apple green (ConCD-ROM)

(195) a. If you mix red and yellow, you get *orange*. (赤と黄色を混ぜれば，オレンジ色になる) (OALD⁵)

b. He should be mostly green but instead he is *a* sickly *yellowish-orange*. (たいていは緑色のはずなのに，[そのイグアナは]薄い黄色がかったオレンジ色だった) (RD 99/9: 83)　類例：a blazing/brilliant orange (CCED³, LDOCE³)

(196) a. The traffic lights have changed (from *red* to green). (交通信号が(赤から青に)変わった) (OALD⁵)

b. When her grandmother painted the little girl's toenails *a* bright *red* to cheer her up, they dubbed her the Sleeping Princess. (おばあさんが元気づけようとして女の子の足の爪を鮮やかな赤に塗ったときから，その子を眠り姫と呼ぶことになった) (RD 00/3: 53)　類例：an angry red (RD 98/9: 61)

(197) a. Pink is a combination of red and *white*. (ピンクは赤と白との混ぜあわせだ) (OALD⁵)

b. Painted *a* brilliant *white*, the 52-metre boat had been afloat for just three years, but she had already steamed through some of the most important currents of American history. (その52メートルの船は，きらきら輝く白に塗られていて，就航からわずか3年だったが，すでにアメリカ史の最も重要な潮流のいくつかを渡っていた) (RD 00/1: 92)　類例：a foul-smelling/ghostly white (RD 02/3: 92; 00/9: 109)

(198) a. (= IV-195, a) If you mix red and *yellow*, you get orange. (OALD⁵)

b. The blood in his contusions, as it broke down, formed the waste product bilirubin, which in large amounts is toxic, and turned his eyes and skin *a* sickly *yellow*. (挫傷箇所の血液は，循環しなくなると，

老廃物のビリルビンを形成した。高濃度では毒性があるので，彼の眼と皮膚は病的な黄色になった) (RD 01/4: 135)　類例：a sooty yellow (RD 02/3: 92); a bright yellow (ConCD-ROM)

NB 7
1) 色彩語＋色彩語
中間色を表すときには色彩語が2つ(以上)並列される。
   i) Less than one metre long, its slender body is *a* speckled *yellow and green*. (1メートルに満たない，[コモドドラゴンの]細身の体は黄緑の斑点がある) (RD 99/6: 27)
2) 非日常的形容詞および動詞
色彩語に形容詞が先行する場合でも，その形容詞が使用頻度の低い，非日常的な語のときは不定冠詞をとらない傾向が強い。イメージを形成しにくいためと思われる。(witに関する形容詞（IV-219）参照)。
   ii) There was a toy lawn mower in hectic *yellow*. (褪せた黄色の，玩具の芝刈り機があった) (RD 99/12: 97) [a hectic yellow も可能だが，無冠詞のほうがふつう]
上の条件に加えて，"形容詞＋色彩語"が不定冠詞をとるためには，動詞の種類にも制限があるようである。手元の資料では"a＋形容詞＋色彩語"に先行する主な動詞は be/turn/paint である。
   iii) The station wagon glowed dull *white* in the overhead fluorescent light. (ステーションワゴンは頭上の蛍光灯に照らされて鈍い白色に輝いていた) (RD 00/1: 62) [a dull white も可能だが，無冠詞のほうがふつう]
3) paleness/pallor
paleness/pallor (青白さ) は，不可算名詞であるが，通例，"a/an＋形容詞"をともなう。これは，これらの語が表す色彩の範囲が狭く限定されているためと推測される。
   iv) His face had *a* deadly *paleness*. (彼の顔は死人のように青白かった) (LDOCE[3])
   v) His usual bright complexion had been replaced by *a* sallow *pallor*. (彼のいつもの明るい顔色は血の気がなく青白くなった) (RD 99/8: 101)　類例：a deathly/sickly pallor (LDOCE[3], OALD[5])

4.4.3.3 挨拶ことば；擬音；発話

筆者の知る限り文法書などで指摘されたことはないが，hello/goodbye など挨拶を表すことばも，通例，形容詞をともなわなければ無冠詞で用いられるが，形容詞をともなえば a/an が必要とされる。挨拶の様態が限定される，つまり，挨拶の仕方に姿かたちが与えられる，ためである。

(199) a. I hugged Auntie Sahru and waved *farewell*. (AS を抱きしめて，手を振って別れを告げた) (RD 99/10: 129)

b. They moved in just in time to spend Christmas 1990 there with their 11-year-old son, Adam, after saying *a* reluctant *farewell* to their native Somerset. (生まれ故郷の S にいやいやいとまを告げたのち，1990 年のクリスマスにちょうど間に合うように，11 歳の息子の A とともに，引っ越ししてきた) (ConCD-ROM)

(200) a. Someone said, "Say *goodbye* to *Orca*." (「O 号 [船名；(VIII-103, b) 参照] に別れを告げなさい」とだれかが言った) (RD 99/8: 22)

b. "Vicky," I said, stopping my car to say *a* final *goodbye*, "look after yourself." (最後の別れを言うために，車を停めて，言った。「V [メギツネの名前]，たっしゃでね」) (RD 99/6: 80)

(201) a. Come and say *hello* to my friends. (来て私の友だちに挨拶しなさい) (CDAE)

b. The salesperson greeted me with *a* warm *hello*. (セールスマンは私に暖かくこんにちはと言って挨拶した) (CCED[3])

(202) a. She penned a few words of *thanks*. (短い感謝のことばを書いた) (OALD[5])

b. "Umm," I said. And I gave *a* silent *thanks* to the person checking quality at the end of this section. (「んー」と言って，この部門の [ベルトコンベヤーの] 終わりで品質検査をしている人に無言の感謝をした) (RD 99/9: 44)

(203) a. It annoys me when people forget to say *thank you*. (人々が謝意を表すのを忘れるとむっとする) (OALD[5])

b. First they look puzzled; then they utter *a* quick *thank you* before setting the thing aside. (最初彼らは当惑した様子だが，そののち急にでありがとうと言い，それをわきに置く) (RD 99/9: 7)

挨拶ことばに限らず，擬音も修飾語句をともなえば，a/an をとる。

(204) a. For instance, if your five-year-old answers with *a* sarcastic *"Duh!"* to everything you've said while you're playing a board game

together, you can say, "I'm too upset by your behaviour to play anymore. You'll have to find something else to do." (たとえば,ボードゲーム中にあなたの言うことすべてに5歳児が意地悪く「ヘーン」と答えるならば,次のように言ってもよい,「お行儀が悪いのでびっくりしたからもうしないよ。何か別のことを探しなさい」と) (RD 99/12: 83)

b. Almost immediately Angela heard *a* faint *"Mee! Mee!"* like the mewing of a kitten. (ほとんどすぐにAは,子猫の鳴き声のような,[新生児の]か弱い「ミー,ミー」という声を聞いた) (RD 99/5: 23)

c. For 30 seconds there is *a* huge *whoosh* and a white cloud, and the flames are smothered. (30秒間ジューと大きな音がして白煙が上がり,そして鎮火された) (RD 97/5: 104)

d. Halfway across, he heard *a* muffled *whump*! (半分行ったところで,押し殺したようなドサッという音を聞いた) (RD 99/4: 136)

NB 8　a thud

例 (204) の擬音が形容詞をともなうときのみ a/an をとるのに対し,thud は,一回きりの擬音を表すので,単独でも不定冠詞をとる。

"I heard *a thud*, as if something fell," he said. (「何かが倒れたようなドスンという音を聞いた」と彼は言った) (RD 99/3: 104)

発話全体も,形容詞をともなうときには,不定冠詞をとる。

(205) a. Since Rae was a toddler, we've told her she was adopted, and she has constantly asked about her birth mother. [. . .] And then, at age ten, after a day of too many stares, *a* teary *"I just want to meet someone I'm related to."* (よちよち歩きのころから,Rには養女だということを言っていたので,彼女はいつも生みの母親のことを尋ねていた。こうして,10歳のとき,1日じゅうしつこいほど何度も見つめて,涙ながらに[言った]「だれか血縁の人にどうしても会いたいの」) (RD 01/7: 106)

b. With *a* curt *"You have a very ill baby here,"* he began his examination. (ぶっきらぼうに「この子はひどく悪化している」と言って,診察を始めた) (RD 99/8: 123)

c. and with *a* commanding *"Forward, march,"* they tramped together around the yard again . . . (命令的な「前へ進め」[の号令]とともに,

彼らはふたたび中庭をズンズンと行進した）(RD 99/8: 128)
d. with *an* affectionate, yet embarrassed, *"Here"*（愛情がこもってはいるが，きまり悪そうに，「はい」と言って）(RD 94/12: 40)

参考：We then exchanged *"I love yous."*（それから互いに「愛してる」と言った）(RD 01/3: 125); We traded *"I love you and miss yous,"*...（「愛してる，恋しいよ」と言い交わした）(RD 02/7: 113) [理論的には，それぞれ，"I love you"s; "I... miss you"s]

ところで，次のように，形容詞がないにもかかわらず hello/OK/thank you に a/an がつけられている例もある。

(206) a. She smiled as our eyes met, and I found myself stammering *a hello*.（眼が会ったとき，彼女は微笑んだ。私は思わず口ごもりながら「こ，こんにちは」と言った）(RD 00/8: 116)
b. Strauss grunts *an OK*. (S はぼそぼそと了承する) (RD 01/4: 122)
c. Reuben murmured *a thank you* and ran home. (R はありがとうとつぶやいて，走って家に帰った) (RD 00/9: 117)

これらの例では stammering/grunts/murmured が発話の様子を具体的に示すので hello/OK/thank you は完結した姿かたちを与えられることになり，それゆえ，不定冠詞が要求されるのである。事実，次例 (207) が示すように，

(207) a. Don't be shy – come and say *hello*.（恥ずかしがらないで，来て挨拶しなさい）(OALD⁶)
b. The lead singer asked me, and I said *okay*.（リードボーカルが尋ねたのでOKと答えた）(CCED³)
c. She did at least write to say *thank you*.（少なくとも礼状は書いた）(OALD⁶)

動詞を無色な，つまり，様態非限定の，say に換えれば，不定冠詞は不要である。不定冠詞の選択には，名詞自体の性質に加えて，形容詞や関係詞節など修飾語句が関与するだけでなく，動詞の意味も関与する，ということである（5.3.3（特に，V-114）も参照）。

4.4.3.4　形容詞による，その他の名詞類の限定

食事名，色彩語および挨拶ことば以外の名詞も，その指示範囲が形容詞など修飾語句により具体的に提示されれば，不定冠詞をとる。この種の例は，本文中に組み込むにはあまりにも多いので，Appendix 2.2 であげることにして，ここでは一般論を述べておきたい。

形容詞により指示範囲が限定されれば a/an をとるということは，逆に言えば，単数形の名詞に形容詞が先行しても，指示範囲が限定されなければ，不定

冠詞はつけられない，ということである。一般論として，a/an がつく場合は当該の"形容詞＋名詞"は完結したものとして認識されているが，a/an がつかない場合は完結性が認識されていない，と言ってよい。たとえば，(208, a-b) において，swift/prompt は行動を実行するまでの時間であり，firm は行為者の態度である。どちらも action の様態そのものを修飾しているのではない。(注：様態 = もののあり方や，行動のありさま。状態。様相。(大辞林).) それゆえ，(208, a-b) の名詞部は指示範囲が限定されないので，冠詞をとらない。これに対し，(208, c-d) が不定冠詞をとるのは，これらの修飾語句は action の様態を限定し，完結した形をもつものとして提示されているからである。同様に，例 (209) の φ forced cheerfulness と a sudden cheerfulness とにおいて，前者は，話し手の態度を表し（つまり，転移修飾と解釈可能），cheerfulness の様態を限定してはいなので無冠詞であり，後者は，一時的な姿かたち，つまり，cheerfulness の１様態を表すので冠詞が必要である。(注：転移修飾 = 形容詞などが本来修飾すべき語ではなく，別の語を修飾すること。たとえば，his *dying* wish（彼の臨終の願い）において，論理的には，dying であるのは wish ではなく，he である。)

(208) a. This problem calls for swift/prompt *action* from the government. (この問題は政府の迅速な行動を要する) (CIDE)

b. The police took firm *action* to deal with the riots. (警察は暴徒の対応に断固とした行動をとった) (LDOCE³)

c. It only needs *a* small wrist *action* to start the process. (その過程を始めるにはちょっと手首を動かすだけだ) (CIDE) [動きの箇所および程度限定]

d. It has *a* very smooth *action*. (とても滑らかな動きをしている) (CCED¹) [動きの様態限定]

(209) a. With forced *cheerfulness*, we told the girls their brother needed a little extra attention at the hospital. (弟はもう少し病院で治療が必要なのだ，と無理して陽気に娘たちに言った) (RD 98/12: 122)

b. Midday sun streamed into the drab little room which gave it *a* sudden *cheerfulness*. (真昼の日光がくすんだ小部屋に射し込み，部屋は不意に陽気になった) (CIDE) [陰気から急転した一時的な陽気]

このように，形容詞の意味解釈は不定冠詞の有無により，一時的様相と非一時的様相（あるいは，抽象概念／転移修飾）という相違が想定可能である。(注：様相 = ありさま。状態。すがた。(小学館 国語大辞典)。) たとえば，例 (IV-152) において触れたように，feel φ great affection for the child における great

は affection の漠然とした分類あるいは評価を表しているのであり，様相とか姿かたちを表しているのではない。つまり，固有名詞との関連において詳述するように (☞ 8.9)，いくつかの形容詞は，後続する名詞の描写・説明というよりも，使用者の感情的もしくは情緒的色彩を表すのである。これに対し，feel a great affection for the old man 中の great は後続する名詞を意味的に限定し，千差万別の affection を 1 様相においてとらえている。つまり，"(形容詞+) 名詞" が不定冠詞をとるということは，その名詞が話し手にとっては特定の姿かたちを有する存在物 (あるいは実現形) として認識されているということを表すのである。

　以上を形容詞を中心に言い換えるならば，形容詞が「情緒的語句」(sentimental epithet) (または，「枕詞」(ornamental epithet)) として名詞に先行するときは，名詞の指示範囲あるいは内容は限定されないので，無冠詞であり，形容詞が「記述的語句」(descriptive epithet) (または「限定的語句」(qualifying epithet)) として名詞に先行するときは，名詞の指示範囲あるいは内容は限定をうけるので，冠詞が必要となる，ということである。次の (210–212, a) は形容詞が主観的評価を，(210–212, b) は範囲限定を表す例である。

(210) a. She has great *determination* to succeed. (成功しようと大決心をしている) (NHD) [great は褒めことば]

　　　b. She has *a* great *determination* to succeed. (成功しようと強固な決意をしている) (CIDE) [great は程度を限定；不定詞による限定 (☞ 4.4.5)]

(211) a. (= III-135, a) She has great *influence* with the manager and could probably help you. (OALD[5]) [不特定の影響力]

　　　b. Freudian theory has had *a* great *influence* on psychology. (フロイト理論は心理学に大きな影響を及ぼした) (LDOCE[3]) [学説史上定説となった影響力]

(212) a. The dining room has lakeside views and offers excellent *cuisine*. (食堂からは湖畔の景色が見え，すばらしい食事が出される) (CCED[3])

　　　b. Where steak and chips was once the primary eating-out fare, *a* sophisticated *cuisine* has evolved, the spices of the world melting with the bounty of the Antipodes. (かつてはステーキチップスが主な外食だったところに，世界じゅうのスパイスが豪州の恵みと混じりあって，洗練された食事が発展した) (RD 99/3: 75)

(213–216, a) の形容詞 (相当語句) は，情緒的語句ではないが，情緒的語句と同

様に漠然とした指示範囲を表し，限定不十分であるため，不定冠詞は不要である。(いくつかは「下位分類」と解釈することも可能 (☞ 8.9.3)。)

(213) a. In America, where action-movie stars are the giants of popular *culture*, a sky walk is often considered a ridiculous stunt. (米では，アクション映画が大衆文化の巨人であるので，空中綱渡りはばかげた曲芸だと思われることがよくある) (RD 97/5: 38)

　　　b. Ten 14-year-olds grouped together will form *a Lord of the Flies culture* — competitive and mean. (同一グループに含められた 10 人の 14 歳児たちは『蠅(はえ)の王』文化——競争的かつ卑劣——を形成するだろう) (RD 99/11: 63) [名詞部の情報完結；*Lord of the Flies* 斜字体は原文]

(214) a. My husband says I have selective *memory*. (夫の言い分では，私の記憶力は選択的だ) (RD 98/3: 13) [selective は対象非限定]

　　　b. She has *an* excellent *memory* for names. (彼女は名前に関して記憶力がいい) (CIDE, CDAE) [対象限定]

(215) a. Growing *unease* at the prospect of an election is causing fierce arguments within the party. (選挙の見込みに関するいや増しつつある焦燥感のため党内で激しい議論が行われている) (CIDE) [unease の様態非限定]

　　　b. 'He'll be alright,' I said to myself, trying to quell *a* growing *unease*. (つのりくる焦燥感を静めようとして，「彼は大丈夫だ」と自分に言い聞かせた) (CCED[1]) [話し手が限定する unease]

(216) a. [T]he author was fond of using archaic *vocabulary* characteristic of that earlier poetry. (著者は以前の詩に特徴的だった擬古体の語彙を好んで用いた) (*CHEL*, III, p. 511) [擬古体の語すべてを指すわけではない]

　　　b. (= II-78, a) Take them each month, and you'll strengthen your immune system against awkward expression, boost your fitness for correct speech and develop *a* healthier, more robust *vocabulary*. (RD 99/10: 7) [形容詞による種類限定；全体的にとらえられた「より健康的で，より逞(たくま)しい語彙」]

"(形容詞+) 名詞" が不定冠詞をとるということは，すでに述べたように，その名詞が話し手にとっては姿かたちを有する存在物 (あるいは実現形) として認識されているということを表す。つまり，話し手にとって姿かたちが認識可能であれば，形容詞はなくても不定冠詞がつけられる，ということになる。事

実，次の b-, c-文は形容詞なしに a がつけられ，話し手による指示範囲限定を含意している。不定冠詞をつけるかつけないかは，話し手／書き手の主観・独断によるところが大きいということである。このように考えれば，(217) 以下のような例は話し手による主観的な範囲限定 (いわゆる，不定冠詞の "specific use") としてとらえることが可能である (文脈に依存することもある；より詳しくは 5.4 参照)。

(217) a. There is considerable *emphasis* on practical work, and students carry out projects in each year (the third-year project counting as a full course). (実践的な仕事にかなりの力点が置かれており，学生たちは毎年自主研究を行う (3 年時は自主研究が全課程である)) (ConCD-ROM) [considerable は漠然とした程度を表すので emphasis の限定不十分]

b. The course puts *an emphasis* on practical work. (その授業は実践的な仕事に力点を置いている) (LDOCE³) [話し手／書き手が独断的に内容を押しつける力点]

(218) a. He tried to ignore the feeling of *emptiness*. (空虚感を無視しようとした) (CDAE)

b. She felt *an emptiness* in her heart when he left. (彼が去ったとき彼女は心に空虚なものを感じた) (LDOCE³)

c. There was *an emptiness* in her heart. (彼女の心には空虚なところがあった) (OALD⁵) [個別事例；話し手の主観的限定]

いま wit を修飾する形容詞と冠詞の有無を見るならば，形容詞にかなりはっきりとした区別が観察される。

(219) a. φ acerbic/broad/devastating/lambent/mordant/native/sarcastic/trenchant *wit* (OALD⁵, LDOCE³)

b. *a* biting/caustic/dry/lively/quick *wit*; *an* acid *wit* (OALD⁵)

(219, a) の無冠詞の例の多くは使用頻度の低い非日常的形容詞と共起しているのに対し，(219, b) の不定冠詞つきの例は日常的形容詞と共起している。この相違は，wit の種類をイメージ化できるか否かから生ずるものである。非日常的形容詞が wit を修飾する場合は，wit はどのような内容か想像しがたいのに対し，日常的形容詞は意味・内容を理解しやすいので，どのような wit であるかが想像可能であり，それゆえ，"日常的形容詞＋wit" はそれ自体で完結した情報をもつのである (4 章 NB7-2 も参照)。

4.4.4　that 節

that 節が内容を明示するため a/an が要求される場合もある。

(220) a. When I'm with women I listen attentively and interrupt only to murmur *agreement*. (女性といるときは注意して話を聴き，割り込むのは賛意を小声で伝えるときだけだ) (CCED[3])

　　 b. We had *an agreement* that Ms Holst would keep me informed of any changes. (何か変わったことがあれば H さんから連絡してもらうという取り決めができていた) (LDOCE[3])

比較：There was general *agreement* that every effort should be made to prevent the war from spreading. (全体的には，戦争の拡大を防ぐためにあらゆる努力がなされるべきだという了解があった) (CCED[3]) [本章 NB 10 参照]

(221) a. Her son's skin improved beyond *belief*. (彼女の息子の皮膚は信じられないくらいよくなった) (CCED[3])

　　 b. As our friendships strengthened, so, too, did *an* unspoken *belief* that we would be here for each other over the long haul. (友情が強まるにつれ，長期間ここに住んで互いに助けあうのだという無言の信頼も強まった) (RD 00/6: 12)

(222) a. Ours is the politics of *conviction*, not of opportunism. (ご都合主義ではなく，確信に基づく政治だ) (CCED[3])

　　 b. She had *a* deep/firm/lifelong *conviction* (that) there would be a better life after death. (死後はもっとよい暮らしがあるという深い／確固とした／生涯にわたる確信をもっていた) (CIDE)

(223) a. a statement based on *fallacy* (誤謬(ごびゅう)に基づく声明) (OALD[5])

　　 b. It's *a* complete *fallacy* that women are worse drivers than men. (女性のほうが男性よりも運転が下手だというのはまったく間違いだ) (CIDE)

(224) a. (= IV-115, a) She spoke with *feeling* about the plight of the homeless. (OALD[5])

　　 b. I had *a feeling* in my guts that something was wrong. (何かがうまくいっていないという胸騒ぎがした) (OALD[5])

(225) a. These can also cause *grief* and exhaustion. (悲しみと疲れも引き起こす) (RD 96/3: 100)

　　 b. It was *a grief* to him that he had never had any children. (子供が 1 人もできなかったのは彼にとって悲しみだった) (LDOCE[3])

(226) a. The watch is still under *guarantee*. (その時計はまだ保証期間中だ) (OALD⁵)

b. The United Nations has demanded *a guarantee* from the army that food convoys will not be attacked. (国連は軍隊に食糧輸送船団を攻撃しないという保証を要求した) (CIDE)

(227) a. *Inconvenience* during a winter ice storm is to be expected. (冬の着氷性悪天のときは不便が予測される) (NTC)

b. It's *a* major *inconvenience* that the bakery went out of business. (パン屋が廃業したのはとても不便だ) (NTC)

(228) a. *Intuition* told him that the future lay in projecting images on a screen ... (未来はスクリーンに映像を映すことにある，と直感した) (RD 96/3: 9)

b. I had *an intuition* that something awful was about to happen. (何か恐ろしいことが起ころうとしていると直感した) (OALD⁵; OALD⁵ (s.v., intuition (b))ではthat節が後続するときintuitionは[C]扱いであることが明記されている)

(229) a. The prisoners pleaded for *mercy*. (囚人たちは減刑を懇願した) (CIDE)

b. It's *a mercy* the accident happened so near the hospital. (事故が病院のすぐ近くで起こったのは幸運だった) (LDOCE³)

(230) a. The soldier climbed the church tower for *observation* of the whole town. (兵士は町全体を見るために教会の塔に上った) (NHD)

b. My friend made *an observation* that I seem nervous today. (友人の発言では，私は今日は神経が高ぶっているように見えるそうだ) (NHD)

(231) a. (= IV-123, a) Perhaps he was not sure whether I had now come as a friend, or out of reluctant duty, or even *pity*. (RD 99/5: 9)

b. It's *a pity* that Jan and George can't make it to the party. (JとGとがパーティに出席できないのは残念だ) (LDOCE³)

(232) a. Where *principle* is involved, be deaf to expediency. (原理原則にかかわるところでは便宜には耳をふさぐがよい) (RD 98/4: 113)

b. It's *a* well-established *principle* that the guilt for war crimes is shared not only by those who pull the trigger but by those who command them. (戦争犯罪の罪は，引き金を引いたものだけでなく，命じたものも共犯だということは定着した原則だ) (CDAE)

(233) a. You cannot prove conclusively that Sellafield caused cancer. You can only work on the basis of *probability*. (S [の核燃料再処理施設] がガンの原因だと決定的に証明することは不可能だ。蓋然(がいぜん)性に基づいて取り組むだけだ) (CCED3)

b. I'm afraid there is *a* high/strong *probability* (that) something has gone wrong. (何かうまく行っていないという見込みは高い/強いと思う) (CIDE)

(234) a. This lack of *recognition* was at the root of the dispute. (この認識の欠如が論争の根底にあった) (CCED3)

b. It sprang from *a recognition* that many things came easily to me. ([その自信は] 私には多くのことが容易だという認識から生じていた) (RD 02/7: 116)

比較 : *Recognition* that the house needed painting badly came when the neighbors complained. (家はどうしてもペンキの塗り換えが必要だという認識は隣人から苦情がきたとき明らかになった) (NTC) [recognition は，動詞との関連において，擬人化されているので無冠詞；本章 NB 9 参照]

(235) a. The best way of finding a solicitor is though [sic; through] personal *recommendation*. (弁護士の１番よい見つけ方は個人的推薦によることだ) (CCED3)

b. There has been *a recommendation* from union leaders that the offer of 5% be rejected. (5 パーセントの申し出は拒否すべきだという勧告が組合の指導者からあった) (OALD5)

参考 : She is likely to make *a recommendation* in a few days time on whether the company should file a law suit. (会社が訴訟を起こすべきか否かに関して数日のうちに勧告しそうだ) (CIDE) [whether 節による詳細限定]

(236) a. *Rumour*/Speculation/Confusion abounds. (うわさ/憶測/混乱に満ちている) (OALD5)

b. *Rumor* has it that the franc will be devalued soon. (うわさによると，フランはじきに切り下げられるとのことだ) (NHD)

c. *A rumour* has surfaced that the company is about to go out of business. (その会社は廃業するといううわさが表面化した) (OALD5)

d. That colonel had been caught and executed – burned alive, according to *a rumour* Kuklinski had heard, and the execution filmed as a warning to others. (大佐は逮捕され処刑された——K が聞いたうわさでは，火刑にされたとのことだった——しかも，その処刑は他の者たちへの警告として録画されたのだった) (RD 00/4: 132) [that 節ではないが，内容明記]

NB 9　擬人的用法
"Rumor has it..." という構文において rumor が必ず無冠詞で用いられるのは，rumor が擬人的に用いられているためと思われる。この見解は，一見，こじつけのように思われるかもしれないが，例 i)–iv) により納得されるであろう。[(IV-131, a; IV-228, a) [instinct/intuition told] も参照]

　i)　*Legend* has it that the lake was formed by the tears of a god. (伝説によると，その湖は神の涙でできたとのことだ)(OALD⁶)
　ii)　*Myth* has it that oysters are the food of love. (神話では，カキは愛の食べ物とされている) (RD 01/10: 50)
　iii)　*Conventional wisdom* has it that riots only ever happen in cities. (世間の通念では，暴動は都市でしか起こらないとされている) (OALD⁶)
　iv)　*Word* has it that she's leaving. (うわさによると，彼女は辞めるそうだ) (OALD⁶)

(237) a. It was *shame* and humiliation, and my heart breaks for him once more. (それは恥辱であり屈辱であった。彼を思うと私はふたたび心が痛む) (RD 99/8: 73)
　　b. It's *a shame* you have to leave so soon. (君がそんなに早く退出しなければならないとは残念だ) (LDOCE³)
(238) a. The atmosphere seemed poisoned with *suspicion* and lack of trust. (そこの空気は疑惑と，信頼感の欠如とに汚染されているようだった) (RD 99/3: 48)
　　b. I had *an* uneasy *suspicion* that all was not well. (万事順調というわけではないのではないかという不安な感じがあった) (OALD⁵)
(239) a. It sounds fine in *theory*, but will it work (in practice)? (理論的にはよさそうだが，(実用上）うまくいくだろうか) (OALD⁵)
　　b. He has *a theory* that wearing hats makes men go bald. (帽子をかぶると禿(はげ)になるという持論だ) (OALD⁵)

以下の例では，ダッシュやコロンなどに後続する箇所が that 節の代用として "a＋名詞部" の内容を説明している。

(240) a. The few houses we have seen are in terrible *condition*. (我々が見た数軒はひどい状態だった) (OALD⁵)

b. They left the flat in *a* terrible *condition* – there was dirt everywhere. (アパートを退去したときはひどい状態だった——どこもかしこもほこりだらけだったのだ) (CIDE)

(241) a. (= II-68) He is very quick-thinking and very much a man of *decision* and action. (CCED³)

b. Later that night we made *an* agonizing *decision*: we wouldn't name the baby Eugene Clifton Stallings III. (その晩遅く苦しい決断をした。新生児に ECS 三世と名づけないことにしたのだ) (RD 98/12: 121)

(242) a. The hunter was filled with *fear* when he saw the bear running toward him. (ハンターはクマが自分に向かって走ってきているのを見て恐怖でいっぱいになった) (NHD)

b. I had *a* new *fear*, and it was now my greatest one: that something might somehow happen to him. (新たな恐怖が生じ，それは今や最大のものになった。すなわち，ともかく彼に何かが起きるのではないかということだ) (RD 98/9: 118)

(243) a. The play seems frighteningly surreal, yet it is based on *truth*. (その劇は怖いほど超現実的に見えるが，事実に基づいている) (OALD⁵)

b. As a result, the billion-dollar cigar industry, which caters to an estimated ten million to 12 million U.S. smokers, has obscured *a* simple *truth*: cigars generally contain more tar and nicotine than cigarettes. (その結果，10億ドルの葉巻産業は，推定1千万ないし1千2百万の米国の喫煙者におもねて，明白な真実をうやむやにしている——葉巻のほうが，通常，タバコよりもタールとニコチンを多く含んでいる，ということだ) (RD 99/3: 53)

(244) a. In short, get the facts. Base worry on reality, rather than on *fantasy*. (要するに，事実を手に入れなさい。心配の根拠は空想よりも現実に置きなさい) (RD 00/7: 94)

b. Romanek allowed himself *a* momentary *fantasy*. Maybe these carbonate globules had been formed when water flowed through cracks in the rock, leaving tiny deposits behind. Maybe, with the right tests, the rock could reveal its past. (R は一瞬空想した。こと

によるとこれらの炭酸小球体が形成されたのは，水が岩の割れ目を流れて，わずかな沈殿物をあとに残したときだったのではないか。ことによると，正しく実験すれば，その岩は過去を示しうるのではないか，と）(RD 97/5: 72)

(245, b) では invention よりもその内容が先行している。(先の (236, d) では内容の途中に rumour が挿入されている。)

(245) a. They subsequently admitted that the story was pure *invention*. (その後，その話はまったく創作だったと彼らは認めた) (LDOCE³) [話の内容には具体的言及なし；ジャンル扱い (☞ 2.2)]

b. His story of being kidnapped and held prisoner was *an invention*. (誘拐され人質にされたという彼の話は作り話だ) (CDAE) [話の内容に言及されているので不定冠詞つき；作品扱い]

以上の例からわかるように，不定冠詞の有無に関して大事なのは，that 節などの位置ではなく，情報の内容が限定されることである。

NB 10   φ information/news that . . .

information/news; agreement/knowledge などは同格の that 節をともなうときでも不定冠詞をとらない。(前2語は不定詞あるいは関係詞節が後続するときも a/an をとらない (☞ 2.3.3.3.6)。)

i) We have *information* that there was such an order. (そのような命令があったという情報を得ている) (ConCD-ROM)

ii) The grieving family of murder victim Julie Dart were last night overjoyed at *news* that police may be a step closer to finding her killer. (殺人事件の被害者である JD の家族は悲嘆に暮れているが，警察は殺人犯の発見に1歩近づいたかもしれないというニュースに昨晩歓喜した) (ConCD-ROM)

iii) It was common *knowledge* that Lucy was superstitious about the number 13. (L が 13 という数字に迷信深いということは常識だった) (CDAE)

agreement も「了解」という意味のときは無冠詞で用いられる。[cf. LDOCE³ (s.v., agreement 2): '[uncountable] a situation in which people have the same opinion as each other']

iv) There is *agreement* among doctors that pregnant women should not smoke. (医者のあいだでは，妊婦は喫煙すべきでないという了解がある) (LDOCE³) [(IV-220) も参照]

「知らせ」という意味のときの word も同様である。

 v) Impatient for *word* that the reactor had been shut down, he turned on the intercom. (原子炉が閉鎖されたという知らせにいらだって，インターホンのスイッチを入れた) (RD 98/3: 135)

4.4.5　不定詞および動名詞

以下は不定詞が名詞の内容を限定するため，a/an が要求される例である。

(246) a. Descriptive *ability* is not important, Wild explains. (記述能力は重要ではない，とWは説明する) (RD 99/10: 118)
  b. Ally McBeal has . . . *an ability* to blend humour and drama . . . (AMにはユーモアとドラマを融合する能力がある) (CCED[3])

(247) a. (= IV-220, a) When I'm with women I listen attentively and interrupt only to murmur *agreement*. (CCED[3])
  b. The two sides have reached *an agreement* to divide the money into two equal parts. (当事者はお金を均等に2分するという同意に達した) (CIDE) [不定詞による内容限定；本章 NB 10 参照]

(248) a. He has *ambition* and works hard to get a salary increase. (志があるので昇給のため一生懸命働く) (NHD)
  b. Every little boy has *an ambition* to be an engine driver. (男の子はみんな機関士になりたいという抱負をもっている) (CCED[3])

(249) a. People experience differences in physical and mental *capability* depending on the time of day. (だれもが経験することだが，肉体的・精神的能力には1日の時刻によって違いがある) (CCED[3])
  b. A willingness and *a capability* to change are necessary to meet the market's needs. (市場のニーズに応じるには意欲と変化する能力とが必要だ) (LDOCE[3])

(250) a. In terrific physical *condition*, Schwartz prided himself on his foot speed. (すばらしい肉体的状態にあって，Sは足の速さを誇りに思った) (RD 00/7: 135)
  b. The ship is not in *a condition* to make a long voyage. (その船は長旅をする状態にはない) (OALD[5])

(251) a. (= IV-112, a) I dreaded going home to face another night of unrelenting *craving*. (RD 97/5: 42)
  b. *a* desperate *craving* to be loved (愛されたいという激しい渇望) (OALD[5])

(252) a. The moment of *decision* has arrived. (決定の瞬間が来た) (OALD⁵)

b. She made *a decision* to go on vacation. (休暇に行くことに決めた) (NHD)

(253) a. They lacked *desire* and, what is infinitely worse, they lacked pride. (希求心がなく，ずっと悪いことに，自尊心に欠けていた) (CCED³)

b. Bill has *a desire* to be a veterinarian. (B には獣医になりたいという願望がある) (NTC)

(254) a. The book's theme is the conflict between love and *duty*. (その本のテーマは愛と義務との葛藤だ) (LDOCE³)

b. Thomson introduced him to the work of a Scottish philosopher, John Macmurray, who wrote that Christians have *a duty* to work toward improving society. (T は彼に S の哲学者，JM の業績を紹介した。彼はキリスト教徒は社会をよくするために働く義務があると述べたのだった) (RD 98/3: 54)

(255) a. USAir ... could be doomed if the public thought its pilots were at *fault*. (パイロットに非があると大衆が思えば USAir は破綻しかねない) (RD 00/2: 90)

b. It is *a* big *fault* to think that you can learn how to manage people in business school. (ビジネススクールで人の管理法を学べると思ったら大間違いだ) (CCED³)

(256) a. Should a soldier value *honour* above life? (兵士は生命よりも名誉を重んじるべきか) (OALD⁵)

b. I deem it *an honour* to be invited. (ご招待いただくのは名誉と思います) (OALD⁶)

(257) a. I don't swim because of *inability*, not because I choose not to. (できないから泳がないのであって，泳がないと選んでいるからではない) (NTC)

b. He's a flawed creature with aggressive tendencies, an enormous ego and *an inability* to listen. (彼は欠陥人間であり，攻撃的傾向があり，自我が大きく，聴く能力に欠ける) (RD 99/6: 44)

(258) a. Balbin was used to hearing tales of *injustice*, but this one was particularly gruesome. (B は不正に関する話を聞くのは慣れていたが，これは特に身の毛もよだつものだった) (RD 99/3: 100)

b. It would be doing Brett *an injustice* to say that he didn't care about other people. (B は他人のことにかまわなかったと言ったら不当な扱

いをすることになるだろう) (LDOCE³)

(259) a. (= IV-131, a) Though she had never migrated before, *instinct* told the flamingo to head for a warmer climate. (RD 99/4: 91)

b. From a book, I learned this was a trait bred into a mastiff, *an instinct* to protect every thing inside its territory. (本で学んだことだが，これはマスチフに生まれつきの特徴，縄張り内のすべてを守るという本能，だった) (RD 97/2: 11)

(260) a. The course gives you basic *instruction* in car maintenance and repairs. (当講座は車の維持と修理に関する基本的な教育を提供する) (CIDE)

b. carry out/ignore *an instruction* to fit a new switch (新しいスイッチを取り付けるようにという指示を実行する／無視する) (OALD⁵)

(261) a. *Kindness* breaks me up; it makes me cry. (優しさには心が乱れる。泣けてくるのだ) (CCED³)

b. It would be *a kindness* to ask her to stay. (彼女に泊まるよう頼むのは思いやりのある行為だろう) (OALD⁵)

(262) a. If a democracy does not preserve *liberty*, that it is a democracy is small consolation. (民主主義国家が自由を守らないのであれば，それが民主主義国家であるということはほんの気休めでしかない) (RD 98/10: 47)

b. What *a liberty*, to refuse the invitation on your behalf, without even asking you! (何て勝手なことを，聞きもしないで，君に代わって招待を断るなんて) (CIDE)

(263) a. The ANC claimed the curfew gave *license* to the police to hunt people as if they were animals. (戒厳令は警察に人を動物であるかのように捕獲する許可を与えた，とANC [アフリカ民族会議] は主張した) (CCED³) [この例の場合 licence が不定詞と離れていることも無冠詞の1因][注：licence は，不定詞が後続しても，必ずしも不定冠詞をとらない；cf. CCED³ (s.v., licence 2): 'If you say that something gives someone licence or a licence to act in a particular way, you mean that it gives them an excuse to behave in an irresponsible or excessive way.']

b. 'Dropping the charges has given racists *a licence* to kill,' said Jim's aunt. (「告訴取り下げは人種差別主義者に人殺しの許可を与えた」とJの叔母は言った) (CCED³)

(264) a. (= IV-120, a) He gazed with *longing* and apprehension into the future. (CCED³)
   b. I felt *a longing* to help. (援助したいという強い願望を感じた) (RD 98/8: 121)
(265) a. I helped you because I wanted to, not out of any sense of *obligation*. (助けたかったから助けたのであって，義務感からではない) (LDOCE³)
   b. College teachers have *a* contractual *obligation* to research and publish. (大学の教師は研究し出版するという契約上の義務を有する) (LDOCE³)
(266) a. It's quite common for little boys to take *pleasure* in torturing insects and small animals. (小さい男の子たちが虫や小動物をいじめて喜ぶのはよくあることだ) (CIDE)
   b. "It was such *a pleasure* to meet you," she said politely. (「お会いできてとてもうれしかったです」と彼女はていねいに言った) (CIDE)
(267) a. The White House said that there will be no change in *policy*. (ホワイトハウスは政策に変更はないと言った) (CIDE)
   b. It is never *a* good *policy* to drive after drinking. (飲酒後車に乗るのは決して得策ではない) (NHD)
   参考 : Rather embarrassed, I explained it was against hotel *policy* to fraternize with the guests. (いささか当惑して，客と親しくなるのはホテルの方針に反すると説明した) (RD 97/5: 64) [to fraternize ... は hotel policy の内容ではない (☞ 4.5.1) ; 類義表現の company policy は会社の方針全般 ('a plan of action chosen by the company' (CIDE)) を指すので，通例，無冠詞]
(268) a. Her words gave me tremendous *relief*. (彼女のことばは私に大きな安堵を与えた) (RD 99/12: 128)
   b. It's *a relief* to get out of the office once in a while. (ときたまオフィスから抜け出るのはいい気晴らしだ) (CCED³)
(269) a. We decided to break with *tradition* and not send any cards this Christmas. (伝統に決別して，今年のクリスマスにはカードを送らないことに決めた) (OALD⁵)
   b. It's *a tradition* to sing 'Auld Lang Syne' on New Year's Eve. (大晦日に「蛍の光」を歌うのは伝統だ) (OALD⁵)
(270) a. He was in *violation* of his contract. (契約に違反していた) (CCED³)

b. To deprive the boy of his education is *a violation* of state law. (少年から教育を奪うのは州法違反だ) (CCED[3])

動名詞が名詞部の内容を限定するため，名詞部が不定冠詞を必要とする場合もある．

(271) a. *Privilege* determined by birth is an offence to any modern sense of justice. (生まれによって決定される特権は現代的な正義感に反している) (CCED[3])

b. It was *a* great *privilege* hearing her sing/to hear her sing. (彼女が歌うのを聞くのは大変名誉なことだった) (OALD[5])

(272) a. Repayments can be made over a long period, without putting undue *strain* on your finances. (家計に過度な負担にならないよう，返済は長期にわたってもよい) (OALD[6])

b. I found it *a strain* making conversation with him. (彼と会話をするのは重荷だった) (OALD[5])

(273) a. Fonda says classmates looked at her as if she should know better, and she endured *humiliation* by a tough teacher. (F が言うには，級友は自分のことを物知らずであるかのように見たし，その上，ひどい教師の屈辱に耐えた，とのことだ) (RD 99/12: 114)

b. Being forced to resign was *a* great *humiliation* for the minister. (詰め腹を切らされるのは大臣にとって大変な屈辱だった) (CIDE)

(274) a. He was allergic to *risk*. (賭けは嫌いだった) (CCED[3])

b. It's always *a risk* starting up a new business. (新しい事業を興すのはいつでも賭けだ) (CIDE)

4.5 否定と存在
4.5.1 否定

文意が肯定か否定かということも冠詞の選択に関与することがある．一般的に言って，肯定は具体的な存在の様態を含意するので冠詞を必要とする傾向が強く，否定は必ずしも存在の様態を含意しないので冠詞がなくてもよいからである．

(275) a. They compared the rent with the mortgage payments and did not feel there was sufficient *difference* ... (彼らは家賃を住宅ローンの支払いと比較してさほど違いはないと考えた) (ConCD-ROM)

b. There is *a* great *difference* between theory and practice. (理論と実践には大きな違いがある) (CIDE)

c. A separation of five years in age makes *a* big *difference* when you're young. (年齢が5歳離れていれば幼いころには大変な違いだ) (RD 00/2: 11)

(276) a. Locking the doors is <u>not</u> *insurance* that your car won't be stolen. (ドアをロックしても車が盗まれないことの保証にはならない) (NTC)

b. I put an extra lock on the door as *an* added *insurance* against burglars. (強盗よけの追加的保証としてドアに余分に錠前をつけた) (LDOCE³)

比較: Do you carry an umbrella as *insurance* against getting wet? (濡れないための保証に傘をもち歩きますか) (NHD) [as のあと無冠詞可 (☞ 3.1)]

(277) a. The two other passengers <u>escaped</u> serious *injury*. (他の2人の乗客は重傷をまぬがれた) (CCED³)

b. They were lucky to <u>escape</u> (<u>without</u>) *injury*. (幸運にも負傷を(しないで)まぬがれた) (CIDE)

c. The pain in his neck signaled to him that he had *a* serious *injury*. (首の痛みは重傷であることを示した) (RD 99/4: 130)

(278) a. We have the ability <u>without</u> *doubt*. We have the market for our movies. (疑うまでもなく我々には能力がある。映画市場があるからだ) (ConCD-ROM)

b. There is just *a* nagging *doubt* about this, however. (しかし、これに関してはどうしてもぬぐいさりがたい疑いがある) (ConCD-ROM)

比較: She is <u>without</u> *(a) doubt* the best student I have ever taught. (彼女は、(1点の)疑いもなく、教えたなかで最も優秀な学生だ) (CIDE) [a の有無による意味の相違なし]

(279) a. Both had died <u>without</u> medical *explanation*. (2人とも医学的説明がつかないまま死んだ) (RD 99/2: 130)

b. I can give you *an explanation* for/of why I'm late. (なぜ遅れたかを説明することができる) (CIDE)

(280) a. We will send you an estimate for the work <u>without</u> *obligation*. (見積書をお送りしますが、責務をともなうものではありません) (OALD⁶)

b. I don't want to be under *an obligation* to anyone. (だれにも借りは作りたくない) (LDOCE³) [個別事例]

(281) a. Atlanta-based CNN is <u>without</u> *peer* as a global television news organization. (Aに拠点をおくCNNは世界規模のテレビニュース機

関としては肩を並べるものがない) (RD [U.S. Edition] 98/9: 211)

 b. Getting help from *a peer* is easier than asking a teacher. (仲間から手伝ってもらうほうが先生に聞くより簡単だ) (CDAE)

(282) a. A heart attack nearly always comes without *warning* and results from an insufficient flow of oxygen via the blood. (心臓発作はほとんどいつも警告なしにやってくるが，原因は酸素が血液中に十分に流れないことだ) (RD 97/2: 82)

 b. (= IV-236, d) That colonel had been caught and executed – burned alive, according to a rumour Kuklinski had heard, and the execution filmed as *a warning* to others. (RD 00/4: 132) [特定の警告]

(283) a. Two teenagers left Sydney, Australia, to hitchhike their way home to Melbourne one summer morning. Then they vanished without *trace*. (2人のティーンエージャーがある夏の朝，ヒッチハイクをしてMに帰省するため，豪のSを出た．その後彼らはなんらの跡形もなく消えてしまった) (RD 99/5: 117) [いかなる痕跡もなく]

 b. The master of suspense had vanished almost without leaving *a trace*. (サスペンスの巨匠は痕跡をほとんど残すことなく消えてしまっていた) (RD 99/11: 61) [よく探せばわかるかもしれない痕跡]

肯定は冠詞をとり，否定は必ずしも冠詞をとらないという傾向により，a little と little との意味の違いが説明される．前者では不定冠詞をつけることにより名詞部を姿かたちをもつ存在物として提示し，後者では不定冠詞をつけないことにより名詞部のイメージ化が抑えられるからである．a few と few との相違もこの傾向により説明可能である（ただし，little と異なり，few は a hundred/thousand years というときと同様に数詞扱いされているという違いがある）．

(284) a. I had little *money* and little free *time*. (お金もヒマもほとんどなかった) (CCED[3])

 b. *A* little *food* would do us all some good. (食料が少しあればみんなに役だつ) (CCED[3])

類例：I felt there was *a* certain ['slight, little'] *coldness* in her manner. (彼女の態度にわずかな冷たさを感じた) (OALD[6])

(285) a. Few *people* understand the difference. (その違いがわかる人はほとんどいない) (OALD[6])

 b. We've had *a* few *replies*. (少しばかり返事があった) (OALD[6])

名詞自体が「非存在」を表すときは a/an の有無は意味の相違に関与しない。母語話者の判断によると，次のいずれの文も話者が含意する欠如を表しているのであり，両者の間には意味的相違はない。この理由は，存在しないもののイメージ化は不可能もしくは困難であることによると解釈してさしつかえない (4 章 NB 5-2 も参照)。

(286) a. The project had hung fire for several years because of *lack* of funds. (そのプロジェクトは資金不足のため数年延び延びになった) (OALD⁵)

b. We aren't having a holiday because of *a lack* of funds. (資金が不足しているため休日をとっていない) (CIDE)

(287) a. Her paper reveals *paucity* of research. (彼女の論文は調査不足であることをさらけだしている)

b. Her paper reveals *a paucity* of research. (同上) [a-文よりふつう]

(288) The shop was forced to close owing to *(a) shortage* of staff. (その店は人手不足のため閉店に追い込まれた) (OALD⁵)

以下の例の否定文では不定冠詞に代わる限定詞として much/little が用いられている。日本人が英文を書くときの参考になるであろう。

(289) a. There isn't much *activity* on the roads after midnight. (深夜以降路上ではあまり活動はない) (NHD)

b. Until the mid-'80s, rock climbing was considered *an* eccentric *activity*, somewhat akin to wrestling alligators. (80 年代半ばまでロッククライミングは常軌を逸した活動，いくぶん取っ組み合い中のワニに似たようなもの，と考えられていた) (RD 98/7: 24)

(290) a. Don't make so much *fuss* over details/the children. (細かいこと／子供に大騒ぎするのはよしなさい) (OALD⁵)

b. The cat loves being made *a fuss* of. (その猫は特別扱いされるのが好きだ) (OALD⁵)

(291) a. "If she gets there early she'll be locked out." "I wouldn't worry — there's not much *possibility* of that!" (「もしも彼女が早く着いたら閉め出されるだろう」「心配してない。その可能性はあまりないから」) (CIDE)

b. The forecast said that there's *a possibility* of snow tonight. (予報によると今晩は雪の可能性がある) (CIDE)

(292) a. There's very little *probability* that anyone will try to escape. (だれも逃げようとする可能性はほとんどない) (OALD⁵)

b. (= IV-233, b) I'm afraid there is *a* high/strong *probability* (that) something has gone wrong. (CIDE)

4.5.2 存在文

前節で述べたように，肯定は具体的な存在の様態を含意するので冠詞をとる傾向が強い。特に，事物や行為などを表す名詞が "There is NP" という存在を表す構文で用いられるときは，不定冠詞をとりやすい。存在物は，通例，話し手／書き手の意識のなかで一定の姿かたちをもっていることと無縁ではない。

(293) a. With oysters, as with all seafood, *freshness* equals quality. (カキに関しては，すべての海産食品と同様，新鮮であることは上質であることだ) (CCED³)

b. There was *a freshness* and enthusiasm about the new students. (新入生たちには初々しさとひたむきさがあった) (CCED³) [意味的には a (freshness & enthusiasm)]

(294) a. There was *frost* on the grass in the early morning. (早朝草の上に霜があった) (CDAE) [様態非限定]

b. There was *a* heavy/hard/sharp *frost* last night. (昨晩ひどく霜が降りた) (OALD⁵, CIDE) [(形容詞をともなって) 個別事例；話し手が限定する昨晩の霜]

(295) a. There is considerable *impatience* with the slow pace of political change. (政治的変化の遅さにかなりのいらだちがある) (CCED³) [considerable は漠然とした程度を表すので a/an をとるには限定不十分]

b. There's *a* growing *impatience* among the electorate with the old two-party system. (選挙民のあいだには古い2党制に対していらだちが募ってきている) (CIDE) [一時的個別事例として提示]

(296) a. The primary cause of failed treatment is *interruption*, which can be caused as easily by a supply failure as by patient non-compliance. (治療の失敗の主原因は中断だ。これは患者が指示を守らないためすぐ生じうるのと同様 [薬の] 供給停止によっても容易に生じうる) (RD 99/10: 91)

b. We forgot to pay our phone bill so there was *an interruption* in our service. (電話代を払い忘れていたため，通信を中断された) (NTC)

(297) a. They were charged with *obstruction* of the police/of justice. (公務執行妨害の罪で告発された) (CIDE) [犯罪名 (☞ 5.1)]

b. There's *an obstruction* in the fuel pipe. (燃料パイプに閉塞箇所があ

る) (LDOCE³) [具体物]

(298) a. *Perfection* was pursued to the tiniest detail. (最も微細な点にまで完璧さが追求された) (RD 99/7: 137)

b. There was a closure, *a perfection*, a beauty about those last days. (最後の日々には終結が, 完璧さが, 美があった) (RD 98/6: 10) [書き手が含意する個別事例]

(299) a. "It was," said McKay with typical *reserve*, "a setback." (「それは逆行でした」と M はいかにも彼らしく控えめに言った) (RD 97/5: 74) [詳細無指定]

b. Having grown up in a military family with five siblings, there is *a reserve* about her, as if she should succeed at a high level but not stand out from the others. (5 人のきょうだいとともにスパルタ的な家庭で育ったので, 彼女には控えめなところがあった。高いレベルで成功しなければならないが, 他から浮き上がってはならないかのようだった) (RD 99/12: 113) [as if 以下による様態限定]

(300) a. *Shortage* of water is a growing problem. (水不足は深刻化しつつある問題だ) (OALD⁶) [慢性的]

b. There is *a shortage* of fresh water on the island. (島では真水が不足している) (OALD⁶) [慢性的不足という解釈も可能だが, 存在文中では一時的不足という読みも可能 (IV-288 参照)]

(301) a. We watched the couple until they disappeared from *view*. (視界から消えるまで夫婦を見送った) (RD 99/1: 132) [抽象概念]

b. There is *a* wonderful *view* from the top of the church tower. (教会の塔の最上部からすばらしい景色が見られる) (OALD⁵) [広がり (または種類) 限定]

(302) a. She's efficient at her job but she lacks *warmth*. (仕事は有能だが, 温かみに欠ける) (OALD⁵)

b. There was *a warmth* in Room 33 as we sat at our desks, quietly poring over classwork while Mr. Mahoney, positioned like a guardian over us, sipped coffee and corrected papers. (33 室には温かさがあった。私たちは机に座って静かに勉強をし, M 先生は, 守護神のように私たちより高い位置を占めて, コーヒーをすすりながら答案を添削していた) (RD 98/3: 48) [書き手が含意する, Room 33 に特有な温かさ]

(303) a. The residents of Monkton Wyld are bound together by 'a search for

wholeness', but there is no single creed.（MWの住民たちは「完全性の追求」によって結びつけられているが，単一の信条というものはない）(CCED³)

b. There is *a wholeness* about the person who has come to terms with his limitations, who has been brave enough to let go of his unrealistic dreams and not feel like a failure for doing so. There is *a wholeness* about the man or woman who has learned that he or she is strong enough to go through a tragedy and survive, who can lose someone and still feel like a complete person.（自分の限界を受け入れ，勇敢にも，非現実的な夢をあきらめ，それを失敗とは思わない人には完全性がある。自分には悲劇を経験しても乗り越える強さがあることがわかった人には，だれかを失っても自分は完全な人間だと感じることができる人には，完全性があるのだ）(RD 98/3: 116)［当該の人に特有な wholeness］

NB 11　there is ɸ N

話し手／書き手の意識のなかで名詞部が一定の姿かたちをもっていなければ，存在文中でも不定冠詞はつけられない（(294-295, a)［frost/impatience］も参照）。

i) He went free because the jury decided there was *(a) reasonable doubt* about his guilt.（有罪にするには道理にかなった疑いがあると陪審員たちが決定したので，自由になった）(CIDE)

ii) There was *silence* for a moment.（一瞬沈黙があった）(RD 01/9: 82)

比較：[T]here was *a silence* for a few seconds . . .（数秒間沈黙があった）(LOB)［上例よりも時間の限定が具体的］

iii) There was *mischief* in her eyes.（彼女の目には悪戯（いたずら）っぽさがあった）(OALD⁵)［「悪戯」という意味のとき mischief は [U]］

不定冠詞の選択が随意的に見える場合に関して注目に値するのは Kałuża (1981: 10) の指摘である。彼は，次の3例をあげて，（特に抽象名詞に）不定冠詞をつけるのは，表現力を高め注意を引くための工夫であり，文学的文体 (literary style) の特徴であると言う。（これは，本書では当該の表現が具象性（つまり，完結性）を得るためであると説明される。）

iv) There was a warmth between them . . .（彼らのあいだには温か

さがあった); Then a loneliness fell upon them. (そして彼らには寂しさが訪れた); She was aware that there was an emptiness in her life. (彼女の人生には空虚さがあることに気づいていた)

第5章　原理 V ——抽象概念と個別事例

5　原理 V ——抽象概念と個別事例

辞書にはしばしば第1義として抽象的語義の定義があげられ，第2義として 'an instance of this' という説明があげられている。たとえば，OALD[5] は antipathy に関して次のように定義している (abstention, ballot, bereavement, betrayal, birth, blasphemy, burglary, etc. も同様)。

(1) (a) [U] a feeling of strong dislike: *She made no attempt to hide her feelings of antipathy.* ((a) [U] 強い嫌悪の感情：...)
(b) [C usually sing] an instance of this: *There exists a profound antipathy between the two men.* ・*He showed a marked antipathy to foreigners.* ((b) [C 通例単数] この個別事例：...)

同様な定義法は他の辞書でも見られる。たとえば，NTC は experience を次のように定義している (一部のみ抜粋)。

(2) 1. knowledge gained from remembering past events and the results of one's actions during those events; ... (1. 過去の出来事とその出来事中の行動の結果を想起することから得られる知識)
2. an event that gives someone ① ... (2. ①を与える出来事)

oscillation に関する LDOCE[3] の定義も同様である (hop 2 (flight), impulse 3, motion[1] 2, pass[2] 3 も参照)。

(3) 1 [uncountable] the regular movement of something from side to side between two limits ([U] 何かが2つの極限点のあいだを端から端に規則的に揺れ動くこと)
2 [countable] a single movement from side to side of something that is oscillating ([C] 揺れ動いているものが端から端へ1回運動すること)

これらの定義に従えば，名詞が個別事例 (個別行為を含む) を表すときは単数形で用いられて a/an をとり，そうでないときは無冠詞で用いられる，ということになる。たしかにそのとおりではあるが，名詞 (部) がどういう場合に個別事例を表し，どういう場合に抽象的意味を表すかは簡単には区別できない。たとえば，上掲 (1) の定義 (b) の例文が形容詞 (profound/marked; ☞ 4.4.3) および前置詞句 (between/to NP; ☞ 4.4.1) をとっていることからわかるように，この区別は前章 (限定と非限定) の原理の上位に位置するものである。本

章では，辞書の第1義と第2義とをまとめて原理 V として提示したい。

> 原理 V：英語の名詞部は，個別事例を表すときは a/an をとり，個別事例を表さないときは a/an をとらない。

5.1 犯罪名と事件

名詞が抽象概念と個別事例とを表す典型的な例として，まず犯罪名と事件（または犯罪行為）とを取り上げたい。筆者の知る限り，これまで文法書で指摘されたことはないが，犯罪名と事件とのあいだには無冠詞と冠詞つきという区別が顕著に見られる。これらの名詞は arrest/charge/convict などにつづくときは，ほとんど常に，無冠詞である。(厳密に言えば，「事件」は個別行為に属するので 5.4.2 に含めることも可能であるが，かなりの語数があるので独立の節を設けることにしたい。)

(4) a. Meanwhile, other investigators were trawling databases of sex offenders, and of people convicted of *abduction* or crimes of violence. (その間，他の捜査官たちは性犯罪者や，拉致あるいは暴行犯罪の前歴者のデータベースを調べていた) (RD 99/5: 130)

b. Singer Fairlie Arrow was fined £10,000 for faking *a* two-day *abduction* to boost her ailing career. (歌手の FA は1万ポンドの科料に処せられた。落ち目の人気を取り戻そうとして2日間の誘拐事件をでっち上げたためだ) (BNC, CBF 14256)

(5) a. A police officer caught the fleeing man and arrested him for *assault* and battery. (警官は逃亡中の男を捕らえ，暴行殴打で逮捕した) (NHD)

b. He had been accused of *a* drunken *assault* on a girl of 15 outside a McDonald's restaurant at Mitcham, Surrey, 13 months ago. (13か月前に，S 州，M 市の M 店の外で，酔っぱらって15歳の少女に暴行した事件で告訴された) (ConCD-ROM)

(6) a. If they fail to deliver the goods, we will sue them for *breach* of contract. (商品をちゃんと配達しなければ，契約違反の罪で訴えるつもりだ) (LDOCE[3])

b. His refusal to work on a Sunday was *a breach* of contract. (日曜日に働くのを拒否するのは契約違反行為だ) (CIDE)

(7) a. He's been arrested for *burglary*. (押込み強盗の罪で逮捕されている) (CCED[3]) [i.e., for the crime of burglary]

b. He was wanted for *a burglary*. (押込み強盗事件でお尋ね者だった) (RD 00/7: 134) [i.e., for the case of burglary]

(8) a. The crime of *carjacking* has claimed numerous lives in America. (米ではカージャックという犯罪で多くの生命が奪われている) (CCED³)

b. The U.S. ambassador to Cameroon was slightly injured in *a carjacking* Friday night in the capital of the Central African country, a U.S. embassy official said. (C駐在の合衆国大使は，金曜日の夜中央アフリカの国の首都におけるカージャック事件の際に軽傷を負った，と合衆国大使館員は述べた) (CNN, Mar. 11, 00)

(9) a. In September 1997 Cheryl pleaded guilty to *conspiracy* to commit credit-card and bank fraud, and was sentenced to 11 months in prison. (1997年9月Cはクレジットカードおよび銀行詐欺の共同謀議の罪を認め，懲役11か月の判決をうけた) (RD 00/4: 86)

b. The generals joined in *a conspiracy* to overthrow their country's dictator. (将軍たちは彼らの国の独裁者を転覆させる陰謀に加った) (NHD)

(10) a. The police fight *crime*, murder, theft, and drug dealing. (警察は，犯罪や殺人，盗み，麻薬取引と闘う) (NHD)

b. Endangering their lives will be regarded as *a crime* against humanity. (彼らの生命を危険にさらすのは人類に対する犯罪行為とみなされる) (CCED³)

(11) a. His wife was a victim of *deception*. (彼の妻は詐欺 [という犯罪] の犠牲者だ) (CIDE)

b. You've been the victim of *a* rather cruel *deception*. (君はとても非道な詐欺事件の犠牲者だ) (CCED³)

NB 1　(a) deception

『新編英和活用大辞典』(研究社) には，次のような例があげられているが，いずれも無冠詞の場合は「詐欺罪」，不定冠詞つきの場合は「詐欺事件」または「詐欺行為」と解釈すべきである。

(a) blatant deception (あくどい詐欺); (a) deliberate deception (計画的詐欺); (a) gross deception (はなはだしい欺瞞); (a) harmless deception (害のないうそ); (an) innocent deception (無邪気なうそ); (an) intentional [unintentional] deception (意図的な [でない] 詐欺)

(12) a. They spent ten years in jail for *fraud*. (詐欺罪で10年間服役した) (CIDE)
　　b. They were sentenced for their part in *a* £14 million *fraud*. (千4百万ポンドの詐欺事件の共犯行為で判決をうけた) (LDOCE³)
(13) a. He was convicted of *homicide*. (殺人罪で有罪とされた) (CIDE, CDAE)
　　b. Her death was *a homicide* from a knife wound to the heart. (彼女の死は心臓に達するナイフの傷による殺人事件だった) (NHD)
(14) a. It could also wipe out bribery, *kidnapping*, extortion and even robbery. (贈賄, 誘拐, 恐喝, さらには強盗 [などの犯罪] も一掃することが可能だろう) (RD 97/2: 63-64)
　　b. report *a* debate/strike/*kidnapping* (討論/ストライキ/誘拐事件を報告する) (OALD⁵)
(15) a. The deputy coroner, Pasul Singleton, recorded a verdict of unlawful *killing*. (副検死官のPSは不法な殺人の答申を記録した) (CIDE) [killing を犯罪名として用いるのはまれ；murder/manslaughter など専門用語があるため]
　　b. The never-ending clan warfare is almost always over pigs and women, and is often payback for *an* earlier *killing*. (部族間の果てしない抗争はほとんどいつもブタと女に関してであるが, 以前の殺人に対する報復であることもしばしばある) (RD 96/10: 31)
(16) a. They have won a reputation worldwide for *massacre* and atrocity. (虐殺と暴虐とで世界的な悪評を得た) (CCED³)
　　b. He told me about the endless wait . . . , the attack seen live on television, the certainty that there would be *a massacre* and the countless calls from distraught family members. (彼が語ったのは, 果てしなく待ったことや, テレビで生で見た攻撃, 虐殺行為が確実にあるであろうこと, 動転した家族からの無数の電話についてだった) (RD 99/6: 143)
　比較：*Genocide* still takes place in many parts of the world. (大量殺りくはいまだに世界の各地で行われている) (NHD) [genocide は, massacre の類義語であるが, 通例, 不定冠詞をとらない]
(17) a. Aguilar was certain that someone was trying to get away with *murder*. (だれか謀殺の罪を逃れようとしている, とAは確信した) (RD 99/3: 101)

第5章 原理 V ——抽象概念と個別事例　*189*

　　　b. I think there could have been *a murder*. Or something. (殺人事件か何かがあったのだと思う) (ConCD-ROM)
(18) a. She was sentenced to twenty years' imprisonment for *poisoning* and attempted murder. (毒物混入と殺人未遂の罪で 20 年の禁固刑を言い渡された) (CCED[3])
　　　b. Call immediately if you suspect *a poisoning*. (中毒ではないかと思ったらすぐに電話しなさい) (RD 96/3: 55) [これは「事件」というよりも「事故」]
(19) a. He served four years in prison for *robbery*. (強盗罪で 4 年間服役した) (CIDE)
　　　b. Within minutes their radios crackled with a report of *a robbery* in the building. (建物内で強盗事件があったことを数分以内に無線は伝えた) (RD 97/6: 79)
(20) a. Prison rarely persuades a criminal of the advantages of honest toil over *theft*. (正直に額に汗するほうが窃盗よりも得策だということを刑務所が犯罪者に納得させることはめったにない) (CIDE) [cf. LDOCE[3] (s.v., theft): '[uncountable] the crime of stealing']
　　　b. I'd like to report *a theft*. (盗難事件について報告したい) (LDOCE[3]) [cf. LDOCE[3] (s.v., theft): '[countable] an act of stealing something']

　　　NB 2　charge someone with a/an N
　　　　　charge (with) に後続する名詞は，犯罪行為を表すこともある。
　　　　　　My brother-in-law was a wildlife officer, and one day he had to attend the hearing of a man whom he had charged with *a fishing violation*. (義兄は野生生物警官だったので，ある日釣魚違反行為で告発した男の聴聞会に出席しなければならなかった) (RD 98/4: 98)　類例：insufficient evidence to charge any person with an offence (CCED)

処刑名と刑罰との関係にも，犯罪名と事件と同様な区別が見られる。
(21) a. Grandison is on death row in Maryland, awaiting *execution*. (G は M 州の死刑囚監房で死刑執行を待っている) (RD 00/2: 36)
　　　b. *a* public [summary] *execution* (公開 [即時] 処刑) (LDOCE[3])
(22) a. *Hanging* is still legal in some countries. (絞首刑はいくつかの国では今でも合法だ) (CIDE)
　　　b. In 24 days, Clappe wrote, we have had murders, fearful accidents,

bloody deaths, a mob, whippings, *a hanging* – and a fatal duel. (Cは書いた。24日のうちに次のようなことがあった：殺人事件，身の毛もよだつ事故，血なまぐさい死，暴徒，むち打ち，縛り首，そして，死にいたる果たし合い) (RD 98/6: 53)

(23) a. There are strong arguments for and against capital *punishment*.（死刑に関しては賛成と反対の激しい議論がある）(OALD⁵)

　　b. But don't impose too harsh *a punishment*, as that might breed resentment.（しかし，厳しすぎる罰を科してはならない。恨みを引き起こしかねないから）(RD 99/12: 83f.)

5.2　治療法と施術

前節と同様に文法書で指摘されたことはないが，治療法と施術とにも，不定冠詞の有無に関する規則的な区別が見られる。治療法は行為者不定であり，かつ抽象概念なので無冠詞で用いられるが，その実現としての施術は個別事例なので冠詞つきで用いられる。

(24) a. *Amputation* of the limb is really a last resort.（手[足]の切断は本当に最後の手段だ）(CIDE)

　　b. Jan had a malignant growth that would require *a* leg *amputation*.（Jには悪性腫瘍(しゅよう)があり，それは脚部切断を要するであろうものだった）(RD 99/6: 76)

(25) a. My youngest daughter was born by *Caesarean*.（末娘は帝王切開で生まれた）(CCED³) [(III-99, a) も参照]

　　b. Not wanting to risk complications from *a Caesarean*, he recommended that I deliver naturally.（帝王切開による合併症の危険を冒したくなかったので，自然分娩をするように勧められた）(RD 98/11: 8)

(26) a. *Massage* and aromatherapy are not just good for relaxing the body, they can also be energising and stimulating.（マッサージやアロマテラピーは体をリラックスさせるのによいだけでなく，活力と刺激も与える）(RD 99/11: 117)

　　b. Would *a massage* do anything for your backache?（マッサージは腰痛に何か役に立つだろうか）(CIDE)

(27) a. When a patient has lost a lot of blood *transfusion* is the only answer.（患者が多量の血液を失えば，輸血法が唯一の解決策だ）(CIDE)

  b. The injured man had lost a lot of blood and had to be given *a transfusion*. (負傷者は多量の血液を失ったので,輸血しなければならなかった) (OALD[5])

(28) a. "If it doesn't [succeed], it will set larynx *transplantation* back 25 years" – and seriously hurt his career. (「うまくいかなければ,喉頭移植術を25年前に戻してしまうだろう」——しかも,彼の経歴に深刻な傷をつけるのだ) (RD 99/7: 60) [transplantation は,通例,「移植(術,療法)」を意味し,無冠詞で用いられる]

  b. For Strome, one of Heidler's biggest advances came when he was able to swallow food, thus proving that *a* larynx *transplant* didn't mean the loss of normal swallowing. (SにとってHの最大の回復の1つは食物を嚥下(えんか)できたことだった。これは,喉頭移植は正常な嚥下能力を失いはしないということの証明なのだ) (RD 99/7: 62) [transplant は,通例,「移植手術(の実施)」を表し,可算名詞;cf. farm [C] / farmland [U]]

(29) a. Standard medical *treatment* is surgery, radiation and chemotherapy. (標準的な医学的治療は手術,放射線投与および化学療法だ) (RD 99/12: 129)

  b. When the cough returned, she visited a herbalist, who specialised in Chinese medicine, and tried *a* herbal *treatment*. (咳がぶりかえしたとき,薬草医を訪ねた。彼は漢方の専門家であり,薬草療法を試みた) (RD 00/7: 84) [分野限定]

  c. *A* single Photofrin *treatment* wiped out the cancer in 79 patients, and the median disease-free survival time was 5.7 years. (1回のP投与で 79 人の患者からガンが消え,無病生存期の平均は 5.7 年だった) (RD 99/2: 14) [個別事例]

  d. Prentiss was taking a drug known as a glucocorticoid, considered *a* near-miracle *treatment* for severe asthmatic attacks, rheumatoid arthritis, inflammatory bowel disease and some kinds of pulmonary disease. (Pはグルココルチコイドとして知られている薬を摂っていた。それは,激しい喘息(ぜんそく)の発作や,リューマチ性関節炎,炎症性の腸疾患,数種類の肺疾患に対する奇跡に近い治療薬と考えられていた) (RD 98/6: 99) [具体物]

  NB 3 therapy は,形容詞をともなって限定された治療法を指すとき

は，不定冠詞をとる。
- i) a. He is having *therapy* to conquer his phobia. (恐怖症を克服するため治療をうけている) (CIDE)
  b. Patients who have failed bone-marrow transplantation, which is as aggressive *a therapy* as you can get for breast cancer, have responded to this antibody with no significant toxicity. (骨髄移植――乳ガンに対してできうる最も積極的な治療――が効かなかった患者でさえ，この抗体に反応し，目立った毒性を示すことはなかった) (RD 98/7: 68)

次例中の therapy は sessions に後続して素材扱いされているので冠詞をとらない (☞ 2.1.2)。
- ii) She signed up for ten sessions of nonsurgical "face lift" *therapy*, performed by a licensed acupuncturist. (有資格の鍼師(はり)によって行われる，手術をともなわない「フェイスリフト」療法10回分にサインした) (RD 98/7: 9)

複合語としての -therapy は治療法を表すので，無冠詞で用いられる。
- iii) (= V-26, a) Massage and *aromatherapy* are not just good for relaxing the body, they can also be energising and stimulating. (RD 99/11: 117)
- iv) After five months of *chemotherapy*, Dorothy would undergo radiation. (5か月の化学療法ののち D は放射線療法をうけることになる) (RD 99/3: 20)
- v) After extensive *physiotherapy* she regained the use of her arm, although she did lose some muscle tissue. (筋肉組織をいくぶん失ったが，大がかりな物理療法ののち彼女はふたたび腕を使えるようになった) (RD 97/5: 35)

abortion/termination の用法も治療法と施術という区別により説明可能である (抽象概念と個別事例と見ることも可; cf. miscarriage)。
- (30) a. Her parents don't approve of *abortion*. (彼女の両親は中絶を認めない) (OALD⁵)
  b. She decided to have/get *an abortion*. (中絶することに決めた) (CIDE)
- (31) a. "Can't you just remove the tumor?" Angela pleaded. "Not without

terminating the pregnancy," Doany said. "But *termination* is the course typically recommended because of the short-term and long-term risks to the mother and the poor prognosis for the fetus." (「腫瘍を除去するだけはできないのですか」Ａは懇願した。「妊娠を終了させずにはできません」とＤは言った。「でも, 人工流産が方針として勧められるのは, 典型的には, 母体が短期的にも長期的にも危険で, 胎児の予後が芳しくないときですわ」) (RD 99/5: 18)

   b. In the end she had to have *a termination*, she was so ill. (最終的に人工流産をせざるをえなかった。それほど具合が悪かったのだ) (CCED[1])

(32)–(34) では「検査法」と「施術」という区別が見られる。

(32) a. "We'll have to do *amniocentesis* to find out for sure," the doctor replied. (「確認のため羊水穿刺をしなければなりません」と医師は答えた) (RD 99/5: 18) [注：羊水穿刺(せんし) = 腹壁より探針を刺して, 妊婦の子宮内の羊水を採取すること (ランダムハウス)]

   b. *An amniocentesis* confirmed the second of the two possible conditions: a tumor was sharing the womb with a co-existing fetus. (羊水穿刺により確認されたのは可能な２つの状態のうちの第２のほうだった。腫瘍は [胎盤の中にはなく] おなかの胎児と子宮を共有していたのだ) (RD 99/5: 19)

(33) a. On September 7, 1988, Balbin wrote to the National Bureau of Investigation (NBI) requesting a new inquiry and asking that the boy's body be exhumed for *autopsy*. (1988 年９月７日, ＢはNBIに新たな調査を依頼する手紙を書いて, 検死のため少年の遺体を掘り出すよう頼んだ) (RD 99/3: 102)

   b. Finally, he recommended an exhumation and *an autopsy*. (ついに彼は死体発掘と検死とを勧告した) (RD 99/3: 102)

(34) a. In 2 cases *biopsy* of a lymph-gland was undertaken and reported as lymphoblastic lymphoma. (２例でリンパ腺の生検が行われ, リンパ芽球性リンパ腫と報告された) (1961 Lancet 5 Aug. 291/2) [OED]

   b. *A biopsy* of her right breast on New Year's Eve, 1992, indicated cancer. (1992 年の大晦日に行われた彼女の右胸の生検でガンと判明した) (RD 98/3: 19)

治療法／検査法と施術との関連において手術名にも言及しておきたい。手術名は, 治療の一環としてとらえられれば, 無冠詞で用いられ, 施術の１種とし

てとらえられれば，不定冠詞をとる。

(35) a. Recovery time averages about a week, compared with four to six weeks for *myomectomy* and *hysterectomy*. (回復期間は，筋腫摘出および子宮摘出の4～6週間に較べ，平均約1週間だ) (RD 01/8: 19)

b. Nevertheless, she suffered through 30 years of incontinence and was correctly diagnosed only last year when she had *a hysterectomy*. (それにもかかわらず，彼女は30年も失禁に苦しみ，昨年子宮摘出手術をうけたとき初めて正確な診断をされた) (RD 99/11: 102)

(36) a. One of my neighbors turned out to be recuperating from *radical prostatectomy*; by coincidence he jogged the road in front of our house every morning. (隣人の1人が前立腺全摘出治療から回復中だとわかった。偶然にも，彼は毎朝わが家の前の道路をジョギングしていた) (RD 97/5: 145)

b. I was at the stage where *a radical prostatectomy* was clearly indicated. (前立腺全摘出手術が明らかに必要とされる段階だった) (RD 97/5: 131)

(37) a. We now know that in stage I and II breast cancer, removing just the cancerous lump and giving radiation produces a survival rate that's equal to *mastectomy*. (今やわかってきたのだが，第1および第2段階の乳ガンでは，ガンのしこり部分のみを取り除いて放射線を投与すれば，乳房切除法に相当する生存率が得られるのだ) (RD 98/11: 84)

b. When told she would need *a* bilateral *mastectomy*, she kept a stiff upper lip. (両方の乳房切除手術が必要だと言われたとき，上唇を固く結んでいた) (RD 98/3: 19)

　surgery は，(38, a-b) が示唆するように，治療法として扱われるため，単数形の場合は (数値により限定される場合を除き) 無冠詞で使われる。ただし，*a surgery とは言わないが，two/three/four surgeries は可能である ((38, e-h) 参照)。

(38) a. The next day, the baby underwent laser *surgery*. It was the first of a series of treatments to repair the vessels in her arm. (翌日新生児はレーザー手術をうけた。それは腕の血管を治すための一連の治療の最初だった) (RD 98/5: 24)

b. They recommended urgent *surgery* to save his life, but the cost

第 5 章　原理 V ——抽象概念と個別事例

was beyond the family's means. (医師たちは彼の命を救うために緊急手術をするように勧めた。しかし、費用は家族の財力を越えていた) (RD 98/12: 9)

c. Without speaking we each knew what the other was thinking: *surgery* will kill him. (ことばに出さなくても互いに相手が考えていることはわかっていた。手術すれば彼は死んでしまう、ということだ) (RD 98/12: 129)

d. In January 1998 *an* 11-hour *surgery* excised the tumour. (1998 年の 1 月、11 時間におよぶ手術で腫瘍は切除された) (RD 01/9: 102) [数値による限定 (☞ 4.4.1.1)]

e. By the time she was 18, Lesia had undergone 17 *surgeries*. (18 歳になるまでに L は 17 回の手術をうけた) (RD 98/11: 18)

f. After two *surgeries*, her knee didn't seem to be healing. (2 度の手術のあとも、彼女の膝は治ってきているようには見えなかった) (RD 98/5: 25)

g. Alan Stoudemire has since developed cancerous tumors, but after several *surgeries* and treatment with an experimental vaccine, his prognosis is hopeful. (AS はその後ガン腫瘍ができたが、数回の手術と実験段階のワクチンによる治療ののち、予後は希望がもてるものである) (RD 98/10: 30)

h. In the month since she arrived in Manila, doctors have begun a series of *surgeries* to reconstruct Rona's shoulder and neck muscles. (M に到着したその月のうちに医師たちは R の肩と首の筋肉を復元するため一連の手術を始めた) (RD 97/2: 22)

surgery に対し、operation は可算名詞である。手術開始から終了までが含意されるからであろう。

(39) a. She had *an operation* to remove her appendix. (虫垂を除去する手術をうけた) (NHD)

b. It would take more than 30 *operations* in all. (全部で 30 回以上手術することになるだろう) (RD 99/4: 10)

NB 4

　　上記以外の、-ectomy に終わる手術名に関しては、手元の資料では、((V-48) [by appendectomy] を除いて) 無冠詞用法はないが、文脈によっては上例と同様に使われると予測可能である。事実、(i−ii, b) は筆

者が母語話者の協力を得て作った文法的な文である。(a-文では，手術名は have の目的語として個別事例を表すので，不定冠詞をとる。)

> i) a. Once a three-year-old arrived to have *a tonsillectomy*, and was quite blasé about the whole affair. (かつて3歳児が扁桃全摘除手術にやってきたことがあったが，すべてにまったく無感動になっていた) (RD 99/12: 92)
>
> b. *Tonsillectomy* is rarely necessary among old people. (扁桃全摘除は老人にはめったに必要でない)
>
> ii) a. Says 48-year-old Katherine Teng of Singapore, who two years ago had *a lumpectomy* for breast cancer and is still undergoing treatment... (S 在住の KT，48歳，は，2年前に乳ガンのため乳腺腫瘤(しゅりゅう)摘出手術をうけ，まだ治療中であるが，次のように言う) (RD 00/1: 108)
>
> b. The young medical student couldn't bear the idea of *lumpectomy*, so she devoted herself to finding a better treatment for breast cancer. (若い医学生は乳腺腫瘤摘出のことを考えると堪えられなかった。それで，より適切な乳ガンの治療法を懸命に模索した)

次の文で一方では冠詞がつけられ，他方では冠詞が落とされているのは文体的変奏 (stylistic variation) のためと思われる。換言すれば，undergo は治療に関しても施術に関しても用いられるということである。

> iii) In addition, the cancer was no more likely to metastasise in women who had undergone *a lumpectomy* than in those who had undergone *mastectomy*. (加えて，乳房切除治療をうけた女性よりも乳腺腫瘤摘出手術をうけた女性のほうがガンが転移しやすいということは決してなかった) (RD 01/9: 16)

5.3 病名と症状

しばしば指摘されているように，病名は通例 [U] である (Berry 1993: 49; Swan 1995: 69)。これは，病気の多くはいつ罹患(りかん)しいつ治癒したかよくわからず，病状も細かな点では患者ごとに異なるからであろう。本書のことばで言い換えれば，病名や体調不良は，多くの場合，完結した姿かたちをもたないので，原理 II (姿かたちの有無) により，無冠詞で用いられる，ということである。英語を母語としないものにとってわかりにくいのは，ある文脈では無冠

詞で用いられる病名が，別の文脈では冠詞つきで用いられるとき，意味に相違があるのかないのか，あるとすれば，冠詞の有無によってどのように意味が異なるのか，ということである。以下，無冠詞で用いられる病名，冠詞つきで用いられる病名（単数形および複数形），冠詞の有無によって意味が異なる病名という順に見ていく（8.2.6; 8.3.3 も参照）。

5.3.1 病名 [U]

(40) a. Taking 150 mg of zinc daily for several months can lead to immune-system problems, *anaemia* and copper *deficiency*. (亜鉛を数か月にわたって毎日 150 mg 摂れば，免疫系統の問題や貧血，銅欠乏症を起こすことがある) (RD 99/9: 6)

b. *Aphasia* is loss of the ability to use language. (失語症とは言語を使用する能力を失うことである) (RD 99/12: 132)

c. Without heat, she could suffer *hypothermia*. (熱がなければ，低体温症になりかねない) (RD 99/2: 108)

d. By now, she was screaming, completely overcome with *hysteria*. (今や，すっかりヒステリーにとらえられて，金切り声を上げていた) (CCED[3]) [(V-76) [hysterics] も参照]

e. If *insomnia* persists, or if daytime drowsiness interferes with work, see a doctor. (もしも不眠症が長引いたり，昼間の眠気が仕事にさしつかえるようなら，医者に相談しなさい) (RD 96/3: 100)

f. Acute *leukemia* was diagnosed, and Bracken was given two weeks to live. (急性白血病と診断され，B は余命 2 週間と告げられた) (RD 97/5: 52)

g. The tourists took medication to protect themselves from *malaria*. (旅行者たちはマラリアの予防に薬を飲んだ) (NTC)

h. Anne's psychiatrist believed she was suffering from *paranoia*. (A の精神科医は，彼女は偏執病だと信じた) (NTC)

i. Long Wolf had been with the show for over a year when he caught *pneumonia*. (LW は，ショーに加わって 1 年以上たったとき，肺炎にかかった) (RD 98/12: 92)

j. *Schizophrenia* runs in families. (統合失調症は遺伝する) (RD 99/12: 76)

(41) a. Severe *diarrhea* struck the orphanage at the end of February, and Tiny was among the children who fell ill. (2 月末，孤児院はひどい下痢に襲われ，T も病気になった子供の 1 人だった) (RD 98/11: 109)

b. Ginger can do more than just add zip to cakes and cookies; the herb can also help relieve *nausea*. (ショウガはケーキやクッキーをピリッとさせるだけではない。この薬草は吐き気を緩和するのにも役立つのだ) (RD 99/3: 115)

(42) a. My uncle suffers from *agoraphobia*, and when he goes out he finds it difficult to breathe. (伯父は広場恐怖症なので，外出すると呼吸困難になる) (CIDE)

b. Anyone with *claustrophobia* had no business in the space program, I thought. (閉所恐怖症のものは宇宙計画には無縁だ，と思った) (RD 99/3: 126)

c. Max was given a series of shots to prevent *hydrophobia*. (Mは恐水病予防のため一連の注射をされた) (NTC)

NB 5　phobia [C]
　　単独の phobia ('fear') は，複合語の agora-/claustro-/hydrophobia などと異なり，可算名詞扱いされる。
　　i) I've got *a phobia* about worms. (私は虫恐怖症だ) (CIDE)
　　ii) Childhood experiences may provide a clue as to why some adults develop *phobias*. (幼児体験は，なぜ一部の大人は恐怖症にかかるかに手がかりを与えるかもしれない) (LDOCE[3])

(43) a. *Arthritis* in her ankles sidelined her. (両くるぶしの関節炎のため出場できなかった) (RD 98/3: 62)

b. More than 60 per cent of the 143 workers in the study had chronic *bronchitis*, and over 13 per cent of them were diagnosed as suffering from *asbestosis*. (調査対象の143人の労働者のうち60％以上に慢性気管支炎があり，彼らの13％以上は石綿症にかかっていると診断された) (RD 99/12: 105)

c. Next morning when I open my eyes, they are stabbed by needles of pain. It's *conjunctivitis*, which grows increasingly more painful. (翌朝目を開けると，針で刺されるような激痛が走る。結膜炎だ。だんだん痛みが増してくる) (RD 99/1: 36)

d. And Dr. David Edelberg recommends that patients with *gingivitis* open a capsule and brush the vitamin on their gums. (DE博士が勧めるのは，歯肉炎患者がカプセルを開いてビタミンを歯肉に塗ること

第 5 章　原理 V ——抽象概念と個別事例　*199*

だ）(RD 98/11: 49)

e. The unsterilised bit could expose him to infections of the brain, like *meningitis* or *encephalitis*. (殺菌していない道具のため，髄膜炎や脳炎といった脳の感染症にかかる危険がある) (RD 99/6: 36)

f. People with *hepatitis*, *liver disease*, cancer, *diabetes*, HIV or chronic stomach upset, or who are pregnant or using steroids for *asthma* or *arthritis*, are at increased risk of serious illness or death from contaminated seafood. (肝炎や肝臓病，ガン，糖尿病，HIV，慢性的腹痛がある人，妊娠中の人，あるいは喘息や関節炎のためステロイド剤を使用中の人たちは，汚染された海産食品のため重病にかかったり死亡したりする危険が増している) (RD 00/3: 57) [cancer に関しては (V-90) 参照]

(44) a. Both said that while *arthrogryposis* was rare, there were surgical procedures to improve the condition of the boy's twisted limbs. (B [医師] が言うには，関節拘縮(こうしゅく)症はまれであるが，少年の歪んだ手足の状態を改善する外科的方法はあるとのことだった) (RD 00/6: 125)

b. He died of *cirrhosis* of the liver. (肝硬変のため亡くなった) (CIDE, NHD)

c. From the day he was born, the fatal disease of *cystic fibrosis* savaged his body daily. (生まれたその日から嚢胞(のう)性繊維症という不治の病が彼の体を日々さいなんだ) (RD 99/8: 121)

d. "In the old days people would have said I was suffering from *neurosis*," says Fujimori. (「昔ならノイローゼだと言っただろう」と F は言う) (RD 01/5: 56)

e. "Not many Asians realize that prevention, early diagnosis and effective treatment are all possible with *osteoporosis*," says Dr. Leong Keng Hong, a rheumatologist and president of the Osteoporosis Society (Singapore). (「アジアの人たちの多くは骨粗しょう症は，予防，初期診断，効果的治療のいずれも可能だということに気づいていない」と LKH 博士——リューマチ専門医で S 骨粗しょう症学会会長——は言う) (RD 98/6: 98)

f. I have multiple *sclerosis*, a degenerative neurological disease. (多発性硬化症がある，退行性の神経病だ) (RD 99/1: 119)

(45) a. He also started Angela on drugs to block premature labor and

avert a cascade of life-threatening events, including seizures and *kidney* and *heart failure.* (A に薬物療法も開始したが，それは早産を阻止し，発作や腎不全，心不全など生命を脅かす諸々の事態を回避するためだった) (RD 99/5: 20) [注：『ランダムハウス』には (a) heart failure という例があるが，手元の資料では heart/kidney/renal failure は無冠詞；『活用』には "a/an＋形容詞＋heart/kidney failure" の例がある]

b. Six months later, when he had painful swelling in his legs, his doctor in Taipei diagnosed chronic *renal failure.* (6 か月後脚がむくんで痛みがあったとき，台北市の主治医は慢性的腎不全だと診断した) (RD 00/7: 86)

(46) a. In addition to *frostbite, altitude sickness* is one of the most common complaints at "Club Med," the research station's sick bay. (凍傷に加えて，高山病はCM，つまり，研究所の診療室，で最もよくある病気の 1 つだ) (RD 98/3: 26)

b. More than 930 local people are registered as suffering from *radiation sickness.* (930 人以上の地元民が放射線病の罹患者として登録されている) (CCED[3])

c. Many deaths from *heart disease* are actually avoidable. (心臓病死の多くは実際には避けることが可能だ) (OALD[6])

d. Donald Hopkins saw his first case of *guinea-worm disease* in Aurangabad, India, 14 years ago. (DH は 14 年前にインドの A でギニア虫病の最初の症例を見た) (RD 87/5: 115) [(V-59) も参照]

e. [Animals] can suffer *mental illness* when kept in inappropriate conditions or mistreated ... (動物は不適切な状況に置かれたり虐待されたりすれば，精神病にかかることがある) (RD 02/2: 21)

(47) a. Johnny has *Down syndrome.* (J はダウン症だ) (RD 98/12: 122)

b. *Aids [Acquired Immune Deficiency Syndrome]* is spread mainly by sexual contact. (エイズは主として性的接触によって広がる) (OALD[5])

c. Their son David was born with *Goltz syndrome*, a rare congenital condition. (息子の D は生まれつきゴルツ症──まれな先天的異常──だった) (RD 96/3: 76)

d. One after another, the Hoyt babies perished, so many and so mysteriously that the case became a crucial part of a landmark medical article on *Sudden Infant Death Syndrome* (SIDS). (次々とH家の乳幼児は死亡した。あまりにも多数であまりにも不可解だったので，その症例は幼児突然死症候群に関する重大な医学論文の中心部分になった) (RD 99/2: 117)

比較： I thought this was our own quirk, but it seems to be *a* common *syndrome* in families. (我々だけの癖だと思っていたが，多くの家庭で共通の特徴のようだ) (RD 98/3: 63) [「特徴」という意味では可算名詞]

(48) "I've had an awful time," a boy told his friends. "First, I got *angina pectoris*, then *arteriosclerosis*. Just as I was recovering, I got *psoriasis*. They gave me hypodermics and, to top it all, *tonsillitis* was followed by *appendectomy*. (ある少年が友人に言った。「ひどい目にあったよ。最初，狭心症，それから，動脈硬化症をやったんだ。もとに戻りかけたとき，乾癬(かんせん)になった。皮下注射をやって，挙げ句の果ては，扁桃腺炎，つづいて虫垂切除だったよ」) (RD 99/11: 114) [病気にかかったように思わせて，実は，これらの単語を勉強したというジョークの一部]

(49) If not treated within hours of the onset of symptoms, *anthrax* is almost always fatal. (徴候が現れて数時間以内に治療されなければ，炭疽病はほとんどの場合，致命的だ) (RD 99/2: 50)

(50) When Emma developed *asthma* and high fever in her fifth month, Zhi Hui was frantic. (Eが5か月目に喘息と高熱を発病したとき，ZHは気も狂わんばかりだった) (RD 98/12: 60) [fever に関しては (V-100) 参照]

(51) *Athlete's Foot* is seen usually between the toes as patches of white flaking skin which can cause itching and burning. (水虫は，通常，足の指のあいだの皮膚が白くなってはがれる部分に見られ，かゆみや痛みを引き起こす) (ConCD-ROM)

(52) The latrines she had installed helped curb *dysentery* and *cholera*. (彼女が設置したトイレは赤痢とコレラを抑えるのに役立った) (RD 99/10: 35)

(53) Typical is a 75-year-old Hong Kong woman with a history of *diabetes* and *hypertension*. (典型的なのは，糖尿病と高血圧の病歴がある，75歳の香港の婦人だ) (RD 99/11: 104)

(54) I felt as if my heart stopped. *Marburg* was lethal, but *Ebola* was

even deadlier. (心臓が止まるかのように感じた。マールブルグ病は致命的だが，エボラ出血熱はさらに命取りだったからだ) (RD 97/6: 123) [もと固有名詞（地名）]

(55) My hands puffed up with *frost nip*, one stage short of *frostbite*. (両手は凍傷一歩手前の凍瘡（とうそう）のため腫れ上がった) (RD 98/11: 96)

(56) You have *gangrene* – a consequence of non-insulin-dependent *diabetes*. (壊疽（えそ）にかかっている。非インスリン依存型の糖尿病のためだ) (RD 99/1: 74)

(57) Marcella, with decades of nursing experience, was familiar with *glioblastoma* – a grade IV tumour. (M は数十年の看護経験があるので，膠芽（こうが）細胞腫――第4段階の腫瘍――をよく知っていた) (RD 99/12: 128)

(58) My neighbor walks with a cane because she's got *gout*. (隣人は，痛風なので，杖をついて歩く) (NTC)

(59) Thanks largely to Hopkins's efforts, experts say, in the next few years *guinea worm* will be a plague of the past everywhere except Sudan, home of three-quarters of the remaining guinea-worm victims. (専門家によれば，主に H の努力のおかげで，数年のうちにギニア虫病はどこでも過去の疫病になるだろう。ただし，ギニア虫病の残存する犠牲者の4分の3の故郷である S は別だ) (RD 97/5: 116) [(V-46, d) も参考]

(60) *Heartburn* is felt in the chest and sometimes the throat. (胸やけは胸で，たまに喉でも，感じられる) (RD 01/7: 80)

(61) With new medical techniques, *incontinence* can usually be cured or, at least, properly managed. (新しい医療技術をもってすれば，失禁はたいてい治癒可能であり，少なくとも適切に管理することは可能だ) (RD 99/11: 99)

(62) To decrease *flatulence* and ease *indigestion*, drink fennel tea. (腹の張りを減じ，消化不良を楽にするためにはウイキョウ茶を飲みなさい) (RD 00/5: 19)

(63) Martini quickly concluded this wasn't *influenza*, but something he'd never seen before. (M はこれはインフルエンザではなくて，今までに見たことのない何かだとすぐに結論した) (RD 97/6: 124)

(64) But before she was a month old, Emma developed *jaundice* and a rash. (生後1か月足らずで E は黄疸と湿疹にかかった) (RD 98/12: 58)

(65) *Leprosy* is usually found in tropical countries. (ライは，通例，熱帯の

国で見られる) (NHD)

(66) His sister, Mary Jean, contracted *lupus*. (妹の MJ は狼瘡(ろうそう)にかかった) (RD [U.S. Edition] 98/9: 66)

(67) Infant *malnutrition* is worse than in famine-stricken North Korea, and infant mortality is the highest in Asia. ([カンボジアでは] 幼児の栄養失調は飢饉に襲われている北朝鮮よりも悪く、幼児の死亡率はアジアで1番高い) (RD 99/11: 22)

(68) The chair was a necessity for Michael, then four, who has *cerebral palsy*. ([車] 椅子は当時4歳だった M には必需品だった。脳性麻痺があったから) (RD 99/5: 112)

(69) An airline passenger could bring *polio* to any nation within 24 hours. (航空機の乗客はどの国にでも24時間以内にポリオを持ち込みうる) (RD 99/2: 15)

(70) Central or abdominal fat has been linked to *heart disease, diabetes, high blood pressure*, strokes and increased risks of some cancers. (中央部や腹部の脂肪は心臓病や糖尿病、高血圧症、脳卒中と結びついており、いくつかのガンにかかる危険も高い) (RD 97/5: 9)

(71) *Rabies* is extremely rare. (狂犬病はきわめてまれだ) (RD 99/11: 59)

(72) She began losing her hair and developed *thrush* in her mouth. (髪が抜けはじめ、口に鵞口瘡(がこうそう)ができた) (RD 98/12: 60)

(73) *Tuberculosis* and *leprosy* were rife, and life expectancy was 53 years. (結核とライが蔓延(まんえん)し、平均余命は53歳だった) (RD 00/6: 47)

(74) *Yellow fever* and *malaria* were among them. (それら [伝染病] のうちには黄熱病とマラリアもあった) (RD 99/11: 59)

(75) After the war, DDT was used throughout the world to combat *yellow fever, typhus* and *elephantiasis*. (戦後 DDT は黄熱病、チフス、象皮病と闘うために世界じゅうで用いられた) (RD 01/7: 99)

以下の病名は歴史的には複数形であるが、現代英語では単数不可算名詞として用いられるほうがふつうである。

(76) The mental patient was overcome with *hysterics*. (精神病患者はヒステリーの発作にとらえられた) (NHD) [(V-40, d) [hysteria] も参照]

(77) If you've already had *measles*, you can't get it again. (すでにはしかにかかっているのなら、2度とかかることはない) (Swan 1995: 138) [単数一致; 8.2.6 も参照]

(78) In 1972, after disappearing from Yugoslavia for four decades,

smallpox broke out. (Yから消滅して40年後の1972年に天然痘が発生した) (RD 99/2: 54)

NB 6   hysterics/measles/smallpox
hysterics/measles/smalllpox [small-pocks] は，現代英語では単数扱いされるが ((V-77) 参照)，歴史的には複数形であり，古い英語では複数扱いされていた。

   i) I found Harriet in *a* strong *hysteric*. (Hが強度のヒステリー状態だと気づいた) (1776, S. J. Pratt *Pupil of Pleasure* II. 76) [OED]

   ii) At that season ther <u>wer</u> the *Meazelles* soo strong, & in especiall amongis Ladies & Gentilwemen, that sum died of that sikeness. (その季節に強烈なはしかが，特に，貴婦人や上流夫人のあいだで，はやったので，幾人かはその病気で亡くなった) (1489, *Plumpton Corr.* (Camden) p. cxiv) [OED]

   iii) The *small-pocks* <u>are</u> often confluent upon the face and head, whilst they are distinct every where else. (天然痘は顔と頭ではしばしば融合的であるが，他の部位では個別的である) (1788, *Med. Comm.* II. 183) [OED]

5.3.2 病名 [C]

(79) a. He had *a cataract* removed. (白内障部分を取り除いた) (CCED[1]) [一方の目の白内障部分]

   b. In one study, light smokers are more than twice as likely to get *cataracts* as non-smokers. (ある研究によると，タバコを少し吸うだけの人でもまったく吸わない人より2倍以上白内障になりやすい) (CCED[3])

   NB 7   φ cataract/a cataract
   ウェブサイト上では，i) のように，cataract の無冠詞の用法も見られるが，これは見出し扱いであるためである (☞ 9.6.1)。文章体では，ii) のように，冠詞がつけられる。

   i) What is *cataract*? [http://www.prevent-blindness.org/eye_problems/cataractFAQ.html]

   ii) What is *a cataract*? [http://www.nei.nih.gov/health/cataract/cataract_facts.htm]

(80) Daniel's growth was *a cavernoma*, a nest of abnormal blood vessels that eventually wear down and haemorrhage. (D の腫瘍はカヴェルノーマだった。異常な血管の巣であり，最終的にはすり減って出血することになる) (RD 99/9: 20)

(81) You can avoid *a hangover* if you don't drink to excess. (飲み過ぎなければ二日酔いにならなくて済む) (NTC)

(82) He had *a hernia* operated on and is now well. (ヘルニアの手術をうけて今は回復している) (NHD)

(83) When the toddler started to vomit repeatedly and developed flu symptoms, doctors first blamed *an intestinal obstruction*. (幼児が繰り返し嘔吐し，インフルエンザの症状が現れたとき，医者たちは最初腸閉塞によるとした) (RD 99/10: 89) [obstruction 単独では，通例，[U]]

(84) I nearly gave myself *a rupture* lifting that bookcase. (あの本箱をもち上げてヘルニアになるところだった) (OALD5)

5.3.3 病名 [U, C]

本節では，無冠詞の場合と不定冠詞つきの場合とで病気を表す名詞にどのような相違があるかを考えたい。

まず，地域差による例をあげておきたい（本章 NB 7 も参照）。たとえば，cramp は冠詞がついていてもついていなくても意味に違いはないように見える。

(85) a. After swimming for half an hour I started to get *cramp* in my legs. (30 分泳いだら脚が痙攣(けいれん)しかけた) (OALD5)

b. After running, he got *a cramp* in his leg. (走ったら脚が痙攣した) (NHD)

この場合，不定冠詞の随意性は地域差によるものである。CIDE は次のように明記している。

(86) I've got (Br and Aus) *cramp*/(esp. Am) *a cramp* in my foot. (脚が痙攣 [〈英・豪〉cramp / 特に〈米〉a cramp] した)

類義語の spasm も go into につづくときは地域差が見られる。

(87) a. (esp. UK and ANZ) If your leg goes into *spasm*, take one of these pills immediately. ((特に〈英・豪 NZ〉)もしも脚が痙攣したら，ただちにこれらのピルの 1 つを摂りなさい) (CIDE)

b. Would my muscles go into *a spasm* as they often did? (よくそうなったように，筋肉が痙攣するだろうか) (RD 98/9: 91)

参考：*A* muscular *spasm* in the coronary artery can cause a heart attack.

(冠状動脈の筋肉が痙攣すれば，心臓発作を引き起こしかねない)
(CCED[3]) [go into (a) spasm 以外では，通例，冠詞つき]
　critical condition の用法にも英米で相違がある．
(88) a. A firefighter tells me Cristine is in *critical condition* and not expected to live. (ある消防士が教えてくれたところでは，C は危篤状態であり，助かるとは思われない) (RD 98/5: 145) [主に〈米〉]
　　b. He remains in *a critical condition* in a California hospital. (C の病院で危険な状態のままだ) (CCED[3]) [主に〈英〉]
　類例：in a parlous/sad/treatable *condition* (いずれも OALD[5]) [主に〈英〉]
　以下，英米共通で冠詞つきでも無冠詞でも用いられる病名を見ていこう．
(89) a. The discomforting symptoms of *allergy* are sometimes relieved by four types of medication: . . . (アレルギーの不快な諸症状は [次の] 4 タイプの薬により緩和されることがある) (GME)
　　b. The body's immune system reacts to an allergen in many different ways to cause the discomforting symptoms of *an allergy*. (体内の免疫組織はアレルゲンに対してさまざまな異なった仕方で反応し，アレルギー反応の不快な諸症状の原因となる) (GME)
　　c. Do you suffer from any *allergies*? (アレルギーの諸症状に苦しんでいますか) (LDOCE[3])

(89, a) が無冠詞であるのは allergy を個々の症例の根本原因として抽象的にとらえているからであり，(89, b) で不定冠詞がつけられているのは，特定のアレルゲンにより引き起こされる特定のアレルギー反応を指すからである．(89, c) の複数形は，くしゃみが出る，涙が出る，鼻水が出る，目がかゆい，といったアレルギーの諸症状を含意している．(一部の辞書 (例：CIDE, CDAE) は allergy の可算性に関して [C] しか表記していないが，実際には，上例のように [U] 用法もある．)

(90) a. No one with *breast cancer* dies from *cancer* in the breast. (乳ガン患者のだれも胸部のガンで死にはしない) (RD 98/7: 66)
　　b. Fortunately for me, I was sitting down in May 1997 when the surgeon called to tell me my biopsy showed *a cancer* of the lymphatic system. (私にとって幸運なことに，1997 年の 5 月腰掛けていたとき，外科の先生が電話してこられて，生検でリンパ組織にガン組織があることがわかったとおっしゃった) (RD 98/6: 8)
　　c. I return to my microscope. In the spread of *a cancer*, I strain to see the leaves of Maine, so fiery when first fallen, then turning

　　　　slowly to compost, to nurture blanketed seeds. (私は顕微鏡に戻る。ガン組織の広がりのなかに，目を凝らして M 州の落葉を見る。最初に落ちたときは紅葉しており，それからゆっくりと堆肥になり，一面[落葉で]おおわれた種子を育てていく) (RD 98/5: 101)
　　d. [W]e think you have something called CML – chronic myelogenous leukemia – *an* adult *cancer* of the blood. (CML, つまり，慢性的骨髄性白血病，大人がかかる血液のガン，というものにかかっていると思う) (RD 98/1: 125)
　　e. Asbestos can cause lung cancer, mesothelioma (*an* always fatal *cancer* of the external lining of the lung or the abdomen) and asbestosis (a scarring of lung tissue that leads to difficulty in breathing). (アスベストは肺ガンや中皮腫 (肺または腹部の外部の膜に生じる常に致命的なガン)，および石綿肺症 (呼吸困難につながる肺組織の傷) の原因となりうる) (RD 99/12: 104)
　類例： *a* dangerous *cancer* (RD 97/5: 131); *a* slow-growing *cancer* that can't be cured (RD 98/6: 8); *a* rare *cancer* of the lung (RD 99/12: 100) [これらの例は「一時性」というより「種類」(☞ 4.3) を表す]
　　f. *Cancers* picked up at their earliest stage are curable in most cases ... (ガンは最も初期の段階で見つかれば，ほとんどの場合治療可能だ) (RD 98/7: 66)
　　g. Ninety per cent of *lung cancers* are caused by smoking. (肺ガンの九割は喫煙が原因だ) (CCED[3])

cancer は，「ガン」という病気を指す場合は，身体部位が先行するときも，進行の程度を表すときも，冠詞をとらない (例：bone cancer (骨ガン); breast cancer (乳ガン); colon cancer (結腸ガン); lung cancer (肺ガン); ovarian cancer (卵巣ガン); pancreatic cancer (膵臓ガン); prostate cancer (前立腺ガン); stomach, breast, prostate and lung cancer (胃ガン，乳ガン，前立腺ガン，および肺ガン) (以上，RD 99/11: 35); stage three cancer (第 3 段階のガン) (RD 00/1: 108))。他方，(90, b-c) の a cancer は「ガンに冒された細胞，ガン組織」を指す。ガンの種類・様態に言及するときは，(90, d-e) のように，a/an をとる (☞ 4.3)。(90, f-g) はさまざまな種類・症例のガンをまとめた表現である (8 章 NB 5 も参照)。(ガンの病巣は正式には malignant tumor [C]と言う。)

(91) a. She caught *cold* yesterday. (きのう風邪を引いた) (NHD)
　　b. A few months ago I came down with *a* whopping *cold*. (数か月前ひどい風邪でダウンした) (RD 99/3: 113)

(91, a) のような無冠詞の cold は諸症状から抽象化された「風邪」という病気を指している。他方，(91, b) のように，形容詞によって修飾されれば，cold は必ず不定冠詞をとる。これは，種類あるいは様態が限定されるため (☞ 4 章)，どのような風邪であるかイメージ化可能になるからである。catch a cold と言うときも，話し手は特定の症状あるいは期間を示唆している。

(92) a. Nicky was rushed to hospital with *concussion*. (N はしんとう症で病院に急送された) (CCED[3])

b. The patient is suffering from severe *concussion* following his fall. (患者は墜落ののち，重度しんとう症を起こした) (OALD[5])

c. Don Collings suffered *a concussion*, severe head lacerations, whiplash, bruising and muscle damage. (DC は脳しんとう，重度の頭部裂傷，むち打ち症，打撲傷および筋肉損傷になった) (RD 00/7: 105)

d. He got *a concussion* while playing football. (フットボールをしていて脳しんとうを起こした) (NHD)

concussion は状態を表すときは無冠詞で用いられるが，一時性が含意されるとき，つまり，意識が戻ることが暗示されるときは，冠詞がつけられる。これは，coma (昏睡); haze (意識混濁); high (恍惚感) が一時性を含意するので a/an をとるのと同様である。(不幸にして，意識不明のまま死亡することもあるが (93, b)，それは言語外の問題である。)

(93) a He was in *a coma* for days, but now he's (fully) conscious again. (数日間昏睡状態だったが，今は (全面的に) 意識が戻っている) (OALD[5])

b. Granny slipped into *a coma* and died peacefully that night. (おばあさんは昏睡状態になり，その晩安らかに亡くなった) (LDOCE[3])

c. After surgery, I was in *a haze* until the anesthetic wore off. (手術後，麻酔がきれるまで私はもうろうとしていた) (NTC)

d. Kids inhale these volatile substances in order to experience *a high*. (子供たちはハイな気分を経験するためにこれらの揮発性の物質を吸入する) (RD 99/7: 43)

(94) a. *Deformation* of her bones was caused by a very poor diet. (彼女の骨の変形は極度の粗食が原因だ) (CIDE)

b. Her own 12-year-old son, David, had already undergone three surgeries for *a heart deformation*. (彼女の 12 歳の息子の D は心臓の奇形のためすでに 3 度の手術をうけていた) (RD 99/1: 18)

(95) a. *Deformity* of fingernails and toenails was common among people

who drank the polluted water. (手足の指の爪の変形は汚染された水を飲んだ人たちのあいだではよく見られる) (CIDE)
   b. She was born with *a deformity* of the spine. (生まれつき脊椎が変形している) (CDAE)

(94-95, a) の φ deformation/deformity は病名，つまり，抽象概念，を指すので，無冠詞であり，(94-95, b) の a deformation/a deformity は冠詞つきで特定の患者に特有の症例，つまり，個別事例を表す。(b-文の主語は患者であることに注意。)

(96, a) では dependency に alcohol/drug が先行しているので dependency は特定の依存症に限定されているように思われるかもしれない。

(96) a. In 1985, he began to show signs of alcohol and drug *dependency*. (1985 年にアルコールおよび薬物依存症の徴候を示しはじめた) (CCED³)
   b. He has *a dependency* on drugs. (薬物への依存症がある) (NHD)

しかし，drug dependency はここでは，signs of に後続して素材扱いであることに加えて，1種の複合語として依存症の下位分類を成しているので (類例：yellow/scarlet fever)，限定をうけてはいない。他方，(96, b) が冠詞をとるのは have と共起して特定の患者の症状を表しているからである ((V-114) [(a) runny nose] 参照)。

(97) a. The doctor is treating him for *depression*. (医者は彼の抑うつ症を治療中だ) (NHD)
   b. She suffered a lot from *depression* after the death of her husband. (夫の死後抑うつ症でとても苦しんだ) (McED)
   c. She's in *a depression* over the death of her husband. (夫の死で悲嘆に暮れている) (NHD) [名詞が一時性を表すときは in のあとでも不定冠詞が必要 (☞ 3 章 NB 8)]
   d. One year, her plans fell through at the last minute, but instead of falling into *a* serious *depression* or taking drugs, she went to three movies in a row. (ある年，彼女の計画は最後の最後で失敗に終わったが，ひどくふさぎこんだり薬物に手を出したりはせず，映画を立てつづけに3本見に行った) (CCED³)

(97, a-b) の depression は「精神の病い」('mental illness') であり，(97, c) の a depression は時間的に限定された「一時的な悲しみの感情」('a feeling of temporary sadness' (NHD)) である。(98, d) の a serious depression は形容詞により抑うつ症の様態 (あるいは，種類) が限定されるため不定冠詞が要求され

る例である (☞ 4.4.3; 4.3).「病名は無冠詞, 一時的症状および様態限定は不定冠詞つき」という区別は, 体調不良全般に当てはまる一般的原則であり, 以下の (98)–(113) にも当てはまる.

(98) a. Many men who suffer from erectile *dysfunction*, or ED, can now restore their virility by taking a prescription drug. (勃起障害 (ED) に悩んでいる多くの男性は今では処方薬を摂ることによって性能力を取り戻すことが可能だ) (RD 98/10: 76) [(V-114) の説明も参照]

b. "One of the great ironies of antidepressants is that they can cause sexual *dysfunction*," says Dr Andrew Leuchter, director of the Division of Adult Psychiatry at the University of California, Los Angeles. (「抗うつ薬の大きなアイロニーの1つは性的機能障害を引き起こすことがあるということだ」と UCLA 成人精神医学科主任の AL 博士は言う) (RD 99/12: 71)

c. There appears to be *a dysfunction* in the patient's respiratory system. (患者は呼吸器系に機能障害があるようだ) (CIDE)

d. The doctor is treating her for *a dysfunction* of the kidneys. (医者は彼女の腎不全を治療中だ) (NHD) [*of*-phrase による限定 (☞ 4.4.1)]

(99) a. Blowing your nose too hard can cause *earache*. (鼻を強くかみすぎると耳が痛くなる) (CCED³)

b. He complained of *an earache*. (耳の痛みを訴えた) (CCED³)

c. When I was a child I used to get terrible *earache(s)*. (子供のころひどく耳が痛くなることがよくあった) (CIDE)

NB 8　toothache/headache/backache

上の (99, a–b) の無冠詞と冠詞つきの例は同一辞書中にあげられていて,「抽象概念」対「個別事例」という相違を示しているが, これは動詞の意味的相違に対応するところが大きい ((V-114) 参照). 一般に, -ache で終わる語は英米で用法に差が見られる. 以下は Swan (1995: 138) からの引用である.

The words for some minor ailments are countable: e.g. *a cold, a sore throat, a headache*. However, *toothache, earache, stomach-ache* and *backache* are more often uncountable in British English. In American English, these words are generally countable if they refer to particular attacks of pain. Compare:

Love isn't as bad as *toothache*. (GB)

Love isn't as bad as *a toothache*. (US)
(いくつかの軽度の病気を表す語は可算名詞である。たとえば, a cold (風邪), a sore throat (喉の痛み), a headache (頭痛)。しかし, toothache (歯痛), earache (耳痛), stomachache (胃痛) および backache (腰痛) は〈英〉では不可算であることのほうが多い。〈米〉では, これらの語が特定の痛みを指すときは, 通例, 可算名詞である。比較せよ:

Love isn't as bad as toothache. 〈英〉
Love isn't as bad as a toothache. 〈米〉
(恋は歯の痛みほど苦しくはない))

別例:
  i) I have a fever and *a* terrible *headache*. (熱があってひどく頭痛がする) (NHD) [形容詞による限定 (☞ 4.4.3)]
  ii) Researchers got the idea to try Botox for head pain when some patients treated for wrinkles reported fewer *headaches*. (研究者たちは頭痛にBを試すことを思いついた。シワ治療をうけた患者の何人かが頭痛の回数が減ったと報告したからだ) (RD 99/11: 64D)
  iii) I had *a stomachache* for four days. (4日間胃が痛かった) (RD 00/3: 134)

(100) a. They described patients suffering from *fever*, myalgia and malaise. (高熱, 筋肉痛, 倦怠感に苦しむ患者の様子を述べた) (RD 97/6: 137)
  b. *A fever* can mean infection. ([一時的な]発熱は感染を表すことがある) (RD 96/3: 99)

(101) a. I notice that Jandu's neck is swollen with *goiter* – the sign of a lack of iodine in her diet. (Jの喉は甲状腺腫——食事にヨウ素が欠乏している徴候——のため腫(は)れているのに気づく) (RD 98/12: 106)
  b. His face was pushed to one side by *an* enormous *goitre*. (彼の顔は巨大な甲状腺腫のため一方にゆがんでいた) (ConCD-ROM) [具体物]

(102) a. He calls infant hearing *impairment* an invisible problem. (幼児の聴覚障害を見えざる問題と呼ぶ) (RD 01/7: 76)
  b. If someone has *an impairment*, they have a condition which prevents their eyes, ears, or brain from working properly. (障害があれば, 目, 耳, 脳がちゃんと働かないという状態だ) (CCED[3])

c. His doctor referred the boy to a specialist, who found that Jing Xian had *a* severe hearing *impairment*. (医者は少年を専門家に紹介し，JX は重度の聴覚障害があることがわかった) (RD 01/7: 76) [種類]

(103) a. (= V-100, b) A fever can mean *infection*. (RD 96/3: 99)

b. When you get *an infection*, you produce proteins called cytokines that help white blood cells devour bacteria and other invaders. (感染症にかかれば，サイトカインと呼ばれるタンパク質が出て，白血球が細菌や他の侵入物を滅ぼすのを助ける) (RD 96/3: 102)

(104) a. But I love it, and just as fulfilling for me is lecturing across the country on head *injury*. (でも，私は気に入っているし，頭部傷害について講演して国じゅうを回るのも充実している) (RD 98/6: 147)

b. He had to limp off with *a* leg *injury*. (脚の怪我のため足を引きずって歩かなければならなかった) (CCED[3])

c. It was clear from his pupils that he had *a* massive brain *injury*. (広範囲に脳に障害をうけていることは瞳孔から明らかだった) (RD 99/6: 74) [様態限定]

(105) a. The rubbing of the strap against the skin had caused *irritation*. (ひもを皮膚にこすりつけたため炎症状態になった) (CIDE)

b. This is *an irritation* and inflammation of the edge of the eyelid which usually affects both eyes. (これはまぶたの端の痛みと炎症であり，たいてい両目に影響する) (ConCD-RO, CCED[3])

(106) a. Do you suffer from *migraine*? (偏頭痛がありますか) (CIDE) [抽象概念]

b. I'm getting *a migraine*. (偏頭痛になりかけている) (OALD[5]) [発話の時点]

(107) a. *Numbness* in the fingers is one of the first signs of frostbite. (指の麻痺は凍傷の最初の兆候の 1 つだ) (CIDE)

b. I came in one morning and heard Rolly mumbling that he had *a numbness* in his left arm and a pain in his chest. (ある朝入室したところ，左手が痺れ，胸が痛いと R がつぶやいているのが聞こえた) (RD 01/5: 132)

(108) a. The baby's got nappy *rash* again. (赤ちゃんはまたおむつかぶれになった) (LDOCE[3])

b. His neck was covered in *(a)* heat *rash*. (首はあせもだらけだった) (CIDE) [無冠詞は状態の記述；冠詞つきは一時的状態であることを含

意]

　　c. I've got *a* strange *rash* all over my chest. (胸全体に妙な発疹ができた) (CIDE) [様態限定]

(109) In fact, Corea was having *a stroke*. *Stroke*, or "brain attack," is Asia's third-leading cause of death (behind cancer and heart disease) and one of the leading causes of adult disability. (事実，Ｃは卒中にかかりかけていた。卒中，つまり「脳卒中」，はアジアで３番目の死因であり（ガンと心臓病につづく），大人の障害の主因の１つである) (RD 02/7: 56)

(110) (medical) *(A) trauma* is also a severe injury, esp. caused by violence or in an accident. ([医学用語] 外傷は，特に，暴力または事故で生じた，重度の損傷のことも指す) (CIDE) [病名または専門用語（無冠詞）vs. 一時的症状（冠詞つき）]

すでに触れたように（☞ V-91; V-97），いくつかの病名は修飾語句なしでは無冠詞で用いられるが，修飾語句により様態（あるいは種類・期間）が限定されれば不定冠詞をとる。たとえば，flu/malaise/paralysis はたいていの辞書では [U] 表記のみであるが，様態が限定される文脈では不定冠詞が要求される。

(111) a. A really shaming incident occurred when our daughter Sal, aged about six, was in bed, slowly recovering from *flu*. (娘のＳが６歳くらいのころ，床についてインフルエンザから徐々に回復中だったとき，まったく赤面するようなことが起こった) (RD 99/12: 62) [病名]

　　b. I was at home with *a* nasty *flu* when the phone rang. (ひどいインフルエンザで家にいたとき電話が鳴った) (RD 98/1: 117) [様態限定；flu/influenza はしばしば the をとる（☞ 8.3.3）]

(112) a. (= V-100, a) They described patients suffering from fever, *myalgia* and malaise. (RD 97/6: 137)

　　b. After his divorce, *an* intense *malaise* confined Bill to his bed. (離婚後，激しい倦怠感のためＢは寝たきりになった) (NTC)

(113) a. At that moment my next appointment was Mrs Patel, an elderly lady with spinal *paralysis* who was in a wheelchair. (そのとき次の予約はＰさんだった。初老の婦人で脊髄麻痺があり，車椅子に乗っていた) (RD 99/6: 72)

　　b. Frederic Cupillard . . . was involved in a road accident at the age of 14 which left him with *a* partial *paralysis* of the face and cost him his right eye. (ＦＣは14歳のとき自動車事故に遭い，そのため顔に部

分的麻痺が残り，右目を失明していた) (ConCD-ROM)

病名と冠詞との関係に関して付言すべきは，動詞も冠詞の選択に関与するという事実である (4.4.3.3 も参照)。病名が "人＋have/get" につづく場合は，ほぼ例外なく，個別の症例を表すので，冠詞をとる。ところが，cause/suffer from につづく場合，全般的体調不良を表すので，病名はしばしば無冠詞で用いられる。次の (114, a) は典型的な例である ((V-98, 100, 106, Ap.3-30) [dysfunction/fever/migraine/mutation], Ap.4, NB2 も参照)。

(114) a. But the immune system would also produce substances such as kinins, which cause *runny nose*, cough and *scratchy throat*. (だが，免疫組織はキニンのような物質もつくりだすので，そのため，鼻水や咳が出て喉がいがいがする) (RD 01/11: 73) [キニンが引き起こす体調不良を総体的に提示；諸症状が同時発生的であることを含意]

b. cold: a common illness that causes sneezing, *a runny nose*, *a sore throat*, etc. (風邪 ＝ よくある病気，くしゃみ，鼻水，喉の痛みなどをともなう) (NTC) [風邪の個別的症状；現れる症状は1つだけの場合もあるということを含意]

c. One of the toddlers was bawling, and the other had *a runny nose*. (幼児の1人は泣きわめき，もう1人は鼻水をたらしていた) (CCED³)

d. She had *a sore throat*. (喉が痛かった) (CCED³)

e. I had to be careful not to get *a sore throat* and lose my voice. (喉を痛めて声が出なくなることがないように注意しなければならなかった) (CCED³)

NB 9　ニキビとしもやけ

1) acne (痤瘡(ざそう)) は皮膚病 (a skin disease) の1種なので，無冠詞で用いられる。「吹き出物」は pimple または spot＜英＞という。日本語では「ニキビ」は主として顔に出た「吹き出物」を指し，両語は下位語と上位語の関係にあるが，英語では acne と pimple/spot とは病名と具体物という相違があり，可算性が異なる。

i) He was about five-foot-nine and had a babyish face riddled with *acne*. (約5フィート9インチになり，童顔はニキビだらけだった) (RD 97/5: 56)

ii) *a pimple* on one's chin (顎に出た吹き出物 [ニキビ]) (OALD⁵)

iii) This cream clears up teenage *spots* in days. (このクリームはティーンエージャーのニキビを数日で治す) (LDOCE³)

2)「凍瘡／凍傷」(frost nip/frostbite) も英語では病名扱いであり，無冠詞で用いられる。

  iv) (= V-55) My hands puffed up with *frost nip*, one stage short of *frostbite*. (RD 98/11: 96)

5.4　その他の個別事例
5.4.1　具体物指示および同定構文
5.4.1.1　具体物指示

 名詞が多義語であり，そのうち1つの意味は，具体的事物を指すため，不定冠詞をとるという場合がある。これらの語は，辞書では，通例，同一語義の下位区分 (1のa, b) あるいは別語義 (1と2) としてあげられている (例: abrasion [摩耗／擦り傷], forgery [詐欺／偽作])。以下の b-文は斜字体の名詞が具体物を指す例である。

(115) a. Amniocentesis involves extracting a small amount of amniotic fluid and analysing foetal cells within for evidence of *abnormality*. (羊水穿刺は，少量の羊水の採取と，異常を見るための胎児の細胞の分析を含む) (CIDE)

  b. "The doctor called this afternoon," he said. "There's *an abnormality* on the scan. They want to do another tomorrow." (彼は言った，「先生から今日の午後電話があった。スキャンに異常箇所があるので，明日また [スキャン] したいとのことだ」) (RD 99/12: 124)

(116) a. Competition is easier to accept if you realize it is not an act of aggression or *abrasion*. (競争は攻撃とか消耗といった行為ではないと悟れば受け入れやすい) (RD 99/3: 105)

  b. She had *a* small *abrasion* on her knee. (ひざに小さな擦り傷をつくった) (CIDE)

(117) a. An hour passed before he admitted he had gone full *circle*. (ぐるっと1周したことに気づくのに1時間かかった) (RD 99/11: 26)

  b. The flag was red, with *a* large white *circle* in the center. (その旗は赤地で，真んなかに大きな白い丸があった) (CCED[3])

(118) a. I almost died of *embarrassment*. (死ぬほどきまりが悪かった) (OALD[5])

  b. He's *an embarrassment* to his family. (家族のもて余しものだ) (OALD[5])

(119) a. Their radical approach to *form* and colour inspired her to break the

rules. (形式と色彩への急進的アプローチに鼓舞されて彼女はルールを破るに至った) (RD 99/11: 76) [抽象概念としての形式]

 b. Next he concentrated the radium and dried it into *a* salt *form*. (次にラジウムを濃縮して乾燥させ塩結晶体にした) (RD 99/6: 62) [物理的な形]

このような例は多数あるので，次節の同定構文の例とともに，Appendix 3 であげることにしたい。

5.4.1.2　同定構文

 "NP₁ is NP₂" という同定を表す構文では NP₂ は不定冠詞をとることが多い。この構文中の NP₂ はしばしば特定の事物・行為など具体物を指示するので (☞ 5.4.1.1)，文脈から情報が完結しうるからである。ここで前節の具体物指示とは別に節を設けるのは，構文的に明白であるという理由によるにすぎない。以下にあげる例以外は Appendix 3 を参照されたい。(意味的には同定構文を具体物指示から区別すべき理由はないので，Appendix 3 では両者の区別はしない。)

(120) a. Claire touched Nyima's arm to comfort her, while the porters murmured *encouragement*. (C は慰めるために N の手にさわり，労働者たちはぼそぼそと励ましを言った) (RD 99/8: 96)

 b. The teacher's words were *a* great *encouragement* to him. (先生のことばは彼には大きな励みだった) (OALD⁵)

(121) a. *Fashion* has never interested me. (流行に興味をもったことはない) (NTC)

 b. This is *a* very popular *fashion* at the moment. (これが現在とても人気のある流行の品 [型] だ) (LDOCE³)

(122) a. The police were able to control the crowd by sheer *force* of numbers. (警察は絶対多数によって群衆を制圧した) (CIDE) [sheer force は，様態の記述よりも，by に後続して手段・方法に重点]

 b. *Would* in a similar sub-clause seems to have temporal *force*. (同様な従節中の would は時間的特徴を有するようだ) (Söderlind, *Verb syntax in John Dryden's Prose*, I, p. 105) [temporal はここでは前後同時などの総称なので force の限定不十分]

 c. My English professor was *an* inspiring *force* in my life. (英語の先生は私の人生においてやる気を引き起こす牽引(けんいん)力だった) (NTC) [具体物]

 d. Deregulation is now *an* unstoppable *force*. (規制解除は今やせき止

められない勢いだ）(RD 99/3: 112)

  e. Everyday English ... looks like remaining *an* effective communicative *force*.（日常の英語は依然として有効な伝達の力であるようだ）(*Oxford Guide*, p. 17)

(123) a. *Help* will be here soon.（じきに援助が来る）(RD 99/3: 70)

  b. I gave my friend *help* with his homework.（友人の宿題を手伝った）(NHD) [cf. support]

  c. Having a word processor would be *a help*.（ワープロをもっていれば助かるだろう）(CIDE)

(124) a. *Innovation* requires a different spirit.（改革は異なった精神を要求する）(RD 99/10: 42)

  b. For people who hate washing dishes, the dish-washer was *a* welcome *innovation*.（皿洗いが嫌いな人にとって皿洗い機は歓迎すべき新製品だった）(NTC)

5.4.2　個別行為

　これまで英語の名詞が個別事例を表す環境を詳しく見てきたが，まだ説明しつくすことはできない。名詞部の完結性は名詞ごとに異なるということに加えて，形容詞や動詞，前置詞の意味的影響もうけるからである。以下，これらの影響も考慮しながら，個別事例を行為，状況および精神活動，内容，その他に分類して（これらの分類は明確な基準があるわけではない）数例ずつあげ，他の例は Appendix 4 に回したい。

　ここで言う個別行為は，本章冒頭の LDOCE³ (s.v., oscillation) の定義のように，完結を含意する 1 回の行為を指す。（特定の様態を含意する行為名詞（例：bite/kiss/nap/run, etc.）はほぼ例外なく常に不定冠詞をとるので，ここでは取り上げない。）

　以下の例の大部分は動詞から派生された名詞であることに注意されたい。これらの行為名詞は，無冠詞で用いられるときは，特定不可能（または特定不要）な行為者による行為を表す。たとえば，"Abortion is restricted." / "delivery at 36 to 38 week" において 'abort' / 'deliver' の論理上の主語は 'women in general' である。これに対し，"She decided to have/get an abortion." / "She had a difficult delivery." では，'abort' / 'deliver' の論理上の行為者は 'she' であり，特定の 1 回の中絶／出産を指している。つまり，無冠詞は抽象的・概念的行為を表し，不定冠詞は個別事例を表すのである。（（段階的）形容詞から派生された名詞に関しては，4 章参照。）

(125) a. The priest gave the woman *absolution* (from/of her sins).（牧師はそ

の女に (罪の) 赦しを与えた) (CIDE) [個人的な absolution ではなく，普遍的概念としての absolution]

b. The sound of it, the emotion of it, washed over Colby like *an absolution*. (その音，その感情は放免 [の行為] のようにCを洗った) (RD 99/4: 142) [it (拍手) が与える個別事例としての absolution]

(126) a. I look outside and feel a sense of *accomplishment*. (外を見て達成感を感じる) (CCED³) ["NP₁ of NP₂" の形式で素材扱い (☞ 2.1.2)]

b. Climbing that high mountain was *an accomplishment* for the hikers. (あんな高い山に登るのはハイカーにとっては偉業だった) (NHD)

(127) a. The house was put up for *auction*. (その家は競売に出された) (LDOCE³)

b. They're holding *an auction* of jewellery on Thursday. (木曜日に宝石類の競売会を開いている) (CIDE)

(128) a. No agreement was reached and both sides prepared to do *battle*. (同意に達しなかったので，両者は戦いの準備をした) (CIDE)

b. The original purpose of trooping the colour was to teach soldiers to recognize their unit's flag in the middle of *a battle*. (軍旗敬礼式のもともとの目的は，戦闘中に兵士たちが所属部隊の旗を識別できるように教えることだった) (CIDE) [cf. combat/conflict/fight/jihad/rebellion/revolt/siege/struggle/war]

(129) a. Cremation is more common than *burial* in some countries. (火葬のほうが土葬よりもふつうな国もある) (OALD⁵)

b. When an Indian baby died, the body was sealed in a box and abandoned overboard. Never had the Lakota witnessed *a burial* at sea. (インディアンの赤ん坊が死んだとき，その遺体は箱に入れられ船から投げられた。ラコタ族は海葬 [の現場] を見たことがなかった) (RD 98/12: 92)

(130) a. He set up *camp* in a flat spot and tried to rest, with little success. (平地にキャンプ [形式の生活方法] を設けて休もうとしたが，ほとんどできなかった) (RD 99/4: 136) [形式]

b. Eventually she had to concede that there were no gorillas on my side of the mountain and established *a* new *camp*, called Karisoke. (ついに彼女は私のいる側の山にはゴリラはいないと認めざるをえなくなり，新しく基地を設けてKと名づけた) (RD 00/3: 134) [具体物]

5.4.3 状態・精神活動

(131) a. And I recalled how he had gone from being a frail child and an object of pity to a man who was loved and valued by countless people, and who had taught me so much about courage, about *empathy* and about being a father. (どのようにして彼が，か弱い子供から，そして同情の対象から，無数の人たちに愛され尊重され，私に勇気と共感と父親であることについて多くを教えてくれる人間になっていったかを思い起こした) (RD 98/12: 142) [抽象概念]

b. The colours of individual costumes serve to break, rather than make choreographic connections, and some of the dancing, particularly the graphic arm movements by the men, lacked *an empathy* with mine. (それぞれの衣装の色は振りつけの関連づけを築くというよりも壊すものでしかなく，踊りのいくつか，特に，男性の写実的な腕の動きは私には共感できなかった) (ConCD-ROM) [筆者のもっている共感] [対象を表す *with*-phrase があっても必ずしも不定冠詞はとらない (☞ 4.4.1.2.4)；例：a doctor who had great *empathy* with her patients (LDOCE[3]) (patients が複数であることに注意)]

(132) a. Another crop failure could result in widespread *famine*. (もう1度穀物の不作があれば広範な飢饉になりかねない) (CIDE) [飢饉状態]

b. It seemed strange, the inspector thought, that North Korea was exporting food in the midst of *a famine*. (北朝鮮が飢饉のさなかに食物を輸出するとは妙だ，と視察官は思った) (RD 99/6: 67) [そのときの飢饉]

(133) a. Georgina was put in his lap – no longer crying, but shaking with *fright*. (G は膝の上にだっこされた。もう泣いてはいなかったが，恐怖で震えていた) (RD 99/11: 47) [抽象概念]

b. The snake picked up its head and stuck out its tongue which gave everyone *a fright*. (蛇は頭をもたげて舌を出したので，みんな怖い思いをした) (CCED[3]) [蛇が引き起こした恐怖]

(134) a. And remember to show *gratitude* when your mate does a kind deed for you. (友だちが親切な行為をしてくれたときは忘れずに感謝の気持ちを示しなさい) (RD 99/3: 63) [一般論]

b. In a country that encourages abortion, even forces it, this woman chose to give our daughter life, a fact that compels *a gratitude* beyond this world's ability to pay. (堕胎を奨励, いや, 強制さえする国で, この女性は私たちの娘に生命を与えたのだ。この世では報いきれない感謝をしないではいられない事実である) (RD 98/6: 84) [個別事例 ; 特定の行為に応じる感謝]

(135) a. Many people are suffering economic *hardship*. (多くの人々は経済的困難に苦しんでいる) (CCED[3]) [具体的状況は無指定 (= 抽象概念)]

  b. It wouldn't be much of *a hardship*, I reasoned ... (たいして困難ではないだろう, と考えた) (RD 00/2: 37) [一時的・個別的]

 参考 : Economic *hardships* are forcing its people to shed old ways and thrive in a competitive world. (経済的困難のため国民は古いやり方を脱して, 競争的世界で成功することを余儀なくされている) (RD 99/12: 45) [多種類]

(136) a. (= IV-239, a) It sounds fine in *theory*, but will it work (in practice)? (OALD[5])

  b. Scientists have advanced *a* new *theory* to explain this phenomenon. (科学者たちはこの現象を説明するのに新理論を提唱した) (OALD[5]) [個別事例]

5.4.4 内容

(137) a. If the three parties cannot reach *agreement* now, there will be a civil war. (3党がいま合意に達することができなければ, 内戦が起きるだろう) (CIDE) [抽象概念 ; 4章 NB 10 参照]

  b. What happens if the warring parties fail to reach *an agreement*? (対立中の政党同士で協定が成立しなければどうなるだろう) (LDOCE[3]) [特定の協定・取り決め]

(138) a. These traditions were deeply rooted in local *custom*. (これらの伝統は地域の慣習に深く根づいていた) (LDOCE[3]) [総体的]

  b. 'Why the pile of salt?' 'It's *an* old Japanese *custom*.' (「なぜ塩を盛るの?」「日本の古い習慣なんだ」) (LDOCE[3]) [個別的 ; 通例, 修飾語句をともなう ; cf. habit/routine/tradition]

(139) a. The first time Fu Manchu broke out, zoo keepers chalked it up to human *error*. (FM [オランウータンの名前] が初めて抜け出したとき, 動物園の飼育係たちは人為的ミスとした) (RD 00/4: 36) [抽象概念 ; どういうミスかには関知せず]

  b. He admitted that he'd made *an error*. (間違いを犯したことを認めた) (CIDE) [特定の間違い ; 内容含意]

(140) a. Contrary to general *expectation*, he announced that all four had given their approval.（大方の予想に反して，4者とも承認してくれたと言った）(CCED3)

b. *a* perfectly legitimate *expectation*（まったく正当な期待）(OALD5)

参考：Last year's predictions fell a bit short of *expectations*.（昨年の予言は少しばかり期待はずれだった）(CDAE) [CDAE の注記によれば，expectation は「期待」という意味のときは 'usually pl']

(141) a. *Fate* brought us something else.（運命はある別のものをもたらした）(RD 99/12: 123) [擬人的]

b. I wouldn't wish such *a fate* on my worst enemy.（最悪の敵にさえもそのような運命は願わないだろう）(LDOCE3) [fate の内容含意；cf. opportunity]

参考：*Fortune* smiled on him.（運命が彼に微笑んだ）/ You're in *luck* – there's one ticket left.（ラッキーですね。チケットは残り1枚です）[fortune/luck は「幸運」の意味では a/an をとらない]

(142) a. Some people find *fault* in everything they see.（見るものすべてに難癖をつける人もいる）(CDAE) [fault の内容非限定（= 抽象概念）]

b. Keri is generous to *a fault*.（K は寛大すぎるのが欠点だ）(CDAE) [fault の内容限定]

5.4.5 その他

(143) a. Paper money replaced all but smaller denominations of *coin*.（紙幣は，より少額の硬貨を除いて，全面的に取って代わった）(CIDE) [制度・形式]

b. Let's toss *a coin* to see who goes first.（硬貨を投げてだれが最初に行くか決めよう）(LDOCE3) [具体物]

(144) a. Actually, Chogali was – is – in the middle of a war. On one side is a military dictatorship that in the past 36 years has killed, tortured and displaced tens of thousands. On the other are ethnic tribes who want autonomy and dissidents who want *democracy*.（実際には，C は，今もそうであるが，戦争中だった。一方には，軍事独裁政権があって，過去 36 年にわたって何万人もを虐殺し，拷問にかけ，退去させた。他方には，自治権を求める民族集団と，民主主義を求める反体制派がいるのだ）(RD 99/10: 32) [次例（V-145）も参照]

b. Americans live in *a democracy*.（米国人は民主主義国家に住んでいる）(RD 98/12: 69)

(145) a. After many years of *dictatorship*, the country is now moving toward democracy. (長年の独裁制ののち，その国は今や民主主義へと動いている) (CIDE) [上例 (V-144) も参照]

b. If a government with limited democracy steadily expands these freedoms, it should not be branded *a dictatorship*. (限定的民主主義の政府がこういった自由を着実に拡げていくならば，独裁国家という烙印を押すべきではない) (RD 98/10: 47)

(146) a. Her economic theories are out of/in *favour* (with the current government). (彼女の経済理論は (現政府に) 気に入られていない／いる) (CIDE)

b. She rang up to ask me *a favour*, but I told her I'll be away all this month. (電話してきてある頼み事をしたが，今月はずっと留守だと答えた) (CIDE)

(147) a. The cockpit was engulfed in *fire*. (操縦室は火につつまれた) (RD 99/10: 67) [形状・範囲非限定]

b. We lit *a fire*, opened a bottle of wine and sprawled in the cooling sand, talking. (たき火をし，ワインの瓶を開け，ひんやりとした砂に手足を伸ばして語りあった) (RD 00/1: 8) [話し手の記憶のなかにある fire；ただし，strike fire では無冠詞]

c. Putting his ear to the door, he heard a muffled voice calling: "There's *fire* in here! There's *a fire* in here!" (ドアに耳をつけて，こもった声が叫んでいるのを聞いた。「ここが燃えている。ここが火事だ」) (RD 00/1: 76) [形状・範囲非限定 vs. 個別事例 (= 話し手の目前の fire)]

(148) a. It's been dry for so long that the forest could burst into *flame*. (長いあいだ乾燥しているので山火事が起こってもおかしくない) (CIDE) [形状・範囲非限定]

b. Gauze is used in chemistry for supporting something above *a flame* while it is being heated. (金網は化学 [の実験] で炎の上のものを熱するとき，それを支えるのに用いられる) (CIDE) [たとえば，アルコールランプが作る 1 つの炎]

参考： An oil heater was knocked over and immediately burst into *flames*. (オイルヒーターが倒され，すぐにぱっと燃え上がった) (OALD[5]) [通例，炎が 1 つだけということはない]

(149) a. Haylee's kidneys began showing *improvement*, and she was taken

off dialysis. (Hの腎臓は回復を見せはじめ，透析をはずされた) (RD 00/3: 55) [行為・過程]

b. So far, 75 per cent have reported *an improvement* in their condition. (これまでのところ，75パーセント[の者]が状態の改善を報告している) (RD 99/8: 69) [結果 ; 類義語の progress は不定冠詞をとらない (☞ 2.3.3.3.7)]

第6章　原理 VI ──a/an＋複数形

6　原理 VI ──a/an＋複数形

　従来の不定冠詞の用法の説明においては無視あるいは例外視されてきた現象であるが，本章中の多数の例が示すように，不定冠詞が複数形を従えることがある。このときの条件は，必ず形容詞(相当語句)と数詞がつく，ということである。この構造においては，形容詞(相当語句)が"数詞＋名詞"という集合を修飾するので名詞部は全体としてひとまとまりの完結した情報をもつことになり，それゆえ，不定冠詞をとることが可能になるのである。言い換えれば，形容詞(相当語句)により当該の名詞部は当てはまる範囲が限定されるので不定冠詞が必要とされる，ということである。したがって，原理 VI は原理 IV (限定と非限定)が複数形名詞に適用されたケースであると言ってよい。a/an は歴史的には one の弱まった形であるが，この構造は現代英語では不定冠詞が数詞の one からは統語的に独立していることを示している。(another ten minutes というパタンも，another は "an＋(形容詞相当語句である) other" から成るので，以下にあげる諸例と同じパタンである。)

> 原理 VI：英語の名詞部は，"形容詞(相当語句)＋数詞＋複数名詞形"という構造のとき，不定冠詞をとる。

以下，この原理によって説明可能な例を列挙する。

(1) After only 11 weeks of taking two O-T pills a day, the documents showed, Gummel increased her throws by *an* amazing two *metres* or more. (1日に[筋肉増強剤の]O-T を2錠摂るようになってわずか11週後に，記録によると，G は驚異的に2メートルあるいはそれ以上も投擲(とうてき)距離を伸ばしたのだった) (RD 99/11: 93)

(2) *An* astonishing 66 million *Asians* have this life-threatening disease – and half of them don't know it. (驚くべきことに6千6百万人のアジアの人々が，生命を脅かすこの病気[糖尿病]にかかっている，しかも，半数はそのことを知らない) (RD 99/1: 73) [複数一致]

(3) By mid-June surface temperatures in an area near the equator had

dropped *an* astounding 14 *degrees* Fahrenheit (7.8 degrees Celsius).（6月中旬までに赤道近くの地域の表面温度は驚くべきことに華氏で14度（摂氏7.8度）も下がった）(RD 98/12: 23)

(4) One chilly day, we all noticed that the thermometer, which was in direct sunlight, read *a* balmy 22 *degrees*.（ある肌寒い日，直射日光の当たるところにあった温度計が，快適な22度を指していることにみんな気づいた）(RD 02/3: 96)

(5) Outside, the temperature was *a* bone-chilling minus 29 *degrees* Celsius, and 12 inches of snow overnight had raised the accumulation to roughly four feet.（外では温度は骨も凍る−29℃であり，12インチの積雪は一晩でおよそ4フィートにまで累積した）(RD 99/2: 106)

(6) With the temperature *a* cool 10 *degrees* Celsius, the Feuchtwangers now prepared to enter the water.（温度が涼しい10℃だったので，F夫妻は今や水に入る用意をした）(RD 98/12: 76)

(7) Huong's message struck a deep chord, and the book sold *an* enormous 60,000 *copies* in Vietnam.（HのメッセージはV深く反響を呼び，その本はVで大量6万冊も売れた）(RD 98/12: 20)

(8) In 1990, *an* estimated 600,000 Asian *women* suffered hip fractures as a result of osteoporosis.（1990年に推定60万人のアジアの女性が骨粗しょう症の結果として骨盤を骨折した）(RD 98/6: 98)

類例： The narrator noted that there are *an* estimated 53 million *dogs* in the United States.（ナレーターは合衆国には推定5千3百万匹の犬がいると言った）(RD 99/6: 13); Over the past 40 years, *an* estimated 6000 *monasteries* have been destroyed.（過去40年で推定6千の修道院が破壊された）(RD 00/3: 20); *An* estimated 15 million *trees* were blown down.（推定千5百万本の木々が吹き倒された）(OALD[5]); Each year, *an* estimated 40,000 *people* in America are potential candidates for heart transplants, but fewer than 2500 organs are available.（アメリカでは毎年推定4万人の人々が心臓移植手術の潜在的候補者だが，提供される臓器は2千5百以下だ）(RD 99/9: 6) [以上すべて複数一致]；an estimated 150,000 [tourists] (RD 99/10: 51) [複数形名詞省略]；an estimated 14,000 discussion forums (RD 97/5: 24); an estimated $260 million (RD 98/8: 84); an estimated 15 million inhabitants (RD 98/3: 69); an estimated 10,000 different scents (RD 98/3: 120); an estimated ten million to 12 million U.S. smokers (RD 99/3: 53); an estimated 4000 chemical compounds (RD 99/3: 57); an estimated 190,000 premature deaths (RD 99/12: 104); an estimated 9200 of the 23,000 American women (RD 99/4: 70); an estimated 5 million people around the world (RD 99/10: 51); an estimated 10,000 people (RD 98/12: 18); an estimated 5000 orangutans (RD 98/12: 8)

(9) On a sunny June day in 1998, Karilyn and her mother, Vivian, spent *an* exhausting 12 *hours* at the world-renowned clinic. (1998年6月の晴れたある日，Kと母親のVとは世界的に有名な診療所で疲れ果てる12時間を過ごした) (RD 01/8: 110)

(10) The goal is *an* extra 150 to 200 *calories* a day – or between 1000 and 1500 a week. (目標は1日にもう150ないし200カロリー，すなわち，1週で千から千5百［カロリー］のあいだだ) (RD 98/10: 43) 類例：an extra five metres (RD 99/12: 58)

> NB 1　数詞＋extra＋名詞
> 上記の語順のときは不定冠詞はつけられない ((VI-29-31) 参照)。
> i) Rankin thinks I'll go through at least 1200 *extra kilojoules* a day. (Rの考えでは，私は1日に少なくとも1,200キロジュール余分に消費する) (RD 01/5: 23)
> ii) Rankin reckons by the time I gain one kilo of muscle, I could start burning about 270 *extra kilojoules* every day, on top of the 630 kilojoules I'll burn on the days I lift. (Rの計算では，筋肉が1キロつくまでには，リフティングをする日に消費する630キロジュールに加えて，毎日余分に約270キロジュール消費できるようになるだろう) (RD 01/5: 22)

(11) When I was asked the surprise question, it was *a* full three *minutes* before I spoke, although my hands were in constant motion, as if their dance could coax my mind to engage. (不意に質問されたとき，口がきけるまでにまる3分もたった。もっとも，両手はずっと動きっぱなしで，その手の踊りは精神をなだめすかして活動させようとしているかのようだった) (RD 98/6: 132)

(12) The bottom step was *a* good two *feet* off the ground. (1番下の段は地面からゆうに2フィートは離れていた) (RD 98/11: 76) 類例：a good 15 seconds (RD 00/5: 54); a good seven miles (Doyle, *Adventures of*

Sherlock Holmes)

(13) We were all extremely weary, and my knee ached appallingly. It had been *a* grueling 200 *miles*. (みな極度に疲労困憊(こんぱい)しており，私の膝はひどく痛んだ．くたくたに疲れる200マイルだった) (RD 97/2: 128)　類例：a grueling nine innings (RD 98/10: 27)

(14) One hot summer day I looked at Giles after he had finished *an* impressive three *hours* of hole-digging and tree-planting. (ある暑い夏の日，Gが3時間も穴掘りと植樹を見事にやったあとで彼を見た) (RD 98/12: 112)

(15) But a Siberian male patrols *an* incredible 400 square *miles*, stalking elk and wild boar for the ten pounds of meat he needs each day. (だが，シベリアン[タイガー]のオスは信じがたいことに400平方マイルも歩き回り，毎日必要とする10ポンドの肉を求めてヘラジカやイノシシを追跡する) (RD 98/9: 30)

(16) None is more enthusiastic than Anselme Selosse, a 44-year-old nonconformist in the town of Avize who produces *a* mere 45,000 *bottles* a year from his six hectares of vines, without benefit of pesticides, synthetic fertilisers or complex modern equipment. (ASほど専念しているものはない．彼はA町の44歳の異端児であり，殺虫剤とか合成肥料，複雑な現代的設備を用いないで，6ヘクタールのブドウ畑から1年にわずか4万5千本しか生産しないのだ) (RD 99/6: 107)

類例：a mere 50 square metres (RD 99/10: 10); a mere 710 square kilometres (RD 00/6: 44); a mere 150 metres (Peter Goldsbury, Chugoku Shimbun, Jan. 15, 00); a mere 5,500 [prospective graduates] (Peter Goldsbury, Chugoku Shimbun, Apr. 3, 99) [複数形名詞省略]

(17) If your timing was absolutely perfect and you jumped exactly when the elevator hit, you might reduce your speed at impact by *a* negligible eight *kilometres* per hour. (タイミングがまったく完璧で，エレベーターがまさにぶつかる瞬間に飛び上がったとしても，衝突のスピードをたかだか時速8キロ分減速させることができるだけだろう) (RD 00/3: 96)

(18) Total seizures in 1997 amounted to *a* paltry 24 *kilos* of heroin and seven *kilos* of cocaine. (1997年の総没収量はわずかヘロイン24キロ，コカイン7キロだった) (RD 00/2: 112) [a paltry (24 kilos of heroin and seven kilos of cocaine)]　類例：a paltry eight kilojoules (RD 00/7: 90)

第 6 章　原理 VI ——a/an＋複数形　*229*

(19) By early afternoon the temperature was *a* perfect 24 *degrees* Celsius, and there was a crystal clarity about the landscape. (午後の早い時点までに温度は申し分ない 24 ℃になり，風景は澄み切ってきた) (RD 97/2: 135)

(20) In all, *a* record 19 *climbers* from Erik's group succeeded that day. (その日，E のグループから全部で記録的な 19 人もの登山者が成功した) (RD 02/2: 39)

(21) Although only four feet, ten inches tall and *a* scant 100 *pounds*, Jackie was a dynamo with big dreams. (わずか 4 フィート 10 インチの身長で，ほんの 100 ポンドだが，J は大きな夢をもった精力家だった) (RD 96/3: 68)

(22) The crest would come in the early morning hours of Tuesday – at *a* staggering 54.35 *feet*. (最高水位——驚異的な 54.35 フィート——に達するのは火曜日の早朝だ) (RD 98/10: 136)　類例: a staggering 57 countries; a staggering 12 times (RD 99/8: 104; 99/9: 111)

(23) After the first 100 metres, my time was *a* terrible 9.9 *seconds*. (スタートから 100 メートルでタイムは最悪の 9.9 秒だった) (RD 95/1: 124)

(24) [H]e won *an* unprecedented four gold *medals* at the Paralympic games in Atlanta. (A でのパラリンピックで前人未到の金メダル 4 個を獲得した) (RD 00/7: 28)

(25) Barely five feet, two inches tall and *a* waifish 90 *pounds*, Flynn suffered from multiple sclerosis. (F は，かろうじて 5 フィート 2 インチで 90 ポンドの細身だが，多発性硬化症を患っている) (RD 97/2: 33)

(26) Eventually, we were *a* whopping $250 *million* in the red. (最終的には，巨額な 2 億 5 千万ドルもの赤字だった) (RD [U.S. Edition] 98/9: 208)　類例: a whopping $467 million (RD 98/10: 101)

　形容詞 (相当語句) は副詞により修飾されることもある。

(27) The airspeed indicator read nearly 225 kilometres an hour, but against the head wind the helicopter could only crawl towards land, averaging *an* agonisingly slow 20 *kilometres* an hour. (対気速度計は時速約 225 km を示しているが，向かい風のためヘリコプターは陸地に向かってやっと這うように進み，平均時速は苦痛なほどのろのろした 20 km である) (RD 01/9: 73)

　例 (8) および (16) [estimated/mere] の類例であげているように複数形名詞は省略されることもある。次は，補うべき名詞があまりにも専門的であるため

省略が一般化した例である。

(28) Sims was examined at the Atlanta Medical Centre and found to be in good condition, his blood pressure *a* solid *120/80*. (S は A 医療センターで診療され、良好であることがわかった。血圧は安定した [最高血圧] 120, [最低血圧] 80だった) (RD 00/5: 45) [医学用語としては mmHg (millimeters of mercury) を補足可]

これまであげてきた例文の語順は "a/an＋形容詞＋数詞＋複数形名詞" であった。これに対し、(29-31, a) が示すように、"数詞＋形容詞＋複数形名詞" という語順のときは a/an はつかない (本章 NB 1 [extra] も参照)。a/an が (hundred/thousand など桁を表す語以外の) 数詞に先行することはないからである。

この構造に関する、より重要な条件は、(31, b) が示すように、about/around/nearly などは現れないということである。名詞部に概略を表す語がつけられれば、名詞部は漠然とした情報となり、もはや完結を表さないからである。((29) および (30) の a-文、b-文とも自然な英語である。)

(29) a. Then we spent eight tense *hours* driving north on icy highways in the midst of a whirling blizzard. (それから緊張して8時間もかけて渦巻くブリザードのなか凍結した道路を北上した) (RD 00/5: 72)

　　 b. Then we spent *a* tense eight *hours* driving north on icy highways in the midst of a whirling blizzard. (同上)

(30) a. But most of all I am doing it for Jock, the husband with whom I spent 32 wonderful *years*. (しかし、何にも増して、私は J―― すばらしい32年をともにした夫――のためにしているのだ) (RD 00/7: 45)

　　 b. But most of all I am doing it for Jock, the husband with whom I spent *a* wonderful 32 *years*. (同上)

(31) a. It was 4.03 p.m. Sims had been trapped for about 90 searing *minutes*. (午後4時3分だった。S は灼熱の90分ぐらいものあいだ、身動きできないでいた) (RD 00/5: 45)

　　 b. *It was 4.03 p.m. Sims had been trapped for about *a* searing 90 *minutes*.

(30) の a wonderful 32 years も 32 wonderful years も正しい英語であるが、a/an をとるタイプは完結を表し、a/an をとらないタイプは必ずしも完結を表さない。このことは (32, a-b) の解釈の相違により裏づけられる。すなわち、(32, a) は20年連続して勤務した場合に用いられるのに対し、(32, b) では途中

(32) a. I spent *a* wonderful 20 *years* working at the office. (その事務所に勤務してすばらしい20年を過ごした) [連続して20年]
　　 b. I spent 20 wonderful *years* working at the office. (同上) [連続または合算して20年; (VIII-53, c) も参照]

NB 2
1) a/an 以外の限定詞
　"形容詞＋数詞＋複数形名詞" は a/an 以外の限定詞をとることもある。
　i) Among the many feelings going through my head during *those* excruciating 20 *minutes* was pride... (この苦しい20分のあいだ, 多くの感情が頭をよぎったが, そのうちの1つはプライドだった) (RD 01/9: 10)

2) a/an＋複数形
　以下の例では a/an に後続する名詞は, -s で終わってはいるが, 単数扱いであるので, 本章であげた例とは異なる。
　ii) The next day I told myself over and over that I was going home soon, and imagined my chest as *a* huge *bellows* that I could open and close at will. (すぐに自宅に帰るのだと翌日繰り返し自分に言い聞かせ, 自分の胸を思いどおりに開閉できる大きなふいごだと想像した) (RD 98/9: 92)
　iii) Around the same time I am also accepted into graduate film school, and find myself at *a crossroads*. (同じころ大学院の映画専攻課程にも入学を認められ, 岐路に立つことになる) (RD 98/5: 123)
　iv) Eventually *a gallows* was built inside the city. (とうとう市内に絞首台がつくられた) (RD 97/5: 62) [単数一致]
　v) "This would go a long way toward guaranteeing *a* clean *Olympic Games*," says former USOC [U.S. Olympic Committee] medical chief Voy. (「これはきれいなオリンピック競技を保証するのにかなり役立つだろう」と合衆国オリンピック委員会の医療主任のVは言う) (RD 96/10: 26) 類例: an Asian/Olympic Games (RD 98/1: 12, 96/10: 27)
　vi) In *a* makeshift *headquarters*, police area commander Charlie

Sanderson explained that at least 11 men and seven women were under the rubble. (仮設本部で，地域警視長 CS は少なくとも 11 人の男性と 7 人の女性が瓦礫(がれき)の下にいると説明した) (RD 00/6: 32)

vii) Bored, the boys reduced my nerves to *a shambles*. (退屈して，少年たちは私の神経をめちゃめちゃにした) (RD 99/8: 126)

3) a/an＋形容詞＋分数

分数に形容詞が先行するときも a/an がつけられる。

viii) We are only two-thirds of what we were, but we will be *a* tight, whole *two-thirds*. (もとの [3 姉妹の] 3 分の 2 だけになったけれど，親密で，すべてがそろった 3 分の 2 となるのだ) (RD 02/4: 80)

第7章　不定冠詞に関するその他の問題

7.1　タイプ：a cup and saucer

and で結ばれた2つ(以上)の名詞が1つの事物として認識されるとき，不定冠詞は最初の名詞の前にだけつけられる。最もわかりやすいのは，次のように2種類の液体がミックスされて1つの製品が作られるときであろう。

(1) He mixed her *a gin and tonic*. (彼女用にジントニックを1人分つくった) (OALD5)

(2) *A whisky and soda*, please. (ウイスキーソーダ1杯お願いします) (OALD5)

類例：a lager and lime (ライム入りラガー); a gin and orange (オレンジ入りジン); a vodka and lime (ライム入りウオッカ)

普通名詞同士が and で結ばれるときも同様であり，2つ(以上)の事物が集まって1つの事物を構成するとみなされれば，a/an は2番目の名詞の前では反復されない。1つの事物であることが統語的に明らかなのは，次のように，combined が用いられるときである。

(3) *a kitchen and dining-room* combined (ie one room used as both) (ダイニングキッチン，すなわち，両方に用いられる1部屋) (OALD5)

しかし，combined は表現されないほうが多い。たいていの場合，不定冠詞が最初の名詞の前に1度だけ用いられることによって，2つ(以上)の名詞が1つのセットであることを表す。

(4) Inside was *a chequebook and card*, which I fenced to my second sister, older by three years. (なかには小切手帳とカードが入っていた。それを3歳年上の次姉に手渡した) (RD 01/7: 54)

(5) *a close ally and friend* of the prime minister (総理の側近にして友人) (OALD5)

(6) Let's arrange *a time and place* for our next meeting. (次回の会議の時間と場所を決めよう) (OALD5)

(7) wear *a suit and tie* (スーツを着てネクタイをする) (OALD5)

(8) build sandcastles with *a bucket and spade* (バケツと手鍬(すき)で砂の城をつくる) (OALD5)

(9) eat with *a knife and fork* (ナイフとフォークで食べる) (OALD5)

(10) Before long, Eilene was in *a leather jacket and vest*, and riding with Hutchinson on weekends. (間もなく E は週末には革ジャンにベスト姿で，H と [オートバイに] 乗っていた) (RD 01/47)

(11) There is *a natural love and empathy* between them. (彼らには生まれつき愛と共感がある) (OALD⁵)

(12) Vern once told me that to write a sentence with *a mismatched noun and verb* was the literary equivalent of going on stage with your fly open. (V がかつて言ったところでは，対応しない名詞と動詞を用いて文を書くのは，文章表現では，ズボンの前ボタンを開けたまま舞台に上がるのに相当する) (RD 97/2: 114)

(13) Then I sold him *a rod and reel*. (その後リールつきの釣り竿を売った) (RD 01/4: 45)

(14) Aaron became *a writer and producer* for such reality-based television shows as "Rescue 911." (A は "R 911" のような事実に基づいたテレビ番組の脚本家兼演出家になった) (RD 01/6: 28)

類例： a cup and saucer (受け皿つきのカップ); a basin and ewer (水差しつきの洗面器); a coach and pair (2 頭立て馬車); a hook and eye (かぎホック); a hook and line (糸のついた釣り針); a horse and cart (荷馬車); a needle and cotton (木綿糸を通した針); a needle and thread (糸を通した針); a shampoo and conditioner (シャンプーとコンディショナーのセット)

and のあとの名詞が修飾語句をともなうこともある．

(15) Al, you know I was *a draft dodger and anti-war demonstrator*. (A, 知ってのとおり，僕は徴兵を忌避して反戦デモをしてたんだ) (RD 01/7: 10)

(16) Each pack contains *a book and accompanying cassette*. (各パックには本と付属のカセットが入っている) (OALD⁶)

NB 1
1) それぞれを個別の事物として提示するときは不定冠詞が反復される．
　i) She's *a career woman* and *a mother*, so she has/gets/enjoys the best of both worlds. (彼女はキャリアウーマンでもあり母親でもあるので，2 つの世界を最高に享受している) (OALD⁵)
　ii) She is doubly gifted: as *a writer* and as *a painter*. (彼女は二重

に才能がある。文筆家として，かつ画家として) (OALD⁵)

iii) The gang did *a warehouse* and *a supermarket*. (ギャングは倉庫とスーパーマーケットを襲った) (OALD⁵)

2) 他の限定詞の場合も，後続する 2 つ (以上) の名詞がセットで用いられるときは，限定詞は最初の名詞にだけつけられる。

iv) Let's drink (a toast) to *the bride and bridegroom*! (新郎新婦に乾杯) (OALD⁵)

v) That actually happened, says *his friend and fellow exile*, poet Bei Ling. (実際にそういうことが起こった，と彼の友人にして共に追放された詩人の BL は言う) (RD 01/5: 24f.)

7.2　一見同義表現

(17)–(60) のように，辞書には a/an がかっこ内に入っている例もある。これは意味に大差がないからではあるが，すでに述べたように (☞ 2.3.2; 4.4)，厳密には，「範囲非限定」対「限定」(=「抽象概念」対「個別事例」) あるいは「物質」対「製品」というような相違があると想定すべきである。(以下の相違に関する注記は，他の例文の場合と同様，英語母語話者の同意を得ている。)

(17) Her theory was quoted without *(an) acknowledgement*. (彼女の理論が感謝 (のことば) なしに引用された) (OALD⁵) [行為と文言]

(18) There is *(a)* close *affinity* between Italian and Spanish. (イタリア語とスペイン語には密接な類似 (箇所) がある) (OALD⁵) [抽象概念と具体物]

(19) Pregnant women over the age of 35 will be offered *(an) amniocentesis*. (35 歳以上の妊婦は羊水穿刺を提案される) (OALD⁶) [検査法と施術；(V-32) も参照]

(20) You'll be under *(an) anaesthetic*, so you won't feel a thing. (麻酔 (薬) をかけられるので，何も感じないだろう) (OALD⁵) [働き (または物質) と製品]

(21) The new laws have *(a)* particular *application* to the self-employed. (新法は自営業者に特に当てはまる) (CIDE) [particular: 漠然とした形容辞 (vague epithet) と記述形容詞 (descriptive adjective) (☞ 4.4.1.2; 4.4.3.4)]

(22) Pretending to faint was merely *(an) artifice*. (気を失った振りをするのは単なる策略だ) (OALD⁵) [抽象概念と内容限定]

(23) You can use *(an) astringent* to make your skin less oily. (オイリースキンを目立たなくするには収れん化粧水を使ったらいい) (CIDE) [働き

(または物質) と製品]

(24) The gentle music was *(a) balm* to his ears. (穏やかな音楽は彼の耳には癒しだった) (OALD5) [働きと製品]

(25) The lizard's light brown skin acts as *(a) camouflage* in the desert sand. (トカゲの明るい褐色の皮膚は砂漠の砂のなかでは迷彩 (色) の役割を果たす) (CIDE) [働きと具体物]

(26) weedkiller: *(a) chemical* used for killing weeds (草枯らし = 雑草を枯らすのに用いられる化学薬品) (CIDE) [物質と製品]

(27) He appealed for *(a) commutation* of the death sentence to life imprisonment. (死刑から終身刑への減刑を求めて上告した) (OALD5) [抽象概念と内容限定]

(28) The two parties have reached *(a) consensus.* (両党は (ある) 合意に達した) (OALD5) [内容非含意と含意]

(29) There's been *(a)* fierce/bitter/heated *controversy* over the policy ever since it was introduced. (導入以来その政策に関しては激論/激しい/激烈な/白熱した議論がなされている) (CIDE) [抽象概念と個別事例 ; cf. war]

(30) I'm afraid my attempts to strike up *(a) conversation* with the exotic-looking man in black came to nothing! (黒い服を着た風変わりな様子の男と話をしようとしたが，だめだったようだ) (CIDE) [行為自体と個別行為]

(31) The country was in the grip of *(an)* economic *depression.* (その国は経済不況に襲われていた) (OALD6) [一時性非含意と含意]

(32) a. *(a) disqualification* for driving while drunk (飲酒運転による資格剥奪) (OALD5) [制度 (= 抽象概念) と個別事例 ; (VII-45) も同様 ; disqualification という用語は主に<英>]

b. Drivers will receive *disqualification/suspension* for driving while drunk/intoxicated. (運転者は飲酒運転をすれば免許停止になる) [制度 (= 抽象概念)]

c. My uncle received *a disqualification/suspension* for driving while drunk/intoxicated. (叔父は飲酒運転のため免許停止になった) [個別事例]

参考：Drivers will be [My uncle was] suspended/disqualified for driving while intoxicated. [(31, b-c) の日常的表現]

(33) There is *(a)* growing *disenchantment* with the way the country/

第7章　不定冠詞に関するその他の問題　237

school/football club is being run. (国家/学校/フットボールクラブの運営方法に関する熱気は冷めつつある) (CIDE) [様態非限定と限定]

(34) serve as *(a) gardener and chauffeur* (庭師兼運転手として勤める) (OALD5) [働きと具体物]

(35) It's a shame – he had *(a) gippy tummy* most of the time he was on holiday. (残念なことに、休暇中の大半下痢をしていた) (CIDE) [病名と一時的症状]

(36) You seem in *(a)* very good *humour* today. (とても機嫌がよさそうだ) (CIDE) [一時性非含意と含意]

(37) have a large family as *(an) insurance* against old age (老いの保証として大家族をもつ) (OALD5) [働きと具体物]

(38) feel/have/show/express *(an) interest* in sth (何かに興味を感じる/もつ/示す/表す) (OALD5) [抽象概念と内容含意]

(39) Applicants will be called for *(an) interview* in April. (応募者は4月に面接を求められる) (OALD5) [制度・形式と実現・個別事例]

(40) a. There was *(an)* immediate *panic* when the alarm sounded. (警報が鳴るとすぐにパニックが生じた) (OALD5) [一時性 (または様態) 非含意と含意]

   b. News of the losses caused *(a) panic* among investors. (損失のニュースは投資家たちにパニックを起こした) (OALD6) [同上]

(41) We spent *(a) part* of our vacation in Maine. (休暇を少しM州で過ごした) (OALD5) [期間非含意と含意；a part は短い期間を含意]

(42) The students spend the third year of the course on *(a) placement* with an industrial firm. (学生たちは課程の3年目を工業会社で職業訓練をして過ごす) (OALD5) [働きと個別行為]

(43) lumps of chalk crushed to *(a) powder* (粉々に砕かれたチョークの固まり) (OALD5) [形状不定と形状特定]

(44) If you beat someone to *(a) pulp*, you seriously injure them by hitting them a lot. (だれかをたたいてぐじゃぐじゃにすれば、何度も殴打して重傷を負わせることになる) (CIDE) [形状不定と形状特定]

(45) get *(a) remission* of six months/get six months' remission (刑期短縮6か月/6か月間分の刑期短縮になる) (OALD5) [制度 (= 抽象概念) と個別事例；(VII-31) も同様]

(46) We tied his feet together with *(a) rope*. (ロープで彼の両足をしばった) (OALD5) [長さ非含意と含意 (☞ 4.1)、または本数非含意と1本だけ]

(47) Her arrest for theft caused *(a) scandal* in the village. (窃盗罪で彼女が逮捕されたことは村ではスキャンダル (の種) になった) (OALD⁵) [内容非限定と限定]

(48) decide on *(a) separation* (別れることに決める) (OALD⁵) [制度としての離婚と個別行為]

(49) We've got a rug made from *(a) sheepskin*. (羊皮で作った敷物を手に入れた) (CIDE) [1 頭分非含意と含意]

(50) They have *(an)* amazing team *spirit*. (驚くべきチームスピリットをもっている) (OALD⁵) [特有性非含意と含意, または amazing = 漠然とした形容辞 (= 枕詞) vs. 記述形容詞 ; (IV-150, a) も参照]

(51) The prisoners have gone on *(a)* hunger *strike* to protest about prison conditions. (囚人たちは刑務所の状態に抗議してハンガーストライキに入った) (CIDE) [様態非限定と限定 ; ハンストは断食という方法に限定されているので不定冠詞をつけても可]

比較 : All 2500 employees have gone on *strike* in protest at the decision to close the factory. (2500 人の従業員すべてが工場閉鎖の決定に抗議してストライキに入った) (CIDE) [ストライキの様態非限定]

(52) The detail of her wildlife paintings is *(a) testament* to her powers of observation. (野生生物の細部にわたる描写は彼女の観察力の証明 (物) だ) (CIDE) [働きと具体物]

(53) The pyramids are *(a) testimony* to the Ancient Egyptians' engineering skills. (ピラミッドは古代エジプトの工学技術の証明 (物) だ) (OALD⁵) [働きと具体物]

(54) a car fitted with *(an)* automatic *transmission* (オートマティック変速機 (能) つきの車) (OALD⁵) [働きと具体物]

(55) The country was in *(a) turmoil* during the strike. (その国はストライキの間, 混乱状態だった) (OALD⁵) [一時性 (または様態) 非含意と含意 ; 2.3.3.3.1 「混乱」) も参照]

(56) Moving to a new house causes such *(an) upheaval*. (新しい家への転居は大変な激変をもたらす) (OALD⁵) [一時性 (または様態) 非含意と含意]

(57) a. The meeting ended in *(an) uproar*. (会議は騒乱状態のうちに終わった) (OALD⁵) [一時性 (または様態) 非含意と含意]

b. There was *(an) uproar* over the tax increases. (増税で大もめした) (OALD⁵) [一時性 (または様態) 非含意と含意]

(58) She is a writer who has lately had/enjoyed *(a)* considerable *vogue* in

France, though she is less well-known in Britain. (近年フランスではかなり売れっ子の作家だが，英国ではそれほど知られていない) (CIDE) [considerable: 漠然とした形容辞と記述形容詞 (☞ 4.4.1.2; 4.4.3.4)]
(59) Job knowledge can be less important than *(a) willingness* to learn. (仕事に関する知識は学習意欲ほど重要ではないことがある) (OALD5) [抽象概念と内容含意]
(60) The element of risk gave *(an)* added *zest* to the whole experience. (危険な要素のため経験全体が刺激的になった) (OALD5) [内容非含意と含意]

NB 2
意味に相違がないと判断される例もある。名詞部の情報が完結か非完結かのボーダーライン上にあるためと思われる。
i) On *(an) impulse*, I picked up the phone and rang my sister in Australia. (衝動的に電話をとって豪の妹に電話した) (OALD5) [Ap.4.2-5 も参照]
ii) He feels/harbours *(a)* deep *resentment* against/at/towards his parents for his miserable childhood. (惨めな子供の頃のため両親に深い恨みを感じて／抱いている) (CIDE)
以下は意味的相違よりもむしろ地域差による。
iii) a. *Gloom* descended on the office when we heard the news. (その知らせを聞いたとき重苦しさが事務所をおおった) (LDOCE3) 〈英〉
   b. *A gloom* descended on the group. (重苦しさが一団をおおった) (CCED3) 〈米〉
iv) Racial prejudice is *(an) anathema* to me. (人種的偏見は大嫌い（なもの）だ) (OALD5) [冠詞をとるのは〈英〉]

7.3 総称用法 (8.6 も参照)

本書では，不定冠詞には総称的「意味」はない，と考える。なぜなら，これまで見てきたように，不定冠詞は名詞がその姿かたちや指示範囲に関してなんらかの限界をもつということを意味するのであって，種全体を指すということは意味しないからである。たとえば，"I like a dog." と言えば，通例，「ある特定の犬が好きだ」という意味であって，「すべての犬が好きだ」という意味ではない。しかし，文脈によっては，"a/an＋名詞"がその名詞の種全体を指すと

解釈可能な場合もある。たとえば，"Vijay has just learnt to ride a bike." は，字義的には，「Vは1台の自転車に乗れるようになったばかりだ」の意であるが，常識的に，1台の自転車に乗れれば他の自転車にも乗れるので，総称的に解釈することが可能である。だが，この例においても，特定の（たとえば，補助輪つき／足が届く）自転車には乗れるが，サドルの高い自転車には乗れないというケースは十分想像可能である。同様に，"A teacher needs to have a lot of patience." における a teacher は，一般論としては，教師全体を指すと解釈されるが，短気な教師への皮肉あるいは当てつけ，忠告，戒告であるかもしれない。これら2例に対し，"A cheetah can run faster than a lion." /"A mule is a cross between a horse and a donkey." は，文の内容（= 命題）が一般論であるので，総称的にとるのが正常な解釈であろう（(68) [cheetahs] 参照）（以上，例文は CIDE および OALD5 による）。これらの例からわかるように，不定冠詞の総称的な「用法」もしくは「解釈」は文脈によって与えられるのであり，a/an に本質的に備わっているのではない。

7.3.1 総称用法の不定冠詞

以下，不定冠詞が総称的に用いられていると解釈可能な例をあげよう。

(61) Overall, *a woman's* brain, like her body, ten to 15 per cent smaller than *a man's*, yet the regions dedicated to higher cognition such as language may be more densely packed with neurons. (全体的に，女性の脳は，体と同様，男性の脳より10〜15％小さいが，高度な認識，たとえば，言語，にかかわる領域はニューロンが [男性よりも] もっと密集しているのかもしれない) (RD 99/7: 76) [(VII-70) 参照]

(62) When *a man* puts his mind to work, neurons turn on in highly specific areas of the brain. When *a woman* does, her brain cells light up such a patchwork that the scans look like a night view of Las Vegas. (男性が精神を活動させればニューロンは脳の限られた特定領域で興奮する。女性の場合は，脳細胞はつぎはぎ状に明るくなるので，そのスキャンは LV の夜景のようである) (RD 99/7: 76) [(VII-70) 参照]

(63) Catholic saints referred to it as "mystical union" with God. *A Buddhist* would call it "interconnectedness." (カトリックの聖人たちは [超越的状態を] 神との「神秘的合体」と呼んだ。仏教徒ならば「融合連結」と呼ぶだろう) (RD 02/3: 25)

(64) For on some level, we all understand that there is still something sacred about *a book*. (というのは，ある段階で，本にはまだどこか神聖なところがあると全員が理解しているからだ) (RD 99/10: 12)

(65) The middle and lower reaches of the Yangtze are the dolphins' habitat. But with more pollution, shipping, and dams, the Yangtze River is no longer a place for *a Yangtze River dolphin*. (揚子江の中流および下流はイルカの生息地であるが、汚染や船舶、ダムの増加につれ、揚子江はもはやヨウスコウカワイルカの住みかではなくなっている) (RD 96/3: 16)

以上の例が示すように、不定冠詞の総称用法は、総称用法であることが明白な文脈中でのみ可能である。

7.3.2 総称用法の複数

不定冠詞の総称用法との関連において、無冠詞複数形の総称用法にも言及しておきたい (the の総称用法に関しては 8.6 参照)。種全体を表すにはこの形式が最も一般的に用いられる。意味的限定をなんら表さないからである。以下、明白な例をあげておきたい。

(66) The 1560 square miles of frozen lakes, snow-clad mountains and old-growth forest are home to *Siberian tigers* as well as *lynx*, *brown bears* and *wolves*. (1,560 平方マイルの氷結した湖、冠雪した山、および原生林がシベリアンタイガーの生息地であり、オオヤマネコ、ヒグマ、オオカミにとってもそうである) (RD 98/9: 26)

(67) *Pigeons*, or *"rock doves,"* can fly up to 75 miles per hour and find their way home from more than 1000 miles away. (ハト、すなわち、「カワラバト」、は時速 75 マイルもの速さで飛行し、1,000 マイル以上離れたところから帰り道を見つけることができる) (RD 96/3: 39)

(68) *Cheetahs* are one of man's oldest animal companions. (チーターは人間にとって最も古いコンパニオン・アニマルのうちの 1 動物である) (RD 00/1: 70)

(69) *Diamonds* are forever tempting people to steal, since a fortune's worth of stones can be stashed in a matchbox. (ダイヤモンドは永遠に人を盗みへと誘惑する、というのも一財産分の宝石をマッチ箱ひとつのうちに隠せるからだ) (RD 98/9: 70)

(70) One possible though controversial explanation: the corpus callosum, the bridge of fibres running down the centre of the brain, is thicker in *females*, which may allow more "crosstalk" between the emotional, intuitive right hemisphere and the rational, just-the-facts left. (議論の余地はあるが可能な説明：脳梁(のうりょう)、つまり、脳の中央を縦に走る神経繊維の連絡部分は女性のほうが密であり、それゆえ、感情的・直感的な右脳と理性的・事実的な左脳との「相互会話」が [男性よりも] 可

能であるのかもしれない) (RD 99/7: 77f.) [(VII-61, 62) [a woman/man] 参照]

(71) *Great whites* are found in all temperate seas, but one of the world's biggest populations is off South Australia. (ホホジロザメは温暖な海ならどこででも見られるが, 世界で最も生息数の多い地域の1つは南豪沖である) (RD 00/5: 94)

(72) In the western Caribbean, where *green turtles* once swam in their millions, only three nesting sites remain and all are threatened. (西カリブ海では, かつてはアオウミガメが何百万と群れていたが, 産卵場はわずか3か所残っているだけであり, いずれも危機に瀕している) (RD 98/4: 122)

(73) *Iguanas* probably weren't what Ellin Prince Speyer envisioned in 1910 when she founded the New York Women's League for Animals, the city's first free clinic for ill, injured and abused animals. (EPSが動物のためのNY女性同盟——病気や怪我の, あるいは虐待をうけた, 動物のためのNY市で最初の無料診療所——を設立した1910年当時, イグアナはたぶん彼女が想定したものではなかっただろう) (RD 99/9: 83)

(74) "*Komodo dragons* are not beautiful," he readily admits. "But they are magnificent, charismatic beasts. They are a living link to a lost world." (「コモドドラゴンは優美ではない」と彼はあっさり認める。「だが, 彼らは雄大で, カリスマ的な獣類であり, 失われた世界につながる現存物だ」) (RD 99/6: 30)

(75) Hunted by man, their habitat shrinking, *pandas* had declined to about 1200 in number. (人間に狩猟され, 生息地は狭められ, パンダは約1,200頭にまで減少していた) (RD 00/2: 24)

(76) *Southern rights* may live to at least 70 years, if they aren't accidentally killed by boats and don't become entangled in fishing gear. (セミクジラは, 船舶のために事故死したり, 漁網にからまったりしなければ, 少なくとも70年は生きるのかもしれない) (RD 99/10: 50)

(77) "*Type E women* are continually anticipating the needs of others at their own expense," Braiker says. (「E型の女性はいつも自分を犠牲にして他人が必要とすることを先回りして考えている」とBは言う) (RD 99/10: 58)

(78) *Whales*, earth's largest mammals, once populated the oceans in their

hundreds of thousands, but man's greed brought many species to the edge of extinction. (地上最大の哺乳動物であるクジラはかつては何十万と海洋に生息していたのだが，人間の貪欲により多くの種が絶滅の瀬戸際に立たされている) (RD 99/10: 48)

NB 3　無冠詞単数形の総称用法か？

　次の例文中では無冠詞の単数形が総称的意味を表すと解釈されるかもしれない。だが，名詞が単独で用いられているのではないことを考えれば，列挙または素材扱いの場合の無冠詞ととるほうが適切であろう（☞ 2.1.2; 8 章 NB 21; 9.1)。

i) endangered species such as *lynx, wolf* and several species of *vulture* (オオヤマネコやオオカミ，ある種のハゲワシのような絶滅危惧種) (CCED³)

ii) Other commercially important furs include the various species of *fox* and *lamb; beaver, marten, raccoon, skunk, otter,* and *seal;* as well as *leopard, lynx, ocelot,* and *wolf.* (他の商業的に重要な毛皮商品は次のようなさまざまな種を含む：キツネ，ラム，ビーバー，テン，アライグマ，スカンク，カワウソ，アザラシ，それに，ヒョウ，オオヤマネコ，オセロット，オオカミ) (EB 01)

iii) In natural outdoor enclosures past and present members of Britain's wildlife are exhibited; these include *otter, lynx, beaver, wild cat, fox* and *snowy owl.* (自然の野外の囲みのなかに英国の過去および現在の野生動物が展示されている。それらには，カワウソ，オオヤマネコ，ビーバー，ヤマネコ，キツネ，シロフクロウが含まれる) (ConCD-ROM)

　他方，無冠詞の物質集合名詞および抽象名詞は，文脈によっては，総称的な読みが可能である。

iv) Families have their problems and jealousies, but *blood* is thicker than *water.* (家族には問題も嫉妬もある。しかし，血は水よりも濃い) (CCED³)

v) *Beauty* is only skin-deep. (美貌も皮一重) [諺]

　しかし，これらの名詞類に総称的意味が内在しているわけではない。なぜなら，vi) では地域限定的であるので，総称的解釈は不適当であるし，vii) でも修飾語句をとる点で，a/an による総称用法とは異なるからである。(the による総称用法に関しては，8.6 参照)

vi) a nationwide system of aqueducts to carry *water* to the arid parts of this country (この国の乾燥地帯に送水するための全国規模の水道システム) (CCED[3])

vii) The scene was one of breathtaking *beauty*. (その景色は息をのむほどの美しさだ) (OALD[6])

第 2 部

定 冠 詞

　　第 2 部では，同定可能性という観点から
英語の定冠詞 (the) が用いられる環境を概説する。
定冠詞の用法は，不定冠詞に較べれば，
英語の非母語話者にも理解できるところが多いので，
あまり知られていないと思われる用法を重点的に記述し，
他はできる限り簡潔に論じたい。

第8章　定冠詞使用の文脈および環境

8　定冠詞の選択原理

　定冠詞 the は名詞部が「同定可能」(identifiable) であることを表す。つまり，the は，話し手/書き手がどれが話題になっているかを指定し，聞き手/読み手がそれを解読可能と予測される場合につけられる，ということである。(注：同定 = 同一であることを見きわめること。(広辞苑).) the の選択原理は次のように述べることができる。

> 原理 VII：英語の名詞部は，同定可能であると判断されるとき，the がつけられる。

　上で言う「同定可能」は，すでに述べられたものを前方照応的に指す場合だけでなく，文化的脈絡において聞き手/読み手に同定可能であることが期待される場合も含む。すなわち，話し手/書き手は，a/an を用いるときは名詞部の情報が完結を表すことを一方的に述べるのに対し，the を用いるときは聞き手/読み手との共同作業を前提とするのである。たとえば，(1) では先行箇所を読むことにより（つまり，前方照応により）"the＋名詞部"が同定され，(2) では文化的了解により "the＋名詞部" が同定される。

(1) A boy and a girl were sitting on a bench. *The boy* was smiling but *the girl* looked angry. (少年と少女がベンチに座っていた。少年のほうは微笑んでいたが，少女のほうは怒っているようだった) (OALD[5])

(2) For centuries *the* Harlech-London *stagecoach* drove along this route, a road constructed by the Romans. (何世紀にもわたって H-L 間の駅馬車はこのルート，つまり，ローマ人が建設した道路，にそって走ったのだった) (RD 96/10: 13)

　第1章で触れた，名詞が冠詞をとる条件——限界を表す——との関連において述べるならば，名詞部が同定可能であるということは，他の解釈の可能性を排除することを意味するので，同定可能であることと限界を表すこととはなんら矛盾するところはない。

8.1 文脈内同定

ここで言う文脈内同定とは，指示物がどれであるかを同定する手がかりが文脈内のどこかに与えられている場合を指す．

8.1.1 形容詞的修飾語句

名詞が前方照応的に用いられるとき ((1), (3))，あるいは形容詞的修飾語句 (4) や最上級 (相当) 語句 (5)，関係詞節 (6)，同格語句 (7) をともなうとき，その名詞の指示物は同定可能なので，通例，*the* がつけられる．

(3) I just bought a new shirt and some new shoes. *The shirt* was quite expensive, but *the shoes* weren't. (先ほど新しいシャツを1着と新しい靴を数足買った．シャツはとても高価だったが，靴はそうでもなかった) (CIDE)

(4) a. Do you like *the food* in this country? (この国の食べ物は気に入っていますか) (OALD⁵)

    b. On April Fools' Day, children make mischief by changing *the salt* and *sugar* on the kitchen table. (エイプリルフールには子供たちは悪戯(いたずら)をして，食卓上の塩と砂糖を取り替える) (NHD)

(5) a. What's *the* highest *mountain* in Europe? (欧州で1番高い山は何ですか) (CIDE)

    b. I shall never forget *the* first *time* we met. (初めて会ったときのことを決して忘れないだろう) (CIDE)

    c. This is *the* only smart *dress* I've got. (私がもっているしゃれたドレスはこれだけだ) (CIDE)

    d. Every time we come to this restaurant, you always have *the* same *thing*. (このレストランに来るたびに，君はいつも同じものをとる) (CIDE)

(6) a. *The people* I met there were very friendly. (そこで出会った人たちはみなとても友好的だった) (OALD⁵)

    b. I really enjoyed *the book* I've just finished reading. (さっき読了した本はとても楽しかった) (CIDE)

(7) a. I am a worker only in *the sense* that I work; I don't get paid for what I do. (働き手と言えるのは働いているという意味でだけだ．することに対して給料はもらっていないのだから) (OALD⁵)

    b. At *the age* of six she could read a newspaper. (6歳という年齢で新聞を読むことができた) (CIDE)

    c. Eric didn't even have *the common sense* to send for a doctor. (E は

医者を呼びにやる常識さえもちあわせていなかった) (LDOCE³)

(7, b) と同様に，固有名詞も内部に同格の *of*-phrase をともなうときは the をとる．これは名詞が同格語句によって同定可能となるためである．例：the Gulf of Mexico, the Isle of Wight. ただし，これらの表現では Gulf/Isle は普通名詞であり，「本来固有名詞」(☞ 1.2) の Mexico/Wight は無冠詞のままである．(固有名詞に関しては後述．☞ 8.7)．

「本来固有名詞」も関係詞節など修飾語句をともなえば，同名の他の固有名詞，あるいは同一物の他の様相，から区別され，どれが話題にのぼっているのか同定されるので the がつけられる (☞ 8.9.1)．

(8) a. *The Diana* I know wouldn't run away. (私が知っている D は逃げたりはしないだろう) (RD 98/3: 22)

b. *The Donald* who had come back from the Japanese prisoner-of-war camp was not the man who went off to war in September 1939. (日本軍の捕虜収容所から帰ってきた D は，1939年9月に出征した男ではなかった) (RD 98/6: 87)

NB 1
1) a/an＋序数詞 (相当語句)

序数詞 (相当語句) と共起しても，指示物が同定不可能 (または同定不要) であるときは，不定冠詞または無冠詞が選ばれることがある (next/following/same を除く (Berry 1993: 33))．

i) She tried the spray *a* third *time*. To her horror the can was empty. (みたび [クマよけ] スプレーを噴霧しようとした．恐怖を感じたことに，カンは空だった) (RD 97/5: 33) [a third time は新情報；聞き手／読み手は何度スプレーしたか知らない；*MEG* (vol. 7, 13.3₂) は "a third time" を 'once more' とパラフレーズしている]

ii) *A* 168th *victim* died while assisting in rescue efforts. (救助活動の援助中に 168人目の犠牲者が亡くなった) (RD 01/6: 116) [文全体が新情報；聞き手には 168人目の犠牲者を同定不可能]

iii) As my boat departs for Hong Kong, I take *a* final *look* at this enchanting city that helped fashion the modern world. (船が香港に向かうとき，現代世界を形成するのに貢献した，この魅力的な都市に最後の視線を投げる) (RD 99/11: 55) [視線を投げる回数を厳密に数えているわけではないので同定不要]

iv) Helping others was φ second *nature* to the couple. (他人を助けるのはこの夫婦にとって第二の天性だった) (RD 99/7: 97) [聞き手/読み手には同定不可能；下位分類とも解釈可 (☞ 8.9.3)]

v) She won φ first *prize* in the competition. (競争で1位になった) (OALD6) [順序というよりも序列もしくは位置づけ (= 体系内の関係、広義の「働き」) を表す；聞き手/読み手には first prize に関する予備知識がないので同定不可能]

vi) I'm in φ fifth *grade*. (5年生だ) (RD 99/2: 80D) [同上]

vii) a hotel on φ Fifth *Avenue* (5番街のホテル) (OALD6) [符帳；8.7.1.10 [道路] 参照]

2) a/an＋名詞＋関係詞節

指示物を同定しないときは、関係詞節に修飾されても、the はつけられない。次例で a がつけられているのは、聞き手/読み手にとっては handbag は初出であるため、どの handbag か同定できないし、買われたのは複数個のハンドバッグだったかもしれないからである。("a/an＋名詞＋関係詞節"の別例は 4.4.2 参照。)

viii) I was working in a shop that sells handbags and luggage, when a woman came in to return *a handbag* she had purchased a few days earlier. (ハンドバッグやトランクを販売する店で働いていたころ、1人の女性が数日前に購入したハンドバッグを返品しにやってきた) (RD 01/3: 67)

3) *of*-phrase

of-phrase が後続しても聞き手/読み手に同定不可能な場合は、定冠詞はつけられない。

ix) *Memories* of that terrible day are forever engraved on my mind. (あの恐ろしい日の記憶は私の胸にいつまでも刻み込まれている) (OALD5) [聞き手が同定することを話し手は期待していない]

8.1.2 関連語句

ある名詞と関連のある名詞が、初出であるにもかかわらず、the をとることがある。これは、文化的連想 (= 常識) により、その名詞が前方照応に準じて扱われるからである。たとえば、(9, a-b) において、the driver は「事故車の運転手」および「停車中の車の運転手」以外ではありえない。

(9) a. There was an accident here yesterday. A car hit a tree and *the driver* was killed. (昨日ここで事故があった。車が木にぶつかって運

転手が死んだ) (OALD⁵)
    b. Then I saw a car parked by the side of the road. *The driver* was asleep. (そのとき道路脇に停めてある車が見えた。運転手は仮眠中だった) (Berry 1993: 26)

上と同様に，(10) の「床／屋根／濡れ縁」は，A large hut の部分を指す。

(10) Two hours later we reach a clearing. A large hut, about 40 feet long and 20 feet wide, is perched 60 feet up in the trees. The decapitated trunk of a massive banyan tree holds up *the floor*, and *the* thatched *roof* rests on slatted walls lined with bark. A notched climbing pole dangles from *the veranda*. (2時間後，空き地に着く。奥行き40フィート，幅20フィートの大きな小屋が樹上60フィートのところに架けられている。上部を切った，巨大なバニヤントゥリーの幹が床を支え，草ぶき屋根をのせている壁は羽根板がつけてあり，樹皮で裏張りされている。切れ込みを入れた登り棒が濡れ縁から垂れている) (RD 96/10: 30)

8.2 複数構成物

　文脈内了解以外の the の用法への導入として，文脈内了解および文脈外了解のいずれにも当てはまる the から始めたい。すなわち，複数形の名詞部につけられる the である。複数形名詞は，前方照応的でない場合も含め，その内容が同定されれば，the が必要とされる。たとえば，φ two books は A 書と B 書を指しても B 書と C 書を指してもかまわないが，the two books は A 書と B 書のように決まった 2 冊を指す。次の (11, a) の the two boats は先行する文脈から密入者を乗せた船と監視船とを指す。他方，(11, b) の the two horns は，牡鹿の頭には，1 本以下でも 3 本以上でもなく，2 本の角 (?) があるという知識に基づいて同定される。

(11) a. (= III-42) At speeds up to 50 knots, *the* two *boats* played cat and mouse for ten minutes across the Adriatic Sea. (RD 99/10: 104)
    b. antler: each of *the* two *horns* with short branches that grow on the head of a male deer (枝角 = 牡鹿の頭に生える，短い分枝のある，2本の角のそれぞれ) (OALD⁵)

以下，(11, b) のように文脈に依存しないで，つまり，「文化」あるいは「常識」に基づいて，複数形に the がつけられる場合を列挙する。いずれも定冠詞がつけられるのは構成物 [構成員] が同定可能であるためである。(構成物 [構成員] が文化的・常識的に同定可能という点で，8.2 節であげる例は，唯一物 (☞ 8.3.2) が複数形である場合と解すことも可能である。)

8.2.1 年代

年代はいつからいつまでかが容易に同定されるので，early/mid/late に修飾される場合も，the がつけられる。

(12) a. Sandy-haired Alan Stoudemire had first met Boyce Blake one summer day in *the 1950s* when both were about five. (砂色の髪の AS が BB に初めて会ったのは 1950 年代の夏の日であり，2 人とも 5 歳ぐらいだった) (RD 98/10: 26)

b. The Mars of 2150 will be as exuberant as the American Wild West of *the 1870s*. (2150 年の火星は 1870 年代の米西部のように活気にあふれているだろう) (RD 98/7: 103)

c. London-based theatre director and film producer Glen Goei grew up in *the '60s* in post-colonial Singapore ... (L を中心に活動中の舞台監督兼映画製作者の GG は 60 年代に植民地後の S で育った) (RD 01/3: 22)

d. By *the* early *1950s*, many of the newly built hospitals featured premature-infant-care centres, which led to the development of the modern incubator. (1950 年代初期までに，新築された病院の多くは未熟児看護センターに力を入れるようになり，現代の保育器の発達へとつながった) (RD 01/4: 131)

e. During the Cultural Revolution in *the* mid-*1960s*, anything that even remotely smacked of ideas, culture or custom was attacked. (1960 年代中葉の文化大革命のころ，ほんのわずかでも思想的，文化的，慣習的なものは攻撃された) (RD 99/7: 84)

f. With the acquisition of other confectionery companies in *the* late *1980s*, Hershey can now boast of having nine of the top 20 confectionery brands in the United States. (1980 年代後期に他の菓子工場を買収したので，今や H は合衆国で上位 20 のブランド銘菓のうち 9 つを所有していることを誇りとしてよい) (RD 99/7: 143)

8.2.2 一族／一門

一家や一族は，そのメンバー数が有限であり全体を同定可能と判断されるので，the をとる (8.2.3 も同様)。

(13) a. Uncle Cecil had lived near *the Presleys*, and he said that Elvis used to get out in the back yard with his guitar and try to sing, and it would stir up all the dogs on the block. (C 伯父さんはプレスリー一家の近くに住んでいた。彼が言うには，エルヴィスはよくギターを

もって裏庭に出てきて歌おうとして，その地区の犬たちを興奮させたとのことだった）(RD 99/5: 38)

b. By 1901, Azerbaijan was producing 51 percent of the world's oil supply, while *the Nobels* and their competitors, *the Rothschilds*, gained control of most of the European market. (1901年までにAは世界の石油供給の51パーセントを産出していた。他方，N家とその競争相手のR家とは欧州の市場の大部分を牛耳っていた）(RD 99/4: 19)

c. [W]e may have found an undiscovered treasure by *the Seymours* of Boston. (BのS父子作の埋もれていた宝物を発見したのかもしれない）(RD 01/3: 110) [the Seymours = John and Thomas Seymour (指物師の父子)]

d. (= VI-6) With the temperature a cool 10 degrees Celsius, *the Feuchtwangers* now prepared to enter the water. (RD 98/12: 76) [この文脈では家族全体ではなく，F夫妻のみを指す]

NB 2　the X family

「～家」の意味では the X family という表現も可。

Members of *the* Gibson *family* traveled the Hume Highway between Melbourne and Sydney . . . (Gさん一家の人たちはMからSまでのH街道を旅した）(RD 99/5: 118)

8.2.3　グループ名／チーム名

(14) a. On the radio at that time you could hear *the Rolling Stones* side by side with Mozart, Beethoven, Glenn Miller, even the blues. (当時ラジオではMやB，GM，さらにはブルースとならんでRSを聞くことができた）(RD 99/9: 62)

b. *The Beatles* came from the same working-class background as I did. (Bは私と同じ労働者階級という背景の出身だった）(RD 99/9: 62)

c. On the bill were *the Four Seasons*, *the Crystals*, Tommy Roe, Fabian and Chuck Jackson. And *the Thornton Sisters*, this time on the marquee. (プログラムにはFS，C，TR，F&CJの名前があった。TSは今回は大看板に書かれていた）(RD 96/3: 131)

(15) a. The owner of *the Braves* became the team's consummate fan. (Bのオーナーはそのチームの熱烈なファンになった）(RD [U.S. Edition]

98/9: 204)

b. One evening I sat in Miami's Pro Player Stadium watching a baseball game between *the Florida Marlins* and *the New York Mets*. (ある日の夕方, M の PP 野球場に座って F マーリンズと NY メッツとの試合を観た) (RD 99/4: 58)

NB 3
1) 単数形のチーム名
同一チームを指すにもかかわらず, (主として地名を表す) 単数形名詞は無冠詞で用いられる。

  i) Craig Counsell blistered an errant fastball for a home run, the first of five runs the Diamondbacks scored against Mussina in his three innings, and *Arizona* crushed the Yankees in Game 1 of the World Series, 9-1. (CC はすっぽ抜けの速球を強打して本塁打にし, これを口火として D は M [投手] から 5 点を奪って 3 イニングで降板させた。A はワールドシリーズの第 1 戦で Y を 9 対 1 で破った) (NY Times, Oct. 28, 01) [the Arizona Diamondbacks = the Diamondbacks = φ Arizona]

2) グループの 1 人
グループの構成員である 1 人は "a＋単数グループ名" で表す。

  ii) [Stella] McCartney was riled by claims that she got the job because she is the daughter of *a Beatle*. (SM は, ビートルズの 1 員の娘なのでその仕事を得たというクレームに立腹した) (RD 99/5: 89)

チームへの所属は次のように形容詞的に表すことができる。(Cardinals/Cubs ではないことに注意。)

  iii) When the 1998 US baseball season was drawing to a close, the staggering home-run totals of *St Louis Cardinal* Mark McGwire and *Chicago Cub* Sammy Sosa were at the centre of attention. (1998 年の米国の野球シーズンが終わろうとしていたころ, SL カーディナルスのマグワイアと C カブスのソーサとの驚異的な本塁打数が注目の的だった) (RD 00/1: 113)

8.2.4　国民；部族／民族

国民全体, 部族や民族を指す名詞も the をとる。いずれも多数ではあるが,

閉じられた集合体を成すので同定可能だからである。(部族名／民族名を表す語は，しばしば語形は単数形のままで集合的に用いられる。)

(16) a. (= VIII-2) For centuries the Harlech-London stagecoach drove along this route, a road constructed by *the Romans*. (RD 96/10: 13) [全体としてのローマ人を指す；LDOCE³ (s.v., the 4) 参照]

b. *The Vikings* discovered Greenland around 950. (ヴァイキングたちは950年ごろGを発見した) (RD 99/9: 24)

c. On my last day among *the Kalash*, I watch an ancient harvest festival. (K族のなかで過ごす最後の日，千古の収穫祭を観る) (RD 00/4: 107)

d. When Long Wolf was born in the 1830s, life was good for *the Lakota*, a branch of *the Sioux*. (LWが1830年代に生まれたころ，S族の一派であるL族の暮らしはよかった) (RD 98/12: 90) [部族全体]

比較：About 300 *Lakota* died, including women and children. (L族に約300人の死者がでた。そのなかには女性や子供も含まれていた) (RD 98/12: 91) [-s なしで複数形]

e. It is also home to *the pygmy* – one of the world's least understood and most endangered peoples. For thousands of years the pygmies were masters of equatorial Africa. (そこはピグミーの住みかでもある。彼らは，世界で最も理解されておらず，最も危機に瀕している種族である。数千年にわたって，ピグミー[の諸グループ]は赤道直下のアフリカの主だった) (RD 98/12: 105f.)

f. The rebellion of 1959 not only brought an end to Tutsi domination, it set the stage for more enmity and future bloodshed between *the Hutu* and *Tutsi* in the decades to follow. (1959年の反乱はT族の支配に終焉をもたらしただけではなかった。それはその後数十年にわたるH族とT族とのさらなる反目と将来の流血のお膳立てをしたのだった) (RD 00/3: 130) [the が Hutu に先行するので，Tutsi の前では省略]

類例：the Bantu (RD 98/12: 106); the Bardi (RD 00/2: 120); the Bayaka (RD 98/12: 107); the Korowai (RD 96/10: 3); the Maori (RD 99/12: 29); the Moriori (RD 99/12: 28)

NB 4

1) the X tribe/people

初出では "the＋民族名" のあとに tribe/people を補うほうが好まれる。次の例のほうが上の引用 (16, c, f) よりもページ数が若いことに注意されたい。(本章 NB 32-3 [Hotel/Restaurant] も参照。)

  i) But deeper in the mountains, I'm told, there is *the Kalash* tribe, whose resemblance to their supposed European ancestors is even more striking. (だが，聞いたところでは，山奥に K 族がいて，彼らのほうが先祖とされる欧州系にさらにもっと顕著に似ている) (RD 00/4: 104)

  ii) Historically, *the Tutsi* people controlled both Rwanda's government and society and subjugated the Hutus, who made up the majority of the country's population. (歴史的には T 族が R の政治も社会も支配し，その国の人口の大半を占める H 族を従えていた) (RD 00/3: 122)

2) 織田 (2002) は定冠詞の用法を「１つの全体を構成するいくつかの下位部分」(p. 113) という枠組みによって説明する。本書も「春夏秋冬」のように下位部分が少数で，かつ，それぞれが単数であるときは基本的に同書と同じ見解であるが (☞ 8.5)，同書はこの枠組みにこだわりすぎているため，たとえば，iii) においても，

  iii) *The Finns* are fond of sport. (フィンランド人はスポーツが好きだ) [原文には訳なし]

「フィンランド人のほかにスウェーデン人やロシア人のグループが想定されて初めて，定冠詞による特定の国民グループへの指示同定が可能になる」と言う (p. 151)。この説に従えば，the Kalash という民族名に初めて遭遇した場合にも，また，the Pearly Gates (VIII-22, b) のように他の Gates が不明な場合にも，枠組みを構成する他の下位部分を想定しなければならないことになる。むしろ，複数構成物に関しては，本書のように，閉じられた集合体を成すので構成物全体を同定可能だから the をとる，と考えるべきであろう。

8.2.5　大陸／国家／山脈／平原／群島

標記の地域や地形を表す語も，複数形の場合は，the をとる（単数形の「平原」に関しては 8.7.2.1 参照）。

(17) a. A sailor on Columbus's second voyage to *the Americas* wrote of

capsicum chilies that the "Caribs and Indians eat that fruit as we eat apples." (ある船員が、Cの[南北]アメリカ大陸への2度目の航海に同行し、唐辛子に関して「カリブ人やインディアンはその実を我々がリンゴを食べるように食べる」と書いている) (RD 98/3: 90)

b. Pygmies in Rwanda, *the* two *Congos*, the Central African Republic and Gabon are treated harshly. (R, 両コンゴ, 中央アフリカ共和国, およびGのピグミーたちは過酷な扱いをうけている) (RD 98/12: 109)

c. *The Balkans* are a mess. (バルカン諸国は混乱状態だ) (RD 00/1: 100)

d. In 1996 Prince Bernhard of *the Netherlands* awarded Pan the Order of the Golden Ark for his unrelenting efforts in fighting for the panda. (1996年オランダのB王子は、パンダ保護のためのたゆまない努力に対してPにゴールデンアーク勲章を授与した) (RD 00/2: 24)

e. The Arabia had ferried soldiers to *the Dakotas* and carried Mormons on their journey toward the promised land of Utah. (A 丸 [船名]は兵士たちを南北ダコタ州に送り、移動中のモルモン教徒たちをユタの約束の地へと運んだ) (RD 00/1: 92)

(18) a. Let others plumb Loch Ness for its monster or climb *the Himalayas* in search of the snow leopard. (怪獣を求めてN湖を調べたり, ユキヒョウを探しにH山脈に登ったりするのはほかの人たちにさせるがよい) (RD 96/3: 38)

b. On a June morning high in *the Rocky Mountains*, snowy peaks rose before me. (6月のある朝R山脈の高所で雪をいただいた峰が目前にそびえた) (RD [U.S. Edition] 98/9: 113)

c. The camp was perched in some of the most rugged terrain in *the Rockies*. (キャンプはR山脈の1番ごつごつした一帯に設けられた) (RD 98/9: 34)

d. The railway line from Leeds to Manchester crosses *the Pennines*. (LからMに至る鉄道路線はP山脈を横断する) (LDOCE[3])

e. And yet the forests of *the Virungas* act as giant sponges, feeding from the streams and rivers during the dry season. (それでいて、V [中央アフリカの火山地帯]の森林は巨大なスポンジのように活動する。乾期の間に小川や大河から水分を吸い上げるのだ) (RD 00/6: 44)

単数形であるが、Range (山脈) も、「山の集合」('a group of mountains or

hills' [CDAE]) を意味し，構成物の数が限定されるので，the をとる。

  f. The small, single-engine Cessna circled the snow-covered summits of *the Alaska Range*. (小さな，単発のセスナ機は A 山脈の雪におおわれた山頂のまわりを回った) (RD 99/4: 120)　類例 : the Cascade/Pennine Range (LDOAE, CIDE)

(19) a. We do know that *the Great Plains*, the upper Mississippi Valley and the Southwest apparently received more rainfall than now. (たしかにわかっているのは，[米西部の] 大平原，M 上流域，および米国南西部は明らかに現在以上に降雨量があった，ということだ) (RD 99/9: 24) [the Southwest に関しては，8.3.1 参照]

  b. For two weeks we drove through rainforests, over washed-out expanses of *the Rwindi plains*. (2 週間，車を走らせて雨林を抜け，R 平原の荒涼とした広がりを越えた) (RD 00/3: 125) [Rwindi plains は Rwanda の平原 ; plains 小文字は原文]

  c. "Each time I visit *the Killing Fields*, I'm reminded of my mother," Chhang says. (「キリング・フィールズに来るたび，母のことを思い出す」と C は言う) (RD 99/11: 23) [Killing Fields は Khmer Rouge による虐殺の場所]

  d. [The Chinese government] claims to own *the Machu grasslands*. (中国政府は M 草原の所有を主張する) (RD 01/9: 126) [grasslands 小文字は原文]

  e. In the south are *the Guiana Highlands* and related mountain areas, which extend along the border with Brazil. ([ガイアナ] 南部には G 高原およびそれと形成を同じくする山地があり，B との国境にまで延びている) (GME)

  f. Beyond *the Pamirs* lay a desert, and beyond that awaited China. (P 高原のかなたには砂漠があり，そのかなたには中国が待っていた) (RD 02/7: 86) [高原名]

(20) a. Twice the 13th-century emperor Kublai Khan sent ships and troops against *the Japanese islands* and twice the typhoon's onslaught wrecked the invader's fleet. (13 世紀の皇帝フビライ・ハンは 2 度日本列島に軍船と軍隊を送ったが，2 度とも台風の襲来のため侵略側の船団は難破した) (RD 96/10: 49)

  b. *The Spratlys,* a group of more than 100 islets, reefs and shoals, may consist of little more than five square kilometres of land, usually visible only at low tide. (南沙群島は100以上の小島，砂礁，砂州(ś)の集合であり，その土地は5平方キロに足りないかもしれないくらいであり，しかも，ふつう引き潮のときにしか見られない) (RD 00/6: 81) [the Spratly Islands とも言う (RD 00/6: 81)]

c. Some of the best whale-watching areas in Asia are round Pamilacan Island in the central Philippines, along Japan's south coast and in *the Maldives* in the Indian Ocean. (アジアでホエールウオッチングができる1番よい場所としては，中央フィリピンのP島周辺，日本の南岸ぞい，およびインド洋上のM諸島がある) (RD 99/10: 52)

以上の名詞の他に，滝も複数形 (Falls) で用いられるが，Falls には必ずしも the はつけられない。単数一致することからわかるように，複数という概念が希薄なためと判断される (8.7.1.5 参照)。

8.2.6　病名 (5.3 および 8.3.3 も参照)

複数形の病名は，通例，the をとる。症状を総体的にとらえているためと思われる。

(21) a. Later that night David began to feel painful twinges in his elbow and ankles – symptoms of *the bends.* (その夜遅くからDは肘とくるぶしに激痛を感じはじめた。潜水病の症状である) (RD 97/6: 96)

b. Don't be surprised if you get *the blues* for a while after your baby is born. (産後しばらく気がふさいでも驚かなくていい) (LDOCE[3])

c. He's got a bad case of *the DTs.* (ひどく悪酔いした) (CIDE)

d. I've got *the hiccups.* (しゃっくりが出はじめた) (CIDE) [しゃっくりの開始と終了を含意し，総体的にとらえる，または現在出ているしゃっくり;『活用』は「<英>では無冠詞」と注記しているが，英国系の辞書も the をつけている]

比較：You can usually get rid of *hiccups* by drinking water very quickly. (水を一気に飲めば，ふつう，しゃっくりをとめることができる) (CIDE) [しゃっくりという反復運動]

e. He had *the shakes* for 12 days. (12日間も悪寒がした) (RD 98/3: 69)

以下の例文中の病名は現代英語では単数扱いされるので，the は，influenza/flu に先行する the と同様に，流行中の病気であることを表す (5章 NB 6; 8.3.3 参照)。

f. Love is like *the measles*; we all have to go through it. (恋ははしかのようなもの。だれもが通らねばならぬ) [Jerome K. Jerome] [単数一

致]
- 比較：*(The) measles* is much less common in Britain now than it used to be. (今日はしかは英国ではかつてよりずっと減っている) (CIDE) (流行中でない病名に the をつけるのは最近ではまれ) [単数一致]
  - g. He's got *the mumps*. ([流行中の] おたふく風邪にかかった) (CIDE)
- 比較：At 15 months a child is injected with a vaccine against *mumps* and rubella. (15 か月で幼児はおたふく風邪と風疹 [という病気] のワクチン注射をうける) (CIDE)
  - h. Jenner . . . had been impressed by the fact that a person who had suffered an attack of cowpox . . . could not become infected whether by accidental or intentional exposure to *the smallpox*. Pondering this phenomenon Jenner concluded that cowpox not only protected against *smallpox* but could be transmitted from one person to another as a deliberate mechanism of protection. (牛痘にかかった人は，偶然であれ意図的であれ，[流行中の] 天然痘に接してもうつることはありえないという事実が J の脳裏にきざみ込まれていた。この現象を熟考し，牛痘は天然痘 [という病気] を防御するだけでなく，防御の周到なメカニズムとして人から人にうつりうるのだと J は結論した) (EB 01) [複数形として扱われていないため (5 章 NB 6 参照)，流行中以外の病気を指すときは無冠詞]
  - i. get/have *the sniffles*: to get/have a slight cold (鼻風邪をひく = 軽い風邪にかかる) (OALD⁵) [流行中の風邪]
- 比較：I had a cold a couple of weeks ago and it's left me with a bit of *a sniffle*. (2，3 週間前に風邪をひいてまだ少し鼻風邪が残っている) (CIDE) [個別事例]

NB 5

病名が複数形ならば自動的に the をとる，というわけではない。i) はガンの種類が複数であることを表し，ii)–iii) は反復を表す ((21, d) 比較 [hiccups] も参照)。

  - i) Other studies are testing the vitamin's effects on colon, lung and breast *cancers*. (他の研究はビタミン [E] の効果を結腸ガン，肺ガンおよび乳ガンに関して試験中である) (RD 98/11: 48)
  - ii) She went into *convulsions* several hours after the accident and had to be rushed to a hospital. (事故の数時間後に痙攣(けいれん)をお

こし，病院に急送された) (CIDE)

iii) He suffered the head injury when he was 4, and he's been having *seizures* ever since. (4歳のとき頭に外傷をうけ，それ以来発作がある) (CIDE)

8.2.7 その他の複数構成物

(22) a. A few months later, in January 1945, German resistance to *the Allies* finally broke down and Krakow was liberated. (数か月後，1945年1月，ついに連合国軍に対するドイツの抵抗はもちこたえられなくなり，Kは解放された) (RD 96/10: 124) [米・英・仏・中など26か国]

b. Three friends arrive at *the Pearly Gates* at the same time. (3人の友人が同時に天国の門に着く) (RD 99/1: 24) [真珠でできた，天国の12の門]

c. At the siege of Badajoz in Spain during *the Napoleonic Wars*, one George Maclachlan of Britain's 74th Highlanders had his rendition of "The Campbells Are Coming" rudely terminated when a bullet hit his bagpipes. (N戦争のころスペインのBを包囲中，英国第74高地連隊のGMという兵隊が「キャンベルがやってきた」を吹奏していたが，バグパイプに弾丸が命中したため，無礼にも中断された) (RD 99/4: 45f.)

8.3 状況的同定

状況的同定とは文脈外了解の1ケースであり，発話の場面において話題になっている事物を指し示すことが可能な場合を言う。

8.3.1 場面依存

場面・状況からどの指示物が言及されているか聞き手にわかるとき，その名詞は同定可能なので the がつけられる。

(23) a. Please would you pass *the salt*. (塩をとっていただけませんか) (CIDE) [食卓上の塩入れ]

b. I'll pick you up at *the station*. (車で駅に迎えに行こう) (CIDE) [相互に了解された駅]

c. Ella's been complaining about *the traffic* keeping her awake at night. (Eは往来の車のため夜眠れないとこぼしている) (LDOCE[3]) [E宅近辺の交通

小説などでは初出であっても名詞(部)にしばしば the がつけられる。その作品の世界に入って名詞部が指示するものを同定することが読者に期待されているからである。

  d. I was walking in *the park* with a friend recently, and his mobile phone rang, interrupting our conversation. (最近友人と公園を散歩中、彼の携帯電話が鳴り、会話は中断された) (RD 01/3: 33) [書き手または友人の居住地近くの公園]

the West/Southwest, the Far/Middle East など本来は位置を表す固有名詞も、場面・状況から指示物が同定されたものである。(このような、普通名詞の意味を残している固有名詞は「転用固有名詞」と呼ぶのが適切であろう。)

8.3.2 唯一物
8.3.2.1 天体／地点；聖典

従来の文法書でも「唯一物」(unique item) として指摘されている、天体・地点と聖典の例から始めたい。sun/moon/earth/sky; north/south pole などが the とともに用いられるのは、指示物が明白であり、同定可能だからである。

(24) a. *The earth* takes a year to make a circuit of *the sun*. (地球は1年かけて太陽を1周する) (OALD⁵)

  b. *The North Star* is a bright star which can be seen in the northern part of *the sky* almost exactly above *the North Pole*. (北極星とは、北極点のほとんど真上の北の空に見られる、明るい星のことだ) (CIDE)

  c. People who said man would land on *the moon* used to be called dreamers. (人類は月に行くだろうと言った人たちは夢想家と呼ばれた) (OALD⁵)

  d. These discoveries may throw some new light on the origins of *the universe*. (これらの発見は宇宙の起源に新たな光を投げかけるかもしれない) (LDOCE³)

  e. Ursa Major, *the Great Bear* (nicknamed *the Plough* or *the Big Dipper*) is high in the north-east, with its curve pointing downwards. (大熊座、(別名、ひしゃく星、北斗七星)は北東の空にあり、曲がった部分は下に向いている) (BNC, EAW 613)

  f. Antares in *the Scorpion* is also the centre of a line of three, but the colour-difference alone means that there can be no confusion; Antares is fiery red. (さそり座のアンタレスは3つの[星を結ぶ]線の中心でもあるが、色が違うので混同されることはありえない。真っ

赤なのだ）(BNC, EAW 757)
g. From the edge of *the Andromeda Galaxy*, Earth would be seen spinning, orbiting and finally spiraling through *the Milky Way* at an average of 530,000 m.p.h. (アンドロメダ銀河の端からは，地球が自転し，公転し，究極的には天の川のなかを平均時速 53 万マイルで回っているのが見られるだろう）(RD [U.S. Edition] 02/8: 100)
h. And this was still summer in *the Southern Hemisphere*. (しかも，これでも南半球ではまだ夏なのだ）(RD 02/3: 110)
i. Singapore is/lies on *the equator*. (S は赤道上にある）(CIDE)

聖典も，当該の宗教においては唯一物であり，同定可能なので，the をとる。

j. However, this is not the case; neither *the Koran* nor *the Bible* makes any mention of female genital mutilation. (しかし，それは事実ではない。コーランも聖書も女性性器切除に関しては言及していないのだから）(RD 99/10: 143)

NB 6

1) a/an＋修飾語句＋唯一物

　　唯一物に修飾語句がつけられて，唯一物の一時的な姿かたちを表すときは，a/an が選ばれる。

　　i) *A* bright *sun* shone as pall-bearers dressed in traditional clothes carried Long Wolf's coffin a half-mile up a hill to the Wolf Creek Cemetery where some family members are buried. (棺搬送者たちが，[米先住民の] 伝統的な衣装をまとい，LW の棺を担って，父祖の眠る WC 墓地へと丘を半マイル登ったとき，太陽がまぶしく照りそそいだ）(RD 98/12: 94)

　　ii) *A* waning *moon* had turned the muddy waters of Oyster Creek to quicksilver. (十七夜ごろの月に照らされて O 川の泥水は水銀色に変わっていた）(RD 99/3: 43)

2) ラテン語と同形の星座名には冠詞はつかない（上例 (24, e) [Ursa Major] も参照）。

　　iii) I was born under *Scorpio*, so I'm supposed to be cunning and ambitious. (さそり座の生まれなので，狡猾(こうかつ)で野心家だとされている）(CIDE) [(VIII-24, f) [the Scorpion] と比較せよ]

　　iv) He was born under *Aquarius*. (水瓶座の生まれだ）(CIDE)

　　惑星名も無冠詞で用いられる。

v) Is there life on *Mars*? (火星に生命はあるか) (CCED³)

vi) *Saturn* is the second biggest planet in the solar system. (土星は太陽系で 2 番目に大きな惑星だ) (CCED³)

「地球」は，原則的に，惑星の 1 つとしてとらえられるときは φ Earth, 人類が住んでいる，同定可能な星としてとらえられるときは the Earth/earth と表される (小文字の earth に関しては 1.7 参照)。[参考：CCED³ (s.v., earth): 'Earth or the Earth is the planet on which we live. People usually say Earth when they are referring to the planet as part of the universe, and the Earth when they are talking about the planet as the place where we live.']

vii) Heavy elements are essential to make planets like *Earth*, and a star with a stable light output is essential for life. (地球のような惑星を造るには重い元素が不可欠であり，生命には恒常的に光を発する星が不可欠である) (CCED³)

viii) We were not altogether sure that the comet would miss *the Earth*. (彗星(すい せい)が [人類のいる] 地球をそれるとは全面的には確信がなかった) (CCED³)

3) 製本された書物を指すときは Bible/Koran なども不定冠詞をとる。

ix) He was sitting there reading, and of all things, he was reading *a Bible*. (座って読書中だった。それも，聖書を読んでいた) (RD 94/5: 99)

8.3.2.2　競技大会

マラソンやゴルフ，テニスなどの競技大会が the をとるのも，それらが唯一物だからである。(同時に，the は他の大会名から区別する機能も果たしている。)

(25) a. And Grete Waitz won the women's division of *the New York City Marathon* nine times. (GW は NY シティマラソンの女子の部で 9 回優勝した) (RD 99/5: 106)

b. *The Hiroshima Men's Relay* took place on January 18. (1 月 18 日，ひろしま男子駅伝が開催された) (Peter Goldsbury, Chugoku Shimbun, Jan. 23, 98)

c. His first move as a pro was to enter, and win, *the Ontario Open*. (プロとしての最初の活動は O オープンに参加して優勝したことだった) (RD 00/2: 78)

d. He twice won *the Missouri Amateur Championship* and even played in *the US Open* in 1955. ([Payne Stewart は] M アマチュア選手権に2度優勝し，1955年には US オープンでもプレーした) (RD 99/11: 81)
e. China will host *the World Cup* for women. (中国は [2003年に] 女性のW杯を主催することになっている) (RD 02/6: 57)
f. Just two weeks earlier his team had won *the Super Bowl* for the first time. (ほんの2週間前，彼のチームはスーパーボウルに初優勝していた) (RD 98/12: 131)
g. The 1991 season ended with a one-point loss to the University of Colorado in *the Orange Bowl*. (オレンジボウルで C 大学に1点差で破れて1991年のシーズンは終わった) (RD 99/6: 53)
h. In March 1993, before practice for *the Brazilian Grand Prix*, Senna invited me to go fishing on his farm in Brazil. (1993年の3月，ブラジルグランプリの練習前にセナは私を招待してくれて，B の彼の農園内に魚釣りに行った) (RD 99/6: 75)
i. Winning *the Tour de France* last July was the ultimate payoff for 28-year-old Lance Armstrong, only the second American to take first place in the world's greatest bicycle race. (昨年7月のツールドフランスでの優勝は28歳の LA にとって究極の快挙だった。世界最大の自転車競技で米人が1位になったのは彼でやっと2人目なのだ) (RD 00/1: 67)
j. *the Champion Hunter Chase* (チャンピオンハンター競馬大会) (CCED[3])

類例：the California International Marathon (RD 99/5: 83); the Pikes Peak Marathon (RD 99/10: 69; RD [U.S. Edition] 98/9: 91); the Canadian Amateur Open (RD 00/2: 77); the French Open (RD 99/4: 30, 00/4: 78); the Los Angeles Open (RD 00/2: 78); the Qatar Open (RD 00/4: 80); the U.S. Women's Open (RD 99/5: 112)

NB 7　似て非なるもの
1) 次の例文中の大会名に the がつくのは，大会名が複数形であるので，ゲーム数や参加者数が有限であることが含意されているからである (☞ 8.2)。

　　i) They were all tired but still excited about the events they had witnessed that day at *the World Rowing Championships* in Cologne, Germany. (みな疲れてはいたが，その日ドイツのケルンを開催地とする世界漕艇選手権大会の際に見た競技でまだ興奮していた) (RD 00/2: 66)

ii) They proved they were on their way when they met in the finals of *the Lipton Championships* last April. ([Williams 姉妹は] 4月に L [テニス] 大会の決勝戦で対戦したとき，力をつけてきていることを証明した) (RD 00/2: 73)

iii) The next day, unable to hold a club, he withdrew from *the Masters*, humiliated. (翌日，クラブを握ることができず，屈辱のうちにマスターズを途中棄権した) (RD 00/2: 78)

2) 次例で the が要求される直接的な理由は，年代に修飾されているためである。ただし，年代なしでも大会名は the をとる。

iv) [T]hey watched a crowd of brightly clad runners warm up for *the 1998 Boston Marathon*. (派手な服装の1団の走者が1998年のBマラソンにそなえてウオームアップするのを見た) (RD 00/4: 66)

v) I was not looking forward to this race, *the 1994 San Marino Grand Prix*. (このレース，1994年の SM グランプリ，を楽しみにしていたのではない) (RD 99/6: 70)

vi) They were competing in *the 1999 ATP* (Association of Tennis Professionals) *Worldwide Senior Tennis Circuit tournament* in Naples, Florida ... (F州Nでの1999年 ATP 世界シニアテニスサーキットトーナメントで競っていた) (RD 00/4: 75)

8.3.2.3 祭り

(26) a. Among his coups, he foiled a 1981 plot to bomb *the Notting Hill Carnival* and use snipers on roofs overlooking the route. (彼の功績の1つは1981年の陰謀の粉砕である。これは NH カーニバルを爆破し，ルートを見下ろす屋根に狙撃者を置こうとするものだった) (RD 出版年月不明)

b. *The Winter Carnival* (February) and an agricultural fair (August) are annual events. (冬のカーニバル (2月) と農業フェア (8月) とは年中行事である) (EB 01)

c. I'd love to go to *the Cannes Film Festival*. (カンヌ映画祭に行きた

い) (CIDE) [the Cannes festival (小文字表記) とも言う]
- d. *The Venice Film Festival* has always been the showcase of Italian cinema. (ヴェニス映画祭は毎年イタリア映画を公開する場だ) (CIDE)
- e. the annual invasion of teenagers and hippies for *the Glastonbury Pop Festival* (G ポップフェスティバルへの毎年のティーンエージャーやヒッピーの侵入) (LDOCE[3])
- f. The lineup for *the Cambridge Folk Festival* looks really interesting. (C フォークフェスティバルの顔ぶれは本当に面白そうだ) (CIDE)
- g. *the Newport Jazz festival* (N ジャズフェスティバル) (LDOCE[3])
- h. But just try to keep from gaping at *the Twins Days Festival* held each August in Twinburg, Ohio. (だが, O 州 T で毎年 8 月に開かれる双生児の祭典では口をあけっぱなしにならないよう気をつけなさい) (RD [U.S. Edition] 02/8: 120) [無冠詞で Twins Days とも言う]

NB 8　祝日名

　Carnival/Festival をともなわない祝日名は, 通例, 無冠詞で用いられる。
- i) He only sees her at *Christmas* and *Easter*. (彼女に会うのはクリスマスとイースターのときだけだ) (CCED[3])
- ii) The children have promised to give up sweets for *Lent*. (子供たちは四旬節のあいだはお菓子断ちをすると約束した) (CIDE)
- iii) On *May Day* we sat as honoured foreign guests in T'ien-an Men Square. (メーデーに外国人貴賓として天安門広場に座った) (CCED[3])
- iv) Do you observe *Passover*? (過ぎ越しの祭りを祝いますか) (CIDE)
- v) On *Valentine's Day*, 1998, Bobbie woke up with Cheryl's heart. (1998 年のヴァレンタインの日 B は [移植された] C の心臓をもって目覚めた) (RD 00/2: 36) [人名の属格があるので無冠詞]

8.3.2.4　賞

(27) a. I was just enjoying a daydream about winning *the Nobel Prize* for literature. (ノーベル文学賞を受賞するという空想を楽しんでいただけだ) (CIDE)

b. During his final year he won *the Rotary Lombardi Award* as the nation's top university lineman. (最終学年のとき国内最高の学生ラインマンとしてRL賞を受賞した) (RD 99/6: 53)

NB 9
1) a+Prize/Award
   賞の1部門を指すときは，不定冠詞が用いられることもある。
   i) His commitment to non-violence led to *a Nobel peace prize* in 1989. (非暴力への貢献により1989年ノーベル平和賞に輝いた) (CCED³)
   ii) In September 1978 she won *an Emmy* for her role in "Holocaust." (1978年9月「ホロコースト」の演技でエミー賞を受賞した) (RD 00/2: 105)
   iii) For her work in the popular series, Manheim was awarded *an Emmy* for best supporting actress. (人気シリーズの役柄により，Mは最優秀助演女優賞を与えられた) (RD 99/11: 82) [best supporting actress が無冠詞である理由に関しては，3章参照]
2) the Oscar
   次は，授与された特定の小像を指す。
   iv) After accepting *the Oscar*, he raised the statuette. (オスカー像をうけとって，その像を高く掲げた) (RD 99/5: 78)

8.3.2.5 単位

単位を表す名詞とともに the が用いられる場合も (例: to sell by the dozen/pound, to pay by the hour/day/week/month)，唯一物 (= 公認された重量・数・長さの単位) と解釈することが可能である。なぜなら，もしも *to be paid by an hour のように不定冠詞を用いるならば，A店の1時間とB店の1時間とは長さが異なることを含意するからである (以下の b-文と比較の文および IV-57-60 参照)。

(28) a. He moved into an apartment and began drinking, buying liquor by *the case*. (アパートに引っ越しして，ケース単位でアルコールを買って飲むようになった) (RD 98/3: 68)
   b. I work freelance and am paid by *the hour/word*. (フリーランサーとして働いており，1時間/1語いくらで報酬を得ている) (OALD⁵)
   [hour = 60分]

比較：I had to drive eight miles at rush *hour*. (ラッシュアワーに8マイル運転しなければならなかった) (CCED³) [rush hour は60分に限定されてはいない；(IV-57, a) も参照]

c. This cloth is sold by *the metre*. (この布は1メートルいくらで売られる) (LDOCE³)

d. Now he trained two hours a day, five, often six days a week, enjoying the feeling that he was growing stronger, and faster, by *the month*. (1日2時間，1週5日，しばしば6日，トレーニングし，1月経(た)つごとにより強く，より速くなってきているという感じを心地よく思った) (RD 01/5: 86)

e. The fire, drafting through the open window, has erupted through the roof of the cabin and is growing by *the second*. (火は開いた窓を通り抜け，小屋の屋根から吹き出て1秒ごとに大きくなっていく) (RD 97/5: 104)

f. sell eggs by *the dozen*/material by *the yard*/coal by *the ton* (卵をダース単位／生地をヤード単位／石炭をトン単位で販売する) (OALD⁵)

g My car does forty miles to *the gallon*. (私の車は1ガロンで40マイル走る) (OALD⁵)

h. There are 2.54 centimetres to *the inch*. (1インチには2.54cm ある) (OALD⁵)

i. Some analysts predicted that the exchange rate would soon be $2 to *the pound*. (アナリストのなかには，交換レートはやがて1ポンド2ドルになるだろうと予測するものもいた) (CCED³)

j (= IV-164, a) *The metre* is a measure of length. (OALD⁵)

上例 (28, i) が示すように，制度としての通貨単位にも the がつけられる。別例をあげよう。

(29) a. By then, the new European currency, *the euro*, will gradually be supplanting *the franc* and other national currencies – electronic transactions in euros began on January 1, and the new coins and bills will follow in three years' time. (それまでには欧州の新通貨であるユーロが徐々にフランや他の国の通貨に取って代わってきているだろう。ユーロによる電子取引はすでに1月1日に始まっており，3年後には新硬貨および新札が発行されることになっている) (RD 99/2: 59)

b. The stock market crashed, and the value of *the ruble* plummeted.

(株式市場は暴落し，ルーブルの価値が急落した) (RD 99/5: 41)
- c. *The pound* has (been) devalued against *the yen*. (ポンドは円に対して安くなった) (OALD5)
- d. (= IV-236, b) Rumor has it that *the franc* will be devalued soon. (NHD)

8.3.2.6 その他

いくつかは唯一物なのか文化的了解なのか区別困難であるが，これは，本来，the の機能が単一であること——同定可能性を表す——から生じる当然の結果と考えるべきであろう。

(30) a. Some 50,000 sympathisers marched through the streets of Macau in 1966, staging daily demonstrations against the government and *the Catholic Church*. (1966年には約5万人の[文化大革命]賛同者たちがMの通りを行進し，政府とカトリック教会に対して毎日デモを行った) (RD 99/11: 54)

 類例：the Linden Baptist Church (RD 00/5: 128); the Open Door Church (RD 00/2: 126); the Presbyterian church (RD 00/4: 59); the Altnewschul (literally the Old-New Synagogue) (RD 00/4: 58)

- b. Even at the height of *the Depression*, their wages rose from six to 30 shillings a week. (世界大恐慌の最中でさえ彼女たちの賃金は週6シリングから30シリングに上がった) (RD 99/11: 77)
- c. Surfing *the Internet* is fun, but it's also a time waster. (ネットサーフィンは面白いが，時間の無駄でもある) (CCED3) [Internet は，電話回線などでつながれた，閉じられた世界を構成しているので，唯一物扱いされる；(III-104) も参照]
- d. Indeed, for a short time during *the Renaissance*, the Prague Ghetto experienced a relatively peaceful time and became a refuge for Jews escaping from persecution elsewhere. (事実，ルネッサンス期に短期間ながらPのゲットーは比較的穏やかな時期を経験し，よそでの迫害から逃れてくるユダヤ人たちの避難場所となった) (RD 00/4: 59)
- e Degas's painting is emblematic of a basic paradox of life in Iran, 20 years after *the Islamic Revolution*. (D の絵画は，イスラム革命から20年後のイランの生活における基本的逆説を象徴している) (RD 00/6: 106) [(VIII-12, e) [the Cultural Revolution] も参照]
- f. Finally, *the Berlin Wall* fell in November. (ついに，Bの壁は11月に

崩壊した) (RD 96/10: 142)

g. Alexander the Great built a Hellenic empire that reached beyond Afghanistan, just as China extended *the Great Wall* to the fringe of the Taklimakan Desert. (A大王はヘレニック帝国を建設し, それはAの彼方にまで達した。中国がT砂漠の縁にまで万里の長城を伸延させたのと同様だった) (RD 99/1: 68)

h. At the stern deck steering station, I braced myself and used all my 54 kilos to wrestle with the helm, heaving the wheel this way and that as I tried to steer *Orca* east, away from *the Great Barrier Reef*. (船尾デッキの操舵室で足を踏ん張り54キロの全体重を使って舵柄(だ)と格闘した。舵輪をあちらにそしてこちらに動かして, O号をGBRから引き離して東に進めようとした) (RD 99/8: 17)

i. Most tourist attractions, such as l'Arc de Triomphe (*the Lark of Triumph*) and the Hunchback of Notre Dame Cathedral, have a lookout point at the top that you – the tourist – are encouraged to climb via a dark and scary medieval stone staircase containing at least 5789 steps and the skeletons of previous tourists. (ほとんどの観光名所, たとえば, 凱旋門やノートルダムのせむし男の [舞台である] 同寺院, は屋上に展望所があり, 観光客は暗く恐い中世の石の階段を——少なくとも5,789段あり, 昔の観光客の骸骨があるにもかかわらず——登ろうという気になる) (RD 00/4: 14)

j. Then she took me shopping at a boutique on *the Left Bank*, where she picked out half a dozen maternity dresses, stylish as could be. (それから, [セーヌ川] 左岸のブティックに連れていき, この上もなくおしゃれなマタニティドレスを6着選んだ) (RD 99/9: 106)

k. In Europe, the Army has sent some 22,000 soldiers on 49 separate deployments outside their home bases since *the Gulf War* – far more than at any time in *the Cold War*. (欧州では, 米軍は湾岸戦争以来およそ2万2千人の兵隊を自国の基地外の49の別々の基地に配備している。冷戦時代のいかなるときよりもはるかに多い数である) (RD 96/3: 121)

類例: the Arctic/Antarctic; the zenith/nadir; the globe; the Indonesian/Malay Archipelago; the Iron Curtain; the Pentagon; the Vietnam War

ここで, 唯一物が a/an をとる例について考えてみたい。supreme pontiff

(ローマ教皇) は 1 人だけなので, これを唯一物と見ることに異論はないであろう。事実, この語は, (31, a) のように, the をとる。ところが, (31, b) のように, 不定冠詞をとる例も見られる。

(31) a. When the notes of the closing hymn fell silent, *the supreme pontiff* broke with tradition and began to reach out to the people around him. (締めくくりの賛美歌の音色が消えたとき, 教皇は伝統に決別して, まわりの人々に手を伸ばしはじめた) (RD 96/10: 130)

b. It would be exhausting work. Officially, they were supposed to trust in the Holy Spirit, but the cardinals knew the process of electing *a supreme pontiff* called forth all the perseverance, cunning and sometimes even the rancor that human being are capable of. ([新教皇の選出は] 疲労困憊(こんぱい)する仕事になるだろう。公的には, 枢機卿たちは精霊に託すとされている。だが, 彼らも知っているように, 教皇を選出する過程は, ありとあらゆる忍耐, 狡猾さ, さらには, ときとして, 人間なら抱きかねない悪意をも引きだすのだ) (RD 96/10: 127)

文脈からわかるように, a-文の the supreme pontiff は現在在位中の教皇であり, b-文の a supreme pontiff はこれから選ぶ教皇である。言い換えれば, 教皇は, ある時代においては 1 人だけであり唯一物であっても, 歴史的には連綿とつづき複数の教皇がいるので, このような文脈においては不定冠詞をとることが可能となる。冠詞の選択も, 究極的には, 「常識」によって決定されると言ってよい。

8.3.3 流行病 (5.3 および 8.2.6 も参照)

いくつかの病名が the をとるのも状況的にどういう病状か理解されることによる。すなわち, the がつけられる病名は流行性の病気だからである (単数扱いの the measles/smallpox も同様)。なお, 流行性の病気にはすべて the がつけられる, というわけではない。the がつけられる単数形の病名は, 潜伏期間が短く, 罹患(りかん)の原因が容易にわかる場合に限られる。common cold および plague は, 便宜上ここに含めるが, むしろ文化的了解 (「だれでも知っている, あの病気」) と見るほうが適切と思われる。

(32) a. He returned home from service abroad with a nasty dose of *the clap*. (ひどい淋病にかかって海外勤務から帰ってきた) (CIDE)

b. Darby's been in bed with *the flu*. (D は [流行中の] 感冒で寝込んでいた) (LDOCE³)

比較: They're both in bed with *flu*. (2 人とも感冒 [という病気] で寝込んで

　　　　いる) (OALD⁵)
　　c. There's no surefire remedy for *the common cold*. (風邪に対する確実な治療法はない) (CIDE)
　　d. *The plague* was greatly feared in the Middle Ages. (ペストは中世にはとても恐れられた) (OALD⁵)

8.3.4　the＋形容詞／分詞

　the rich/poor, the young/old, the dead/living など "the＋形容詞／分詞" で用いられるタイプの特徴は，名詞が表現されないことである。つまり，指示物が何であるかは，文脈に依存して推測されるのである。指示物が文脈依存であることは，(33) のように指示物が単数のときも複数のときもあること，および，(34) のように，補いうる名詞として people/thing(s) 以外のものも可能であることによって証明される。the young は，日本語に直訳するならば，「若者／若い人たち」というよりも，「若いの」に対応する。

(33) a. *The deceased* left a large sum of money to his children. (死者は子供たちに多額のお金を残した) (LDOCE³) [単数]
　　b. *The accused* was/were acquitted of the charge. (被告は無罪を言い渡された) (OALD⁵) [単数または複数]
　　c. *The military* was/were called in to deal with the riot. (暴動の処理に軍隊が召集された) (OALD⁵) [単数または複数]
　　d. *The rich* get richer and *the poor* get poorer. (富者はより豊かに，貧者はより貧しくなる) (OALD⁵) [複数]
　　e. Alexander/Charles *the Great* (A大王／Ch大帝) [the Great one/King/Emperor と解釈可能]

(34) a. Mothers with babies, *the elderly*, *the disabled* are all fair game. (赤ん坊づれの母親，老人，障害者はみなかっこうのカモだ) (RD 01/7: 55) [the elderly/disabled people]
　　b. I suppose we'll just have to wait for *the inevitable* (= the particular thing that is certain to happen). (不可避 [なことが起こるの] を待つほかなさそうだ) (CIDE) [the inevitable thing]
　　c. Imagination allows us to escape *the predictable*. (想像力により予測可能なことは回避できる) (S. Johnson, quoted in RD 99/12: 99) [the predictable things/events]
　　d. Then Saddam Hussein did *the unthinkable*: he ordered his troops to invade Kuwait. (その後，SH は思いもつかないことをした。軍隊にクエート侵攻を命じたのだ) (RD 99/7: 122) [the unthinkable

thing/action]
    e. Her behaviour is verging on *the manic.* (彼女の行動は狂気の沙汰と紙一重だ) (LDOCE³) [the manic behaviour]
    f. Poultry books say "never interfere" because "no hatch" is often nature's way of ridding a species of *the weak* and *the imperfect.* (鳥に関する本は「かまうな」と書いている。「非孵化(ふか)」は，ふつう，弱いのや欠陥があるのを淘汰する自然の方法だからだ) (RD 99/12: 32) [the weak/imperfect birds]
    g. the survival of *the fittest* (適者生存) [the fittest bioform/living thing]

NB 10
1) 所有格＋形容詞
the の代わりに所有格が用いられることもある。
For Jack Preger, a British physician helping *Calcutta's poor*, the struggle is everything (JP, Cの貧者を救済している英国人医師，にとっては闘いこそがすべてだ) (RD 00/9: 90, caption)
2) the *happy
すべての形容詞が"the＋形容詞"というパタンをとるわけではない。このパタンに関して，Swan (1980, §14.2) は，たとえば，foreign/happy/disgusting は用いられないと述べている。(Swan (1995) ではこの説明は削除されているが，そのような表現法がないという事実には変わりない。)

8.4　文化的了解
前節の状況的同定によって説明されたのは，指示物が，いわば，眼前にある場合の the の用法であった。しかし，同定すべき対象を理解するには語の意味や背景知識が必要とされることもある。以下，そのような場合を指して文化的了解と呼ぶことにしたい。
8.4.1　換喩的同定
8.4.1.1　内面的特徴
「換喩的同定」とは，指示物の属性 (attribute) に焦点を当てる用法である。典型的には，次のような表現に見られる。
(35) a. *The pen* is mightier than *the sword.* (文は武よりも強し) [諺]
    b. She lived in the same village from *the cradle* to *the grave.* (揺りか

ごから墓場まで同じ村で暮らした) (CIDE)

これらの例では pen/sword/cradle/grave の属性のうち，「円筒型である／鉄[青銅]製であり，細長い／乳児を入れる／石で作られている」といった外面的特徴ではなく，「表現行為／武力行使／乳児期／死」といった内面的（もしくは，機能的）特徴が the によって喚起されている．以下，類例をあげる．

c. Rupert took to *the bottle* (= began to drink a lot of alcohol) after his wife died. (細君の死後，R は酒びんに手を伸ばすようになった) (LDOCE[3])

d. In school, you knew if you misbehaved you would get *the cane*. (学校では，ご存じのように，行儀が悪ければ，鞭(むち)[打ちの罰]をくらった) (CCED[3])

e. She's been called the queen of *the catwalk*. (ファッション界の女王と呼ばれている) (CCED[3])

f. Some people think *the Church* (= Christian religious organizations) shouldn't interfere in politics. (教会 [= 宗教界] は政治に介入すべきでないと思う人もいる) (CIDE)

g. He's already been under *the knife* (= had a medical operation) twice this year. (今年すでに 2 回体にメスを入れた) (LDOCE[3])

h. It's hard to be anonymous when you are in *the limelight*. (脚光を浴びているとき匿名でいるのは困難だ) (RD 99/10: 27)

i. I spent 300 days a year on *the road* performing one-nighters, but I had a dream. (1 年に 300 日も巡業して一晩興行を演じたが，夢があった) (RD 00/7: 6)

j. Jim was back in the *spotlight*. (J は注目を浴びる場にもどった) (RD [U.S. Edition] 02/8: 110)

k. It's not a good idea to spend more that [sic; than] three hours at *the wheel* (= driving a vehicle) without a break. (休憩なしで 3 時間以上もハンドルを握るのはいい考えではない) (CIDE)

l. One of China's biggest traffic problems is the bitter clash between the present and the past – between *the automobile* and *the bicycle*. (中国の最大の交通問題の 1 つは，自動車と自転車という現在と過去との激しい衝突である) (RD 98/10: 22) [発明品 (☞ 8.6.3) と解釈することも可能]

換喩的同定は婉曲表現に利用される．

m. "We're both quite shy in *the bedroom*," Larry, 75, explains. (「2 人

とも寝室ではとてもシャイなので」と L, 75 歳, は説明する) (RD 02/3: 134)

n. [T]housands of racehorses are destined for *the slaughterhouse* after their racing days are done. (何千頭もの競走馬は，競走の日々が終われば，と畜場に行く運命にある) (RD [U.S. Edition] 02/8: 26)

8.4.1.2　娯楽

Berry (1993: 43) は娯楽 (entertainment) を表す名詞は the をとると述べ、次の例をあげている。

(36) a. You have seen things. You have been to *the opera, the ballet, the theatre.* (あなたは見聞が広い。オペラにもバレエにも映画にも行っているから)

本書では，この用法は上記の内面的特徴を表す用法と同じものであると考える。なぜなら，(36) は，特定の歌劇／バレエ(曲)／劇場ではなく，歌／踊り／映像による表現行為，つまり，当該の語に内在する表現方法を表すからである。類例：

b. Her ambition is to write for *the screen* (= for television and films). (彼女の大望は銀幕用に [台本を] 書くことだ) (CIDE)

c. Although acting took a back seat as he pursued his corporate career, Cheong says he often longed to return to *the stage*. (会社員として働いていたころ副次的に俳優業をしていたが，舞台に帰りたいと何度も思った，と C は言う) (RD 00/2: 71)

d. Even after stunningly successful film performances, Australian actress Cate Blanchett is always happy to return to *the theatre*. (映画の演技ですばらしい成功を収めたあとでさえ，豪の女優 CB はいつも喜々として芝居に戻る) (RD 00/7: 20)

e. It was February 23, 1996, a Friday night, and Margaux was going to *the movies* at the mall with a friend, Crystal Cordes. (1996 年 2 月 23 日，金曜日の夜，M は友人の CC と映画を見に繁華街に行くところだった) (RD 98/12: 34)

NB 11

娯楽などの形式あるいはジャンルを表すときは無冠詞で用いられる (2.2; (II-89) [opera] 参照)。

Before long, Ora and about 40 other kids were coming every day after school for tutoring and lessons in *art, ceramics, photography, dance* and *theater*. (間もなく O といっしょに 40 人ぐ

らいの子供が毎日放課後やってきて，美術，陶芸，写真，ダンス，芝居の個人指導とレッスンをうけた）(RD 98/6: 108)

8.4.1.3　タイプ：play the clown

典型的な役割，つまり，プロトタイプ，が演じられるとき，act/play は "the ＋名詞" を従える。"play ϕ 名詞"（☞ 3.4）においては「役割」に重点が置かれているのに対し，"play the 名詞" においては，だれもが連想する，特定の「特徴」(＝プロトタイプ) に重点が置かれる。(注：プロトタイプ ＝ ある意味範疇に属するもののうち，典型的・中心的と考えられるもの。(広辞苑))

(37) a. In those days, the first baseman on a team in the Negro League often played *the clown*. (当時黒人リーグに所属するチームの1塁手は道化を演じることがよくあった) (CCED³)
   b. Stop acting *the fool*, I'm trying to talk to you. (ばかな真似はやめろ。話し合おうとしているのだ) (CIDE)
   c. That woman there, she is playing *the lady*. (あそこの女性，彼女は淑女を気取っている) (RD 97/2: 99)
   d. (＝ II-122, a) The *Rules* advised modest dress, and undue attention to appearance was deplored: "Play not *the peacock*." (RD 99/2: 114)

8.4.1.4　タイプ：the perfect pizza

名詞部が ideal/perfect などを含むときは，しばしば the をとる。形容詞によりプロトタイプが喚起されるからである。

(38) a. Borkowski has been bitten and scratched by a wider variety of animals than *the* average *vet*. (B は平均的獣医よりももっと多種多様な動物に噛まれたり引っかかれたりしている) (RD 00/9: 131)
   b. She was *the* ideal *American teenager*, both on and off screen. (スクリーン上でもスクリーンを離れても，アメリカの理想的ティーンエージャーだった) (CCED³)
   c. As more and more students seek out the secrets of *the* perfect *pizza*, the Neapolitans are planning a "Pizza University," with intensive on-the-job training at the city's historic pizzerias. (より多くの研究家が完璧なピザの秘密を見つけだすにつれて，ナポリの人たちは「ピザ大学」を計画している。ナポリの歴史的ピザ店で集中的な現場訓練をともなうものである) (RD 99/2: 96)
   d. Pick up *the* typical *celebrity magazine* and you'll read this about Mel Gibson: (典型的な芸能雑誌を手に取れば，MG に関して次のよう

な記事を読むだろう）(RD 98/11: 39)

このタイプでは the は名詞の属性というよりも名詞部全体の属性に関してつけられることに注意されたい。すなわち、the は pizza の特徴ではなく、perfect pizza の特徴を同定するのである。しばしば斜字体で書かれる「強調の the」も、通例、名詞部全体の特徴を同定する。

(39) a. Harry's Bar is *the place* to go. (H のバーは行くのに最適な場所だ) (CIDE)
　　 b. Camden Market is *the place* to be on a Saturday or Sunday. (CM こそ土日に行く場所だ) (CCED³)
　　 c. "Most of us in the field consider him *the expert* on rhinovirus colds," says Dr Robert Couch . . . (「この分野にいるほとんどの者は彼こそライノウイルス風邪の第一人者だと思っています」と RC 博士は言う) (RD 01/11: 72) [*the* 斜字体は原文]

ちなみに、perfect など上記の形容詞を含む名詞部が多数のうちの1つを表すときは a/an がつけられる。

(40) a. the size and composition of *an* average *class* (平均的なクラスのサイズと構成) (OALD⁶) [任意の平均的クラス]
　　 b. At first he seemed to be *an* ideal *husband*. (最初のうちは理想的な夫のように見えた) (CIDE)
　　 c. A spider had spun *a* perfect *web* outside the window. (クモが窓の外に完璧な巣を張った) (OALD⁶)
　　 d. She's *a* typical *Taurus*. (典型的な牡牛座の女だ) (CIDE)
　　 比較：She was the incarnation of perfect *wisdom*. (完璧な智慧の化身だった) (LDOCE³) [抽象名詞が後続するときは無冠詞]

8.4.1.5　タイプ：the Mona Liza

有名な固有名詞が the をとることがあるのは、その固有名詞がなんらかの属性を獲得し、語と指示物との関係が先に述べた図2から図1へと変化したためである。(☞ 1.2)。

(41) a. "Apparently Paul McCartney's singing at the club tonight." "Not *the Paul McCartney* surely!" (「どうも今晩 PM がクラブで歌うらしい」「絶対あの［ビートルズのメンバーの］PM ではないよね」) (LDOCE³)
　　 b. 'Olympia is in America, where K Records was founded.' 'No! Surely you don't mean THE K Records?' (「O は米国内にあり、KR が設立された場所だ」「ウソッ、まさかあの［インターネット音楽店

の] KR のことではないだろう」) (CCED³) [K Records に関しては http://www.kpunk.com/ 参照)

    c. You cannot paint *the "Mona Lisa"* by assigning one dab each to a thousand painters. (千人の画家に一刷毛(ひとはけ)ずつ割り当てて「モナリザ」[に匹敵する名画] が描けるわけではない) (William Buckley, Jr. quoted in RD 00/5: 81)

8.4.2 その他の文化的了解
8.4.2.1 同格

Edward the Confessor (E 告解王) のような同格の名詞句に the がつけられるのは，その名詞句を典型的代表 (= プロトタイプ) として提示するためであると解釈してさしつかえない。

(42) a. The Berkeleys must be considered the oldest hunting family in England, as there have been hounds kept at Berkeley Castle in Gloucestershire since Roger Berkeley was given the land by William *the Conqueror*. (B 家が英国で狩猟を職業とする最も古い一家だと想定されなければならない。RB が征服王 W から土地を与えられて以来 G 州の B 城ではずっと猟犬が飼われているからである) (CCED³)

    b. Alexander *the Great* ruled over a large empire. (A 大王は大帝国を支配した) (LDOCE³) [the Great (King) に関しては 8.3.4 参照]

類例： Charles the Bold (勇胆公シャルル); King Alfred the Great (A 大王); Julian the Apostate (背教者ユリアヌス); a barefoot St. John the Baptist (裸足の洗礼者聖ヨハネ [の像]) (RD 96/3: 88)

文化的に有名でない場合にもこのパタンが用いられ，the をともなう同格語句がその類の代表として説明的に付加される。

(43) a. But when it ran into a problem at its new Year 2000 missile-warning centre, it turned to Misty *the ferret*. (だが, [米宇宙司令本部は] 新 2000 年問題ミサイル警報センターの問題に直面すると，白イタチの M に任務を依存した) (RD 00/3: 89)

    b. Hammie *the hamster* had crawled inside our bathroom wall. (ハムスターの H はわが家の風呂の壁に入りこんでいた) (RD 00/1: 37)

    c. They had transformed me. Instead of Waris *the maid*, I was Waris *the model*. (私は変身していた。私はメードの W ではなく，モデルの W になっていた) (RD 99/10: 133)

    d. One day, Lynch recalls, "I found myself in my office looking at

Shakey *the Robot* firmly blocking my exit ..."(ある日，Lは思いだして言う，「事務所にいてロボットのSが私の出口をすっかり塞いでいるのを見つめていた」)(RD 99/10: 42)

 e. Once there was a little cheat called *Crooky the Goblin*. (昔々小さなごまかし屋がいて，こそどろ小鬼と呼ばれていました) (Blyton, "The Enchanted Button")

同格語句が主要部より前に置かれることもある。

(44) a. *The co-author of Eccentrics*, Weeks, a genial man of about 50, described his study as an effort to examine a phenomenon that science had never paid much attention to. (『奇人』の共著者のW，50歳くらいの気さくな男，が述べるところでは，彼の研究は科学があまり注意を払ったことのない現象を検討するための努力だ) (RD 99/9: 115)

 b. One fine May morning in 1819, *the poet* John Keats sat under a tree in a north London garden and wrote his great ode to the "immortal bird" in two or three hours. (1819年のある晴れた5月の朝，詩人のキーツはL北部の庭園の木の下に座って，2, 3時間で「不滅の鳥」によせるオードの名作を書いた) (RD 97/5: 67)

類例：The Reverend John-Paul Tan (RD 97/5: 25); the Ayatollah Khomeini (RD 00/4: 77); the Prophet Muhammad (NY Times, Nov. 13, 01)

同格語句が同定可能で，かつ主要部または同格語句が長い場合は，通例，"the ＋同格語句" の前後をコンマで囲む。

(45) a. Charles Ewing, *the psychologist*, had seen Waneta a total of 21 hours. (心理学者のCEは全部で21時間Wと面接をした) (RD 99/2: 137) [主要部が full name]

 b. Adam Sapieha, *the metropolitan bishop* of Krakow, was a patrician, a patriot and a politician. (AS，Kの首都大司教，は貴族，愛国者，政治家だった) (RD 96/10: 123)

 c. Thelma Schneider, *the head nurse*, took Molly from her mother's arms and smiled serenely, an offer of comfort from one mother to another. (看護師長のTSは母親の腕からMをとって，穏やかに微笑んだ．母親から母親へ安心感を与える行為である) (RD 99/2: 123)

 d. Twelve miles west of the Harbour Bridge is Homebush Bay, *the main site* for the Sydney Olympics in September 2000. (H橋の12

マイル西に HB がある。2000 年 9 月の S オリンピックの主会場である）(RD 99/3: 77)

上例に対し，主要部に関して，地位・機能（つまり，「働き」）よりも個体として補足するときは，同格語句は a/an をとる。

(46) a. "Curitiba is a model for the first world, not just for the third," says Michael Cohen, *a senior advisor* to the World Bank in Washington, D.C. (「C は第 3 世界だけでなく，第 1 世界でもモデルだ」と MC, W 州の世界銀行の主席顧問，は言う) (RD 98/6: 60)
  b. I started taking Proscar, *a drug* intended to shrink the prostate. (P を摂りはじめた。前立腺を縮小させるための薬である) (RD 97/5: 129)
  c. But I am in Cabramatta, *a suburb* of Sydney. (ところが，私は S の郊外の C にいる) (RD 99/3: 72)
  d. Then he spoke to John Walker, *a special agent* with the South Dakota Division of Criminal Investigation and *an expert* in thermal imagery. (それから彼は JW に話しかけた。彼は犯罪捜査 SD 支部の特別職員であり，放熱像の専門家である) (RD 99/2: 110)

> **NB 12** a/an つき名詞部＋主要部
> 次の例は同格語句が主要部に先行しているように見えるかもしれないが，being の省略と考えるほうが妥当であろう。
> *A self-made man*, Kwok-Chi Tam was the first in his family to get a university education. (KCT は独学の人であり，彼の一族では最初に大学教育をうけた) (RD 99/3: 5) [(He being) a self-made man, . . .]

同格語句が主要部の「働き」を補足するときは，無冠詞で用いられる。

(47) a. John Gottman, *author* of Why Marriages Succeed or Fail (JG,『なぜ結婚は成功または失敗するか』の著者) (RD 99/1: 115) [主要部の業績を補足]
  b. Stanford, J. Newman, *chairman* of J. C. Newman Cigar Co. (SJN, JCN 葉巻会社会長) (RD 99/3: 56) [地位・身分]
  c. Dr. Adriane Fugh-Berman, *chairperson* of the U.S. National Women's Health Network, (AFB 博士，合衆国女性健康ネットワーク会長) (RD 99/3: 115)
  d. Dr. Robert Voy, former medical *chief* for the U.S. Olympic Com-

mittee (USOC) (RV 博士，合衆国五輪委員会前医学主任) (RD 96/10: 24)
  e. Hun Sarin, *dean* of the music department at the city's University of Fine Arts (HS, 市立の芸術大学の音楽学科長) (RD 99/2: 29)
  f. Jim Riggleman, *manager* of the Chicago Cubs baseball team (JR, CC 野球チーム監督) (RD 99/4: 107)

次例が無冠詞であるのは，同格語句が「関係」(「働き」の下位区分) を表すからである。

(48) a. On June 11, 1889, Raffaele Esposito was invited to cook pizza for Queen Margherita, *wife* of King Umberto of the newly unified kingdom of Italy. (1889 年 6 月 11 日 RE は M 女王にピザをつくるため招待された。彼女は新しく統一されたイタリア王国の U 王の妃だった) (RD 99/2: 94) [a をつければ妃が複数いたことになる]
  b. "But you can be indoors for only so long," says Geoff Carroll, *father* of two boys, nine and three. (「だが，屋内にいることができる時間はその程度だ」と GC，9 歳と 3 歳の 2 人の少年の父親，は言う) (RD 99/3: 14)
  c. The child is *father* of/to the man. (子供は成人の父) (Wordsworth) [原文では of であるが，father が関係を表すので前置詞はしばしば to が用いられる；(III-26) 参照]

次の例が無冠詞であるのは，文学史上の業績という「働き」を表すためであるが，同時に，a/an をつけるには主要部があまりにも有名であり，だからといって，すべてに the をつけるのは断定的すぎるという意味的・文体的理由もあるであろう。

(49) The patient was Edgar Allan Poe, *poet* and *author*, *master* of the macabre, *inventor* of the modern detective story, *creator* of one of the world's best-known poems, "The Raven." (その患者は E. A. ポーだった。詩人であり文筆家，怪奇作品の巨匠，現代探偵小説の創案者，世界でも最もよく知られた詩の 1 つ，『大鴉』，の創作者である) (RD 99/11: 60)

8.4.2.2 ダンス名／泳法名

ダンスは振りつけが定まっているので，通例，the をとる。

(50) a. I tell her *the fox-trot*, waltz and swing. (彼女にフォックストロット，ワルツ，スイング [に興味がある] と答える) (RD 00/4: 110) [ダンス名が連続するので後 2 者の前では the 省略]

b. *The waltz* would be easy, *the cha-cha* a bit complicated, *the swing* hard, and *the tango* – ah, *the tango*. (ワルツは簡単で，チャチャはちょっと複雑で，スイングはむずかしくて，そしてタンゴは，ああ，タンゴは [愛のダンスだ]) (RD 01/7: 35)
c. Her father taught her how to dance *the polka*. (父親は彼女にポルカの踊り方を教えた) (CIDE)
d. dance/do *the rumba* (ルンバを踊る) (OALD5)
e. She waterskied, she danced *the twist*, and she listened to the bossa nova on her White House hi-fi. ([Jackie は] 水上スキーをし，ツイストを踊り，大統領官邸のハイファイでボサノバを聴いた) (RD 01/12: 47)

NB 13　a/an＋ダンス名
　１曲分の踊り（またはダンス音楽）を指すときはダンス名に不定冠詞がつけられる。
　　We start with *a waltz*, followed by *a fox-trot* and *a swing*. (ワルツから始め，次にフォックストロット，それからスイングだ) (RD 00/4: 111)

文法書で指摘されたことはないが，泳法にも the がつけられる。正式な泳ぎ方ならば，手足などの動きが決まっているからである。

(51) a. Jimmy likes *the backstroke* because he doesn't like to put his face in the water. (J は顔を水に浸けたくないので背泳が好きだ) (NTC)
b. Jane did *the breaststroke* so she wouldn't get her hair wet. (J は髪を濡らさないように平泳ぎで泳いだ) (NTC)
c. I could never do *the butterfly*. (バタフライはどうしてもできなかった) (CCED1)
d. Can you do *the crawl*? (クロールができますか) (OALD5)

NB 14　φ 泳法名
　〈英〉では泳法名には the がつかないことがある。the の有無は，意味的相違よりも，文体的相違に関与している。すなわち，無冠詞のほうが口語的である。
　　i) When I get to the next one, I'll start swimming *backstroke*. At the one after that, I'll rest, take a break, then switch to

       breaststroke.(次[のカニ捕りの罠かご]に着いたら，背泳ぎで泳ごう。その次では休もう。休憩して，そのあとは平泳ぎに切り替えよう) (RD 00/3: 71)

   ii) Can you do *(the) backstroke*? (背泳ぎができますか) (CIDE)

   iii) do *(the) breaststroke* (平泳ぎで泳ぐ) (OALD[5])

   iv) *Butterfly* is the only stroke I can't do. (バタフライは私に唯一できない泳法だ) (OALD[6])

8.5 対立

8.5.1 二項対立

　in the light/dark, in the right/wrong などにおける名詞は同定不可能であるように思われるかもしれない。しかし，これらの表現は二項対立を成しているので，一方は他方との対立において，つまり，他方を排除することによって，同定可能となる。(52) は文脈内で二項対立が明示されている例である。

(52) a. To learn from the old, we must love them – not just in *the abstract* but in *the flesh* – beside us in our homes, businesses and churches. (老人から学ぶためには，自宅や職場や教会で身のまわりにいる老人を愛さねばならない。抽象的にだけでなく生身の人間として) (RD 99/11: 64)

   b. In one class, an older professor was having difficulty controlling some boys sitting in *the back* who were making a racket. As usual, the girls were quietly seated in *the front*. After a particularly loud noise, the professor angrily yelled, "The pants at *the back* come down and skirts in *the front* go up!" (ある授業で年輩の教授が，後ろに座って騒いでいる男子たちを従わせるのに苦労していた。いつものように，女子は前に座って静かにしていた。特にうるさかったとき，教授は怒って叫んだ。「後ろのズボンは出てきて，前のスカートはさがりなさい」) (RD 99/11: 65)

   c. What the wise do in *the beginning*, fools do in *the end*. (賢者が最初にすることを愚者は最後にする) (Warren Buffett, quoted in RD 98/11: 37)

   d. The work was good for *the career*, but bad for *the soul*. (その仕事は経歴にはよかったが，精神的には悪かった) (RD 00/6: 5)

   e. He had cut away every bit of visible tumor, and it appeared that Dorothy was in *the low-risk category*. [...] Now she was in *the*

  high-risk category.（目に見える腫瘍はすべて切除していたので，D は
  ローリスクの範疇内だと思われた。今や彼女はハイリスクの範疇内だ
  った）(RD 99/3: 19)
 f. Michelangelo died at nearly 90 in 1564, a creative genius and a
  savvy executive, a man equally at home in *the mundane* and *the
  sublime.*（M は 1564 年に 90 歳近くで亡くなった。創造的天才であり，
  やり手の管理職でもあり，通俗にも崇高にも同様に通じた人だった）
  (RD 97/6: 106)

次の例ではペアの他方は明記されてはいない。

(53) a. Death is easier to bear in *the abstract.*（死は抽象的には堪えやすい）
  (RD 99/11: 63) [in the concrete/flesh と対立]
 b. I tried to look on *the bright side.*（明るい面を見ようとした）(RD
  98/6: 135)
 c. On Alaska's Bering Sea, a crab fisherman works 20 frantic hours
  at a stretch, mostly in *the dark.*（A の B 海ではカニ漁師は，たいて
  い暗闇のなかで，20 時間連続で一心不乱に働く）(RD 99/2: 72)
 d. Certain types of crime seem to be on *the decrease.*（ある種の犯罪は
  減りつつあるようだ）(OALD[5])
 e. Kibo looms in *the distance.*（遠くに K 峰が見えてくる）(RD 99/11:
  72)
 f. Diseases like TB and pneumonia are on *the increase.*（結核や肺炎
  のような病気が増えている）(LDOCE[3])
 g. Giuliani's welfare reforms were not popular on *the political left*,
  and his "workfare" programme was compared to slavery. (G [前市
  長] の福祉改革は政治的左翼側には不評であり，彼の「勤労福祉」プ
  ログラムは奴隷制にたとえられた）(RD 99/7: 74)
 h. The word 'teeth' is plural – in *the singular* it's 'tooth'. ('teeth' とい
  う語は複数だ——単数では 'tooth' だ) (CIDE)
 i. But in the hit TV show "The Practice," her role is exactly that – the
  feisty Ellenor Frutt, a lawyer who fights for *the underdog* and has
  romantic relationships. (TV のヒット番組の『ザ・プラクティス』[ボ
  ストン弁護士ファイル] では, 彼女の役はまさにそれだ。決然たる EF，
  つまり，弱者のために闘い，ロマンチックな関係もある弁護士役であ
  る) (RD 99/11: 81) [the topdog と対立]
 j. "I think you had *the wrong name*," I informed him.（「名前をお間違

いだと思います」と彼に教えた) (RD 00/7: 7) [間違いの名前は多々あるが, the correct/right name と対立させて the wrong name を用いる。類例: (have) the wrong number]

NB 15

1) in the night は, in the day(time) と対立を成して1日の区分としての「夜間」に力点が置かれ, at night は夜の「働き」(=暗闇) を表すので, 「夜陰」に力点が置かれる。

   i) She was ill *in the night*. (夜のあいだ具合が悪かった) (OALD5)

   ii) Bats and owls generally hunt *at night*. (コウモリやフクロウは一般的に夜陰に乗じて獲物を捕る) (CIDE)

2) 一方向の二項対立

いくつかの語では対立する表現が明白でない。

iii) Several metres above me, Graham Ussher, a 26-year-old University of Auckland ecologist, is negotiating a tangle of branches in *the moonlight*. (私より数メートル上にいる, A大学の26歳の生態系学者, GUは月光の中, 絡まった枝を乗り越えている) (RD 99/11: 108) [反意表現は in φ daylight]

iv) These felons may still be on *the run*, but starting now they will find it harder to hide. (これらの凶悪犯たちはまだ逃走中であるかもしれないが, 今後は隠れるのは困難になるだろう) (RD 99/10: 5) [反意表現は in φ custody]

v) "In *the wild*, the eggs swell as they absorb moisture from the soil, helping to hydrate the embryo," says Nelson. (「野生では卵は土中の湿気を吸収して膨らみ, 胚に水分を供給する」とNは言う) (RD 99/11: 110) [反意表現は in the brooder/poultry house/ chicken coop など]

次は三項対立の例である。

(54) a. If we establish officially that these shameful acts did happen, we might help clean up high-level sport in *the future*. (このような恥ずべき行為が実際に起こったと公式に認めるならば, 将来ハイレベルのスポーツを浄化するのに役立つかもしれない) (RD 99/11: 96) [past/present/future] (特に<米>;<英>では, 通例, in future. Cf. OALD6, s.v., future (idioms); CCED3, s.v., future 7)

b. Before we left our home in Jerusalem, her obstetrician had given her *the green light* to fly overseas. (J の自宅を出る前，飛行機で海外に飛ぶことに産科医からゴーサインを得ていた) (RD 99/9: 106) [green/yellow/red]

Quirk et al. (1985: 279) によると，(55) の The winter は暦の上での冬を指し，(56) の Winter は気候を表す。この相違の理由に関して彼らの説明はないが，本書の考えでは，「対立」対「働き」という区別により説明可能である。すなわち，(55) では winter は spring/summer/autumn との四項対立においてとらえられ期間が画定されているのに対し，(56) では，winter と他の季節との対比は考慮されず，冬の寒さに力点が置かれているのである。

(55) *The winter* in 1963 was an exciting time. (1963 年の冬期は胸がときめくひとときだった)

(56) *Winter* in 1963 was an exciting time. (1963 年の厳冬は胸がときめくひとときだった) [1963 年 (= 昭和 38 年) は日本では三八(さんぱち)豪雪の年として知られる]

上の考えにそって，次の 2 例における the の有無の理由を考えてみよう。

(57) My friend Mike and I were home from university for *the summer*. (友人の M と私とは夏休みで大学から帰省していた) (RD 99/5: 47)

(58) Sperm whales visit in *summer* and *autumn*. (マッコウクジラは夏から秋にやってくる) (RD 99/10: 52)

(57) の例では夏期休暇中に帰省したのだから，期間を表すために the が必要である。もしも the がなければ，休みとは関係なく，暑さを求めて帰ったことになる。他方，(58) では，クジラは，暦とは無関係に，水温に従って回遊するのだから，the は不要である。

8.5.2 身体部位

二項（あるいは多項）対立という観点に立てば，身体部位につけられる the の用法も他の部位との対立を表すと解釈される。この解釈は，(59, e) のように，複数の部位に関しても "the＋単数形" が用いられるという事実によって支持される。この例では，the knee は「腿(もも)」(thigh) あるいは「脛(すね)」(shin) との対立においてとらえられているのであり，「両足の膝」であることは文脈および人間には 2 つ膝があるという常識に基づいて推論されるのである。

(59) a. The cause of incontinence can lie anywhere in the body's complex waste-disposal system: in *the bladder* and the muscle that controls it; *the urethra*, the tube that takes urine away from *the bladder*; *the urethral sphincter*, a valve-like mechanism that opens and

closes *the bladder outlet*; the pelvic floor muscles that support *the bladder*; or the spinal nerve pathways that carry signals between bladder and brain. (失禁の原因は人体の複雑な排泄組織のどこにでもありうる。膀胱とそれを制御する筋肉；尿道，すなわち，膀胱から尿を運ぶ管；括約筋，すなわち，膀胱の出口を開閉する弁のような装置；膀胱を支える骨盤底筋；それに，膀胱から大脳にシグナルを伝達する脊髄神経路）(RD 99/11: 101f.)

b. Kitty had malignant tumours in *the retina*, the inner lining of *the eye*, which receives images formed by the lens and transmits them through *the optic nerve* to *the brain*. (K は網膜に悪性腫瘍があった。網膜は，眼の内部の膜であり，レンズで作られた像をうけとって，視神経をとおして大脳に伝える) (RD 00/7: 26)

c. She carefully isolates *the crucial phrenic nerve* from *the pericardium*, then enters the sac, releasing the fluid that has been compressing *the heart*. (注意深く十字横隔神経を心膜から分離し，囊を挿入し，心臓を圧迫していた液体を出す) (RD 99/9: 82)

d. (= V-60) Heartburn is felt in *the chest* and sometimes *the throat*. (RD 01/7: 80)

e. Both legs had to be amputated near *the knee*. (両足ともひざ近くで切断されねばならなかった) (RD 01/9: 5)

上の諸例のように，身体部位に the がつけられることが理解されるならば，pat one on the shoulder のような表現における the も対立から生じることが理解されるであろう。すなわち，the の用法に関する限り，このパタンは「(頭や背中ではなく) 肩を軽くたたく」の意味であり，the が his の代用をしているのではない。((60, a) の the = his という書き換えは外国人や初心者用の便宜的な説明にすぎないことを心得ておかなければならない。)

(60) a. She hit him on *the* (= his) *ear*. (彼女は彼の耳をたたいた) (LDOCE[3])

b. One hit Zora square in *the face*, and Chris saw a tear roll down her cheek. (1つ[の雪の玉] がまともにZの顔に当たり，Cは涙が頬をつたうのを見た) (RD 99/6: 51)

c. Later, Patricia claps me on *the back* and says, "Good job, for an idiot." (あとで，P は背中をたたいて言う，「よくやったじゃない，アホにしては」) (RD 98/5: 133)

d. He had been shot in *the head* and chest. (頭と胸を撃たれていた) (RD 99/10: 22) [最初の身体部位にのみ the]

e. Despite his slight stature, the 13-year-old ran at the creature and kicked it in *the face*. (小柄ではあるが，13歳児はその生物 [クマ] に駆けより，顔を蹴った) (RD 99/9: 71)
f. I took her by *the shoulders*. (彼女の両肩をつかんだ) (RD 01/8: 59)
g. Gangs operating on the local buses feel no compunction about shooting recalcitrant passengers in *the head*. (地元のバスを襲うギャングたちは抵抗する乗客に対しては呵責(かしゃく)の念もなく頭に銃弾を撃ち込む) (RD 98/3: 112) [V＋pl.＋in＋sg.]
h. Then, recalling that the snout is the bear's most sensitive spot, she gave the grizzly a swift, solid kick in *the nose*. (それから，鼻がクマの最大の弱点だということを思い出して，グリズリーの鼻を素速くしたたかに蹴った) (RD 97/5: 33) [V＋IO＋DO＋prep-phrase]
i. Joce-Lyne Grand'Maison, a 44 year-old journalist at the *Journal de Quebec*, whose love of the esoteric earned her two bullets in *the head*. (JLGM, 44 歳，Q 誌勤務のジャーナリスト，秘儀への好奇心のため頭部に 2 発被弾) (RD 98/3: 33) [V＋IO＋DO＋prep-phrase]
j. The patient, Tom Long, had been stabbed in *the heart*, stomach and spleen during a domestic dispute. (患者の TL は，家庭争議中に心臓，胃，脾臓(ひぞう)を刺されていた) (RD 01/9: 99) [最初の身体部位にのみ the]

NB 16　タイプ：pat one's shoulder
　所有格を用いる表現も頻度は高い。意味的には，pat one on the shoulder は「人」に，pat one's shoulder は「身体の部分」に力点を置いた言い方である（安藤 1969: 25）。
　　i) My crewmate James Frank reaches over and pats *my* shoulder encouragingly before I move forward. (同僚の乗務員の JF が手を伸ばして，私が前進する前に，励ますように肩をポンとたたく) (RD 98/5: 135)
　　ii) Someone grabs *my* shoulder and I turn to see another chief, his white helmet gleaming against the flames, beckoning. (だれかが私の肩をつかむので振り向いて見ると，別の上司が，白いヘルメットを炎に光らせながら，手招きをしている) (RD 98/5: 140)
　　iii) The woman kept running her hands down the man's arms and massaging his shoulders and neck while kissing *his* ear. (女は，

両手で彼の両腕をなで，両肩と首を揉みつづけながら，男の耳に口づけをしていた) (RD 00/7: 7)

iv) With a strength born of anger, he smashed at *the bear's* head, all the while screaming for help. (怒りから生じた力でもって彼はクマの頭を殴りつけ，その間ずっと大声で助けを求めた) (RD 99/9: 71)

下の例 v) は grasp the raven by the legs と grasp the raven's legs との混交 (blending) と思われる。Quirk et al. (1985: 271) はこのタイプに関して前置詞句内に形容詞を含まない例のみあげて,「ときとして非慣用的」(sometimes unidiomatic) と述べているが，安藤 [上掲書] は，このタイプは身体部分に「性質形容詞 (Qualifying adjective) が付いている場合，特にふさわしい表現法となってくる」と指摘している。

v) Very gently, I grasped the raven by *its legs*. (非常にそうっとカラスの両足を捕まえた) (RD 01/3: 128)

vi) I kissed my uncle on *his* bald *forehead*. (おじさんのはげた額に口づけした) (Maugham, *Cakes and Ale*) [安藤]

"the＋身体部位" はしばしば「機能」を含意する。(この意味で「対立の the」は内面的特徴を表す「換喩的限定の the」(☞ 8.4.1) と連続している。) "the＋身体部位" が機能を含意することは，名詞自体が機能・役割を有するときに顕著である。

(61) a. But I couldn't resist the chance to discover the truth at last about *the pituitary gland* in the centre of my head. It has never worked. I've had treatment for the last 30 years, but no-one has ever been able to tell me exactly what is wrong with it – or whether I have a pituitary gland at all. (だが，私は頭の真んなかにある下垂体についてやっと事実を突き止めるという機会に逆らうことができなかった。ちゃんと働いたことはないのだ。過去 30 年間治療をうけてきたが，厳密にどこが悪いのか，そもそも私に下垂体があるかどうかさえ，だれも言うことができなかった) (RD 01/3: 81) [下垂体のホルモン分泌機能；姿かたちを表す a pituitary gland と対立的に用いられている]

b. His songs seem to contain whatever *the ear* could then wish ... (彼の歌は耳がそのときに求めることができたものはなんでも含んでいるようだ) (CCED³) [作曲のための機能・感受性]

c. The room was painted in soft pastels that were easy on *the eye*. (部屋は目にやさしい穏やかなパステル調に塗られていた) (OALD⁶) [視覚機能]

次例のような部品名も身体部分に準じて用いられていると考えてよいであろう。

d. Many things can make a plane do that, but one was most likely: a sudden move by *the rudder*. (飛行機がそうなるには多くの原因があるが, あることが特に見込みが高かった。方向舵の突発的な動きである) (RD 00/2: 91)

e. After her conversation, she turned to me mechanically and explained that a drunk-driver had lost control at *the wheel*. (会話ののち, 機械的に私の方を向いて, 酔っぱらい運転者がハンドルの制御を失ったのだと説明した) (RD 00/2: 81)

8.5.3　交通機関

Berry (1993: 42) は (62) の諸例をあげて, the plane/train などは特定の事物を指すのではなく, 輸送制度 (transport system) を指す, と言う。

(62) a. She sent a cable to her husband and caught *the plane* back to New York. (彼女は夫に電報を打ち, 飛行機で NY に戻った)

b. How long does it take on *the train*? (電車でどのくらい時間がかかりますか)

c. Then I saw him get into a cab, although *the subway* was good enough as a rule. (彼がタクシーに乗るのを見た, ふつうは地下鉄で十分なのに)

d. I walked to *the tube* instead of spending money on a taxi. (地下鉄まで歩いて, タクシーにはお金を使わなかった)

次の the bus/ferry も同様である。

e. We left our apartment to take *the bus* to town, but we didn't have exact change, so my husband ducked into a shop to break a few dollars. (アパートを出て市街地行きのバスに乗ろうとしたが, 運賃きっかりの小銭がなかったので, 夫は数ドルくずすため店に入った) (RD 00/1: 102)

f. When I was single, I played tennis at an island resort, catching *the ferry* almost every day. (独身のころ, 島のリゾート地でテニスをして, ほとんど毎日フェリーに乗った) (RD 99/10: 44)

(62) にあげたもの以外に, このような用いられ方をするのは次のような語であ

る : boat, hovercraft, tram, (Br) underground。これらに対し, taxi/car/bicycle は,「輸送の組織的方法を提供するものではないので」(Berry, ibid), つまり, 公共輸送機関ではないので, (62) の諸例のようには用いられない。もしも the がつけられれば, 特定の taxi ほかを指すことになる ((62, c−d) [cab/taxi] 参照)。

　本書では, "the＋交通機関名" は, 特定の地域内における他の交通機関名と対立関係にあると考える。つまり, take the bus は do not take the train/tube/plane を含意するのである。この見解は (63, a-b) によって裏づけられる。

(63) a. Riding *the SkyTrain* high above Vancouver, Emory Georges, 21, pitched his video-game idea. (スカイトレインに乗って V 市の上で, EG, 21 歳, は彼のビデオゲームのことを考えた) (RD 98/11: 85) [SkyTrain は Vancouver の地下および地上を通る電車]

　　　b. *SkyTrain* runs along a scenic 28 kilometer track from Vancouver to Burnaby, New Westminster, and Surrey in just 39 minutes. (スカイトレインは, V から B, NW を経由し, S に至る景色のよい 23 キロの軌道をわずか39分で走る) [http://www.translink.bc.ca/Schedules_and_Fares/SkyTrain/]

(63, a) では, EG が乗っていたのは, バスや汽車など他の交通機関ではなく, SkyTrain だという意味なので the がつけられ, (63, b) では SkyTrain そのものの説明なので, 他の交通機関と対立させる必要はないため無冠詞で用いられている。

8.6　総称

8.6.1　総称用法 (7.3 も参照)

　すでに述べたように (☞ 7.3), 本書では不定冠詞に総称的「意味」はないと考える。定冠詞にも, 総称的意味はなく, 次のような文脈において総称的な「解釈」が可能なのである。

(64) a. *The panda* is becoming an increasingly rare animal. (パンダはますます希少動物になりつつある) (CIDE)
　　　b. Exercise is good for *the circulation*. (運動は血行によい) (CIDE)
　　　c. *The car* is responsible for causing a lot of damage to our environment. (車が多くの環境破壊の原因だ) (CIDE)

では, 総称的解釈はどこから生じるのか。1 つの考えとしては,「総称の the」は「対立の the」の一部であると考えることも可能であろう。たとえば, (64, a) 中の the panda は「パンダでないものすべて」と対立すると考えるのである。

(理論的には，(64, a) の panda は他のすべての動物 (cat, bear, lion, tiger, etc.) と対立していると仮定できるかもしれないが，実際には，the panda と聞いて／読んで，他のすべての動物との対立を想起するということはありそうにない。) 第2の，より有力と思われるのは，「総称の the」はプロトタイプ (☞ 8.4.1.3; 8.4.1.4; 8.4.2.1) を表すとする見方である。この見方に立てば，the panda は英語話者の意識のうちに典型として存在する panda を表すことになる。つまり，個別性を切り捨てた，最大公約数的な panda が想定されるのである。

総称用法の the が特に多用されるのは，動植物に関する記述においてである。

(65) a. Yudin is one of a team of American and Russian scientists working to save *the Siberian tiger*. (Y は米ロ科学者チームの1員であり，シベリアンタイガーの保存に取り組んでいる) (RD 98/9: 26)

b. Before the dawn of human history, the ancestors of *the Komodo dragon* thrived in great numbers from Mongolia to Australia. (有史以前，コモドドラゴンの祖先は M から A にかけて多数の群れで生息していた) (RD 99/6: 26)

c. In the 1860s, Jonathan Couch described *the white shark* in *A History of the Fishes of the British Islands* as "the dread of sailors, who are in constant fear of becoming its prey . . ." (1860 年代に JC は『英諸島の魚類史』のなかでホホジロザメについて「船乗りの恐怖——船乗りはその餌食になることをいつも恐れている」と書いた) (RD 00/5: 92)

d. Numerous studies show that *the leaf* of *the ginkgo tree* appears to alleviate some age-related memory loss. (多くの研究が示すところでは，銀杏の葉は加齢による物忘れを緩和するようだ) (RD 00/3: 27)

e. Pandas were known to feed almost exclusively on bamboo, and researchers working in Sichuan had found that they favoured the leaves and young stems of *the arrow bamboo*. (パンダがほとんど竹しか食ないことは知られていたが，四川省で調査中の研究者たちの発見によると，パンダは arrow bamboo [日本語名未詳] の葉と若い茎を好む) (RD 00/2: 25)

動植物以外の例：

(66) a. (= VIII-49) The patient was Edgar Allan Poe, poet and author, master of the macabre, inventor of *the modern detective story*, creator of one of the world's best known poems, "The Raven." (RD

99/11: 60)

b. Tornadoes are mongrel cousins of the more sedate storm known as *the hurricane*. In most cases, *the Atlantic hurricane* is precisely bred off the coast of Africa and has a rather predictable gestation period. (竜巻は, ハリケーンとして知られている, より穏やかな嵐の遠い親戚である。たいてい, 大西洋ハリケーンはアフリカ沖で同一条件下で発生し, かなり予測可能な胚胎期間がある) (RD 00/2: 128)

c. "We knew for a long time, in *the test tube*, that vitamin E prevents several types of cancer," Kucuk says. (「試験管内ではずっと前からわかっていたが, ビタミンEはある種のガンを阻止する」とKは言う) (RD 98/11: 48)

the による総称用法に関してあまり知られていないのは, (i) 修飾語句がつきうること (例 (67); このとき総称用法は状況から指示物が理解される用法 (☞ 8.3) といくぶん重なる), (ii) 複数形による総称表現に切り替え可能であること (68), その結果として, (iii) 数の一致がしばしば無視されること (69), である。

(67) a. But Pulau Selingaan is a thriving nesting place for the green turtle, which, with an adult weight of 200 to 300 pounds, is the largest hard-shelled sea turtle, and for smaller numbers of *the more threatened hawksbill*, once hunted widely for its lustrous shell. (だが, PSはアオウミガメと, それよりは少数だが, より絶滅の恐れがあるタイマイとがたくさんやってくる産卵場である。前者は成長すれば体重は200～300ポンドになり, 最大の甲羅をもつウミガメである。後者は光沢のある背甲のため以前は広く捕獲されたのだった) (RD 98/4: 122)

b. Producer Mike Salisbury and camerawoman Justine Evans spent days in New Zealand stalking *the elusive kakapo*, a burrowing parrot, and talk about it like children recalling a birthday party. (プロデューサーのMSと写真家のJEとは幻のフクロウオウム——土穴を掘るオウム——を追ってNZで何日も過ごしたので, そのことを語るときは誕生パーティを思いだす子供のようだ) (RD 98/9: 59)

c. That very day commenced my love affair with the king of fruit, *the smelly, mace-like durian*. (まさにその日, 果実の王との恋愛関係が始まった。強烈なにおいの, 鎚矛(つちほこ)のごときドリアンである) (RD 99/7: 53)

(68) a. Many concern a creature that looks like a transparent lobster, but with six claws, which sucks human blood – *the head louse*. [改行] *Head lice*, about three millimetres long, can live for up to a month. (多くはある生物と関係がある。それは，形は透明なロブスターのようだが，足は6本あり，人間の血を吸う。すなわち，頭ジラミだ。頭ジラミは，体長約3ミリであり，最大1か月生存する) (RD 99/8: 69) [改行後，複数形で言い換え]

b. Like all reptiles, *tuatara* <u>are</u> cold-blooded, and their metabolism speeds up as the temperature rises. [. . .] Courtship is an especially slow affair for *the tuatara*. [. . .] *The tuatara* <u>was</u> a scientific enigma until last century. (すべての爬虫類と同様，ムカシトカゲは冷血であり，温度の上昇にあわせて代謝は速まる。求愛はムカシトカゲにとって特に時間のかかる仕事である。ムカシトカゲは前世紀まで科学上の謎だった) (RD 99/11: 110) [the による総称表現で言い換え]

c. After dogs, *the horse* has had the closest relationship with man. (犬の次には，馬が人間と最も親密な関係をもってきた) (CCED[3])

(69) a. Says Mark Marks, a research biologist at the South African Museum in Cape Town, "I believe *the white shark* to be cognisant and aware. I have seen some of <u>them</u> make decisions and change behaviours to suit circumstances." (CT の南ア博物館の生物学研究者，MM は次のように言う，「私の確信ですが，ホホジロザメは認識力・理解力があります。彼らの何頭かが，状況に適応するように決定して行動を変えたのを見たことがあります」と) (RD 00/5: 92)

b. No bugs I ever encountered prepared me for *the arctic mosquito*. [改行] At <u>their</u> worst, there are millions per square kilometre, rising in huge vortexes to engulf any unfortunate mammal, including humans. They can take half a litre of blood *a day* from a single moose, or stampede entire herds of caribou into panicky, aimless gallops. (これまでも虫には出くわしたが，ホッキョクカには用意ができていなかった。最悪の場合，1平方キロに何百万匹もいて，大きく渦を巻きながら，人間を含む不幸な哺乳動物をのみこむ。彼らは1頭のヘラジカからわずか1日に半リットルもの血を吸いとったり，カリブーの群全体をパニック状態で目的もなく駆けださせたりするのだ) (RD 99/9: 12) [改行後，複数形でうける] [*a day* 斜字体は原文]

c. Even *the humpback's* ordinary qualities have a touch of the fantastic about them. Their common name comes from the high curve of their backs as they dive, accentuated by the hump on the forward part of the dorsal fin. (ザトウクジラの日常的な特徴さえも彼らの物珍しさを少しばかり示している。彼らの呼び名は，彼らがダイブするときの背中の大きな曲線に由来するものであり，それは背びれの前面のふくらみにより強調されるのだ) (RD 01/8: 63)

比較：*The tuatara* was a scientific enigma until last century. Before 1867, some experts believed it was a lizard. (ムカシトカゲは19世紀までは科学上の謎だった。1867年以前には，トカゲだと信じる専門家もいた) (RD 99/11: 110) ["the＋単数形" を単数代名詞でうけるほうが正式]

次は総称的意味を表すために必然的に the が選ばれる例である。

(70) Then he heard the whir of *the diamondback snake* underneath the truck. He reached for the shovel he kept in the rear of the truck. [改行] A few minutes later, Bill laid nine snake rattles on the kitchen table. "Scared the hell out of me," he said. (そのとき，彼はトラックの下にガラガラヘビの音を聞き，トラックの後部に置いていたショベルに手を伸ばした。数分後，Bは食卓上に9匹のガラガラヘビを並べて，「肝をつぶしたよ」と言った) (RD 97/2: 13)

上例では文体的効果のために the による総称用法が選ばれている。もしもa/an による総称用法を選べば，あとで述べられる「9 匹」と矛盾するし，複数形による総称用法を選べば，蛇が複数匹いることを明示するので，後半部分はある程度予測されることになる。つまり，この例は，the による総称用法を選択することによって蛇の数が単数か複数かを伏せてあるので，意外性を高めるのに成功しているのである。

8.6.2 （play＋）楽器名 (2.1.1.4 および 3.5 参照)

play に piano/guitar/violin/flute など楽器名がつづくときしばしば the がつけられるのは，演奏者は自分が所有している楽器に限らず，同種の楽器ならどれでも演奏する能力があるはずだからである。念のため付言するならば，"the＋楽器名" は play 以外の動詞とも用いられる。

(71) a. *The cello* produces lower sounds than *the viola*, and higher sounds than *the double bass*. (チェロはビオラよりも低く，ダブルベースよりも高い音を出す) (NHD) [i.e., the instrument called cello]

b. He learned to play *the clarinet* at the age of ten. (10歳でクラリネッ

トの演奏を習得した）(CIDE)
- c. Fiona's learning *the flute*. (F はフルートを習っている) (LDOCE³) [i.e., learning to play the flute, 上例参照]
- d. I've been learning how to play *the guitar*. (ギターの弾き方を習っている) (CIDE)
- e. Learning *the piano* is definitely something best done in later life. (ピアノを学ぶのは老後にするのに絶対 1 番よいことだ) (RD 99/1: 109)

8.6.3 発明品

the motor car, the radio, the (tele)phone など発明品に the が冠せられるのも，楽器の場合と同様，その製品全般に当てはまるからである。

(72) a. For many people, avoiding *the computer* isn't an option. (多くの人にとってコンピュータを避けて通るという選択の余地はない) (RD 98/9: 7)
- b. *The crossword puzzle* was invented in 1913 by Arthur Wynne, an editor at the old New York *World*. (クロスワードパズルは，AW，かつて刊行されていた NY の W 紙の編集者，により 1913 年に考案された) (RD 98/9: 114)
- c. Patented by American Thomas Alava Edison . . . , the machine was dubbed *the kinetoscope*. (米国人のエジソンが特許を取り，その機械はキネトスコープ [無声映写機] と名づけられた) (RD 96/3: 8)
- d. (= VIII-12, d) By the early 1950s, many of the newly built hospitals featured premature-infant-care centres, which led to the development of *the modern incubator*. (RD 01/4: 131)
- e. That evening we got through to Barney on *the radio*. (その晩 B に無線がつながった) (RD 97/2: 132)
- f. Invention such as *the radio* and *the dishwasher* brought communications and automation to the ordinary home. (ラジオや皿洗い機のような発明は一般家庭に通信と自動化をもたらした) (CIDE)
- g. In the kitchen of the future at the Massachusetts Institute of Technology (MIT), I meet *the Talking Oven Mitt*. (MIT にある未来の台所で，話すオーブン手袋に出会う) (RD 01/9: 50)
- h. As a purchasing agent I use *the telephone* a lot. (買い付け代理人をしているので，私は電話をよく使う) (RD 00/2: 47)

NB 17　watch TV
　　TV が，発明品であるにもかかわらず，無冠詞で用いられるのは，画面が変化するので画定不可能と判断されるためであろう．次のように the が TV に先行する場合は，その家／部屋の TV を指す．
　　Turn off *the TV* and radio for at least two hours a day. (1日に少なくとも2時間はテレビやラジオを消しなさい) (RD 01/9: 116)

8.7　the＋固有名詞

　ある固有名詞は the をとり，別の固有名詞は the をとらない理由に関して，Quirk et al. (1985: 295) は，「その名称が英語話者にとってどの程度制度化された名称であるかという問題のようである」と言う (a matter of how far the name is an institutionalized name)．しかし，これは the の有無によって「制度化」の程度が判断されるのであるから，循環論であり，外国人にはなんの役にも立たない．

　他方，Hewson (1972: 109) は，the がつけられる地名とつけられない地名とに関して，概略，はっきりした境界が認識されない Category (a) には the がつき，境界が認識される Category (b) には冠詞はつかない，と指摘した．(これは，名詞が冠詞をとるのは，なんらかの限界を表すときであるという条件 (☞ 1.1) と矛盾するものではない．Pellatt Lake/Tokyo Bay などの固有名詞は符帳扱いであるため冠詞をとらないが，普通名詞の lake/bay は冠詞をとるからである．)

　　Category (a): ocean, sea, river, canal, isthmus, peninsula, gulf
　　Category (b): street, avenue, square, road, place, crescent, bridge, mount, cape, lake, island, county, parish, point, bay, part

この指摘は原則的に正しいが，地名以外の固有名詞をほとんどカバーしていないという点で不十分である．本書では，天然の地形であれ人工の建造物であれ，固有名詞につけられる the は「文化的了解の the」であると考える．なぜなら，見渡せないほど広い場所や巨大な建造物は多くの人々に知られているはずであり，それゆえ，同定可能であるのに対し，狭い場所や小規模の建造物はその土地の人々のみが用いる符帳 (☞ 1.2) にすぎず，他の土地の人々には同定不可能だからである．やや比喩的に言えば，「全国区」の固有名詞には the がつき，「地方区」の固有名詞には the がつかない，ということである．以下，この区別を実証する例をあげていきたい．

8.7.1　同定可能性と the の有無

　まず，上記の Hewson の指摘に従って，天然の地形およびそれに準じるも

のと the との関係を見て，つづいて人口の建造物と the との関連を見よう。
8.7.1.1 海
よく知られているように，海 (Ocean/Sea) の名称には規則的に the がつけられる。

(73) a. *the Atlantic/Pacific/Indian/Arctic/Antarctic Ocean* (大西洋／太平洋／インド洋／北氷洋／南氷洋) (OALD[5])

b. Moonlight twinkled off *the Indian Ocean* as Chandrasiri Abrew walked along Kosgoda Beach. (CAがKビーチを散歩したとき月光がインド洋沖でまたたいた) (RD 99/5: 49) [Sri Lanka]

c. (= III-42) At speeds up to 50 knots, the two boats played cat and mouse for ten minutes across *the Adriatic Sea*. (RD 99/10: 104)

d. Centuries ago, travelers in Central Asia observed with wonderment a sticky black liquid oozing from the earth along the shores of *the Caspian*. (何世紀も以前，中央アジアの旅人たちは，カスピ海の海岸ぞいにねばねばした黒い液体が地中からにじみ出るのを見て驚異の念をもった) (RD 99/4: 18) [Sea の省略]

e. Before entering Zurich University to study biology, she worked for a year in the Camargue, the flat, marshy delta in the south of France where the Rhône River runs into *the Mediterranean*. (生物学を研究するためにZ大学に入学する前，彼女はCで1年間働いた。そこは，フランス南部の平坦な湿地のデルタであり，R川が地中海にそそぐ場所である) (RD 96/10: 90) [Sea の省略]

類例：the Baltic Sea (RD 96/10: 131); the Bering Sea (RD 99/2: 74); the Kara Sea [east of Novaya Zemlya] (RD 97/6: 72); the South China Sea (RD 99/9: 123)

他方，湖や池には the はつけられない。この相違は，Ocean/Sea には形容詞が先行し Lake/Pond には名詞が先行しているという構造的な理由よりも，後者は前者よりもずっと狭いので，同定不可能とみなされるという理由のほうが大きい。(the Black Canyon vs. φ White Canyon を比較せよ (☞ 8.7.1.8)。)

(74) a. Whiteouts are another hazard. In the winter of 1993, 13 trucks were caught in a blinding, swirling curtain as they were crossing *Pellatt Lake*, 160 kilometres south of the Arctic Circle. (別の危険はホワイトアウトだ。1993年の冬，13台のトラックが，北極圏から160キロ南のP湖を横断中，視界ゼロの，渦巻く[雪の]カーテンに巻き

b. [T]he parts of his boyhood that mattered most were summers spent with his family on *Walloon Lake* in upper Michigan. ([Hemingway の] 少年時代のうち最も重要なのはM州北部のW湖畔で家族と過ごした夏だった) (EB 01)

c. A fiercely competitive ice hockey player, she loved nothing more than to skate with her younger brothers on *Snow Pond* at their home in Princeton, Massachusetts. (彼女は競争心旺盛なアイスホッケー選手なので，M州Pの自宅のS池で弟たちとスケートをするのが何より好きだった) (RD 00/4: 66)

d. In the spring he picked a spot by *Walden Pond*, a small glacial lake located 2 miles (3 km) south of Concord on land Emerson owned. ([1845年の] 春 [Thoreau は] W池——Eの所有地内の小さな氷河湖であり，Cから3km南に位置する——近くの場所を選んだ) (EB 01)

NB 18

1) 次の湖名に the がついているのは，字義どおりの意味が残っているためである。

  i) [T]o the northwest is *the Great Salt Lake*, one of the world's largest salt lakes ... (北西にはGSL，世界最大の塩湖の1つ，がある) (RD 02/2: 88)

2) Lake が肩書き扱い (☞ 1.3) されるときは the はつけられない。

例：Lake Michigan/Victoria.

3) 海に対して，大陸 (Continent) は無冠詞で用いられる。大陸に限らず平地にある地名は，無標であるため（つまり，当然すぎて）同定可能性が問題にされることなく，符帳として扱われるためと推測される。(複数形の大陸名に関しては，8.2.5 参照。)

  ii) This is roughly as difficult as melting *Antarctica*. (それは南極大陸を溶かすのと同じくらいむずかしい) (RD 98/7: 102)

  iii) *Europe* and *Asia* are sometimes considered a single continent, *Eurasia*. (ヨーロッパ大陸とアジア大陸とは単一の大陸，ユーラシア大陸，と考えられることがある) (EB 01)

8.7.1.2 湾／海岸

(75) a. In August 1990 Dion was sent to *the Persian Gulf*. (1990年の8月 D

はペルシャ湾に派遣された) (RD 96/3: 106)
　b. It's a brisk winter's morning on *the Great Australian Bight*. (GA 湾上のひんやりとした冬の朝のことだった) (RD 99/10: 47) [豪南部]

(76) a. *Kuwait Bay* is one of the world's most important wintering grounds for wading birds. (K 湾は渉禽(しょうきん)にとって世界で最も大事な越冬地の 1 つだ) (CIDE)
　b. Then the sun, a brilliant disk, rises above *Mirs Bay*. (ときあたかも，まばゆい円盤の太陽が M 湾に昇る) (RD 97/5: 120) [香港]
　c. a hillside overlooking *Fairview Cove* (F 湾を見下ろす丘の斜面) (CCED[3])

同じような地形でも，"X Gulf/Bight" は the をとり，"X Bay/Cove" は the をとらない。前者が広大であるのに対し，後者は狭小であるという区別が見られる。たとえば，McED では，これらの語は次のように定義されている：

(77) a. gulf: a <u>large area</u> of ocean that is almost surrounded by land
　b. bight: a <u>long</u> curved part of the coast or a large river
　c. bay: an area of the coast where the land curves inward
　d. cove: a <u>small area</u> of ocean that is partly surrounded by land

「湾」に先行する the の有無は，広い湾 (gulf/bight) はその名前が多くの人に知られていて同定可能であるのに対し，狭い湾 (bay/cove) は地元の人にしか知られておらず，多くの人には同定不可能であるという相違に帰せられるのである。

NB 19
1) Dublin/Hudson Bay のように "NP＋Bay" という構造のときは冠詞は不要であるが，the Bay of Naples/Bengal のように "Bay of NP" という構造のときは the が必要である。(本書ではこのような固有名詞を「派生固有名詞」と呼ぶ。)
2) the Moray Firth (マリ湾；スコットランド北東岸の入り江) は例外的に the がつけられる。

Gulf と Bay の相違から予想されるように，Coast (海岸) が the をとるのに対し Beach (浜辺) は無冠詞で用いられる。
(78) a. New York is the busiest port on *the East Coast*. (NY は東海岸で 1 番繁華な港だ) (McED)
　b. His plan was to take a boat to Brewers Lagoon, a town in the

northwest of *the Mosquito Coast* . . . (彼の計画は乗り合いボートで，M 海岸の北西の町である BL にまで行くことだった) (RD 02/4: 67) [Honduras]

類例： the Gold/Ivory/Slave Coast (EB 01) [φ Ivory Coast は国名]

(79) a. A soft breeze cooled Lesia Stockall's face as she emerged dripping from the blue waters of *Carlsbad Beach* in San Diego. (LS が SD の C ビーチの青い海から水をしたたらせながら出てきたとき，そよ風が顔に涼しかった) (RD 98/11: 16)

b. My wife and I were lunching at a sidewalk café in *Huntington Beach*, California. (妻と私とは C の H ビーチの路上カフェテラスで昼食中だった) (RD 00/2: 51)

c. Nearing *Virginia Beach*, Stubbs descended and slowed. (V ビーチに近づくと，S は下降し速度を落とした) (RD 97/6: 31)

類例： Cable Beach (RD 00/2: 122); Kosgoda Beach [Sri Lanka] (RD 99/5: 49); Miami Beach (RD 99/9: 132); Riviera Beach, Florida (RD 99/4: 103)

比較： On another occasion we went for a walk on a bike path near *a Santa Monica beach*. (別の機会に SM の海岸近くの自転車道を散歩した) (RD 99/10: 26) [普通名詞；8.7.2.1 [an Arizona desert] も参照]

港や波止場，埠頭(ふとう) (Harbor/Pier/Quay) の名称も無冠詞で用いられる。

(80) a. On December 7, 1941, the Japanese bombed *Pearl Harbor* and hours later Britain joined the United States in declaring war on Japan. (1941 年 12 月 7 日 [日本時間 8 日] 日本軍は真珠湾を爆撃した。数時間後，英国は合衆国に加担して日本に宣戦布告した) (RD 98/6: 88)

b. In *Dutch Harbor*, halfway out on the Aleutians, more tons of seafood are unloaded than anyplace else in North America. (D 港──アリューシャン列島の真んなかあたり──では，北米のどこよりも何トンも多い海産物が水揚げされる) (RD 99/2: 75)

c. Hike from Tai Long Wan or take the local ferry from *Wong Shek Pier* across the inlet to Ko Lau Wan, then walk up to the nearby headland. (TLW から徒歩で行くか，WS 桟橋から KLW まで地元のフェリーに乗って入り江を横断したのち歩いて近くの岬に登りなさい) (RD 97/5: 124) [香港の Sharp Peak への行き方]

d. At *Circular Quay*, where the passenger fleet docks, I board the

Manly ferry.（乗客用の船が泊まる C 埠頭で M フェリーに乗船する）(RD 99/3: 76) [Sydney]

類例：New York Harbor (RD 99/5: 95); Victor Harbor (RD 99/10: 51); [小文字] Hong Kong harbour (RD 99/9: 123); Tacoma harbour, south of Seattle (RD 99/9: 126)

8.7.1.3 海峡

(81) a. In the spring of 1940, Adolf Hitler's tanks smashed through the Belgian Ardennes on the way to *the English Channel*. (1940 年春，ヒトラーの戦車は英仏海峡に向かう途中 B のアルデンヌ [の森] を突き抜けた) (RD 96/3: 89)

b. They lobbed missiles into *the Taiwan Strait* when the Taiwanese dared to organize open national elections. (台湾の人々が国民投票を組織しようとしているとき，台湾海峡にミサイルを発射した) (RD 98/12: 71)

(82) a. *Menai Strait*, the narrow strip of sea that separates the island from the mainland, is barely 200 yards wide in places. (メナイ海峡は [英国] 本土と [Anglesey] 島とを分かつ狭い瀬戸であり，場所によってはわずか 200 ヤードしかない) (RD 96/10: 12)

b. This slow-moving creature about the length of a fore-arm, is now found only on about 30 remote islands off the North Island and in *Cook Strait*. (この，前腕ほどの長さの，動きの遅い生物 [tuatara] は [ニュージーランドの] NI 島沖とクック海峡内とのおよそ 30 の離れ小島で見られるだけだ) (RD 99/11: 108)

英和辞典には Menai/Cook Strait には the が必要と注記されているが（『ランダムハウス』，『リーダーズ・プラス』），実際には無冠詞で用いられている。これら無冠詞の海峡と the English Channel/Taiwan Strait との主要な相違は知名度である。客観的な広さは，それぞれ，最狭部 200 メートル弱／23 キロ；34 キロ／134 キロであるが，重要なのは文化的・主観的な位置づけである。つまり，知名度の高い海峡は同定可能性が高く，知名度の低い海峡はその可能性が低いのである。

8.7.1.4 河川／運河

河川名に the がつくことはよく知られているが，これが当てはまるのは大きな川のときだけである。これまで指摘されたことはないと思われるが，(84) のように，きわめて限定された地域内の川に関しては無冠詞で用いられる。

(83) a. Of all America's Western rivers, *the Missouri* was probably the

b. After a wonderful Saturday evening dining on *the Seine*, Nicola, Jenny and I had taken a taxi back to our hotel. (すばらしい日曜日の夕べS河畔で食事をしたのち，NとJと私はタクシーでホテルに帰った) (RD 00/7: 40)

c. The long, still canal stretched along to our right, and the fresh brown water of *the Potomac River* glimmered to our left. (右手には長い穏やかな運河が広がり，左手にはP川の初春の[雪解けで]土色の水が光っていた) (RD 99/12: 131)

d. She is in the United States illegally, like many in this border town on *the Rio Grande*. (合衆国に不法滞在しているが，RG川ぞいのこの国境の都市の多くの居住者と同様だ) (RD 99/11: 120)

e. The Oxford and Cambridge boat race takes place on *the River Thames*. (O大学とC大学とのボートレースはテムズ川で行われる) (CIDE)

f. On a warm sunny day there are few things more pleasant than a gentle boat trip down *the Thames*. (暖かくて日当たりのよい日には，テムズをゆっくりと船で巡るよりも心地よいことはほとんどない) (CIDE)

(84) a. I swear this litany was in my head when, as we drew abreast of *Indian River* on Princess Royal, a roundish white boulder suddenly grew a head and turned to stare at our boat. (誓って言うが，PR島のインディアン川に接近しながら，この呪文を頭のなかで唱えていたとき，突然丸い白い巨岩から頭が生え，振り向いて我々のボートを見たのだ) (RD 97/3: 10) [白い岩だと思っていたものが実は白クマだったの意；Indian River は British Columbia (Canada) の Princess Royal Island にある川の名前]

b. *Granite Rapid* lies just downstream. (G急流はすぐ川下にある) (RD 00/2: 58)

c. At *Wounded Knee Creek*, on December 29, 1890, some 450 soldiers prepared to disarm a group of Lakota. (1890年12月29日，WK川で約450人の兵士はラコタ族の1団に武装解除させる準備をした) (RD 98/12: 91)

d. Follow *Austin Creek* for a few miles. (A細流にそって数マイル行き

なさい）(CCED³) [本章 NB 6, ii) [Oyster Creek] も参照]
e. Her gang prospected up and down *Mangahouanga Stream*, dragging rocks from the icy water, working like convicts to split them with hammer and chisel or a petrol-driven masonry saw. （一団はM川の上流下流を調査した。冷たい水底から岩をさらいだし，囚人のように働き，ハンマーと鑿(のみ)で，あるいは油動式の石切りのこで，岩を割った）(RD 01/9: 111)

運河名にも the がつけられる。大河に準じて扱われているためと考えられる。

(85) a. *The Erie Canal* connects the Great Lakes with New York Harbor. （E運河は五大湖とNY港とを結ぶ）(NHD)
b. *The Panama Canal* provides a crucial shipping link between the Atlantic and Pacific oceans. （P運河は大西洋と太平洋との海運の重要な連絡路だ）(CIDE)
c. Egypt has lost out on revenues from *the Suez Canal*. （EはS運河からの収益で損をした）(CCED³)

次は運河名ではあるが，the Great Wall（万里の長城）と同様に，唯一物（または文化的了解）(☞ VIII-30, g) と見るほうが適切であろう。

d. Many of these cities were strung along *the Grand Canal*, which stretched 1800 kilometres south from Daidu to Hongzhou. （これらの都市の多くは，大都から杭州まで南に 1,800 キロ延びる，大運河ぞいに連なっていた）(RD 02/7: 89)

NB 20
1) 意味的根拠

gulf/bight 対 bay/cove（☞ 8.7.1.2）と同様な相違が，river 対 rapid/creek/stream にも見られる。

river: a natural flow of water that continues in a <u>long</u> line across land to the sea/ocean (OALD⁶) [(84, a) は例外的用法]
rapid: A <u>part</u> of a river where the bed forms a steep descent, causing a swift current. (OED) [通例，複数形で使用]
creek: a <u>small</u> river or stream (OALD⁶)
stream: a <u>small</u> <u>narrow</u> river (OALD⁶)

2) 所有格＋河川名

河川名に所有格が先行するときは，他の限定詞と同様，the は落とされる。

i) Instead, sitting at the computer in my den overlooking London's *River Thames*, I sent an e-mail. (その代わりに，Lのテムズ川を見渡す自室のコンピュータに向かって座り，Eメールを送った) (RD 00/7: 31)

3) River を含む地名

次例は，川を指すのではなく，地名なので，the は不要である。つまり，the Mississippi (M川) 対 φ Mississippi (M州) の場合と同様な区別が見られる。

ii) By then my father had moved our family from the Bronx to *Pearl River*, a suburb north of New York, seeking more room and a safe haven. (そのときまでに，広さと安全な土地を求めて，父はBからPR，NYの北部の郊外，に家族を引っ越しさせていた) (RD 00/7: 123)

4) 表記法

river が小文字で書かれるときは普通名詞と区別不可能である (8.7.1.7 [peninsula] も参照)。

iii) Some weeks later, the teenager was driven across Poland, then smuggled across *the Neisse river* into Germany. (数週間後，十代のその娘は車に乗せられてPを越え，N川を渡ってドイツに密入国させられた) (RD 99/10: 107)

8.7.1.5 滝

(86) a. They went on a day trip to *the Niagara Falls*. (日帰り旅行にN瀑布(ばくふ)に行った) (CIDE)

b. The Zambezi ... includes along its course *the Victoria Falls*, one of the world's greatest natural wonders, and the Kariba and Cahora Bassa dams, two of Africa's largest hydroelectric projects. (Z川ぞいには世界最大の天然の驚異の1つであるV瀑布や，アフリカ最大の水力発電計画の2つであるKダムおよびCBダムがある) (EB 01)

(87) a. Charles Blondin crossed *Niagara Falls* on a tightrope in 1859. (CBは1859年N瀑布の上を綱渡りした) (CIDE)

b. The volume of flow at *Victoria Falls* is relatively large, approximately 1,080 cubic metres per second, but *Guaira Falls*... had the largest known average discharge – 13,300 cubic metres per second. (V瀑布の水量は相対的に多く，毎秒約1,080立方メートルであるが，

知られている限りで最大の平均放水量を記録したのはG滝であり，1秒につき13,300立方メートルであった) (EB 01)

c. Tom Feuchtwanger . . . paused to admire the beauty of *Virginia Falls*, one of the highest in Canada. (TFは立ちどまって，Cで最も高所にある滝の1つである，V滝の美しさに見とれた) (RD 98/12: 76)

d. *Angel Falls* (Spanish: Salto Angel) is the highest waterfall in the world. (A滝 (S語で SA) は世界で1番高所にある滝だ) (GME) [単数一致]

『ランダムハウス』は Niagara Falls に関して「((英)) では the をつけて用いる」と注記している。しかし，上例 (87, a) や "Niagara Falls" (OALD⁵); "Niagara Falls is worth seeing (NOT . . . to be seen)." (LDOCE³) のように，英国系の辞書でも the なしの例があげられているという事実は，the の選択は地域差に帰せられるのではないということを示している。本書では，滝の名前に the がつけられるときは，当該の滝は知名度の高い存在ととらえられ，the がつけられないときは，知名度の低い存在ととらえられている，と考える (the が先行しうるのは Niagara/Victoria Falls のように有名な滝のみである)。

8.7.1.6 環礁

(88) The explosion of nuclear devices in *the Bikini Atoll* was stopped in 1958. (ビキニ環礁での核装置爆発は1958年に中止になった) (CIDE)

(89) a. an atomic bomb detonated on *Bikini Atoll* in the Pacific (太平洋上のビキニ環礁で炸裂した原子爆弾) (LDOCE³)

b. France has carried out an underground nuclear explosion on *Murruroa Atoll* in the south Pacific. (仏は南太平洋のムルロワ環礁で地下核爆発を行った) (CCED³)

c. And the Chinese have built a satellite tracking station on *Tarawa atoll* to keep their eyes on America's Kwajalein Missile Range, 800 kilometres to the north. (中国はタラワ環礁に衛星追跡所を建設した。800キロ北方にある米のKミサイル試射場を監視するためである) (RD 00/6: 83) [atoll 小文字は原文]

Bikini Atoll はよく知られているので the がつけられることもあるが，他の環礁は知名度が低く同定可能性が低いので無冠詞で用いられる。

8.7.1.7 半島

半島 (peninsula) は the をとるが，しばしば小文字で書かれるので，普通名詞と区別困難である。事実，同一の辞書内でも不統一が見られる (the Arabian Peninsula/peninsula (CIDE); 本章 NB 20-4 [river] も参照)。

(90) a. He would map all the potential sources of radioactive pollution in *the Kola Peninsula*. (K 半島の放射線汚染の恐れのある箇所すべてを地図上に描くことにした) (RD 97/6: 72) [Russia]

b. The Japanese Maritime Safety Agency, roughly the equivalent of the U.S. Coast Guard, said it spotted one ship on Tuesday morning 28 miles east of *the Noto Peninsula* in central Japan, on the side facing *the Korean peninsula*. (日本の海上保安庁──合衆国沿岸警備隊にほぼ相当──によると，同庁は，火曜日の朝，朝鮮半島に面する側の中部日本にある能登半島の 28 マイル東で1隻の [不審] 船を発見したとのことである) (NY Times, Mar. 24, 99)

類例：the Korean / Arabian / Florida Peninsula (CIDE); the Arabian Peninsula/peninsula (CCED³; OALD⁶, CIDE); the Baja peninsula (RD 99/3: 128); the Iberian Peninsula/peninsula (CIDE; CCED³, OALD⁶, LDOCE³); the Sai Kung peninsula (RD 97/5: 119)

半島に対し，岬 (point/head) は，半島よりずっと小さいため他地区の人々には同定不可能なので，無冠詞で用いられる。cape は，肩書き扱いされるときは無冠詞であり (☞ 1.3)，*of*-phrase をともなうときは the がつけられる。

(91) a. Mark . . . was rushing to greet me as I rounded *Acacia Point* several hundred yards from camp. (キャンプから数百ヤード離れたA岬を回っていたとき M が私を迎えに駆けてきていた) (ConCD-ROM) 類例：Pagoda Point (OALD⁵)

b. I am walking to *Beachy Head* from the nearby resort town of Eastbourne, a journalist on assignment to write about one of Britain's worst suicide spots. (近くのリゾート地の E から B 岬へと歩いているところだ。ジャーナリストとして英国で最悪の自殺名所の1つに関する記事を書くという任務を帯びているのだ) (RD 01/6: 67) [地名；本章の例 (123, k) と比較せよ]

比較：The ship sank off *Cape Horn*. (H 岬沖で沈没した) (OALD⁵) 類例：Cape Cod (NHD); Cape Columbia (CIDE) [肩書き扱い]

比較：the Cape of Good Hope (喜望峰) (LDOCE³) [派生固有名詞；the がつけられるのは構造的理由による]

8.7.1.8 峡谷／渓谷；海溝

多くの峡谷／渓谷には，(92) のように，the がつけられるが，(93) のように無冠詞で用いられるものもある。この相違は渓谷の知名度 (主として，規模に基づく)，つまり，同定可能性の程度に帰せられる。

(92) a. To most of its 5 million yearly visitors, *the Grand Canyon* means breath-taking vistas.（年間の訪問客500万人の大半にとってGキャニオンは息をのむような眺めである）(RD 00/2: 54) [Arizona]

b. One day she climbed into her Jeep and drove hard for the Rocky Mountains, intending to jump into *the Black Canyon* of the Gunnison River.（ある日ジープに乗ってR山脈へと飛ばして行った。G川のBキャニオンに飛び込むつもりだったのだ）(RD 98/3: 20) [Nevada, Arizona,]

c. We are passing through *the Inner Gorge*, the dark heart of the canyon.（[グランド]キャニオンの深奥部である，奥部峡谷を通過中だ）(RD 00/2: 58)

d. In my memory, the hilly landscape, with the zipper-like Jiange range to the north and *the Wu Gorge* that all but closed like a locked door to the east, confined me in a large basin.（記憶しているところでは，その丘陵地の地形は私を大きな盆地のなかに閉じ込めるものだった。北にはジッパーのような剣閣の山並みが広がり，東には錠をかけた扉のようにほとんど閉鎖された烏江峡谷があったのだ）(RD 00/9: 47) [四川省]

e. In 1997 a record amount of snow fell in *the Red River Valley*.（1997年RRバレーでは記録的な降雪があった）(RD 98/10: 122) [North Dakota]

f. Kilimanjaro lies at the heart of *the Rift Valley*, a great chasm stretching 5600 kilometres across Africa from Mozambique in the south to the Red Sea in the north.（KはRバレーの中心部にある。それは南はMから北は紅海まで5,600 kmにわたってアフリカを走る巨大な地溝である）(RD 99/11: 68)

類例： Ambler, a small Eskimo village in the Kobuk Valley (RD 99/9: 11); the upper Mississippi Valley (RD 99/9: 24); the Redstone Valley [northwest Alaska] (RD 99/9: 11); the Rhone Valley (RD 00/7: 72); the San Gabriel Valley [Los Angeles suburbs] (RD 99/4: 107); the San Joaquin Valley (RD 02/2: 12); the Stour Valley in Suffolk, England (RD 97/5: 64)

g. Your navigator announces you are over the deepest point, *the Mariana Trench*.（航海士が最深部，つまり，M海溝，の上にいると告げる）(RD 97/2: 23)

(93) a. We step out of the truck at *White Canyon*, Utah, and peer over the landscape. (U 州の W キャニオンでトラックから降りて景色を見渡す) (RD 96/10: 77)
  b. *Olduvai Gorge* is in Tanzania. (O 峡谷は T にある) (CIDE)

NB 21 列挙
次の例で冠詞が落とされているのは，地名が列挙されているので，省略的文体が選ばれているためである (☞ 9.3)。
That's where the canyons of the Colorado Plateau run from the middle of Utah south to the middle of Arizona – *Grand Canyon, Glen Canyon, Grand Gulch* and thousands of others. (そこは，C 高原の峡谷——G キャニオン，G キャニオン，G 峡谷，他に何千も——が U 州中央部から南に A 州中央部へと連なっているところだ) (RD 96/10: 77)

8.7.1.9　山／峰

(94) a. Their attempt to climb *the Eiger* ended in failure. (E 峰登攀(とうはん)の試みは失敗に終わった) (CIDE)
  b. *The Matterhorn* rose proudly in the background. (M 峰が背後に雄壮にそびえていた) (OALD[6])
  c. The scenic mountain separates the cantons of Bern and Valais and is in the Bernese Alps, two other peaks of which (*the Finsteraarhorn* [14,022 feet] and *the Aletschhorn* [13,763 feet]) surpass it in height. (その秀峰 [the Jungfrau] は B アルプス中にあり，B 州と V 州を分かっている。B アルプスの他の 2 つの峰 (F 峰と A 峰) のほうが [ユングフラウより] 高い) (EB 01)
  d. The town is a year-round resort near many Alpine peaks, including *the Jungfrau* (13,642 feet [4,158 m]). ([Lauterbrunnen の] 町は 1 年をとおしてリゾート地であり，近くにはアルプスの峰々があり，J 峰もその 1 つだ) (EB 01)

参考：Snacks and afternoon tea can be enjoyed on the sun terrace facing *the Jungfrau mountain*. (軽食と午後のティーを J 峰を見渡す屋外のテラスで楽しむことができる) (BNC, AMD 489)

(95) a. A mountain in the Rockies became the location for a film about *Everest*. (R 山脈中のある山が E に関する映画のロケ地になった)

(OALD⁶)

b. *Kilimanjaro* was finally at peace. (K峰は [火山活動が終わって] やっと穏やかになった) (RD 99/11: 68)

c. To mould his officers, Sarakikya turned to his beloved mountain, introducing an annual military march to *Uhuru Peak*. (将校たちを一人前にするため，S は彼の好きな山に目を向けて，U 峰への毎年の軍事行進を導入した) (RD 99/11: 70) [Tanzania]

d. *Kibo* looms in the distance. (K峰が遠くに見えてくる) (RD 99/11: 72) [Tanzania]

e. Why does *Galeras* seem to be producing so much gold? (なぜ G 火山はそんなにも金を産出しているように見えるのか) (RD 96/3: 16)

参考： When actively erupting, *the Galeras volcano* in the Andes spews more than a pound of gold each day into the atmosphere and could be depositing 45 pounds of gold a year into rocks lining its crater. (活発に噴火すれば，A 山脈中の G 火山は毎日 1 ポンド以上の金を大気中に噴出し，クレーター内の岩に 1 年に 45 ポンドもの金を堆積させることになる) (RD 96/3: 15)

世界最高峰の Everest に the がつけられず，Eiger/Matterhorn などに定冠詞がつけられるという事実は，高さが the の選択要因ではないことを示している。同定可能性という観点から考えるならば，(94) の Eiger などはヨーロッパの山であり，しかも，ゲルマン系の名称であるので英語話者には同定可能性が高く，(95) の Everest などは遠隔地の山なので同定可能性が低い，と言ってさしつかえない。山の名前につく the は，本来は，原語の冠詞の翻訳であるが (der Eiger; das Matterhorn; die Jungfrau)，現代英語でも the が保たれているのは，the が同定可能性を示すという機能を有しているからであると推測される。なぜなら，もしもなんらの機能も果たしていないのであれば，Road につけられていた the のように (本章 NB 23-4 参照)，落とされていくはずだからである。ちなみに，ゲルマン系以外の山の名前は，無冠詞で用いられるか，Mount/Mt がつけられるかのいずれかである (例：Mount Vesuvius; Mt McKinley; Mont Blanc; BNC では *the Kilimanjaro/McKinley/Vesuvius という連語は検出できない)。

NB 22　(the) X crater

火山との関連において crater に言及しておくならば，「火口」を指すときは，地域限定的な符帳として扱われるので無冠詞で用いられる。

i) *Haleakala Crater*, on the Hawaiian island of Maui, is one of the world's largest volcanic craters. It is about 32 km (20 mi) in circumference, and the floor lies about 825 m (2,700 ft) below the peak (3,055 m/10,023 ft). (HクレーターはハワイのM島にあり，世界最大の噴火口の1つである。周囲は約32kmであり，底は山頂 (3,055m) からおよそ825m下ったところにある) (GME)

これに対し，隕石によるクレーターは巨大であり，他地区の人々にも同定可能であるので，the をとる。

ii) Many large impact structures have been recognized in Canada since the discovery of *the New Quebec Crater* in northern Quebec.（北QのNQクレーターの発見後，多数の巨大衝撃構造がカナダで認められている）(GME) [小文字表記のほうがふつう：the Kaalijarv crater in Estonia; the El Aouelloul crater in Mauritania; the Wabar crater in the Empty Quarter of Saudi Arabia (GME)]

8.7.1.10　道路

(96) a. I formed a support party of six and equipped them with two six-wheel-drive vehicles to travel along *the Silk Road* up to 200 miles to our south.（6人から成る支援隊をつくり，6輪駆動車を2台配備した。シルクロードを駆けて我々のいるところから200マイル南にまで来るためだ）(RD 97/2: 123)

b. For a thousand years, *the Silk Route* spun the thinnest of links between China and the Mediterranean.（1千年にわたって絹の道は中国と地中海との最もか細いつながりを紡いだ）(RD 99/1: 67)

c. From Dali we followed Marco's footsteps to a village, along what [is] now known as *the Burma Road*. (DからMポーロの足跡に従って，現在ビルマルートとして知られている道ぞいに，ある村に入った) (RD 02/7: 88) [原文　誤植]

d. A sign announced that this was no ordinary footpath, but part of *the Appalachian Trail*. It wanders across 14 American states from Georgia to Maine and through comely hills whose names – Blue Ridge, Smokies, Catskills – seem an invitation to amble.（道路標識の示すところでは，ここはありきたりの歩道ではなく，A自然歩

道の一部だった。それは米国の 14 の州を巡って，G 州から美しい丘陵地帯を抜けて M 州に至るのであり，BR, S, C といった [山脈の] 名前は歩いてみようという気持ちを起こさせるように思われた）(RD 99/6: 108)

e. At night they lay awake and listened to the rumble of trucks on *the Trans-Canada Highway*, just a few streets away. (夜間目覚めたまま横になって，わずか数本道路を隔てた，カナダ横断道のトラックの音を聞いた) (RD 00/1: 132)　類例：(VIII-112, c) [the Alaska Highway]

f. In the Chugoku region all the interchanges on *the Sanyo Expressway* will have the system and also some interchanges on *the Chugoku Expressway*, with consequent savings of time during the rush hours. (中国地方では，山陽自動車道のすべてのインターチェンジと中国自動車道のいくつかのインターチェンジでその [ETC] システムが導入され，結果的に，ラッシュ時に時間の節約になる) (Peter Goldsbury, Chugoku Shimbun, Mar. 11, 99)

(97) a. I'd start walking along *Second Avenue* at a brisk pace. (2 番通りをきびきび歩くことから始めよう) (RD 98/6: 128)

b. Actress Diane Keaton, he explained, discovered Karina on *Hollywood Boulevard*. (彼の説明によると，女優の DK は H ブールバールで K を見つけた) (RD 99/10: 27)

c. I am about to run my first New York City Marathon, the annual 26.2-mile footrace through all five boroughs of the city, ending on *West Drive* at *67th Street* in Central Park. (初めての NY シティマラソンを走ろうとしている。これは，毎年恒例の 26.2 マイル走るレースであり，市の 5 区すべてを走り抜けて C パークの 67 番通りの W ドライブをゴールとする) (RD 99/1: 117) [(III-108, b) [Cross Street] も参照]

d. A few days later David Jones turned right onto *West End Lane*, a tree-lined street of large brick houses, shops and apartments. (数日後 DJ は右折して WE レーンに入った。大きな煉瓦(れんが)造りの家や商店，アパートが並んだ，街路樹のある通りである) (RD 99/9: 136)

e. When he heard the school bus coming down *South Curtis Road* around 11 a.m., 49-year-old Wayne Barrett headed out the door. (午前 11 時ごろスクールバスが SC 道路をやってきているのを聞くと，49 歳の WB はドアから飛び出ていった) (RD 99/1: 91) [(III-108, a)

[Owlstone Road] も参照)
 f. He lives at 9, *Acacia Gardens*. (A 通り 9 番地に住んでいる) (CCED³)
以上の諸例が示すように，道路名も，河川名と同様に，長距離の場合は他地区の住人にも同定されるので the がつけられ，市内の通りの場合は他地区の住人には同定しがたいので無冠詞で用いられる。

NB 23
1) "名詞＋数字"という構造の道路名は，長距離でも，冠詞をとらない (☞ 1.5)。
 i) McVeigh rolled on through the countryside along *Interstate 35*. (MV は州際高速道 35 号線ぞいに田園を走っていった) (RD 01/6: 117)

次は，数字つきであるが，highway が後続し，かつ長距離の道路であるので，the がつけられる。

 ii) The man turned onto *the Interstate 75 highway* – known as Alligator Alley where it crosses the Everglades, home to many thousands of alligators and hundreds of crocodiles. (その男は州際高速道 75 号線，通称，ワニ道路，に入った。E 湿地と交差し，何千ものアリゲータや何百ものクロコダイルが生息しているところだ) (RD 00/6: 54)

2) the Mall/Strand; the Champs-Élysées
Mall/Strand (ロンドン市内) には the がつけられる (Berry 1993: 59)。それぞれ，「ペルメル球技が行われた道」(OED, s.v., mall¹)，「州(＋)」という本来の意味が残っているためと思われる。

 iii) I saw Sally last Saturday at *the Mall*. (先週の土曜日マル通りで S を見かけた) (LDOCE³) [(VIII-107, a) も参照]
 iv) Police closed *the Strand* because of smoke billowing over the road. (警察は煙が路上に充満したためストランド通りを封鎖した) (CCED³)

Champs-Élysées も定冠詞をとる。これはフランス語 (les Champs-Élysées, 「エリゼの野，極楽」の意) の逐語訳である。

 v) Most people look silly jogging, but . . . one can feel like General de Gaulle parading down *the Champs-Élysées* . . . (ほとんどの人はジョッギング中は愚者のような様子だが，ドゴール将軍がシャンゼリゼ通りをパレードしているかのような気分になることが

できる) (RD 91/7: 39)
3) 外国語の長距離道路にも the がつけられる.
 vi) Unlike the highway connecting Honshu and Shikoku via the Seto Ohashi, which is a road and rail bridge, the entire length of *the Setouchi Shimanami Kaido* has special lanes set aside for pedestrians and cyclists. They can use all the bridges on the route except for the Shin Onomichi Ohashi. (瀬戸大橋を経由して本州と四国を結ぶ交通路は,車と列車用の橋であるが,これと異なり,瀬戸内しまなみ街道は全体にわたって歩行者とサイクリストのために特別のレーンが設けられており,彼らは新尾道大橋を除いて途中のすべての橋を通行できる) (Peter Goldsbury, Chugoku Shimbun, Apr. 17, 99)

4) the X Road
　informal な話しことばでは,市内の道路でも the がつけられることがある (LDOCE³, s.v., the [usage note]). 次は書きことばからの例である.
 vii) Fitzwilliam College is located on *the Huntingdon Road* (A1307) and is approximately one mile North West of the city centre. (F コレッジは H 通り (A1307) に面し, シティセンターからおよそ 1 マイル北西です) (Guest Information of Fitzwilliam College)
比較: The College car parks are on *Huntingdon Road*, (Porters' Lodge entrance) and on Storey's Way. (コレッジの駐車場は H 通り (守衛室入り口) と S 道路にあります) (Guest Information of Fitzwilliam College) [上例と同じ道路；英国 Cambridge 市内]
 viii) I remember the first, on *the Albert Embankment* in central London. (最初 [のスリ] をよく覚えている, L 中心部の A 河畔通りでだった) (RD 01/7: 54) [もとスリによる文章]
 ix) Following my map, I strolled along *the Arbat*, a pedestrian street dotted with stalls, souvenir shops, street acts and restaurants. (地図に従って, [Moscow の] A 通りを散策した. これは歩行者用の通りであり, 露店や, 土産物店, 大道芸[人], レストランが点在している) (RD 02/3: 137)

　MEG (vol. 7, 16.2₄–16.2₅) は, Street/Lane は無冠詞であるが, Road は the をとると述べ,豊富な例をあげている. しかし,筆者が集めた,教養ある (と思われる) 母語話者による 2000 年前後の英語の

例ではこの傾向は見られない。例：((VIII-97, e) に加えて) Cavanagh Road (RD 99/5: 7-8); Madison Road (in Culpeper, Virginia) (RD 91/7: 113); Malcolm Road (RD 99/2: 81); McKnight Road (RD 01/8: 123); Ridge Road (RD 99/4: 115); Phahon Yothin Road (in Bangkok) (RD 02/8: 26); Rolling Hills Road (in the town of Mount Mason, N.Y.) (RD [U.S. Edition] 02/8: 168)

　Quirk et al. (1985: 294) は，記述的名詞と固有名詞との段階を (i) the Oxford road → (ii) the Oxford Road → (iii) Oxford Road → (iv) Oxford と表しているが，少なくとも road/Road の用法に関しては，この段階表記にはなんの根拠もない。なお，この4段階は Jespersen (*MEG*, vol. 7) の唱える「親密度の度合い」(stages of familiarity) に基づくと思われるが，この理論自体に問題があることはすでに触れたとおりである (☞1章 NB 1)。

8.7.1.11　トンネル

(98) a. *The Seikan Tunnel* is the longest tunnel in the world; it is 33.4 miles (53.8 km) in length ... (青函トンネルは世界最長であり，全長53.8km である) (EB 01)

b. *The Channel Tunnel* goes under the sea. (英仏海峡トンネルは海底を通過する) (OALD5) [全長 50km]

c. The blaze in *the Mont Blanc tunnel*, which broke out Wednesday on a Belgian truck carrying flour and margarine, was not extinguished until Friday afternoon. (MBトンネルの火災は，小麦とマーガリンを輸送中のBのトラックで水曜日に発生したが，金曜日の午後になってようやく鎮火された) (NY Times, Mar. 27, 99) [全長 12km；tunnel 小文字表記は原文]

d. *The Merstham Tunnel*, on the London-to-Brighton line, is approximately one mile long ... (Mトンネルは，L－B線にあり，長さおよそ1マイルである) (LOB)

e. Later, as we bounced through *the Lincoln Tunnel* back to New Jersey, I was so excited I hardly noticed the rough ride. (のちに，揺られながらLトンネルを抜けて NJ 州に戻ったとき，あまりにも興奮していたので乗り心地の悪さにはほとんど気づかなかった) (RD 98/9: 91) [全長 2,504 m；ハドソン湾底]

(99) a. He ... remembered that when they reached Redhill, after passing

through *Merstham Tunnel*, a man who might have been the companion of the girl had left the train. (少女の連れのようだった男が, Mトンネルを過ぎてRに着いたときには, 列車を降りていたのを思い出した) (LOB) [符帳扱い (☞ 1.2); (98, d) と比較せよ]

b. The accident occurred at about 8.25 am on Saturday, March 4, in *Gobun Tunnel*, one of a series of tunnels situated between Fukuyama-Nishi and Fukuyama-Higashi interchanges on the Sanyo Expressway. (この事故は3月4日の土曜日, 午前8時25分ごろ, 山陽自動車道の福山東と福山西インターチェンジ間にある連続したトンネルの1つ, 郷分トンネル内で起きた) (Peter Goldsbury, Chugoku Shimbun, Mar. 11, 00) [870メートル]

　長大トンネルのほか, LondonやNew Yorkなど大都市近くのトンネルには定冠詞がつけられるが, ローカルなトンネルは無冠詞で用いられる。トンネルの同定可能性は, 当該トンネルの長さと所在地とにより決定されると言ってさしつかえない。

8.7.1.12　橋

(100) a. Nine months later, Collins rolled across *the Sydney Harbour Bridge*, having raised $30,000. (9か月後, 3万ドル集めて, CはSH橋を自転車で渡った) (RD 01/6: 8)

b. Snug in this anchorage, we could still hear a surf thundering just beyond the low span of *the Denton Bridge*. (この船泊りでくつろいでいると, D橋の低いスパンのすぐ向こうから波音がとどろいてくるのをまだ聞くことができた) (RD 99/3: 43)

c. The next day, a body later identified as Sopha's was found by a tourist trekking near *the Golden Gate Bridge*, about 80 kilometres from the Wonggoun home. (翌日, 金門橋近くをトレッキング中の旅行者によって遺体が発見され, のちにSと確認された。そこは [容疑者の] Wの自宅から約80キロ離れた場所だった) (RD 01/5: 36)

d. Among the first of these was a twinning ceremony with *the Normandy Bridge*, which, until the opening of *the Tatara Bridge*, was the longest cable-stay bridge in the world. (最初 [の行事] はN橋との姉妹橋式だった。N橋はたたら橋開通までは世界最長のケーブルステー橋だった) (Peter Goldsbury, Chugoku Shimbun, May 8, 99)

(101) a. Many expatriate Australians like myself see *Sydney Harbour*

  Bridge as the signature of home. (私のように豪を離れたものの多くは SH 橋を故国の署名だと見る) (RD 00/3: 40)
- b. About 100 feet behind them loomed *Denton Bridge*. (およそ 100 フィート後ろに D 橋が姿を現した) (RD 99/3: 44)
- c. The slightly built, 46-year-old teacher hurries to her other work – with street children at *Memorial Bridge*. (やせ気味の 46 歳の教師は別の仕事へと急ぐ，M 橋の浮浪児たちを連れて) (RD 99/3: 82)
- d. an old engraving of *London Bridge* (L 橋の古い銅板刷り) (CIDE)

上の例が示すように，長大で有名な橋には the がつけられ，短い，あまり知られていない橋には the はつけられないという傾向がある。同一の橋名に the がつけられたりつけられなかったりするのは，意図的な文体的変奏 (stylistic variation) を除けば，ひとつには，話し手の判断に「揺れ」(fluctuation) があるためであり，ひとつには，話し手が愛称 (符帳) 扱いしているためである。

NB 24
1) 外国語の長大橋にも the がつけられる。
  i) (= 本章 NB 23, vi) Unlike the highway connecting Honshu and Shikoku via *the Seto Ohashi*, which is a road and rail bridge, the entire length of the Setouchi Shimanami Kaido has special lanes set aside for pedestrians and cyclists. They can use all the bridges on the route except for *the Shin Onomichi Ohashi*. (Peter Goldsbury, Chugoku Shimbun, Apr. 17, 99)

2) Coat Hanger は the をつけて，Sydney Harbour Bridge の別称として用いられるが，これは「コート掛け」という原義を残しているので，普通名詞が大文字表記され，転用的に固有名詞扱いされている，ととるべきである。
  ii) *"The Coat Hanger"* is to Sydney what the Eiffel Tower is to Paris. (S に対する CH は，P に対する E タワーと同じだ) (RD 99/3: 77)

8.7.1.13 船
(102) a. *The Kinbasket Princess* – a 23-foot aluminum cab boat – wasn't built for speed, but that day Gustafson shaved precious minutes off the hour-long trip back to Bush Harbour. (KP 丸──23 フィートの

アルミニウム製の遊覧ボート——はスピード用には建造されていなかったが，その日 G は B 港に戻る 1 時間の航行を急いで貴重な数分を捻出した) (RD 98/9: 38)

b. As *the Malkerry* sailed into port, Copik could see a police car on the quayside. (M 丸が入港するとき，C はパトロールカーが岸壁に停まっているのを見た) (RD 00/1: 124)

c. A memorable typhoon in 1906 wrecked the ferry piers, and another in 1908 carried *the Morning Star* onto the rocks at Lai Chi Kok. (1906 年に忘れがたい台風がフェリー桟橋を破壊し，1908 年には別の台風が MS 丸を LCK の岩礁に乗り上げさせた) (RD 99/6: 41)

(103) a. One night in New York, in 1980, he was flicking through a boating magazine when he saw an advertisement for *Delfino II*, a 40-metre motor yacht costing $1.1 million. (1980 年のある夜 NY でボート誌をめくっていたところ，D 二世号——40 メートルのモーターヨットで 110 万ドル——の広告を見た) (RD 99/9: 132) [本章 NB 25-2 と比較せよ]

b. We named her *Orca*. We sailed *Orca* from the Caribbean across the South Pacific to Australia, revelling in remote sun-drenched islands and coral atolls along the way. (彼女を O 号と命名し，O 号でカリブ海から南太平洋を横断し豪まで航海した。途中では，太陽がいっぱいの離れ小島やさんご環礁で楽しんだ) (RD 99/8: 17)

c. *Exide Challenger* has capsized. (EC 号は転覆した) (RD 98/7: 122)

船名に the がつくことはよく知られているが, (103) のように，個人的または家族・友人で私的に使用されるボートやヨットは，原則的に，無冠詞で用いられる。これは，知名度が低いことに加え，愛称（符帳）扱い（☞ 1.2）されているためである（本章 NB 37 も参照）。

NB 25
1) 同格

　Berry (1993: 60) は，船名に the がつけられることを指摘したのち，「小さい船の名前には，ふつう，冠詞はつかない」と述べ，次の例をあげている。

　　i) The front runner will undoubtedly be Richard Matthews's converted America's Cup 12-metre yacht, *Crusader*. (最有力候補は，疑うまでもなく，RM 所有の改造されたアメリカズカップ

用の 12 メートルのヨット，C 号，だろう）

しかし，この例では Crusader は yacht と同格であるので，小さい船が the をとらない例としては不適切である。次の例のように，同格の場合は the が落とされることがあるからである。(ただし，(122, c) [the V-S Orient Express] のような例もある；下記 v) [the Queen Elizabeth 2] も参照。)

    ii) Several kilometres out to sea, the *Conifer* stopped. The Sea World staff finished saying their goodbyes. (数キロ沖に出て，C は停船した。SW のメンバーはさよならを言い終えた) (RD 99/8: 49)

    iii) She was then taken to the US Naval Station San Diego and hoisted onto the Coast Guard cutter *Conifer*. (その後，SD 米海軍基地に搬送され，沿岸警備艇 C に引き上げられた) (RD 99/8: 49)

2) 大型船の名前は，数字つきの場合でも the がつけられる (1.5 参照；私的に使用される船に関しては (VIII-103, a) [Delfino II] 参照)。

    iv) The Soviet Northern Fleet was scrambling to maintain the constant submarine patrols, even sending out such aging vessels as *the K-219*. (ソ連軍北方艦隊は潜水艦による常時偵察を継続するため緊急発進をかけ，K-219 のような古船まで送り出した) (RD 98/3: 124) [潜水艦]

    v) Its successor, *the Queen Elizabeth 2*, launched in 1967, made its maiden voyage in 1969. ([Queen Elizabeth 号の] 後継である QE 二世号は 1967 年に進水し，1969 年に処女航海をした) (EB 01)

3) 船名に外国語の冠詞が含まれるときは，英語の冠詞はつけられない。

    vi) Four years later, *La Jonque* was raised and French judicial authorities hired Grafeille to inspect and analyse the wreck in dry dock. (4 年後，J 丸は引き上げられ，仏司法当局は，難破船を乾ドックで調査分析するため G を雇った) (RD 00/3: 78)

8.7.1.14 塔

(104) a. *The Eiffel Tower* stands 300m high. (エッフェル塔は高さ 300 メートルだ) (LDOCE[3])

    b. At one point today, government officials said they had acquired information pointing to a possible attack on *the Sears Tower* in

Chicago. (本日のある時点で, 政府関係筋は, C の S タワーへの [テロ] 攻撃もありうることを示唆する情報を得た, と発言した) (NY Times, Oct. 13, 01)

c. I'm standing in a packed elevator with my wife and two kids, shooting skyward at 1800 feet per minute in a 113-story-high observation tower called *the Stratosphere*. (妻と 2 人の子供といっしょにぎゅうぎゅう詰めのエレベーターに乗っている。S という 113 階の展望台を分速 1,800 フィートで昇っているところだ) (RD 99/2: 39)

d. At 120,000 tonnes, *the Pearl Tower* is the heaviest in the world – *the Eiffel Tower* at just over 10,000 tonnes is a light-weight by comparison. (パールタワーは 12 万トンあり, 世界で 1 番重い。エッフェル塔は 1 万トン強なので較べれば軽量だ) (RD 02/9: 104) [上海；展望台の高さ 263m；the Oriental Pearl Tower とも言う]

e. [The middle manager] was happy, in author Tom Peters's words, to "sit on the 37th floor of *the General Motors tower* passing memorandums from the left side of the desk to the right side of the desk for 43 years." (中間管理職は満ち足りて, 著述家 TP の言葉で言えば, 「43 年間, GM タワーの 37 階に座って, メモを机の左側から机の右側に移していた」) (RD 99/10: 43) [tower 小文字表記は原文]

(105) a. *Carfax Tower*, constructed in local rubble stone, is the only surviving part of the later medieval church and probably dates from the 13th century. (C 塔は地元の割栗石で建造されている。中世後期の教会 [St Martin's Church] のうち現存する唯一の部分であり, たぶん 13 世紀にまでさかのぼる) (Information board in Carfax Tower)

b. *Bell Harry*, the great tower over the crossing, was built at the end of the 15th century in late perpendicular Gothic. (BH は交差部上の高塔であり, 垂直な後期ゴシック様式で 15 世紀末に建設された) (GME) [カンタベリ寺院内；Bell Harry tower とも言う]

(104) の塔は知名度の高い高層建築であり, 同定可能であるのに対し, (105) の φ Carfax Tower/Bell Harry (tower) は Oxford/Canterbury にある, 中世の教会の一部であり高さも低く, エッフェル塔などよりずっと知名度も低く, したがって, 同定可能性も低い。この違いによりタワー名の前の the の有無が決定されるのである。

NB 26　表記法

2001年9月11日,テロリストによって破壊された世界貿易センタービルの twin towers は *The Times* においては次のように表記されている (peninsula/desert の表記法 (VIII-90; VIII-120) も参照)。

(9月11日) the north tower/the south tower
(9月12日) the north tower/the south tower
(9月13日) the north tower/the south tower
(9月14日) the North Tower/the south tower

事件後3日目に「北側の塔」という普通名詞から「北塔」という固有名詞へと転用されたのである。(ただし,south tower は14日も小文字であるし,north tower という小文字の表記は14日以後も現れることがある。Washington Post 紙は初めから大文字で表記している。)

8.7.1.15　宮殿

宮殿名 (Palace) は the がつけられることも,つけられないこともある。手元の資料では,the をとらないのは英王室関係の Palace である。城郭名 (☞ 本章 NB 27-1) と同様に扱われるためであろう。

(106) a. Life in *the Apostolic Palace* was thrown into utter disarray. (A宮殿の生活は大混乱に陥った) (RD 96/10: 118) [バチカン]

　　b. the vast unsupported wall of *the Ajuda Palace* in Lisbon (LのA宮殿のつっかいのない長大な城壁) (CCED³)

　　c. The president also meets ministers at inter-ministerial councils held at *the Elysee Palace*. (大統領はE宮で開かれる省間の会議でも大臣と会う) (CCED³) [仏大統領官邸]

　　d. *the Pitti Palace* (begun 1458) in Florence (FのP宮殿 (1458年建築開始)) (EB 01)

類例: the Nymphenburg Palace, near Munich (GME)

参考: the Vatican (バチカン宮殿) も the をとる; ベルサイユ宮殿は the Palace of Versailles (le Château de Versailles) という言い方が一般的である。

(107) a. The celebrations in London, UK, were particularly spectacular, with a huge fun fair on the Mall, the avenue leading to *Buckingham Palace*, the London residence of Queen Elizabeth. (英連合王国のLでの式は特にすばらしかった。マル通り——E女王のLの住居であるB宮殿につづく通り——では大きな市が設けられた)

(Peter Goldsbury, Chugoku Shimbun, Jan. 15, 00)
b. He also received a studio on the Thames at Blackfriars . . . plus a summer apartment at *Eltham Palace*. ([Van Dyck は] T 河畔の B にアトリエを授かり, さらに, E 宮殿内にも夏用の部屋を授かった) (RD 99/12: 111)
c. Its southern part contains *Fulham Palace* (early 16th century), the residence of the bishops of London until 1973; the palace is now a museum. ([ロンドンの Fulham 地区の] 南側には F 宮殿 (16世紀初期) がある。当宮殿は1973年まで英国国教会主教の住居であったが, 現在は記念館になっている) (EB 01)

例外： In 1852 he supervised the decorations for *the Crystal Palace*. (1852年には C パレスの装飾を監督した) (EB 01) [Hyde Park に建設された宮殿； (107, a-c) が所在地を表すのに対し, これは形容詞的性格が強いので the がつけられる (☞ 8.3.1 [転用固有名詞])]

参考： the Brighton/London Pavilion (B/L離宮) は the をとる ((Ap. 2.1-10, a) 参照)。

NB 27

1) 城郭名は, 無冠詞で用いられる。本来, 私的所有物であるためであろう。

　i) Some two kilometres north was *Tintagel Castle*, the legendary birthplace of King Arthur, whose golden round table was said to lie deep under the mound of *Bossiney Castle*, just across the fields from the hotel. (およそ2キロ北には T 城, A 王の伝説上の生誕地, があった。彼の黄金の円卓は, ホテルの庭地のすぐ向かいの B 城の土塁の奥深くに眠っていると伝えられていた) (RD 99/12: 55)

　ii) A few days before, a fire had devastated large parts of *Windsor Castle*. (数日前, 火事で W 城のかなりの部分が焼け落ちた) (CCED[3])

　類例： Manorbier Castle in Wales (RD 99/7: 38); Picton Castle in Wales (RD 99/7: 40); Leeds Castle in Kent (CCED[3]); Himeji Castle in Harima province (EB 01)

2) 教会名 (Church) は the をとるが, 建物というよりも, 組織としての教会を指す。

iii) (= VIII-30, a) Some 50,000 sympathisers marched through the streets of Macau in 1966, staging daily demonstrations against the government and *the Catholic Church*. (RD 99/11: 54)

3) Abbey/Cathedral/Chapel など寺院名は，通例，その利用者が地域限定的であるため，the をとらない．

iv) Elizabeth was crowned in *Westminster Abbey* on 2 June 1953. (Eは1953年6月2日W寺院で戴冠(たいかん)された) (CCED³)

v) At 21, he talked his way into a job at *Wells Cathedral*, where they were pioneering a rebirth of old building methods. (21歳のとき話をつけてW大聖堂に職を得た．そこでは他に先駆けて古い建築方法が再生されつつあった) (RD 99/7: 39f.)

vi) Looking down from the hilltop where the church had stood, it seemed like a giant weed eater had attacked the community of *McDonald Chapel* and its surrounding hills. (教会がかつて建っていた丘の上から見下ろすと，まるでマリファナ常用の巨人がMD分会堂のあった共同体とそのまわりの丘を攻撃したかのようだった) (RD 00/2: 126)

類例：Wawel Cathedral (RD 96/10: 126)

上記の Abbey などが the をとらないことを考えれば，次例中の Temple は，厳密には，小文字で表記すべきである（本章 NB 35-2, v [airport] 参照）．事実，*Encyclopaedia Britannica*（2001年版）では小文字で表記されている．

vii) We enter *the Wannian Temple*, but nowhere can we see a monk to show us a place to sleep. (W寺院に入るが，寝場所を教えてくれる僧侶をどこにも見つけることができない) (RD 99/7: 85)

参考：To the north in Rajasthan, *the Mahanalesvara temple* at Menal (c. 11th century), *the Sun temple* at Jhalrapatan (11th century), *the Siva temple* at Ramgarh (12th century), and *the Endesvara temple* (12th century) at Bijolian are important examples. (Rの北方では，MのM寺（11世紀頃），JのS寺（11世紀），RのS寺（12世紀），およびBのE寺（12世紀）が重要な代表例である) (EB 01) [インド北西部]；*the Angkor Wat temple* (= Angkor (Wat) [Ap.2.2-23 (参考) 参照]) (CCED³)

4) Alhambra / Taj Mahal は外国の palace 扱いされているため定冠詞をとる．

viii) Today the red-and-yellow flag of Spain flies above the battlements of *the Alhambra.*（今日Ａの塔上狭間胸壁の上にはＳの赤と黄色の国旗がひるがえる）(RD 02/6: 104)

ix) "*The Taj Mahal* is dying and no-one cares," he said ...（「ＴＭは壊れかけているのに，だれも気にかけていない」と彼は言った）(RD 99/9: 49)

x) He had never visited *the Taj* ...（１度もタージ[マハル]を訪れたことはなかった）(RD 99/9: 50)

8.7.1.16 公園／庭園；植物園

植物園は (i) X Gardens または (ii) X Garden という構造で表される。公園・庭園は，これらに加えて，(iii) X Park という構造もとる。(i) は複数構成物（☞ 8.2）なので原則的に the をとる（例外：Kensington Gardens ((113, a) 参照)。(ii) の場合も the をとる。

(108) a. He had almost reached the turn-off to *the Hanging Gardens* when someone yelled: "A bear's coming! Run for your lives!"（Ｈ庭園への枝道にほとんど着いたとき，だれかが叫んだ，「クマだ，逃げろ」）(RD 99/9: 73) [カナダ西部]

b. *the Japanese Tea Gardens* in Golden Gate park（金門公園内の日本茶庭園）(LDOAE) [San Francisco]

c. *the Botanic Gardens* at Kew（Ｋの植物園）(LDOCE³) [London]

類例：the Longwood Gardens near Kennett Square, Pa.; the U.S. National Gardens; the Boboli Gardens (begun 1560) of the Pitti Palace in Florence; the Hanging Gardens of Babylon（以上 GME）

(109) a. Soon afterward we got a call from the White House inviting us to the signing ceremony in *the Rose Garden.*（まもなくホワイトハウスから電話をうけ，Ｒ庭園での調印式に招待された）(RD 98/9: 136)

b. Stroll through the pathways of *the Flora Garden* with its abundant flowers, aviary of native birds, and recreation areas.（Ｆ植物庭園の小道を散策してごらんなさい。たくさんの花，地鳥の飼育場，休養所があります）(RD 98/6: n.p. (after 80))

c. He ... took them to places he loved that they otherwise might never visit, like *the Chicago Botanic Garden.*（[生徒たちを] Ｃ植物園のような，自分の好きな所に連れていったが，そうしなかったら彼らは自分では訪れることはないだろう）(RD 00/2: 12)

類例：the Royal Botanic Garden in Edinburgh; the Chelsea Physic Garden in London; the Brooklyn Botanic Garden in New York City; the Fairchild Tropical Garden in Miami, Fla.; the Petrozavodsk University Botanical Garden in Karelia, Russia; the M. M. Grishko Central Botanical Garden in Kiev, Ukraine; the Kirstenbosch National Botanical Garden in Cape Town (以上 EB 01, s.v., Botanical Gardens)

(iii) の X+Park という構造に関しては，まず (110)-(111) の諸例を観察されたい。(これらの例文はいずれも Peter Goldsbury (Chugoku Shimbun) による〈英〉用法である。掲載日のみ記す。)

(110) a. There is a famous monument in *the Peace Memorial Park* dedicated to children.（平和記念公園には，子どもたちに捧げられた有名な記念碑がある）(Apr. 15, 00)

b. Hiroshima City is soliciting donations to replace the benches in *the Peace Park*.（広島市は平和公園内のベンチを取り替えるため寄付を募っている）(Sep. 12, 97)

c. A shuttle bus service will operate between Hiroshima Castle and *the Forest Park* until Dec 14.（12月14日まで広島城と森林公園間にシャトルバスが運行される）(Apr. 18, 97)

d. It will be very close to *the Hiroshima Regional Park* and the A-City.（そこは広島広域公園やA-CITYにとても近い位置にある）(May 1, 98)

(111) a. An observation platform constructed like a mountain castle of the Warring States era has been constructed in *Hiroshima City Forest Park* (Fukuda-cho, Higashi-ku).（戦国時代の山城を復元した展望台が広島市森林公園（東区福田町）に建設された）(Apr. 11, 97)

b. The new proposals all involve building extensions to the Astramline, which runs from Hondori to *Hiroshima Regional Park*.（新提案は，すべて現在本通りから広島広域公園を結んでいるアストラムラインを延伸する案である）(Jun.13, 97)

c. Hijiyama Skywalk is an escalator and elevated walkway affording access to *Hijiyama Park* from Danbara.（比治山スカイウオークはエスカレーターと高架式歩道であり，段原から比治山公園に登ることができる）(May 8, 98)

d. There are many other sports facilities at *Senogawa Park*, which can be used for a fee, also a sports ground and forest park with free access. (瀬野川公園には，他にもたくさん，有料のスポーツ設備があり，無料で利用可能な運動場つきの森林公園もある) (Apr.11, 97)

広島市内の公園のうち，原爆投下跡地に造られた，知名度の高い Peace (Memorial) Park (平和(記念)公園) には the がつけられ，知名度が高いとも低いとも断定しがたい公園には the がつけられることもつけられないこともあり，知名度の低い公園には the がつけられていない。この事実は，the の有無に同定可能性が関与していることを示している。(ただし，〈米〉では公園名に the はつけられない。本節では主として〈英〉用法に関して述べる。)

だが，ここで問題を複雑にしているのは，Hyde/Regent's Park がかつては the Hyde/Regent's Park と呼ばれていたが，のちに定冠詞が落とされたという歴史的経緯である (*MEG* (vol. 7, 16.2₃); Christophersen (1939: 178))。このことは，当該の Park が多くの人々に知られてくるにつれて，単なる「符帳」となり (☞ 1.2)，無冠詞で用いられるようになるということを示唆しているのかもしれない。あるいは，*MEG* があげている the Hyde Park の例は1例だけなので，それは偶発的な例であり (道路名に関する「誤例」(本章 NB23-4) 参照)，本来は無冠詞の Hyde Park が一般的であったのかもしれない。(現在でも (the) Forest/Regional Park (110, c—d; 111, a—b) のような揺れの例がある；Regent's Park は，もともと「Prince Regent (= George IV) の公園」の意なので文法的に the が必要。) あるいは，公園名は，同定可能性が低いので，全国区扱いよりも地方区扱いのほうが適切であると再解釈されたのかもしれない。もっとも，いずれの理由によるにせよ，現代英語の話者にとって，ある固有名詞が歴史的にどういう経過をたどったかは重要な問題ではない。現代英語の観点から見れば，公園名に先行する the の有無は，同定可能性の程度に関する話者の判断を反映していると考えるべきである。(the Regent's Park が無冠詞になったのは，他の多くの無冠詞の公園名にならった結果であると推測される (文法用語で言えば，「類推」(analogy) である)。*MEG* (vol. 7, 16.2₃) が the Hyde/Regent's Park 以外には the のつく公園名をあげていないことから推測すると，(112) の公園は比較的新しく造られたのではないであろうか。もしもそうであれば，(112) の公園名には，同定可能性が高い固有名詞には the をつけるという話者の意識が反映されていると見ることが可能である。

(112) a. I wander along my last length of drovers' road in *the Brecon Beacons National Park* in South Wales. (南ウエールズにある BB 国立公園内の牛追いの道の最後の箇所を歩く) (RD 96/10: 14)

b. "This isn't *the Chitwan National Park*," said Beryl, gazing round at the scrubby undergrowth and distant village. (低木の茂みや遠くの村を見渡しながら，Bは言った，「ここはC国立公園ではないな」) (RD 00/6: 45) [Nepal]

c. Having delivered the last of his explosives to seismic crews working on the Alaska Highway in Canada's far north-west, Ray Kitchen, a 56-year-old truck driver from Fort Nelson, British Columbia, decided to stop off at *the Liard River Hotsprings Provincial Park*. (カナダの最北西のAHで作業中の地震調査隊に最後の爆薬を届けたのち，BC州のFNからやってきた56歳のトラック運転手であるRKは，LRH州立公園に立ち寄ることに決めた) (RD 99/9: 69) [カナダ西部]

類例：the Mountain Zebra National Park [South Africa] (RD 01/10: 142); the Snowdonia national Park [Wales 北西部] (RD 96/10: 13); the Wildlife Safari park, near Winston, Oregon (RD 00/1: 70)

(113) a. A few minutes from my house in Bayswater, I can enter *Kensington Gardens* at Notting Hill Gate and walk across the grass all the way through *Hyde Park*, *Green Park* and *St. James Park* to Westminster, scarcely setting foot on a sidewalk. (BのわがHPから数分でNHGのK庭園に入り，ほとんど歩道に足を降ろすことなく，HP，GP，聖JPの芝生を横切ってW寺院へと歩いていくことができる) (RD 96/3: 115)

b. It was only 9 a.m., but already Camden Lock, just north of *Regent's Park* in London, was its usual frenetic mix of clothes stalls, bookshops, tarot readers and pavement artists. (まだ9時だが，LのRPのすぐ北側のCLでは，すでにいつものように衣料品の露店，本屋，タロット占い師，大道芸人が雑然と入り乱れている) (RD 99/9: 137)

c. The day, our first full one in *Rocky Mountain National Park*, had started out well. (その日，R山脈国立公園での最初のまる1日は無事に始まった) (RD [U.S. Edition] 98/9: 113)

類例：Andrew Haydon Park, along the Ottawa River (RD 99/4: 94); Big Lake Park [Council Bluffs, Iowa] (RD 99/8: 117); Centennial Park [Australia] (RD 00/3: 45); Central Park [New York City] (RD 96/3: 116); Jasper Country Park, Alberta [Canada] (CCED[3]); Komodo National Park [Indonesia] (RD 99/6: 29); Kruger National Park

[South Africa] (RD 02/2: 45); Ku-ring-gai Chase National Park [Sydney] (RD 99/3: 77); Shenandoah National Park [Virginia] (RD 99/6: 112); Yosemite/Yellowstone National Park (EB 01/GME 01) [以上，英国以外の公園であることに注意]

NB 28
1) Garden(s)/Park をともなわない公園名
    i) *The Tuileries, the Élysée, the Luxembourg, Monceau* and so on are dainty, artificial, ornamental. (チュイルリー宮[跡公園]，エリゼ宮，リュクサンブール宮庭園，モンソー公園，等々は優美で，人工的で，装飾的だ) (RD 96/3: 116)
2) 普通名詞扱い
    park (小文字表記) が普通名詞のときは，不定冠詞をとる。
    ii) Within hours investigators were reading reports about five badly charred bodies discovered in a shallow grave in *a North Carolina park*. (数時間のうちに調査官たちは，NC 州内のある公園の地中に浅く埋められているところを発見された黒こげの5体に関する報告書を読んでいた) (RD 99/10: 17)
3) 外国語の公園名
    外国語の公園名も，同定可能性に応じて，the の有無が決定される。
(次の例はいずれも Peter Goldsbury (Chugoku Shimbun) による。)
    iii) *The Kokuei Bihoku Kyuryo Koen* is a large open space situated near the city of Shobara in the north of Hiroshima Prefecture. (国営備北丘陵公園は広大な野外広場であり，広島県北部の庄原市の近くにある) (May 1, 98)
類例：the Chibori Koen (May 1, 98); the Higashisenda Koen (Sep. 25, 98); the Innoshima Amenity Koen (Jun.12, 99); the Karuga Kaihin Koen (Jun. 6, 97); the Kyuryo Koen (May 1, 98)
    iv) The street is almost adjacent to *Fukuromachi Koen*, a park where young people congregate. (その通りは，若者が集まる袋町公園とほとんど隣接している) (Nov. 13, 98)
類例：Chuo Koen (Jun. 26, 98); Noborimachi Koen (May 22, 98)
4) φ X Square
    公園名は〈英〉用法では the をとることがあるが，広場 (Square/Circus) の名称は〈英・米〉とも無冠詞で用いられる。海に対し湖や池

が狭小であるため the をとらないのと同じ原理が観察される。

- v) Arriving in *Castle Square*, at the entrance to Warsaw's Old Town, the pope's vehicle drove across cobble-stones strewn with garlands of flowers. (ワルシャワの旧市街地の入り口にあるC広場に到着したとき，教皇の車は花束が撒(ま)かれた玉石の上を過ぎていった) (RD 96/10: 131)
- vi) In the predawn hours of June 4, Yeh awakened to the roar of tanks and the rattle of rifle fire in *Tiananmen Square*. ([1989年]6月4日の夜明け前，Yは戦車の轟音(ごうおん)と天安門広場でのライフルの発砲音で目を覚ました) (RD 98/6: 106)
- vii) For the first time in years, *Trafalgar Square* was empty of pigeons. (数年ぶりにT広場にハトがいなくなった) (OALD⁶)
- viii) Its headquarters are located in Burlington House, near *Piccadilly Circus*, London, England. ([RAS (王立天文学会) の] 本部所在地は英国，LのP広場近くのBHである) (EB 01) [単にPiccadilly とも言う]

類例：Herald Square (RD 00/7: 127); Red Square (RD 02/3: 137); San Gabriel Square (RD 99/4: 107); St. Peter's Square (RD 96/10: 135); Victory Square (RD 96/10: 131); Cuscatlan/George/Leicester/Manchester/Parliament Square (CCED³)

8.7.1.17 病院

病院名 (Hospital) に関しては，原則的に，〈英〉用法では the がつけられ，〈米〉用法では，公園の場合と同様，無冠詞で用いられる（本章 NB 35 参照）。

(114) a. Ladan Bijani died at 2.30pm at *the Raffles Hospital*, Singapore, after huge blood loss. Her sister, Laleh, died 90 minutes later. ([結合双生児の] LB はSのR病院で大量失血後，午後2時半に死亡。姉のLも90分後に死亡した) (Daily Telegraph, July 9, 03) 〈英〉
- b. Next, Hindley called *the Sir Charles Gardner Hospital* in Perth. (次に，HはPのSCG病院に電話した) (RD 99/6: 34)
- c. One day when I was in the operating room, a message came for me to call *the Monmouth Medical Center*. (ある日手術室にいたとき，M医療センターに電話するようにとの伝言をうけた) (RD 96/3: 140)

類例：the National Hospital (RD 01/9: 137); the North Devon Hospital (RD 99/12: 60); the Philippine General Hospital in Manila (RD

99/11: 100); the Royal Edinburgh Hospital (RD 99/9: 115); the Royal Orthopaedic Hospital in Birmingham, England (RD 02/3: 20); the Singapore General Hospital (RD 02/3: 20); the Vejthani Hospital in Bangkok (RD 99/7: 55); the Metro Specialist hospital in Sungai Petani, Malaysia (RD 00/7: 85); the Perth hospital (RD 99/6: 37); the Shriners hospital (RD 00/6: 132) [後3例中の小文字は原文]; the New York City Poison Center (RD 96/3: 54); the Royal Victoria Infirmary (RD 01/8: 18)

(115) a. The 29-year-old Iranian women died 90 minutes apart early yesterday at *Raffles Hospital* in Singapore ... (Washington Post, July 9, 03) 〈米〉[(114, a) と比較せよ］
　　 b. After I finished at Columbia, I started my postgraduate training at *Roosevelt Hospital*. (C 大学を修了したのち, R 病院で大学院課程の訓練を始めた) (RD 96/3: 140)
　　 c. His radiation treatment had begun at *Washington Hospital Centre* and was to continue every weekday for seven weeks. (放射線治療はW 病院センターで始まり, 7 週間にわたって平日は毎日行われることになった) (RD 99/12: 134)

　類例：Arlington Hospital in Virginia (RD 01/9: 101); Barnes Hospital in St Louis (RD 99/12: 76); Canberra Hospital (RD 00/6: 36); Columbia Presbyterian Hospital (RD 00/7: 125); Danbury Hospital (RD 00/3: 52); Kuala Lumpur General Hospital (RD 99/11: 99); Kunde hospital (RD 99/8: 95); Mercy Hospital in Laredo, Texas (RD 99/11: 120); Nawaloka Hospital in Colombo (RD 99/8: 29); Queen Elizabeth Hospital (RD 01/5: 33); Queen Mary hospital in nearby Pokfulam (RD 00/7: 26); Ragama Rehabilitation Hospital on the outskirts of Colombo (RD 00/1: 17); Ravensthorpe Hospital (RD 99/6: 37); Royal Adelaide Hospital (RD 00/9: 27); Royal Prince Alfred Hospital in Sydney (RD 99/6: 37); Tung Wah hospital in Hong Kong (RD 00/7: 88); United Christian Hospital in Hong Kong (RD 99/11: 104); Yale New Haven Hospital (RD 00/3: 52); Shriners (= the Shriners hospital) (RD 00/6: 138); Hospital Permai in Johor Baharu, Malaysia (RD 00/3: 87) [Hospital は肩書き扱い]; Beth Israel Medical Centre (RD 99/9: 108); Columbia-Presbyterian Medical Center (RD 96/3: 126); Makati Medical Centre in Manila

(RD 00/1: 107) [Kunde hospital など小文字は原文]

Clinic には the がつけらる。

(116) a. Nineteen years after the accident, on an afternoon in July 1997, Heidler sat nervously in a conference room in *The Cleveland Clinic* of Ohio. (事故から19年後，1997年7月のある日の午後，HはO州のCクリニックの会議室に不安そうに座っていた) (RD 99/7: 58)

b. At *the Gemelli Clinic* the pope was rushed first to a tenth-floor room reserved for a papal emergency and then to an operating room. (Gクリニックで教皇は，まず10階の病室——教皇の緊急事態用に用意されている——に大急ぎで運び込まれ，その後，手術室に移された) (RD 96/10: 138)

c. [A]nxiety-ridden and depressed, he was twice hospitalized at *the Mayo Clinic* in Rochester, Minnesota, where he received electro-shock treatments. (不安に襲われ，鬱(?)状態になり [Hemingway は] M州，RのMクリニックに2度入院し，電気ショック療法をうけた) (EB 01)

8.7.1.18　一般化困難な固有名詞

上記の一般的傾向にもかかわらず，個別的にはなお一般化しがたい場合がある。以下は情報収集が困難なため the の有無の理由を判断しがたい例である。

the をとる地名・施設：

(117) a. (=8章 NB 6-1, i) A bright sun shone as pall-bearers dressed in traditional clothes carried Long Wolf's coffin a half-mile up a hill to *the Wolf Creek Cemetery* where some family members are buried. (RD 98/12: 94) [墓地名；(118, a) と比較せよ]　類例：the Wounded Knee memorial cemetery in South Dakota [小文字表記] (RD 98/12: 94)

b. For all his wealth, the primary home for him and his wife is a surprisingly modest two-story log house on *the Flying D Ranch* near Bozeman, Mont. (裕福であるにもかかわらず，彼と妻との本宅は，驚くほど質素な2階建てのログハウスであり，モンタナ州のB近くのFD牧場にある) (RD [U.S. Edition] 99/9: 216) [牧場名；(118, b) と比較せよ]　類例：the Porter ranch (RD 97/2: 14); the Montana ranch (RD 99/2: 103) [小文字表記]

c. East of *the Kyber Pass*, in the North-West Frontier Province of Pakistan, sits a school called the Haqqania *madrassa*. (Pの北西国

境地域にある，K 峠の東方に，H 校という学校がある）(RD 02/3: 48)
[峠名；(118, c) と比較せよ；英和辞典では Bolan/Brenner/Chilkoot
Pass には the がつけられている；*madrassa* 斜字体は原文]

d. (= VIII-73, e) Before entering Zurich University to study biology, she worked for a year in *the Camargue*, the flat, marshy delta in the south of France where the Rhône River runs into the Mediterranean. (RD 96/10: 90) [デルタ名；(118, d) と比較せよ] 類例：the Zhujiang Delta in southern China's Guangdong province (RD 02/8: 93)

e. Dorine shuddered as she arrived at *the Castelsarrasin airfield*, north of Toulouse, in May 1996. (1996 年 5 月，D は T の北部の C 飛行場に着いたとき身震いした) (RD 00/7: 76) [飛行場名；小文字表記；(118, e) と比較せよ]

f. On December 27, 1994, four-and-a-half months after my return to Rwanda, *the Imbabazi* officially opened with Sembagare as the co-director. (1994 年 12 月 27 日，R に帰って 4 か月半後，S を共同院長として I 孤児院は正式にオープンした) (RD 00/3: 142) [(118, f) と比較せよ]

g. On holiday in southwestern France, the ten-year-old and her parents soon arrived at *the Lascaux Cave*. (南西フランスでの休暇中，10 歳児と両親はすぐに L 洞窟に到着した) (RD 96/10: 89) [洞窟名] 類例：the Paviland/Worms Head Cave (CCED[3])

h. Nine years after he filed the Taj Mahal case, the Supreme Court banned all coal-based factories in *the Taj Trapezium*, a nearly 10,000-square-kilometre environmental sanctuary created around the mausoleum. (TM の訴訟から 9 年後，最高裁は TT——霊廟(れいびょう)のまわりに造られた約 1 万平方キロの聖域環境——内の石炭関連の工場すべてを操業禁止にした) (RD 99/9: 52) [聖域名]

i. After travelling the interior, we finally reached our destination – *the Kivu*. [. . .] Kivu, unlike many African waters, was crystal-clear and uninhabited by crocodiles, hippopotamuses or parasites, making it ideal for swimming and recreation. (内陸部を移動して，やっと目的地の K に着いた。K[湖] は，多くのアフリカの湖水と異なって，透明であり，ワニやカバ，寄生動物はいなくて，泳いだりくつろいだりするのに理想的だった) (RD 00/3: 125) [the Kivu (地域名)

は (Lake) Kivu と弁別的]

j. Suddenly, as if the Red Sea had parted, Johnson stepped from the dense forest of *the Northwest Angle* and stood atop a roadway. (突然まるで紅海が裂けたかのように，JはNAの密林から抜け出て，路上に立っていた) (RD 99/11: 30) [Minnesota 州内の地名]

比較 : Minnesota's remote *Northwest Angle* (RD 99/11: 25) [所有格が先行すれば，the は落とされる]

the がつけられる，その他の地名 : the Bronx (RD 97/6: 80); the Hollywood Bowl (RD 00/4: 8); the Ensanche, Bilbao's centre [Spain] (RD 02/3: 92); the Josefov [Prague's Jewish Quarter] (RD 00/4: 59); The Hague, The Strand, The Sudan (LDOCE³); the Alamo (アラモの砦) (RD 99/4: 47)

the をとらない地名・施設 :

(118) a. Three days later the family gathered for a service at *Highland Cemetery*. (3 日後家族はH墓地での式に集まった) (RD 99/2: 120) [墓地名 ; (117, a) と比較せよ]　類例 : Arlington National Cemetery (RD 01/12: 48); Brompton Cemetery [London 郊外] (RD 98/12: 92)

b. Word travels fast along the Arizona-Mexico border, and *Singing Valley Ranch* would soon become the place where *el buen perro grande* (the nice big dog) lived. (うわさはすぐにAとMとの境界にそって広まり，SV牧場は間もなくすばらしい大型犬がいる場所になることだろう) (RD 97/2: 12) [牧場名 ; (117, b) と比較せよ]

c. After a short drive south, they had been dropped off at a service station near the coast at *Bulli Pass*. (南に少し行ったのち，B峠の海岸近くのガソリンスタンドで降ろされた) [豪州] (RD 99/5: 123) [峠名 ; (117, c) と比較せよ]

d. About 13 kilometres later, time takes on a more human scale at *Unkar Delta*. (約 13 キロ下流のUデルタでは，時間は少しばかり人間的な規模になる) (RD 00/2: 56) [デルタ名 ; (117, d) と比較せよ]

e. They drove past *Aulnat airfield*. (A 飛行場を車で過ぎた) (RD 00/7: 73) [飛行場名 ; 小文字表記 ; (117, e) と比較せよ]

f. An hour earlier he'd been singled out from the other orphans in *Crèche Maison d'espoir* in Port au Prince . . . (1 時間前に，ポルトープランス [ハイチ共和国の首都] にある希望の館の孤児のなかから選ばれたばかりだった) (RD 02/4: 23) [孤児院名 ; (117, f) と比較せよ]

これまであげてきた 8.7.1 の諸例は，墓地名など少数を除き，固有名詞が the

第 8 章　定冠詞使用の文脈および環境　335

をとるかとらないかは指示物の大きさや広がりなど知名度と関係があること，つまり，the の有無は同定可能性によって決定される傾向が強いことを示している．

ここで墓地名など，一見，無秩序に見える例について考えるならば，これらは現代英語における「揺れ」であり，遅かれ早かれ，同定可能性に基づいて the の有無が決定されることになると予測される．なぜなら，過去の揺れは類似物の用法にならって安定化されてきているからである．例：the X Road → φ X Road (狭い地域内の道路；本章 NB 23-4); the Hyde Park → φ Hyde Park (☞ 8.7.1.16); the Paddington Station → φ Paddington Station (*MEG*, vol. 7, 16.3₅); φ Drury Lane → the Drury Lane (劇場；本章 NB 32-5); φ Tigrys and Eufrates (Chaucer, Bo, V, m. 1, 1) → the Tigris (River)/the Euphrates (River)

8.7.2　the をとる固有名詞

前節では，類似の形でありながら the をとる場合ととらない場合とがある地名および建造物を見た．本節では，the をとるのが通例である固有名詞を項目ごとに列挙したい．

8.7.2.1　砂漠／荒野；高原；森林

上記の地名は the をとる．LDOCE³ からの次の定義が示すように，これらはすべて大規模であり，それゆえ，同定可能だからである．

(119) a. desert: <u>a large area</u> of sand where it is always very hot and dry.
　　　b. wilderness: <u>a large area</u> of land that has never been developed or farmed.
　　　c. plateau: <u>a large area</u> of flat land that is higher than the land around it.
　　　d. forest: <u>a large area</u> of land that is thickly covered with trees.

定義上，小規模な砂漠や荒野，高原，森林は，ありえない．固有名詞扱いでない場合は desert は小文字で書かれる．(複数形の「平原」(Plains/Fields) に関しては 8.2.5 参照．)

(120) a. Now her expertise is sought out by scientists planning the return of the Mongolian horse to its last wild home – *the Gobi Desert*. (今こそ彼女の専門知識が科学者たちに求められている．蒙古馬を彼らの最後の野生の故郷であるゴビ砂漠に帰そうと計画しているからだ) (RD 96/10: 94)
　　　b. China has a nuclear test site in *the Lop Desert* at the eastern end of *the Taklimakan*... (中国はタクラマカン砂漠の東端にあるロプ砂

c. And in Africa there is some evidence that *the Sahara* shrank in response to the increase in rain. (アフリカでは，雨量の増加に呼応してサハラ砂漠が縮小したというかなりの証拠がある) (RD 99/9: 24)

d. Below was nothing but the craggy, forested mountain ridges and steep canyons of *the Pecos Wilderness*. (眼下には，植林されてはいるが岩肌のむきでた山の尾根とペーコス荒野の急峻な峡谷以外には何もなかった) (RD 99/10: 67)

e. (= III-36) *The Gila*, a rugged wilderness in south-west New Mexico, was a perilous place to play cowboy. (RD 99/8: 60)

f. (= 本章 NB 21) That's where the canyons of *the Colorado Plateau* run from the middle of Utah south to the middle of Arizona – Grand Canyon, Glen Canyon, Grand Gulch and thousands of others. (RD 96/10: 77) [高原名]

g. Just before the clouds roll across *the Nullarbor* to jostle away the last rays of sunlight, I look out once again over the glinting water. A mother whale is bonding with her newborn, a white calf, 15 metres offshore. (入り日の最後の光線を押しのけて雲が N 平原に広がる直前，きらきら光っている水面をもう 1 度見る。15 メートル沖合で母クジラが生まれたばかりの白い子クジラを連れている) (RD 99/10: 53) [the Nullarbor Plain]

比較：At *Nullarbor*, some 18,000 spectators each year trod a special walkway to a narrow, wooden platform at the base of the cliffs. (N では毎年およそ 1 万 8 千人の観光客が特別の歩道を歩いて，崖の基部に設けられた狭い木製の展望所を訪れた) (RD 99/10: 48) [町名]

参考：When I was a teenager, a young hotshot test pilot named Chuck Yeager first cracked the sound barrier over *the California desert*, starting a new era for aviation. (私が十代のとき，やり手の若いテストパイロットの CY が C の砂漠地帯で初めて音速の壁を破り，航空術の新時代を開いた) (RD 99/3: 120) [小文字表記]

類例：the Somalian desert (RD 99/10: 122); the Tibetan plateau (RD 00/1: 66); the remote Gobi Desert in Mongolia (RD 96/10: 90) [形容詞つき]

比較：(= IV-6, b) It now looked almost as if we were flying over *an Arizona desert*, but no desert has ever had such terrain. [月面上で

の描写；アリゾナ州（特に，南部）にある多くの砂漠のうちの任意の1つを指す〕(RD 99/3: 133)

NB 29　φ Saudi desert
　次の例で Saudi desert が無冠詞であるのは，the one million square kilometres の素材（☞ 2.1.2）として扱われているためである。
　Davies pointed out that Mars was the only company that operated a refrigerated warehouse and controlled an enormous fleet of air-conditioned trucks, a boon to troops scattered throughout the one million square kilometres of *Saudi desert*. (D の指摘では，M［チョコレート］会社だけが冷凍倉庫を稼働し，空調器つきのトラックを大量に管理しているので，百万平方キロの S の砂漠に点在している部隊には大助かりだった) (RD 99/7: 123)

森林の名前も the をとる。
(121) a. I'd like to report a body in *the Belanglo State Forest*. (B 国立森林の遺体についてご報告いたしたく存じます) (RD 99/5: 121)
　　　b. In *the Belanglo Forest*, a massive search was under way. (B 森林では大がかりな捜索が進行中だった) (RD 99/5: 122)
　　　c. Yet those living near *the Belanglo* continued to feel alarm at the possibility of a killer in their midst. (しかし，B の森近くの住人は彼らのなかに人殺しがいるのではないかという可能性にずっと不安を感じていた) (RD 99/5: 124)
　　　d. *Marka* is a Norwegian word for forest. *The Oslomarka* is actually seven adjoining forests that cover an area twice as large as the city of Chicago, where I live. (M は森を表すノルウエー語である。オスロの森は，実際には，近接した 7 つの森林であり，私が住んでいる C 市の 2 倍の広さがある) (RD 99/5: 107f.)〔外国語の森林名にも the がつけられる；*Marka* 斜字体は原文〕
　類例：the Angeles National Forest; the New Forest; the Savermake Forest（以上 CCED[3]）

NB 30　外国語の定冠詞
　次の例で森林名が the をとっていないのは，the foothills の素材であると同時に，外国語の定冠詞があるためであろう。

Vineyards cover close to 10,000 acres, from near the coast to the foothills of *Los Padres National Forest*, often following the flowing contours of the land. (ブドウ園はほとんど1万エーカーの面積があり，海岸近くからLP国立森林の麓に及び，しばしば土地にそってうねっている) (CCED[3])

8.7.2.2　電車／バス／宇宙船

船名が，私的に用いられるものを除いて，the をとるのと同様に，電車，バス，ヘリコプターなどが固有の名称をもつ場合も the をとる。電車・バスは公共の乗り物であり，同定可能だからである。ヘリコプター・宇宙船も公共の乗り物に準じて the をとる。

(122) a. Welcome to *the Thames Express*. (T急行をご利用いただきありがとうございます) [Thames Express は Brighton と Stratford-upon-Avon 間を走る急行]

b. Let us hope you will not be snowed up in *the Taurus*! (雪のためT号に閉じ込められないよう祈りましょう) (Christie, *Murder on the Orient Express*)

c. He's the man who recreated the world's most celebrated passenger train, *the Venice-Simplon-Orient Express*, reassembling old coaches that had lain in goods yards throughout Europe. (彼は世界で最も有名な旅客列車，V-S オリエント急行を再現した男だ。欧州じゅうの貨物操車場にあった古い列車を再結集したのだった) (RD 00/5: 69)

d. Next week will see the operation of *the Green Mover* on the streets of Hiroshima. This is the name for the new fleet of articulated tramcars to be operated by the Hiroden company on the Miyajima route. (来週には広島の通りで「グリーン・ムーバー」が走っているのが見られるだろう。これは，広島電鉄が宮島線に走らせる新しい連結車両の名前である) (Peter Goldsbury, Chugoku Shimbun, Jun. 5, 99) [路面電車名]

e. Passengers travelling to and from the airport to places not served by the limousine bus will be able to transfer to various highway buses at the Takasaka Parking Area on the Sanyo Expressway. The highway buses, which all operate from Hiroshima are *the Flower Liner*, to Innoshima City; *the Reed Liner*, to Fuchu City and Kannabe-cho; and *the Peace Liner*, to Konu-cho. (空港へ，また

第 8 章　定冠詞使用の文脈および環境　*339*

は空港からリムジンバスのない地域へ向かう乗客は，山陽自動車道の高坂 PA で様々な高速バスに乗り換えができるようになる。高速バスはすべて広島発で，因島市行きのフラワーライナー，府中市・神辺町行きのリードライナー，および甲奴町行きのピースライナーである) (Peter Goldsbury, Chugoku Shimbun, Nov. 14, 98) [バス名]

f. Hanging ten feet below *the Blackhawk*, he slung a harness around the nearest man and they were winched, face to face, into the helicopter. (B 号の下 10 フィートにぶらさがって，彼は 1 番近くの男に背負いひもを降ろした。2 人は向き合ったまま巻き上げられてヘリコプターに入った) (RD 97/5: 115) [ヘリコプター名]

g. Ten minutes later, *the Starlifter* came by for a second pass, dropping four more packages, and its job was over. (10 分後，S は戻って再度通過して，もう 4 袋落とし，仕事を終えた) (RD 02/3: 108) [飛行機名]

h. A single B-29 bomber, named *the Enola Gay*, flew over Hiroshima, Japan, on Monday, Aug. 6, 1945, at 8:15 in the morning, local time. (単発の B-29 爆撃機，EG 号，が現地時間で 1945 年 8 月 6 日 8 時 15 分，日本の広島上空を飛行した) (EB 01) [飛行機名]

i. Houston, Tranquility Base here. *The Eagle* has landed. (H，こちら静かの基地。E 号着陸しました) (RD 99/3: 134) [Apollo 11 号の月着陸船]

j. Unlike *the Challenger*, which exploded over the ocean, *the Columbia* fell to earth this morning in fiery and potentially toxic bits over the cities and towns of Mr. Bush's home state, like a scene from "War of the Worlds." (Ch が [太平] 洋上で爆発したのと異なり，C は今朝 B の故郷の都市の上空で，「世界戦争」の 1 シーンのように，有毒ガス発生の恐れのある猛火の破片となって落下した) (NY Times, Feb. 1, 03) [スペースシャトル名]

比較 : Also, *Challenger* blew up while still within sight of the Florida launching pad, where long-range cameras recorded many details of its fiery destruction. By contrast, *Columbia* experienced its problem high in the atmosphere... (それに，Ch の爆発は F の打ち上げ台からまだ見えるところで起き，望遠カメラにより炎上損壊の細部が大量に記録された。これに対し，C は大気圏上層で問題が生じた) (NY Times, Feb. 1, 03) [愛称扱い（☞ 1.2)]

比較：The space shuttle *Columbia* broke up this morning on re-entry into the earth's atmosphere … (スペースシャトル C は今朝大気圏への再突入の際分解した) (NY Times, Feb. 1, 03) [同格構文 (☞ 本章 NB 25-1)]

NB 31
1) 人工衛星名は the をとらない。利用者が限られているので，私的に使われる船と同様な扱いをされるためであろう。
    i) Peering out of a porthole, he watched as *Atlantis* slowly approached *Mir*. (機窓から覗(の)いて，A が M に近づくのを見た) (RD 98/6: 68)
    ii) (= I-25) Four months after *Sputnik* the United States responded with *Explorer 1*. (RD 99/3: 120)
2) 飛行機は，一般的には，固有の名称は与えられず，iii) のように「製品」扱いされるか，iv) のように，"Flight＋数字" で呼ばれるかのいずれかである。
    iii) He circled the plane – *a Boeing 737* – twice, inspecting tyres, wings, rudder. (搭乗機である B737 を 2 度旋回させて，タイヤや翼，方向舵を調べた) (RD 00/2: 89)
    iv) Eighteen minutes later *United Airlines (UA) Flight 175*, hijacked from Boston en route to Los Angeles, slammed into the south tower. (18 分後には，UA Flight 175 便が B を発って LA に向かう途中ハイジャックされ，南側の塔に突っ込んだ) (Times, Sept. 11, 01) [(I-11) も参照]
3) 英仏共同開発の超音速旅客機であるコンコルドは，フランス語では定冠詞をつけて le Concorde と呼ばれるが，英語では無冠詞で用いられることもある (機体を指すときは可算名詞扱いされる: a Concorde/Concordes)。
    v) *The Concorde* has a maximum cruising speed of 2,179 km (1,354 miles) per hour, or Mach 2.04. (C の最大飛行速度は時速 2,179 km，すなわち，マッハ 2.04 だ) (EB 01)
    vi) *Concorde* was the first passenger aircraft to fly at supersonic speed. (C は超音速で飛ぶ最初の旅客機だった) (CIDE) [愛称扱いと解釈可能 (☞ 1.2)]
次の例は事故を起こした，特定の Concorde を指す。(コーパスから

例を探すときはこのような例を誤読しないよう注意が必要である。)

vii) When *the Concorde* came down it hit a low-rise hotel. (墜落の際、コンコルド機は低層のホテルに衝突した) (Japan Times, July 27, 00)

4) トラックは名前がつけられている場合でも，通常は私的に使用され他人には同定不可能なので，無冠詞で用いられる。

viii) After eating in the mine's dining room, Paul returns to *Maybelline* to help load her for the return trip. (鉱山の食堂で食事を済ませたあと，PはMに戻って帰りの荷物を積み込むのを手伝う) (RD 00/3: 108)

8.7.2.3 ホテル／レストラン／パブ；劇場／映画館

ホテルや劇場などの名前には the がつけられる。集客施設なので，だれにでも同定可能なはずだからである。

(123) a. His Orient Express Hotels Inc. now has four luxury trains, a luxury cruise ship and 22 international hotels that include *the Cipriani* in Venice, *the Observatory* in Sydney and *the Bora Bora Lagoon Resort* in Tahiti. (彼のOEH会社は今では4台の豪華列車に，1艘の豪華クルーズ船，22館の国際ホテルを所有している。そのなかにはVのCホテルや，SのOホテル，TのBBLRホテルが含まれている) (RD 00/5: 69)

b. He soon found a job as a porter at *the Theresa*, one of the biggest and finest hotels in Harlem. (間もなくTホテルのポーターという仕事を見つけた。Hで1番大きく1番立派なホテルの1つだ) (RD 96/3: 125)

c. On Thursday, April 20, the evening after the bombing, they hit pay dirt at *the Dream Motel*. (4月20日，木曜日，爆破の夕方，Dモーテルで捜していたものを見つけた) (RD 01/6: 137)

d. On April 13, 2000, Karilyn faced an audience of 600 at *the Hotel Vancouver*. (2000年4月13日，KはホテルVで600人の聴衆と向き合っていた) (RD 01/8: 112) [Hotel が名詞に先行する場合も the がつけられる]

e. The Ford is at the rear of *the Railway Inn* in Watling Street ... (F宅はW通りのRIの裏にあった) (RD 99/11: 46)

f. Leaning across the table at *the Hi Boy restaurant* in Independence, Missouri, Harlond "Bob" Hawley listened to his son David with growing excitement. (M州, IのHBレストランで, HBHはテーブルから身を乗り出して, 息子のDが言うことをだんだん興奮しながら聞いた) (RD 00/1: 89)

g. Everyone – Bob, David and his younger brother Greg, and their old friend Jerry Mackey, owner of *the Hi Boy* – began talking all at once. (みんなが一斉に話しはじめた。BもDも, 彼の弟のGも, 彼らの旧友であるHB[レストラン]のオーナーであるJMも) (RD 00/1: 90)

h. It was Jenny Schueneman's day off from her job as a restaurant cashier at *the Stardust Resort and Casino* in Las Vegas, and she wasn't enthused about spending it at a car-mechanic's garage. (その日JSはLVにあるSRC[レストラン]のレジの仕事が休みだった。自動車修理工場でその日を過ごしたいとは思わなかった) (RD 00/2: 5)

i. She took the next day off, then returned to work at *the Stardust*. ([上例中のJSは]翌日休暇を取って, S[レストラン]の仕事に戻った) (RD 00/2: 8)

j. Since he moved to San Antonio, he has frequented the city's Eastside, attending church there, getting haircuts at Sam's Barber Shop and lunch at *the N'Awlin's Creole Kitchen*. (SAに引っ越して以来, その街のイーストサイドによく足を運び, 教会に出入りしたり, S理髪店で散髪したり, NC食堂で昼食をとったりした) (RD 01/7: 51) [食堂名]

k. Lights appear in the distance and turn out to be a large, lonely pub called *The Beachy Head*, so the cliffs can't be far away. (灯りが遠くに現れ, 人気(ひとけ)のない大型パブ, BH, だと判明する。断崖は遠くないはずだ) (RD 01/6: 67) [パブ名]

比較: (= VIII-91, b) I am walking to *Beachy Head* from the nearby resort town of Eastbourne, a journalist on assignment to write about one of Britain's worst suicide spots. (RD 01/6: 67) [地名]

l. When Harry came home drunk at 3 a.m., his angry wife screamed, "Where have you been?" "At this fabulous bar, *the Golden Saloon*," he told her. (Hが酔っぱらって午前3時に帰ったとき, 妻は怒って叫んだ, 「どこに行ってたのよ。」「ここのすばらしいバーのGS

第8章　定冠詞使用の文脈および環境　*343*

だよ」と彼は答えた) (RD 00/2: 60) [同格でも the つき]

m. We're down here at *the Sydney Opera House* having a look around. (S オペラハウスに来て，見て回っている) (RD 99/5: 121)

n. My love of theater began on the night that he took a group of us to Shakespeare's *Coriolanus* at *the Young Vic theater*. (演劇を好きになったのは，Sh の C を観に YV 劇場に連れていってもらった夜からだ) (RD 97/5: 107)

o. The sounds coming out were so ghastly that Mommy and Daddy, who both had an ear for music and a strong memory of Dizzy Gillespie at *the Savoy Ballroom*, felt they would go crazy if she didn't get some lessons. (漏れてくる音があまりにもひどかったため，父と母はどちらも音楽鑑賞の耳があり，SB [Harlem にあったダンスホール] での DG [米のジャズトランペット奏者] の強烈な記憶をもっていたので，彼女にレッスンをしなければ自分たちのほうが発狂してしまうと思った) (RD 96/3: 128)

p. In Hiroshima, the pioneer of this type of mini-theatre is *the Salon Cinema* in Ote-machi. [. . .] A third cinema, *the Cine-Twin*, is in Hondori.　Later this month *the Yokogawa Cinema* . . . will open its doors again as a mini-theatre. (広島では，このようなミニシアターの先駆けは，大手町の SC だ。3つ目の映画館 CT は本通りにある。今月末には，YC がふたたびミニシアターとしてオープンする) (Peter Goldsbury, Chugoku Shimbun, Nov. 6, 99)

類例: the Do Duck Inn (RD 00/3: 119); the New Victoria hotel in Watford (RD 99/11: 45); the New Victoria (RD 99/11: 45); the Sunrise Restaurant in Pailin (RD 99/11: 21); the Warren House motel in Pikesville, Maryland (RD 00/2: 35) [Victoria hotel など小文字は原文]

NB 32

1) ホテル名などが他の名詞の同格であるときは，通例，the は落とされる（船名に関する注（本章 NB 25-1）参照；ただし，上例 (123, 1) [bar] のような例もある）。

   i) One of the newest hotels, *New York-New York*, reproduces the Manhattan skyline, including a 150-foot replica of the Statue of Liberty. (最新のホテルの1つ，NYNY，は M の鳥瞰図(ちょうかんず)を

再現し，自由の女神像の，150 フィートのレプリカも含んでいる）(RD 99/2: 40)

2) 外国語の定冠詞がつけられているときは the は不要。(CIDE (s.v., playhouse) には "*the La* Jolla Playhouse in San Diego, California" という例があるが，これは英語の Playhouse が後続するためであると思われる。)

  ii) He walked over, kissed me, and said, "Surprise. We couldn't go to *L'Auberge*, so *L'Auberge* came to us." *L'Auberge* is a fabulous French restaurant, one of the best in the area. (歩いて来て，口づけをして言った。「びっくりパーティだよ。[病気のため] A に行けないので，A のほうがここに来たんだ。」A は豪華フランス料理店であり，近隣では最高級店の 1 つだ) (RD 99/12: 136; http://www.beyondbook.com/pages/book/wholeformat.19.html)

  iii) (= III-98, b) So, if I've got this right, a scent that doesn't work is the national anthem sung by Roseanne, and an aroma that sings is Pavarotti at *La Scala*. (RD 99/10: 119)

3) 初出では Hotel/Restaurant などを明示するほうがわかりやすい。上例 (123, f–g) および本章 NB 4 [tribe/people] 参照。

4) チェーン店形式のホテルなどには a/an がつけられる。

  iv) Just before 12:30 p.m. they checked in to their hotel, *a Days Inn*. (12 時半直前に宿泊ホテルである DI にチェックインした) (RD [U.S. Edition] 98/9: 118)

  v) She told him the man had struck up a conversation with her and a girlfriend outside *a 7-Eleven*. (彼女が言うには，その男はセブンイレブンの外で彼女とガールフレンドと話をしたとのことだった) (RD [U.S. Edition] 98/9: 120)

  vi) (= V-5, b) He had been accused of a drunken assault on a girl of 15 outside *a McDonald's restaurant* at Mitcham, Surrey, 13 months ago. (ConCD-ROM)

5) Drury Lane は劇場を指すときは，原則的に，the がつけられ，同劇場の所在地区を指すときは無冠詞で用いられる (8.7.1.10 も参照)。

  vii) On May 7, 1963, *the Drury Lane* celebrated its tercentenary. (1963 年 5 月 7 日 DL 劇場は 300 年祭を祝った) (EB 01) [*MEG*, vol. 7, 16.3$_1$ は無冠詞用法のみあげている]

  viii) *Drury Lane*, redecorated, reopened in September 1747 . . . (DL

第8章　定冠詞使用の文脈および環境　*345*

　　　　[劇場] は改築され，1747年9月に再開された）(EB 01)
　　ix) Rebuilt on its present site in *Drury Lane* in 1674 with Sir Christopher Wren as its probable architect, the second Theatre Royal soon featured the works of William Congreve. (1674年たぶんレンの建築でDL地区の現在の場所に再建されてすぐ第2王立劇場はコングレーヴの作品を興行した）(EB 01)

8.7.2.4　動物園；博物館／図書館；研究所／大学

動物園名は英語圏では，通例，the がつけられるが，非英語圏の動物園は無冠詞で用いられる。これは，同定可能性の程度の相違に帰せられるであろう。

(124) a. Marker ultimately resigned a prestigious position at *the National Zoo* in Washington, moving to Namibia in 1991. (Mは最終的にWの国立動物園の要職を辞して，1991年にNに移動した）(RD 00/1: 73)
　　b. It was a balmy day, and the orangutans at *the Omaha Zoo* had been playing in their big outdoor enclosure. (さわやかな日だった。O動物園のオランウータンたちは戸外の広い囲い地で遊んでいた）(RD 00/4: 36)
　　c. Papago Park, which contains the Desert Botanical Garden and *the Phoenix Zoo*...(P公園には，砂漠植物園やP動物園がある）(EB 01)
　類例：the American National Zoo (RD 01/9: 41); the Columbus Zoo (RD 00/4: 38); the Indianapolis Zoo (RD 98/9: 32)

(125) a. Ciofi vividly remembers his first glimpse of a Komodo, at *Surabaya Zoo* in Indonesia five years ago. (Cは5年前にIのS動物園で初めてコモドドラゴンを見たときのことを鮮明に思い出す）(RD 99/6: 26)
　　b. As a biology student at Beijing University, Pan saw the world's first captive-born panda during a visit to *Beijing Zoo*. (Pは，北京大学の生物学専攻生のとき，北京動物園訪問中に世界初の動物園生まれのパンダを見た）(RD 00/2: 24)
　　c. Indeed, when I caught up with the orangutan at *Zoo Atlanta*, where he now lives, I saw an example of sharing that a robber baron might envy. (事実，いま飼育されているA動物園でオランウータンと再会したとき，追いはぎ貴族がうらやむような [食物を] 分かち合う実例を見た）(RD 00/4: 39) [Zooが肩書き扱いのため無冠詞（☞ 1.3); cf. Lake Michigan; Mt Fuji]

博物館／記念館／美術館，図書館，研究所の名前も定冠詞をとる。
(126) a. In 1992 his job counselor recommended him to work at *the Bear Bryant Museum*. (1992 年彼の仕事の助言者は BB 博物館で働くよう勧めた) (RD 98/12: 109)
　　b. When in Paris, you should visit *the Louvre*. (パリに行ったら，L 美術館を訪れるべきだ) (CCED³)
　　c. This autumn *the Ashmolean* goes Brazilian! (今秋 A 美術館はブラジル展を行う) (Information sheet of the Ashmolean Museum, 2001 September-November)
　　d. *The Lincoln Library* reopened on August 12, upstairs at Burnham Hall, with about 2000 books. (8 月 12 日に L 図書館は B ホールの 2 階で約 2,000 冊の本を備えてリオープンした) (RD 99/10: 11) [(IX-25, d) と比較せよ]
　　e. On August 10, 1846, President James K. Polk signed the bill creating *the Smithsonian Institution*. (1846 年 8 月 10 日，JKP 大統領は S 研究所を設立する法案に署名した) (RD 96/10: 58)
　　f. In 1858 Congress appropriated funds for a national museum as an adjunct to *the Smithsonian*. (1858 年，議会は S 研究所に国立博物館を付設する基金を認可した) (RD 96/10: 59) [初出では Institution が補われ，2 度目からは省略可；本章 NB 4 参照]
類例：the Guggenheim (Museum) [Bilbao, Spain] (RD 02/3: 92); the Huntington Museum of Art [West Virginia] (RD 00/4: 82); the Peace Memorial Museum [広島市] (Peter Goldsbury, Chugoku Shimbun, Jun. 20, 97); the Southland Museum and Art Gallery [New Zealand's South Island] (RD 99/11: 112); the Titanic Museum [Massachusetts] (RD 00/2: 8); the Van Gogh Museum (RD 02/7: 66); the Boston Public Library (RD 99/10: 10); the Detroit Public Library (RD 01/8: 6); the Richard Nixon Library & Birthplace [Yorba Linda, California] (RD 99/11: 79); [the＋所有格] the Smithsonian's Natural History Museum in Washington (RD 95/5: 24)

大学名が the をとるかとらないかは構造的に決定される。地名／人名で始まる大学名は無冠詞であり，*of*-phrase をともなう大学名は the をとる。(書きことばでは the University of X のパタンが好まれる (Heaton & Turton 1987: 281)。) 他方，研究所名は "地名＋Institute" という構造でも the をと

る。
(127) a. (= IV-20, i) He's been offered a place at *York University*. (LDOCE[3])
   b. (= 1章 NB 2-1, i-b) "Parents who are not educated may feel they cannot approach a teacher, who seems to know everything," says Anthony Lim, an award-winning teacher and now principal of *Stanford College* in Petaling Jaya, Malaysia. (RD 99/9: 89)
  類例：Cambridge University (RD 97/5: 108); Edinburgh University (OALD[5]); Duke University (RD 96/3: 108); Gadjah Mada University, Yogyakarta (RD 01/6: 8); McGill University [Montreal, Canada] (RD 99/12: 70); New York University (RD 99/12: 114); Pacific Western University [Los Angeles] (RD 00/5: 18); Princeton University (RD 99/8: 105); Singapore National University (RD 01/5: 57); Sydney University (RD 99/10: 48); Victoria University (RD 99/11: 110); Washington University (RD 99/8: 108); Baylor College of Medicine [Houston] (RD 99/3: 8); Middlebury College [Vermont] (RD 00/3: 18)

(128) a. After graduation, Zeke went to *the University of North Carolina*, then on to medical school and a residency at *the University of Colorado Medical Center*. (卒業後ZはNC大学に進学し，それからCMC大学の医学部に行き，実習生になった) (RD 98/10: 28)
   b. (= V-98, b) "One of the great ironies of antidepressants is that they can cause sexual dysfunction," says Dr Andrew Leuchter, director of the Division of Adult Psychiatry at *the University of California*, Los Angeles. (RD 99/12: 71)
   c. *the California/Massachusetts Institute* of Technology (C/M工科大学) (RD 88/6: 102; 99/9: 5)
  類例：the Chinese University of Hong Kong (RD 97/2: 72); the State University of New York at Buffalo (RD 99/12: 72); the University of Florida College of Medicine in Gainesville (RD 99/12: 70); the University of Illinois at Chicago (RD 99/10: 93); the University of Melbourne (RD 99/5: 118); the University of Miami Mailman Centre for Child Development (RD 99/10: 74); the University of Michigan (RD 98/10: 104); the University of Surrey in southeast England (RD 98/6: 86); the University of Utah School of Medicine (RD 96/10: 45); the Queensland Institute of Medical Research (RD

02/9: 18)

大学以外の学校名も，しばしば the をとる（ただし，例外もある）。学校名が the をとるかとらないかは慣用によるところが大きいが，the がつけられる場合は広範囲から生徒が集まる，有名な（つまり，同定可能な）学校という含みがあると思われる。

(129) a. Colby Coombs today works as a guide on Mount McKinley and teaches climbing at *the Alaska Mountaineering School*, which he opened in Talkeetna. (CC は今日では M 山のガイドとして働き，彼が T で開学した A 登山学校で登山術を教えている) (RD 99/4: 142)

b. His thoughts naturally turned to *the Hershey Industrial School*. (彼の思いはおのずと H 実業学校に戻っていった) (RD 99/7: 143)

c. But Jewel's life took yet another new turn when a teacher from *the Interlochen Arts Academy* in Michigan heard her sing at a summer music festival. (しかし，M 州の I 芸術学院の教師が夏の音楽祭で J が歌うのを聞いたとき，彼女の人生は，さらに別の新たな展開を迎えた) (RD 00/1: 44)

d. (= III-44, c) Invited to study cello at *the Moscow Conservatory* at the age of seven, Nina practised endlessly, until her fingers bled and her head pounded. (RD 01/10: 108)

類例：the Albuquerque Indian School (RD 02/7: 70); the Hershey School (RD 99/7: 143); the Juilliard School (RD 99/4: 79); the Lee Strasberg Theatre Institute (RD 99/12: 114); the Robert Wood Johnson Medical School Centre for Sexual and Marital Health in New Jersey (RD 99/12: 72); the Sandhurst Royal Military Academy in England (RD 99/11: 70); the State Academy of Fine Arts in Stuttgart (RD 99/4: 74); the Sunethra Devi School in Pepiliyana, Sri Lanka (RD 99/12: 66)

例外：David Forte, an Islamic law expert at *Cleveland Marshall Law School* (DF, C 軍法学校のイスラム法の専門家) (RD 99/12: 20)

類例：Angolo Primary School in Otwal subcounty of northern Uganda (RD 01/8: 43); Holy Cross Catholic School in Kemptville, Ontario (RD 01/8: 38); Lawrence Heights Middle School [Toronto] (RD 02/1: 69)

第8章　定冠詞使用の文脈および環境　*349*

NB 33
1) 肩書き
　"University of X" が肩書きの一部として名詞の前におかれるときは，the はつけられない。
　i) "In the Middle East, odd numbers tend to be regarded as good," says *University of Toronto anthropology professor* Janice Boddy.（「中東では奇数は吉だと考えられる傾向がある」とT大学人類学教授のJBは言う）(RD 02/3: 21)
2) (the) Ohio State University
　オハイオ州立大のURL (http://www.osu.edu/index.php) には the Ohio State University と表記されているが，*Encyclopaedia Britannica* (2001年版) では一貫して無冠詞で用いられている。
　ii) *Ohio State University*, founded in 1870, is the largest state-assisted university.（O州立大，1870年設立，は最大の州立大学である）(EB 01)
　iii) Schlesinger graduated from *Ohio State University* in 1910.（ShはO州立大を1910年に卒業した）(EB 01)
3) 外国語の学校名
　学校名が外国語の場合もしばしば the がつけられる。
　iv) Given a smelling test, Bell did well and was sent to *the École de Parfumerie Roure Bertrand Fils et Justin Dupont*, in Grasse, France.（嗅覚テストをうけて，Bは成績がよかったので，仏のGにあるRBF&JD芳香学校に送られた）(RD 99/10: 118)
　v) After Aranas' wife died and his children had grown up, his priest told him about *the La Salle Green Hills night school.*（Aは奥さんが亡くなり，子供たちが成長したのち，牧師からラサールGH夜間学校のことを教えてもらった）(RD 00/9: 6)
4) the がつかない施設
　本節で見た「知的」設備に対し，遊園地，テーマパークなど「娯楽」施設や刑務所名，駅名，空港名は，通例，無冠詞で用いられる（☞ 8.8）。

8.7.2.5　新聞／雑誌
　人工の建造物ではないが，出版物も人の手によるものなので，ここで見ておきたい。
(130) a. *The Daily News* has the largest circulation of any Sunday

newspaper. (DN 紙は日曜紙では最大の発行部数だ) (RD 99/3: 55)

b. Brenda contacted *the Los Angeles Times*. (B は LA 紙に連絡した) (RD 99/1: 21)

c. In a June 7, 1984, letter to *the New York Times*, Jonathan M. Weisberg wrote:... (1984 年 6 月 7 日付けの NY 紙への手紙で JMW は次のように書いた) (RD 99/3: 54)

d. He may not be "lovable," one writer declared in *the New York Post*, "but he certainly has made the city more livable." (NYP 紙にだれかが書いていたように，彼は「好かれやすく」はないかもしれないが，「[NY] 市を住みやすくしてくれたのはたしかだ」) (RD 99/7: 74)

e. They point to an interview in *the Observer* in which Blair said:... (O 紙のインタビューのことを指す。そこで B は次のように述べている) (RD 98/3: 57)

f. In one provocative study reported in *The American Journal of Clinical Nutrition*, diet relapsers tended to deal with their personal problems by trying to escape them. (AJCN 誌に報告された刺激的な研究では，ダイエットを守れないものは個人的問題から逃避しようとする傾向がある) (RD 97/5: 12) [以下の例で雑誌名に the がつけられるのは構造的理由による。すなわち，普通名詞が *of*-phrase により限定されているためである]

g. Eating yogurt can help reduce yeast infections, according to a study in *the Annals of Internal Medicine*. (AIJ 誌の研究によると，ヨーグルトを食べれば酵母菌感染を減じる効果がある) (RD 99/3: 114)

h. (= VIII-60, i) Joce-Lyne Grand'Maison, a 44 year-old journalist at *the Journal de Quebec*, whose love of the esoteric earned her two bullets in the head. (RD 98/3: 33)

NB 34   φ 雑誌名
新聞名には，次の i)–ii) のような場合を除いて，the がつけられる。

i) His presence by Gorbachev's side at international summits happened so quickly that, according to *Washington Post* writer Jim Hoagland, the British security service code-named him Harrier, after their fast-rising vertical takeoff jet. ([Primakov が] 非常に短期間で国際的首脳会議の際に G の傍らに付き添うよ

うになったので，WP 紙の記者 JH によると，英国安全保障機関は彼に H という暗号をつけた。急速に垂直離陸するジェット機からとったものだ）(RD 99/5: 44) [肩書きの一部のとき冠詞不要（☞ 1.3）]

ii) In a recent survey by *the Far Eastern Economic Review* and *Asia Business News*, Asian business leaders ranked Changi the No. 1 airport for security. (FEER 誌と ABN 誌との最近の調査で，アジアの実業界のリーダーたちは C を安全面でナンバーワンの空港だと評価した) (RD 98/3: 78) [新聞・雑誌名が連続するとき the は最初の新聞・雑誌名にだけつけられる]

新聞が日刊であるのに対し，雑誌の多くは月刊または季刊であるため，新聞に較べ同定可能性が低いので，雑誌名には必ずしも the はつけられない。当該の定期刊行物が the をとるかとらないか不明な場合は現物や大型の辞書，検索サイトなどで調べればよい。

iii) Taufik and several former *Tempo* journalists launched *Independen*, a crusading monthly that continued to expose corruption and nepotism in Suharto's government. (T はもと T 誌のジャーナリスト数人とで I 誌，改革キャンペーンの月刊誌，を発刊し，S 政権の腐敗と情実を暴きつづけた) (RD 99/3: 39)

iv) Muhammad Ali would talk to *Reader's Digest* on the morning of September 11 at his home, a 35-hectare farm in Berrien Springs, Michigan. (M アリは M 州 BS の 35 ヘクタールの農園である自宅で [2001 年] 9 月 11 日の朝 RD 誌 [記者] とインタビューすることになっていた) (RD 02/1: 36)

類例：*Cigar Aficionado* (RD 99/3: 55); *Nintendo Power* magazine (RD 98/11: 86); *Rolling Stone* magazine (RD 98/11: 43); *Extension Magazine* (RD 03/6: 127) [新聞・雑誌名は，通例，斜字体で表記される]

Christophersen (1939: 181) および *MEG* (vol. 7, 16.3$_7$) は，概略，雑誌の名称が質量名詞 (mass-word)，複数形あるいは固有名詞である場合は無冠詞であると指摘している。これらのほかに，無冠詞の雑誌名はタイトルが単数形普通名詞である場合にも見られる。例：φ *Business Week*, φ *Editor & Publisher*, φ *Modern Bride*, φ *National Review* (*Chaucer/Kenyon/Transatlantic Review* は the をとる)

8.8　the をとらない施設
8.8.1　刑務所
　刑務所名は，通例，the をとらない。この事実の背後には，刑務所は地域限定的な施設であるため他地方の人々には同定可能性が低いという理由に加えて，「矯正・贖罪(しょくざい)のための施設」という機能・目的を有するという理由もあるかもしれない（原理 III 参照）。

(131) a. (= III-126, d) Instead, she was taken to *prison*, where she spent five months before Chinese authorities charged her with "spying and illegally providing state secrets." (RD 99/3: 36)

b. Her husband spent three years in *prison*. (彼女の夫は3年間服役した) (OALD⁶)

(132) a. In December 1995, Donato "Donnie" Lama was charged with preaching Christianity and moved to *Al-Malaz Prison*, an expanse of low-lying, white-washed buildings deep in the desert outside Riyadh. (1995年12月，DDLはキリスト教伝道の罪で告発され，AM刑務所に移送された。R郊外の砂漠の奥地にあり，低層の水しっくいの建物が広がるところである) (RD 99/12: 19)

b. He is currently in *Frankland Prison*, County Durham. (現在 CD の F 刑務所にいる) (CCED³)

c. A dozen inmates have escaped or absconded from *Forest Jail* in the past year. (この1年で12人もの収容者がF刑務所から脱走もしくは失踪した) (CCED³)

類例：Long Lartin maximum-security prison in England (RD 00/1: 142); San Quentin prison (RD 99/10: 26) [小文字は原文]; Woodhill Prison in Milton Keynes; Leeds Prison; Wandsworth Prison, South London; Camp Hill Prison on the Isle of Wight (以上 CCED³)

例外：Most of the other 12,000 inmates in *the New Bilibid Prison* live in cramped cells. (NB刑務所の他の1万2千人の受刑者の大半は狭苦しい監房にいる) (RD 99/9: 65) [Manila; the new Bilibid Prison と表記すべきか]; *The Terrell County Jail* is unsanitary, and a fire hazard. (TC 刑務所は不衛生であり，火事の危険もある) (CCED³)

8.8.2　駅／空港
　駅名および空港名も the をとらない。この理由としては，これらの施設は，地図なしではその位置も規模も同定不可能な場合が多いという事実のほか，「陸路（または，空路／海路）移動」という機能を有するという事実も関与して

いるかもしれない。

(133) a. *Victoria Station* was a welcome sight to me after my long journey. (長旅のあと，V 駅はうれしい光景だった) (OALD5)
   類例：Basildon/Broad Street/Penn/Pennsylvania/Union/Waterloo Station (CCED3); (link) JR Hiroshima Station with JR Nishi-Hiroshima Station (Peter Goldsbury, Chugoku Shimbun, Jun. 26, 99); Seno Station and Hachihonmatsu Station (Ibid, Sep. 11, 98); Kasumigaseki subway station (RD 97/2: 50)

   b. (= I-42, 参考) At *Algiers Airport* an Air France Airbus was about to take off for Paris. (RD 99/6: 124)
   類例：Berlin-Tegel Airport (RD 99/11: 89); Brussels Airport (RD 99/3: 106); Changi Airport (RD 98/3: 74); Christopher Columbus Airport (RD 01/5: 87); Guernsey Airport (RD 99/1: 27); Halifax International Airport (RD 00/9: 56); Heathrow Airport (RD 99/9: 143); Kennedy Airport (RD 99/9: 106); Richmond International Airport (RD 00/2: 93); Orly Airport (RD 99/5: 85); [小文字表記] Algiers airport (RD 99/6: 127); Heathrow airport (RD 96/3: 23)

   c. Officials at *Luke Air Force Base* in Phoenix, *Nellis Air Force Base* in Las Vegas and *Edwards Air Force Base* in Rosamund, California, all denied that any of their planes were responsible for the sightings. (P の L 空軍基地でも，LV の N 空軍基地でも，C 州 R の E 空軍基地でも当局者は目撃 [された UFO] に対する彼らの飛行機の関与を否定した) (RD 99/8: 116)　類例：Andrews Air Force Base (RD 99/1: 107; 00/4: 138)

8.8.3　娯楽施設

娯楽施設名（例：テーマパーク）が本来固有名詞の場合，冠詞をとらないのは，愛称（符帳；☞ 1.2）扱いされることに加えて，「娯楽」という機能を有するためとも考えられる。

(134) a. Other officials said there were threats against *Disney World* in Florida or *Disneyland* in California ... (別の政府筋によると，F の DW や C の D にも [テロの] 脅威がある) (NY Times, Oct. 13, 01)

   b. Our seven-year-old daughter was thrilled when we took her to *Disney World* for the first time, and headed straight for *Space Mountain*. [. . .] Next year we returned to *the Magic Kingdom*, and my daughter, now eight, again dragged me to *Space Mountain*.

(DW に初めて連れていったとき7歳の娘はわくわくして，まっすぐ SM に行った。翌年 MK を再訪すると，娘は8歳になっていたが，また私の手を引いて SM に行った) (RD 99/8: 56) [the Magic Kingdom (park) は Disneyland/Disney World の別称；Space Mountain はジェットコースター (roller coaster) がある施設] 類例：Walt Disney World (RD 97/5: 40)

c. It would soon occur to Yip and the staff that this fragile creature needed a name, just like the other animals that populated the aquarium at *Sea World*. (間もなく Y や [他の] 職員も気づくことになったのだが，SW の水槽にいる他の動物と同様に，このか弱な生き物も名前が必要だった) (RD 99/8: 42)

d. But the last time I went to *Red Rolfe Field* to see the Darmouth College team play baseball, I got lucky. (ところが，前回 D 大学チームが野球の試合をするのを見に RR 球場に行ったときはラッキーだった) (RD 99/8: 83)

NB 35

1) (the) Hospital

　Prison などを含む固有名詞が無冠詞で用いられるのは「働き」(機能・目的) を含意することも1因であると考えるならば，Hospital の無冠詞用法 (☞ 8.7.1.17) も同じ理由によると考えてよいかもしれない。ただし，この場合は英米の用法に違いがあるため複雑である。すなわち，〈英〉では，普通名詞のとき「働き」を表せば冠詞をとらない，固有名詞の大病院は the をとる，〈米〉では普通名詞のとき「働き」を表す場合でも the をとる，固有名詞のときは the をとらない，という4条件が拮抗しているのである。

　　i) a. 〈AmE〉 I've been in *the hospital* for the last five weeks.
　　　b. 〈BrE〉 I've been in *hospital* for the last five weeks.
　　　　(この5週間入院していた) (Heaton & Turton 1987: 114)
　　ii) a. My friend's warning was also borne out by Dr Saiyud Niyomviphat during a seminar on diabetes mellitus at *the Vejthani Hospital* in Bangkok. (友人の警告は，B の V 病院での真性糖尿病に関するセミナー中に SN 博士によっても支持された) (RD 99/7: 55)
　　　b. (= VIII-115, b) After I finished at Columbia, I started my

postgraduate training at *Roosevelt Hospital*. (RD 96/3: 140)

2) 筆の誤り

　上述のように，駅名は無冠詞で用いられる。次例中の the は不要である（執筆者本人に確認済み）。

iii) Except for the western end, the second stage, called the Tozai-sen, will be underground and will connect *the JR Nishi-Hiroshima Station* with *the JR Hiroshima Station.*（「東西線」の2期［工事］は，西端を除き，地下鉄であり，JR 西広島駅と JR 広島駅が結ばれる予定である）(Peter Goldsbury, Chugoku Shimbun, Apr. 18, 97)

次の例文における定冠詞も不要である。

iv) for $1.25, the A train takes travelers from subways stations ... to *the Howard Beach Station* where a free shuttle bus to JFK terminals is provided. (A トレインを利用すれば，旅行者は 1.25 ドルで地下鉄駅から HB 駅に着く。そこからは終点の JFK まで無料シャトルバスが出ている) (CCED[3])

他方，次の例では，the をつけるのであれば，International Airport は小文字で表記するのが正用法である。

v) After Armenian terrorists set a bomb in *the Los Angeles International Airport*, police, acting on FBI intelligence, arrived to snuff it with only minutes to spare. (A のテロリストが LA の国際的な空港に爆発物を仕掛けたあと，警察は FBI の情報に基づいて行動し，到着して処理するのにわずか数分の余裕しかなかった) (RD 97/2: 53); [RD 99/3: 121; 99/4: 27 では φ Los Angeles International Airport (LA 国際空港)]

8.9　修飾語句＋人名／地名

　修飾語句をともなうとき，固有名詞は冠詞をとることがある。本節では，定冠詞，不定冠詞および無冠詞の順に論じたい。

8.9.1　定冠詞（8.1.1 も参照）

　同一人物（または場所，事物）の別の姿（様相，側面）との比較対照（あるいは，区別）が含意されるとき，固有名詞は the をとる。（同名異物のときも同様。）

(135) a. *The Samantha Hunter-Allen* I had just seen was starkly different from the woman I'd interviewed just six days earlier. (会ったばかりの SHA は，ほんの6日前にインタヴューした女性とはまったく違っ

ていた) (RD 01/5: 42)
b. *The Rwanda* that I had once known was gone for ever... (私がかつて知っていた R は永遠に消えてしまった) (RD 00/3: 124)
c. Irish Republican Army (IRA) activities were at their peak in *the Belfast* of 1972, and temporary disappearances were common. (IRA の活動は1972年の B で最も激しかった。一時的行方不明は日常茶飯だった) (RD 98/3: 84) [*of*-phrase による限定；現在または1972年以外の Belfast と区別]
d. In *the* brave new *Ireland* of today, it is hardly a far-fetched dream. (今日のすばらしい新しい I では, それは突拍子もない夢物語とばかりも言えない) (RD 99/8: 36)
e. (= VIII-12, b) *The Mars* of 2150 will be as exuberant as the American Wild West of the 1870s. (RD 98/7: 103)

8.9.2 不定冠詞

人物 (または場所, 事物) が形容詞など修飾語句をともなって, その一時的な姿 (様相, 側面) を表すときは a/an をとる。

(136) a. Several hours passed before I remembered to telephone *a* very angry *Barbara*. (数時間後に思い出して電話したところ B はとても怒っていた) (RD 99/3: 122)
b. Minutes later headlights appeared round a bend in the track and *an* elated *Moloney* shook his head. (数分後曲がり角にヘッドライトが現れ, M がうれしそうに首を振った) (RD 00/7: 105)
c. At one point *an* exasperated *Adams* said he would rather have "the whole money thrown into the Potomac" than entertain some particularly narrow scheme that had been suggested. (あるとき A は怒って言った, 提案されている特に融通のきかない計画を考えるぐらいなら「お金をみな P 川に投げ捨てる」ほうがましだ, と) (RD 96/10: 58)
d. *A* grinning *Shawn Becker* poked his head through my door. (SB がにやにやしながらドアから頭を出した) (RD 01/5: 136)
e. *A* smiling *Trish* announced, "I've spoken with Mr Ryan, and he said he will write you a personal cheque for $5000 to help with the adoption." (T はにこにこしながら告げた, 「R 氏と話をしたら, 養子縁組の支援に 5 千ドルの個人用小切手を切ろうと言ってくれた」と) (RD 00/6: 126)

f. *This cannot be*, *a* stunned *Belo* thought as he studied the telegram. (こんなことはあってはならない,電報を検討しながらベロ神父は愕然(がくぜん)として思った) (RD 96/3: 31) [*This . . . be* 斜字体は原文]
g. *A Poland* Free From Jews Is *a* Free *Poland*. (ユダヤ人のいない P こそ自由な P だ) (RD 01/7: 122) [前半は関係詞節 (☞ 4.4.2) による限定に準ずる]

類例： an amused Vonnegut (RD 98/9: 93); an astonished Choi Hyun-shi (RD 98/8: 49); a baggy-eyed but wary Ryszard Kuklinski (RD 00/4: 131); a barefoot Nielsen (RD 99/10: 18); a computer-age Confucian (RD 01/4: 6); a concerned Renke (RD 99/12: 105); a crying, hungry Timmy (RD 00/4: 12); a deadpan Gavaskar (RD 00/5: 34); a desperate Zhi Hui (RD 98/12: 61); a disappointed McVeigh (RD 01/6: 128); a disbelieving Bartlett (RD 99/9: 127); a discouraged Jyp (RD 99/8: 60); an emotional Forden (RD 00/4: 141); an enraged Belo/Preger (RD 96/3: 32; 00/9: 95); an exhausted Marker/Dave (RD 00/1: 70; 00/1: 79); a wide-eyed and exhausted Zach (RD 01/4: 40); a free China/Tibet (RD 98/12: 73; 00/3: 23); a furious Little Bit (RD 96/10: 84); a frustrated Fregonese (RD 99/1: 141); a grateful Hayden (RD 99/6: 37); a groggy Shirley (RD 99/4: 9); an independent Tibet/Poland (RD 00/3: 21; 00/4: 135); an insistent Claudia Feh (RD 96/10: 92); a jubilant Sembagare (RD 00/3: 129); a nervous Kuklinski (RD 00/4: 127); a nervously grinning Zeke (RD 98/10: 28); a new Silicon Valley (RD 98/7: 103); a pregnant Phoebe (RD 00/3: 13); a real ER (RD 98/10: 64); a remorseful Amy Pestor (RD 98/12: 33); a shaken Boyes (RD 00/1: 129); a silent and despondent Lee (RD 99/8: 135); a shaken Tran/Maggie (RD 97/2: 56; 97/5: 84); a shrieking Christina (RD 00/9: 38); a skeptical David (RD 98/8: 19); a sleepy-sounding Milat (RD 99/5: 138); a spirited Blanca (RD 99/11: 130); a stunned and devastated Daddy (RD 96/3: 137); a surprised Bychkov (RD 99/4: 56); a sympathetic Moore (RD 00/9: 127); a thunderstruck Bahrami (RD 00/4: 77); a young Sembagare (RD 00/3: 129); a youthful Hogan (RD 00/3: 41); a weary Sembagare (RD 00/3: 141); a worried Stoudemire/Deborah Helms (RD 98/10: 30; 00/2: 130); a shirt-sleeved Prince (RD 00/3: 61); an unfathomable God (RD 00/2: 143)

NB 36

上記の a/an の用法は普通名詞の前にも現れる。

i) Half an hour later *a* ringing *telephone* roused me from sleep. (30分後，電話が鳴って眠りから起こされた) (RD 99/12: 94) [ringing がなければ the (tele)phone (次例参照)]

比較：Then one Friday morning *the phone* rang. (それから，ある金曜日の朝電話が鳴った) (RD 99/12: 130) [書き手の家の電話]

ii) A half-hour later, *a* flustered *deliveryman* arrived, shaking his head and holding up a sheep with some scribbled directions. (30分後，配達員が面食らった様子でやってきた。首をひねりながら，羊を抱えて，なぐり書きの説明書きを何枚かもっていた) (RD 00/6: 39) [(Ap.2.2-29, b) [seat belt] も参照]

他の限定詞の例：

iii) (= VIII-123, 1) When Harry came home drunk at 3 a.m., *his* angry *wife* screamed, "Where have you been?" "At this fabulous bar, the Golden Saloon," he told her. (RD 00/2: 60)

8.9.3　無冠詞

"φ＋修飾語句＋固有名詞" という構造には2つの場合がある。1つは，修飾語句が固有名詞の本来的・恒常的な特徴を述べるときである。つまり，(137) におけるように，無冠詞のときの修飾語句は，人物（または場所，事物）の，いわば，枕詞として（☞ 4.4.3.4），よく知られている特徴を装飾的・感情的に述べるものである。

(137) a. Hazel-eyed *Jamie* was baby-sitting her cousin, Donald Joseph, or DJ, as he was called. (うす茶色の瞳の J は従弟のドナルド・ジョーゼフ，通称 DJ，のお守りをしていた) (RD 00/1: 76) [(VIII-12, a) [Sandy-haired A. S.] も参照]

b. Except for plucky *Richard*, who was still suffering badly from dysentery but refused to ride a camel and tottered along some distance behind us, we slid down the slope gleefully. (勇者 R を除いて——まだひどく下痢をしていたが，ラクダに乗るのを拒んでかなり後方を歩いていた——我々ははしゃいで坂を滑りおりた) (RD 97/2: 126)

c. Fat *Benjamin Harrison* of Virginia, so the story goes, told tiny *Elbridge Gerry* of Massachusetts: "I shall die in a few minutes, but from the lightness of your body, you shall dance in the air for an hour or two before you are dead." (V 出身のデブの BH は, 話によると, M 出身のチビの EG に言った.「[絞首刑になれば] おれは数分で死ぬが, おまえは体が軽いので, 死ぬまで 1, 2 時間空中でダンスをすることになるぜ」) (RD 99/5: 95)

d. Young *Bill* was watching us like a hawk. (若き B はタカのように我々を見ていた) (RD 99/6: 126)

e. For Boyes, who had lived almost all of her life in gentle, leafy *Harrogate*, Calgary in February was a harsh introduction to a new country. (B は人生の大半を温暖青葉の H で暮らしてきたので, 2 月の C は新しい国への厳しい序章だった) (RD 00/1: 132)

類例: avant-garde Paris (RD 99/11: 76); big Zhang (RD 97/2: 142); charming, lovable Moe (RD 00/2: 79); dynamic Singapore (RD 96/10: 86); ebony-skinned, white-bearded Richard Donation (RD 00/2: 120); frenetic Kowloon (RD 97/5: 122); Italian-born Franco Mancassola (RD 99/3: 110); little David (RD 97/6: 91); little flu-stricken Sal (RD 99/12: 62); low-crime Singapore (RD 99/4: 82); quietly spoken Conor (RD 00/3: 109); Rome-based Matthews (RD 00/4: 4); shy Bill McVeigh (RD 01/6: 123); status-conscious South Korea (RD 99/12: 45); steamy Kota Kinabalu (RD 98/6: 78); tiny Andrea Mongiardo (RD 97/5: 86); vintage Bombeck (RD 97/6: 34); young America (RD 00/1: 94)

第 2 は, (138) のように, 修飾語句が歴史的・地理的な区分を表す場合である. このとき, "修飾語句+固有名詞" は複合語の固有名詞を形成して, もとの固有名詞の下位分類を表していると言ってよい (4 章 NB 6-4 も参照).

(138) a. "The Lamb" rested on its pedestal until 1794, when troops from revolutionary *France* swarmed into Ghent. (「神の子羊」[の像] は 1794 年まで台座にあったが, その年, 革命フランスの軍隊が G に乱入した) (RD 96/3: 89)

b. What really sets Mr Thaksin apart is that he comes not from Southern *China*, but from northern *Thailand*. (本当は, T 氏が異質であるのは, 南中国ではなく, タイ北部の出身だということだ) (CCED[3])

類例: gold rush California (RD 98/6: 53); pre-revolutionary France (RD 99/4: 53); Victorian England (RD 00/2: 85); war-torn Germany (RD

96/3: 90); war-ravaged Burma (RD 99/10: 1); central Birmingham (RD 00/2: 143); suburban Washington (RD 97/2: 57)

以上の考察に基づいて，次の例がなぜ無冠詞で用いられているのか考えてみたい。

(139) But the impact flung unbelted *Mike* halfway through the windshield, police said. (だが，衝撃のためシートベルトをしていなかったMはフロントガラスから半分投げ出された，と警察は言った) (RD 96/3: 71)

この例に関しては，一時的な状態を表すので，an が必要であると思われるかもしれない。だが，実は，Mike は遺体としての Mike を指すので，an をつければ，遺体がシートベルトをつけている場合とつけていない場合とがあることになり，事実に反する。他方，the をつければ，シートベルトをつけた遺体との対照を含意するので，これも事実に反する。したがって，無冠詞用法だけが適切な選択である。

8.9.4　年齢＋人名

年齢が付加されるときは the がつけられる場合とつけられない場合がある。("a/an＋年齢＋人名" という構造は (同一人物に関しては) 用いられない。) 一般に知られていない事実であるが，the がつけられれば現在との対照を表すので，「当時」何歳であったかを明示する。

(140) a. Five-year-old *Mesa* was telling our other daughter, two-year-old *Molly*, that she planned to grow peas and carrots in her garden. (5歳のMがわが家の別の娘の2歳のMに，お庭で豆とニンジンをつくることにしてるのよと言っていた) (RD 98/9: 73)

b. Afternoons I could find 83-year-old *Margaret Harris* perhaps, or 66-year-old *Darlene Simmons*. (午後にはことによれば83歳のMHに，あるいは66歳のDSに会えた) (RD 99/10: 11)

c. Ten-year-old *Ann* was shouting at the back door. (10歳のAが裏のドアで叫んでいた) (RD 98/10: 115)

d. Pretty 16-year-old *Lyudmila* is a typical victim. (16歳のかわいいLは典型的な犠牲者だ) (RD 99/10: 107)

(141) a. Thirty minutes later, the 20-year-old *Perez* was dead. (30分後，Pは20歳で亡くなった) (RD 98/5: 32)

b. Entering the crumbling church of San Damiano near Assisi, *the* 24-year old *Francis* heard Christ on the crucifix speaking to him. (A近くのSDの崩れかけた教会に入ったとき，当時24歳のFは十字

架上のキリストが話しかけるのを聞いた) (RD 01/4: 80)

c. Like Dyer, *the* 40-year-old *Jones* was a policeman who knew the value of detail. (当時40歳のJは, Dと同様, 緻密さの価値を熟知している警官だった) (RD 99/9: 134)

d. All of this was done to help him offer his team the most insightful summary on *the* 28-year-old *Matsui* in case he declared himself a free agent. (以上すべては, 現在28歳の松井がFA宣言をした場合, 最も洞察にみちた報告を [スカウトの] 所属チームに提出するためだ) (NY Times, Nov. 2, 02)

e. If you could go back in time and meet *the* 12-year-old *Paul McCartney*, what advice would you give him? (もしも時間をさかのぼって12歳当時のPマカートニー少年に会うことができるとしたら, どんなアドバイスを与えますか) (RD 01/11: 59)

8.10 *the* が随意的に見える場合

すでに見たように, 同一の固有名詞が *the* をとったりとらなかったりする場合がある (例：(the) Bikini Atoll (VIII-88; 89, a); (the) Sydney Harbour/Denton Bridge (VIII-100, a–b; 101, a–b); (the) Hiroshima Regional Park (VIII-110, d; 111, b))。この区別は, 話し手/書き手が当該の事物を同定可能なものと判断するか, それとも符帳扱いするか, という選択による。次の諸例も同様である。

(142) a. The days were quite long in *the Biomed*, so I tried to get outside whenever I could. ([南極基地内の] B診療所での日々はとても長かったので, 可能なときはいつでも外に出るようにした) (RD 02/3: 112) [正式名称]

b. Unlike the average American hospital, *Biomed* didn't have special pumps to administer drugs at the prescribed rates . . . (米の平均的な病院と異なり, Bには, 処方した割合で薬品を投与する特殊ポンプはなかった) (RD 02/3: 121) [愛称扱い]

(143) a. "Houston, *the Challenger* has landed!" I reported joyfully and pried my cramped hands from the controls. (「H, C号 [月面に] 着陸」と喜々として報告して, 痙攣(けいれん)した手を操縦装置から離した) (RD 99/3: 137) [正式な報告では *the* つき]

b. We spent over seven hours on the surface before going back inside *Challenger*, filthy and exhausted. (月面で7時間以上過ごして, 汚れ

疲れてCの内部に戻った) (RD 99/3: 139) [愛称扱いのときは無冠詞]

(144) a. When Bijan asked *the Givaudan Roure* to develop the Michael Jordan fragrance, Bell's perfumery team identified five themes ... (BがGR社にMジョーダンの香りの開発を依頼したとき、Bの香水調合チームは5つのテーマを設定した) (RD 99/10: 118) [正式名称]

b. Today, Bell is vice president of *Givaudan Roure*. (今日BはGRの副社長である) (RD 99/10: 118) [通称]

(145) a. He resigned as pastor of *the Providence Baptist Church*. (PB教会の牧師の職を辞任した) (RD 92/8: 137) [組織名]

b. The people at *Providence Baptist Church* were in a hurry ... (PB教会の人々は急いでいた) (RD 92/8: 123) [通称]

(146) a. It won't be easy, but if the people come together, we can defeat *the Shining Path*. (容易ではないだろうが、団結すればセンデロ・ルミノソを打倒できる) (RD 92/9: 112) [組織名] [注:Shining Pathはスペイン語 Sendero Luminoso (ペルーの左翼ゲリラ組織) の英訳]

b. The coup has done little to erase the specter of *Shining Path*. (そのクーデターはセンデロ・ルミノソの亡霊を消し去るにはほとんど役に立たなかった) (RD 92/9: 111) [通称]

NB 37 φ 船名

MEG (vol. 7, 16.3₆) は、Collinson の説を引用して、英国海軍の海戦に関する公式文書では船名に the がつかない例が多いと述べている。同書はこの理由を説明していないが、本書の立場からは、船名が仲間内で愛称 (部外者から見れば「符帳」) 扱いされることによる、と説明可能である。

8.11 タイプ：this the 最上級／序数

MEG (vol. 7, 14.7₁₀) には this the greatest faculty of the human mind (人間精神のこの最も偉大な能力) (Coleridge); this the last night of his being with us (彼が我々のもとに滞在するこの最後の夜) (Black); This the first private house (この最初の個人住宅) (Galsworthy) という例が記録されている。次例中の this the fourth day は現代英語では誤用であるが、由緒ある誤用と言ってよいのかもしれない。

(147) As the sun began to rise, on *this the* fourth day since the tornado wreaked its devastation, Pastor Rick Cooper reminded his

congregation that the presence of each person who was in the church on Wednesday night represented one of God's miracles. (竜巻が破壊をもたらして4日目に太陽が昇りはじめたとき，RC 牧師は信徒たちに，水曜日の夜教会にいたものたちが生存しているのは神の奇蹟だ，と言った) (RD 00/2: 141)

第3部

限定詞の省略

　第3部では，冠詞あるいは他の限定詞が期待される箇所で
それが省略される場合を概観する。
ここでは主として構造的および文体的な理由による省略を取り上げる。
素材や働き，符帳扱いなど意味的な理由により
名詞部が無冠詞で用いられる場合に関しては，
第1部および第2部で論じたので，当該の箇所を参照されたい。

第9章　限定詞の省略

9.1　等位接続詞のあと
9.1.1　and による並列
　すでに述べたように (☞ 7.1)，同一の人物もしくは事物が2つ (以上) の役割を「兼任」あるいは「兼用」するときは，通例，最初の名詞の前にだけ a/an がつけられる。
(1) a. "Games – really fun, captivating games – are the mental counterpart of physical exertion," explains Cohen, *a 54-year-old game inventor, geriatric psychiatrist* and *former director* of the U.S. National Institute of Mental Health's Center on Aging. (「ゲームは，本当に面白くて夢中にさせるようなゲームなら，肉体運動に対応する精神的運動だ」と C，54歳，は説明する。彼はゲーム開発者であり，老人精神科医であり，合衆国加齢精神健康センター研究所の元所長である) (RD 99/2: 98)
   b. Another showed us a perfectly preserved wine jug some 18 inches high, with *a fine handle* and *curved spout*. (別の人は，申し分のない保存状態のワイン・ジャグを見せた。高さは18センチぐらいで，立派な取っ手がつき注 (っ) ぎ口は湾曲していた) (RD 97/2: 134)
   c. Instead, residents used the nearby Brantas River as *a bath, toilet* and *source of water*. (その代わりに，住民たちは近くの B 川を風呂兼トイレ兼水源として使っていた) (RD 99/12: 65)
　2つ (以上) の名詞が and によって並列または列挙されるときは，兼任や兼用を表さない場合でも，2番目 (以後) の名詞部の前ではしばしば冠詞 (または他の限定詞) は省略される。別物であることが明白だからである。
(2) a. Here there's a one-roomed bank and post office, *a police station, hotel, café*, and *general store*, all within a stone's throw of each other. (ここには1部屋の銀行兼郵便局 [のほか]，警察署，ホテル，カフェ，雑貨店が互いに石を投げれば届く距離にある) (RD 99/12: 28)
   b. Because the community is so interdependent, the Chathams are virtually crime-free. Every three months, *a judge, prosecutor, defence lawyer* and *clerk* fly from Wellington to Waitangi for a

one-day court sitting. (共同体は互いに依存しあっているので C 群島には犯罪はほとんどない。3 か月ごとに裁判官，検察官，弁護士，事務官が 1 日の開廷のため W から W に飛行機でやってくるにすぎない) (RD 99/12: 31) [1 人が裁判官ほかを兼任しているのではない；動詞が複数一致していることに注意]

c. Brandishing *a baseball bat* and *knife* at one robbery, they told victims, "You'll never look the same again after tonight." (ある強盗事件のとき野球バットとナイフを振り回しながら，「今晩からは 2 度と同じ顔ではないぞ」と犠牲者たちに言った) (RD 99/11: 44)

d. In it two bunk beds, lockers, and *a toilet, sink* and *shower* are shoe-horned into a space roughly three metres square. ([私の部屋では] 2 段ベッド 2 台，ロッカー，トイレ，流し，シャワーが約 3 メートル四方のなかに詰め込まれている) (RD 99/6: 90)

e. Hershey left wide-open space – 60 hectares – for an enormous park, equipped with *a band shell, dance hall* and *baseball diamond.* (H は 60 ヘクタールもの広い土地を空けておいて，巨大パークにして，野外音楽堂，ダンスホール，野球場を設置した) (RD 99/7: 129)

f. Zhi Hui was allowed to go into the isolation unit, but first she had to go through an anteroom where she put on *a sterile green gown, surgical cap* and *mask.* (ZH は隔離室に入るのを許可されたが，まず予備室に入って滅菌した緑色のガウン，手術用帽子，それにマスクをつけなければならなかった) (RD 98/12: 61)

g. He had dressed for the role in *an expensive leather jacket, gold watch* and cuff links – a touch of flamboyance to convince Woodward that he really was a prosperous antiques dealer. (その役割のため高価な皮ジャケット，金時計，それにカフスを身につけた。繁盛している古美術商だというのは本当だと W に納得させるための派手めな装飾である) (RD 99/1: 29)

h. My parents had come to Britain from Grenada before I was born and made a good life for themselves, with my mother working as a nurse and my father as *a mechanic*, and then *civil servant.* (両親は，私が生まれる前に，G から英国に移住して自力でいい暮らしをしていた。母は看護師，父は修理工，のちに公務員として働いたのだ) (RD 97/5: 107)

名詞部が並列されるときは，最初の名詞部に a/an がつかないときでも，後続の名詞部はしばしば限定詞なしで用いられる (9.5 も参照)。

(3) a. In some ways, cancer has allowed me to focus on the things that actually matter: my wife, three daughters and *son*, the smell of flowers. (いくつかの点では，ガンのおかげで本当に大事なことに集中できた——妻，3人の娘，息子，花の香りである) (RD 00/6: 25) [(my) son]

b. Eager to impress paying guests, the crew had pursued one mother and *calf* to within metres. (有料乗客に印象づけようとして，乗組員たちは [クジラの] 母子を数メートルにまで追いつめた) (RD 99/10: 52) [one (mother & calf)]

c. Waterside apartment blocks and stylish marinas were built, while beside the old harbor arose a gleaming $163 million office complex called Europort, with apartments, shops and *16-story hotel*. (水辺のマンションやしゃれた遊歩道が建設され，古い波止場の隣には1億6千3百万ドルのぴかぴかのオフィスビルがそびえ立った。それはEと呼ばれ，アパート，商店，16階のホテルが入っている) (RD 98/11: 29) [複数形連続のあと]

d. (= VIII-60, j) The patient, Tom Long, had been stabbed in the heart, *stomach* and *spleen* during a domestic dispute. (RD 01/9: 99) [the の省略]

NB 1 冠詞の反復

名詞部が並列あるいは列挙されるときは無冠詞でなければならない，というわけではない (7章 NB 1 も参照)。

i) If you're eating out, have *a salad* and *an appetiser* instead of a full entree. (外食するのなら，フルアントレではなく，サラダと食前酒をとりなさい) (RD 00/7: 90)

ii) Even when we moved 20 miles down the road to Odessa, oil was part of our lives. That was where *the drillers* and *the roughnecks* lived. (道路を20マイル移動してOまで行っても，石油は生活の一部だった。削岩者や採掘労働者の居住地だったからだ) (RD 97/6: 132)

9.1.2　or による並列

類義の名詞部が or によって並列されるとき、後ろの名詞部はしばしば限定詞なしで用いられる。

(4) a. Leave a telephone number so they can find you, or, if you're in a high-rise apartment block, send *a family member* or *neighbor* down to street level to direct them. ([救急隊員が] 見つけることができるように電話番号を伝えておきなさい。あるいは、高層マンションに住んでいるのであれば、隊員の誘導のため家族か隣人を路上に降りさせておきなさい) (RD 97/2: 83)

b. If you get *a rip* or *tear* and blood leaks in, you could be in big trouble. (もし裂き傷や引っかき傷をして血液が体内に流れたら、非常に面倒なことになりかねない) (RD 97/6: 129)

c. The hyenas would sneak up and snatch *a lamb* or *kid* that had wandered off. (子ヒツジや子ヤギがはぐれれば、ハイエナが忍び寄ってかっさらうだろう) (RD 99/10: 124)

d. In the four years of fighting in Kabul until 1996, 40 per cent had lost *a mother* or *father*, another 25 per cent had lost *a brother* or *sister*, 95 per cent had witnessed fighting, with two-thirds seeing someone killed by rockets and half seeing someone killed by bombs. (K での 1996 年までの 4 年間の戦闘で 40 パーセントは父親か母親かを失い、別の 25 パーセントはきょうだいを失った。95 パーセントは戦闘を目撃し、3 分の 2 はロケット弾によりだれかが殺されるのを見、半数は爆撃によりだれかが殺されるのを見た) (RD 99/7: 22)

e. What would happen if Johnny had to have *an appendectomy* or *tonsillectomy* or was seriously injured? (もしも J が虫垂切除あるいは扁桃摘除をしなければならないなら、あるいは重傷を負ったなら、どうなるだろう) (RD 98/12: 124)

f. Verbs in this pattern are followed by *a noun* or *pronoun* which is the indirect object, and *a noun, pronoun,* or *noun phrase* which is the direct object. (この型の動詞には間接目的語である名詞または代名詞、および、直接目的語である名詞、代名詞、または名詞句が後続する) (Hornby, *Guide to Patterns and Usage in English*, p. 49)

g. *The end* or *breakup* of a marriage changes not only your future but also your past ... (結婚の終了もしくは解消は本人の未来だけでなく過去をも変える) (RD 99/4: 110)

  h. Ask *your pediatrician* or *family doctor* for an assessment. (判定に関しては小児科医または家庭医に尋ねなさい) (RD 98/9: 83)

 類義でない名詞部が or によって並列されるときは，冠詞が反復される。

(5) a. The adverbial particle may precede the direct object when this object is *a noun* or *a short noun phrase*. (直接目的語が名詞あるいは短い名詞句のときは，副詞的不変化詞はその目的語に先行することがある) (Hornby, *Guide to Patterns and Usage in English*, p. 59) [noun と noun phrase とが並列されれば後者の前では a は不要であるが（上例 (4, f) 参照），ここでは short があるため文体的並行性に欠けるので a がつけられる]

 b. "You have what it takes to become anything you want in life," he told the boy, who scored high on I.Q. tests but flunked courses. "*A doctor, lawyer, teacher* or *a bum*. It's your choice." (「人生でなりたいものになるために必要なものは何でも備わっているのだよ」と，IQ テストではいい成績をあげていながら不合格になった少年に言った。「医者でも弁護士でも先生でも，あるいは浮浪者でも。選ぶのは君なのだ」) (RD 99/3: 90) [前 3 者は類似の職業として並列されているので無冠詞，or のあとは前 3 者と異なるので冠詞がつけられる]

9.2 ペア

 名詞同士が，修飾語句をともなわないで，ペアもしくは対(?)を成すときは，本来，「関係」を表すので（親族関係，心的関係，位置的関係など；「関係」は「働き」の下位区分；第 3 章および例 (VIII-48, a–b) [wife/father] 参照)，a/an や他の限定詞はつけられない。Quirk et al. (1985: 280) は both A and B および neither A nor B における名詞の無冠詞用法は「生産的」(productive) であると述べているが，筆者の観察では，最も生産的なのは between のあとである (9.4.1 も参照)。

9.2.1 between; both; neither ... nor

(6) a. It became a battle of wits between *student* and *teacher*. (生徒と教師との知恵比べになった) (LDOCE³)

 b. Western civilization has given the relationship between *human* and *dog* great importance ... (西欧文明はヒトとイヌとの関係を非常に重視してきた) (EB 01)

 c. When a lucky match is made between *pet* and *owner*, the results can be truly life-changing. (ペットと飼い主とのあいだが幸運にもし

っくりいけば，その結果として本当に人生を変えることもある) (RD 01/4: 96)

d. She answered before he had picked up the receiver, so he was unaware she was on the other end of the line and continued to work with the receiver tucked between *shoulder* and *ear*. ([発信者が机上の]受話器を持ち上げるより先に彼女が電話に出た。彼は，彼女と電話がつながっていることを知らないまま，受話器を肩と耳のあいだに挟んで仕事をつづけた) (RD 00/5: 59)

e. When he got near the end of his cigarette, he pinched the butt between *thumb* and *forefinger*, took a final drag and then flicked it away. (タバコの終わり近くになると，親指と人差し指のあいだに挟んで最後の一服を吸って吸い殻を放り捨てた) (RD 97/5: 42)

f. It was 8:20 the next evening when Constable A. Wilson, in the garage at Hedge End, heard voices and the sound of feet jumping over the gate into the alley between *garage* and *house*. (翌日の夕方の8時20分，AW巡査はHEの駐車場で話し声と足音を聞いた。足音はゲートを跳び越えて駐車場と家とのあいだの路地に入っていった) (RD 99/1: 30)

類例：between church and lab (RD 01/9: 100); between immigrant and native (RD 99/4: 107); between spirit and body (RD 01/9: 100)

(7) a. He gave Jen a huge hug, and both *father* and *daughter* plunged into the cold, turbulent water. (Jをしっかり抱いて，父娘は冷たい濁流のなかに飛び込んだ) (RD 01/6: 94)

b. Both *mother* and *daughter* knew the chances of survival were slim. (母娘とも生存のチャンスはわずかだということがわかっていた) (RD 00/2: 31)

c. Both *teacher* and *student* learn from each other and develop each other's potential. (師弟とも互いから学び，互いの可能性を伸ばす) (RD 99/9: 1)

d. More generally, my conclusion will be that the correct approach to language is both *formalist* and *functionalist*. (より一般的に言えば，私の結論は言語への正しいアプローチは形式主義者と機能主義者との両方だ，ということである) (Leech, *The Principles of Pragmatics*, p. 46)

e. The birth took place this morning, and both (the) *mother* and (the) *child* are doing well. (今朝出産し，母子とも順調だ) (Quirk et al. 85: 280) [無冠詞ならば「(親子)関係」(あるいは続柄)(☞ 3 章)を表し，the をつければ特定の母子を指す]

(8) a. To attain ability to catenate properly requires neither *book* nor *teacher*; it is a matter of private practice on the part of the student. (きちんと [音を] つづけて発音できるようになるには本も教師も要らない。これは生徒が個人的に練習するかどうかという問題だ) (Jones, *An Outline of English Phonetics*, p. 10)
  b. [H]is accompanist ... used neither *mike* or *amplifier*. (伴奏者はマイクもアンプも使わなかった) (CCED³)
  c. They pitched camp between a small winding river and a ridge covered with brushwood; but neither (the) *river* nor (the) *brushwood* afforded the protection they needed in the event of attack. (小さな曲がりくねった川と茂みにおおわれた尾根とのあいだに陣営を張ったが，攻撃をうけた際には，川も茂みも必要な防御にはならなかった) (Quirk et al. 85: 280) [the をつければ前方照応；無冠詞のときは「防御機能」を表す]

NB 2

1) between＋単数形＋複数形
   between のあとに無冠詞で"単数形＋複数形"がつづくこともある。(本章 NB 3 および NB 5 も参照。)
   i) I had wanted to start a garden, but the fear of getting between *mother* and *cubs* was a deterrent. (庭仕事を始めたかったが，母[グマ]と子[グマ]とのあいだに割り込むのではないかという恐れのためできなかった) (RD 99/1: 128)
2) between/both＋冠詞つき名詞部
   冠詞つきの名詞部が between/both/neither ... nor ... と共に現れることもまれではない ((IX-7, e) および (IX-8, c) も参照)。
   ii) On one occasion I witnessed an argument between *a shopper* and *a produce manager*. (あるとき買い物客と青果店の店長とが言い争っているのを目撃した) (RD 99/7: 7) [独立の個体]
   iii) Cheryl's story was both *a shock* and *a comfort* to the children. (C の話は子供たちにとってショックでもあり慰めでもあった) (RD 00/2: 36)

iv) I have received neither *an acknowledgment* nor *a reply*. (承認も返事も受け取っていない) (CCED³)

9.2.2 その他の文脈

2つの名詞部が and で結ばれてペアを構成するときは，しばしば無冠詞で用いられる。(三幅対の場合も同様；(9, o) 参照。) 本節の例は最初の名詞部にも限定詞がつかない点で 9.1 の例と異なる。

(9) a The boy loved to look at huge cranes in books, so after school *father* and *son* would drive around town looking at and sketching cranes. (少年は本で巨大なクレーンを見るのが好きだったので，放課後，父子は車で市街を回ってクレーンを見たりスケッチしたりした) (RD 99/10: 75) [主語 (a-j)]

比較： Could *a father* and *his son* make an impossible dream real? (父親と少年は不可能な夢を現実にすることがはたしてできるだろうか) (RD 99/10: 73) [個人としてとらえれば，限定詞をとる]

b. It was the eighth medical facility *mother* and *daughter* had visited that hazy spring afternoon in 1993. (母娘が 1993 年の霞のかかった春の午後に訪れた医療機関は 8 番目だった) (RD 00/1: 42)

c. Explains psychologist Evelyn Bassoff, "In the course of protecting, nurturing, worrying about, disciplining and rejoicing in their children, *husband* and *wife* are drawn into a daily intimacy from which a strong marital love can grow." (心理学者の EB は次のように説明する。「子供を守ったり，育てたり，心配したり，しつけをしたり，嬉しがったりしているうちに，夫婦は日々親しくなり，そこから結婚生活の強い愛情が育つのです」) (RD 98/3: 94) [複数一致]

d. *Man* and *machine* were bound together. (ヒトと機械とが合体された) (RD 00/5: 44)

e. "Corky's in love," said a trainer when *dog* and *master* met (「C は気に入っています」と，犬と主人が会ったとき，調教師は言った) (RD 99/11: 41, caption)

f. The feat was shown on TV and *man* and *beast* soon had invitations to hunts all over England as well as to many agricultural shows. (妙技はテレビで放映され，間もなく人と動物は，多くの農業ショーのほか，英国全土で狩猟に招待されるようになった) (RD 99/9: 118)

g. Locked in a fatal embrace, *man* and *crocodile* sank into deeper water.（死の絡みあいのまま，ヒトとワニは深水へと沈んでいった）(RD 98/11: 33)

h. *Man* and *cub*, named Globus, became inseparable, playing tag and wrestling in the snow.（ヒトとトラの子——名前はG——とは離れがたくなり，雪のなかで鬼ごっこをしたり組みあいをしたりした）(RD 98/9: 32)

i. The impact knocked him right through the railing, *bear* and *man* tumbling into the bush.（衝撃で柵のあいだを抜けて，クマとヒトは茂みのなかに倒れ込んだ）(RD 99/9: 71f.)

j. So intent were *mother* and *son* on identifying the exotic plants, they paid no attention to a rustling in the bushes beside the boardwalk.（母と息子はそれらの外来植物が何であるかを知るのに夢中になっていたので，遊歩道脇の茂みの物音にはほとんど注意を払わなかった）(RD 99/9: 70)

k. We must talk and act and think as though we are *pianist* and *composer*.（私たちはピアニストと作曲家のつもりで話し行動し考えなければなりません）(Dahl, "Mr Botibol") [補語]

l. Then they bundled *mother* and *baby* into the ambulance.（その後，母子をいっしょに救急車に乗せた）(RD 99/2: 122) [動詞の目的語 (l–o)]

m. The saddle twisted sideways, and the bull dragged *horse* and *rider* through the rocks and brush.（鞍は横にねじれた。牡牛は馬と乗り手一体のまま岩場や茂みのなかを引きずっていった）(RD 99/8: 62)

n. They wielded *bow* and *arrow*, reliving the Battle of Little Bighorn.（[米先住民たちは] 弓矢を振り回して，LBの闘いを追体験した）(RD 98/12: 92)

o. Today, Dr Purification Tumbaga, wearing *surgical gown, mask* and *gloves*, is absorbed in the delicate task of inserting a catheter through the umbilical cord of the new patient on a warming table before her: Baby Boy Allman.（今日，PT博士は，手術着にマスク，手袋を身につけて，目前の暖房手術台上にいる新米患者——新生児のA君——のへその緒からカテーテルを入れるというむずかしい施術に没頭している）(RD 01/4: 122) [複数形を含めて三幅対]

p. But it was locked from the inside by *key* and *deadbolt*, and it held tight.（だが，[裏口は] 内側からキーと安全錠とでロックされていたの

で，びくともしなかった) (RD 95/5: 37) [前置詞の目的語 (p-t); 9.5.1 も参照]

q. It is designed above all to be really useful to *student* and *teacher*. (とりわけ，[本書は] 学生にも教師にも真に有益であるように意図されている) (*Collins Cobuild English Grammar*, p. x)

r. Now, after three years of imprisonment and torture by the junta that seized power in Chile in 1973 and three years of exile to Denmark, Lee is broken in *mind* and *body*. (1973 年に権力を握ったCの臨時政府に3年間収監され拷問をうけ，3年間Dに追放され，現在ではLは精神も肉体もボロボロになっている) (RD 99/6: 18)

s. These were the hands that had reached out to Stoudemire when he'd been crippled in *body* and *spirit*. (これこそSが身も心も萎えていたころに差し延べられた手だった) (RD 98/10: 30)

t. Yuengben, his wife and his sister are Buddhists in *heart* and *soul*. (Yも彼の妻も妹も心底仏教徒だ) (RD 99/7: 86)

比較：They threw themselves *heart* and *soul* into the project. (心底その企画に打ち込んだ) (OALD⁶) [副詞用法]

NB 3　無冠詞単数形＋無冠詞複数形

無冠詞単数形に無冠詞複数形が後続することもある。(本章 NB 2-1 および NB 5 も参照。)

i) *Father* and *children* walked down to a shady tree on a grassy bank sloping steeply toward the river. (父親と子供たちは，草の生い茂る急坂の川岸にある木陰へと歩いていった) (RD 96/10: 18)

ii) One night *father* and *sons* built three big fires to keep watch over cattle they had penned in a canyon. (ある晩，父親と息子たちは渓谷に閉じ込めた牛の番をするため3か所で火をおこした) (RD 99/8: 64)

iii) "It helps the child if he sees *teacher* and *parents* working together," he explains. (「教師と親たちがいっしょに仕事をしているのを見れば子供のためになります」と彼は説明する) (RD 99/9: 88)

iv) There isn't much – just *skull* and *antlers*. (たいして残っていない，頭骨と枝角だけだ) (RD 99/6: 30)

ペアが or/nor によって結ばれるときも，しばしば，無冠詞で用いられる。

(10) a. It was his self-appointed mission to ensure that no one, *friend* or *foe*, approached within 100 yards of Breath without a warning. (自らに課した任務だったが，味方であれ敵であれ，だれも予告なしに B から百ヤード以内に近づかないようにした) (RD 99/3: 44)

  b. Except for dehydration, nothing was seriously wrong with *mother* or *child*. (脱水症状以外には，母子ともどこもひどく悪いところはなかった) (RD 02/2: 123)

  c. I couldn't make *head* nor *tail* of the damn film. (あのボロ映画はさっぱりわからなかった) (CCED³)

ペアをなす 2 語 (以上) が副詞的に用いられるときも冠詞をとらない (3.11; 9.5.3 も参照)。

(11) a. A few years later, under Forrest's leadership, his firm was running *neck* and *neck* with its competitor. (数年後 F の指導の下に，彼の会社は競争相手と横一線で競り合っていた) (RD 99/7: 138)

  b. He dedicated himself *body* and *soul* to the education of young men. (若者の教育に全身全霊を捧げた) (CCED³)

  c. [Dana Morosini] wore an off-the-shoulder dress and sang "The Music That Makes Me Dance." I went down *hook, line* and *sinker*. ([DM は] ノースリーブのドレスをまとって，"The Music" を歌った。私はすっかりとりこになった) (RD 98/9: 88) [三幅対]

9.3 列挙

冠詞など限定詞は，名詞部がペアを構成するときだけでなく，3 つ以上の項目が列挙されるときも，しばしば省略される。列挙に関して注意すべきことは，名詞 (部) だけでなく，(12, g) のように，文の連続においても観察されるということである。

(12) a. *Fox, badger, weasel* and *stoat* are regularly seen here. (キツネ，アナグマ，イタチ，それにシロテンはこのあたりでは定期的に見られる) (CCED³)

  b. Meanwhile, I think about the weight I am wearing. *Airpack, turnout coat, crash ax, flashlight.* Fifty or so pounds extra. (その間，背負っている重量のことを考える。酸素ボンベ，リバーシブルのコート，粉砕用斧，懐中電灯。余分に 50 ポンドかそれ以上だ) (RD 98/5:

143)

c. One night he came to my room and asked to borrow *mop, bucket, vacuum* and *broom*. (ある晩, 私の部屋に来て, モップ, バケツ, 掃除機, ほうきを貸してくれと言った) (RD 94/3: 117)

d. Dashing toward my train one morning, hair, *coat* and bags flying behind, I heard an announcement boom out: "Stand clear on Platform Five – express passenger passing through." (ある朝, 髪もコートもカバンも後ろにふっ飛ばしながら, 私の [乗る] 列車に突進していたとき, 構内放送が響くのを聞いた。「5番フォームから離れてください。特急乗客が通過中です」) (RD 98/7: 112) [複数形と並列；express passenger が無冠詞であることに関しては 9.6.2 参照]

e. Every living thing around us – *man, woman* and *child, dog, cat* and *chicken* – was running too. (まわりの生きとし生けるものすべて——男に女, 子供, 犬に猫, 鶏——が駆けていた) (RD 94/8: 67)

f. He followed the same routine: *coat* from the cupboard, *hat* from the stack of hats on the shelf, his walking stick from the stand. (いつもの手順に従った。クロゼットからコート, 棚の帽子の山から帽子, 杖立から杖 [を取り出した]) (RD 00/3: 112) [前置詞句つき]

g. *Liver* looks OK ... *Spleen* looks good ... *Stomach* looks good. (肝臓 OK, 脾臓異常なし。胃も異常なし) (RD 00/9: 122) [文単位] [省略記号 (...) は原文]

h. Since our inception in 1976, our purpose has been constant: we will only use ingredients that make our products effective, practical, honest and exciting without harming *man, woman, animal* or *planet*. (1976年の創業以来, 弊社の目的は一貫しています。素材には, 製品を効率的, 実用的, 純正, かつエキサイティングにし, 男性も女性も動物も惑星も傷つけることのないもののみを用いるということです) (ConCD-ROM) [or による列挙]

9.4 構造的省略

9.4.1 タイプ：three times a day

a/per day/cup などという表現では, 何月何日とか, どんな色のカップかという特定のものを指すのではないので, 冠詞はとらない (a/per *a day)。歴史的には, このパタン中の a は前置詞であるが (OED, s.v., a *prep 1*, 8b; a *a 2*, 4), 現代では, 不定冠詞と同様, 母音の前では an が用いられる。

(13) a. It was her job to make tea three times a *day*. (1日に3度お茶を入れるのが彼女の仕事だった) (CCED³)
　　 b. The helicopter can zip along at about 150 kilometres an *hour*. (そのヘリコプターは時速約150キロで飛行できる) (CCED³)
　　 c. How many hours do you work per *day*? (1日に何時間働きますか) (CIDE)
　　 d. Check for added sugar – 66 to 400 kilojoules' worth per *cup*. (入れた砂糖をチェックしなさい——1カップにつき66〜400キロジュール相当分あるので) (RD 01/4: 21)

9.4.2　文頭
9.4.2.1　タイプ：Fool as [that, though] I am
「譲歩」を表す as/though に名詞部が先行するとき，名詞部は無冠詞で用いられる。"名詞部＋that 節" という構造も同様である。

(14) a. In parenthetic affirmations, e.g. '*fool* as I am,' *that* is more common than *as*. ('fool as I am' [私は愚かだが] のような挿入的断言では，as よりも that のほうが普通である) (OED) [that/as 斜字体は原文]
　　 b. *Astute bargainer* that she was, Colo then broke the key chain and gave Jendry a link, perhaps reckoning *Why give her the whole thing if I can get a bit of pineapple for each piece?* (抜け目のない交渉人なので，C [牝ゴリラの名前] はそののちキーチェーンを壊して，輪を1つだけJに渡した。1つごとにパイナップルを1切れもらえるのに，どうして全部渡すことがあろうか，とひょっとすると計算したのかもしれない) (RD 00/4: 38) [*Why . . . piece?* 斜字体は原文]
　　 c. By this time, anyone else might have given up. But, *smart turkey hunter* that he was, Goodloe had spent too many hours to be deterred. (このときまでに他の人ならあきらめていただろう。だが，鋭い不正追跡者なので，Gは断念するにはあまりにも長時間を費やしていた) (RD 00/5: 131)
　　 d. *Rich man* though he was . . . the High Sheriff must have faced a staggering bill. (金持ちの男だったが，州長官は莫大な請求書とご対面したにちがいない) (1978 *Lancashire Life* July 55/4) [OED]

9.4.2.2　タイプ：Fact is,
"Fact/Problem/Trouble is/was" など名詞節を導入する語句は，しばしば冠詞なしで用いられる。この構文では，通例，is/was のあとにコンマが置かれ，名詞節を導くための that は省略される。

(15) a. He chuckled. "*Fact* is, you may not have much choice in the matter." (彼は笑って言った。「実は，その件ではあまり選択の余地はないかもしれないよ」) (RD 01/5: 132)
　　b. *Problem* was, the captain had a parrot who saw each show and had figured out how the magician did his tricks. (問題は，船長が連れていたオウムがショーを見て，マジシャンのトリックを見破っていたのだ) (RD [U.S. Edition] 98/9: 110)
　　c. *Funny thing* was, it didn't feel all that good. (奇妙なことに，それほど気持ちよいとは感じなかった) (RD 01/7: 49)
　　d. *Trouble* was he didn't care much for work. (困ったことに，彼はあまり仕事が好きでなかった) (RD 99/10: 23) [原文でコンマなし]

　　NB 4　The fact is
　　　　正式な文体では fact などの前に the がつけられる。
　　　i) *The fact* is, in the vast majority of cases, treatment of depression does work. (事実は，ほとんどの場合，鬱(うつ)の治療は効果があるということだ) (RD 01/5: 58)
　　　ii) *The trouble* is that these restrictions have remained while other things have changed. (困ったことに，まわりは変わったのに，これらの規制だけは残っている) (CCED[3])

9.4.2.3　タイプ：Same＋名詞／副詞的語句
same を含む名詞部が文頭に現れるとき，しばしば，the は落とされる。
(16) a. When I stepped into Dr Cynthia's clinic in Mae Sot after ten months away, it seemed nothing had changed. *Same* stoop covered with thongs. *Same* ceiling fan, still broken. (10か月間不在ののち，MS の C 先生の診療所に足を踏み入れたとき，何も変わっていない様子だった。同じ玄関にはゴム草履がいっぱいだったし，同じ天井扇風機があり，まだ壊れたままだった) (RD 99/10: 36)
　　b. The two small children fared well – even Margaret, who had been taken on such a remarkable ride. *Same* with little John Michael. Neither sustained any life-threatening injuries. (2人の幼い子供たちは無事だった。[竜巻に]乗って運ばれるという特異な目に遭った，Mでさえも。幼い JM も同様だった。2人とも命にかかわるような怪我はしていなかった) (RD 00/2: 140)

    c. 'I can't wait to see it.' '*Same* here.' (「見たくてたまらない」「私も」) (OALD⁶)

    d. *Same* again, please! (もう 1 度お願いします) (OALD⁶)

    e. 'Get lost!' '*Same* to you!' (「消えちまえ」「そちらこそ」) (OALD⁶)

比較：'Happy Christmas!' 'And *the same* to you!' (「楽しいクリスマスを」「あなたにも」) (OALD⁶) [and が先行しているので the をつけるほうがふつう]

9.4.2.4　間投詞扱い

発話中で名詞が間投詞的に用いられるときは，通例，冠詞をとらない．

(17) a. *Advantage* Agassi. ([テニスで] アドバンテージ, A) (LDOCE³)

    b. *Blast* for Ormrod. ([クリケットで] O にブラスト) (CCED³)

    c. Meikle cried, "*Man* overboard!" [...] Skipper Peter Joubert called on the radio, "Mayday! Mayday! We have <u>a man</u> overboard" (M は「人が落ちた」と叫んだ．PJ 船長は無線で連絡した「M, M, 人が船外に投げだされた」) (RD 01/9: 71)

    d. The boys scrambled out of the water and up on the muddy banks, crying, *"Shark! Shark!"* They ran naked into the heart of town, shouting that <u>a shark</u> had taken young Lester Stilwell. (少年たちはあわてて水から出て，ぬかるんだ土手を登りながら，「サメだ，サメだ」と大声で言った．裸のまま町の中心部に走っていき，サメが LS 兄さんをとっていったと叫んだ) (RD 02/8: 121)

    e. *"Speech! Speech!"* the chant went up. "<u>A speech, a speech</u>," he mused, and something dawned in his eyes. (「スピーチ，スピーチ」と一斉に声があがった．「スピーチ，スピーチか」と彼は考え，何か思いついたらしいことが目に現れた」) (RD 01/8: 81)

9.4.2.5　その他の文頭位置

上記以外に，(18) のように "It is/was a" が省略される場合もある (*MEG*, vol. 7, 12.3₄; 12.7₈ も参照)．

(18) a. *Pity* he hadn't thought of that a long time ago. (彼がずっと以前にそれに思いいたらなかったのは残念だ) (RD 02/7: 5)

    b. *Pity* you haven't got your car, isn't it. (車がないのは残念だね) (CCED³)

9.5 付帯的表現

9.5.1 タイプ：with pen and notebook

and で結ばれた2語(以上)が with に後続するとき，しばしば，限定詞なしで用いられる (9.1.1; 9.2 参照)。

(19) a. I sat by the door with *pen* and *notebook*, wishing I could will time to move in reverse, or at least stand still. (ペンとノートをもってドアのところに立ち，意のままに時間を逆行させることができたら，せめて，止めることができたらと願った) (RD 99/12: 124)

b. I was fitted out in a new cowboy suit, with *hat* and *bandanna*. (帽子とバンダナつきで，新品のカウボーイスーツをあつらえてもらった) (RD 99/5: 37)

c. a modern reception desk with *telephone* and *fax* (電話とファックスを備えた近代的な受付カウンター) (CCED³)

d. I attacked them with *broom* and *water pistol*. ([ハトを]ほうきと水鉄砲で攻撃した) (RD 96/3: 37) [(19, a–c) の with は「随伴」(concomitance) を表すのに対し，(19, d–e) では「道具」(instrument) を表す]

with A and B にさらに別の名詞句が後続することもある。

e. (= VIII-84, e) Her gang prospected up and down Mangahouanga Stream, dragging rocks from the icy water, working like convicts to split them with *hammer* and *chisel* or a petrol-driven masonry saw. (RD 01/9: 111)

次は，and NP が後続するため and が省略された例である。(最後の名詞部が冠詞をとるのは *of*-phrase により限定されるため (☞ 4.4.1)。

f. Five minutes later I left the house, burdened with *briefcase, purse* and a box of files, looking forward to climbing into a warm car. (5分後，暖かい車に乗るのを楽しみにしながら，重いブリーフケースとハンドバッグ，それに書類の入った箱をもって，家を出た) (RD 01/9: 79)

NB 5　無冠詞単数形＋無冠詞複数形

with に"無冠詞単数形＋無冠詞複数形"が後続することもある。(本章 NB 2 および NB 3 も参照。)

i) But as he read the pathologist's report, the 48-year-old father of four, six feet, six inches tall with graying *mustache* and watchful *eyes*, knew this was going to be one of the worst. (だが，病理学者の報告を読むにつれて，その4児の父親——48歳，上背6フィート6インチ，白髪になりかけの口ひげを生やし，鋭敏な目つきである——は，これは最悪のものになりそうだと察した) (RD 99/5: 122)

比較：As he bought himself a cold drink at a newsagent, a stocky man with *a* bushy *mustache* standing next to him asked genially, "Need a lift?" (新聞スタンドで冷たい飲み物を買ったとき，もじゃもじゃの口ひげをたくわえた，がっしりした男が隣に立っていたが，「乗るかね」と愛想よく尋ねた) (RD 99/5: 136) [ペアを成さないので，冠詞をとる；上例中の mustache と意味が異なるわけではない]

次例では with につづく3項目（うち2つは複数形）が限定詞なしに and で結ばれている。

  ii) Robin sloshed across the floor to his tool cupboard and returned with *hand drill, screws* and *wooden battens*. (Rは水をはねながら床を歩いて道具棚まで行き，ハンドドリル，ねじ，目板をもって戻ってきた) (RD 99/8: 20)

9.5.2 タイプ：pen in hand

「Xを手にもって」という意味を表す "X(s) in hand" は，通例，冠詞をとらない。この構文では hand はしばしば単数形で用いられる。

(20) a. She turns in triumph, holding her little arms like a bird against the wind, *bag* in hand. (得意そうに振り向き，手にはカバンをもって，風に向かう小鳥のように小さい腕を差し出す) (RD 01/5: 135)

 b. Returning home from a business trip, my husband Wayne, *bags* in hand, was slowly making his way to his vehicle in a crowded airport parking lot. (出張から帰って，夫のWは，手にカバンをもち，飛行場の混んだ駐車場の自分の車へとゆっくり向かっていた) (RD 99/5: 5)

 c. A light rain was falling as Kuklinski waited on the street corner, *briefcase* in hand, consulting his watch. (小雨が降るなか，Kはブリーフケースを手にして時計を見ながら，街角で待っていた) (RD 00/4: 130)

 d. *Chisel* in hand, Eddy again wormed on his belly through the puddled fuel. (鑿(のみ)を手に，Eは燃料のぬかるみのなかをふたたび腹ばいで進んでいった) (RD 98/3: 45)

e. "Can I sit by you?" John stood in front of me, *lunch tray* in hand and a grin on his face. (「隣に座ってもいい？」とJは私の前に立って言った．手にはランチトレーをもって，にやにやしていた) (RD 96/3: 18)

f. "I never forget A. A. Milne," she says, *pen* in hand. (「A. A. ミルンのことは忘れはしない」と，ペンを手に，彼女は言う) (RD 01/4: 53)

g. *Torch* in hand, I kick snow from the door, prise it open enough to pass through into a tiny veranda, then wrestle open a second frozen door. (懐中電灯を手に，ドアの雪を蹴落とし，通れる程度に押し開けて狭いベランダに出て，別の凍ったドアと格闘してこじ開ける) (RD 00/6: 73)

類例：guitar case in hand (RD 99/5: 37); plane tickets in hand (RD 97/2: 88); shotgun in hand (RD 99/6: 43); walking stick in hand (RD 99/11: 71); files in hand (RD 97/5: 131)

次も同じパタンである．

h. But one Mormon's website says, *tongue* in cheek, that the reason polygamy is no longer practised is "simple. Having multiple wives also means having multiple mothers-in-law." (だが，あるモルモン教徒のウエブサイトは，冗談っぽく，次のように言う．多妻が行われていない理由は「単純だ．妻をたくさんもてば，姑もたくさんもつことになるからだ」) (RD 02/2: 86)

まれに動詞に後続するときも無冠詞で用いられることがある．

i. He had *leash* in hand, while the dog trotted happily away on the treadmill. (彼は引き綱を手にもち，犬は喜んでトレッドミルの上を走りつづけていた) (RD 01/8: 37)

NB 6 類似タイプ

1) with a/an X in hand

  i) With *a* written *map* in hand, however, you'll enjoy the trip and arrive at your destination in the shortest possible time. (しかし，地図を書いてもっていれば，旅を楽しみ，しかも最短時間で目的地に着くだろう) (RD 99/12: 42)

2) with φ X in hand

ii) When the Vatican's refurbished Sistine Chapel was unveiled in 1994, it called to mind a common image of Michelangelo: the lonely genius trapped between agony and ecstasy, isolated on his back on a scaffold, with *paintbrush* in hand. (1994年にV宮殿の改装なったシスティナ礼拝堂が公開されたとき，Mのよく知られた姿が思いだされた——[天井画を描くため] 足場の上で独り仰向けになり，手には絵筆をもって，苦悶と恍惚に囚われた孤独な天才 [の姿] である) (RD 97/6: 104)

iii) Then, the night before Christmas, I found myself in the sitting room, armed with *pen* in hand, scribbling down an inventory of my life. (その後，クリスマスの前夜，気づくと居間で手にペンをもって，自分史の目録を走り書きしていた) (RD 02/7: 123)

3) a/an X in hand

iv) On a rainy Sunday morning in May 1998, Kuklinski was in the nave of the Cathedral of St Mary, *a microphone* in hand. (1998年5月，雨の日曜日の朝，Kは，マイクを手に，聖マリア聖堂の本堂にいた) (RD 00/4: 142)

4) X in hands

両手にもっていることを明示するときは hands を用いる。

v) At my desk, *head* in hands, I would wait for classwork to begin. (自分の机で，両手でほおづえをついて，授業が始まるのを待った) (RD 98/3: 48)

次は限定詞つきの例である。

vi) Addled, Johnson paused and leaned against a fallen tree, his *head* in his hands. (混乱して，Jは立ち止まり，倒木に寄りかかって頭を両手に抱えた) (RD 99/11: 27)

9.5.3　タイプ：belly down/up

名詞部が文中で副詞的に用いられるときは限定詞をとらない (3.10, 3.11 も参照)。

(21) a. The soft-looking, chocolate-coloured creature lay motionless, *belly* down on an examining table. (チョコレート色の，柔らかそうな動物 [porcupine] は身動きせず，うつぶせに診察台に横たわっていた) (RD 00/9: 129)

b. Anaesthetised, Misty is lying *belly*-up on the table. (麻酔をかけら

れMは腹を上にして手術台に横たわっていた) (RD 00/9: 122)
   c. Then he collapses on the hot yellow sand of the great Madrid arena, *face* down in his own blood. (そして，自分の血のなかに顔を埋めてMの大闘牛場の熱い黄色の砂の上に倒れる) (RD 02/9: 46) 類例: face down in a rice paddy (IV-46, a)
   d. He walked with a limp, *head* down. (うなだれて，足を引きずりながら歩いていった) (RD 99/3: 47)

比較: Watching him walk through the school door, *his head* down, my heart ached. (彼がうなだれて校門から出ていくのを見ると心が痛んだ) (RD 99/8: 135)

   e. The 35-year-old monarch is shown in profile, *head* on, and three-quarter-profile, showing off his straight nose, hooded eyes and sensitive lips. (35歳の国王は真横，正面，および斜め横から描かれていて，まっすぐな鼻筋と半ば閉じた目，敏感そうな口元を誇示している) (RD 99/12: 112)
   f. He looked down at his hands; they lay *palm*-up and useless in his lap. (自分の両手に視線を落とした。手のひらを上にして為すすべもなく膝の上にあった) (RD 00/1: 19)

   NB 7　複数形
   　down/up の意味上の主語が複数形のときも限定詞なしで用いられることがある。

   Thinking he was going to be attacked, Stallone went into a crouch, *fists* up, to defend himself. (やられると思って，Sは防御のため両拳(こぶし)をあげてうずくまった) (RD 99/10: 25)

9.5.4　タイプ：engine running
分詞構文の意味上の主語も，しばしば，無冠詞で用いられる。
(22) a. "There were no children," he says, *chin* quivering. (「子供たちはなくなっていました」と，あごを震わせながら，彼は言う) (RD 02/2: 112)
   b. Special agent Michael Pelonero of the American Drug Enforcement Administration (DEA) sat waiting in a utility, *engine* running. (米麻薬取締局の特別局員MPは，エンジンをかけたまま，小型トラックのなかで待っていた) (RD 99/10: 21)

c. Having said that, my preferred target was the lone female, *handbag* dangling my side – the right side, to be exact, so if I'm next to her I can reach it discreetly with my right hand across my body. (ここまで言ったついでに、私の好みのカモは、ハンドバッグを私の側、正確に言えば、右側、に掛けている、連れのいない女性だった。隣に並べば、体の前を交差して右手でそうっとそれに触ることができるからだ) (RD 01/7: 55)

d. For a moment he rested on all fours, *head* hanging down between his arms. (しばらく四つんばいのまま両腕のあいだに頭を垂れていた) (RD 99/8: 130)

e. I trudged perhaps 30 metres up, then stopped, bug-eyed, *heart* kabooming. (たぶん30メートルは登って、立ち止まった。目は飛び出て、心臓は大きな音を立てていた) (RD 99/6: 111)

f. *Heart* pounding wildly, he groped round and touched the frame of the stroller. (激しく心臓が高鳴るなか、手探りであたりを探したところベビーカーのフレームに手が触れた) (RD 96/10: 20)

g. A tractor-trailer blasted past, *horn* blaring, as it swerved to avoid collision. (トラクタートレーラーが、クラクションを鳴らしながら、通り過ぎていった。衝突を避けようとして進路からそれたのだ) (RD 98/8: 28)

h. *Siren* blaring, the ambulance sped through the hilly streets of Tegucigalpa. (サイレンを鳴らしながら、救急車はTの起伏の多い通りを駆け抜けた) (RD 99/7: 102)

i. He wriggled with delight, *tail* thumping, eyes bright. ([犬は] 喜んで体をくねらせ、しっぽをバタバタ振り回し、目を輝かせた) (RD 01/6: 86)

次のような例も、being が省略されていると考えられるので、このタイプに含めることが可能である。

(23) a. *Body* bent by the cave into an agonizing, near-fetal position, I waited in the darkness wondering how much longer our luck could hold out. (洞窟の [形の] ため体を胎児のような苦痛の姿勢に曲げたまま、暗闇のなかで待ちながら、あとどのくらい運がもつだろうかと思った) (RD 98/11: 95) [i.e., (My) Body (being) bent . . .]

b. *Eyebrow* raised, she said, "That's my jacket." ([片方の] 眉を上げて言った、「あれは私のジャケットよ」) (RD 01/8: 105)

c. He was lying on his stomach *face* buried in his arms when he dropped his bombshell. (爆弾を落としたとき, 腹ばいになって両腕に顔を埋めていた) (RD 99/8: 132)

d. Now his teeth were set in rage, *face* flushed, arteries bulging. (今や怒りのため歯を食いしばり, 顔は紅潮し, 血管は浮き出ていた) (RD 98/3: 70)

e. *Gun* drawn, Pelonero entered the garage. (銃を抜いて, Pは駐車場に入った) (RD 99/10: 22)

f. It's Rodney sitting on the boat, his back to the camera, *head* turned. ([写真中で] Rはボートに乗って, カメラに背中を向け, 顔だけ振り向いている) (RD 01/6: 89)

g. *Face* scarlet, eyes black with anger, he demanded, "Tell her she's a liar!" (顔は紅潮し, 目は怒りで黒ずみ, 声を荒らげた, 「嘘つきめとあいつに言え」と) (RD 99/8: 129) [eyes black に関しては, 下記 NB 8 参照]

h. The first real gorilla up on the screen was a frightening portrait: a head-and-shoulders shot of an adult male, *mouth* open in what appeared to be a scream of rage. (スクリーンに映った最初の本物のゴリラはぞっとする顔つきだった。成獣のオスの肩から顔の写真であり, 怒りの雄叫びと思われる様子で口を開いていた) (RD 00/6: 42)

i. *Treatment* over, I gave him a hug and left the room. (治療が終わると, 彼を抱きしめ, それから部屋を出た) (RD 99/8: 133)

比較: Talking always seemed easier when I was giving him *a treatment*. (治療中はいつも話すのが容易であるように見えた) (RD 99/8: 130) [省略構文でないときは, 限定詞が必要]

NB 8 複数形

分詞構文の意味上の主語が複数形のときも限定詞なしで使われることがある。

i) They jump feet first and immediately thrash their way to the surface, *hands* flailing, *eyes* wild. (足から飛び込み, すぐに水面に上がってくる。両手を振り回し, すごい目をして) (RD 01/5: 112) [i.e., their hands failing, their eyes wild]

ii) As I read it, the little girls appeared again, *shoulders* hunched, scared. (読んでいるうちに, あの少女たちが, 肩をすぼめて怖が

っている姿がまたまぶたに浮かんだ) (RD 99/10: 36)

9.6 省略的文体
9.6.1 見出し／キャプション／ト書き／かっこ内／注
見出しおよびキャプションでは，冠詞など限定詞はしばしば省略される。

(24) a. Inhalation Anthrax Is Diagnosed in Connecticut *Woman*, 94 (C 州 94 歳の女性に呼吸器炭素病の診断) (NY Times, Nov. 21, 01) [見出し]

比較： *A* 94-year-old *woman* from Oxford, Conn., appears to have contracted the inhaled form of anthrax, the rarest and most deadly form of the disease, state and federal officials said late yesterday afternoon. (C 州 O の 94 歳の女性が，最もまれで最も死亡率の高い病気である，呼吸器系の炭素病に感染した模様である，と州および連邦政府筋は昨日午後遅く発表した) (NY Times, Nov. 21, 01) [本文]

b. In Final *Address*, Giuliani Envisions Soaring *Memorial* (G [市長] 最終演説で天にも届く記念碑を構想) (NY Times, Dec. 28, 01) [見出し]

比較： In *his* official farewell *address* to New Yorkers after eight years in office, Mayor Rudolph W. Giuliani promised yesterday that he would push for *a* "soaring, monumental" *memorial* to be built at the World Trade Center site. (8 年間在職ののち，昨日 G 市長は NY 市民へのお別れの公式演説において，世界貿易センター跡地に「天にも届く大型」記念碑の建設を押し進めることを約束した) (NY Times, Dec. 28, 01) [本文]

c. Doctor Becomes *Patient* (医師が患者になる) (RD 98/6: 123) [小見出し]

比較： "You are *the patient*," she replied. (「あなたが患者なのよ」と彼女は答えた) (RD 98/6: 123) [本文]

d. John Paul wounded in assassination *attempt* (暗殺計画のため負傷したヨハネ・パウロ [二世]) (RD 96/10: 139) [キャプション]

比較： CIA director Casey always believed that the Soviets were responsible for *the* assassination *attempt* and was impressed with Sterling's account. (CIA 局長の C はソ連政府が暗殺計画にかかわっていると当初から信じており，S の報告に関心をもった) (RD 96/10: 139) [本文]

e. Making the Maple Sing – Rena uses an aluminum template to trace and carve the violin's neck. After gluing the maple together, she hollows the back with spoon-shaped *chisel*. (カエデに歌わせる：R はアルミニウムの型板を使ってバイオリンのネックをトレースして彫る。カエデを接合したあと，スプーン型の鑿(のみ)で裏側にくぼみをつける) (RD 98/9: 44 [キャプション])

かっこ内，注，ト書きなどの補足的説明でもしばしば冠詞など限定詞は省略される。

(25) a. (see *box* on page 102) (102 ページの囲み記事を見よ) (RD 01/9: 100)
   b. (see previous *page*) (前ページを見よ) (RD 01/8: 23)
   c. (like when *hammer* meets *thumb*) (たとえば，金槌(かなづち)で親指をたたいたとき) (RD [U.S. Edition] 02/8: 29)
   d. *Lincoln Library* has now replaced its collection of books, and is raising money for a new building. (現在 L 図書館は蔵書を入れ替え，新館のための拠金を応募中です) (RD 99/10: 12) [巻末注]
   比較：(= VIII-126, d) *The Lincoln Library* reopened on August 12, upstairs at Burnham Hall, with about 2000 books. (RD 99/10: 11) [本文]
   e. *Name* has been changed to protect privacy. (プライバシー保護のため名前は変えてあります) (RD 01/11: 46) [脚注]
   f. *Man* on bended *knee* to fortune-teller *girlfriend*: "Cynthia, will I marry you?" (男性がひざまづいて占い師のガールフレンドに：C，僕は君と結婚するだろうか) (RD 98/3: 29) [ト書き]
   g. *Employer* to job *candidate*: "I hire only married people. They're less likely to go home early." (雇用者が求職者に向かって：既婚者しか採用しません。早く帰宅しそうにないからです) (RD 99/10: 71) [ト書き]

9.6.2 その他の省略構文

書き手が省略的な文体を選べば，しばしば限定詞は省略される。前節の見出しやかっこ内の表現と同様に扱われるからである。

(26) a. *Problem* again: wiggle *line* under *came*. "Verb confusion (no suggestions)," says GC's warning box. (またも問題 [が指摘される]：came の下に波線だ。「動詞の混乱 (候補なし)」とグラマーチェックの警告ボックスは表示する) (RD 00/5: 88) [省略的文体；*came* 斜字体は原文]

比較：I can already see *a* wiggly green *line* under *writers* in my previous sentence. (すでに前文中の writers の下に緑色の波線が見える) (RD 00/5: 87) [非省略的文体] [*writer* 斜字体は原文]

b. The Siamese purred like a chain saw, hot glitter blazing in his eyes. The young chicken approached, bewitched by Ping's strange vibration. *Nose* met *beak*, and Sam stabbed. Ping recoiled, instantly subdued. (シャム猫はチェーンソーのように喉を鳴らし, 眼をギラギラと光らせた。ひな鳥は, P の奇妙な振動音に引かれて, 近づいてきた。鼻がくちばしに触れ, S は突いた。P はあとずさりして, 即座に家来になった) (RD 99/12: 39) [glitter に関しては, 9.5.4 参照]

c. Tendons and muscles tore as the rider, now sans *bike*, tumbled down Dawnhill Road, staining it red. (腱も筋肉も裂け, 乗り手は, 今や自転車から放りだされ, D 道路を赤く染めながら転がり落ちた) (RD [U.S. Edition] 02/8: 21) [挿入的；かっこ内に準じる]

d. Eventually the angel turned into a female fairy, complete with *wand*. (やがて天使 [の人形] は, 魔法の杖をもった妖精の女の子になった) (RD 98/12: 55) [同上]

省略的文体はしばしば決まり文句となる。

(27) a. *Case* closed. (これにて一件落着) (RD 00/3: 79)

比較：The *case* is closed. (本件はこれにて終了とする) [活用]

b. *Case* in point: ... (要点) (RD 00/4: 94)

c. *Court* adjourned! (これにて閉廷) (CIDE)

d. *Joke*'s on you, boys. (かついだんだよ) (RD 94/11: 36)

e. *dog* eat *dog* ... (骨肉相食 (は) む世のなかだ) (N. Lewis, *Word Power Made Easy*) [*MEG*, vol. 7, 12.8$_7$ に類例多数]

f. *Paddles* up! (パドル用意) (RD 02/9: 50) [複数形]

Appendix 1
(a/an ＋物質名詞)

(1) a. The thieves had thrown *acid* in his face, which would have blinded him. (泥棒たちが彼の顔に酸を投げたため，視力を失いかねなかった) (CIDE) [物質；以下，注記のない場合，a-文の例は「物質」を表す]

  b. Because the pH of this liquid is less than 7・0 we can say it is *an acid*. (この液体の pH は 7 未満なので，酸だ) (CIDE) [液体の種類；以下，注記のない場合，b-文の例は「種類」を表す]

(2) a. I put salve in the male's eyes, while Mark injected him with *antibiotic*. (私はその男の目に軟膏を塗り，M は抗生物質を注射した) (ConCD-ROM)

  b. He said there might be some infection, so I was to take *an antibiotic*, drink fluids and have plenty of sex. ([前立腺に] 感染症があるかもしれないので，抗生物質をとり，流動物を飲み，たっぷりセックスをするようにと言われた) (RD 97/5: 129) [医者が処方する，特定の抗生物質]

(3) a. Seated at small Formica tables, they swab an arm or leg with *antiseptic*, slide the needle into a vein and inject a preloaded syringe of pure heroin. (小さなフォーマイカのテーブルに座って，腕か脚に消毒液を塗り，静脈に針を刺し込み，注射器にすでに入っている純粋ヘロインを注入する) (RD 99/1: 97)

  b. Veronica from the herb garden was also used to stop bleeding, and rue was *an antiseptic*. (薬草園のヴェロニカは止血にも用いられたし，ヘンルーダは消毒薬だった) (Brown)

(4) a. The sky was white, ash floated in the air, *bamboo* exploded like artillery, and now there were real gunshots too. (空は白く，空中には灰が漂い，竹が大砲のように破裂した。今や本物の砲撃も始まった) (RD 99/10: 38) [通例，bamboo は，grass と同様に，一定の姿かたちをもたないものとして扱われる (☞ 2.3.1)]

  b. In the Himalayas there is *a bamboo* with each section of a different colour. (II 山脈には，それぞれの節が別々の色のタケがある) (BNC, B1F 698) [種類限定]

(5) a. The one from the first floor, she must be stingy; she doesn't use *bleach* at all. (一階の住人，あれはケチにちがいない。漂白剤をぜんぜん使っていないから) (RD 97/2: 99)

b. Remove the fungus as soon as possible and treat the area where it was growing with *a* strong *bleach*. (大急ぎでカビを取り除いて，生えていた場所に強力な漂白剤を施しなさい) (ConCD-ROM)

(6) a. *Bourbon* is made by distilling maize and rye. (バーボンはトウモロコシとライ麦を蒸留してつくられる) (CIDE)

b. (= II-113, b) I'll have *a bourbon* on the rocks/and water/and soda. (CIDE) [グラスなど容器に入ったバーボン；意味的には a (bourbon on the rocks)/(bourbon & water/soda)]

(7) a. She likes Cheddar *cheese*. (チェダーチーズが好きだ) (NHD) [下位分類 (☞ 8.9.3)　類例：V-96, a; Ap.2.2-93, a; Ap.4.1-32, c; 55, a; 78, a]

b. I've bought *a* large Stilton *cheese* to eat over the Christmas holidays. (クリスマス休暇中に食べるのに大きなスティルトンチーズを買った) (CIDE) [製品]　類例：a lower-fat cheese; a lovely Spanish cheese [２例とも ConCD-ROM]

(8) a. I always use *deodorant* after I've had a shower. (シャワーのあとはいつもデオドラントを使う) (CIDE)

b. Someone should tell him that he needs *a deodorant*. (彼にはデオドラントが必要だとだれかが言ってやるべきだ) (CIDE) [製品]

(9) a. When Esther asked what she could do, they told her to bring laundry *detergent*; the family was always running out of it. (何かできることはないかと E が尋ねたところ，洗剤をもってきてくれと彼らは言った。いつも切らしていたのだ) (RD 99/11: 125)

b. As true porcelain is non-porous, it can be washed in water and a mild dishwashing *detergent*. (本物の磁器は水を通さないので，真水や刺激の少ない台所洗剤のなかで洗ってもよい) (ConCD-ROM)

(10) a. "If you're so worried about viruses," one committee member replied, "why don't you just spray the computers with *disinfectant*?" (委員会のメンバーの１人が言った，「そんなにウイルスが心配なのならコンピュータに消毒液をスプレーしたらどうだい」) (RD 99/5: 92)

b. If a family member is sick, take the added precaution of wiping commonly touched surfaces (faucets, phones, refrigerator-door handle, etc.) with *a disinfectant*. (家族のだれかが病気なら，いっそ

う予防するため，だれもが触るものの表面（蛇口，電話，冷蔵庫のドアの握りなど）を消毒液で拭きなさい）(RD 98/12: 85) [任意の製品]

(11) a. *Fertilizer* promotes leaf growth. (肥料は葉の成長を促す) (LDOCE³)
 b. Work in *a* balanced *fertiliser* before planting. (植え付け前にバランスのとれた肥料を施しなさい) (CCED³) [複数の肥料を混合した製品]

(12) a. I bought some new *film* for my camera. (私のカメラ用に新しいフィルムを買った) (NTC)
 b. *a* 24 exposure/16mm/high-speed *film* (24枚撮りの／16ミリの／高速フィルム) (CIDE) [数値による限定 (☞ 4.4.1.1) および種類限定]

(13) a. I bought ice cream with natural chocolate *flavoring*. (天然のチョコレート風味のアイスクリームを買った) (NTC)
 b. At once I smell the strong citrus aroma used as *a flavoring* in food and beverages. (ただちに，飲食物の香料に用いられている柑橘類が強烈に匂ってくる) (RD 99/3: 76) [製品]
 c. I try not to buy foods with too many artificial *flavourings*. (人工調味料が多すぎる食物は買わないようにしている) (CIDE)

(14) a. *Food* generates waste. (食物は排泄物を作り出す) (RD 99/11: 116) [食物全般 (= 抽象概念)]
 b. In time the sweet came to be considered by some as more of a medicine than *a food*. (やがてその甘菓子[チョコレート]は一部の人によって食物よりも薬と考えられるようになった) (RD 99/7: 128) [個別事例 (the sweet を指す)]

(15) a. *Frost* can kill young plants. (霜で若い植物は枯れることがある) (OALD⁵)
 d. *A* late *frost* killed the flowers' blooms. (遅霜のため花の蕾が枯れた) (NTC) [特定の日の遅霜]

(16) a. They ran out of *fuel*. (燃料切れになった) (CCED³)
 b. Diesel *fuel* was puddling under his face. (ディーゼル燃料が彼の顔の下にたまっていた) (RD 98/3: 43) [物質]
 c. coke: a solid black substance produced from coal and burnt as a *fuel* (コークス = 石炭からつくられる黒い固形物，燃料として燃やされる) (OALD⁵; 以下の項目も参照：alcohol, butane, ethanol, methylated spirit, paraffin, peat, plutonium, propane) [製品]
比較： Charcoal is used esp as *fuel* or for drawing. (木炭は，特に，燃料もしくはデッサンに用いられる) (OALD⁵) [as のあとで「働き」を表す]

(17) a. When heated, the mixture would produce deadly formaldehyde *gas*. (熱せられれば，その混合物は命にかかわるフォルムアルデヒドガスを発する) (RD 97/6: 131)

b. Many tombs also contain high levels of radon, *a* radioactive *gas*. (多くの墓は高レベルのラドン，放射性ガス，も含んでいる) (RD 00/4: 27) [ガスとしてのラドンの種類]

(18) a. Jane prefers organic food and refuses to use *herbicide* in her garden. (J は無農薬食品を好むので，自分の庭では除草剤を使用しない) (NTC) [cf. insecticide/pesticide]

b. Scientists can now take a gene for resistance to *a* particular *herbicide* and transfer it to a crop: when these plants are sprayed with weedkiller, the weeds are destroyed while the crop is unharmed. (今や科学者たちは特定の除草剤に対して抵抗力のある遺伝子を取り出して農作物に移植することができる。これらの植物に除草薬を噴霧すれば，雑草は枯れるがその農作物には無害である) (RD 00/2: 63)

(19) a. Certain mosquitoes become resistant to *insecticide*. (ある種の蚊は殺虫剤に抵抗力ができる) (NTC) [cf. herbicide/pesticide]

b. But treating my hair with a lotion containing *an insecticide*, like malathion or permethrin, usually gets rid of them. (しかし，マラチオンとかペルメトリンといった殺虫剤入りのローションで髪を消毒すれば，たいてい[シラミを]駆除できる) (RD 99/8: 69) [製品 ; (IV-76) 参照]

(20) a. Do you think pencil *lead* will wash out of this white shirt? (洗えばこの白いシャツから鉛筆の黒鉛が落ちると思いますか) (CIDE)

b. I need a pencil with *a* softer *lead*. (もっと柔らかい芯の鉛筆が要る) (NHD)

(21) a. I don't usually wear *lipstick*. (ふだん口紅は塗らない) (CIDE)

b. There was only her driving licence, *a lipstick* and some tissues in the handbag. (ハンドバッグには彼女の免許証と口紅1本，ティッシュペーパー数枚しかなかった) (ConCD-ROM) [製品]

(22) a. She poured clear *liquid* and passed him a glass. He sniffed. Vodka. (彼女は透明な液体をそそいで彼にグラスを渡した。彼はにおいを嗅いだ。ウオッカだ) (ConCD-ROM)

b. Milk is *a liquid*; cheese is a solid. (ミルクは流動物であり，チーズは

固形物だ) (OALD5)

(23) a. Elaine smeared sun tan *lotion* liberally on her body. (E は日焼けローションを体にたっぷり塗った) (LDOCE3)

　　 b. *a* suntan *lotion* with a high protection factor (強力な保護作用のある日焼けローション) (OALD5) [種類 (または製品)]

(24) a. I spread *margarine* onto my toast. (トーストにマーガリンを塗った) (NTC)

　　 b. *A margarine* derived from a pine-tree extract blocks cholesterol absorption in the digestive tract. (マツエキスからつくられたマーガリンはコレステロールが消化管に吸収されるのを阻止する) (RD 00/1: 28)

(25) a. He has to take *medication* for high blood pressure twice a day. (高血圧の薬を1日に2度摂らなければならない) (NHD)

　　 b. Five of the children were treated with *a* similar *medication*. (子供のうち5人が同様な医薬品で治療された) (CIDE) [製品]

(26) a. She gave her baby cough *medicine*. (赤ちゃんに咳どめ薬を与えた) (NHD)

　　 b. *a medicine* compounded from various herbs (様々な薬草から合成された薬) (OALD5) [種類 (または製品)]

　参考：She's studying *medicine* at Edinburgh University. (E 大学で医学を勉強中だ) (OALD5) [学問名は無冠詞 (☞ 2.3.3.2)]

(27) a. *Metal* rang on *metal*. (金属が金属に当たって音を立てた) (RD 99/9: 41)

　　 b. Mercury is *a* liquid *metal*. (水銀は液体金属だ) (RD 99/8: 13)

(28) a. *Oil* and water do not blend (together). (油と水は混じりあわない) (OALD5)

　　 b. Neroli is *an oil* derived from orange blossom. (ネロリ[油]は橙花(とうか)から採った油だ) (CCED3)

(29) a. Workers find gold in *ore* taken from deep in the earth. (作業員たちは，地下深くで採取された原鉱のなかに金を見つけ出す) (NHD)

　　 b. David had located some pitch-blende, *an ore* containing tiny amounts of uranium, and pulverised it with a hammer. (D は瀝青(れきせい)ウラン鉱——少量のウランを含む鉱石——を発見し，ハンマーで粉々にした) (RD 99/6: 62)

(30) a. Jimmy used *paste* to stick the drawing to the poster. (J は絵画をポ

スターに貼るのに糊(のり)を用いた) (NTC)

b. I made *a paste* of flour and water to use as glue. (接着剤として使うために小麦粉と水で糊を作った) (NTC) [製品]

(31) a. She put a few drops of *perfume* on the back of her neck. (香水を数滴うなじにつけた) (CDAE)

b. She was wearing a filmy dress which suited her slender figure, and *a* delicate *perfume*. (すらっとした容姿によく似合う薄地のドレスをまとい, 微妙な香りの香水をつけていた) (ConCD-ROM) [特定の香水]

(32) a. Soon we were both drenched with *perspiration*. (間もなく2人とも汗びっしょりになった) (RD 99/8: 125)

b. *A* cold *perspiration* began to bespangle my brow. (冷や汗で額が光りはじめた) (ConCD-ROM)

(33) a. The local health authority had sent them for analysis because it feared they might have grown resistant to *pesticide*. (地元の衛生局はそれら[頭ジラミ]を分析に出した。殺虫剤に抵抗力をつけたのかもしれないと恐れたからだ) (RD 99/8: 70) [cf. herbicide/insecticide]

b. Pyrethrum is a plant of the chrysanthemum family that resembles the common white field daisy and contains *a* powerful *pesticide* safe for all mammals. (除虫菊は, どこにでもある白い雛菊(ひなぎく)に似た, キク科の植物であり, 強力な殺虫剤を含んでいるが, すべての哺乳類には安全だ) (RD 00/3: 126)

(34) a. The farmer put rat *poison* under the barn. (農夫は納屋の床下に殺鼠(さっそ)剤を置いた) (CDAE)

b. These fruits contain *a* deadly *poison*. (これらの果実は命取りの猛毒を含む) (LDOCE³) [名称指定可能な特定の猛毒]

参考: They distilled out deadly *poison* from the plant. (その草から猛毒を抽出した) [活用; cf. OALD⁵ (s.v., deadly) [どういう猛毒か非限定]

(35) a. I'm a vegetarian, so I eat a lot of cheese and eggs for *protein*. (菜食主義者なのでタンパク質にチーズと卵をたくさん食べる) (CIDE)

b. The gene is activated by *a* specific *protein*. (遺伝子は特定のタンパク質によって活性化される) (OALD⁵)

(36) a. Unlike white wine, *red* is made with not just the juice, but also the skins and pips of grapes, which contain tannin. (白ワインと異なり, 赤[ワイン]はブドウの果汁だけでなく, 皮や種も成分であり, それらはタンニンを含んでいる) (RD 00/2: 113)

  b. But you serve them *a* cheap and very odious Spanish *red*. (それなのに，安物でまったく不味いスペイン産の赤を出していらっしゃいます) (Dahl, "The Butler")

(37) a. Use insect *repellent* to avoid getting bitten. (刺されないように防虫剤を使いなさい) (CIDE)

  b. He sprayed *a repellent* all over his body so mosquitoes wouldn't bite him. (蚊に刺されないよう体じゅうに防虫剤をスプレーした) (NHD) [特定の防虫剤 (= 製品)]

(38) a. That late in the evening, all they could offer me was cold chicken *salad*. (あんなに夜遅かったので，彼らが私に出すことができたのは冷えたチキンサラダだけだった) (CIDE) [不定形の物体としてのサラダ]

  b. It only takes a minute to make *a salad*. (サラダを作るには1分もかからない) (OALD[5]) [完成品 (= 製品) としてのサラダ]

(39) a. He puts tomato *sauce* on everything he eats. (彼は食べるものすべてにトマトソースをかける) (CIDE)

  b. *A* tomato-based *sauce* on pasta or chicken is less fattening than a cream-based white one. (パスタやチキンにかける，トマトを基調とするソースはクリームを基調とするホワイトソースよりも太らない) (RD 99/3: 10) [製品]

(40) a. Three times he lunged at the rocks, but it was worse than gripping wet *soap*. (3度岩めがけて突進したが，濡れた石鹸をつかむよりやっかいだった) (RD 99/12: 57)

  b. Regular cleansing with *a* medicated *soap* or lotion will remove surface dirt and oil . . . (薬用石鹸またはローションで定期的に洗えば，表面のほこりと油が取り除かれる) (ConCD-ROM)

  c. I was told not to use *a soap* as it is too drying, and to try a facial wash instead. (乾燥しすぎるので石鹸は使わないで，代わりに洗顔料を使うように言われた) (ConCD-ROM) [facial wash と対照的に用いられているので指示範囲が限定されるため不定冠詞をとる (☞ Ap. 2.2-56, b; 75, b)]

(41) a. Do you want *soda* in your Scotch? (スコッチにソーダを入れるほうがいいですか) (LDOCE[3])

  b. When I arrived home from work, my housemate, Marcia, also a doctor, was sitting at the kitchen counter sipping *a soda*. (仕事から

帰宅したところ, 同居人でやはり医者のMが台所のカウンターに座ってソーダを飲んでいた) (RD 98/6: 123) [(グラス／瓶に入れられ) 姿かたちをもつソーダ]

(42) a. We had vegetable *soup*/curry for dinner. (夕食に野菜スープ／カレーを食べた) (CIDE) [vegetable/carrot/celery/chicken soup などは soup の下位分類 (☞ 8.9.3) として, 不定形の物体を指すので無冠詞]

　　b. I had *a* delicious *soup* with vegetables and thin strands of pasta in it. (野菜と細いパスタが入った美味しいスープを食べた) (CIDE) [味覚限定]

(43) a. Shall we have *steak* for dinner? (夕食はステーキにしようか) (CIDE) [大きさ・量など非限定]

　　b. Lisa bought *a* large *steak* for dinner. (Lは夕食に大きなステーキを買った) (NTC) [種類 (または製品)]

　　c. I've ordered *a steak*. (ステーキを注文した) (OALD⁵) [その店のメニューにあるステーキ；製品扱い]

(44) a. She played a really nasty trick on me – she put *syrup* in my shampoo bottle! (まったく意地の悪い悪戯(いたずら)をしてくれた。シャンプーの瓶にシロップを入れたのだ) (CIDE)

　　b. The high concentration of sugars forms *a syrup* when the sap evaporates. (糖類が高濃度なので, 樹液が蒸発すれば, シロップができる) (CIDE) [製品]

　　c. *A syrup* that contains a suppressant is best for dry, hacking coughs. (咳どめ入りのシロップが, 乾いた空咳には1番よい) (RD 98/12: 86) [関係詞節による種類限定 (☞ 4.4.2)]

(45) a. It is rich in minerals, *timber* and hydroelectric potential. ([チベットは] 鉱物や材木, 水力発電の潜在力に富んでいる) (RD 00/3: 19)

　　b. The main beam is *a* very sturdy *timber*. (主柱は非常に頑丈な材木だ) (NTC)

(46) a. It also vaccinated the whole country, using *vaccine* supplied by the World Health Organization. (WHOから供給されたワクチンを用いて, 全国民に予防接種も行った) (RD 99/2: 54) [ワクチンの種類非限定]

　　b. The discovery of *a vaccine* was the turning-point in the fight against smallpox. (天然痘に対する戦いにおいてワクチンの発見は転

換点だった) (OALD⁵) [天然痘用のワクチン]
(47) a. *Whisky* can be good for you if taken in moderation. (ウイスキーは適度に飲めば体によい) (OALD⁵) [物質；量・種類非限定]
   b. What would you say to *a* whisky? (ウイスキーを 1 杯いかがですか) (OALD⁵) [製品；量限定]
   c. He ordered himself *a* double *whisky*. (ウイスキーのダブルを注文した) (OALD⁵) [製品；量限定]
   d. 'That must be *a* treble *whisky*,' my mummy said. (「トレブルのウイスキーだわ」とお母さんは言った) (Dahl, "The Umbrella man") [製品；量限定]
   d. This is *a* very good *whisky*. (これはとても上質のウイスキーだ) (OALD⁵) [品質限定]
(48) a. *Yoghurt* is obtained by fermenting milk with bacteria. (ヨーグルトは牛乳をバクテリアで発酵させて作られる) (CIDE)
   b. I only had *a yogurt* (= a container of this) for lunch. (昼食にはヨーグルトを 1 カップ食べただけだ) (CIDE) [製品]

Appendix 2
(a/an＋修飾語句＋名詞)

Ap. 2.1 関係詞節

(1) a. *Disability* increases with age.（障害は加齢とともに増加する）(OALD[6])

  b. At age eight, for instance, she was diagnosed with dyslexia, *a disability* that affected her reading and coordination.（たとえば，8歳で難読症――読書と筋肉協調能力に影響する障害――だと診断された）(RD 00/1: 43)

(2) a. *Dryness* of the skin can also be caused by living in centrally heated homes and offices.（皮膚の乾燥は集中暖房の家や会社で過ごすことによっても引き起こされる）(CCED[3])

  b. The song has *a* wry *dryness* you won't recognise.（その歌にはひねった乾きがあるが，理解されないだろう）(CCED[3])

(3) a. It was the voice of a woman speaking with breathless *eagerness*.（息もつかぬほど熱を込めて話している女性の声だった）(CCED[3])

  b. He was cautious and conservative, but something about the rock made him feel *an eagerness* he had not experienced since he held the first moon rocks in his hands.（慎重で保守的だったが，その岩の何かに，最初の月の岩を手にもって以来経験したことのない熱い気持ちを感じた）(RD 97/5: 72)

(4) a. Anne was intelligent and capable of passing her exams with *ease*.（Aは頭が良いので，試験に楽々と合格できた）(CCED[3])

  b. She moved among the children with *an ease* that Andrea admired.（Aが感心するほど楽々と子供たちのあいだを移動した）(RD 99/4: 28)

(5) a. (= IV-218, a) He tried to ignore the feeling of *emptiness*. (CDAE)

  b. I felt *an emptiness* in my soul that could not be filled.（満たされることのない空虚さを心に感じた）(RD 98/6: 110)

(6) a. For the bishop still trusts that *freedom* will come, that Indonesia will one day grant East Timor self-rule.（というのも，神父はまだ信じているのだ，自由は来る，インドネシアはいつの日か東ティモールの自治を認める，と）(RD 96/3: 34)

b. It was *a freedom* the fashion community quickly fell in love with. (ファッション界が一目惚れした自由だった) (RD 00/5: 22)

(7) a. Workaholics can only find *fulfillment* in their work. (仕事中毒者は仕事のなかにしか充足感を見いだせない) (CDAE)

b. And at the end, if we are . . . generous enough to rejoice in another's happiness, and wise enough to know there is enough love to go around for us all, then we can achieve *a fulfillment* that no other living creature will ever know. (最後に，他人の幸せを喜ぶほど広量であり，愛はだれにでも行き渡るほど十分にあると理解するほど賢明であるならば，他のどの生命体も知ることのない充足感に達することができる) (RD 98/3: 116)

(8) a. (= IV-141, a) In Arab countries *generosity* must be boundless because your honour is at stake. (ConCD-ROM)

b. There is *a generosity* and a self-sufficiency about the Inupiat that attracted me when I first moved here more than 15 years ago. (イヌピアト族には気前のよさと自給自足の精神とがあり，15年以上前に初めてここに来たとき私の注意を引いた) (RD 97/5: 105) [that 以下は a generosity にもかかると解釈可能]

(9) a. We study *grammar* in order to write good sentences. (よい文を書くために文法を勉強する) (NHD)

b. *A grammar* which puts together the patterns of the language and the things you can do with them is called a functional grammar. (言語のパタンと，パタンを用いてできることとをまとめた文法は機能文法と呼ばれる) (*Collins Cobuild English Grammar*, p. v)

(10) a. Even if you don't like it, you have to admit that the Brighton Pavilion has (a certain) *grandeur*. (たとえ好みでなくても，B 離宮には (ある種の) 壮麗さがあることを認めざるをえない) (CIDE)

b. Van Dyck painted them and their children to brilliant effect, giving to these worthies *a grandeur* and elegance money alone could not buy. (VD は彼らと子供たちを描いてめざましい効果を添え，名士たちに金銭だけでは買うことのできない壮麗さと優雅さとを付与した) (RD 99/12: 111) [意味的には a (grandeur & elegance)]

(11) a. *Happiness* comes from giving *happiness*. (幸せは幸せを与えることによってもたらされる) (de Zubiliaga, quoted in RD 99/12: 62)

b. He . . . had *a happiness* that I didn't. (彼には私にはない幸せがあっ

た) (ConCD-ROM)

(12) a. He defines *hardiness* as a conglomeration of characteristics that make people try to solve stressful problems rather than fall victim to them. (彼は逞(たくま)しさを定義して、人々をして、ストレスに満ちた問題の犠牲となるよりもそれらを解決しようという気持ちにさせる特徴の集合である、と言う) (RD 99/10: 57)

b. There's *a* psychological and physical *hardiness* that comes about with a regular exerciser that you simply don't see with a couch potato. (規則的に運動をする人にはカウチポテトにはまったく見られない心理的かつ肉体的な逞しさが生じる) (RD 00/9: 23)

(13) a. When the water subsided, he put his hands under his armpits to conserve *heat*. (水が引いたとき、体温を保つために手を脇の下にはさんだ) (RD 00/6: 32)

b. The canyons radiated *a heat* that left the horses flecked with foam and the riders in a sweat. (峡谷は熱を放射し、そのため馬も騎手も汗をかいた) (RD 99/8: 64)

(14) a. (= IV-118, a) "Jump!" Gorrell yelled. Horton looked toward him and saw *horror* on his face. (RD 98/9: 34)

b. Nuclear war is *a horror* that people hope to avoid. (核戦争はだれもが避けたい恐怖だ) (NTC)

(15) a. Do hedgehogs have *intelligence*? (ハリネズミには知性がありますか) (CCED[3])

b. [Y]et he shows *an intelligence* and sensitivity that hasn't been seen in a rock star since pre-punk days. (それでいて、彼は前パンクロック時代からロックスターには見られない知性と感性を示している) (ConCD-ROM) [意味的には an (intelligence & sensitivity)]

(16) a. Bill's eyes glittered with *irritation*. (Bの目はいらだちで光を放った) (McED)

b. Smoking is *an irritation* that I cannot endure. (喫煙には我慢できないほどいらだつ) (NTC)

(17) a. *Knowledge* itself is power. (知は力なり) (Francis Bacon in *Religious Meditations*, 1597) (CIDE)

b. I got to know which stairs creaked or groaned when stood on, *a knowledge* which much later proved useful to me when I wanted to sneak silently out of the house at night. (上に立ったときどの階段が

ミシミシ, ギーギーいうかがわかってきた。この知識はずっとあとになって夜中に家をそっと抜け出したいとき役に立った) (ConCD-ROM)

(18) a. Once you get your computer home, learn just enough basic *lingo* to get going. (いったん自宅にコンピュータを置いたら, [操作に] まごつかない程度に基本的用語を勉強しなさい) (RD 98/9: 8)

b. The computer experts spoke to each other in *a lingo* I couldn't decipher. (コンピュータの専門家たちは私には解読不可能な業界用語で互いにしゃべった) (NHD)

(19) a. (= V-41, b) Ginger can do more than just add zip to cakes and cookies; the herb can also help relieve *nausea*. (RD 99/3: 115)

b. Polly looked away, her stomach churning with *a nausea* that couldn't be blamed solely on hunger or seasickness. (P は遠くに目をやった。彼女の胃は吐き気で七転八倒していたが, 空腹や船酔いのせいだけではなかった) (BNC, H7W 2221)

(20) a. *Politeness* prevented me from asking the actress her age. (礼節から女優に年齢を聞くのははばかられた) (NTC)

b. Edward said, turning his august profile with *a politeness* that Emily didn't believe necessarily to be lasting. (荘厳な横顔を向けて E は丁重に言ったが, その丁重さは必ずしも長つづきするとは E には思われなかった) (BNC, FRH 3507)

(21) a. Do you have *resentment* for your parents? (両親に対して恨みをもっていますか) (NTC) (7 章 NB 2 [(a) deep resentment] も参照)

b. I have *a resentment* I would like to talk to you about. (聞いてもらいたい恨みがある) (NTC)

(22) a. It is with great *sadness* that we announce the death of Wilfred White. (大きな悲しみをもって WW が亡くなったことをご報告します) (McED)

b. A deep, heavy sigh rumbled inside him, and suddenly he looked up at me with *a sadness* in his eyes that will haunt me for the rest of my life. (深く重い溜息が彼 [飼い犬] のなかで音を立てた。そして, 突然視線を上げて, 生涯忘れることのない悲しみを目に浮かべて私を見た) (RD 97/2: 14)

(23) a. We aim to give full *satisfaction* to all our customers. (私どもはすべてのお客様に全面的にご満足していただくことを目指しております)

(CIDE)

b. Traveling abroad was *a satisfaction* John enjoyed once a year. (海外旅行はJが1年に1度享受する満足だった) (NTC)

(24) a. While *skill* is certainly needed for success, it can never guarantee happiness and fulfillment. (技術はたしかに成功に必要だが，決して幸福と充足感を保証することはできない) (RD 99/3: 49)

b. Sewing is *a skill* that I don't possess. (裁縫は私にはない技術だ) (CIDE)

(25) a. The constant travel and training, under incredible *tension*, were taking a physical, emotional and mental toll. (信じられないほどの緊張のもとでたえず移動し，かつトレーニングしていたので，肉体的，感情的，精神的に参ってきていた) (RD 99/3: 132)

b. Searching long and hard for something creates a restless suspense, *a tension* that is wonderfully relieved when the lost item is finally found. (何かを長時間一生懸命探せば，不安な緊迫感が生まれるが，その緊張は探し物がついに見つかればものの見事に取り除かれる) (RD 99/1: 65)

(26) a. (= IV-127, a) The news of the epidemic struck *terror* into the population. (OALD[5])

b. Still, his thoughts filled him with *a terror* that quickened the movements of his arms and legs. (それでも，そう考えると恐怖でいっぱいになり，手足の動きが速くなった) (RD 00/3: 71)

(27) a. The main symptom of anorexia is a relentless pursuit of *thinness* by starving yourself. (拒食症の主な兆候は絶食してまでも容赦なくやせようとすることだ) (CIDE)

b. Her cropped, blond hair has *a thinness* that suggests chemotherapy; her face is gaunt and pale. (短く刈られた金髪が薄くなっていて，化学療法を[受けていることを]示している。顔はやつれて青白い) (RD 98/5: 98)

(28) a. Margaret's voice was shrill in *tone*. (Mの声は調子がかん高かった) (CIDE)

b. "Dad!" she snapped in *a tone* he hadn't heard before. (「お父さん」と彼女は彼がそれまで聞いたことのない調子でいきなり言った) (RD 99/5: 29)

(29) a. Her healthy figure radiates *vitality* and her deep blue eyes glint

vivaciously. (彼女の健康な姿は生命力を放射し，濃紺の瞳は生き生きと輝く) (RD 00/2: 17)

 b. She had *a* glowing *vitality* that immediately made her seem out of place, impolite even, ... (彼女には輝くばかりの活力があり，そのため，すぐに彼女は場違い，いや，無礼にさえ見えた) (ConCD-ROM)

(30) a. The symptoms of potassium deficiency include *weakness*, listlessness and drowsiness. (カリウム欠乏の兆候としては虚弱，倦怠感，眠気がある) (CIDE)

 b. Metal fatigue is *a weakness* which develops in a metal structure that has been subjected to many repeated stresses. (金属疲労とは，何度も繰り返し変形作用にさらされた金属構造に生じる弱体化のことだ) (CIDE)

Ap. 2.2 形容詞

(1) a. The pub was really humming (with life/*activity*) last night. (パブは昨晩まったく (活気/活力に) あふれていた) (CIDE) [抽象概念]

 b. (= IV-289, b) Until the mid-'80s, rock climbing was considered *an* eccentric *activity*, somewhat akin to wrestling alligators. (RD 98/7: 24) [個別事例 (rock climbing に限定)]

(2) a. Again, these results were found even after *adjustment* for other risk factors. (また，これらの結果は他の危険因子に対して調整したあとでも見られた) (RD 99/11: 8)

 b. Though symptoms can persist into adulthood, experts say, many ADHD [attention-deficit hyperactivity disorder] children make *a* satisfactory *adjustment* in adult life. (兆候は大人になっても残ることがあるが，専門家によれば，多くの注意欠陥多動障害児たちは成人後の生活において満足のいく適応をすることができる) (RD 00/3: 87)

(3) a. I have great *admiration* for the way he plays football. (彼のフットボールのプレーぶりにとても感心している) (NHD) [great は枕詞的 (☞ 4.4.3.4)]

 b. Tippett later developed *a* deep *admiration* for Wagner. (T はのちに W に深い敬服の念をもつようになった) (LDOCE[3]) [deep は admiration の様態を限定]

(4) a. Unlike a pregnancy, *adoption* has no natural terminus. (妊娠と違って，養子縁組は自然に終わることはない) (RD 98/6: 83)

b. Diana and I had completed lengthy adoption applications before, but those were nothing compared with what was required for *an* international *adoption*. (Dと私とは以前にも長々しい養子縁組依頼書を書いたが，それらは国際養子縁組みに要求されるものに比べれば何でもなかった) (RD 00/6: 124) [個別事例 (計画中の養子縁組)]

(5) a. Saturday *afternoon* is for recreation and outings. (土曜日の午後は気晴らしと外出のためのものだ) (CCED³) [一般論]

b. She arranged an appointment for Friday *afternoon* at four-fifteen. (予約を金曜日の午後4時15分に取り決めた) (CCED³) [次の金曜日 (=「身近」な金曜日なので無冠詞 (☞ 1.7))]

c. The interview took place on *a* Friday *afternoon*. (インタビューはある金曜日の午後行われた) (CCED³) [特定の金曜日]

(6) a. All the negotiators have expressed considerable *ambivalence* about the prospects for peace. (交渉者は全員平和の見込みにかなりのためらいを表した) (CIDE) [considerable は限定不十分なので無冠詞]

b. Once this realization sunk in, I felt *a* curious *ambivalence*. I had longed to have the staff reassure me I wasn't injured enough to require their high-level care, but now I became anxious about getting help. (いったんこの認識が理解されると，私は奇妙な相反する感情をもった。私の怪我は高度なケアを必要とするほどではないとスタッフが安心させてくれるのを望んでいたのに，今や援助が得られるのだろうかと心配になったのだ) (RD 98/6: 129) [後続の文が ambivalence の内容を限定しているので冠詞をとる]

(7) a. Like other women in the department, I have met with *antipathy* from certain firefighters, simply because I'm a woman. (部署の他の女性と同様，女性だというだけの理由で，私も何人かの消防士の敵意に遭った) (RD 98/5: 133)

b. His letters show *a* deep and intense *antipathy* toward workers. (彼の手紙は労働者に対する深く激しい敵意を示している) (CDAE) [antipathy の程度限定]

(8) a. Although there was nothing haughty about him, his demeanour could have been mistaken for *arrogance*. (不遜なところはなかったが，彼の振る舞いは傲慢ととられかねなかった) (RD 99/6: 129)

b. There is *a* cruel *arrogance* about their actions. (彼らの行動には残酷な傲慢さがある) (ConCD-ROM)

(9) a. I did feel a certain sense of *attachment* for the strange old guy.（その見知らぬ老人にある種の愛情を感じた）(LDOCE³)［"NP₁ of NP₂"の形式で素材扱い（☞ 2.1.2）］

　b. She had *a* special *attachment* to these students.（これらの生徒たちに特別な愛情をもった）(CDAE)　類例：a close/deep/particular/strong attachment［attachment が a/an をとるときは，通例，修飾語句をともなう］

(10) a. He seems to have undergone a change in/of *attitude* recently, and has become much more co-operative.（最近態度が変化したらしくて，ずっと協力的になった）(CIDE)

　b. "The chemotherapy made me feel terrible, but I knew *a* positive *attitude* was important," says Ng.（「化学療法は恐かったけれど，積極的な態度が大事だってことはわかっていた」と N は言う）(RD 00/1: 110)［種類限定（☞ 4.3）］

(11) a. We are always plagued by wasps in *autumn*.（秋にはいつもスズメバチに悩まされる）(CCED³)

　b. We enjoyed *a* very warm *autumn* last year.（昨年はとても暖かい秋を楽しんだ）(CIDE)［種類限定（☞ 4.3）］

(12) a. In a country where class can be rigid and accents betray economic and regional *background*, Blair speaks in standard upper-class English.（階級が固定し，言葉づかいから経済的地域的背景が知られる国で，B は標準的な上流階級の英語を話す）(RD 98/3: 54)［ここでは economic and regional background は特定の人物の生い立ちを指すわけではないので冠詞は不要］

　b. She came from *a* working-class Yorkshire *background*.（Y 地方の労働者階級という背景の育ちだ）(CIDE)［特定の人物の生い立ちを指すので冠詞が必要］

　c. The meeting takes place against *a background* of continuing political violence.（会議は政治的暴力がつづいているという背景の下で行われる）(CIDE)［*of*-phrase による限定（☞ 4.4.1）］

(13) a. There's nothing better than a good hot bath before *bedtime*.（就寝前の熱めの風呂ほどいいものはない）(OALD⁵)

　b. By the time your baby is 9 or 10 months old, he may still be having two long naps a day and need *an* early *bedtime*.（9～10 か月になるころまでは，赤ちゃんはまだ 1 日に 2 回長い昼寝をし，早く寝るのが

必要かもしれない) (ConCD-ROM)
(14) a. His body is being brought back to his birthplace for *burial*. (彼の遺体は埋葬のため生まれ故郷に戻ってきているところだ) (OALD5)
   b. I just want to find where my mom's buried and give her *a Christian burial*. (お母さんがどこに埋められているのか見つけだして，キリスト教の埋葬をしたいだけなのです) (RD 98/3: 87) [様態限定；具体的手順含意] 類例：give her a proper Muslim burial (RD 00/3: 80)
(15) a. Community and church leaders have appealed for *calm* and no retaliation. (共同体と教会の指導者たちは冷静にし報復しないよう訴えた) (CCED3)
   b. *An* uneasy *calm* is reported to be prevailing in the area. (その地域には不安な静けさが広まっていると報告されている) (CCED3) 類例：an emotional calm (RD 99/10: 56)
(16) a. She had never felt such *calmness* before. It was as if all her worries had disappeared. (そのような落ち着きを以前に感じたことはなかった。心配事がすべて消えたかのようだった) (CIDE)
   b. *An* eerie *calmness* settled over him as he thought again of his wife and daughter. (妻と娘のことをふたたび考えたとき不気味な冷静さが彼に訪れた) (RD 00/3: 72) 類例：an inexplicable calmness (RD 00/4: 69)
(17) a. "For women, the risk of developing incontinence increases with *childbirth*," explains urologist Dr Marie Lapitan of the Philippine General Hospital in Manila. (「女性にとって失禁になる危険は出産とともに増える」とM市にあるP総合病院の泌尿器科医ML博士は説明する) (RD 99/11: 100)
   類例：Her mother had bled to death during *childbirth*. (彼女の母親は出産時に出血多量のため死亡した) (RD 99/10: 38)
   b. Because of a weakening of the sphincter, often after *a* difficult *childbirth*, any pressure on the bladder forces some urine through. (しばしば難産のあとでは括約筋が弱まるため，膀胱に少しでも圧力がかかると尿が漏れることになる) (RD 99/11: 102) [様態限定]
(18) a. *Childhood* is not always a happy time. (幼年時代が幸せなときだとは限らない) (CIDE) [抽象概念]
   b. I didn't want to have kids as I didn't have *a* happy *childhood*. (幸せ

な幼年時代ではなかったので子供をもちたくなかった) (RD 99/1: 111) [特定の個人の幼年時代]

(19) a. Environmental crises triggered by changing *climate* will also create a new class of 'environmental refugee', whether from permanent drought in Africa or coastal flooding in Bangladesh, carrying their diseases with them. (Aの慢性的旱魃(かんばつ)であれ, Bの暴風津波であれ, 気候の変化をきっかけとする環境危機は「環境難民」という新しい階級をも生み出し, 彼らとともに病気を伝染させることになるだろう) (ConCD-ROM) [変化の内容は非限定]

b. *A* warm *climate* was chosen for the cars' debuts: cold weather severely compromises their performance. (その車のデビューには暖かい気候が選ばれた。天候が寒いと性能にひどく悪影響をうけるからだ) (RD 98/6: 114) 類例: a balmy/stable/temperate/tropical climate (RD 99/3: 74; ConCD-ROM; OALD[5]; LDOCE[3]); an extreme climate (CIDE)

(20) a. The soldiers were trained for *combat*. (兵士たちは戦闘の訓練をうけた) (NTC)

b. It was the end of *a* long *combat*. (長い戦いの終わりだった) (CCED[3]) [cf. battle/war]

(21) a. Had he not shown such remorse, would I have been able to forgive? I'll never know. But I do know that in that moment, *compassion* won out over revenge. (彼があのような悔恨を見せなかったとしても赦すことができただろうか? わかることはないだろう。だが, あの瞬間共感が復讐心に打ち勝ったことはたしかにわかる) (RD 99/12: 96)

b. Mr Major won the election because people believed he had *a* rare *compassion*. (M氏が選挙で勝ったのは彼には類いまれな思いやりがあると人々が信じたからだ) (ConCD-ROM) [M特有のcompassion]

(22) a. I could not in *conscience* refuse to help. (道義上援助を断ることはできなかった) (OALD[5]) 類例: a matter/pang of conscience (OALD[5]; LDOCE[3])

b. Self-respect and *a* clear *conscience* are powerful components of integrity and are the basis for enriching your relationships with others. (自尊心と清らかな良心とが清廉潔白さの強力な要素であり, 他人との関係を豊かにする基盤である) (RD 00/1: 51) 類例: a guilty conscience (CDAE)

(23) a. Familiarity breeds *contempt*. (慣れすぎは侮りのもと) [諺]
   b. His remarks betray *a* staggering *contempt* for the truth. (彼の発言は真実に対する突拍子もない軽蔑を示している) (OALD5) [記述的形容詞]　類例：a complete contempt for other people's feelings (McED)
  参考：The scholar had great *contempt* for his lazy colleagues. (その学者は怠け者の同僚を大いに軽蔑していた) (NTC); The Communist zealots also showed raw *contempt* for Angkor. (狂信的共産主義者たちはA遺跡に露骨な軽蔑を示した) (RD 98/7: 74) [感情的形容詞]

(24) a. Dr Gillett regrets that she cannot enter into *correspondence* with readers of her column. (G博士は残念ながらコラムの読者に [個人的には] お答えできません) (CIDE)
   b. Although he was far away, we never lost touch and kept up *a* steady *correspondence* over the years. (遠く隔たっていたが，音信不通になることはなく，長年にわたって間断なく文通をつづけていた) (RD 00/3: 135)　類例：a long/regular correspondence (CCED3, RD 00/6: 46)

(25) a. They knew the forest abounded in wildlife, yet *curiosity* drew them to an overhang on the far side of the rock. (森には野生動物が多くいることはわかってはいたが，好奇心から岩の向こう側の張り出し部分に引き寄せられた) (RD 99/5: 120)
   b. He showed *a* childlike *curiosity* and meticulously examined my hair, face and clothing and pawed through my backpack. (彼 [ゴリラ] は子供のような好奇心を示し，私の髪や顔，服を入念に調べ，バックパックのなかを掻き回した) (RD 00/3: 135)

(26) a. "This is not just a technical change of *currency*," he says. (「これは単に通貨の技術的な変更ではない」と彼は言う) (RD 99/2: 61)
   b. And, like Major, Blair refused to take a stand on *a* common European *currency*. (Mと同様，Bもヨーロッパ共通の通貨の側に立つことを拒否した) (RD 98/3: 56) [特定の通貨制度]　類例：a national currency (RD 99/2: 59)

(27) a. The road sign was obscured by *darkness*. (道路標識は暗さのため見えなくなった) (NTC)
   b. Diane ran out of the house and saw that *an* unusually heavy *darkness* cloaked everything. (Dは家から駆け出て，異常に重苦しい

暗闇がすべてを包んでいるのを見た) (RD 00/2: 131)

(28) a. Many of the 22 members sent their photos before *deadline*, and a reminder brought in all but the last six. (22人のメンバーのうちの多くは締め切り前に写真を送り，督促状により，最後の6人を除いて，全員が提出した) (RD 00/6: 38)

    b. We're working to *a* tight *deadline*. (厳しい締め切りに合わせて働いている) (CIDE)

(29) a. The moment of *decision* has arrived. (決定の瞬間が来た) (OALD⁵)

    b. A moment's inattention, *a* rash *decision*, a forgotten seat belt, a sense of invincibility – that's all it took. (一瞬の不注意，性急な決定，シートベルトの閉め忘れ，死ぬことはないという思い――起こったことはこれだけだ) (RD 96/3: 73)　類例：a firm decision (LDOCE³)

(30) a. *Defeat* is something that our team is quite used to. (敗戦にはわがチームは慣れっこだ) (NTC)

    b. The government has suffered *a* serious *defeat*. (政府は深刻な敗北を喫した) (LDOCE³) [個別事例]

(31) a. *Dependence* is not the answer. (依存が解決策ではない) (RD 00/1: 21)

    b. She has developed *a* deep *dependence* on him. (彼に強く依存するようになった) (CIDE)

(32) a. It bursts through on *descent* to reveal an ocean covered with whitecaps and a low-lying island whose cliffs are surrounded by a rim of white foam. ([機体が] 急降下すると海と島が見えてきた。海は白い波頭におおわれ，島は低く横たわり，その崖は白い泡の環(わ)に囲まれていた) (RD 99/12: 27)

    b. The pilot took *a* lazy *descent* around the mountain, spiraling over the slopes where we'd be climbing the next day. (操縦士は山のまわりをゆっくりと降下しながら，翌日登る斜面の上を旋回した) (RD [U.S. Edition] 98/9: 132)

(33) a. (= IV-175, b) My daily walk, lengthened every day, saved me from *despair* and fueled my recovery. (RD 97/5: 143)

    b. Sleepy and stiff, he felt *a* suffocating *despair* as he realised help was not on its way – and might never come. (眠気と体の硬直のなかで，救援は来ていないのだ，しかも，まったく来ないかもしれないのだ，と気づくと息のつまるような絶望を感じた) (RD 00/3: 71)

(34) a. A hurricane causes great *destruction* to buildings and trees. (ハリケーンは建物や樹木に大きな被害を生じさせる) (NHD) [destruction は形容詞をともなうときも不定冠詞をとらないことが多い；1度破壊すれば別の破壊はないためと思われる。cf. give (*a) birth] 類例：threaten the enemy with near-instant destruction (RD 98/3: 124)

b. It is world-wide knowledge that any power which might be tempted today to attack the United States by surprise, even though we might sustain great losses, would itself promptly suffer *a* terrible *destruction*. (周知のことであるが、今日どんな大国が米国を奇襲しようという気になっても、米側が大損害をこうむるにせよ、その国自体がすぐに恐ろしい破壊に苦しむことになるだろう) (Brown)

(35) a. The most urgent problem was *deterioration*. (最も差し迫った問題は劣化だ) (RD 00/1: 95)

b. There has been *a* continuing/serious *deterioration* in the relations between the two countries. (2国間の関係は悪化の一途をたどっている／深刻に悪化している) (CIDE, OALD⁶) 類例：a progressive deterioration (CCED³)

(36) a. They are pursuing their aims with dogged / relentless *determination*. (頑強な／たゆまない決意をもって目的を追求している) (CIDE) [dogged/relentless は枕詞的 (☞ 4.4.3.4)]

b. Within minutes, however, his despair gave way to *a* fierce *determination*. (しかし、数分以内に絶望は断固とした決意へと変わった) (RD 00/6: 31) [記述的]

(37) a. The wind has changed *direction*. (風は向きを変えた) (OALD⁵)

b. We walked (flew, ran, drove) in *a* northerly *direction*. (北の方向に歩いた (飛行した、走った、運転した)) (NHD)

(38) a. But we suffered bitter *disappointment*. (にがい失望を味わった) (RD 97/2: 132) [bitter は枕詞的 (☞ 4.4.3.4);『ジーニアス』(大修館) には a bitter disappointment という例がある]

b. Ream reached for the photos, but several minutes later felt *a* keen *disappointment*. (Rは写真に手を伸ばしたが、数分後には激しい失望を感じた) (RD 97/5: 58) 類例：betray a keener disappointment (RD 00/3: 62)

(39) a. She thought with *dread* of the cold winters to come. (これからの厳

寒の冬のことを考えてぞっとした)(CCED³)

b. Though I've chosen to be here to observe the great whites' behaviour firsthand, I experience *a* sudden, primal *dread*. (ホホジロザメの行動をじかに観察するためにここに来ることを選んだのだが, 突然原始的な恐怖を感じる)(RD 00/5: 92) 類例: a deep-seated dread of marital relations (Brown)

(40) a. He turned over the pages with *eagerness*, but after a short intent perusal he threw down the great book with a snarl of disappointment. (一生懸命ページをめくり, しばらく熱心に黙読していたが, 失望の声をもらして分厚い書物を投げだした)(Doyle, *Case Book*)

b. As it is, by *an* indiscreet *eagerness*, which was taken advantage of with extraordinary quickness and energy by our opponent, we have betrayed ourselves and lost our man. (あのとおり, 軽率にも熱心にやりすぎたため, 実に早々と, しかも激しく相手につけこまれて, 正体を見破られ, 逃げられてしまった)(Doyle, *Hound*) 類例: a subdued eagerness (Doyle, *His Last Bow*)

(41) a. *Education* should accustom children to thinking for themselves. (教育は子供たちに自分で考えることを習慣づけるべきだ)(OALD⁶)

b. My goal is to give them *a* practical *education*, to give them self-respect. (私の目的は彼らに実践的教育をし, 自尊心を授けることだ) (RD 99/12: 67) 類例: a classical / private-school / university education (Boulton, *Anatomy of Poetry*; RD 99/9: 96; 99/3: 5)

比較: It was hard for me to believe he would finally be going to a real school, one that offered special *education* for disabled kids. (彼がついに本当の学校, 障害児に特別教育をしてくれる学校, に行くことは信じがたいことだった) (RD 98/12: 133) [教育内容非限定]

(42) a. They had to wait ten minutes for the anaesthetic to take *effect* before they stitched up the cut. (傷を縫合するに先立って, 麻酔が効くまで10分待たなければならなかった) (CIDE)

b. The radiation leak has had *a* disastrous *effect* on/upon the environment. (放射線漏れは環境に壊滅的影響を与えた) (CIDE) 類例: (have) a strong/decongestant effect (NHD; RD 99/3: 113)

(43) a. His voice quavered with *emotion*. (感情で声が震えていた) (OALD⁵)

b. burn: to be filled with *a* strong *emotion* (燃える = 強い感情で満たされること) (OALD⁵) [程度限定]

比較： have, etc a lump in one's/the throat: to feel pressure in the throat as a result of strong *emotion* caused by love, sadness, etc (喉をつまらせる = 愛情，悲しみなどによって引き起こされた強い感情の結果として喉に圧迫を感じること) (OALD⁵) ["NP₁ of NP₂" の形式で素材扱い (☞ 2.1.2)]

(44) a. *Waiting for Godot*, by Samuel Beckett and *The Bald Soprano* (1950; Eng. trans., 1965), by Eugène Ionesco . . . treat spiritual *emptiness* and pessimism with comic absurdity. (SB 作『ゴドーを待ちながら』および EI 作『禿の女歌手』はコミカルな不条理によって精神的虚無感と厭世主義とを扱う) (GME) [抽象概念]

b. Forty years of the totalitarian system have left behind *a* material and spiritual *emptiness*. (40 年の全体制度は物質的・精神的な空虚さを残した) (CIDE) [様態限定]

(45) a. It is important to conserve *energy*. (エネルギーを節約するのは大事なことだ) (LDOCE³)

b. He was a thief, a con man and worse, driven by *a* malignant *energy* fuelled by anger and hate. (泥棒であり，ペテン師であり，より悪いことに，怒りと憎しみに補給された悪意の原動力に駆り立てられていた) (RD 00/6: 53)

(46) a. The moral characters of men are formed not by heredity but by *environment*. (人間の道徳的性格は，遺伝ではなく，環境によって形成される) (CCED³)

b. Office buildings with poor air circulation are *a* high-risk *environment* because cold viruses can't escape. (換気が悪いオフィスビルは，風邪のウイルスが出ていかないので，危険度の高い環境だ) (RD 98/12: 84)

(47) a. It is a hallucinatory land of *euphoria*. (幻覚的な幸福の土地だ) (RD 99/2: 80)

b. I changed my name to Jake Jonathan Zebedee Mangle-Wurzel, and I just surged off on *a* self-induced manic *euphoria*. (名前を JJZMW と変えて，自分で作り出した，躁(そう)状態の幸福感に浸った) (RD 99/9: 119) [一時的幸福感；種類 (☞ 4.3) と見ることも可能]

(48) a. This is the oldest Hebrew manuscript in *existence*. (これは現存するうちで最古のヘブライ語の写本だ) (OALD⁵)

b. My new husband had been accustomed to *a* completely independent existence. (新しい夫は完全に独立した生活になれていた) (RD 00/3: 124) [「暮らし(ぶり)」という意味のとき existence は，通例，"a/an ＋形容詞" をともなう]

(49) a. I know this from *experience*. (このことは経験から知っている) (RD 98/10: 86)

b. What could have been *a* horrible *experience* turned into one I will never forget. (恐ろしい経験になりかねなかったことが，決して忘れることのないものになった) (RD 98/3: 76) [experience が a/an をとるときは，通例，修飾語句をともなう]

(50) a. His research team, studying thousands of people since 1984, has compiled powerful evidence that religious *faith* not only promotes overall good health, but also aids in recovery from serious illness. (彼の研究チームは1984年から数千人を調査して強力な証拠をまとめた。宗教的信仰は健康全般を促進するだけでなく，重病からの回復も助長する，ということである) (RD 99/2: 86) [抽象概念]

b. But one thing Rose and Al shared was a set of values – *an* unshakable *faith*, a belief in the duty of people to offer a hand to those who need one, and trust in the power of love. (だが，RとAとが共有していたのは価値観だった——揺らぐことのない信仰，必要とする人々に手を差し出すのは人間としての義務であるという信念，および愛の力への信頼) (RD 99/11: 123) [2人に共通な個別的信念]

c. England shifted officially from a Catholic to *a* Protestant *faith* in the 16th century. (英国は16世紀に正式にカトリックから新教に改宗した) (CCED³) [faith は「宗派」という意味では可算名詞]

(51) a. Children of twelve up must pay full *fare*. (12歳以上の子供は全額料金を払わなければならない) (LDOCE³) [全額料金がいくらかはノーコメント；cf. full price]

b. stage: a section of a bus route for which there is *a* fixed *fare* (同一料金区間 ＝ 運賃が一定であるバス路線区間) (OALD⁵) [特定の金額]

(52) a. He watched the snake in horrified *fascination*. (怖いながらも魅了されて蛇を見つめた) (OALD⁵) [in と共起して状態 (☞ 3章 NB 8)]

b. I've had *a* lifelong *fascination* with the sea and with small boats. (海と小型船舶に一生つづく興味を抱いた) (CCED³) [have と共起して個別事例]

(53) a. Daniel, who dismounted in similar *fashion* [＝ similarly], later

declared himself the victor by virtue of having spent more time on the track. (D も同様に落馬したのだったが，走路にもっと長くいたという理由で，のちに勝利宣言をした) (RD 99/2: 105)
b. There is another drug called DHE that works in *a* similar *fashion*. (DHE という別の薬物も同様な仕方で作用する) (CCED³)

NB 1　fashion 補説
　　fashion が明白に「仕方，様式」という意味を表すときは冠詞をとり，fashion の意味が希薄なときは無冠詞で用いられる。
i) To Shortridge and Webster, Hong Kong's poultry markets held the key to why the cases of H5N1 were spread in haphazard *fashion* [= haphazardly]. (S と W にとって，なぜ H5N1 の症状が無方針に広がったかの鍵は香港の養鶏市場が握っていた) (RD 98/10: 112)
ii) In true fairy-tale *fashion*, they lived happily ever after. (本当のおとぎ話のように，彼らはその後ずっと幸せに暮らした) (OALD⁵)
iii) In true polar *fashion*, we turned my ultimate haircut into an event. (いかにも南極式に，最後の剃髪(ていはつ)をお祭りにした) (RD 02/3: 122)
iv) The rebel army behaved in *a* brutal *fashion*. (反乱軍は残忍なやり方をした) (CIDE) [様態・期間・頻度など限定的；brutally に書き換え不可]
v) The criminal was executed in *a* merciless *fashion*. (犯罪者は無慈悲な方法で処刑された) (NTC) [同上；mercilessly に書き換え不可]
　　類義語の style も同様に用いられる。
vi) He won the championship in fine/great *style*. (堂々と制覇した) (CCED³)
vii) Over the years he'd let his beard grow, tied back his dark hair in a ponytail and got tattoos in proper biker *style*. (長年月のうちにバイク乗り風にひげを伸ばし，黒髪を後ろで束ねてポニーテールにし，入れ墨をしていた) (RD 01/9: 46)
viii) The girl was well dressed, as usual, though in *a* more conservative *style*. (少女は例によってちゃんと着飾っていた。も

っとも，いつもより地味な服装だったが) (CCED³)

(54) a. (= IV-115, a) She spoke with *feeling* about the plight of the homeless. (OALD⁵)

　　 b. And then I started getting *a* strange *feeling*. (そのとき奇妙な感情が湧きはじめた) (RD 98/9: 120)

(55) a. A pinch of herbs will add *flavour* to any dish. (ハーブをひとつまみ加えればどんな料理も風味が増す) (LDOCE³)

　　 b. The wine has *a* light, fruity *flavour*. (そのワインは軽く，フルーティな香りがする) (CIDE) [flavour は不定冠詞をとるとき，通例，修飾語句をともなう]　別例：This brief description should give you *a flavour* of what the book is like. (この短い記述からどんな本であるかの概略がわかるはずだ) (CIDE) [*of*-phrase による限定]

(56) a. *Freedom* is the natural birthright of every human. (自由はすべての人間の生まれながらの権利である) (CCED³) [抽象概念]

　　 b. The result has been a kind of chaos. One day *a* new *freedom* is granted; the next day *an* old *freedom* is rescinded. (結果は一種の混沌だった．ある日新しい自由が認められ，翌日古い自由が撤回された) (RD 00/6: 110) [同一文内で対照的に用いて自由の範囲あるいは様態限定；(Ap.1-40, c; Ap.2.2-75, b) 参照]　類例：a basic/fundamental/ unaccustomed freedom (ConCD-ROM)

　参考： Such an income gave them unprecedented *freedom* and the paintresses became the fashionable girls of Stoke. (そのような収入はかつてなかった自由を与え，塗り子たちはS市のハイカラ娘になった) (RD 99/11: 77) [unprecedented はそのときの freedom の様態に関しては非限定]

(57) a. The massive, unmanaged influx, however, swamps welfare systems, exhausts goodwill and threatens social *harmony*. (しかし，大量の無規制な[移民の]流入は福祉制度を破壊し，善意を枯渇させ，社会的調和を脅かす) (RD 99/10: 110)

　　 b. The castle is a mass of medieval improvements, extensions and additions, creating *a* haphazard *harmony*. (その城は中世の改装，拡張および増築の集合体であるが，無作為の調和を作り出している) (ConCD-ROM)

(58) a. (= IV-143, a) The bonds between immigrant and native are forged

in the workplace, Salins says, where hard work counts for more than *heritage*. (RD 99/4: 107)

 b. The country has *a* rich cultural *heritage*. (その国は豊かな文化的遺産がある) (CDAE) [個別事例 (その国特有の遺産)]

(59) a. Ever since her friend was killed in a plane crash, the idea of flying fills Lisa with *horror*. (友人が飛行機の墜落で死んで以来、Lは飛ぶことを考えると恐怖でいっぱいになる) (NTC)

 b. We shivered with *a* delicious *horror* at the opportunity, the life – our lives – that would have been missed. (その奇縁に，誕生しなかったかもしれない，私たち [兄弟] の生命に，心地よい恐れをもって震えた) (RD 98/8: 8) [horror の種類限定]

(60) a. Susan shows *imagination* in her writing style. (Sの文体には想像力が見られる) (NTC)

 b. Rafael has *a* very active *imagination*. (Rはとても活発な想像力の持ち主だ) (CDAE)

(61) a. Four hours later mother *instinct* pulled me from sleep. (4時間後母性本能により眠りから引き起こされた) (RD 00/4: 12)

 b. I didn't have as strong *a* maternal *instinct* as some other mothers. (ほかの母親ほど強い母性本能はもっていなかった) (CCED³) [様態限定]

(62) a. Some of the earliest evidence that play can influence *intellect* came from neuroanatomist Marian Diamond. (遊びが知力に影響を与えうるという最も初期の証拠のいくつかは神経解剖学者のMDにより報告された) (RD 99/2: 99) [抽象概念]

 b. The professor had *a* very sharp *intellect*. (その教授は非常に鋭い知力をもっていた) (NTC) [様態限定]

(63) a. One by one the group were taken for *interrogation*. (1人また1人とそのグループは尋問に連れて行かれた) (CIDE)

 b. Police brought in the suspect for *a* lengthy *interrogation*. (警察は容疑者を長い尋問に連行した) (CDAE)

(64) a. He was always polite, but he shunned *intimacy*. (いつも礼儀正しかったが親交は避けた) (CDAE)

 b. The couple shared *a* romantic *intimacy* that they decided was love. (その夫婦はロマンチックな親しさを共有し，それは愛情だと結論した) (NTC) [関係詞節による修飾も a をとる一因 (☞ 4.4.2)]

(65) a. After long *introspection*, we decided to have a baby. (長考ののち赤ちゃんを産むことに決めた) (NHD) [長さの程度非含意；a をつければ，集中的に数時間熟慮したことを含意]

b In subsequent films, reviewers noted *a* new *introspection* and restraint in Williams's acting. (批評家たちはのちの映画で W の演技に新たな内省と抑制があることに気づいた) (RD 99/5: 78) [種類限定；意味的には a new (introspection & restraint)]

(66) a. For the first time Leonard felt *irritation* at her methods. (L は彼女のやり方に初めていらだちを感じた) (CCED[3])

b. He felt *a* sudden *irritation* against Percival . . . (P に突発的ないらだちを感じた) (ConCD-ROM)

(67) a. At the medical center the doctor told me there was a high probability that I would go into early *labor*. (医療センターで医師は早産の可能性が高い，と言った) (RD 98/11: 8) [下位分類 (☞ 8.9.3) 類例：block premature labor (RD 99/5: 20)；V-96, a; Ap.1-7, a; Ap.2.2-93, a; Ap.4.1-32, c; 55, a; 78, a も参照；病名または専門用語と解釈することも可能 (☞ 5.3; 1.7)]

b. When she emerged after *a* long, hard *labour*, I asked for her to be placed skin-to-skin on my chest. (長い難産ののち彼女が生まれてきたとき，肌と肌が触れるよう私の胸の上に置いてほしいと依頼した) (RD 00/5: 74) [個別の陣痛・出産；cf. birth/delivery]

(68) a. When *La Nina* develops, the trade winds that normally push warm water toward Indonesia and Australia are stronger and faster. (ラニーニャが発生すると，通常は暖流を I および豪方向に押している貿易風が，より強力でより速くなる) (RD 98/ 12: 24)

b. Even without *an* active *La Nina*, for example, Southeast Asia would return to wetter conditions with El Nino's departure. (活発なラニーニャがなくても，たとえば，東南アジアでは，エルニーニョが去れば，湿気が多い状態に戻るだろう) (RD 98/12: 25)　類例：a major La Nina (RD 98/12: 26)

(69) a. Decisions are made at local and not national *level*. (決定は，全国的ではなく，地方レベルでなされる) (LDOCE[3])

b. It's a children's story but adults can appreciate it at/on *an*other/*a* deeper *level*. (児童書ではあるが，大人も別の／より深いレベルで鑑賞することができる) (CIDE) [種類限定]

(70) a. *Libido* can wax and wane for any number of reasons. (ありとあらゆる理由で性欲は満ちたり引いたりする) (RD 99/12: 68) [抽象概念]
　　 b. She seems to be suffering from *an* overactive *libido*. (彼女は性欲が強すぎるようだ) (NTC) [様態限定；個別事例]
参考： If you suspect that stress is causing low *libido*, find time to decompress by taking a bath or a long walk early in the evening. (ストレスが性欲低下の原因になっていると思うならば，時間を見いだして，入浴するとか夕方早く長い散歩をするとかしてリラックスしなさい) (RD 99/12: 72) [様態非限定；cause に後続して抽象概念 (☞ 5.3.3)]

(71) a. "The village was born because of the brokenness of *life* here," she said. (「その村が生まれたのはここでの暮らしが成り立たないからだ」と彼女は言った) (RD 98/6: 104) [生活全般]
　　 b. To achieve *a* happier *life*, it's necessary to overcome some stumbling blocks. (より幸せな生活を得るためにはいくつかの障害物を乗り越えることが必要だ) (RD 98/7: 38) [種類限定；cf. retirement]

(72) a. Scientific experiments show that although moths fly towards *light* from a distance, when they get nearer, their behaviour becomes confused and they often veer off or settle away from it. (科学的実験の示すところでは，ガは遠くから光に向かって飛んでくるが，近づくと彼らの行動は混乱し，しばしば方向を変えたり，光から離れたところに止まったりする) (RD 99/10: 79) [抽象概念]
　　 b. When the moth comes across *a* bright *light*, only the ommatidia directly facing the light source respond. (ガはまぶしい光に出くわすと，じかに光源に向いている個眼だけが反応する) (RD 99/10: 79) [個別事例]

(73) a. This music has *majesty*, power and passion. (この音楽には威厳，力強さ，情熱がある) (CIDE)
　　 b. It's the world's biggest cat and possesses *a* compelling *majesty* and charisma. ([Siberian tiger は] 世界最大のネコ科動物であり，人を引きつける威厳とカリスマ性とがある) (RD 98/9: 1) [意味的には a compelling (majesty & charisma)]

(74) a. Lazy people with slow *metabolism* tend to gain weight. (代謝の遅いものぐさな人は体重が増えがちだ) (NTC) [lazy people 全般の代謝]
　　 b. He says he's got *a* fast *metabolism*, so he can eat a lot without

putting on weight. (彼が言うには，代謝が早いのでたくさん食べても体重が増えない，とのことだ) (CIDE) [彼固有の代謝]

(75) a. Instantly the world's busiest international airport swung into crisis *mode*. (世界で最もにぎやかな国際空港はただちに危機モードへと急回転した) (RD 99/5: 28) [危機モードの範囲非含意]

b. "The animals switch from *a* growth *mode* to *a* survival *mode*," Roth says. (「動物は成長モードから生存モードに切り替える」とRは言う) (RD 97/6: 25) [対照的に使用して，成長／生存モードの範囲含意；(Ap.1-40, c; Ap.2.2-56, b) も参照]

(76) a. Clinical depression is thought by many to result from an imbalance in the brain chemicals (such as serotonin and norepinephrine) that influence *mood* and behavior. (臨床的うつ病は，多くの [専門家の] 考えでは，気分と行動に影響を与える大脳化学物質（たとえば，セロトニンやノルエピネフリン）の不均衡によって生じる) (RD 96/3: 101)

b. She's in *a* good/bad *mood* today. (今日は機嫌がいい／悪い) (CDAE)

(77) a. For children to take *morality* seriously they must see adults take *morality* seriously. (子供が道徳を真剣に受け取るためには大人が道徳を真剣に受け取るのを見なければならない) (RD 99/12: 73) [抽象概念]

b. A life of principle, of not succumbing to the seductive sirens of *an* easy *morality*, will always win the day. (安易な道徳という誘惑的な魔女に屈しない，規範に基づく生活が常に勝利するだろう) (RD 00/1: 51) [種類限定]

(78) a. Then I heard a low, grinding rumble as the big rocket started to lift away from Earth in slow *motion*. (大きなロケットがゆっくりと動いて地球から離れはじめたとき，ゴーという低い轟音を聞いた) (RD 99/3: 118) [ゆっくりの程度は非含意]

b. He rocked the cradle with *a* gentle backwards and forwards *motion*. (揺りかごを穏やかに前後に動かして揺すった) (CIDE) [様態限定]

(79) a. I spent the afternoon listening to *music* and writing letters. (音楽を聴いたり手紙を書いたりして午後を過ごした) (CIDE)

b. It is possible that up there in those high-pitched inaudible regions there is *a* new exciting *music* being made, with subtle harmonies and fierce grinding discords, *a music* so powerful that it would drive us mad if only our ears were tuned to hear the sound of it. (聞こえない高周波の領域で新しい刺激的な音楽が創られているかもしれません。微妙な調和と激しい耳障りな不調和をともなうものであり，その音が聞けるように耳が調整されさえすれば，非常にパワーにあふれていて我々を発狂させるであろうような音楽なのです) (Dahl, "The Sound Machine") [種類限定]

(80) a. It's human *nature*. (それは人間の本性だ) (RD 96/3: 131)
   b. Marker . . . was surprised to learn that they have *a* timid *nature*. (M は [チーターが] 臆病な性質だと知って驚いた) (RD 00/1: 70)

(81) a. The soldier climbed the church tower for *observation* of the whole town. (兵士は町全体を観察するために教会の塔に上った) (NHD) [様態非限定]
   b. *A* quick *observation* of the room revealed a broken window and a rock on the floor. (部屋を急いで見ただけで窓が割れて床の上に岩があることがわかった) (NTC) [様態限定；一時的行為]

(82) a. He has, on *occasion*, had too much to drink. (ときおり飲み過ぎた) (CDAE) [抽象概念]
   b. She had met Zahid on *an* earlier *occasion*. (Z には以前会っていた) (LDOCE³) [時期限定]

(83) a. The train gathered *pace* as it went down the hill. (列車は丘を下るにつれて速度を増した) (CIDE) [様態非限定]
   b. Work continued at *a* frenetic *pace* throughout the weekend. (週末のあいだじゅう仕事は狂乱的なペースでつづいた) (RD 98/6: 61) [様態限定]

(84) a. Passion, not *pedigree*, will win in the end. (最後に勝つのは，家柄ではなくて，情熱だ) (Jon Bon Jovi, quoted in RD 02/1: 99)
   b. A leading specialist in what gases tell us about the volcano's behaviour, Igor had *a* superb geochemical *pedigree*. (ガスから火山活動を読みとる指導的専門家である I は，超一流の地球化学研究一家の出身だった) (RD 02/1: 113)

(85) a. It was a florist's shop, exuberant with late spring flowers, a riot of colour and *perfume*. (それは花屋であり，晩春の花，さまざまな色彩と芳香に満ちていた) (ConCD-ROM)
   b. The flowers had *a* strong *perfume*. (その花は強い香りがあった) (NHD) [その花に特定の香り]

(86) a. When I get really sick, I told myself, I want the smartest doctor, regardless of *personality*. (自分に言い聞かせたのだが, 本当に具合が悪くなると, 性格はさておき, 1番優秀な医者に診てもらいたい) (RD 99/2: 143)

b. She has *a* very warm *personality*. (とても暖かい性格をしている) (CIDE) [個別事例]

(87) a. (= IV-266, a) It's quite common for little boys to take *pleasure* in torturing insects and small animals. (CIDE) [抽象概念]

b. Patti and I took *a* special *pleasure* in seeing what a good mother Little Bit had become. (PとPとはLBがなんと立派な母[グマ]になったかを見て特にうれしく思った) (RD 99/1: 138) [種類限定；個別事例]

(88) a. The White House said that there will be no change in *policy*. (ホワイトハウスは政策に変更はないと言った) (CIDE)

b. The company operates *a* very strict *policy* on smoking. (その会社は喫煙に対して非常に厳しい方針をとる) (LDOCE³) [種類限定；個別事例]

(89) a. For the first time in years, the old body had *power*. (数年ぶりに老身は力を得た) (RD 99/5: 83) [抽象概念]

b. Babies have *an* amazing *power* to comfort and heal. (赤子は慰め癒すのに驚くべき力をもっている) (RD 99/11: 64) [種類限定]

(90) a. (US) The play has had good/bad *press*. 〈米〉(その芝居は好評/不評だった) (CIDE)

b. (UK and ANZ) The play has had *a* good/bad *press*. 〈英・豪 NZ〉 (CIDE)

(91) a. (= IV-86, a) She didn't care to pay full *price* because she didn't really want such a large tree. (RD 99/12: 9) [cf. full fare]

b. We thought they were asking *a* very high/low *price*. (とても高い/安い料金を要求していると思った) (CIDE) [そのとき要求された価格]

(92) a. *Prosperity* stimulated an outpouring of creativity – in architecture, art and practical invention. (繁栄に刺激されて創造性が一気に開花した――建築, 芸術, 実用的発明において) (RD 99/9: 24)

b. Social planning has led to greater equality and *a* more diffused *prosperity*. (社会計画により, いっそう平等になり, 繁栄がより浸透した) (OALD⁵) [繁栄の1様相]

(93) a. This permissiveness was a reaction against Victorian *puritanism*. (この寛容さはヴィクトリア朝清教主義に対する反動だった) (OALD5) [下位分類 (☞ 8.9.3)　類例: V-96, a; Ap.1-7, a; Ap.4.1-32, c; 55, a; 78, a]

　b. With Iran's Islamic revolution, *a* fanatical *puritanism* swept the lands; its leader, the Ayatollah Khomeini, practically banned tennis, seeing it as ungodly. (Iのイスラム革命とともに狂信的な潔癖主義がその地を襲った。指導者のK師は, 神に背くと見て, テニスを事実上禁止したのだ) (RD 00/4: 77) [様態限定]

(94) a. In *pursuit* of a healthier diet, Americans are eating more fish than they used to. (より健康的な食生活を求めて, 米国人たちは以前よりも多く魚を食べている) (CIDE)

　b. (= Ap.2.1-27, a) The main symptom of anorexia is *a* relentless *pursuit* of thinness by starving yourself. (CIDE) [様態限定]

(95) a. Our company puts the emphasis on *quality*. (わが社は品質に力点を置いている) (OALD5) [「品質」という意味のとき形容詞をともなっても無冠詞；類例: φ good/high/inferior/poor/low/merchantable/uneven quality]

　b. His poems have *a* surreal *quality*. (彼の詩には超現実的な特徴がある) (OALD5) [「性質・特徴」という意味のとき, 通例, "a/an＋形容詞"をともなう；類例: a dreamlike/fruity/rich melodic/spellbinding/timeless/whimsical quality]

(96) a. Over the next 20 years, candlelit trees became popular, the lights symbolizing *rebirth*. (それから20年かかって木にロウソクを灯すことが一般的になった。灯りは再生を象徴するのだ) (RD 98/12: 54)

　b. Cigar smoking in America was poised for *a* spectacular *rebirth*. (米では葉巻の喫煙がめざましく再生するための準備がなされていた) (RD 99/3: 55) [様態限定]

(97) a. The President is to launch a blitz on teenage crime accompanied by drastic *reform* of the police and prison services. (大統領は十代の犯罪に対し電撃作戦を行う予定だ。警察と刑務所の勤務に関する抜本的改革をともなうものだ) (CIDE) [改革の詳細無指定]

　b. This is *a* major, but long overdue *reform* which will benefit around 4 million low-paid people. (これは重要であるにもかかわらず, 長く延び延びになっていた改革であり, 約4百万人の低所得者に利するも

のだ) (LDOCE³) [修飾語句をともなって，特定の改革 (= 個別事例)]

(98) a. His new book bears suspicious *resemblance* to a book written by someone else. (彼の新書は，疑惑をもたせるほど，別人によって書かれた本に類似性がある) (CIDE) [この例では suspicious は心的判断を表す転移修飾語句 (☞ 4.4.3.4)；a をつければ程度・様相限定]

b. She bears *a* striking *resemblance* to her mother. (彼女は母と著しく類似点がある) (CIDE) [striking は記述的に resemblance の程度・様相を限定する]

(99) a. *Resentment* is like taking poison and waiting for the other person to die. (恨みは毒を飲んで他人が死ぬのを待つようなものだ) (Malachy McCourt, quoted in RD 99/1: 55) [抽象概念]

b. She felt *a* deep-seated *resentment* at/of/over the way she had been treated. (自分がうけた仕打ちに根深い恨みをもっていた) (OALD⁵) [様態限定；7 章 NB 2, ii) [(a) deep resentment] も参照]

(100) a. He's living happily in *retirement*, with his retirement pension. (退職年金を受け取って幸せに隠居生活を送っている) (CIDE) [様態非限定]

b. We all wish you *a* long and happy *retirement*. (長くお幸せな引退後の生活を一同お祈り申し上げます) (OALD⁵) [特定の生活；cf. life]

(101) a. This is the story of how a woman exacts grim *revenge* on the man who murdered her husband. (これは，どのようにしてある女性が夫を殺した男に容赦なき復讐をするかという物語だ) (CIDE) [grim は枕詞的 (☞ 4.4.3.4)；限定不十分]

b. The film recounts the story of a woman who plots *a* dastardly *revenge* on her unfaithful lover. (その映画は，不実な恋人に陰険な復讐を企てる女性の物語を描いている) (CIDE) [様態限定]

(102) a. She has/shows/feels great *reverence* for her professors. (彼女は指導教授に大いなる敬意を抱いている／示す／感じている) (CIDE) [great は枕詞的 (☞ 4.4.3.4)]

b. Fred had *an* enormous *reverence* for life. That basic philosophy underlay everything he did. (F は人生に特大の敬意をもっていた。その基本的哲学は彼の行動すべての根底にあった) (RD 98/10: 74) [enormous は程度記述] 類例：a deep/special reverence (OALD⁵, LDOCE³)

c. I stand for a moment in silent *reverence*, to marvel at my unforgettable brush with these majestic creatures of power and grace. (一瞬沈黙して尊敬の念をもって佇(たたず)み，強力で優雅な，これらの雄大な生物［クジラ］との忘れえぬ出会いに感嘆した) (RD 99/10: 53) [silent は転移修飾 (☞ 4.4.3.4)]

(103) a. I've got no sense of *rhythm*, so I'm a terrible dancer. (私はリズム感がないのでダンスが下手だ) (CIDE) [抽象概念]

b. Defibrillators are used to restore normal *rhythm* to the heart. (細動除去器は心臓に正常なリズムを取り戻すために用いられる) (CIDE) [a をとるには限定不十分]

c. The music suddenly changed from a smooth melody to *a* staccato *rhythm*. (音楽はなめらかなメロディから突然スタッカートのリズムに変わった) (CIDE) [様態限定]

d. His belief is that some babies don't establish *a* reliable circadian *rhythm*, the hormonal process that "tells" our bodies it's day or night. (彼が信じているのは，きちんとした日周リズム，つまり，体に昼とか夜とかを「告げる」ホルモンの過程，を確立できない赤ちゃんもいる，ということだ) (RD 99/11: 112) [様態限定]

(104) a. The winner was beaming with *satisfaction*. (勝者は満足で輝いていた) (OALD⁵)

b. She takes *a* quiet *satisfaction* in her work. (自分の仕事に静かな満足を得ている) (OALD⁵) [種類限定]

(105) a. The boat broke its moorings and drifted out to *sea*. (船は係留器具が破損して海へ漂い出た) (OALD⁵)

b. Each morning pairs of fishermen in oilskins haul their long black canoes, or *curraghs*, down to *a* fickle *sea*. (毎朝防水服を着た漁師が2人1組で長い黒いカヌー，［現地語で］curragh, を曳いて変わりやすい海に降ろす) (RD 99/9: 33)

(106) a. Bill meditates to achieve *serenity*. (B は不動心に到達するために瞑想する) (NTC)

b. Inisheer exudes *a* calm *serenity*. (I の村は静かな落ち着きを醸(かも)し出す) (RD 99/9: 34)

(107) a. It was *shame* and humiliation, and my heart breaks for him once more. (それは恥辱であり屈辱であった。彼を思うと私は再び心が痛む) (RD 99/8: 73)

b. Many people were filled with *a* deep (sense of) *shame* at the actions taken by their government. (多くの人々は政府が取った行動に対し深い恥辱(感)でいっぱいになった) (CIDE)

(108) a. *Shyness* is a nearly universal human trait. (はにかみはほとんど普遍的な人類の特徴だ) (RD 00/6: 66)

b. Seeing that their mother trusted us, the cubs soon got over *an* initial *shyness*. (母[グマ]が我々を信頼しているのを見て、子グマたちは間もなく当初の用心深さを克服した) (RD 99/1: 137) [一時的]

(109) a. Quakers emphasize the importance of *simplicity* in all things. (クエーカー教徒たちはすべてにおいて質素であることの重要性を強調する) (CIDE)

b. Asked about her extraordinary bravery, she speaks with *a simplicity* as profound as her mother's faith. (並はずれた勇気について尋ねられると、彼女は母親の信仰に匹敵する深さの素朴さで話す) (RD 97/2: 22) [程度限定]

(110) a. The priest was a man of deep *sincerity*. (牧師は非常に誠実な人だった) (CIDE) ["NP$_1$ of NP$_2$" という形式で素材扱い (☞ 2.1.2)]

b. His every word and gesture is expressive of *a* powerful *sincerity*. (彼のことばと身振りのことごとくが強固な誠実さを示している) (OALD[5]) [様態限定]

(111) a. *Size* isn't important; it's the quality that counts. (大きさは重要ではない。大事なのは質だ) (OALD[5])

b. Certain trees grow to *a* huge *size*. (ある種の木々は巨大な大きさになる) (CIDE) [大きさ限定]

(112) a. She has beautiful *skin*. (きれいな肌をしている) (OALD[5]) [修飾語句が beautiful だけでは限定不十分と判断されるので無冠詞]

b. She has *a* beautifully clear *skin*/complexion. (きれいな澄んだ肌をしている). (CIDE) [beautifully clear は skin に関して完結した情報を表すと判断されるので冠詞をとる]

(113) a. (= IV-38, a) All we could see was blue *sky*. (RD 99/3: 126)

b. This mall is modeled on a Roman village – you follow narrow "streets" under a ceiling painted like *a* blue Tuscany *sky*. (この商店街はローマの村をモデルにしている。トスカナの青い空のように描かれた天井の下の狭い「通り」をめぐるのだ) (RD 99/2: 45) [上例の skin に関する注記参照]

(114) a. He was extremely tired but *sleep* eluded him. (極度に疲れていたが

　　　　眠れなかった) (OALD⁶)
　　b. To my surprise, he fell into *a* deep *sleep*, allowing me to nod off comfortably too. (驚いたことに，彼は深い眠りに落ち，私も心地よくうたた寝をすることになった) (RD 00/7: 98) [程度限定；個別事例]
　比較： Afterward your body will cool down, which may be associated with deeper *sleep*. (その後身体は冷めていき，それはより深い眠りと結びつくかもしれない) (RD 99/3: 114) [深さ非限定；抽象概念]
(115) a. Heavy *snow* has caused the cancellation of several matches. (豪雪のため数試合がキャンセルされた) (OALD⁵) [降雪の期間や場所は非含意] 類例： blinding snow (RD 01/9: 8)
　　b. *A* steady *snow* was now covering the roof of their lodge, and as Stuart slept, the first warning sign came: a sudden thundering roar. (間断のない雪が今や小屋の屋根を覆おうとしていた。Sの睡眠中，最初の警告の兆候があった，突然の耳をつんざく轟音である) (RD 00/6: 30) [降雪の期間や場所を含意；cf. fog/haze/mist]
(116) a. We were full of *sorrow* when we learned our favorite uncle had died. (好きな伯父が亡くなったのがわかったとき悲しみでいっぱいになった) (NHD)
　　b. Anna felt *a* suffocating *sorrow*, but she kept thinking, *John is with Ali*. (Aは息もつまるほどの悲しみを感じたが，[夫の] Jは [先に亡くなった娘の] Aのところに行ったのだ，と考えた) (RD 00/4: 69)
(117) a. The job brings with it *status* and a high income. (その仕事は地位と高収入をもたらす) (OALD⁶) [抽象概念]
　　b. As an ambassador, she enjoys *a* very privileged *status*. (大使として非常に特権的な地位を享受している) (CIDE) [種類限定]
　比較： John Lennon gained iconic *status* following his death. (JLは死後偶像的な地位を獲得した) (CIDE) [iconic の様態・程度など非限定]
(118) a. (= IV-238, a) The atmosphere seemed poisoned with *suspicion* and lack of trust. (RD 99/3: 48)
　　b. He has *a* profound *suspicion* of anyone in authority. (権力の座にあるだれにでも深い疑いをもっている) (CIDE) [形容詞および *of*-phrase による限定 (☞ 4.4.3; 4.4.1)]
　比較： "I'm arresting you on *suspicion* of illegally possessing drugs," said the police officer. (「薬物不法所持の容疑で逮捕する」と警官は言った) (CIDE) [on に後続して「根拠」を表すので無冠詞]

(119) a. The Chinese thought the kebabs in poor *taste* and none of them would eat the meat. (中国人はケバブ[の串焼き]をまずいと思い、だれもその肉を食べようとしなかった) (RD 97/2: 138) [抽象概念；poor は情緒的]

b. This not only gives the pizza *a* delicate smoky *taste* but also spots the edges with the necessary scorch marks. (これはピザに微妙な燻製(くんせい)の味を与えるだけでなく，端に必要な焦げあともつける) (RD 99/2: 96) [様態限定]

(120) a. Just 53 minutes after *takeoff*, veteran pilot Urs Zimmerman and copilot Stephan Loew have noticed smoke in the cockpit. (離陸からわずか53分後、ベテラン操縦士のUZと副操縦士のSLは操縦室内の煙に気づいた) (RD 00/9: 56)

b. Our flight attendants were trying to help us passengers get settled into our seats for *an* on-time *takeoff*. (フライトアテンダントたちは定刻の離陸にそなえて乗客が席に着くよう手助けしようとしていた) (RD 98/6: 101) [様態限定]

(121) a. The incident has further increased *tension* between the two countries. (その事件のため2国間の緊張がさらに高まった) (OALD6) [限定不十分]　類例：incredible tension (☞ Ap.2.1-25, a) (RD 99/3: 132)

b. For more than a decade we've enjoyed an easy friendship, but on this cold and clear December afternoon in 1991, *a* disquieting *tension* separates us. (10年以上気楽な友情を楽しんできたのだったが，1991年のこの寒い晴れた12月の午後，不穏な緊張が私たちを離ればなれにすることになる) (RD 99/12: 93) [程度・種類限定；書き手が経験した tension]

(122) a. They lost their way in the desert and died of *thirst*. (砂漠で道に迷って渇きのため死んだ) (OALD5)

b. I woke up with a thumping headache and *a* raging *thirst*. (ずきずきする頭痛と激しい渇きで目が覚めた) (CIDE)

(123) a. War had given to the community a greater sense of *togetherness*. (戦争でその共同体はより強力な一体感を得た) (CIDE)

b. There's never much conversation, just *a* peaceful *togetherness*. (たいして会話はなく，ただ安らかな一体感だけがあった) (RD 00/1: 87)

(124) a. (= Ap.2.1-28, a) Margaret's voice was shrill in *tone*. (CIDE)

b. "You have a choice," Archie said in *a* faintly threatening *tone* of voice. (「選べるんだよ」とＡは少しばかり威嚇的な調子の声で言った) (RD 99/5: 67) [様態限定]

(125) a. It is likely that he was paid more for the sequel *Babe: Pig in the City*, released last year, in which the talented sheep-pig goes on *tour* to raise money to save his injured owner's farm. (昨年公開された続編の『ベイブ　都会へ行く』のほうが高収入だったようだ。それは有能な牧羊ブタが，負傷した飼い主の牧場を救うために資金集めの旅に出るという物語だ) (RD 99/10: 101f.) [期間・様態非限定 (= 抽象概念)] [cf. travel/journey]

b. We went on *a* guided *tour* of / (UK also) round the cathedral/museum/castle/factory. (寺院／博物館／城郭／工場を巡るガイドつきの旅に出た) (CIDE) [様態限定]

(126) a. In 1997, she undertook computer *training* and is now a computer operator. (1997年にコンピュータ訓練をうけ，現在はコンピュータ操作士だ) (RD 99/12: 67) [training の下位分類；複合語扱い]　類例：military training (軍事訓練) (RD 96/3: 119); first-aid training (救急訓練) (RD 97/5: 35); emergency medical training (緊急医療訓練) (RD 98/5: 125); professional training (職業教育) (OALD5); technical training (専門教育) (RD 99/9: 18)

b. We aim to provide *a* thorough *training* in all aspects of the work. (仕事のあらゆる面で徹底的な訓練を施すことを目的とする) (OALD5) [複数の主語が一体として授ける単一の training]

(127) a. The microphone converts acoustic waves to electrical signals for *transmission*. (マイクロホンは送信のため音波を電気信号に変換する) (CIDE) [抽象概念]

b. Please be aware that certain faxmachines will print a transmission report after *a* successful *transmission*. (ある種のファックスは送信に成功すると送信録を印刷することをご承知ください) (RD 99/11: 49) [個別事例]

(128) a. *Twilight* merged into total darkness. (薄暮は漆黒(しっこく)の闇へと変わっていった) (OALD5)

b. Then the lights flickered and died, and the house was smothered in *an* eerie *twilight*. (そのとき明かりがチカチカして消え，家は不気味な薄暗がりにおおわれた) (RD 00/2: 131) [様態限定]

(129) a. The footballer scored with such *velocity* that the goalkeeper didn't stand a chance of saving the goal. (そのフットボール選手はすごい早さで得点したのでゴールキーパーは失点を阻止するチャンスはなかった) (CIDE)
   b. Gazelles can move with *an* astonishing *velocity*. (ガゼルは驚くほどの速度で移動することができる) (OALD5) ［様態限定］ 類例 : at a high velocity (NHD)

Appendix 3
(具体物指示および同定構文)

(1) a. She was surprised that he had no words of blame or *accusation* for her.（彼が咎めや非難のことばを言わなかったので彼女は驚いた）(CCED³)

　　b. *An*other *accusation* levelled at the Minister is that he does not understand ordinary people.（大臣に向けられた別の非難［のことば］は一般庶民のことをわかっていないということだ）(CCED³) ［ジャンルと作品（☞ 2.2）と見ることも可能］

(2) a. (= IV-7, a) Feminine forms – circles and ovals that suggest completeness, receptiveness and *enclosure* – provide the underlying theme for many packages, because these forms have the most positive associations. (RD 96/3: 27)

　　b. The report is *an enclosure* with the letter explaining it.（レポートは説明書といっしょに同封してある）

(3) a. Life beyond our solar system was great *entertainment*, but it was dubious science.（太陽系の彼方の生命は娯楽としてはよくできていたが，科学としては胡散（うさん）くさかった）(RD 00/6: 6)

　　b. She wrote, "Crosswords are *an entertainment*."（「クロスワードは娯楽物だ」と書いた）(RD 98/9: 113)

(4) a. It's no surprise, then, that the diamond trade is a tight-knit family affair so exclusive that *entrance* is almost impossible unless you're born into the business.（だから，驚くにはあたらないが，ダイヤモンド取り引きは結束の強い家庭の仕事であり非常に排他的なので，その業界に生まれなければ参入はほとんど不可能だ）(RD 00/2: 42)

　　b. He was driven out of *a* side *entrance* with his hand covering his face.（横の入り口から追い出されたとき，手で顔を隠していた）(CCED³)

(5) a. There was little possibility of *escape*.（脱出の可能性はほとんどなかった）(OALD⁵)

　　b. He desperately looked for *an escape*.（必死で避難出口を探した）(RD 00/5: 40)

参考： Ironically, food became *an escape* for Chris. (皮肉なことに，食物はCにとって逃避手段となった) (RD 99/6: 52) [個別事例]

(6) a. She accused the Foreign Office of disgraceful *failure* to support British citizens arrested overseas. (外務省を非難したのは，海外で逮捕された英国市民を支持できなかったという恥ずべき失態の故だ) (CCED3) [抽象概念]

   b. Does that mean you're *a failure*? (君が落ちこぼれだということなのか) (RD 00/2: 93)

参考： The meeting was *a* complete/utter/total *failure*. (会議は完全な失敗だった) (CIDE) [個別事例 ; cf. success]

(7) a. He spent 5 years in prison for *forgery*. (文書偽造罪で5年間服役した) (OALD5) [犯罪名 (☞ 5.1)]

   b. Close scrutiny of the document showed it to be *a forgery*. (文書を精査したところ偽作だと判明した) (LDOCE3)

(8) a. The horse reared (up) in *fright*. (馬は驚いて後足立ちした) (OALD5)

   b. She thinks that dress is pretty – I think she looks *a fright* in it. (彼女はそのドレスをかわいいと思っているが，私は彼女がそれを着れば化け物のようだと思う) (OALD5)

(9) a. The waves were topped with white *froth*. (波の上は白く泡立っていた) (NTC) [広がりの範囲には関知せず]

   b. Tom served some sort of fruit drink with *a* sweet *froth* on top. (Tは，上に甘いフロスを浮かべたある種のフルーツドリンクを出した) (NTC) [製品 ; 具体物]

参考： He broke the surface in *a froth* of his own blood with an arm almost torn off. (腕をほとんど喰いちぎられて自分の血で泡だっている海面に浮かび出た) (RD 99/12: 30) [製品 (＝血でできた泡) ; 広がりの範囲含意 (☞ 4.1)]

(10) a. And they worry about side-effects, such as slower *growth*. (副作用，たとえば，成長の遅れ，を心配している) (RD 99/6: 84)

   b. During surgery doctors found *a* large, potentially malignant *growth* spread over almost her entire uterus. (手術中医師たちは大きな，悪性かもしれない腫瘍がほとんど子宮全体に広がっているのを発見した) (RD 98/3: 20) [cf. mass]

(11) a. [T]he book sold 372,775 copies in *hardback*. (その本はハードカバーで372,775冊売れた) (RD 01/4: 48) [形式]

b. *A hardback* is a book which has a stiff hard cover. (ハードカバーとは堅固な堅いカバーがついている本のことだ) (CCED³)
(12) a. But Dana was looking in *horror* at the windowsill behind me. (しかし，D は恐れて私の後ろの窓の下枠を見ていた) (RD 96/3: 37)
  b. Peter was *a* (real) little *horror* when he was four. (P は 4 歳のころは (ほんとに) 悪ガキだった) (CIDE)
(13) a. In a way, Diana gained *identity* through her illness: She became obsessive about skiing and racing. (ある意味で D は病気によって自分を取り戻し，スキーとレースに病みつきになった) (RD 98/3: 18)
  b. In the early 1990s he got his first fake licence so he could get a new job – and was surprised at how easy it was to obtain *a* false *identity*. (1990 年代初めに新しい職に就くために最初の偽免許証を入手し，虚偽の証明書を得るのがいかに簡単であるかに驚いた) (RD 00/4: 82)
(14) a. *Illustration* can be more useful than definition for showing what words mean. (語の意味を示すには定義よりも例示 (法) のほうが有益なことがある) (OALD⁵)
  b. She looked like a princess in *a* nineteenth-century *illustration*. (彼女は 19 世紀の挿し絵のお姫さまのようだった) (CCED³)
(15) a. *Imperfection* in diamonds reduces their value. (ダイヤの欠陥は価値を減じる) (NTC)
  b. "But the stone has *an imperfection*!" she exclaims. (「でも，その宝石にはきずがあるわ」と彼女は声をあらげる) (RD 00/2: 41)
(16) a. *Impurity* of the mind leads to moral errors. (精神の不純は道徳的過ちにつながる) (NTC)
  b. For instance if a stone has been drilled more than once to remove *an impurity*, she'll make an unflattering remark about it being an "oil well." (たとえば，不純物を取り除くために宝石が 2 回以上穴をあけられていれば，彼女は歯に衣着せずそれは「油井」(ゆせい)だと言う) (RD 00/2: 44)
(17) a. Heavy *indulgence* in alcohol should be avoided. (アルコールにひどくふけるのは避けるべきだ) (CDAE)
  b. She regarded expensive lingerie as *a* gross and unjustifiable *indulgence*. (高価なランジェリ類はとんでもない，不当な贅沢 (ぜいたく) 品だと思った) (CIDE)

(18) a. The incident provided *inspiration* for a novel. (その出来事が元で小説のインスピレーションを得た) (OALD[5])

b. She has been *an inspiration* to us all. (彼女は我々全員にとって激励してくれる源だった) (CIDE, CDAE)

(19) a. (= Ap.2.2-62, a) Some of the earliest evidence that play can influence *intellect* came from neuroanatomist Marian Diamond. (RD 99/2: 99)

b. My boss isn't *a* great *intellect*. (私の上司はさほど知恵者ではない) (CCED[3])

(20) a. He lived a life of complete *irregularity*. (まったく不規則な生活をした) (LDOCE[3])

b. We can't use the lens in the camera if it has even *a* single *irregularity*. (1箇所でもでこぼこがあれば，そのレンズはカメラに使うわけにはいかない) (CIDE)

(21) a. (= Ap.2.2-66, a) For the first time Leonard felt *irritation* at her methods. (CCED[3])

b. My little brother is *an irritation* at times, but I still love him. (弟はときどきイライラの原因だが，それでもかわいい) (NTC)

(22) a. *Luxury* is something I will never have to get used to. (贅沢は私には慣れる必要のないものだ) (NTC)

b. A dishwasher is *a luxury* many families cannot afford. (皿洗い機は多くの家庭では買う余裕のない贅沢品だ) (NTC)

参考：It would be *a luxury* to be able to have a day off work. (休暇をとれるのは贅沢だ) (CIDE) [不定詞による内容限定 (☞ 4.4.5)]

(23) a. The talk in the Olympic village was of pills called anabolic steroids that increased body *mass* and strength. (オリンピック村での話題はアナボリックステロイドと呼ばれるピルだった。これは体格と筋力を増大させるのだ) (RD 99/11: 90)

b. She learned the result ten minutes later: *a* benign *mass*. (10分後に結果を聞いた。良性のしこりだった) (RD 98/7: 66) [cf. growth]

(24) a. He stood gazing into the water, lost in *meditation* (瞑想にふけって，水を見つめながら立っていた) (LDOCE[3]).

b. I read *a* Buddhist *meditation*... (仏教徒による瞑想録を読んだ) (RD 99/12: 139)

(25) a. *Memory* is what makes us who we are. (記憶こそが我々を我々たら

しめているものだ) (T. Sowell, quoted in RD 99/4: 89) [抽象概念]
    b. School is just *a* dim/distant *memory* for me now. (学校は今や私にとってはかすかな／遠い記憶にすぎない) (CIDE) [個別事例]
(26) a. She made *mention* of how much she likes living in Florida, but didn't give any details. (Fに住むのがどんなに気に入っているか述べたが，詳しいことは何も言わなかった) (NHD) [様態非限定]
    b. Did the concert get *a mention* in the paper? (コンサートのことは新聞に載っていたか) (OALD[5]) [具体物 (「記事」) (または，個別行為)]
(27) a. Oh, Lord, have *mercy* on us sinners. (主よ，我ら罪人たちにお慈悲を) (LDOCE[3])
    b. After months of suffering, his death was *a mercy*. (何か月も苦しんだあとだったので彼の死は救いだった) (CIDE)
(28) a. (= VIII-4, b) On April Fools' Day, children make *mischief* by changing the salt and sugar on the kitchen table. (NHD)
    b. Whenever something goes wrong in our office, we all blame Bob because he's *a mischief*. (職場で何かうまくいかないことがあれば，やっかい者なのでみんながBを悪人にする) (NTC)
(29) a. *Misfortune* follows her wherever she goes. (どこに行こうと彼女には不幸がついて回る) (NHD)
    b. The earthquake was *a misfortune* for thousands of people. (地震は何千人もの人にとって災難だった) (NHD)
(30) a. It is well-known that radiation can cause *mutation*. (よく知られていることだが，放射線は突然変異を起こすことがある) (CIDE)
    b. The chance of a woman in the general population having *a mutation* in either gene is only one in 800. (一般住民の女性がいずれかの遺伝子に突然変異体を生じる確率はわずか800分の1だ) (RD 99/4: 71)
(31) a. With a personal fortune of six million pounds she certainly doesn't work out of *necessity*. (600万ポンドという個人資産があるので必要に迫られて働くことがないのはたしかだ) (CIDE)
    b. (= V-68) The chair was *a necessity* for Michael, then four, who has cerebral palsy. (RD 99/5: 112)
(32) a. Kim Jung Mi . . . was fired without *notice* in June 1998; she had held her job for five years. (KJMは1998年6月に予告なしに解雇された。5年間その職にあったにもかかわらずである) (RD 99/12: 51)

[cf. information/news/rumour]

b. There was *a* large *notice* on the wall saying 'No Parking'. (塀に大きな掲示板があって「駐車禁止」と書かれていた) (CIDE)

(33) a. A static, technocratic order, by contrast, requires a very different sort of personality: a drone who does what he is told and shuns *novelty*, someone who avoids facing, or posing, challenges. (これに対し，変化のない，技術官僚的秩序は非常に異なった種類の人物を要求する。言われたことを行い，斬新さを避ける，面白みのない人であり，チャレンジしたり，それに直面したりするのを避ける人だ) (RD 99/10: 43)

b. A car that can run on electricity is still something of *a novelty*. (電気自動車はまだ珍奇なものだ) (OALD⁵)

(34) a. More than once Dr Standish had *occasion* to warn his son about his irresponsible behaviour. (1度ならずS博士は無責任な行動に関して息子に警告せざるをえなかった) (LDOCE³) [「原因・理由，必要」という意味のとき無冠詞]

b. Sara's party was quite *an occasion* – there were hundreds of people there. (Sのパーティはとても盛大だった——何百人もの人が出席していたのだ) (CIDE) [a-文以外の意味では，on occasion を除けば，通例，限定詞が必要 (☞ Ap.2.2-82)]

(35) a. *Opposition* to companies that pollute comes from environmental groups. (汚染する会社への異議は環境保護団体から出される) (NHD)

b. The source of Banda's money is the target of *an* increasingly powerful *opposition* pressing for early elections. (Bの財源は，早期選挙を迫り勢力を増しつつある反対勢力の標的だ) (ConCD-ROM)

(36) a. We've been in *partnership* for five years. (5年前から提携関係にある) (LDOCE³)

b. "A wife needs a sense that her marriage is *a partnership*," says Piorkowski. (「結婚は共同事業なのだという感覚が妻には必要だ」とPは言う) (RD 99/10: 94)

(37) a. *Passage* through the Panama Canal will take a number of hours. (P運河の通過には何時間もかかる) (CDAE)

b. *A* narrow *passage* led through the house to the yard. (狭い通路は家を抜けて中庭につづいていた) (CDAE)

(38) a. (= Ap.2.2-62, a) Some of the earliest evidence that *play* can influence

intellect came from neuroanatomist Marian Diamond. (RD 99/2: 99)

b. The word for monkey (*saru* or *zaru*) sounds the same as the verb-ending *zaru*, so to represent the phrase with the three monkeys in the appropriate poses is *a play* on words. (猿を表す語 (サルまたはザル) は「[見／聞か／言わ]ざる」という動詞語尾と同音なので，当該の警句をそれに相応するポーズの3匹の猿によって表すのはことば遊びだ) (RD 00/3: 95) [個別事例]

(39) a. (= IV-266, a) It's quite common for little boys to take *pleasure* in torturing insects and small animals. (CIDE)

b. The adulthood to be conferred by staying up was *a pleasure* beyond the reach of ordinary mortals. (夜更かししてもよいということによって与えられる大人の世界は普通の者には手の届かない喜びだった) (RD 99/12: 9)

(40) a. This drug is available only on *prescription*. (この薬品は処方によってのみ入手可能だ) (OALD⁵) [方法・形式]

b. The doctor gave me *a prescription* for antibiotics. (医者は抗生物質の処方箋をくれた) (OALD⁵) [具体物 (書類)]

(41) a. The government should give top *priority* to rebuilding the inner cities. (政府は都心部の再建を最優先すべきだ) (OALD⁵)

b. Improved housing is *a* (top) *priority*. (住宅事情の改善は(最)優先事項だ) (OALD⁵)

(42) a. (= IX-21, e) The 35-year-old monarch is shown in *profile*, head on, and three-quarter-profile, showing off his straight nose, hooded eyes and sensitive lips. (RD 99/12: 112) [角度に重点が置かれているので無冠詞]

b. Dani has *a* lovely *profile*. (D はかわいい横顔をしている) (LDOCE³) [具体物]

(43) a. We need more *proof* before we can accuse him of stealing. (窃盗で彼を告訴する前にもっと証拠が必要だ) (OALD⁵) [cf. evidence]

b. A cheque card is not *a* valid *proof* of identity. (チェックカードは有効な身分証明書ではない) (OALD⁵)

(44) a. When Bill was away, my two young children and I needed *protection*. (B の不在中，2人の幼い子供と私とは庇護(を)を必要とした) (RD 97/2: 10)

b. I also found, perhaps for the first time in my life, a certain kind of peace that was *a protection* against the everyday stress of work. (たぶん生まれて初めて，ある種の安らぎをも見いだした。それは日々の仕事上のストレスから守ってくれるものだった) (RD 97/5: 147)

(45) a. In February last year, two months before *publication* of the report, Nikitin was arrested. (昨年2月，報告書公表の2か月前，Nは逮捕された) (RD 97/6: 74)

b. The annals of the British Parliament are recorded in *a publication* called Hansard. (英国国会の年報はH［英国国会議事録］と呼ばれる出版物に収録されている) (CIDE)

(46) a. *Redundancy* is both wasteful and inefficient. (重複は不経済にして非効率的だ) (NTC)

b. To say "cease and desist" is *a redundancy*. (「やめて終える」と言うのは重複表現だ) (NTC) [ジャンルと作品（☞ 2.2) 参照］

(47) a. At first I thought her ideas were crazy, but on *reflection*, I realize there was some truth in what she said. (最初は彼女の考えは狂気の沙汰だと思ったが，よく考えれば，彼女の言ったことに幾分の真実があったということがわかる) (LDOCE[3]) [cf. examination/inspection]

b. The article is *an* accurate *reflection* of events that day, in my opinion. (その記事は，私の見解では，その日の出来事を正確に映すものだ) (OALD[5])

c. The light is causing *a reflection* on my computer screen. (光のためコンピュータ画面に映り込みができている) (CIDE)

(48) a. He began to withdraw into himself, seeking *refuge* in books and prayer. (自分自身に引き込もり，本と祈りに逃避を求めた) (RD 96/10: 120)

b. (= VIII-30, d) Indeed, for a short time during the Renaissance, the Prague Ghetto experienced a relatively peaceful time and became *a refuge* for Jews escaping from persecution elsewhere. (RD 00/4: 59)

(49) a. Hindus and Buddhists believe in *reincarnation*. (ヒンズー教徒および仏教徒は輪廻転生を信じている) (CIDE)

b. Di Mambro claimed to be *a reincarnation* of Moses. (DMはモーゼの生まれ変わりだと主張した) (RD 98/3: 34)

(50) a. If you are not satisfied, return the goods within 14 days for

　　　　replacement or refund! (ご満足いただけない場合は，交換または返金のため 14 日以内に商品をご返品ください) (OALD⁵)

　　b. The Internet is not *a replacement* for your doctor, who knows the details of your specific case. (インターネットは主治医の代替物ではない。医者はあなた特有の症状を細部まで知っているのだから) (RD 98/5: 27)

(51) a. The author whom you criticized in your review has written a letter in *reply*. (書評で君が批判した著者が返答に手紙を書いた) (OALD⁵)

　　b. I'm composing *a* formal *reply* to the letter. (その手紙に正式な返事を書いているところだ) (OALD⁵)

(52) a. More interesting, his results hint at reasons why vitamin E cuts cardiac *risk*. (より興味あることに，彼の調査結果はビタミン E がなぜ心臓病の危険を下げるかを示唆している) (RD 98/11: 47)

　　b. In that kind of weather, death from exposure was *a* real *risk*. (その種の天候では，外気にさらされることによる死亡は現実の危険だ) (RD 99/4: 127)

(53) a. The house has fallen into *ruin* through years of neglect. (その家は何年もほうっておかれたため荒れ果てた) (OALD⁵)

　　b. The abbey is now *a ruin*. (その寺院は今では廃墟だ) (OALD⁵)

(54) a. This belief was irreconcilable with the Church's doctrine of *salvation*. (この信仰は救いに関する教会の教義と相いれなかった) (LDOCE³)

　　b. The guide dog's *a salvation*. (盲導犬は救いだ) (RD 99/11: 39)

(55) a. Suddenly his investigation took new *shape*. (突然彼の調査は新しい姿をとった) (RD 99/11: 59) [形状非限定；cf. form]

　　b. *A* huge *shape* loomed up out of the fog. (大きな姿が霧のなかから浮かび出た) (OALD⁵)

(56) a. It is with great *sorrow* that I inform you of the death of our director. (大きな悲しみをもって重役の逝去をお知らせいたします) (CIDE)

　　b. Her death was *a* great *sorrow* to everyone. (彼女の死はだれにとっても大きな悲しみの種だった) (OALD⁵)

(57) a. Now we knew for sure: our cause had strong *support*. (今や確実にわかった。我々の目的には強力な支援があるのだ) (RD 99/2: 83) [「支援・援助」の意味では画定不可能なので無冠詞；cf. help]

　　b. When my father died, Jim was *a* great *support*. (父が亡くなったと

き，Jが大きな支えだった) (OALD⁵) [特定の人物]

(58) a. In the wild, cockatoos learn *survival* from their parents and other members of the flock. (野生のなかで，コカトゥー [豪の大型オウム] は親や群の他の仲間から生存方法を学ぶ) (RD 98/7: 87)

　　 b. The ceremony is *a survival* from pre-Christian times. (その儀式は紀元前のころからの名残だ) (OALD⁵)

(59) a. Those around him saw he was in obvious *torment*. (まわりのものは彼が明らかに苦しんでいることを見てとった) (RD 99/2: 141)

　　 b. The tax forms were *an* annual *torment* to him. (納税用紙は彼にとって毎年の苦しみの種だった) (CIDE)

(60) a. *Uncertainty* again hangs over the project. (不確実性がその計画にふたたび垂れ込めている) (CIDE)

　　 b. The weather is always *an uncertainty*, especially when planning a picnic. (天候はいつも不確定要素だ。特に，ピクニックの計画を立てるときは) (NTC)

(61) a. (= IV-95, a) Shares can go down as well as go up in *value*. (CIDE)

　　 b. These shoes were *a* real *value* because I bought them on sale. (この靴は本当に掘り出し物だった。特売で買ったのだから) (NTC)

　　 c. I thought the offer was good *value* (for money) / (US also) *a* good *value*. (その提案は値打ちがあると思った) (CIDE) [英米での相違]

(62) a. *Worry* is an emotional response that is stressful and draining. (心配は感情的反応であり，ストレスに満ちていて人を消耗させる) (RD 00/2: 99)

　　 b. Water is *a* serious *worry*. (水は深刻な心配の種だ) (RD 97/2: 125)

　　 c. Simply by explaining *a worry* to another person, you can begin to regain perspective on it. (心配事を他人に説明するだけで，その全体的視野を取り戻すことができるようになる) (RD 00/7: 94) [特定の心配事]

Appendix 4
(個別行為など)

Ap. 4.1 個別行為

(1) a. He had been trying to make *conversation*. (会話を始めようとしていた) (CCED³)

　b. I'd finally had *a conversation* with Diane. (ついに D と話をした) (RD 99/5: 39) [cf. dialogue/debate/monologue/talk]

(2) a. Under *cross-examination*, she admitted she'd lied. (反対尋問により嘘をついたことを認めた) (CDAE) [形式・方法]

　b. When Mrs Powell sat down opposite me, I felt that *a cross-examination* was about to begin. (P 女史が向かいに座ったとき, 反対尋問が始まるのだと思った) (ConCD-ROM)

(3) a. Interlochen gave Jewel formal training in *dance*, writing and theatre and broadened her artistic horizons. (I 学院は J にダンス, 文章表現および演劇の正式な訓練を与え, 彼女の芸術的地平を拡げた) (RD 00/1: 44) [舞踏法]

　b. Let's have *a dance*. (一曲踊ろう) (OALD⁶)

(4) a. Sleep was sometimes held to be analogous to *death*. (眠りはときおり死に似ているとされた) (OALD⁵)

　b. After a tragedy such as *a death* in the family, it's normal to be tired. (家族の死といったような悲劇的事件のあとでは疲れるのは正常だ) (RD 96/3: 100)

(5) a. Education is the current focus of public *debate*. (教育が公的論争の目下の焦点だ) (CIDE)

　b. There was *a debate* during the committee meeting about the new budget. (新しい予算に関して委員会の会議で論争があった) (RD 97/5: 110) [cf. conversation/dialogue/monologue/talk]

(6) a. Premature birth is three times more likely for twins, and *delivery* at 36 to 38 weeks is normal. (双生児の場合, 早産は 3 倍の確率であり, 36〜38 週での分娩は通常だ) (CCED³) [cf. birth/labor]

　b. She had *a difficult delivery*, but the baby is fine. (難産だったが, 赤ちゃんは元気だ) (NHD) [形容詞をともなうとき, 通例, 冠詞つき]

(7) a. For the first few hours, *dialogue* with the tower was carried out in Arabic. (最初の数時間, 管制塔との会話はアラビア語で行われた) (RD 99/6: 127)

  b. Act Two begins with *a* short *dialogue* between father and son. (第2幕は父と息子の短い対話で始まる) (CIDE) [cf. conversation/debate/monologue/talk]

(8) a. *Divorce* is bad for children. (離婚は子供によくない) (CCED[3])

  b. It takes quite a long time to get *a divorce*. (離婚するにはかなり時間がかかる) (CCED[3]) [cf. marriage/separation]

(9) a. (= Ap.2.2-41, a) *Education* should accustom children to thinking for themselves. (OALD[6])

  b. "You're very lucky to have been born in a country where the government guarantees each child *an education*," I told him. (「政府がどの子供にも学校教育を保証している国に生まれてお前は幸せだ」と私は彼に言った) (RD 00/2: 87) [国家で決められた教育]

(10) a. If you can't excel with talent, triumph with *effort*. (才能で抜きんでることができないなら, 努力で勝利を得よ) (Dave Weinbaum, quoted in RD 98/8: 23) [抽象概念]

  b. With *an effort* she contained her irritation. (努力して怒りを抑えた) (CCED[3]) [彼女の, そのときの努力]

(11) a. He's standing for *election*. (選挙に立候補中だ) (OALD[5]) [選出手順]

  b. The Government is expected to call *an election* very soon. (政府は近日中に選挙をすると予想されている) (CIDE) [選挙の実施]

(12) a. He finally gained *entry* to the hotel by giving some money to the doorman. (ドアマンに金を握らせて, とうとうホテルに入る機会 [権利] を得た) (OALD[5])

  b. The thieves had forced *an entry* into the building. (泥棒たちはその建物に押し入った) (OALD[5])

(13) a. "I planted them years back to prevent *erosion*," Malnati said. (「浸食作用を防ぐために何年も前に植えたのです」とMは言った) (RD 99/7: 32)

  b. *an erosion* of academic standards (学問的水準の弱体化) (CDAE) [通例, "a/an+erosion" は比喩的意味を表す]

(14) a. with Mount Vesuvius in full *eruption* at the back of the stage, and streams of lava pouring down towards the auditorium (舞台の背後

でV火山が大噴火し,溶岩流が観客席のほうに流れ) (LOB) [噴火状態]

b. *a* major volcanic *eruption* (火山の大噴火) (OALD⁵) [1回の噴火]

c. Because of the imposition of martial law there was *a* violent *eruption* of anti-government feeling. (戒厳令が敷かれたため,反政府感情が激しく爆発した) (CIDE) [比喩的個別事例]

(15) a. "You will never get away," said the prison-camp commander. "*Escape* is impossible." (捕虜収容所の所長が言った「絶対出ることはない,逃亡は不可能だ」と) (CIDE) [様態非限定 (＝抽象概念)]

b. The criminal made *an escape* from prison. (犯罪者は脱獄した) (NHD) [make に後続して個別事例を表す；Ap.4.1-27, e; 46, b; 47, b; 49, b; 56, b も参照]]

(16) a. He left the court under police *escort*. (警察の護衛の下に裁判所を出た) (CIDE) [働き]

b. It took *a* police *escort* to lead them to the hospital. (彼らを病院に誘導するのに警察の護衛が必要だった) (RD 98/10: 135) [個別行為]

(17) a. He assembled a group of 25 men, composed of wounded troopers awaiting *evacuation*, the company clerk, supply men, cooks and drivers, and led them to the hill. (25人の1団を集めて丘に導いた。彼らは,撤退を待っている負傷兵,それに会社員,配達員,料理人,運転手だった) (LOB) [撤退の様態非限定]

b. Fearing another earthquake, local officials ordered *an evacuation*. (地震がまた起きるのを恐れて,地元の当局者は避難を命じた) (LDOCE³) [一斉避難]

(18) a. *Evaluation* of this new treatment cannot take place until all the data has been collected. (この新治療法の評価はすべての資料が集められるまではできない) (CIDE)

b. My boss did *an evaluation* of my job performance. (上司が私の仕事の成績を評価した) (NHD)

(19) a. On closer *examination*, the father turned out to be Billy Joel. (もっとよく調べてみると,その父親はBJだった) (RD 00/6: 50) [形式・方法；cf. inspection/reflection/watch]

b. But *a* closer *examination* reveals that . . . he has lifted his right heel off the ground to the extent that he is almost on tiptoe! (だが,もっとよく調べたところ,彼は右足のかかとを地面から上げてほとんどつま先立ちだったことがわかった) (ConCD-ROM)

(20) a. Regular *exercise* is just as important as eating the right type of food. (正しい食事と同程度に規則的な運動が大切だ) (OALD5)

　　b. The firm I work for has *an* annual *exercise* in which its emergency procedures are observed by inspectors. (勤務先の会社は毎年 [避難] 訓練をし，調査官が緊急処置を監察する) (RD 98/9: 95)

参考 : Exercise slowly at first. Focus on gentle *exercises* that you can do repeatedly. (最初はゆっくり運動しなさい。反復可能な穏やかな運動に集中しなさい) (RD 98/9: 52) [exercise は「運動」という意味のとき a/an はとらないが，複数形はとる。類例 : research/surgery/water]

(21) a. Her fascination with space *exploration* began as she was growing up. (宇宙探検への彼女の情熱は成長途中に芽生えた) (RD 98/11: 80)

　　b. Livingstone was the first European to make *an exploration* of the Zambezi river. (L は Z 川の探検をした最初のヨーロッパ人だった) (CIDE)

(22) a. Some workers had developed cancer after *exposure* to radioactive substances. (数人の労働者は放射性物質に被曝(ひばく)後ガンを発病した) (McED) [多人数の別々の被曝を抽象化]

　　b. Even *a* brief *exposure* to radiation is very dangerous. (短時間の放射線被曝でも非常に危険だ) (CIDE) [1 人 1 回の被曝]

参考 : Avoid prolonged *exposure* to sunlight. (長時間日光に身を曝すのは避けなさい) (CDAE) [一般論 (= 抽象概念)]

(23) a. (= Ap.3-6, a) She accused the Foreign Office of disgraceful *failure* to support British citizens arrested overseas. (CCED3)

　　b. Of course, if there were *an* overall power *failure*, elevators would stop operating. (もちろん，全面的停電があれば，エレベーターは作動を止めるだろう) (RD 99/4: 35) [一時的]

(24) a. The team came out on the court full of *fight*. (チームは闘争心むきだしでコートに来た) (CIDE)

　　b. He had had *a fight* with Smith and bloodied his nose. (S とけんかをして鼻血を出した) (CCED3) [cf. battle/war]

(25) a. Some people thought that too much money was spent on space *flight*. (宇宙飛行にお金をかけすぎると思った人もいる) (CIDE)

　　b. The plane was hijacked while on *a flight* to Delhi. (その飛行機は D へのフライト中ハイジャックされた) (OALD5)

(26) a. Samples must be taken from the sick for *identification* and

submitted for laboratory analysis. (鑑識のため病人からサンプルを採って，実験室での分析に回されなければならない) (RD 99/2: 52)

b. He concentrated on the distance between the eyes and the bridge of the nose, a characteristic often used by police to make *an identification*.　It was a match. (両目と鼻梁(びりょう)とのあいだの距離を特に調べた。しばしば身元確認のため警察に用いられる特徴である。一致だった) (RD 00/2: 7) [個別事例；*of*-phrase (e.g., of the body/ criminal) を補足可 (☞ 4.4.1.2)]

(27) a. (= VI-17) If your timing was absolutely perfect and you jumped exactly when the elevator hit, you might reduce your speed at *impact* by a negligible eight kilometres per hour. (RD 00/3: 96)

b. At this sink-rate, they had only minutes before *impact*. (この降下率では衝突までわずか数分だった) (RD 98/10: 35)

c. The front passenger door and the sliding side door popped open on *impact*. (前部の乗客ドアと横のスライドドアは衝撃でパッと開いた) (RD 98/12: 34) [以上，前置詞に後続して，広がりをもたない，行為の１点を表すので無冠詞；cf. high tide]

d. These chemicals have *a* detrimental effect/*impact* on the environment. (これらの化学薬品は環境に悪い影響を与える) (CIDE)

e. The anti-smoking campaign had had/made quite *an impact* on young people. (禁煙キャンペーンは若者にかなり効果があった) (CIDE) [have/make に後続して個別事例を表す]

(28) a. On (closer) *inspection* the notes proved to be forgeries. ((いっそう)精査したところそのメモは偽物だと判明した) (OALD⁵) [形式・方法；cf. examination/watch]

b. *Inspection* of the kitchen is required every six months. (台所の点検は６か月ごとに必要だ) (NTC) [半年ごとに反復]

c. But suddenly he turned round and went back for *a* closer *inspection*. (だが，急に向きを変えて，もっとよく調べるために戻っていった) (RD 01/6: 108) [個別行為]

d. *An inspection* of the suitcase revealed a crudely made bomb. (スーツケースを調べたところ粗雑な作りの爆弾があることがわかった) (NTC) [１回きり]

(29) a. troops sent to guard against *invasion* (侵略から防御するために送られた軍隊) (OALD⁵)

b. Who knew of the secret plans to mount *an invasion* of the north? (北部侵略を開始するという秘密計画をだれが知っていただろうか) (CIDE)

(30) a. *Investigation* confirmed that the call was the one made inviting the healer to Canada. (調査により確認されたところでは，電話は祈祷(きとう)師をカナダに呼ぶためにかけられたものだった) (RD 98/10: 66) [調査という手段・方法]

b. *An investigation* followed, and eventually the spacecraft was completely redesigned. (検討が行われ，最終的に宇宙船はまったく設計を変更された) (RD 99/3: 130) [特定の調査]

(31) a. He said it was necessary to wage *jihad* against America for "occupying" Saudi Arabia. (米のSA「占拠」に対して聖戦を遂行することが必要だと言った) (RD 02/3: 55)

b. *A jihad*, then, is compulsory. (したがって，聖戦は必須だ) (RD 02/3: 55) [cf. battle/war]

(32) a. The plane had been cleared for *landing* at Brunswick's Glynco Airport. (飛行機はBのG空港への着陸許可を与えられた) (CCED[3]) [着陸の様態非限定 ; cf. takeoff]

b. And then as quickly as it had come, the scene dissolved as a jetliner roared down for *a landing* at Kansas City International Airport. (それから，現れたときと同じようにあっという間に，その光景は消え，ジェット機がKC国際空港に爆音をとどろかせて到着した) (RD 00/1: 96) [個別行為 ; そのときの着陸の様態含意]

c. Moncton air-traffic control clears them for emergency *landing* at Halifax International Airport. (Mの航空交通管制はH国際空港に緊急着陸の許可を与える) (RD 00/9: 56) [着陸の下位分類 (☞ 8.9.3) 類例: V-96, a, Ap.1-7, a; Ap.2.2-93, a; Ap.4.1-55, a; 78, a]

d. One person has died after the pilot of a light aircraft was forced to make *a* crash/emergency *landing* in a field. (軽飛行機のパイロットがやむをえず野原に胴体／緊急着陸をしたとき1人死亡した) (CIDE) [個別行為]

(33) a. *Leakage* from the broken pipe made the floor slippery. (破損したパイプからの漏出(ろうしゅつ)のため床が滑りやすくなった) (NTC) [漏出の様態非限定 ; 因果関係としてとらえられた漏出]

b. *A leakage* of kerosene has polluted water supplies. (灯油が漏れたた

め上水道を汚染した) (CCED[3]) [個別事例としてとらえられた漏出]

(34) a. This exhibit is on *loan* from/to another museum. (この展示物は別の博物館から借り出し中だ/博物館に貸し出し中だ) (CIDE) [期間等非限定]

b. Stained records make it difficult for the victim to rent an apartment, get phone services, cash a cheque, qualify for *a loan*. (経歴が汚されれば，犠牲者はアパートを借りたり，電話を引いたり，小切手を換金したり，ローンの資格を得たりするのがむずかしくなる) (RD 00/4: 82) [個別のローン]

(35) a. Mild cases can improve with weight *loss*. (軽度の症状は体重を減らせば改善できる) (RD 96/3: 101)

b. Evans couldn't fathom how he'd deal with such *a loss* himself. (E は自分ならそのような喪失にどのように対処するかわからなかった) (RD 00/3: 34) [特定の喪失]

c. For a moment I was at *a loss* for words. (一瞬ことばにつまった) (RD 00/5: 35) [個別事例 ; cf. clutter]

(36) a. If *marriage*, as Woody Allen once claimed, is the death of hope, then what is divorce – the hope of death, and end to the inevitable and sometimes unbearable pain? (結婚が，WA がかつて言ったように，希望の死であるならば，離婚は何であろう。死の希望であり，不可避的な，ときとして耐えがたい，苦痛の終わりであろうか) (RD 99/4: 10) [制度としての結婚 ; cf. divorce]

b. (= IX-4, g) The end or breakup of *a marriage* changes not only your future but also your past ... (RD 99/4: 110) [個別事例]

c. Instead, she found herself in *an* abusive *marriage*. (そうはならず，彼女の結婚は暴力をともなうものとなった) (RD 00/4: 30) [様態限定]

(37) a. I'd conceived several times, but the pregnancies had ended in *miscarriage*. (数回妊娠したことはあったが，流産してしまった) (RD 98/11: 7) [cf. pregnancy]

b. She had *a miscarriage*. About a year later *a* second *miscarriage* sent her into an emotional tailspin. (彼女は流産した。約 1 年後に 2 度目の流産をして，気分的に落ち込んでしまった) (RD 99/5: 18)

(38) a. In chapter 12 ... there was only *monologue*. (第 12 章では，独白のみだった) (BNC, ACG 209) [cf. conversation/debate/dialogue/talk]

b. The comedian gave *a* long *monologue* of jokes. (喜劇役者はジョーク

を1人で長々と述べた) (NHD)

(39) a. He pulled the lever and set the machine in *motion*. (レバーを引いて機械を作動させた) (OALD⁶)

　　 b. He summoned the waiter with *a motion* of his hand. (手を動かしてウエイターを呼んだ) (LDOCE³) [様態限定；個別事例]

(40) a. Loose clothing gives you greater freedom of *movement*. (ゆったりした衣服は運動がより自由だ) (OALD⁵)

　　 b. As she turned back, *a movement* across the lawn caught her eye. (振り向いたとき，芝生を横切る動きが目にとまった) (CCED³)

　　 c. A patient who suddenly complains of either an increase or decrease in *bowel movement* would have to be evaluated thoroughly. (患者が突然便通の増加または減少を訴えれば，徹底的に検査されなければならない) (RD 02/2: 93) [様態非限定 (= 抽象概念)]

　　 d. [S]ome people have *a bowel movement* once a day, some more, some less, which may all be perfectly normal. (便通が1日1回の人も，もっと多い人も，少ない人もいる。それでまったく正常かもしれない) (RD 02/2: 93) [have と共起して個別事例]

(41) a. A drop in the levels of oestrogen can also cause vaginal dryness and decrease the ability to reach *orgasm*. (エストロゲンのレベルが下がると膣の乾きも引き起こし，オルガスムに達する能力を減少させかねない) (RD 99/12: 70) [reach/achieve と共起するときは様態非限定なので無冠詞]

　　 b. Annie is a Republican who has never had *an orgasm*. (A はオルガスムを1度も感じたことがない共和党員だ) (ConCD-ROM) [have と共起するときは個別事例を表すので冠詞をとる；5.3.3 および pain に関する注 (Ap.4, NB 2) も参照]

(42) a. Reacting to international *outrage*, Jakarta set up a 25-member National Commission on Human Rights to monitor abuses. (国際的な憤りに反応して，インドネシア政府は虐待を監視するため25人のメンバーから成る人権に関する国家委員会を発足させた) (RD 96/3: 34) [詳細非限定 (= 抽象概念)]

　　 b. These terrorist attacks are *an outrage* against society. (これらのテロ攻撃は社会に対する暴力行為だ) (LDOCE³) [事件 (☞ 5.1)]

(43) a. A back injury prevented active *participation* in any sports for a while. (背中の怪我のためしばらくスポーツに積極的に参加できなか

った) (OALD[6]) [抽象概念]

  b. All theatrical events . . . can produce *an* emotional *participation* from the audience, who become actors in the drama. (すべての演劇行為は観客からの感情的参加を引きだすことができる。彼らはドラマ中の役者になるからだ) (Brando, quoted in RD 99/6: 87) [それぞれの公演における参加]

(44) a. (= VIII-25, h) In March 1993, before *practice* for the Brazilian Grand Prix, Senna invited me to go fishing on his farm in Brazil. (RD 99/6: 75) [抽象概念]

  b. The players will meet for *a practice* in the morning. (演奏者たちは午前中練習に集まる) (OALD[5]) [一時的行為]

 参考: OALD[5] (s.v., practice): '2(a) [U] regularly repeated exercise or training done in order to improve one's skill at sth . . . (b) [C] <u>a period of time</u> spent doing this.'

(45) a. Many women experience feelings of nausea during *pregnancy*. (多くの女性は妊娠中に嘔吐(おう と)感を経験する) (CIDE)

  b. It is better to abort *a pregnancy* in its early stages rather than later on. (遅くなってからよりも初期のうちに妊娠を中絶させるほうがよい) (CIDE) [cf. miscarriage]

(46) a. John waited for her under *pretence* of tying his shoelaces. (J は靴ひもを結ぶふりをしながら彼女を待った) (LDOCE[3])

  b. Welland made *a pretence* of writing a note in his pad. (W はメモ用紙にメモを書いているふりをした) (CCED[3])

(47) a. It was one of those stunning California days, full of hope and *promise*. (希望と期待に満ちた, すばらしいカリフォルニアの日々のころのことだった) (RD 98/11: 16)

  b. If I make *a promise* I like to keep it. (約束をしたら守りたい) (CIDE) [個別事例]

 参考: They've given *a promise* to introduce equal pay for women. (女性に均等な給与を導入すると約束した) (LDOCE[3]) [不定詞による限定 (☞ 4.4.5)]

(48) a. Then he learned he'd been passed over for *promotion*. (それでやっと昇進からはずされたことがわかった) (RD 99/10: 17) [昇進全般]

  b. It took me ages to summon/pluck up the courage to ask for *a promotion*. (昇進を要求する勇気を奮い起こすのに長年かかった)

(CIDE) [自分の昇進]
(49) a. The receipt is your proof of *purchase*. (レシートは購入の証拠だ) (OALD⁵)
   b. He was seen making *a purchase* at the station bookstall. (駅の本屋で買い物をしているところを見られた) (OALD⁵)
(50) a. *Reaction* to the visit is mixed. (訪問に対する反応は賛否両論ある) (CCED³)
   b. They finally succeeded in extorting *a reaction* from the audience. (ついに聴衆から反応を引き出した) (CIDE)
(51) a. The Russian people rose in *rebellion* in 1917. (ロシア人民は1917年に [反乱という形で] 蜂起した) (LDOCE³) [形式; cf. revolt]
   b. Open *rebellion* finally erupted in Gdansk's huge Lenin Shipyard. (公然たる反乱がついにGの巨大なL造船所で勃発した) (RD 00/4: 133) [様態非限定 (あるいは, 下位分類)]
   c. The slave leader Nat Turner led *an* 1831 *rebellion*. (奴隷の指導者のNTが1831年の反乱を導いた) (CDAE) [個別事例; cf. battle/war]
(52) a. The oil price increases sent Europe into deep *recession*. (石油価格の値上げのため欧州はひどい不況になった) (CCED³) [期間非限定]
   b. The president's policies led the country into *a recession*. (大統領の政策がその国を不況に陥らせた) (NTC) [一時的]
   参考: NTC (s.v., recession): '1. *n*. backward movement or direction. (No plural form in this sense.); 2. *n*. a time when the economy is shrinking rather than growing.'
(53) a. Fears are growing that a tax increase may stall economic *recovery*. (増税は経済の回復を失速させるかもしれないという恐れが増大している) (CIDE) [様態・時期など非限定 (= 抽象概念)]
   b. Hopes of *an* economic *recovery* have been dashed by the latest unemployment statistics. (経済的回復の希望は失業に関する最新の統計により打ち砕かれた) (CIDE) [特定時期の経済的回復]
(54) a. (= IV-105, a) *Reduction* in government spending will necessitate further cuts in public services. (CIDE)
   b. If the government deflates the economy, that will cause *a reduction* in the country's economic activity, which will lead to lower prices. (政府が経済を縮小すれば, 国の経済活動の減少を引き起こし, 低価格につながるだろう) (CIDE) [一時的な経済活動の減少]

(55) a. For anyone trapped on the roof, air *rescue* was the only hope. (屋根の上に取り残された人には空中救出が唯一の希望だった) (RD 97/5: 115) [救出の下位分類 (☞ 8.9.3)　類例: V-96, a; Ap.1-7, a; Ap.2.2-93, a; Ap.4.1-32, c; 78, a]

　b. Ten fishermen were saved in *a* daring sea *rescue* off the Welsh coast. (10人の漁師たちはWの海岸から勇敢な海上救出によって救助された) (OALD⁵) [様態限定]

(56) a. Advance *reservation* of seats for the train is recommended. (列車の座席はあらかじめ予約されることをお勧めします) (CIDE)

　b. I'd like to make *a* table *reservation* for two people for 9 o'clock. (9時に2人用の席を予約したい) (CIDE)

(57) a. But if you wait, you're going to meet *resistance*. (しかし，もし待てば抵抗に遭うだろう) (RD 99/2: 69)

　b. She'd snuggle with pleasure in my arms. But as the weeks passed, I noticed *a resistance* each time I carried her off. (彼女 [鶏] は私の腕のなかで喜んで身を丸めていた。しかし，数週間たつうちに，抱いて移動させるたびに抵抗に気づいた) (RD 99/12: 40) [その鶏に特有な抵抗]

(58) a. Management have granted a 10% pay rise in *response* to union pressure. (経営側は組合の圧力に応じて10パーセントの賃上げを認めた) (CIDE) [抽象概念]

　b. produce *a response* to a stimulus (刺激に対して反応を起こす) (OALD⁵) [一時的；開始と終了含意]

(59) a. Enemy soldiers are now in (full) *retreat*. (敵兵は今や (全面) 撤退している) (CIDE)

　b. She burst into tears, so I beat *a* (hasty) *retreat*. (彼女が急に泣き出したので (急いで) 退却した) (CIDE)

(60) a. The peasants rose up in armed *revolt*. (農民は武装蜂起した) (CIDE) [形式；cf. rebellion]

　b. It was undeniably *a revolt* by ordinary people against their leaders. (それが，指導者に対する一般大衆による反乱だったことは否定できない) (CCED³) [cf. battle/war]

(61) a. The country seems to be heading towards *revolution*. (その国は革命へと向かっているようだ) (CIDE)

　b. The nineteenth century witnessed *a revolution* in ship design and propulsion. (19世紀は船舶のデザインと推進力において革命を見た) (CCED³) [cf. battle/war]

(62) a. After Schmidt and Squires had searched for an hour and a half, the blizzard was at full *roar*, and the deputies couldn't see past their vehicle's hood. (SとSによる1時間半の捜索ののち、ブリザードは激しく唸り、代理保安官たちは車のボンネットより先は見ることができなかった) (RD 99/2: 108)

b. The stadium shook with *a roar* as the winning goal was scored. (勝ち越しのゴールが得点されたときスタジアムは歓声で揺れた) (CIDE)

(63) a. The couple put up their flat for *sale*. (夫婦は彼らのアパートを売りに出した) (RD 00/1: 131)

b. I got it for next to nothing in *a sale*. (安売りでただ同然で入手した) (OALD⁵) [時間・場所が限定された sale]

(64) a. Lynn, who was experienced in *search* and rescue, mentally prepared herself for the worst. (Lは、捜索と救出の経験があったので、心の内で最悪の覚悟をした) (RD 99/10: 67)

b. The police had run *a search* and discovered only one David Walliss Davis. (警察は捜索を行って、ただ1人のDWDという人物を発見しただけだった) (RD 00/1: 136)

(65) a. In June 1176 King Richard laid *siege* to Limoges. (1176年6月R王はLを包囲した) (LDOCE³) [cf. battle/war]

b. A mother is suing police for negligence over the death of her daughter who was used as a human shield at the end of *a siege* 10 years ago. (10年前の包囲の末期に娘が人間の盾として使われ死亡したのは過失だとして母親が警察を訴訟中だ) (ConCD-ROM)

(66) a. *Sleep* is important for good health. (睡眠は健康にとって重要だ) (NHD) [抽象概念]

b. I think he may be ready for *a sleep* soon. (彼はもうすぐ寝る用意ができると思う) (CCED³) [個別事例；一時的]

参考：LDOCE³ (s.v., sleep): '1 [uncountable] the natural state of being asleep: . . . 2 [singular] <u>a period</u> of sleeping: . . .'

(67) a. According to Marxists, class conflict/*struggle* is a continuing fight between the capitalist class and the working class for political and economic power. (マルクス主義者によれば、階級闘争は資本家階級と労働者階級との、政治的・経済的権力を求める絶えざる戦いだ)

(CIDE) [抽象概念 ; the capitalist/working class に関しては 8.5 参照]

 b. The room bore evidence of *a struggle*. (部屋には争った痕跡があった) (OALD5) [特定の争い ; cf. battle/war]

(68) a. The proposals deserve careful *study*. (その提案は注意深く調査するに値する) (OALD5) [内容非限定]

 b. The information in this book is taken from *a* long and careful *study* of present-day English. (本書中の情報は現代英語に関する長期にわたる注意深い調査から得られている) (*Collins Cobuild English Grammar*, p. v) [書き手たちが行った調査]

(69) a. Many have come to believe that the only things we need for *success* are talent, energy and personality. (多くの人たちが信じるようになったことだが，成功するために必要なのは，才能，体力および個性だけだ) (RD 99/3: 49)

 b. The program was pronounced *a success*. (そのプログラムは成功 [の事例] だったと公表された) (RD 99/1: 99) [cf. failure]

(70) a. We had a fine dinner on the first night of our visit. *Talk* was newsy and amiable. (訪問した最初の夜，すばらしい夕食をした。語らいは話題豊富でなごやかだった) (RD 00/1: 62)

 b. I asked him to have *a talk* with his mother about his plan. (彼の計画のことで母親と話をするよう彼に頼んだ) (CIDE) [個別事例 ; cf. conversation/debate/dialogue/monologue]

(71) a. The car in front of us is (UK) on/(US) in/(ANZ also) under *tow* – that's why we're going so slowly. (前の車が牽引されている。だからノロノロなのだ) (CIDE)

 b. When my car broke down, a police car gave me *a tow* to the nearest garage. (車が故障したとき，パトカーが最寄りの修理工場まで牽引してくれた) (CIDE)

(72) a. His eyes gleamed with/in *triumph*/pleasure. (彼の目は勝利／喜びで輝いた) (CIDE)

 b. Samuel Johnson described marrying for a second time as *a triumph* of hope over experience. (SJ は再婚を経験に対する希望の勝利だと述べた) (CIDE) [cf. victory]

(73) a. This machine has been specially adapted for *use* under water. (この機械は水中で使用されるように特別に改造されている) (OALD5)

 b. Don't throw that cloth away, you'll find *a use* for it one day. (その布

は捨ててはならない。いつか使い道が見つかるだろうから) (CIDE) [個別事例；「使い方・使い道」の意のとき use は [C]]

(74) a. The epidemic was held in check by widespread *vaccination*. (伝染病は広範な予防接種により食い止められた) (OALD5)

b. A complete cure requires *a vaccination*, too, after infection. (完治には感染後にワクチン接種することも必要だ) (RD 99/2: 54)

(75) a. His persistence gained him *victory*. (彼の勝利はねばり強さのたまものだ) (OALD5) [抽象概念；cf. triumph]

b. Consider every accomplishment, no matter how small, *a victory* to be rewarded. (成し遂げたことすべてを、たとえどんなに小さくても、報奨すべき勝利だと思いなさい) (RD 97/5: 54) [個別事例]

(76) a. We watched the couple until they disappeared from *view*. (視界から消えるまで夫婦を見送った) (RD 99/1: 132) [働き (視覚)]

b. You'd have a good *view* of the sea from here except for the hotels in between. (あいだにあるホテルがなければ、ここから海がよく見えるのに) (OALD5) [空間限定]

(77) a. *War* broke out between the two countries after a border dispute. (国境紛争ののち2国間で戦争が勃発した) [抽象概念；戦争行為自体に重点] (CIDE)

b. If *a war* breaks out, many other countries will be affected. (戦争が起これば他の多くの国も影響をうけることになる) (OALD5) [個別事例；特定の国による特定時期の戦争；cf. battle/combat/conflict/fight/jihad/rebellion/revolt/siege/struggle]

(78) a. Atomic *warfare* could destroy the entire earth. (核戦争は全地球を破滅させうるだろう) (NTC) [下位分類 (☞ 8.9.3) 類例：V-96, a; Ap.1-7, a; Ap.2.2-93, a; Ap.4.1-32, c; 55, a]

b. These drugs prevent cell reproduction, destroying the rapidly growing cancer cells, the hair cells, bone-marrow cells and cells lining the gastrointestinal tract. Hence the tumor destruction, hair loss, reduction of blood cells, nausea and vomiting. It's *a* supervised chemical *warfare*. (これらの薬は細胞の再生を阻止し、急速に成長するガン細胞、毛髪細胞、骨髄細胞、および胃腸の管の内側の細胞を破壊する。そのため、腫瘍の破壊や脱毛、血液細胞の減少、吐き気、嘔吐が生じる。これは管理された化学戦争なのだ) (RD 98/5: 99) [様態限定；個別事例；cf. battle/war]

比較： A leading scientist has warned that protective suits and gas masks will not guard troops against prolonged chemical and biological *warfare*. (指導的科学者の警告によると，防御服やガスマスクは長期の化学・生物戦争に際しては部隊を守ることはできない) (CIDE) [下位分類 (☞ 8.9.3)　類例：V-96, a; Ap.1-7, a; Ap.2.2-93, a; Ap.4.1-32, c; 55, a; 78, a]

(79) a. Global *warming* may be coming, but if it does, it won't necessarily be extreme. (地球温暖化がやってくるかもしれないが，たとえ来ても，必ずしも極端ではないだろう) (RD 99/9: 23) [global とはいっても模糊（ｂ）としているので完結した姿かたちは形成されない]

　　 b. It may seem paradoxical, but *a* modest *warming* in the normally cold and dry polar regions will actually mean more arctic ice, not less. (逆説的に聞こえるかもしれないが，通常は寒く乾燥した極地が適度に温暖化されれば，実際には，北極の氷が減少ではなく，より増加するという事態を引き起こすだろう) (RD 99/9: 25) [程度限定]

(80) a. Her condition is improving but we want to keep close *watch* on her for a few days just to be safe. (彼女の健康状態は回復してきているが，安全のため数日よく観察したい) (CIDE) [一般的観察；cf. examination/inspection/reflection]

　　 b. Once your name has been linked with a drug offence, the police keep *a* close *watch* on you. (いったん名前が薬物犯罪と結びつけられれば，警察は厳重に監視する) (CIDE) [個別的監視]

Ap. 4.2 状況および精神活動

(1) a. *Hurry* is the enemy of careful people. (急ぎは慎重な人たちにとって敵だ) (NTC) [抽象概念]

　　 b. We left in such *a hurry* that we forgot our tickets. (とても急いで出たので切符を忘れた) (CIDE) [そのときの状態；類義語の haste は無冠詞 (☞ 3 章 NB 8)]

(2) a. *Illness* has curtailed her sporting activities. (病気のためスポーツ活動が縮小された) (OALD[5]) [病気という状態；病名・症状には関知せず]

　　 b. How can you tell whether your fatigue is due to depression and not to *an illness* like the flu? (どうして疲れがふさぎの虫のためであって，感冒のような病気のためではない，と言えるだろうか) (RD 96/3: 101) [特定の病気；cf. sickness]

(3) a. Postnatal depression is usually due to hormonal *imbalance*. (産後の鬱(うつ)状態はふつうホルモン失調による) (OALD[6]) [抽象的病名]

　　b. *A* chemical *imbalance* in Bob's brain caused his seizures. (B は大脳内の化学的不均衡のため発作が起きた) (NTC) [特定の (一時的) 症状]

(4) a. Birds in outside cages develop *immunity* to airborne bacteria. (屋外のかごにいる鳥は空気によって運ばれる細菌に対して免疫ができる) (CCED[3]) [免疫一般]

　　b. People don't realise that many adults develop *an immunity* and may never know they still have lice. (認識している人はいないが、多くの大人は免疫ができてしまって、まだシラミがいるということに気づかないかもしれない) (RD 99/8: 70) [特定の (この場合, シラミに対する) 免疫；NTC は定義 1 で免疫一般に関する解説をし, 定義 2 では 'immunity ① to a specific disease' と定義している]

　　c. Exposure to many diseases gave the doctor a number of specific *immunities*. (多くの病気に接したのでその医者は多くの特定の免疫ができた) (NTC)

(5) a. On *impulse*, I chose *The Story of My Life* by Helen Keller. (衝動的に HK の『自叙伝』を選んだ) (RD 99/3: 10) (7 章 NB 2 参照) [抽象概念]

　　b. She had invited Joseph on *a* sudden *impulse* but was now regretting it. (一時の衝動で J を招待したが、今では後悔している) (LDOCE[3]) [on が先行する場合, 形容詞をともなえば不定冠詞をとる]

　　c. *An* electrical *impulse* shocked Mary when she touched the electric fence. (M は電流の流れているフェンスにさわったらビリッときた) (NTC) [種類限定]

(6) a. (= IV-227, a) *Inconvenience* during a winter ice storm is to be expected. (NTC) [抽象概念]

　　b. I work in a busy office where a computer going down causes quite *an inconvenience*. (忙しい会社で働いているのでコンピュータがダウンすれば相当な不便が生じる) (RD 98/3: 99) [一時的；仕事上の不便という内容も含意]

(7) a. If there has been a betrayal, such as *infidelity*, don't expect the wounds to heal quickly. (不倫といったような裏切りがあったならば、傷がすぐに癒えるとは期待すべきでない) (RD 99/1: 116)

　　b. He's only committing *a* normal *infidelity*.　Tell me ... who do you know who doesn't cheat, given the opportunity? (彼はただよくある

不倫をしているだけだ. いいかい, チャンスがあったとして, 浮気をしないものを知っているか) (1967 E. Lindall, *Time too Soon*, vii. 81) [OED] [種類限定]

(8) a. Teenagers often go through periods of emotional *instability*. (ティーンエージャーはしばしば情緒不安定の時期を経験する) (CDAE)

b. The vast majority of headaches – tension-type, migraine and cluster – involve *an instability* of chemical messengers known as neurotransmitters. (頭痛の大半——緊張型, 偏頭痛, 群発性——は神経伝達物質として知られる化学メッセンジャーが不安定であることと関連がある) (RD 99/8: 85) [種類限定；一時性含意]

(9) a. But now he and Han Dan cried with unbridled *joy*. (だが今や彼とHD は心おきなくうれし泣きをした) (RD 99/1: 22)

b. My child's birth was *a joy*. (子供の誕生は慶事だった) (NTC)

(10) a. Linda can't stand *mess*. (L は散らかっている状態に我慢できない) (CCED3) [様態非限定]

b. My brother's house is always in *a mess*. (兄の家はいつも散らかっている) (CIDE) [in に後続して範囲限定；cf. clutter (☞ 3 章 NB 8)]

c. I always make *a mess* when I try to cook anything. (料理をしようとするといつも散らかしてしまう) (CIDE)

(11) a. You may examine the books in your own home for ten days without cost or *obligation*. (書籍は自宅で 10 日間無料で, 責任を負うことなく, 審査することができる) (OALD5) [抽象概念；without に後続することも無冠詞の 1 因 (☞ 4.5.1)]

b. I don't want to be under *an obligation* to anyone. (だれにも借りは作りたくない) (LDOCE3) [一時性含意]

(12) a. That man experienced far more *pain* than most of us could ever imagine. (その人はほとんどのものが想像もできないほどの苦痛を味わった) (RD 00/6: 58)

b. Two weeks later, when Lesia regained consciousness, she felt *a shocking pain* throughout her body. (2 週間後意識を回復したとき, L は体じゅうに衝撃的な痛みを感じた) (RD 98/11: 18)

NB 2　have a pain / cause φ pain

病名と動詞 (☞ 5.3) との関連において述べたのと同じ傾向が pain (「肉体的・精神的苦痛」) の用法に関しても見られる. この語が個

人的知覚を表す動詞（例：feel/give/get/have）に後続するときは，通例，不定冠詞をとる。

    i) But now I've got *a* terrible *pain* in my gut. (しかし，いま腹部がひどく痛んでいる) (RD 98/12: 111)

    ii) All that heavy lifting has given me *a pain* in the back. (重いものをもちあげて背中が痛くなった) (OALD⁵)

    iii) have *a pain* in the gut(s) (腹部が痛む) (OALD⁵)

これに対し，cause/suffer from につづくときは無冠詞で用いられる。

    iv) Wasp stings cause swelling and sharp *pain*. (ハチに刺されると腫(は)れて激しく痛む) (OALD⁵)

    v) suffer from acute back *pain* (背中の激痛に苦しむ) (OALD⁵)

(13) a. *Panic* spread through the crowd as the bullets started to fly. (弾丸が飛びはじめたとき群衆にパニックが広がった) (CIDE) [panic の期間非含意；状態に重点；(VII-40) も参照]

    b *Will I even recognize him?* she thought in *panic*. (「いったい彼がわかるかしら」と彼女はパニック状態で考えた) (RD 98/6: 90) [*Will ... him?* 斜字体は原文]

    c. He got in(to) *a panic* that he would forget his lines on stage. (舞台で台詞を忘れるのではないかとパニックに陥った) [内容限定；一時性含意] (CIDE)

    d. In *a panic*, Alistair lurched backward into clear water and went under again. (パニックになって，Aは透明な水のなかに後ろ向きに倒れて再び沈んだ) (RD 98/11: 33) [一時性含意]

(14) a. Primakov's foreign policy, they say, endangers U.S.-Russia relations and poses a threat to world *peace* and stability. (彼らの言い分では，Pの外交政策は米露関係を危険にし，世界の平和と安定に脅威となる) (RD 99/5: 45)

    b. After *a peace* was established and the UN had collected its weapons, a potential force would always still be in Bosnia, and it could be quickly re-equipped in case the peace was violated. (平和が確立され国連が武器を回収したあとも，潜在的軍隊はつねに依然としてBに存在し，平和が破られれば即座に再軍備されうるであろう) (ConCD-ROM) [一時的平和；cf. LDOCE³ (s.v., peace): 'a period of time in which there is no war']

参考： Negotiating *a truce* will not be an easy task. (休戦の交渉は容易な仕事ではないだろう) (McED) [truce (休戦) は一時的であることを含意するので不定冠詞をとる；cf. OALD⁶ (s.v., truce a): 'an agreement between enemies or opponents to stop fighting for an agreed period of time; <u>the period of time</u> that this lasts']

(15) a. Standing 196 centimetres tall, with sloppy *posture* and a goofy laugh, Smith lacked the confidence to be much of a teacher and regarded himself as just a "kitchen chemist." (上背が196センチあり，だらしない姿勢で，笑えばそっ歯が出る，S はひとかどの教師としての自信に欠け，自分を単なる「台所の化学者」だとみなしていた) (RD 99/12: 75) [他の姿勢と対比せず，漠然とした姿勢を指す]　類例： φ good/bad posture (CIDE)

b. If you stand above him, he thinks you want to fight. Scientists call that *an* aggressive *posture*. (彼 [ゴリラ] の上に立てば，戦うつもりでいると彼は思う。攻撃の構えと科学者に呼ばれているものだからだ) (RD 00/6: 43) [他から区別可能な，型にはまった posture]　類例： an angular/awkward/inelegant posture (OALD⁵, CIDE)

(16) a. *Prejudice* is often based on fear or ignorance. (偏見はしばしば恐怖もしくは無知に基づく) (NTC)

b. There was *a* deep-rooted racial *prejudice* long before the two countries became rivals and went to war. (2つの国が敵対し戦争状態になるずっと以前から深く根ざした民族的偏見があった) (CCED³)

参考： NTC (s.v., prejudice): '1. n. opinion formed about someone or something before learning all the facts. (No plural form in this sense.) . . . 2. n. <u>an instance</u> of ①.'

(17) a. She takes *pride* in doing a job well. (ちゃんと仕事をすることに誇りをもっている) (LDOCE³) [pride に "in＋-ing" 形が後続するときは無冠詞；cf. show/feel/take pride in (doing) sth (LDOCE³)]

b. Scott takes *a* great *pride* in his appearance. (S は自分の容姿にとても誇りをもっている) (LDOCE³) [pride に "in＋名詞" が後続するとき不定冠詞は随意的；cf. show/feel/take (a) pride in sth (LDOCE³)]

(18) a. The most obvious sources are those pursuits that give our lives *purpose* – anything from studying insects to playing baseball. (最も明らかな [エネルギー] 源は人生に意欲を与える楽しみだ――昆虫の研究から野球をすることに至る何でも) (RD 98/7: 39)

b. "Having *a purpose* in your life is the most important element of becoming a fully functioning person," says Wayne Dyer, author of the best-selling *Your Erroneous Zones*. (「人生に目的をもつことこそが十全に本務を果たす人間になるための最重要な要素だ」とベストセラーの [邦訳]『自分のための人生』の著者であるWDは言う) (RD 99/12: 42) [特定の目的]

(19) a. Hal was beside himself with *rage* and grief. (Hは激怒と悲しみのため我を忘れた) (RD [U.S. Edition] 98/9: 119-20)

   b. He was in *a rage*. (激怒していた) (OALD⁵) [一時的; cf. clutter/hurry]

(20) a. In April 1998, *reconciliation* was complete when Kuklinski was invited back to Poland as a guest of Solidarity and the cities of Krakow and Gdansk. (1998年4月和解は完成し，Kは連帯，K市およびG市のゲストとして招待されてPに帰国した) (RD 00/4: 142)

   b. It took hours of negotiations to bring about *a reconciliation* between the two sides. (両者に和解をもたらすには何時間もの交渉が必要だった) (CIDE)

   参考： CCED³ (s.v., reconciliation): 'Reconciliation between two people or countries who have quarrelled is the process of their becoming friends again.　A reconciliation is <u>an instance</u> of this.'

(21) a. The President doesn't have much time for *relaxation*. (大統領には息抜きの時間はあまりない) (OALD⁵)

   b. On the other hand there are many more amateur hand-turners about, men who do wood turning as *a relaxation* from their normal jobs. (他方，手作業でろくろ回しをするアマチュアがもっとたくさんいる，つまり，普段の仕事の息抜きにろくろ細工をする人たちだ) (ConCD-ROM)

(22) a. The villagers had no experience with a hatchery, but they did have *respect* for Similus. (村人たちは孵化(か)場の経験はなかったが，Sに尊敬の念をもっていた) (RD 99/5: 52)

   b. inculcate (in young people) *a respect* for the law ((若者に)順法精神を教え込む) (OALD⁵) [特定の内容をもった敬意]

(23) a. Now that the job is truly his, Bill takes full *responsibility*. (今やその仕事は真に彼のものなので，Bは全面的に責任を引きうける) (RD 98/3: 95)

   b. Disgusted but still feeling *a responsibility* to the man, Bien-Aimé led him to the spot where he'd taken Maria Puras. (うんざりしたが，それでも，その男に責任を感じて，BA は MP を連れていった場所に彼を案内した) (RD 99/3: 68) [限定的な責任]

(24) a. Soon it seemed that the cage had become her den, the place she returned to for *security*. (間もなく鳥かごが彼女の住みか――安全のために戻ってくる場所――になったようだった) (RD 99/6: 79)

b. In the sense that knowing God is the meaning of life and gives the believer *a security* and a peace, a Christian faith should help in all aspects of life. (神を知ることは，人生の目的であり，信ずるものに安心と安らぎを与えるという意味で，キリスト教の信仰は人生のあらゆる面で役に立つ) (ConCD-ROM) [信者個々人が得る security]

(25) a. The disease causes a loss of *sensation* in the fingers. (その病気にかかると指の感覚がなくなる) (CIDE)

b. Recovering from anesthesia produced *a sensation* like drowning, but peacefully, if there is such a thing. (麻酔からの覚醒は溺れるような，ただし，もしもそのようなものがあるとすれば，穏やかに溺れるような，感覚だった) (RD 97/5: 138) [特定の感覚]

(26) a. The wave and curl of her blonde hair gave her *sensuality* and youth. (彼女の金髪のウエーブとカールは彼女に性的魅力と若々しさを与えた) (CIDE) [様態非含意]

b. McCartney has big photogenic eyes and *a sensuality* beyond her years. ([Stella] M は写真写りのよい大きな目をしていて，年齢以上の性的魅力をそなえている) (RD 99/5: 88) [M 特有の性的魅力]

(27) a. *Shock* registered on everyone's face. (全員の顔にショックが浮かんだ) (OALD[6]) [様態非限定 (= 抽象概念) ; cf. Ap.4.4-28]

b. She told me she had some bad news for me and I braced myself for *a shock*. (私に悪い知らせがあると言ったので，ショックに対し心の準備をした) (CIDE) [特定のショック]

(28) a. They were absent because of *sickness*. (病気のため欠席した) (OALD[5]) [病名非限定の体調不良]

b. They died within a few days of each other, probably from *a sickness* like the plague. (互いに数日以内に死亡した。多分ペストのような病気のためだろう) (LDOCE[3]) [特定の病気 ; cf. illness]

(29) a. (= Ap.2.2-109, a) Quakers emphasize the importance of *simplicity* in all things. (CIDE)

b. There was something about him – a solidity, a sincerity, *a simplicity* – that opened doors. (彼には扉を開く何かがあった――堅実さ, 誠実さ, 素朴さである) (RD 96/3: 135) [当該の少年に特有な, 個別事例としての simplicity]

(30) a. They expressed *surprise* at the result. (結果に驚きを表わした) (CIDE)

b. What *a* nice *surprise*! (なんてうれしい驚きでしょう) (OALD⁵)

(31) a. The factory is under *threat* of closure. (工場は閉鎖の脅威にさらされている) (OALD⁵) [抽象概念]

b. He lived under *a* constant *threat* of his health problems returning. (健康問題がぶり返すのではないかという絶えざる脅威のもとで暮らしていた) (CIDE) [内容限定]

c. (= Ap.4.2-14, a) Primakov's foreign policy, they say, endangers U.S.-Russia relations and poses *a threat* to world peace and stability. (RD 99/5: 45) [特定の脅威]

(32) a. *Wisdom* and maturity don't necessarily go together. (知恵と成熟とは必ずしも両立しない) (CIDE)

b. He was right, with *a wisdom* all his own. (彼は正しく, 独自の知恵を備えていた) (RD 96/3: 144) [彼の知恵に限定]

Ap. 4.3 内容

(1) a. Jo's English teacher puts/places/lays great *emphasis* (up)on written work and grammar. (Jの英語の先生は書かれた作品と文法とにとても重点をおく) (CIDE) [emphasis の内容非含意]

b. (= IV-217, b) The course puts *an emphasis* on practical work. (LDOCE³) [話し手はどのような emphasis かを承知]

(2) a. There is nothing more influential in a child's life than the moral power of quiet *example*. (無言のお手本という道徳的な力ほど子供の生活に影響を与えるものはない) (RD 99/12: 73) [内容非含意 (= 抽象概念)]

b. (= III-86, b) Let me give you *an example* of what I mean. (CDAE) [内容限定 (= 特定の例)]

(3) a. (= IV-225, a) These can also cause *grief* and exhaustion. (RD 96/3: 100)

b. The letter carrier brought *a* new *grief* into my life. The tax bill came! (郵便配達人は私の人生に新たな悲しみをもたらした。納税請求書が来たのだ) (NTC) [内容後続 (☞ 4.4.4)]

(4) a. The small amount of compensation is a further source of *grievance* to the people forced to leave their homes. (わずかな補償額は家を追い出される人々にとってはさらなる不満のもとだ) (CIDE) ["NP₁ of NP₂" の形式で素材扱い (☞ 2.1.2)]

b. Bill still harbours/nurses *a grievance* against his employers for not promoting him. (昇進させなかったことでBは雇い主にまだ不満をもっている) (CIDE)

(5) a. What begins as great effort will eventually become *habit*. (始めるときは非常に努力しても最終的には習慣になるだろう) (RD 99/3: 50) [内容非限定]

b. It's all right to borrow money occasionally, but don't let it become *a habit*/ make *a habit* of it. (たまに借金するのはかまわないが、くせにしてはならない) (OALD5) [内容限定; cf. custom/routine/tradition]

(6) a. As a journalist you simply cannot tolerate *inaccuracy*. (ジャーナリストとして不正確を許すことはどうしてもできない) (LDOCE3)

b. It is unfortunate that Jonathan Coe had to quote *a* gross *inaccuracy* in his review of *A Fool's Alphabet* (July 12). (JC が『愚者のアルファベット』の書評中で甚だしい間違いを引用せざるをえなかったのは不幸なことだ) (ConCD-ROM)

(7) a. Then *inspiration* hit. (そのとき考えが閃(ひら)いた) (RD 00/1: 12) [内容非限定]

b. Married for eight years and the parents of a five-year-old girl, Dana and John Terry had little time for romance until Dana had *an inspiration*. One Friday she told John she was going to pick him up at work and take him to lunch. (結婚後8年たち、5歳の娘の親なので、DとJTとはほとんど恋愛気分の時間がなかったが、ある考えがDに閃いた。ある金曜日、彼女はJに言った、彼を職場に迎えに行くからいっしょに昼食に行こう、と) (RD 98/7: 81) [内容後続]

(8) a. But I began to answer Sister's letters, more out of politeness than *interest*. (それでも、シスターの手紙に返事を書くようにはなったが、関心よりも礼節からだった) (RD 98/11: 53)

b. I have *an interest* in learning about computers. (コンピュータについて勉強することに関心がある) (NHD) [対象を示す *in*-phrase をと

もなって個別的内容を表す (☞ 4.4.1.2)]

(9) a. *Interpretation* is often as important as the text itself. (解釈は本文自体と同程度に重要なことがよくある) (CIDE) [抽象概念]

b. The opposition Labour Party put *a* different *interpretation* on the figures. (野党の労働党はその数値に関して異なる解釈をした) (CCED[3]) [特定の解釈]

(10) a. The lack of a superpower enemy, after the fall of Soviet communism, has reduced *justification* of military spending in the public mind. (ソビエト共産主義の崩壊後, 超大国の敵がいなくなったので, 一般人の考えでは軍事費を正当化する根拠が低下した) (RD 96/3: 119) [抽象概念]

b. We expect you to provide *a justification* of/for your actions. (君の行動に関して納得のいく説明をしていただきたい) (CIDE) [個別的内容を含む justification]

(11) a. On November 14, 1986, President Ronald Reagan signed the HCQIA [Health Care Quality Improvement Act] into *law*. (1986年11月14日 RR 大統領は健康管理の質向上法案に署名して立法化した) (RD 99/9: 109) [制度としての法]

b. Don't forget there's *a law* about exporting certain antiques. (ある種の古美術品の輸出に関しては法律があることを忘れてはならない) (CIDE) [特定の法律]

c. She's going to study *law* at university. (大学で法学を専攻するつもりだ) (CIDE) [学問名 (☞ 2.3.3.2)]

(12) a. Her writing came to *maturity* in the 1960s. (彼女の書き物は1960年代に成熟に達した) (CIDE)

b. Iqbal possessed *a maturity* beyond his years and a precocious sense of justice. (I は年齢以上に成熟しており早熟な正義感をもっていた) (RD 97/5: 21) [I に特有な maturity; このあとに具体的特徴が詳述されているので内容限定でもある (長すぎるため引用割愛)]

比較 : At times, she seems to have *maturity* beyond her years. (ときどき彼女は年齢以上に成熟しているように見える) (CIDE) [内容非限定 (= 抽象概念)]

(13) a. The play has several layers of *meaning*. (その戯曲には幾層もの意味がある) (OALD[5]) ["NP$_1$ of NP$_2$" の形式で素材扱い (☞ 2.1.2)]

b. His words had *a* hidden *meaning*. (彼のことばには隠された意味が

あった) (OALD⁵) [特定の意味]

(14) a. The details of the scandal remain cloaked/shrouded/wrapped in *mystery*. (スキャンダルの詳細は謎に包まれたままだ) (CIDE)

　　b. How the massive stones were brought here from hundreds of miles away is/remains *a mystery*. (巨石群が何百マイルも離れたところからどうやってここまで運ばれたかは謎だ／のままだ) (CIDE)

(15) a. His love for her turned to *obsession*. (彼女への愛は強迫観念となった) (CDAE) [抽象概念]

　　b. He's convinced he was unfairly treated and it's become *an obsession*. (彼は不公平な扱いをうけたと確信しており, それは強迫観念になった) (LDOCE³) [内容限定]

　参考： NTC (s.v., obsession): '1. feeling or thought that completely fills one's mind. (No plural form in this sense.)　2. <u>an instance or case</u> of ①.'

(16) a. *Opinion* is shifting in favour of the new scheme. (世論は新しい計画の支持に回りつつある) (OALD⁵) [抽象概念； cf. information/news/rumour]

　　b. Most who expressed *an opinion* spoke favorably of Thomas. (見解を述べたものの大半はTのことを好意的に話した) (CCED³) [個別事例]

(17) a. I have good *reason* to be suspicious. (疑うべきちゃんとした根拠がある) (OALD⁵) [「根拠」という意味のとき [U]; evidence と同様に抽象概念を表す(☞ 2.3.3.3.5)]

　　b. Only human beings are capable of *reason*. (人間だけが理性的思考能力がある) (OALD⁶) [「判断力・理性」という意味のとき [U]；「能力・機能」を表す (☞ 3.9)]

　　c. There has to be *a reason* for his strange behaviour. (彼の奇妙な行動には理由があるはずだ) (OALD⁵) [「理由・説明」(= 根拠あるいは判断力・理性の個別事例) という意味のとき [C]]

(18) a. *Revelation* of the truth about the murder came out in court. (殺人に関する真実の暴露が法廷で行われた) (NHD) [行為]

　　b. It was *a revelation* of the President's involvement in secret arms deals that shocked the nation. (国民を驚かせたのは大統領が秘密軍事協定に関与していたという新事実だった) (CIDE) [個別情報]

　参考： NTC (s.v., revelation): '1. revealing something; making something known. (No plural form in this sense.)　2. something that is made known; <u>a piece</u> of information that is learned by someone.'

(19) a. You've got to enjoy life and not get bogged down with daily *routine*, or your existence becomes dull. (日々の決まりきった仕事にはまりこまず，人生を楽しむべきだ。さもなければ，生きているのが退屈になってしまう) (RD 00/7: 22) [仕事・行為全般]

  b. *A routine* was quickly established. (すぐに日常の仕事となった) (RD 00/7: 28) [特定の仕事・行為 ; cf. custom/habit/tradition]

(20) a. The coach called a time-out to discuss *strategy*. (コーチは戦略を論じるためにタイムアウトをとった) (CIDE) [内容非限定]

  b. to develop *a strategy* for dealing with unemployment (失業に対処するため戦略を展開する) (OALD[6]) [特定の戦略]

(21) a. (= IV-269, a) We decided to break with *tradition* and not send any cards this Christmas. (OALD[5]) [抽象概念]

  b. To abandon such *an* old *tradition* is unthinkable. (そのような古い伝統を捨てるなんて考えられない) (OALD[5]) [個別事例 ; 通例，修飾語句をともなう ; cf. custom/habit/routine]

(22) a. Rusted ships stuffed with radioactive *waste* and spent nuclear fuel were docked at Murmansk's piers. (錆びた船が，放射性廃棄物と使用核燃料を積んで，Mの波止場に入っていた) (RD 97/6: 73) [物質]

  b. Takahito Koya, a retired newspaper editor, and several friends in the central Japanese city of Ikeda thought it was *a waste* when they noticed their neighbors discarding books. (日本中部の池田市在住の，引退した新聞編集者TK氏と彼の友人数名は，隣人が本を捨てているのを知ってもったいないと思った) (RD 99/3: 81) [内容限定]

Ap. 4.4 その他

(1) a. (= IV-52, a) You're grounded for three weeks for staying out after *curfew*. (RD 99/1: 54) [効力・制度]

  b. "Are you saying I have *a curfew*?" she asked with horror. (「門限があるってことなの？」彼女は恐怖を浮かべて尋ねた) (RD 98/3: 15) 類例 : to impose/enforce/lift a curfew (CIDE)

(2) a. The children's faces are badly out of *focus* in the photograph. (写真中の子供たちの顔はひどくピンぼけだった) (OALD[5])

  b. Term one introduces feminist theory and politics with *a focus* on the family. (1学期は，家族に焦点をあてたフェミニスト理論および政治学を紹介する) (ConCD-ROM)

(3) a. Thick / Heavy / Swirling *fog* has made the driving conditions dangerous. (濃霧のため運転するには危険だ) (CIDE) [広がり・期間には関知せず]
　　b. They went about their duties that day in *a fog*. (その日は霧のなかで業務に取りかかった) (RD 99/2: 129) [そのときの霧 ; (IV-39) も参照 ; cf. haze/mist/rain]
(4) a. *Fragrance* . . . is our strongest link to the past, our closest fellow traveller to the future. (においは最も強力に過去に結びつけるものであり，未来に旅する最も親密な仲間だ) (CCED³)
　　b. Lavender has *a* delicate *fragrance*. (ラベンダはほのかな香りがする) (OALD⁵) [特定の芳香 ; cf. odour]
参考 : Balsam firs sprouted fresh boughs, filling the air with tart *fragrance*. (バルサムモミは若枝を広げ，大気を酸っぱい芳香で満たした) (RD 99/11: 25) [非日常的形容詞 (☞ 4 章 NB 7-2; 4.4.3.4)]
(5) a. Her suggestion: consider *friendship* an honour and a gift, and worth the effort to treasure and nurture. (彼女の提言：友情とは名誉であり贈り物であり，尊び育(はぐく)む努力に値するものだと考えなさい) (RD 99/8: 39) [抽象概念]
　　b. Bob Coleman and Scott Sterritt forged *a friendship* through adversity (BC と SS とは逆境をとおして友情を築いた) (RD 99/10: 70, caption) [特定の 2 人のあいだの友情]
　　c. "*Friendships* change as our needs and lifestyles change," Wilmot observes. (「我々の必要や生活様式が変化するにつれて付き合いも変化する」と W は言う) (RD 99/8: 39) [いろいろな種類の友情]
(6) a. *Government* is expensive but necessary. (政治はカネがかかるが必要だ) (NTC) [制度・体制 (a-d)]
　　b. What this state needs is really strong *government*. (この国が必要とするのは真に強力な政治形態だ) (CIDE)
　　c. How long have the Christian Democrats been in *government*? (キリスト教民主党はどのくらい政権にあるか) (LDOCE³)
　　d. The 1990s have seen a shift to democratic *government* in Eastern Europe. (1990 年代東欧では民主的政治体制への移行が見られた) (CIDE)
　　e. *a* democratic *government* (民主的政府) (LDOCE³) [個別事例 (e-g)]
　　f. For *a government* to give up this kind of power is unusual. (政府が

この種の権力を放棄するのはまれだ）(RD 98/3: 57)

 g. When President Peron fell from power in Argentina, *a* provisional military *government* took office. (AでP大統領が失脚したとき，暫定軍事政府が発足した) (CIDE)

(7) a. New tax incentives will be introduced in the hope of stimulating future *investment*. (将来的な投資の刺激を期待して新しい減税措置が導入されるだろう) (CIDE)

 b. Paying the gypsy woman for this circumcision is one of the greatest expenses a household will undergo, but is considered *a* good *investment*. (陰核切除手術に対するジプシーの女への支払いは家庭がする最大の出費の1つだが，よい投資対象だと思われている) (RD 99/10: 125)

(8) a. (= V-134, b) In a country that encourages abortion, even forces it, this woman chose to give our daughter *life*, a fact that compels a gratitude beyond this world's ability to pay. (RD 98/6: 84)

 b. But don't be too quickly repulsed – after all *a life* is at stake. (しかし，[mouth to mouth の人工呼吸法を] 早くあきらめすぎてはいけない。人ひとりの命がかかっているのだから) (RD 97/2: 83)

(9) a. *Living* is easy in the summertime. (夏期には暮らしは楽だ) (NTC) [全般的]

 b. The teacher announced that each member of the class would say what their father did for *a living* and then spell the occupation. (先生はクラスの一人ひとりが，父親が生計のために何をしているのか言って，その職業の綴りを書くように告げた) (RD 99/4: 25) [個別事例]

(10) a. Still, when people brought up the Olympics, I could see only *mockery* in their smiles. (それでも，人々がオリンピックを話題にするとき，彼らの笑いにはあざけりしか見られなかった) (RD 99/5: 82)

 b. The continued flouting of Security Council resolutions is making *a mockery* of the UN. (安全保障理事会の決議の継続的な無視は国連をあざ笑っている) (LDOCE[3]) [個別事例]

 c. The trial was *a mockery* – the judge had decided the verdict before it began. (裁判は茶番だった。裁判官は開始前に判決を決めていたのだから) (CIDE) [cf. failure/success]

参考：There was an element of *mockery* in the politeness he showed the inspector. (彼が調査官に示した慇懃（いんぎん）さにはいささかあざけりが

あった) (LDOCE³) ["NP₁ of NP₂" の形式で素材扱い (☞ 2.1.2)]

(11) a. Trees along the sides of roads can reduce traffic *noise*. (街路樹は交通騒音を減少させる) (CIDE) [交通騒音一般]

  b. She'd been working in her room till *a noise* had disturbed her. (自分の部屋で働いていたが, 物音で妨げられた) (CCED³) [特定の騒音 ; cf. sound]

(12) a. *Odour* (= Smells generally) can become a problem if the ventilation in a room is inadequate. (部屋の換気が不十分だとにおい (= におい全般) が問題になることがある) (CIDE) [におい全般]

  b. Homing pigeons can be disoriented when the direction of *an odor* is shifted. (においの方向が変えられると伝書バトは方向がわからなくなることがある) (RD 96/3: 39) [特定のにおい ; cf. fragrance]

 比較: What *a stink*! (なんという臭気だ) (LDOCE3) [stink は 'terrible/unpleasant' という意味限定が組み込まれているので, 不定冠詞をとる ; cf. grin/laugh/smile (☞ 2.3.3.3.2)]

(13) a. Sometimes facing *opportunity* is like staring at the knees of a giraffe. (幸運に出くわすのはキリンの膝を見つめるのに似ているようなことがある) (L. B. Jones, quoted in RD 99/2: 115) [cf. fate]

  b. *An opportunity* like that doesn't often come my way. (そのような好機に巡り会うことはめったにない) (OALD⁵) [特定の opportunity]

(14) a. We swept behind the moon and into lunar *orbit* on December 10. (12月10日, 月の裏側を回って月の軌道に入った) (RD 99/3: 136) [高度・形状など非限定]

  b. The space vehicle settled into *an orbit* around Mars. (宇宙船は火星を回る軌道に定着した) (NHD) [話し手の描く高度・形状をもつ軌道]

  c. In April of 1961 the ante went up when Russian cosmonaut Yuri Gagarin . . . flew *a* single *orbit* of Earth in 108 minutes, becoming the first man in space. (1961年の4月に [宇宙開発の] 先行投資金が増額された。その年, ロシアの宇宙飛行士YGが108分で地球を一周して, 宇宙に出た最初の人間になったのだ) (RD 99/3: 121) [軌道1周]

(15) a. During the novel, there is a shift in *perspective* from an adult's view of events to a child's view. (その小説では, 出来事に対して大人の見方から子供の見方へと視点の移動がある) (CIDE)

  b. He writes from *a* Marxist *perspective*. (マルクス主義的視点から書く) (CIDE) [特定の視点]

(16) a. It is not beyond the bounds of *possibility* that he'll win the match. (彼が試合に勝つのは可能性の範囲外ではない) (OALD5) [抽象概念 ; i.e. 'choice; likelihood' (NTC)]

b. Defense Secretary William S. Cohen fears a biological attack on U.S. soil "is not *a* remote *possibility* but a real probability in the present." (WSC 国防長官が恐れるのは，合衆国の土壌への生物学的攻撃が「現時点では遠い可能性ではなく現実的見込みである」ということだ) (RD 99/2: 50) [個別事例 ; i.e, 'something that is possible' (NTC); cf. probability/reality]

(17) a. (= IV-232, a) Where *principle* is involved, be deaf to expediency. (RD 98/4: 113)

b. *A principle* does not cease to be *a principle* because it coincides with a legitimate interest. (正当な利益と重なるという理由で原則が原則でなくなるということはない) (CIDE) [個別の原則]

(18) a. (= IV-233, a) You cannot prove conclusively that Sellafield caused cancer.　You can only work on the basis of *probability*. (CCED3) [抽象概念]

b. Formal talks are still said to be a possibility, not *a probability*. (公式な会談はまだ可能性であり，見込みではないと言われている) (CCED3) [個別事例 ; cf. possibility/reality]

(19) a. A garden design should reflect nature in shape, *proportion* and size. (庭の設計は形，比率，大きさにおいて自然を映すべきだ) (OALD5)

b. As people accumulate more wealth, they tend to spend *a* greater *proportion* of their incomes. (富を蓄えるにつれて，収入のうちより多くの部分を消費する傾向がある) (CIDE) [全体における位置づけ限定 ; 通例，形容詞をともなう]

(20) a. *Rain* still slashed in from all sides. (依然として雨は四方八方から降り込んだ) (RD 99/3: 91)

b. She was a child of the desert, as tenacious and beautiful as the flowers that bloom there after *a rain*. (彼女は砂漠の子であり，雨のあとそこに咲く花のように力強く美しいのだ) (RD 99/10: 120) [一時的 ; cf. fog/frost/haze/mist]

(21) a. His answer jarred me back to *reality*. (彼の答えは私を現実に引き戻した) (RD 99/3: 41)

b. Now my dreams had finally become *a reality*. (今や私の夢はついに

現実のものになった) (RD 98/12: 120) [cf. possibility/probability]

(22) It's not enough to belong to *a religion*. You also have to put it into practice. *Religion* is like a medicine. You have to ingest it to combat the illness. (宗派に属しているだけでは不十分だ。実践もしなければならない。宗教は薬のようなものであり，病気と闘うためには摂取しなければならないからだ) (The Dalai Lama, quoted in RD [U.S. edition] 00/1: 107)

(23) a. *Romance* inspired me to buy my date a dozen roses. (恋心からデートの相手にバラを1ダース買った) (NTC)

    b. That offer blossomed into *a romance*, and eventually Jeff asked Shirley to be his wife. (その申し出はロマンスへと開花し，ついにJはShに妻になってくれるよう申し込んだ) (RD 99/4: 8)

参考: There was an air of *romance* about the old castle. (その古城にはロマンの雰囲気があった) (OALD⁵) ["NP₁ of NP₂" の形式で素材扱い (☞ 2.1.2); 4.4.1.3「助数詞」扱い] も参照]

(24) a. Resilient couples view their marriage as sacred, worthy of *sacrifice*. (立ち直りができる夫婦は結婚を聖なるもの，犠牲に値するものと見ている) (RD 00/1: 119) [抽象概念]

    b. Now marriage no longer feels like *a sacrifice*. (もはや今では結婚は犠牲行為のようには思われない) (RD 99/2: 36) [個別事例]

(25) a. She was one day ahead of *schedule*. (予定より1日進んでいた) (RD 98/10: 135) [抽象概念；詳細には関知せず]

    b. Write *a* daily *schedule*. (毎日の予定を書きなさい) (RD 00/7: 95) [具体的予定]

(26) a. Archie is on full *scholarship* and has to live on what he makes from a part-time job and on what his grandmother can share of her welfare cheque. (Aは奨学金を満額貸与されており，彼のアルバイト収入と祖母が生活保護の小切手から分けてくれる額とで暮らさなければならない) (RD 99/12: 90)

    b. Paula went up to Oxford on *a scholarship*. (PはOに奨学金で大学に行った) (CIDE) [特定の財団から貸与される奨学金]

(27) a. Apart from heart attacks, people die every day from suffocation, drowning, choking, electric *shock* or drug overdose. (心臓発作のほか，人は窒息したり，溺れたり，喉にものを詰まらせたり，感電したり，薬物を取りすぎたりして毎日死んでいる) (RD 97/2: 82) [様態・

回数など非限定 (= 抽象概念); cf. Ap.4.2-27]
    b. I got *an* electric *shock* from that faulty light switch. (電灯の欠陥スイッチで感電した) (OALD⁵) [個別事例]

(28) a. *Sound* travels more slowly than light. (音は光よりも進むのが遅い) (OALD⁵)
    b. (= III-100, b) There was not *a sound* from Jimmy. (RD 99/2: 122) [特定の音; cf. noise]

(29) a. She has a lot of personal problems and is under great *strain*. (個人的な問題が多々あって，とても [精神的に] 緊張している) (OALD⁵) [抽象概念; great は情緒的 (☞ 4.4.3.4)]
    b. Big meals put *a* great *strain* on the body's digestive processes, and this can rob the rest of the body of energy. (大食は身体の消化過程に大きな負担をかけるので，身体の他の部分のエネルギーを奪いかねない) (RD 99/11: 115) [一時的な strain]

(30) a. Periods of great *surplus* were followed by periods of shortage. (大変なもの余り期間のあとにはもの不足の期間がつづいた) (OALD⁵)
    b. The chemical industry has *a* large and growing trade *surplus*. (化学産業は多額な，しかも増加中の，貿易黒字を抱えている) (CIDE) [分野限定 (= 個別事例)]
    c. There is *a surplus* of staff in some departments of the company. (会社のいくつかの部門ではスタッフが余っている) (CIDE) [*of*-phrase による限定 (☞ 4.4.1)]

(31) a. *Tax* will be deducted automatically from your salary. (税金は給与から自動的に天引きされる) (CIDE) [制度]
    b. *A* sales *tax* is chargeable on most goods. (ほとんどの商品に売上税が課せられる) (OALD⁵) [個別の税]
    c. It is a common fallacy that *a* heavy *tax* on cars will solve all London's transport problems. (車への重税が L の輸送問題をすべて解決するというのはよくある間違いだ) (OALD⁵) [種類]

(32) a. We set sail (for France) at high *tide*. (満潮時に (フランスに) 出帆した) (OALD⁵) [at noon/midnight と同様に１点ととらえ，時間的広がり非含意]
    参考: High tide or high water is <u>the time</u> when the sea or a river reaches its highest level and comes furthest up the beach or the bank. (満潮または高潮とは，海あるいは川が最高の水位に達し，岸や土手の１番

上にあがるときのことだ) (CIDE)

    b. *A* flood *tide* is the movement of the sea inwards to the coast. (満ち潮とは海岸内部への海水の移動のことだ) (CIDE) [開始と終了を含意する, 個別的な潮の移動]

(33) a. (= IV-56, a) For a girl who had never been aware of *time*, I learned to watch the clock closely – and live by it. (RD 99/10: 130) [抽象概念]

    b. At Christmas he found *time* to have a cup or two of holiday cheer and don his hollyshaped bow tie. (クリスマスには暇を見つけて, 祝い酒を１, ２杯楽しみ, ヒイラギ型のボータイを締めた) (RD 97/2: 77) [開始・終了は非含意]

    c. I was at the library every evening until closing *time* at ten. (毎夕 10 時の閉館時間まで図書館にいた) (RD 96/3: 137) [１点ととらえ, 時間的広がり非含意；cf. high tide]

    d. Standing outside, staring at the summit, it is *a* long *time* before I have calmed my thoughts enough to realise that the General is right. (外に立って山頂を眺め, 長い時間ののち, 考えが落ち着いてきて, 将軍は正しいのだとわかった) (RD 99/11: 73) [期間含意]

(34) a. Short hair has come back into *vogue*. (ショートヘアが復活して流行している) (OALD⁵)

    b. The film created *a vogue* for 1950s-style rock 'n roll. (その映画は 50 年代式のロックンロールの流行を作り出した) (CIDE) [一時的]

(35) a. There isn't enough *wind* to fly a kite. (凧揚げができるほどは風がない) [風力に重点] (CIDE)

    b. There was *a* light *wind* blowing. (微風が吹いていた) [一時的現象；通例, 形容詞をともなう] (CIDE) [cf. fog/rain]

参考文献

【辞書・事典】
Cambridge Dictionary of American English (CDAE)
Cambridge International Dictionary of English (CIDE)
Collins Cobuild English Dictionary (CCED, 第1版および第3版)
Longman Dictionary of American English (LDOAE)
Longman Dictionary of Contemporary English (LDOCE, 第3版)
MacMillan English Dictionary (McED) [本書ではMcEDと略す；MEDは，本来，Middle English Dictionary の省略形]
Newbury House Dictionary (NHD)
NTC's American English Learner's Dictionary (NTC)
Oxford Advanced Learner's Dictionary (OALD, 第5版および第6版)
Oxford English Dictionary 2 (OED, 第2版)
Encyclopaedia Britannica 2001 (EB 01)
Grolier Multimedia Encyclopedia (GME)
(以上の辞書・事典は，CCED[1] と NHD を除いて，CD-ROM で利用可能)

【コーパス】
The British National Corpus. [http://sara.natcorp.ox.ac.uk/lookup.html] (BNC)
COBUILD English Collocations on CD-ROM. 1995. London: HarperCollins. (ConCD-ROM)
ICAME Collection of English Language Corpora. 2nd ed. 1999. CD-ROM. The HIT Centre University of Bergen. [Brown, LOB を含む]

【言及した著書・論文】
安藤貞雄. 1969. 『英語語法研究』 東京：研究社出版.
Berry, Roger. 1993. *Articles*. London: HarperCollins. [英語冠詞論への入門書として最適]
Biard, A. 1908. *L'Article Défini dans les principales langues européennes* I. *L'Article "the" et les caracteristiques différentielles de son emploi*. Bordeaux: Gounouilhon. (厨川文夫 (抄訳). (1936) 1957. 『定冠詞論』 東京：研究社)
Christophersen, Paul. 1939. *The Articles: A Study with Their Theory and Use in English*. Copenhagen: Einar Munksgaard.
Heaton, J. B. & Turton N. D. 1987. *Longman Dictionary of Common Errors*. London: Longman.
Hewson, John. 1972. *Article and Noun in English*. The Hague: Mouton.

樋口昌幸. 1993. 「冠詞の説明文法：一試案」（『近代英語研究』編集委員会（編）．『近代英語の諸相』所収）. 東京：英潮社.

樋口昌幸. 1998. 「英語の論文における冠詞の用法について」（『広島外国語教育研究』, Vol. 1, pp. 105-120; 樋口・ゴールズベリ. 1999.『英語論文表現事典』（東京：北星堂書店）に再録）

広瀬泰三. (1955) 1973. 『名詞』（大塚高信ほか（編）『英文法シリーズ』（第一集）所収）. 東京：研究社出版.

石田秀雄. 2002. 『わかりやすい英語冠詞講義』 東京：大修館書店.

Jespersen, Otto. (1947) 1965. *A Modern English Grammar.* Part VII. London: George Allen & Unwin. [*MEG*] [用例豊富；冠詞の用法の史的変化にも言及がある]

Kałuża, Henryk. 1981. *The Use of Articles in Contemporary English.* Heidelberg: Groos.

金口儀明. 1970. 『英語冠詞活用辞典』 東京：大修館書店.

Langacker, Ronald W. 1991. *Concept, Image, and Symbol: The Cognitive Basis of Grammar.* New York & Berlin: Mouton de Gruyter.

松本安弘・松本アイリン. 1976. 『あなたの英語診断辞書』 東京：北星堂書店.

織田稔. 1982. 『存在の様態と確認——英語冠詞の研究』 東京：風間書房.

織田稔. 2002. 『英語冠詞の世界——英語の「もの」の見方と示し方』 東京：研究社.

Ogden, C. K. & I. A. Richards. (1923) 1969. *The Meaning of Meaning.* London: Routledge & Kegan Paul. (石橋幸太郎（訳）. 1972. 『意味の意味』 東京：新泉社)

Quirk, Randolf. et al. 1985. *A Comprehensive Grammar of the English Language.* London: Longman.

Swan, Michael. 1980, 1995. *Practical English Usage.* Oxford: Oxford University Press.

Ullmann, Stephen. 1962. *Semantics: An Introduction to the Science of Meaning.* Oxford: Basil Blackwell. (池上嘉彦（訳）. 1969. 『言語と意味』 東京：大修館書店)

安井稔. 2000. 「関係詞節とその先行詞」（『英語青年』, Vol. CXLVI, No. 9 (2000年, 12月号), pp. 22-26)

山梨正明. 1995. 『認知文法論』 東京：ひつじ書房.

索引

→ に先行される数字は関連の章または節を示す。
→ に先行されない数字はページを示す。

【欧文索引】

A
a（前置詞） → 9.4.1
Abbey　324
abduction　186
ability　40, 173
abnormality　215
abortion　192
abrasion　215
absence　130
absolution　217, 218
abstract　284, 285
abundance　148
Academy　348
accomplishment　218
accordion　34
accusation　435
accused　273
-ache　210
acid　393
acknowledgement　235
acne　214
acquaintance　144
act
　　act the fool　277
action　40, 163
activity　180, 408
adjustment　408
admiration　408
adoption　408, 409
advice　→ 2.3.3.3.4

affection　147
affinity　235
after
　　A after A　108
afternoon　409
against
　　A against A/B　108, 109
age　126, 127
agility　150, 151
agony　140
agoraphobia　198
agreement　167, 172, 220
Aids　200
air　149
airfield/Airfield　333, 334
Air Force Base　353
airport/Airport　22, 353
Alexander the Great　279
Alhambra　325
allegory　42
allergy　206
Allies　261
alligator　32
altitude　137
altitude sickness　200
ambition　173
ambivalence　409
ambulance　77
Americas　256
amniocentesis　193, 235
amputation　190
anaemia　197

anaesthetic 235
analogy 327
anarchy 60
anathema 239
anchor 104
and → 9.1.1
  and の省略 382
Andromeda Galaxy 263
angina pectoris 201
Angkor Wat 324
anthrax 201
antibiotic 393
antipathy 185, 409
antiseptic 393
aphasia 197
appendectomy 201
apple 27, 34
application 235
appointment 83
aptitude 143
Aquarius 263
area 134
aromatherapy 192
arrangement 83
arrest 186
arrogance 409
art 276
arteriosclerosis 201
arthritis 198, 199
arthrogryposis 199
artifice 235
as
  譲歩 → 9.4.2.1
  前置詞 66
  as much as 71
asbestosis 198
ascent 37
ash 31
asparagus 48, 49
aspirin 52
assault 186

asthma 199, 201
astringent 235
astrology 60
astronomy 60
athlete's foot 201
Atoll 307
attachment 410
attitude 410
auction 83, 218
autobiography 42
automobile 38, 275
autopsy 193
autumn 103, 287, 410
Avenue 250, 313
average 134, 277, 278
Award 268

B

baby 70
back 284, 288
backache 210
background 410
backstroke 283, 284
bagpipe 76
Balkans 257
ballet 276
balm 236
bamboo 393
banana 27, 34
banjo 34
Bank 271
barge 78
baseball 57
basketball 57
bass 73, 296
basset hound 38
bat 104
battle 218
Bay 301
be 41
beach 37

Beach 302
Beatle 254
Beatles 253
beauty 151
bed 104
bedroom 275
bedtime 410
beech 32
beef 35
beer 52
beginning 284
belief 167
bends 259
bergamot orange 29
Berlin Wall 271
Berry (1993) 88, 132, 196, 249, 251, 276, 291, 314, 319
between → 9.2.1
   between sg and pl 373
Biard (1957) 49
bias 144
Bible 263, 264
bicycle 78, 275, 292
Big Dipper 262
Bight 301
Bikini Atoll 307
bingo 58
biography 42
biology 60
biopsy 193
birth 80, 177, 445
   → childbirth
bite 58
   throat bite 58
bladder 287
bleach 394
blending 290
bloom
   in bloom 110
blossom
   in blossom 110

blue 157
blues 259
boar
   wild boar 32
boat 78, 292
bone 51
boredom 151
botany 60
both → 9.2.1
bottle 148, 275
Boulevard 313
boundedness 11
bourbon 53, 394
Bowl
   Super Bowl 265
brain 288
Braves 253
breach 186
breakfast 153, 154
breaststroke 283, 284
brick 32
bridge 58
Bridge 317, 318
brilliance 151
broccoli 48
bronchitis 198
brunch 153, 155
bud
   in bud 110
burglary 186
burial 218, 411
bus 66, 78, 291
business 125
butterfly 283, 284
by 66, 77
   by＋名詞句 → 3.7

C
cab 78
cabbage 27
Caesarean 190

C/caesarean section   86
cake   36
calm   411
calmness   411
camel   79
camera   87
camouflage   236
camp   218
campus   91, 95
Canal   305
cancer   206, 207
   cancers   260
cane   275
canvas   104
Canyon   309, 310
capability   173
capacity   134, 143
Cape   308
cappuccino   53
car   292
car park   125
cards   60
career   284
carjacking   187
Carnival   266
carpet   36
carrot   28, 30, 49
cart   79
carving   47
case   268
cassette   104
Castle   323
casualty   91, 92
cat   33
catalogue   83
cat and mouse   72
cataract   204
catch   58
category
   low-/high-risk category   284, 285
Cathedral   324

Catholic Church   270, 324
cat's cradle   58
catwalk   275
cauliflower   28, 48
cause   214, 423, 462
Cave   333
cavernoma   205
cedar   32, 36
cello   74, 296
Cemetery   332, 334
Center   347
ceramics   276
cerebral palsy   203
cha-cha   283
Championship   265
Championships   266
Champs-Élysées   314
Channel   303
chaos   61
chapel   92, 95
Chapel   324
charades   60
charge   186, 189
chauffer   237
check   → cheque
checkers   60
cheerfulness   163
cheese   394
chemical   236
chemistry   60
chemotherapy   192
cheque   83
chess   58
chicken   30, 32
child   104
childbirth   411
childhood   411
chilli   28
chocolate   53
cholera   201
chorus   45, 46

Christmas 267
Christophersen (1939) 11, 327, 351
chronology 42
church 92, 95
Church 270, 275, 324
Cinema 343
circle 215
Circus 330
cirrhosis 199
clap 272
clarinet 74, 296
class 90, 91
claustrophobia 198
clearance 134
climate 412
Clinic 332
cloth 53
cloud 51
clove 28
clown 277
clutter 110, 149
　in a clutter 110f.
coach 79
coal 51
coast 38
Coast 301
Cockney 63
cocktail 57
coconut 28
coffee 53
cognac 53, 54
coin 221
cold 207
　common cold 273
Cold War 271
collage 47
college 92, 95
College 347
coma 208
combat 412
comedy 43

command 150
commander 67
commission 24, 25
common cold 273
community 122
commutation 236
compassion 412
composer 375
computer 82, 87, 88, 297
　PC 82
conception 144
concomitance 382
concussion 208
condition 144, 171, 173, 206
confidence 151
confusion 61
Congos 257
Congress 23
conjunctivitis 198
conscience 412
consensus 236
conspiracy 187
consultant
　management consultant 71
contempt 413
contrast 144
controversy 236
conversation 236, 445
convict 186
conviction 167
convoy 148
convulsions 260
cook
　second cook 66
cop 71
cord 114
correct 286
correspondence 413
costume 54
countenance 41
court 92, 93, 95, 104, 105

486

Cove   301
cow   35
cowboy   72
crab   30
cradle   274
　cat's cradle   58
cramp   205
Crater   312
craving   140, 173
crawl   283
cream   57
creek/Creek   304, 305
cribbage   58
crime   187
critical condition   206
cross-examination   445
crossword puzzle   297
crow   63
cuisine   164
culture   165
Cup
　World Cup   265
cup and saucer   234
curfew   127, 470
curiosity   413
currency   413
curry   54
custom   220
cystic fibrosis   199

D

Dakotas   257
dance   276, 445
dark   285
darkness   413
day   128, 129
deadline   414
death   445
debate   445
debt   137, 144
deceased   273

deception   187
decision   40, 171, 174, 414
deck   22
decrease   285
defeat   414
deficiency   144, 197
definition   83
deformation   208, 209
deformity   208, 209
delivery   445
democracy   221
deodorant   394
dependence   414
dependency   209
depression   209, 236
Depression   270
depth   134, 151
descent   414
desert   114, 115, 336, 337
Desert   335
design   47
desire   174
despair   414
desperation   151, 152
dessert   153, 155, 156
destruction   415
detergent   394
deterioration   415
determination   40, 164, 415
determiner　→　限定詞
diabetes   199, 201, 202, 203
dialogue   446
diameter   134
diamond   54
diarrhea   197
dictatorship   222
diet   156, 157
difference   177
dinner   153, 155, 156
direction   415
director   66

disability 403
disabled 273
disappointment 415
disease
  guinea-worm disease 200
  heart disease 200, 203
  liver disease 199
disenchantment 236
dishwasher 107, 297, 438
disinfectant 394
Disney World 353
Disneyland 353
disqualification 236
dissatisfaction 140
distance 121, 122, 123, 285
divorce 446
doctor 23, 72
dog 33, 70
donkey 71
double bass 296
doubt 178, 183
down
  belly down → 9.5.3
Down syndrome 200
downtown 24
dozen 269
drama 43
dread 415, 416
dress 54
drink 54
Drive 313
dryness 403
DTs 259
duty 174
dysentery 201
dysfunction 210

E
eagerness 403, 416
ear 288, 290
earache 210

earn
  earn IO DO in 身体部位 289
earshot 123
earth 23, 262, 264
Earth 23, 264
ease 403
Easter 267
Ebola 201
editor 66
education 416, 446
effect 416
effort 446
egg 30
Eiger 310
elderly 273
election 446
elephantiasis 203
Élysée 329
embarrassment 215
emerald 57
emergency 38
Emmy 268
emotion 416, 417
empathy 219
emphasis 166, 466
emptiness 166, 403, 417
encephalitis 199
enclosure 115, 435
encouragement 216
end 105, 284
energy 417
enough → 3.3
ensign 67
enterprise 125
entertainment 435
entrance 435
entry 446
environment 417
equator 263
erection 96, 97
erosion 446

error 220
eruption 446, 447
escape (n.) 435, 436, 447
escape (v.) 178: → 否定
escort 447
estimate 84
estrangement 127
eternity 127
euphemism 43
euphoria 417
euro 269
evacuation 447
evaluation 447
Everest 310
evidence → 2.3.3.3.5
examination 447
example 84, 466
excursion 131
execution 189
exercise 448
exile 131
existence 417, 418
expectancy 134, 135, 138
expectation 221
expedition 131
experience 185, 418
explanation 178
exploration 448
exposure 448
Express 338
expression 43, 145
Expressway 313
extension 84
extra 227
eye 288, 291

F
face 97, 288, 289
fact
  Fact is → 9.4.2.2
failure 436, 448

kidney/heart failure 200
  renal failure 200
faith 418
fallacy 167
Falls 306
familiarity
  stages of familiarity 12, 316:
  → *MEG*
family 23, 253
famine 219
fantasy 171
farce 43
fare 418
farewell 160
farm 115
farmland 115
fascination 418
fashion 216, 418, 419
fate 221
fault 174, 221
favo(u)r 222
fax/facsimile 82
fear 140, 171
feeling 140, 167, 420
ferocity 152
ferry 291
fertilizer 395
Festival 266, 267
fever 211
  yellow fever 203
few/a few 179
fiction 45
field 115
Field(s) 258, 354
fight 448
film 395
fire 222
firefighter 67
fish 30
fittest 274
flame 222

flatulence 202
flavo(u)r 420
flavo(u)ring 395
fleece 52
flesh 284
flight 448
Florida Marlins 254
flower
　in flower 110
flu 213, 272: → influenza
fluctuation 318: → 揺れ
flute 34, 297
focus 470
fog 124, 149, 471
food 395
fool
　act the fool 277
　fool as I am → 9.4.2.1
football 58, 59
force 216
forest 116
Forest 337
forgery 436
form 215, 216
　a form of 39
fortune 221
fox 5, 34
fox-trot 282, 283
fragrance 471
franc 269
fraud 188
freedom 403, 404, 420
freshness 181
friendship 471
fright 219, 436
from
　from A to B 107, 108
front 284
frost 181, 395
frost nip 202, 215
frostbite 200, 202, 215

froth 436
fuel 395
fulfillment 404
function 97
fur 54
fuss 180
future 286

G
Galaxy 263
gallon 269
gangrene 202
Garden 325
　Botanic Garden 325
　Gardens 314, 325
gardener 237
garlic 49
gas 396
Gates 261
generosity 145, 404
genius 143
genocide 188
get 214, 462
gift 143
gin and tonic 233
ginger 49
gingivitis 198
gippy tummy 237
give
　give IO DO in 身体部位 289
glacier 36
gland
　pituitary gland 290
glass 52, 148
glioblastoma 202
gloom 239
goiter 211
golf 58
goodbye 160
Gorge 309, 310
gout 202

government   471, 472
gown   36
grade   250
grammar   404
Grand Canal   305
Grand Canyon   309, 310
Grand Prix   265, 266
grandeur   404
grasslands   258
gratitude   219
grave   274
gray   157
Great
   Alexander the Great   273, 279
Great Barrier Reef   271
Great Bear   262
Great Plains   258
Great Wall   271
green   158, 159
green light   287
grief   167, 466
grievance   467
grin   61
ground   116
growth   436
grunt   162
guarantee   138, 145, 168
guard   97, 139
guinea worm   202
   guinea-worm disease   200
guitar   73, 74, 297
Gulf
   Persian Gulf   300
Gulf War   271

H
habit   467
habitat   116
hagiography   43, 44
half   → 3.3
halibut   31

hand   84
   pen in hand   → 9.5.2
handball   59
hanging   189
hangover   205
happiness   404
harbo(u)r   97
Harbo(u)r   302
hardback   436, 437
hardiness   405
hardship   220
harmony   420
hatred   140
have   214, 449, 452, 462
haze   124, 208
head   288, 289
Head   308
headache   211
heart   105, 288, 289
   heart and soul   376
heart disease   200, 203
heart failure   200
heartburn   202
heat   405
Heaton & Turton (1987)   75, 346
heaven   124
height   135
heir   66, 67
helicopter   81, 87
hell   124
hello   160, 162
help   71, 217
Hemisphere   263
hepatitis   199
herbicide   396
heritage   145, 421
hernia   205
Hewson (1972)   298
hiccups   259
high   208
high blood pressure   203

Highlands 258
high-risk category 285
Highway 313
Himalayas 257
hiss 47
history 44, 60, 130, 145
hockey 59
holiday 129
homicide 188
honour 174
hope 141
horn 35, 251
Horn 308
horror 141, 405, 421, 437
horse 71
   horse and buggy 79
hose 114
hospital 93, 95, 96
Hospital 330, 331, 354
host 72
hostage 67
hour 128, 268, 269
house 6, 37, 88
humiliation 177
humour 237
hunger 141
hurry 459
hurt 36
Hutu 255
Hyde Park 328
hydrophobia 198
hyperbole 44
hypertension 201
hypothermia 197
hysterectomy 194
hysteria 197
hysterics 203, 204

I
ideal 277, 278
identification 62, 145, 146, 448, 449

identity 146, 437
illness 38, 459
   mental illness 200
illustration 146, 437
imagination 421
imbalance 460
immunity 460
impact 449
impairment 211
impatience 181
imperfect 274
imperfection 437
importance 40, 41
improvement 222, 223
impulse 239, 460
impurity 437
in 127, 130, 140, 142, 144, 146, 461
   A in A 109
   in a clutter 110
   in bloom/blossom etc. 110
   in-phrase 467
   pen in hand → 9.5.2
inability 174
inaccuracy 467
inch 269
incontinence 202
inconvenience 168, 460
increase 285
incubator 297
indigestion 202
indulgence 437
industry 126
inevitable 273
infection 212
infidelity 460
infinity 149
influence 97, 98, 164
influenza 202: → flu
information 172: → 2.3.3.3.6
informer 77
inhaler 84

inheritance 84, 85
injection 85
injury 178, 212
injustice 174
Inn 341
innovation 217
insecticide 396
insight 98
insomnia 197
inspection 449
inspiration 438, 467
instability 461
instinct 143, 175, 421
Institute 347
institution 88
Institution 346
instruction 175
instrument 382
insurance 178, 237
intellect 41, 421, 438
intelligence 6, 405
interest 237, 467
Internet 270
interpretation 468
interrogation 421
interruption 181
interview 237
intestinal obstruction 205
intimacy 421
introspection 422
intuition 168
invasion 449, 450
invention 172
investigation 450
investment 472
iron 52
irregularity 438
irritation 212, 405, 422, 438
Islamic Revolution 270
islands 258

J
jail 93, 95
Jail 352
jam 132
Japanese islands 258
jaundice 202
jaunt 131
Jeep 79
Jespersen → *MEG*
jihad 450
job
　the job of 67
joker 69
Journal 350
journey 131
joy 461
judgment 98
juice 55
Jungfrau 310
jungle 116
justification 468

K
Kałuża (1981) 183
Kensington Gardens 328
kick
　give IO a kick in 身体部位 289
kidnapping 188
kidney failure 200
Kilimanjaro 311
killing 188
Killing Fields 258
kindergarten 93
kindness 175
knee 288
knife 275
knife and fork 233
knowledge 150, 172, 405
Koran 263

L

labo(u)r 422
Labrador 38, 39
lack 150, 180
ladder 79
lady 69
   play the lady 277
Lake 299, 300
Lakota 255
lamb 5, 31
land 116, 117
landing 450
Lane 313
Langacker (1991) 11
La Nina 422
laugh 61
laughter → 2.3.3.3.2
law 468
lawn 117
lead 396
leakage 450
left 285
Left Bank 271
legend 44, 170
lemon 33, 37
length 135, 149
Lent 267
leprosy 202, 203
leukemia 197
level 422
liberty 175
libido 423
library/Library 96, 346
licence/license 175
lieutenant 67
life 423, 472
light 423
   green light 287
limelight 275
limit 11
line 390, 391
   telephone lines 87
Liner 338
lingo 406
linguistics 60
lipstick 396
liquid 396
little/a little 179
living 472
loan 451
lobster 31
loin 33
longing 141, 176
loss 451
lotion 397
love 141, 147
low-risk category 284
loyalty 141
luck 221
lumpectomy 196
lunch 153, 154, 156
lupus 203
Luxembourg 329
luxury 438

M

machine 69, 85
mahjong 59
mahogany 32
main street 22
majesty 423
make 447, 449
malaise 213
malaria 197, 203
Maldives 259
Mall 314
malnutrition 203
management consultant 71
manager 65, 66
   general manager 65
manic 274
Marathon 264, 265, 266

Marburg   201
margarine   397
market   96, 105
marriage   451
Mars   252, 264
marsh   117
mass   438
massacre   188
massage   190
mastectomy   194
Masters   266
math   60
Matterhorn   310
maturity   468
May Day   267
mayor   66
meadow   117
meal   155
meaning   468
measles   203, 204, 259
medication   397
medicine   397
meditation   438
MEG   12, 22, 39, 249, 315, 316, 327, 335, 344, 351, 362, 381, 391
melon   28
memory   138, 165, 438, 439
meningitis   199
mental illness   200
mention   439
mercy   168, 439
mess   461
metabolism   423
metal   397
metaphor   44
metre   269
migraine   212
military   273
Milky Way   263
mink   34, 35
miscarriage   451

mischief   183, 439
misfortune   439
mist   124
mistake   85
mockery   472
mode   424
Mona Lisa   279
Monceau   329
monologue   451
month   269
mood   424
moon   262, 263
moonlight   286
morality   424
more   → 3.3
  more NP_1 than NP_2 71
mosaic   47
mosque   91
Motel   341
motion   424, 452
motorbike   79
mountain   117
Mountains   → 8.2.5
mouth   69, 85
movement   98, 452
movies   276
mumps   260
mundane   285
murder   188
murmur   162
muscle   52
Museum   346
music   424
mustache   382, 383
mutation   439
myalgia   213
myomectomy   194
mystery   469
myth   170

索引 *495*

N

name 146
nature 425
  second nature 250
nausea 198, 406
necessity 439
need 146, 147
neither A nor B → 9.2.1
nerve 288
Netherlands 257
neurosis 199
New York Mets 254
news 172: → 2.3.3.3.6
Niagara Falls 306
night 129, 286
nightcap 156
Nobel Prize 267
noise 473
nominal part 5
nor 377: → 9.2.1
North Pole 262
North Star 262
nose 33, 214, 289
notice 439, 440
novel 45
novelty 440
Nullarbor 336
numbness 212
nurse 72

O

oak 32
obligation 176, 178, 461
oboe 75
observation 168, 425
obsession 469
obstruction 181, 205
occasion 425, 440
occupation
  by occupation 68
Ocean 299
octopus 31
odo(u)r 473
odyssey 131
of-phrase 40, 41, 42, 46, 108, 148, 150, 249, 250, 308, 346, 350, 382: → 4.4.1
office 90
officer 18
  patrol officer 66
Ogden & Richards (1969) 11
oil 397
OK 162
onion 28, 29
Open 264
opera 45, 46, 276
operation 195
opinion 469
opportunity 473
opposition 440
or 377: → 9.1.2
orange 29, 158
orbit 473
ore 397
orgasm 452
orphanage 96: → 孤児院名
orthography 39
Oscar 268
oscillation 185
osteoporosis 199
outrage 452
owner
  part owner 67

P

pace 425
paddle steamer 80
paddy 125
pain 461, 462
Palace 322, 323
paleness 159
pallor 159
palsy 203

Pamirs 258
pandemonium 61
panic 111, 237, 462
paradise/Paradise 125
paralysis 213
paranoia 197
park
　car park 125
Park 326, 327
parking lot 125
Parliament 23
part 117, 118, 237
participation 452, 453
partnership 440
Pass 332, 334
passage 440
passion 148
Passover 267
paste 397, 398
patchwork 47, 48
paucity 180
Pavilion 323, 404
PC 82: → computer
peace 462
peach 29
peacock
　play the peacock 277
Pearly Gates 261
pearwood 32
pedigree 425
peer 178
pen 274
pencil 55
Peninsula 308
people 256
peppermint 34
per → 9.4.1
perception 98
perfect 277, 278
perfection 182
performance 99

perfume 398, 425
personality 426
perspective 473
perspiration 398
pesticide 398
philosophy 60
phobia 198
phone 82: → telephone
photography 276
physics 60
physiotherapy 192
pianist 375
piano 74, 75, 297
Piccadilly 330
pie 55
piece
　a piece of 37
Pier 302
pig 35
pilgrimage 132
pimple 214
pine
　pitch pine 32
pineapple 29
pipe 114
pituitary gland 290
pity 141, 142, 168
pizza 55
place 118, 119
placement 237
plague 273
plains/Plains 258
plane 291
Plateau 336
play (n.) 440, 441
play (v.) 296
　play φ doctor → 3.4
　play φ 楽器名 → 3.5
　play the clown → 8.4.1.3
　play the 楽器名 → 8.6.2
pleasure 176, 426, 441

Plough   262
pneumonia   197
poetry   51
Point   308
poison   398
poisoning   189
poker   59
Pole   262
policy   176, 426
polio   203
politeness   406
politics   60
polka   283
polo   59
Pond   300
pontiff
   supreme pontiff   272
pony   78
pool   59
poor   273, 274
pork   35
port   99
position   119
   the position of   67
possibility   180, 474
posture   463
potato   30
pound   269, 270
poverty   150
powder   237
power   426
practice   453
prairie   119
prayer   46
predictable   273
preference   142
pregnancy   453
prejudice   148, 463
prescription   441
present   127, 128
preservative   133

preserver   133
president   65
press   426
pressure   203
pretence   453
price   135, 426
pride   463
principle   168, 474
priority   441
prison   93, 94, 95, 352
Prison   352
privilege   177
prize/Prize   250
   Nobel Prize   267
   Nobel peace prize   268
probability   169, 181, 474
problem
   Problem is   → 9.4.2.2
professor   67
profile   441
profit   135, 138
progress   → 2.3.3.3.7
promise   453
promotion   453
proof   61, 441
property   119
prophecy   99
proportion   474
prosperity   426
prostatectomy   194
protection   441, 442
protein   398
psoriasis   201
publication   442
pulp   237
punishment   190
purchase   454
puritanism   427
purpose   463, 464
pursuit   427
pygmy   255

Q

quality 427
Quay 302
queen 65
Queen Elizabeth 2 320
Quirk et al. (1985) 107, 298, 371

R

rabies 203
racquetball 59
radio 82, 297
raft 80
rage 464
rain 474
rainfall 135
Ranch 332, 334
range 136
Range 258
rank
   the rank of 67, 68
ransom 136, 138
rapid/Rapid 304, 305
rash 56, 212
reach 123(n.), 452(v.)
reaction 454
reality 474
reason 69, 469
rebellion 454
rebirth 427
reception 99
recession 454
recognition 169
recollection 100
recommendation 169
reconciliation 464
recovery 100, 454
red 158, 398, 399
Red River Valley 309
reduction 138, 454
redundancy 442
reflection 442
reform 427
refuge 442
Regent's Park 327, 328
reincarnation 442
relaxation 464
Relay 264
relief 176
religion 475
remission 237
Renaissance 270
renal failure 200
repellent 399
replacement 443
reply 443
reputation 85
rescue 455
resemblance 428
resentment 239, 406, 428
reservation 125, 455
reserve 182
resistance 455
resolution 100
respect 464
response 455
responsibility 464
restaurant 341
retina 288
retirement 428
retreat 455
revelation 469
revenge 428
reverence 428
Review 351
revolt 455
revolution 455
Revolution
   Cultural Revolution 252
   Islamic Revolution 270
rhubarb 49
rhyme 45
rhythm 429

ribbon 37
rich 273
risk 13, 177, 443
river 85
River 304
road 37, 85, 275
Road 313, 315
roar 456
robbery 189
rock 32
Rockies 257
Rocky Mountains 257
role
   the role of 68
Rolling Stones 253
romance 45, 475
Romans 255
room 119
root 100
rope 114, 237
Route 312
routine 470
ruble 269
rudder 291
ruin 443
rumba 283
rumo(u)r 169, 170
run 286
runny nose 214
rupture 205
Russian roulette 59

S
sacrifice 475
sadness 406
safari 132
sage 69
salad 399
sale 456
salmon 31
salvation 443

same → 9.4.2.3
sanctuary 119
satellite 82
satisfaction 406, 407, 429
Saturn 264
sauce 399
saxophone 75
scandal 238
scent 86
schedule 475
schizophrenia 197
scholar 71
scholarship 475
school 94, 95
School 348
sclerosis 199
Scorpio 263
Scorpion 262
scrap
   scraps/a scrap of 36, 38
screen 120, 276
sculpture 48
sea 429
Sea 299
Sea World 354
search 456
season 129
second 269
security 465
Seine 304
seizures 261
sensation 465
sensibility 100
sensor 87
sensuality 465
separation 238
serenity 429
sergeant 66
service 126
shade 120
shadow 120

shakes 259
shame 170, 429
shape 443
sheepskin 238
shelter 100, 101
sheriff 66
shift 138
ship 23, 79, 80: → 船名
shipment 149
shock 465, 475, 476
shop 89
shore 120
shortage 180, 182
shoulder 289
shyness 430
sickness 465
   altitude sickness 200
   radiation sickness 200
side
   bright side 285
siege 456
sign
   V/victory sign 47
signal 101
silence 8, 130, 183
Silk Road/Route 312
simplicity 430, 465, 466
sincerity 430
singular 285
Sioux 255
siren 69
site 105, 106
size 430
skill 407
skin 430
skunk 33
sky 124, 262, 430
SkyTrain 292
slaughterhouse 276
sleep 130, 430, 431, 456
sleep debt 137

slice
   a slice of 36, 37
smallpox 204, 260
smell 101
smile 61
smoothness 6
snake 69
sniffle(s) 260
snow 431
soap 399
society 122, 123
sociology 60
soda 399
song 46
sorrow 431, 443
soul 284
   heart and soul 376
sound 86, 476
soup 400
space 122
spasm 205
speech 101
speed 136
spider 33
spirit 147, 238
spot 214
spotlight 275
Spratlys 258
spring 103
Square 330
staff 136
stage 106, 276
stages of familiarity 12, 316
stammer 162
Star
   North Star 262
Station 335, 353, 355
statistics 60
status 431
steak 35, 400
stink 473

stomachache 211
stone 32
stop 101
storm 86
strain 177, 476
Strait 303
Strand 314
strategy 470
strawberry 33
stream/Stream 101, 102, 305
Street 313
strength 152
stretch
　this stretch of 37
stretcher 80
strike 238
stroke 213
struggle 456, 457
study 457
　study φ 楽器名 → 3.5
style 419
sublime 285
subtype 86
subway 291
success 457
suffer from 214, 462
summer 103, 287
sun 262, 263
Super Bowl 265
superintendent 66
supper 153, 154
support 443
surgery 194, 195
surplus 476
surprise 466
survival 444
suspension 236
suspicion 170, 431
swamp 120
Swan (1980) 274
Swan (1995) 76, 96, 196, 210, 274

sweat 55
swing 282, 283
sword 274
synagogue 91
syndrome 200, 201
syrup 400

T
table 106
Taj Mahal 325
takeoff 432
talent 143
talk 457
tango 34, 283
target 106
taste 142, 432
tax 476
taxi 292
tea 49, 154, 155
teacher 71
telephone 83, 297: → phone
telephone lines 87
temperature 136
Temple 324
tenderness 142
tennis 59
tension 407, 432
termination 193
territory 121
terror 142, 407
testament 238
testimony 238
Thames 304
thank you 160, 162
thanks 160
that 節 → 4.4.4
theater/theatre 106, 276, 343
theft 189
theory 170, 220
therapy 192
thickness 136, 137

thinness 41, 407
thirst 432
though
　譲歩 → 9.4.2.1
thought 102
thread 114
threat 466
throat 210, 214
throat bite 58
thrush 203
thud 161
thunder 149
thyroid 24
tide 476, 477
tile 32
timber 52, 400
time 128, 477
tin 56
to
　A to A 109
togetherness 432
tomato 29
ton 269
tone 407, 432, 433
tonsillectomy 196
tonsillitis 201
toothache 210
torment 444
touch 102
tour 106, 131, 433
Tour de France 265
tow 457
towel 56
Tower 320, 321
town 22
trace 179
trade 42
　by trade 68
tradition 176, 470
Trafalgar Square 330
traffic → 2.3.3.3.3

Trail 312
train 78, 80, 291
training 433
traitor 77
transfusion 190
transmission 102, 238, 433
transplant 191
transplantation 191
trauma 213
travel 131
treatment 191
Trench 309
trial 139
tribe 256
trip 131
triumph 457
trouble
　Trouble is → 9.4.2.2
trout 31
truce 463
truck 80
trust 147
truth 171
tube 114, 291
tuberculosis 203
Tuileries 329
tummy 238
Tunnel 316
turbulence 61
turkey 33
turmoil 238
turn → 3.6
Tutsi 255
TV 298
twilight 433
twist 283
type → 4.3；種類
　a type of 37
typhus 203
typical 277, 278

U

Ullmann (1962)   11
uncertainty   444
underdog   285
understatement   45
unease   165
universe   262
university   95, 96
University   347, 349
unthinkable   273
up
  belly up   → 9.5.3
upheaval   238
upon
  A upon A   109
uproar   239
urethra   287
urethral sphincter   287
use   457
utopia   125

V

V/victory sign   47
vacation   129, 130
vaccination   458
vaccine   400
Valentine's Day   267
Valley   309
value   40, 41, 137, 139, 444
vanish   179
velocity   434
veterinarian   68
via   87
victim   67
victory   458
view   182, 458
Vikings   255
viola   74, 296
violation   176, 177, 189
violin   74, 75
vision   102, 103
vitality   407, 408
vocabulary   137, 165
vocation
  by vocation   68
vogue   238, 477
volleyball   59

W

wait   139
Wall
  Berlin Wall   270
  Great Wall   271
waltz   282, 283
war   86, 87, 458
War
  civil war/Civil War   45, 86, 220
  Cold War   271
  Gulf War   271
  Napoleonic Wars   261
warfare   458, 459
warming   459
warmth   182
warning   179
waste   470
wasteland   121
watch   459
way   107
weak   274
weakness   408
wealth   149
weather   → 2.3.3.3.8
weedkiller   133
week   128
weight   137, 139
wheel   275, 291
whirl   132
whisky   401
whisky and soda   233
white   158, 159
wholeness   183
wild   286

wild boar   32
wilderness   121
Wilderness   336
William the Conqueror   279
willingness   239
wind   477
wine   132
wing   103
winter   103, 287
wisdom   170, 278, 466
wit   166
with   41, 382: → 9章 NB 6
　　with pen and notebook   → 9.5.1
　　with-phrase   146, 219
without   178, 461: → 否定
wizard   71
wood preservative   133
word   170, 173, 268
World Cup   265
worry   444
wrong   285

Y
yacht   319, 320
yard   269
year   128
yellow   158, 159
yellow fever   203
yen   270
yoghurt/yogurt   401

Z
zest   239
Zoo   345

【和文索引】

あ

挨拶ことば → 4.4.3.3
愛称 12, 22, 318, 319, 339, 340, 353, 361, 362: → 符帳, 通称
アメリカ用法 → 〈米〉用法
安藤 (1969) 289, 290
イギリス用法 → 〈英〉用法
池 299
石田 (2002) 11
一族 → 8.2.2
一門 → 8.2.2
一家 → 8.2.2
一致 18, 294
　単数一致 60, 203, 231, 259, 260, 307
　複数一致 225, 226, 368, 374
移動手段 → 3.7.1
意味 8, 11, 12, 21, 22, 33, 42, 47, 61, 66, 77, 111, 133, 150, 162, 166, 178, 179, 180, 210, 215, 235, 239, 262, 289, 300, 305, 314, 383, 419, 473: → 1章
イメージ化 8, 113, 166, 179, 208
宇宙船 → 8.7.2.2
海 → 8.7.1.1
運河 → 8.7.1.4
映画館 → 8.7.2.3
泳法名 → 8.4.2.2
〈英〉用法 6, 75, 89, 93, 100, 117, 125, 129, 206, 211, 214, 236, 239, 259, 283, 286, 326, 327, 329, 330, 354, 426, 457
駅 → 8.8.2
織田 (1982) 35
織田 (2002) 7, 35, 256
音 → 2.1.1.4
泳ぎ方 → 泳法名

か

海岸 → 8.7.1.2
海峡 → 8.7.1.3
海溝 → 8.7.1.8
外国語 315(長距離道路), 318(長大橋), 320(船名), 329(公園名), 337(森林名), 338(森林名), 344(レストラン名・劇場名), 349(学校名)
下位分類 156, 165, 209, 250, 359, 394, 400, 422, 427, 433, 450, 454, 455, 458, 459
画定 11, 62, 128, 129, 287, 298: → 囲い込み／囲い込む
学問名 → 2.3.3.2
囲い込み／囲い込む 11, 96, 97, 99, 114, 115, 116, 125: → 画定
加工前の複数 30, 34
河川 → 8.7.1.4
肩書き 349: → 1.3
楽器名 → 3.5; 8.6.2
学校名 348
かっこ内 → 9.6.1
金口 (1970) 8
川 → 河川
関係 65, 69, 71, 108, 118, 250, 282, 371, 373: → 9.2
　主語―述語関係 39
関係詞節 6, 54, 126, 128, 172, 248, 249, 250, 400: → 4.4.2; Ap.2.1
完結 5, 6, 7, 8, 11, 51, 113, 134, 162, 163, 166, 217, 225, 230, 239, 430
環礁 → 8.7.1.6
感情 → 4.4.1.2.1
感情的色彩 164
換喩的限定 → 8.4.1
慣用的表現 → 3.10; 3.11
関連語句 → 8.1.2
擬音 → 4.4.3.3
記号 → 1.6
擬人 (化／的) 169, 170, 221
季節名 103
擬態普通名詞 → 1.7
記念館 346
機能 24, 65, 66, 68, 96, 101, 102, 104, 105, 281, 290, 291, 352, 353, 354, 373,

索引 *505*

469: → 3.9; 働き
技法　47, 73
決まり文句　391: → 慣用的表現
キャプション　→ 9.6.1
宮殿　→ 8.7.1.15
急流　304: → rapid/Rapid
境界 (性／領域)　11, 298
教会名　323
競技大会　→ 8.3.2.2
峡谷　→ 8.7.1.8
強調の the　278
空間的限定　→ 4.1
空港　→ 8.8.2
具体物指示　→ 5.4.1.1; Ap.3
グループ名　→ 8.2.3
　　グループの1員　254
クレーター　312
群島　→ 8.2.5
渓谷　→ 8.7.1.8
形式　48, 218, 221, 237, 276, 436, 441, 445, 447, 449, 454, 455
刑罰　189
刑務所　→ 8.8.1; jail; prison
形容詞　8, 83, 103, 150, 159, 160, 161, 164, 166, 191, 208, 209, 225, 230, 277, 278, 356: → 4.4.3; Ap.2.2
　　the＋形容詞　→ 8.3.4
　　記述的語句　164
　　形容詞的修飾語句　→ 8.1.1
　　限定的語句　164
　　情緒的語句　164
　　所有格＋形容詞　274
　　性質形容詞　290
　　段階的形容詞　113
　　日常的形容詞　166
　　非日常的形容詞　159, 166, 471
　　枕詞　147, 150, 164, 238, 358, 408, 415, 428
ゲーム名　→ 2.3.3.1
毛皮　→ 2.1.1.5
劇場　→ 8.7.2.3

決定詞　→ 限定詞
限界　11, 247
研究所　→ 8.7.2.4
言語　→ 2.5
　　メタ言語　→ 2.4
限定　11: → 4章
　　換喩的限定　→ 8.4.1
　　空間的限定　→ 4.1
　　時間的限定　→ 4.2
　　指示範囲限定　96
　　数値による限定　→ 4.4.1.1
限定詞　5, 78, 180, 231, 235, 358
　　限定詞の省略　→ 9章
公園名　→ 8.7.1.16
高原　→ 8.7.2.1
構成物　31
交通機関　→ 8.5.3
肯定　→ 4.5.1
荒野　→ 8.7.2.1
効力　65, 470
国籍名　16
国民　→ 8.2.4
孤児院名　333, 334: → orphanage
個体　31, 32, 35, 39, 49, 51, 63, 65, 66, 70, 82, 83, 88, 281, 373
国家　→ 8.2.5
個別行為　→ 5.4.2; Ap.4.1
個別事例　→ 5章
固有名詞　11, 12, 249, 335: → 1.2; 8.7
　　固有名詞化　22
　　派生固有名詞　12, 301
　　本来固有名詞　12, 249, 353
　　転用固有名詞　262, 323
娯楽　→ 8.4.1.2
娯楽施設　→ 8.8.3
混交　290
混乱　→ 2.3.3.3.1

さ
最上級　248: → 8.11
細流　304: → creek/Creek

作品　→ 2.2
雑誌　→ 8.7.2.5
砂漠　→ 8.7.2.1
三項対立　286; → 8.5.1
山脈　→ 8.2.5
寺院名　324
時間的限定　→ 4.2
色彩語　→ 4.4.3.2
指示
　具体物指示　215
指示範囲　150
指示範囲限定　96; → 4章
指示物　11
施術　→ 5.2
施設名　→ 3.8
しもやけ　→ frostbite/frost nip
ジャンル　276; → 2.2
集合名詞
　物質集合名詞　→ 2.3.1
修飾語句　6, 16, 51, 83, 113, 133, 137, 152, 160, 163, 213, 263, 294, 356, 358, 359; → 8.1.1; 8.9; Ap.2
祝日名　267
主語−述語関係　39
手術名　193
主要部　280, 281
種類　→ 4.3
準補語　→ 3.1
賞　→ 8.3.2.4
城郭名　323
状況的同定　→ 8.3
称号　→ 1.3
常識　250, 251, 272, 287
症状　→ 5.3
状態　→ 5.4.3
情緒の色彩　164
情報　6, 8, 113, 134, 166, 172, 216, 225, 230, 239, 249, 430
省略　226, 228, 229, 255, 281, 282, 299, 346; → 9章
　構造的省略　→ 9.4

省略的文体　→ 9.6
食材　→ 2.1.1.1
食事名　→ 4.4.3.1
食堂名　342
植物　→ 2.3.1.1
植物園名　→ 8.7.1.16
処刑名　189
叙述用法　→ be, *of*-phrase, 補語
序数(詞)　72, 249; → 8.11
助数詞　→ 4.4.1.3
所有格
　pat one's shoulder　289
　所有格＋河川名　305
　所有格＋形容詞　274
城　→ 城郭名
人工衛星名　340
身体部位　→ 8.5.2
新聞　→ 8.7.2.5
親密度の度合い　12, 316; → *MEG*
人名　11, 63, 346; → 8.9
森林　→ 8.7.2.1
随伴　382
数字つき　314, 320; → 1.5
数値　121, 127, 131, 139, 195, 395
　数値による限定　→ 4.4.1.1
姿かたち　→ 2章
スペースシャトル名　339
聖域名　333
星座名　263
性質　6, 57, 63, 65
性質形容詞　290
精神活動　→ 2.3.1.2; 5.4.3; Ap.4.2
聖典　→ 8.3.2.1
制度　48, 221, 236, 237, 238, 269, 413, 451, 468, 470, 471, 476
　輸送制度　291
製品(名)　20, 35, 50, 51, 52, 55, 56, 57, 102, 133, 155, 233, 235, 236, 297, 340, 394, 395, 396, 397, 398, 399, 400, 401, 436; → 2.3.1.3
施術　→ 5.2

接続詞 → 9.1; 9.4.2.1
前置詞 24, 41, 78, 80, 87, 282, 376, 378, 449
前置詞句 290, 378: → 3.11; 4.4.1
前方照応 247, 248, 250, 373
船名 319, 320, 362: → 8.7.1.13
専門用語 24, 213, 422
創作物 → 2.3.1.3
総称用法 → 7.3; 8.6.1
属性 274, 275, 278
素材 71, 114, 116, 117, 121, 146, 158, 192, 209, 218, 243, 337, 410, 417, 430, 467, 468, 473, 475: → 2.1.1
存在文 → 4.5.2

た
大学 → 8.7.2.4
対照 81, 355, 360, 399, 420, 424
対象
　感情の対象 → 4.4.1.2.1
　能力の対象 → 4.4.1.2.2
大陸 300: → 8.2.5
対立
　三項対立 286
　二項対立 → 8.5.1
滝 → 8.7.1.5
多義語 215
タワー名 321: → 塔; Tower
単位 → 8.3.2.5
段階的形容詞 113, 150
単数一致 → 一致
ダンス名 → 8.4.2.2
地位 107, 281: → 身分
チーム名 → 8.2.3
　所属チーム 254
　単数形 254
チェーン店 344
血筋 70
地点 → 8.3.2.1
地名 11, 16, 22, 254, 298, 306, 332, 334, 346: → 8.9

注 → 9.6.1
抽象概念 → 5 章
抽象名詞 6, 113, 243: → 2.3.3
治療法 → 5.2
対 → 9.2; ペア
通貨 269
通称 362: → 愛称, 符帳
通信手段 → 3.7.2
月着陸船 339
庭園名 → 8.7.1.16
テーマパーク 353
デルタ名 333, 334
転移修飾 163, 428, 429
電車(名) → 8.7.2.2
天体 → 8.3.2.1
転用固有名詞 262
塔 → 8.7.1.14
等位接続詞 → 9.1
同格(語句／構文) 17, 20, 172, 248, 249, 319f., 340, 343: → 8.4.2.1
道具 382
洞窟名 333
峠 333, 334
動詞 81, 159, 162, 210, 214, 217, 384, 462: → be, act, cause, get, grunt, have, murmur, play, stammer, suffer from
同定 247
　状況的同定 → 8.3
　文脈内同定 → 8.1
同定可能 247
同定可能性 → 8.7.1
同定構文 → 5.4.1.2; Ap.3
動物園 → 8.7.2.4
動名詞 → 4.4.5
道路 → 8.7.1.10
ト書き → 9.6.1
図書館 → 8.7.2.4
トラック名 341
トンネル → 8.7.1.11

な

内面的特徴 → 8.4.1.1
内容 167: → 5.4.4; Ap.4.3
におい → 2.1.1.3
ニキビ 214
二項対立 → 8.5.1
日常的形容詞 166
　→ 形容詞, 非日常的形容詞
人称
　2人称 18
年代 266: → 8.2.1
年齢 → 8.9.4
能力 → 3.9; 4.4.1.2.2
乗り物名 81

は

場／場所 96
博物館 → 8.7.2.4
橋 → 8.7.1.12
バス → 8.7.2.2
派生固有名詞 12
働き 62, 63, 119, 120, 127, 129, 235, 236, 237, 238, 281, 282, 286, 287, 354, 395, 447, 458: → 3章; 関係, 機能, 効力, 地位, 身分, 役割
発明品 → 8.6.3
発話 → 4.4.3.3
波止場 302
パブ → 8.7.2.3
浜辺 301
場面依存 → 8.3.1
犯罪(行為／名) → 5.1
半島 → 8.7.1.7
樋口(1993, 1998) 11
飛行機(名) 339, 340
飛行場名 333, 334
否定 → 4.5.1
非日常的の形容詞 159, 166, 471: → 形容詞, 日常的形容詞
病院(名) 354: → 8.7.1.17
表現 42, 62, 63: → 慣用的表現, 付帯的表現
病名 272: → 5.3; 8.2.6
　流行病 → 8.3.3
広瀬(1973) 48
広場 329
副詞的(語句／用法) 107, 377, 385: → 9.4.2.3
複数(形) 7, 16, 18, 20, 30, 34, 39, 42, 59, 67, 73, 76, 87, 203, 204, 206, 219, 241, 251, 256, 294, 351, 369, 373, 376, 382, 386, 388, 448: → 8.2
　a/an＋adj＋複数形 → 6章
　加工前の複数 30
　総称用法の複数 → 7.3.2
複数一致 → 一致
複数構成物 325: → 8.2
部族 → 8.2.4
付帯的表現 → 9.5
符帳 11, 12, 19, 24, 250, 298, 300, 311, 317, 318, 319, 327, 361, 362: → 愛称, 通称
普通名詞
　擬態普通名詞 → 1.7
普通名詞化 → 2.3.2
物質集合名詞 48, 244
物質名詞 113: → Ap.1
　普通名詞化 → 2.3.2
不定詞 → 4.4.5
埠頭 302
船 → 8.7.1.13
プロトタイプ 277, 279, 293
文化的了解 247, 270, 272, 298, 305: → 8.4
文化的連想 250
分詞
　the＋分詞 → 8.3.4
分詞構文 386
分数
　形容詞＋分数 232
文体
　省略的文体 → 9.6

文体的効果　296
文頭　→ 9.4.2
文脈内同定　→ 8.1
ペア　72, 235, 285, 377, 383: → 9.2; 対
　副詞的用法　377
〈米〉用法　30, 75, 80, 91, 96, 125, 205,
　206, 211, 239, 286, 327, 330, 331, 354,
　426, 444, 457
平原　→ 8.2.5; 8.7.2.1
並列　159, 378: → 9.1.1; 9.1.2; 列挙
ヘリコプター名　339
牧場名　332, 334
補語　41, 375: → 3.1
補足的説明　390
墓地名　332, 334
ホテル　→ 8.7.2.3
本来固有名詞　12, 249

ま

枕詞　147, 150, 164, 238, 358, 408, 415,
　428
祭り　→ 8.3.2.3
岬　308
湖　299
見出し　→ 9.6.1
港　302
峰　→ 8.7.1.9
身分　65, 66, 67, 107, 281: → 地位
民族　→ 8.2.4
名詞
　間投詞扱い　→ 9.4.2.4
　固有名詞　11, 12, 249, 335: → 1.2; 8.7
　抽象名詞　6, 113, 243: → 2.3.3
名詞部　5
命題　241

メタ言語　→ 2.4
文字つき　→ 1.5
森　→ 森林

や

役割　65, 67, 71, 72, 73, 74, 75, 76, 97,
　100, 104, 277, 290
安井 (2000)　113
山　→ 8.7.1.9
山梨 (1995)　11
唯一物　251, 305: → 8.3.2
輸送手段　→ 3.7.1
輸送制度　291
揺れ　318, 335
様相　152, 163, 164, 249, 355, 356, 426,
　428
様態　6, 57, 61, 101, 113, 126, 147, 160,
　163, 165, 177, 181, 182, 207, 208, 209,
　210, 212, 213, 217, 237, 238, 408, 411,
　417, 419, 420, 421, 423, 424, 425, 427,
　428, 429, 430, 431, 432, 433, 434, 447,
　450, 451, 452, 455, 458, 461, 465, 475
呼びかけ　→ 1.4

ら

流行病　→ 8.3.3
類推　327
レストラン　→ 8.7.2.3
列挙　243, 310, 367, 369: → 9.3; 並列
連想　277
　文化的連想　250

わ

惑星(名)　24, 263
湾　→ 8.7.1.2

■著者・協力者紹介

<著者>
樋口 昌幸（ひぐち　まさゆき）
1974年広島大学大学院文学研究科博士課程単位取得退学
現在，広島大学名誉教授　博士（英語学）
著書等：『言語学・英語学小事典』（共著，北星堂書店，1990），『英文法小事典』（共著，北星堂書店，1991），*Studies in Chaucer's English*（英潮社，1996），『英語論文表現事典』（共著，北星堂書店，1999），『英語の冠詞―歴史から探る本質』（広島大学出版会，2009）［英語コーパス学会賞受賞］

<協力者>
Michael Gorman（マイケル・ゴーマン）
2005年タルサ大学大学院博士課程修了
現在，広島市立大学准教授　Ph.D.
編著書・論文等：*Guide to Japanese Women Writers and Their Culture, 1892-1992*（共著，University of Wisconsin System, 1993），*Thinking and Writing about Literacy*（共編，Orlando: Harcourt Brace, 1999），'Versed in Country Things': Pastoral Ideology, American Identity, and Imperialism（博士論文，提出先 University of Tulsa, 2005）

［例解］現代英語冠詞事典

© Masayuki Higuchi, 2003　　　　NDC835/xiii,510p/21cm

初版第1刷　──── 2003年11月10日
第5刷　　　──── 2014年9月 1日

著　者 ──── 樋口昌幸
発行者 ──── 鈴木一行
発行所 ──── 株式会社大修館書店
　　　　　　〒113-8541 東京都文京区湯島 2-1-1
　　　　　　電話 03-3868-2651（販売部）03-3868-2293（編集部）
　　　　　　振替 00190-7-40504
　　　　　　［出版情報］http://www.taishukan.co.jp

装丁者 ──── 井之上聖子
印刷所 ──── 壮光舎印刷
製本所 ──── 三水舎

ISBN978-4-469-04166-8　　Printed in Japan

回本書のコピー，スキャン，デジタル化等の無断複製は著作権法上での例外を除き禁じられています。本書を代行業者等の第三者に依頼してスキャンやデジタル化することは，たとえ個人や家庭内での利用であっても著作権法上認められておりません。